THE ART OF
INTERPRETATION

THE ART OF INTERPRETATION

Third Edition

WALLACE A. BACON
Northwestern University

HOLT, RINEHART AND WINSTON
New York   Chicago   San Francisco
Atlanta   Dallas   Montreal   Toronto

Library of Congress Cataloging in Publication Data
Bacon, Wallace A.
    The art of interpretation.

    Includes indexes.
    1. Oral interpretation.   I. Title.

PN4145 . B15   1979   808 . 5'4   78-22101

ISBN 0-03-089958-3

For Robert S. Breen
with whom, for half a lifetime,
I have explored the many mansions
of interpretation

PREFACE TO THE THIRD EDITION

The word *art* in *The Art of Interpretation* is used in its classic sense to mean both a discipline to be studied so that it can be applied (e.g., the art of arithmetic) and the principles of an esthetic endeavor. Interpretation is an art of performance; this book is an attempt to set forth for students ways in which that art can be examined and practiced.

In this third edition, I have tried to take into account the suggestions of those who have used earlier editions, and I have carried out more fully commitments that began with the first edition and grew with the second. The sense of becoming, the notion of the act, and of embodiment—the creation of tensive presence—these have grown increasingly important with each edition, and there are constant large and small changes in the body of the text to support their growth. Many of the terms which in the first edition seemed new have worked their way into the critical vocabulary of teachers and students; their adoption has thus testified to their usefulness. The concepts of *matching,* of *locus,* of *presence,* of *tensiveness*—the concept of the literary act which conjoins with, shapes, and is shaped by the body act of the performer in the creative endeavor—these and other views seem to point usefully to ways in which the performing art itself can be seen anew.

Commitment to the literary work remains squarely at the heart of interpretation—not apart from concern with the performer, but as the reason for the study of performance. The third edition continues the belief of the first and second editions that it is through the process of matching, through leading the self or selves of the performer to an engagement with works of literature, that growth occurs in interpretation. A sense of the *other* is here a crucial concern. A new section of the text is devoted to the audience, which in its turn becomes *another* in the triad of text, performer, listener.

Embodiment, enactment, is to be seen *not* as the *literalizing* of the words of a text (as if one were to point when a text says "He pointed") but as the enactment of the felt sensing of a text, the process in which feeling/meaning constitutes an act, with a beginning, middle, and end.

Literalizing frequently destroys this sense of process, leads the attention to what is done rather than to the reason for its being done. This is not to deny that literalizing may have *specific* effects which may be useful.

Just as we read literary texts, we "read" the body, too, as it engages in process. There are psychological acts to which words point, which words seek to express, within which words prosper. Birdwhistel tells us in fascinating detail of the sounds, gestures, postures, expressions by which the human body seeks to encompass the communicative acts that constitute life. He tells us, for example, that there are some 250,000 different expressions of which the human face alone is capable.[1] A human being is a *moving* creature; through the body a being participates in the world. Interpretation is vitally concerned with the ways in which the expressive capacities of the body are engaged with language in the esthetic experience of literature. As students of interpretation, we engage in descriptive criticism to sharpen our awareness of these ways; we engage in evaluative criticism to say how effective we take these ways to be with respect to texts. Always the interest should be in this cooperation of literature and the living body of the student. Always, we think, humility toward the literary text is a good guide; one grows inwardly by taking the time to seek outward, toward the text to be performed. Interpretation is a study for all readers, whether silent or oral.

As in earlier editions, we try to be wary of rules, though mindful of helpful suggestions. Teachers and students are again urged to use the book in whatever ways may be most profitable. Literary selections are not tied to the chapters in which they are found, but may be useful at many points. The glossary is meant to be helpful both in conjunction with the text and apart from it.

The book is written for students, and I have tried to share with students as much as I can of my own understanding both of literature and of interpretation. In the process of that sharing, I have learned much from colleagues both at Northwestern University and elsewhere, much from students both here and abroad, much from what others have written about the various phases of the art forms that here conjoin. To the readers of earlier editions, I continue to be thankful.

To my colleagues and students in the Department of Interpretation at Northwestern I owe more than I can comfortably acknowledge. Finally, to the teachers who constituted that department when I first joined it—Alvina Krause, Charlotte Lee, and Robert Breen—I wish to pay particular tribute. While the point of view of this text is essentially my own, I have listened to them as carefully as I could, and from them I have learned more than I can say. To one of them, who has shared with

---

[1] Ray L. Birdwhistel, *Kinesics and Context: Essays on Body Motion Communication* (Philadelphia: University of Pennsylvania Press, 1970), p. 8.

me in an especially full way his rich experience in interpretation, I have taken the liberty of dedicating this third edition.

—W.A.B.

January 1979
Evanston, Illinois

In accordance with contemporary usage, I have attempted to change the singular pronoun "he" to an equivalent term indicating both male and female. However, this was not always possible. For these instances, please read "he" as the general pronoun referring to both sexes.

CONTENTS

TO BEGIN WITH...

We shall be seeking answers to the question, How does a literary work feel when it speaks? This is the basic question for interpreters, who must put themselves in the position of the poem [1] rather than in that of viewers of the poem if they are to let us see and hear the poem rather than themselves. They must have some sense of the "antecedents" of the poem, the state of mind out of which it arises, so that even at the outset they give us not themselves but the work. In this respect, they are much like the writer who, as Eliot has said, escapes from the confines of his own personality by entering into the thing being created. It is a paradox, and a happy one, that our growth results in part from this concentration on growth outside us. It is not alone the writer who aspires, nor the reader; literature itself aspires, speaks, and the interpreter becomes language in its full and most significant sense—not a horn through which the poet calls, not a vacuum transmitting speech, but the embodiment of speech.

Emphasis will be on the process of becoming. For a time during the process, the tensions observable in the experience of interpreting will seem more the tensions of the reader than of the poem; the presence and perspective frequently will be those of the reader. But practice will help the interpreter to channel these tensions into the tensions of the poem—or, where they are not functional within the poem, to eliminate them. It is a difficult and demanding art, the art of interpretation, but it has rich rewards including, but certainly not stopping with, the pleasure of reading.

A literary structure, within the limits of its materials, is what it is because it tries to become what it wants to be. Emphasis here too is on the process of becoming. Once *becoming* has ripened into full *being*, once the realization is complete, no more is to be done. Some literary works set their goals very low, and we find it difficult to sustain interest in them; other works set their goals very high—sometimes so high that they are doomed to defeat. Sometimes the goal is barely beyond reach and constantly exhilarating; sometimes the goal is almost fully achieved. Almost. It is never completely achieved; complete ripeness is possible

---

[1] *Poem* is used to mean any work of literature, whether in verse or in prose. This use of the word is both convenient and traditional.

only on the verge of decay—and, indeed, some poems are overripe. The readers, too, may set their goals too high or too low, but their overripeness is likely to be an overripeness of techniques thought of as ends in themselves, a lack of congruence between their bodies and the body of the poem—all the virtues of life except significant purpose.

Like a poem, interpreters, within the limits of their capacities, are what they are because they try to become what they want to be. Hence our emphasis is first on what we should want to be and second on the means by which we try to achieve this goal. We shall look first at the body of the poem (what the interpreter wants to be), then at the interpreter (who wants to be the poem). This is not to say that our primary interest is the poem, for the two things together ultimately constitute our single interest; the ultimate goal can be achieved more completely by looking first at the poem rather than at the student.

We shall be wary of rules, though not of suggestions. It is better to say "Let's see whether" than to say "You must never." We are not so much interested in confining as in defining possibilities. Our responsibility, finally, is to be *responsive*.

This view hopefully places the art of interpretation in the liberal arts context. Interpretation is the study of literature through the medium of oral performance, where the medium is itself a process of defining. This indicates interest in both the reader and the thing read, but what—all those voices cry—about the audience?

In a class in interpretation, the audience is a special audience—students who are interested in the whole process, from the poem in print to the poem in oral performance. The only way in which interpreters can demonstrate their degree of achievement is by performing before the class and the instructor, who are mutually interested in being helpful by applauding what is good and pointing constructively to things that can be made better. If the reading cannot be heard, it cannot be judged; if it is not projected, it cannot engage the hearers so that they can participate; if it is defective in articulation, pronunciation, level of pitch, patterns of intonation, rate of utterance, it will set up barriers to effective response. But the reading may be adequate in all these respects and still not embody the text that is its subject—and these additional matters (at which we shall look throughout the book) are of the utmost importance both to the reader and to the audience. The students listening are also learning. It is often easier to understand a difficulty of one's own if it can be pointed to objectively in the reading of another. The audience, then, is never left out in the classroom situation.

What about the "public audience"? Need the study of interpretation in the classroom result in public performance? We think the answer is no, though clearly the successful reader *ought* to be able to perform in public and should be encouraged to take advantage of opportunities to do so. The class in interpretation achieves its primary goal within the classroom; public performance is an additional, somewhat different matter. At this point, distinctions between liberal and professional training begin to arise. This is not in any sense a judgment against public performance, an undervaluing of the worth of fine public reading; it is simply a recognition that the value of a course in interpretation cannot reasonably be held to lie in the number of its graduates who read in public. The essential educational value of interpretation as a separate and distinct aspect of speech and of literary study lies in its emphasis on the bringing together into an organic relationship of student and poem. Interpretation shares with many other branches of speech the further problem of the public audience. The relationship between interpreter and audience is complex, even when the interpreter is his or her own auditor and no other person is present. While some of the issues arising from this interrelationship lie beyond the scope of this book, others will be treated in Chapters 4, 5, and 7. *The art of interpretation is an art of performance;* we must be clear about that. A performance involves an audience, and the audience becomes, in its way and in its turn, a participant in the total act of interpretation. There is no question that an audience brings to the total environment of performance many considerations that relate the study of interpretation to other aspects of speech and communication. These matters deserve close and careful study and a large body of writing is devoted to them, but they are outside the province of this particular text in the same way that extended study of the vocal mechanism and body mechanics are outside it. The text does not pretend to be complete, nor is it simply a composite account of the subject. It provides a rationale for interpretation; it tries to define the centrally significant concerns of the subject; it suggests a direction of study that sees the art as an art of enactment, of embodiment, of becoming. The poem is active, the reader active; the art of interpretation aims at establishing in oral performance a congruence between these two sets of acts.

The pleasures of interpretation, like the pleasures of literature, are many, varied, and richly rewarding, but they do not come automatically. The reader who wants to become an interpreter must actively *try* to become the interpreter he or she wants to become.

THE HOUSE WAS QUIET
AND THE WORLD WAS CALM

—Wallace Stevens
from Collected Poems[1]

The house was quiet and the world was calm.
The reader became the book; and summer night

Was like the conscious being of the book.
The house was quiet and the world was calm.

The words were spoken as if there was no book,
Except that the reader leaned above the page,

Wanted to lean, wanted much most to be
The scholar to whom his book is true, to whom

The summer night is like a perfection of thought.
The house was quiet because it had to be.

The quiet was part of the meaning, part of the mind:
The access of perfection to the page.

And the world was calm. The truth in a calm world,
In which there is no other meaning, itself

Is calm, itself is summer and night, itself
Is the reader leaning late and reading there.

THE ACT OF PERFORMANCE

Part **1**

Chapter **1**

GENERAL INTRODUCTION

We often act as though the written word were primary in the act of communication, but carefully collected evidence suggests that individuals spend the major part of their lives with the spoken word, as speakers or as listeners. Speech is concerned not only with diction, pronunciation, pitch and volume, not only with delivery; it is intimately concerned with all that is meaningful to the human being as a communicating agent—with his heart, mind, voice, reason, feelings, and gestures.

Speech cannot be divorced from subject matter, for a man speaking is a man speaking something, and the "something" is what concerns him. Indeed, it is profitable to look upon the study of speech as the study of man as a gesturing creature. Sounds, words, movements, ideas, dreams, hopes—all are gestures by which man seeks to convey to those around him the secrets that must otherwise die within him. The function of the study of speech is to help men to gesture successfully. Written words are signs of gestures; they are symbols that seek to make gestures meaningful. Writing is often a preliminary to oral utterance, a way of trying to make the act of oral utterance more precise, more meaningful, by sub-

SPEECH AS GESTURE

jecting it to an ordering process through the formal organization of the gesture.

DEVELOPMENT OF INTERPRETATION

One of the oldest forms of speech is concerned with the oral performance of literature. Now called *interpretation,* this branch of speech is also called oral reading or interpretative reading. During the eighteenth and nineteenth centuries it was usually called *elocution;* early in the twentieth century it was often called *expression.* In Greece during the Golden Age the reader or interpreter was called a *rhapsode.*

While interpretation may be thought of, broadly, as including any kind of reading aloud of written material, and hence may include the oral reading of radio or television commercials, of expository papers, of announcements, and so on, it is by long tradition associated primarily with the oral reading of literature.

It was once assumed that literature was meant to be read aloud. Before the invention of printing, the oral reader was often the means by which written materials were "published." The Greek historians, for example, read their works aloud to audiences. Poets gathered together to hear their poems. Playwrights were heard almost solely at the great dramatic festivals, where their plays competed for prizes. The rhapsode traveled about to the Greek games and festivals (where the literary arts were part of the contests) reciting from his favorite poets, and he delighted his listeners by his ability to bring written words to life.

All through the Middle Ages, we are told, reading was more oral than silent. Even in the monasteries, the monks who sat in the libraries reading to themselves read aloud. St. Augustine reports the following story about St. Ambrose, for example, as if the conduct of Ambrose were strange and unusual:

> But when he was reading, he drew his eyes along over the leaves, and his heart searched into the sense, but his voice and tongue were silent. Oftentimes when we were present (for no man was debarred of coming to him, nor was it his fashion to be told of anybody that came to speak with him) we still saw him reading to himself; and never otherwise: so that having long sat in silence (for who durst be so bold as to interrupt him, so intentive to his study?) we were fain to depart. We conjectured that the small time which he gat for the repairing of his mind, he retired himself from the clamour of other men's businesses, being unwilling to be taken off for any other employment; and he was wary perchance too, lest some hearer being struck into suspense, and eager upon it, if the author he read should deliver anything obscurely, he should be put to it to expound it, or to discuss some of the harder questions; so that spending away his time about this work, he could not turn over so many volumes as he desired: although peradventure, the preserving of his voice (which a little speaking used to weaken) might be a just reason for his read-

ing to himself. But with what intent soever he did it, that man certainly had a good meaning in it.[1]

The habit of hearing language is reflected in the formulas found scattered through classical and medieval literature—"Of arms and the man I *sing*," or "Listen while I *tell* you," or "Now you must *hear*. . . ." One of the most famous stories of a medieval singer is the story of Caedmon, the simple English singer who sang of the glory of God, as it is told by the Venerable Bede (see Appendix A).

In Teutonic history oral readers are called bards, and so great was their importance that they were sometimes the givers of laws. In Wales the bards became so powerful at one point that they had to be driven from the country. The power of the spoken word before the invention of printing was at times magical. To the medieval and early Renaissance mind, reason was the attribute that most clearly distinguished man from animal, and man's capacity to reason was best demonstrated through his power of speech.

After the invention of printing, the written or printed word gradually became more powerful. Today, while it is still said that literature is meant to be heard, we are not really accustomed to listening to literature. As a result, we miss what Henry James has called the most rewarding test of literary excellence, the test by which literary forms are subjected to the "close pressure" of oral performance. For it is only under such pressure, says James, that literature gives out "its finest and most numerous secrets. . . ."[2]

It is with the oldest of the speech arts (antedating formal study of rhetoric, antedating the actor) that the present volume is concerned. While it is perfectly true that not all literature can profitably be read aloud to all audiences, it is nevertheless safe to say that, granted the right audience, most literature still gains by being read aloud. Interpretation, however, remains a mystery to many people. Part of the problem arises from the fact that authorities in the field have viewed the subject in diverse ways.

INTERPRETATION AS A STUDY: DEFINITION

What is the primary object of study in interpretation? Is it delivery? Is it communication to an audience? Is it the student? Is it the writer? Or is it the literary work? At times the study has been defined as the study of delivery, and the chief attention of teachers and students has gone to such matters as diction, enunciation, pitch, volume, timbre, pause, emphasis, and tempo. The quality of the vocal instrument is important because flexibility of the instrument increases the range of things it can encompass. Experience has shown, however, that too narrow a focus on

[1] From St. Augustine's *Confessions*.
[2] Henry James, From the preface to *The Golden Bowl*.

such matters often produces an interpreter more concerned with his instrument than with his music. Such a single interest in the techniques of delivery led to the worst excesses of the elocutionary movement, to too much emphasis on the *way* things were said and too little on the things themselves. As a result, readings were often "brilliant" but hollow and shallow. Long ago Aristotle pointed out the dangers of too exclusive an interest in delivery, and experience has constantly reaffirmed his view. Delivery is important as a tool, but it is not (in its ordinary sense) the center of study in interpretation.

Surely communication is important. What is the good of reading literature aloud if it does not communicate? But communicate to whom? For what end? If it is true that the study of literature itself is valuable, and that literature gives forth its fullest secrets when it is articulately sounded, then the study of interpretation is valuable for the student because the literature that is sounded gives forth its secrets to him or her, whether or not others are listening. The interpreter cannot ultimately overlook the fact of the larger audience. In the classroom where we are practicing and learning, the auditors too perform; in their turn, they become a part of the matching process that brings together reader and work. But the problem of the larger audience is not specific to interpretation alone; it is a complex problem shared with all the performing arts and is in part beyond the scope of this volume.

Does this mean, then, that the student is the primary object of interest in interpretation? No, not quite, although it is perfectly true that the education of the student is the end of all academic work. In our view, interpretation as an academic discipline may best be defined as the study of literature *through the medium of oral performance where the medium is itself a process of defining.* As a performing art, it is the actualization or realization of literature through its embodiment in the performer. In interpretation the performer is led, in a process of matching, through one of the most profoundly civilizing of all processes—the education of the senses, in the richest sense of the phrase—through the experience of literature. By "education of the senses" we do not mean indulgence in emotion. The senses are educated when they are made not only finely operative but also perceptive and are coordinated with taste and judgment. Sensory experience underlies all thought; indeed, thinking has been described as the flow of *felt sensing,* and feeling (about which more will be said in Chapter 6) as "a living texture of environmental interaction."[3] One's "feelings" about a thing or an issue or a person or an attitude involve all of one's responses; they are the focusing of one's living self on a context.

For the interpreter, the life of literature exists in such felt sensing. The separation of words from felt sensing destroys literature; the separa-

---

[3] See Eugene T. Gendlin, "The Discovery of Felt Meaning," in *Language and Meaning,* ed. James B. Macdonald and Robert R. Leeper (Association for Supervision and Curriculum Development, NEA, 1966), pp. 45-62.

tion of emotionality from words and concepts destroys literature. It is in the controlled interplay of both concepts and felt sensing that the life of literature resides. A developed sensory apparatus is essential for the interpreter. There is, then, no quarrel between the senses and sense, except when one fails to remain in balance with the other. By nature, men and women seem to be creatures who must forever struggle to establish the delicate balance between ideas and feelings, so that they can give themselves wholly to their problems.

It is sometimes thought that science develops the reason and that literature develops the emotions, but no serious person can long believe in so simple a dichotomy. At the topmost levels, the theoretical scientist is a poet and the poet is a philosopher.[4] Science is not poetry and poetry is not philosophy, yet both science and poetry seek to sharpen our perceptions of the world in which we live. Science seeks to establish truth objectively, though it must work through processes that are in part always subjective; poetry seeks to establish not "truth" but rather "what is true," because it believes that the world is as we perceive it and takes as its central subject matter the states of human perception. Poetry (that is, imaginative literature in general) explores relationships between language and the lived world. Plays, poems, stories want, by and large, to embody *both* the processes of thought and the processes of lived experience—to get the feel of the lived world into the process of thought about that world. Thus poets in fact *create* experience. The experiences of poems become part of our experience of the world itself—the poem lives in the world, and it changes our lives.[5]

Interpretation is an excellent way of studying literature because it demands that the student perceive. The oral process involves active participation in the perceptions of the poem. Passivity is a completely impossible state for the oral reader.

[4] Here and frequently elsewhere *poet* is used in its classic sense to mean "maker" or "creator" and *poem* to mean "the work of literature—i.e., the thing made by the poet." English does not have available to us a *single* term as a synonym. The word *writer,* for example, is too broadly inclusive, and it is cumbersome to keep using phrases such as "the literary artist," "the work of literature," and so on.

[5] See my brief essay "Language and the Lived World," in *Representative American Speeches 1976-1977,* ed. Waldo W. Braden (New York: H. W. Wilson Company, 1977), pp. 174–180.

Chapter 2

TEXT AND BODY AS ACTS

Literature is a part of life. What we read in books becomes as much a part of us as the food we eat—provided we really read it. Literature, like food, needs to be digested to be useful.

THE USES OF
LITERATURE

Historically, two functions have been ascribed to literature: to give pleasure and to instruct. The Roman poet Horace expressed these functions in the words *dulce* and *utile,* "sweet" and "useful." There are people who think that poetry that only entertains is not very important, not really worth the consideration of mature minds. But all history is against them. Readers have always enjoyed what has given them pleasure, whether or not it seems in any particular way useful. They have usually, on the other hand, rejected as literature what has been too narrowly didactic. A textbook, for example, no matter how literate its author, is not literature in the usual sense. (One may define *literature* to include anything in words or in print, but this makes the definition so broad as to be almost shapeless.) Indeed, imaginative literature is sometimes defined as that use of language which has for its end pleasure, not truth. Literature is true (true to life), but it is not truth. It is true to life because it can spring only from the experience of the writer, and in its own way (often indirect) it must reflect his or her being.

But in the final analysis, there is no conflict between *pleasure* and *profit* as the ends of literature, for the acquisition of experience through reading may be useful because it is pleasurable and pleasurable because it is useful. Insight combines pleasure and profit.

THE PLEASURES OF LITERATURE

Literature involves both the head and the heart—the mind and the emotions, if we may be permitted to separate what actually function as one in the human being. *Emotion* means "outward movement"; it is a response to a stimulus which, involving physiological changes in the body preparatory to acts (which may or may not be performed), renders the body itself *active* as opposed to quiescent. Properly used, literature stimulates us to respond imaginatively to things outside ourselves. It is not the purpose of literature to make us wallow in emotional states in which we are already involved. The individual who reads only to excite movement inward (pornography, for example, does this) is misusing literature; such a reader is like the glutton who converts all things into flesh. Properly, literature leads us from ourselves, and its pleasure is the pleasure of adventure. But the wonderful thing about the journey is that it ultimately brings us back home; we can say of an experience that we have had for the first time in reading, "How true!"

LITERATURE AS TRANSLATION

To be enjoyed and to be profitable, literature must make some contact with the reader. No reader can profit from literature containing an experience completely unrelated to his own. Literature does not ask for identification (no reader's experience can actually be identical with that in a poem), but it does ask for participation in the ongoing feelings of the poem. Poems name and define feelings and provide new contexts for them. They give us words for feelings, and, in a sense, knowing the word for it makes a thing intelligible. As one critic put it, "You see so much more of the forest when you know the names of trees."[1]

If literature is experience, it is also translation—the translation of the experience of the writer into the experience of the reader, and vice versa. Every book must be thus translated. Since the study of interpretation demands by its very nature that the student actively translate literature, it must begin with literature that in some clear way involves the experience of the student.

THE PROCESS OF INTERPRETING

Our minds are teeming storehouses, filled with the memories (some conscious, some subconscious) of our past. Literature recalls these memories, activates them, shapes them anew by combining them with new images, and then lets them, in the shape of poems, settle back into the storehouse. Literature, when used fully, is thus assimilated.

[1] L. C. Knights, in "The Place of English Literature in a Liberal Education," *The Use of English,* 4, No. 3 (Spring 1958): 157.

Silent readers, who often skim and skip and scavenge for particular ideas or images, frequently do not assimilate whole pieces of literature, but only taste them. But interpreters cannot so read. They must bring the whole poem close to themselves, recalling memories, translating the poem into themselves and themselves into the poem. The memories, together with the stimulus that is the poem, lead to emotions, to outward responses, to audible and visible signs (words, gestures, tones, glances) that are part of the process of assimilation. The act of oral reading before an audience (though that audience may be a single listener or, indeed, the reader alone) is a way of making objective, of testing the accuracy of the interpreter's measure of the poem. Listening to a student's reading of a poem, the audience knows—often more clearly than by questioning him or her about it—what the poem means to the reader.

EMPATHY, KINESTHESIS, KINESICS

An ineffective reader is sometimes said to read from the neck up, as if there were a divorce between mind and body. While of course no one performs without a body, a reader may do so little to reinforce concepts with feelings that the reading will appear lifeless and inert—will seem not to mean what is said.

One may, for example, say very matter-of-factly "I hear a bell tolling" with a minimum of felt sensing. Now imagine that you are in a situation (devise one) in which you are waiting anxiously to hear a bell tolling because the bell will announce something important you. Suddenly you hear the bell. How will your saying of the line "I hear a bell tolling" differ from the matter-of-fact statement? Describe as specifically as you can your body response to the bell. How does it affect your eyes, shoulders, neck, arms, chest, trunk, or legs? Imagine a variety of kinds of situation with a variety of kinds of bell—a death knell, a fire alarm, a bell announcing the birth of a prince, a bell summoning people to a church service. How do your responses to the various bells differ? Remember, be as *specific* as possible in describing actual (not imaginary) body sensations of which you are aware. Try out some of these responses on the class and see whether they can identify the kind of situation you have in mind and can feel with you.

The process of "feeling with" or "feeling into" is known as *empathy*. Readers empathize with persons and things within the poems they read. Audiences empathize with readers; if the reader is uncertain, frightened, or distressed, audiences are likely to empathize with that state and to miss a good deal of the poem because the reader is missing much of it. If the reader is sure, controlled, attentive to the text, the audience often seems able to empathize with the poem itself. In this sense people sometimes say that a good interpreter seems to disappear or to become transparent. Nothing that he or she does interferes with the experience of the poem. Hence, the interpreter should devote attention as completely as possible to the felt sensing of the poem to avoid the projection of irrelevant feelings with which the audience will empathize.

Empathy involves *kinesthesis,* which is the sensation of body movement, position, and tension. Kinesthetic activity is as vital an aspect of reading as it is of daily living. *Kinesics* is the science devoted to study of body movement in relation to speech; it is concerned with all movement that accompanies, reinforces, complements, and otherwise extends spoken language. What, for example, may be intended when a speaker stamps his foot, shrugs his shoulders, grits his teeth, clenches his fist, turns up his lip, extends his nostrils? More than one thing, to be sure—each action must be taken in context before the full meaning can be felt. Kinesthetic behavior and the related (but not identical) phenomenon empathy are essential in full interpretation. While we shall not attach the label *empathy* or *kinesthesis* to every aspect of interpretation to which we turn, in almost everything we say of oral reading the importance of body movement and tension is vital.

Here are additional exercises:

1. Imagine that you are scraping your fingernail on a blackboard. What do you hear? What do you feel? Are the sensations of which you are aware centered in your feet? Your stomach? Your neck and shoulders? Or where? Try to locate and describe them accurately. (If you have never had the experience of scraping your fingernail on the blackboard, try it!)

2. Imagine that you are standing alone in a classroom looking out the window and that suddenly, without looking around, you sense that someone has come up behind you. What sensations do you feel? Try to be specific in naming your body responses.

3. Now read the following:

from THE WHITE OLD MAID[2]
—Nathaniel Hawthorne

The moonbeams came through two deep and narrow windows and showed a spacious chamber richly furnished in an antique fashion. From one lattice the shadow of the diamond panes was thrown upon the floor; the ghostly light through the other slept upon a bed, falling between the heavy silken curtains and illuminating the face of a young man. But how quietly the slumberer lay! how pale his features! And how like a shroud the sheet was wound about his frame! Yes, it was a corpse in its burial clothes.

Suddenly the fixed features seemed to move with dark emotion. Strange fantasy! It was but the shadow of the fringed curtain waving betwixt the dead face and the moonlight as the door of the chamber opened and a girl stole softly to the bedside. Was there delusion in the moonbeams, or did her gesture and her eye betray a gleam of triumph as she bent over the pale corpse, pale as itself, and pressed her living lips to the cold ones of the dead?

[2] From *Twice-Told Tales,* originally published in 1851.

Can you see the moonlit room, the shadows of the diamond panes on the floor, the curtained bed—and the corpse of the young man? Watch the movement of the fringed curtain. Does the door of the chamber make any noise as it opens? Do you dare follow the young girl to the bedside and bend with her over the corpse? Read the passage aloud. Imagine that you are in the room with the narrator, discovering with him the fact that the young man is dead and being startled, with him, at the seeming movement on the face of the dead. Then watch the girl come into the room. Can you describe any of the physical sensations you feel as you read? (If you feel *nothing,* it is *you* who are dead!)

Notice that as you particularize your responses, you begin to fill in details not literally supplied by the author. Hawthorne says only "the door of the chamber opened and a girl stole softly to the bedside." But the door must have been a door of *some sort,* and the girl must have been of some certain size, shape, coloring and in some sort of clothing. How many details do you add to the literal words of the text? All readers fill in details from clues presented by the author; so long as they do not run *counter* to the text, such additions are a natural and useful part of the *actualization* or *realization* of the language. In this sense, you as reader become a participant in the writing of the poem, and your contribution will always be in some ways distinct from that made by other readers. It is because readers value their *own* contributions to stories that publishers have generally foregone, nowadays, the once-common practice of illustrating novels. Illustrations often violated reader responses.

4. Here is the opening of:

THE LAGOON[3]
—*Joseph Conrad*

The white man, leaning with both arms over the roof of the little house in the stern of the boat, said to the steersman:

"We will pass the night in Arsat's clearing. It is late."

The Malay only grunted, and went on looking fixedly at the river. The white man rested his chin on his crossed arms and gazed at the wake of the boat. At the end of the straight avenue of forests cut by the intense glitter of the river, the sun appeared unclouded and dazzling, poised low over the water that shone smoothly like a band of metal. The forests, somber and dull, stood motionless and silent on each side of the broad stream. At the feet of big, towering trees, trunkless nipa palms rose from the mud of the bank, in bunches of leaves enormous and heavy, that hung unstirring over the brown swirl of eddies. In the stillness of the air every tree, every leaf, every bough, every tendril of creeper and every petal of minute blossoms

[3] By permission of J. M. Dent & Sons Ltd. and the Trustees of the Joseph Conrad Estate.

seemed to have been bewitched into an immobility perfect and final. Nothing moved on the river but the eight paddles that rose flashing regularly, dipped together with a single splash; while the steersman swept right and left with a periodic and sudden flourish of his blade describing a glinting semicircle above his head. The churned-up water frothed alongside with a confused murmur. And the white man's canoe, advancing upstream in the short-lived disturbance of its own making, seemed to enter the portals of a land from which the very memory of motion had forever departed.

The white man, turning his back upon the setting sun, looked along the empty and broad expanse of the sea-reach. For the last three miles of its course the wandering, hesitating river, as if enticed irresistibly by the freedom of an open horizon, flows straight into the sea, flows straight to the east—to the east that harbors both light and darkness. Astern of the boat the repeated call of some bird, a cry discordant and feeble, skipped along over the smooth water and lost itself, before it could reach the other shore, in the breathless silence of the world.

Read the passage aloud, trying to feel the details of the scene. The sun is *dazzling,* making an *intense glitter* on the water of the river. The forests edging the river are *somber* and *dull, motionless* and *silent;* the nipa leaves are *enormous* and *heavy* in the heat, hanging *unstirring* over the swirling brown water. Everything is still (notice the repetition of *every*)—*an immobility perfect and final*—except for the boat and the muddy water stirred by the boat and paddles. It seems too hot for speech; the Malay only grunts. We get only the confused murmur of the frothing river, and the *feeble, discordant* cry of a bird, too feeble to reach the river's other side in this *breathless silence* of the world. Look closely at the clues to muscular tension and relaxation, and see whether you can sense in your own body muscular responses to the images. (Notice that an image is more than a picture.) Try to feel the heaviness of the heat, cut only by the sounds of the paddles in the water. Once you have captured the feel of the whole scene, remembering these sensations, these images to which you respond, try to put them all in place as you lean, with the white man, over the roof of the little house in the stern of the boat while you read the very opening sentence of the passage. Then continue. The sense of the whole passage hangs over each sentence. Take whatever time you need to keep the images alive as you read.

Now, with the image content and the movement of the whole passage in mind, pick up your book and, standing at one end of the room, try to imagine that the scene you are describing is taking place before you, at the opposite end of the room. Look all the way across the room and read the paragraph aloud as you look at the scene. Resist the temptation to keep your eyes on the book. Watch the scene just as carefully as you can. Fill the room with the river and the forest and the heat and the boat. Rehearse this process until you persuade yourself that the scene is *true,* and does not merely exist in words. Do not forget that the passage is not simply a collection of pictures: It has a meaning that all the images converge to convey, and the total meaning is what you are asked to interpret.

It is very important that you *accept* the room you are in as the space to be filled. While you speak them, Conrad's words *live* in that room. The river, the forest, the sun expand beyond the limits of your four walls, to be sure, but your consciousness of them must move outward to fill your own space. Walk about in that space; examine it. Speak to it. Then, with the sense of that space fully established, read the passage again with your mind's eye on the *scene.*

5. Now read the following poem aloud. As you did with the passage from Conrad, stand at one end of the room and picture the pears all the way at the other end of the room. Look at their yellowness, their bulging bases, their touches of red and citron and orange and green. Do you see the way they taper at the top? Do you see in their shaped surfaces the hints of blue? See the single dried leaf at the top? Notice that they have been placed on a green cloth. Keep every detail in the poem alive in your imagination as you watch and read. Remember that Stevens tells you that "The pears are not seen / As the observer wills"! Let them exist in their own right. *Try reading very slowly.* This will give you time to absorb all the details and keep your senses open.

Let the line lengths guide you, too. Take the lines one by one; resist the temptation to ignore line endings and to finish sentences as if they were prose sentences. Don't read "They are yellow forms composed of curves bulging toward the base," but follow Stevens' divisions of the images: "They are yellow forms / Composed of curves / Bulging toward the base." These are *temporal* markings, intended to modify rate of speaking and hence to call attention more deliberately to images. But while you take time to focus on details, remember that the image is ultimately a complete one, not simply parts seen in isolation.

STUDY OF TWO PEARS[4]
—*Wallace Stevens*

I

Opusculum paedagogum.[5]
The pears are not viols,
Nudes or bottles.
They resemble nothing else.

[4] Copyright 1942 by Wallace Stevens and renewed 1970 by Holly Stevens. Reprinted from *Collected Poems of Wallace Stevens* by permission of the publisher.

[5] The first line of the poem (*Opusculum paedagogum*) may be translated "A little book of instruction." What do you take to be the "lesson" the poet has in mind?

II
They are yellow forms
Composed of curves
Bulging toward the base.
They are touched red.

III
They are not flat surfaces
Having curved outlines.
They are round
Tapering toward the top.

IV
In the way they are modelled
There are bits of blue.
A hard dry leaf hangs
From the stem.

V
The yellow glistens.
It glistens with various yellows,
Citrons, oranges and greens
Flowering over the skin.

VI
The shadows of the pears
Are blobs on the green cloth.
The pears are not seen
As the observer wills.

6. Finally, we come to a longer poem. Try again to "feel your way into" the experience described. We understand others and get the feel of things by empathizing with them, a process that involves many separate muscular responses, all of them affecting the tonality of the body. An oral reader may find that many of these responses will ultimately come automatically or unconsciously, but until you are able to respond in this fashion, you may need to make the responses deliberately and consciously. It is important to take all the time you need, at first, to make these responses. And remember that it is not what you are *doing* but what you are *watching* that is important. Keep your attention off yourself as much as possible and on the objects of the poem. You are trying not to dramatize yourself but to be an accurate observer. Watch and listen! Your own feelings are important only insofar as they help you to respond fully to the poem.

You will find these suggestions useful in your oral reading:

a. Hold the book high enough that you do not have to bend your head down to see the page. You should be able to see the text simply by lowering your eyes without spending much of your time looking down at your book and then up at the back of the room.

b. Hold the book out in front of you, not close to your body. Let it rest easily in the palm of one hand. The whole movement of the poem from the page to the back of the room is a movement *forward*. Don't hug the poem to you! Project it! (Even if your room has a lectern, or reading stand, try this exercise with the book in your hand rather than on the lectern.) Don't ever think of yourself as standing with the poem on a platform. Even when your eyes are on the page, keep your imagination active and out in front of you. This will require some hard work at first. Keep trying until you manage it.

c. Look up words and references you do not understand.

d. There are many additional kinds of detail, which we will examine later on in our study, but for now try to get into your reading of them some sense of the words *haunchy, jabbing, infringe, bobbingly, parades, darkly, strangled, vast black, floats, shuddering, cold, vague, superb, timeless, clocking, vulgar joy, acclaim.* Such words underscore that contrast between the simple, pecking white chickens and the dying (though he doesn't know it) turkey-cock in his dark and pompous grandeur. Life and death exist in strong tension in Wilbur's poem. You must feel this tension in your *actualizing* of his language.

A BLACK NOVEMBER TURKEY[6]
—*Richard Wilbur*

> Nine white chickens come
> With haunchy walk and heads
> Jabbing among the chips, the chaff, the stones
> And the cornhusk-shreds,
>
> And bit by bit infringe
> A pond of dusty light,
> Spectral in shadow until they bobbingly one
> By one ignite.
>
> Neither pale nor bright,
> The turkey-cock parades
> Through radiant squalors, darkly auspicious as
> The ace of spades,
>
> Himself his own cortège
> And puffed with the pomp of death,
> Rehearsing over and over with strangled râle
> His latest breath.

The vast black body floats
Above the crossing knees
As a cloud over thrashed branches, a calm ship
    Over choppy seas.

Shuddering its fan and feathers
In fine soft clashes
With the cold sound that the wind makes, fondling
    Paper ashes.

The pale-blue bony head
Set on its shepherd's-crook
Like a saint's death-mask, turns a vague, superb
    And timeless look

Upon these clocking hens
And the cocks that one by one,
After mortal dawn, with vulgar joy
    Acclaim the sun.

It is important, once you have found yourself responsive to the separate details in the poem, to remember always that the details do not exist as separate entities. Each one has a place in something the whole poem is trying to say and each one is part of the continuing felt sensing. The poet has chosen carefully the *proportion* each detail is to assume in the total poem; the reader must not blow up or warp single details so that it is impossible for a listener to follow this proportioning.

GESTURE AND ATTITUDE

We have discussed people as gesturing agents. Literature, because it is made up of language, is an art of gesture. Gestures in literature may be verbal or nonverbal. Empathy is a kind of gesturing of the reader in response to language signs. On a certain level, we like to feel words themselves. C. E. Montague has said that the mind will "finger single words and caress them, adoring the mellow fullness or granular hardness of their several sounds, the balance, undulation or trailing fall of their syllables, or the core of sun-like splendour in the broad, warm, central vowel of such a word as 'auroral.' Each word's evocative value or virtue, its individual power of touching springs in the mind and of initiating visions, becomes a treasure to revel in."[7]

There is a danger in Montague's view. It is more often than not an error to attribute innate qualities to individual sounds. Nevertheless, if one starts with what words mean, it is possible to say words in such a way that we show how the speaker feels. Sounds can be manipulated for specific effects in terms of meaning—not only can be, but must be.

[7] C. E. Montague, *A Writer's Notes on His Trade* (New York: Doubleday & Company, 1930), p. 30.

The term given to such manipulation is *tone color.* A line from Tennyson's "The Lotos-Eaters" which reads "Here are cool mosses deep" can be spoken in such a way as to underscore the coolness, the depth, the softness of the mosses, and this is the right way to read the line. But one can also read the line flatly, with no attention to tone color at all, though this is the wrong way to read the line. Most readers at first do not pay enough attention to tone color, to the gestures or tensiveness of the language. However, some experienced readers overemphasize tone color—at the expense of other elements in the language—and produce readings that are too ornate, and in which the sense itself may be lost. Tone coloring has a purpose: to arouse feelings necessary to the conveyance of meaning; it is not something valuable entirely of itself.

Language, then, has a kind of action built into it, if the reader will observe it. There is also often an action implied in words. A character in a story may say "I wouldn't give a snap of my fingers for him," and in real life such an individual might well accompany the statement with a snap of the fingers. Or a narrator in a story may say of a character "He lifted his eyes and looked longingly into the distance." An oral reader may make use of the literal actions suggested in such cases, being careful not to produce comic effects in serious literature by trying to reproduce literally *every* action suggested. When a writer summarizes a series of actions, this use of summary often indicates that he does not want the reader to linger over specific actions. For example, if a text reads "She got out of bed, put on her slippers, and went out into the kitchen to make the coffee," it would be ludicrous for the reader to try to *do* in a literal fashion each of these actions, though is useful to *imagine* them.

If, on the other hand, in a highly exciting scene (not in a summary), the writer suddenly says of a character "He glared at her," the reader may wish to make something of the implied action. It is important to resist the temptation to "act out" every word in the text; it is the feeling-state of the *whole* we are after, and too much pressure on individual words can destroy total effects. In such a sentence as "First she laughed and then she cried," for example, unless one is reaching for comic effects it would be ludicrous to laugh with the word *laughed* and cry with the word *cried.* The embodiment of the feeling-state of such a sentence does not call for such acting out of *words.* It is again, a matter of economy. The reader will observe the proportions that the writer has carefully indicated. Robert Breen has said it this way:

> Some gestures will illustrate or imitate, others will point or indicate, still others will emphasize; always they are to be regarded as intimately related to verbal speech. It is important to realize . . . that not all the gestures in a literary text . . . are necessarily the overt gestures apparent in real interpersonal communication.

> Gestures in literature range from the nervous behavior of some character in a story to the more highly symbolic gesticulation of the mouth in sounding a line of poetry. Properly, our interest has been

in the question of how these gestures in the literature affect the behavior of the reader. The hope is that the reader's imitation of the gestures expressed in the text will lead him to an understanding of those whose gestures he successfully imitates. A gesture transmits subconsciously a quality of thought or feeling which can be satisfactorily appreciated only if the observer imitates the gesture. This does not mean that a full overt expression of anguish on the part of a character in a novel must be *duplicated* by the reader if he is to understand the anguish fully. It is perfectly possible to imitate certain tensions characteristic of the original gesture and still inhibit the cry of anguish which was part of the original gesture.[8]

A helpful distinction has been made by both psychologists and literary critics. The interpreter need not carry out all the acts suggested in literature; nevertheless, it is necessary that he develop attitudes that show his understanding of the acts implied or expressed. Such attitudes involve tensions, empathy, and kinesthesis. The interpreter's participation in the literary text must be active, a reaching into the experience of the language.

MATERIALS FOR PRACTICE

In the following selections try to determine as accurately as you can the specific attitudes being conveyed. What overt gestures (if any) would you employ in your reading of the selections? Point out ways in which tone coloring will help the expression of the experience being described. Remember that your reading should also illustrate what you have learned in the entire chapter about kinesthesis, empathy, imagery, visualization, projection, management of the book. Try very hard to keep from concentrating on the printed page; look at the page as you need to (you will not need to look at it as often as you think), but focus your *attention* out in the room. The effort to project what you are reading ought to produce a kind of tension between you and the place in the room where you are imagining the scene to be, almost as if a string were stretched taut between you and the projected poem. When that tension is lost, projection fails.

from **ETHAN BRAND**
—*Nathaniel Hawthorne*

Bartram and his little son . . . sat watching the same lime-kiln that had been the scene of Ethan Brand's solitary and meditative life, before he began his search for the Unpardonable Sin. . . . The kiln . . . stood unimpaired, and was in nothing changed since he had thrown his dark thoughts into the

[8] Bacon and Breen, *Literature as Experience* (New York: McGraw-Hill Book Company, Inc., 1959), p. 302.

intense glow of its furnace, and melted them, as it were, into the one thought that took possession of his life. It was a rude, round, tower-like structure, about twenty feet high, heavily built of rough stones, and with a hillock of earth heaped about the larger part of its circumference; so that the blocks and fragments of marble might be drawn by cartloads, and thrown in at the top. There was an opening at the bottom of the tower, like an oven-mouth, but large enough to admit a man in a stooping posture, and provided with a massive iron door. With the smoke and jets of flame issuing from the chinks and crevices of this door, which seemed to give admittance into the hillside, it resembled nothing so much as the private entrance to the infernal regions, which the shepherds of the Delectable Mountains were accustomed to show to pilgrims. . . .

The man who now watched the fire . . . troubled himself with no thoughts save the very few that were requisite to his business. At frequent intervals, he flung back the clashing weight of the iron door, and, turning his face from the insufferable glare, thrust in huge logs of oak, or stirred the immense brands with a long pole. Within the furnace were seen the curling and riotous flames, and the burning marble, almost molten with the intensity of heat; while without, the reflection of the fire quivered on the dark intricacy of the surrounding forest, and showed in the foreground a bright and ruddy little picture of the hut, the spring beside its door, the athletic and coal-begrimed figure of the lime-burner, and the half-frightened child, shrinking into the protection of his father's shadow. And when again the iron door was closed, then reappeared the tender light of the half-full moon, which vainly strove to trace out the indistinct shapes of the neighboring mountains; and, in the upper sky, there was a flitting congregation of clouds, still faintly tinged with the rosy sunset, though thus far down into the valley the sunshine had vanished long and long ago.

AFTER APPLE-PICKING[9]
—Robert Frost

My long two-pointed ladder's sticking through a tree
Toward heaven still.
And there's the barrel that I didn't fill
Beside it, and there may be two or three
Apples I didn't pick upon some bough.
But I am done with apple-picking now.
Essence of winter sleep is on the night,
The scent of apples: I am drowsing off.
I cannot rub the strangeness from my sight
I got from looking through a pane of glass
I skimmed this morning from the drinking trough

And held against the world of hoary grass.
It melted, and I let it fall and break.
But I was well
Upon my way to sleep before it fell,
And I could tell
What form my dreaming was about to take.
Magnified apples appear and disappear,
Stem end and blossom end,
And every fleck of russet showing clear.
My instep arch not only keeps the ache,
It keeps the pressure of a ladder-round.
I feel the ladder sway as the boughs bend.
And I keep hearing from the cellar bin
The rumbling sound
Of load on load of apples coming in.
For I have had too much
Of apple-picking: I am overtired
Of the great harvest I myself desired.
There were ten thousand thousand fruit to touch,
Cherish in hand, lift down, and not let fall.
For all
That struck the earth,
No matter if not bruised or spiked with stubble,
Went surely to the cider-apple heap
As of no worth.
One can see what will trouble
This sleep of mine, whatever sleep it is.
Were he not gone,
The woodchuck could say whether it's like his
Long sleep, as I describe its coming on,
Or just some human sleep.

A YOUNG BIRCH[10]
—Robert Frost

The birch begins to crack its outer sheath
Of baby green and show the white beneath,
As whosoever likes the young and slight
May well have noticed. Soon entirely white
To double day and cut in half the dark
It will stand forth, entirely white in bark,
And nothing but the top a leafy green—
The only native tree that dares to lean,
Relying on its beauty, to the air.
(Less brave perhaps than trusting are the fair.)

And someone reminiscent will recall
How once in cutting brush along the wall
He spared it from the number of the slain,
At first to be no bigger than a cane,
And then no bigger than a fishing pole,
But now at last so obvious a bole
The most efficient help you ever hired
Would know that it was there to be admired,
And zeal would not be thanked that cut it down
When you were sick in bed or out of town.
It was a thing of beauty and was sent
To live its life out as an ornament.

from GRASMERE JOURNAL
—*Dorothy Wordsworth*

[April] 15th, Thursday. . . . When we were in the woods beyond Gowborrow
Park we saw a few daffodils close to the water-side. We fancied that the lake
had floated the seeds ashore, and that the little colony had so sprung up. But
as we went along there were more and yet more; and at last, under the
boughs of the trees, we saw that there was a long belt of them along the
shore, about the breadth of a country turnpike road. I never saw daffodils so
beautiful. They grew among the mossy stones about and about them; some
rested their heads upon these stones as on a pillow for weariness; and the
rest tossed and reeled and danced, and seemed as if they verily laughed with
the wind, that blew upon them over the lake; they looked so gay, ever
glancing, ever changing. This wind blew directly over the lake to them.
There was here and there a little knot, and a few stragglers a few yards
higher up; but they were so few as not to disturb the simplicity, unity, and
life of that one busy highway.

I WANDERED LONELY AS A CLOUD
—*William Wordsworth*

I wandered lonely as a cloud
That floats on high o'er vales and hills,
When all at once I saw a crowd,
A host, of golden daffodils;
Beside the lake, beneath the trees,
Fluttering and dancing in the breeze.

Continuous as the stars that shine
And twinkle on the Milky Way,
They stretched in never-ending line
Along the margin of a bay:
Ten thousand saw I at a glance,
Tossing their heads in sprightly dance.

The waves beside them danced; but they
Outdid the sparkling waves in glee:
A poet could not but be gay
In such a jocund company:
I gazed—and gazed—but little thought
What wealth the show to me had brought:

For oft, when on my couch I lie
In vacant or in pensive mood,
They flash upon that inward eye
Which is the bliss of solitude;
And then my heart with pleasure fills,
And dances with the daffodils.

SHAKING HANDS
—Leigh Hunt

Among the first things which we remember noticing in the manners of people, were two errors in the custom of shaking hands. Some, we observed, grasped everybody's hand alike—with an equal fervour of grip. You would have thought that Jenkins was the best friend they had in the world; but on succeeding to the squeeze, though a slight acquaintance, you found it equally flattering to yourself; and on the appearance of somebody else (whose name, it turned out, the operator had forgotten), the crush was no less complimentary:—the face was as earnest, and beaming, the "glad to see you" was syllabical and sincere, and the shake as close, as long, and as rejoicing, as if the semi-unknown was a friend come home from the Deserts.

On the other hand, there would be a gentleman, now and then, as coy of his hand, as if he were a prude, or had a whitlow. It was in vain that your pretensions did not go beyond the "civil salute" of the ordinary shake; or that being introduced to him in a friendly manner, and expected to shake hands with the rest of the company, you could not in decency omit his. His fingers half coming out and half retreating, seemed to think that you were going to do them a mischief; and when you got hold of them, the whole shake was on your side; the other hand did but proudly or pensively acquiesce—there was no knowing which; you had to sustain it, as you might a lady's in handling her to a seat; and it was an equal perplexity to know whether to shake or to let it go. The one seemed a violence done to the patient, the other an awkward responsibility brought upon yourself. You did not know, all the evening, whether you were an object of dislike to the person; till, on the party's breaking up, you saw him behave like an equally ill-used gentleman to all who practised the same unthinking civility.

Both these errors, we think, might as well be avoided; but, of the two, we must say we prefer the former. If it does not look so much like particular sincerity, it looks more like general kindness; and if those two virtues are to be separated (which they assuredly need not be, if considered without spleen), the world can better afford to dispense with an unpleasant truth than a gratuituous humanity. Besides, it is more difficult to make sure of the one than to practise the other, and kindness itself is the best of all truths. As long as we are sure of that, we are sure of something, and of something pleasant. It is always the best end, if not in every instance the most logical means.

This manual shyness is sometimes attributed to modesty, but never, we suspect, with justice, unless it be that sort of modesty whose fear of committing itself is grounded in pride. Want of address is a better reason; but this particular instance of it would be grounded in the same feeling. It always implies a habit either of pride or mistrust. We have met with two really kind men who evinced this soreness of hand. Neither of them, perhaps, thought to think highly of themselves, but both had been sanguine men contradicted in their early hopes. There was a plot to meet the hand of one of them with a fish-slice, in order to show him the disadvantage to which he put his friends by that flat mode of salutation; but the conspirator had not the courage to do it. Whether he heard of the intention we know not, but shortly afterwards he took very kindly to a shake. The other was the only man of a warm set of politicians who remained true to his first hopes of mankind. He was impatient at the change in his companions, and at the folly and inattention of the rest; but though his manner became cold, his consistency remained warm, and this gave him a right to be as strange as he pleased.

WHAT IS POETRY[11]
—John Ashbery

> The medieval town, with frieze
> Of boy scouts from Nagoya? The snow
>
> That came when we wanted it to snow?
> Beautiful images? Trying to avoid
>
> Ideas, as in this poem? But we
> Go back to them as to a wife, leaving
>
> The mistress we desire? Now they
> Will have to believe it
>
> As we believe it. In school
> All the thought got combed out:
>
> What was left was like a field.
> Shut your eyes, and you can feel it for miles around.
>
> Now open them on a thin vertical path.
> It might give us—what?—some flowers soon?

[11] From *Houseboat Days* by John Ashbery. Copyright © 1975, 1976, 1977 by John Ashbery. First appeared in *Vanderbilt Poetry Review*. Reprinted by permission of the author and The Viking Press.

THE MASQUE OF THE RED DEATH
—*Edgar Allan Poe*

The "Red Death" had long devastated the country. No pestilence had ever been so fatal, or so hideous. Blood was its Avator and its seal—the redness and the horror of blood. There were sharp pains, and sudden dizziness, and then profuse bleeding at the pores, with dissolution. The scarlet stains upon the body and especially upon the face of the victim, were the pest ban which shut him out from the aid and from the sympathy of his fellowmen. And the whole seizure, progress and termination of the disease, were the incidents of half an hour.

But the Prince Prospero was happy and dauntless and sagacious. When his dominions were half depopulated, he summoned to his presence a thousand hale and light-hearted friends from among the knights and dames of his court, and with these retired to the deep seclusion of one of his castellated abbeys. This was an extensive and magnificent structure, the creation of the prince's own eccentric yet august taste. A strong and lofty wall girdled it in. This wall had gates of iron. The courtiers, having entered, brought furnaces and massy hammers and welded the bolts. They resolved to leave means neither of ingress or egress to the sudden impulses of despair or of frenzy from within. The abbey was amply provisioned. With such precautions the courtiers might bid defiance to contagion. The external world could take care of itself. In the meantime it was folly to grieve, or to think. The prince had provided all the appliances of pleasure. There were buffoons, there were improvisatori, there were ballet-dancers, there were musicians, there was Beauty, there was wine. All these and security were within. Without was the "Red Death."

It was toward the close of the fifth or sixth month of his seclusion, and while the pestilence raged most furiously abroad, that the Prince Prospero entertained his thousand friends at a masked ball of the most unusual magnificence.

It was a voluptuous scene, that masquerade. But first let me tell of the rooms in which it was held. There were seven—an imperial suite. In many palaces, however, such suites form a long and straight vista, while the folding doors slide back nearly to the walls on either hand, so that the view of the whole extent is scarcely impeded. Here the case was very different; as might have been expected from the duke's love of the *bizarre*. The apartments were so irregularly disposed that the vision embraced but little more than one at a time. There was a sharp turn at every twenty or thirty yards, and at each turn a novel effect. To the right and left, in the middle of each wall, a tall and narrow Gothic window looked out upon a closed corridor which pursued the windings of the suite. These windows were of stained glass whose color varied in accordance with the prevailing hue of the decorations of the chamber into which it opened. That at the eastern extremity was hung, for example, in blue—and vividly blue were its windows. The second chamber was purple in its ornaments and tapestries, and here the panes were purple. The third was green throughout, and so were the casements. The fourth was furnished and lighted with orange—the fifth with white—the

sixth with violet. The seventh apartment was closely shrouded in black velvet tapestries that hung all over the ceiling and down the walls, falling in
heavy folds upon a carpet of the same material and hue. But in this chamber
only, the color of the windows failed to correspond with the decorations.
The panes here were scarlet—a deep blood color. Now in no one of the
seven apartments was there any lamp or candelabrum, amid the profusion of
golden ornaments that lay scattered to and fro or depended from the roof.
There was no light of any kind emanating from lamp or candle within the
suite of chambers. But in the corridors that followed the suite, there stood,
opposite to each window, a heavy tripod, bearing a brazier of fire that projected its rays through the tinted glass and so glaringly illumined the room.
And thus were produced a multitude of gaudy and fantastic appearances.
But in the western or black chamber the effect of the firelight that streamed
upon the dark hangings through the blood-tinted panes, was ghastly in the
extreme, and produced so wild a look upon the countenances of those who
entered, that there were few of the company bold enough to set foot within
its precincts at all.

It was in this apartment, also, that there stood against the western wall,
a gigantic clock of ebony. Its pendulum swung to and fro with a dull, heavy,
monotonous clang; and when the minute-hand made the circuit of the face,
and the hour was to be stricken, there came from the brazen lungs of the
clock a sound which was clear and loud and deep and exceedingly musical,
but of so peculiar a note and emphasis that, at each lapse of an hour, the
musicians of the orchestra were constrained to pause, momentarily, in their
performance, to hearken to the sound; an thus the waltzers perforce ceased
their evolutions; and there was a brief disconcert of the whole gay company;
and, while the chimes of the clock yet rang, it was observed that the giddiest
grew pale, and the more aged and sedate passed their hands over their brows
as if in confused revery or meditation. But when the echoes had fully ceased,
a light laughter at once pervaded the assembly; the musicians looked at each
other and smiled as if at their own nervousness and folly, and made whispering vows, each to the other, that the next chiming of the clock should
produce in them no similar emotion; and then, after the lapse of sixty minutes (which embrace three thousand and six hundred seconds of the Time
that flies,) there came yet another chiming of the clock, and then were the
same disconcert and tremulousness and meditation as before.

But, in spite of these things, it was a gay and magnificent revel. The
tastes of the duke were peculiar. He had a fine eye for colors and effects. He
disregarded the *decora* of mere fashion. His plans were bold and fiery, and
his conceptions glowed with barbaric lustre. There are some who would have
thought him mad. His followers felt that he was not. It was necessary to hear
and see and touch him to be *sure* that he was not.

He had directed, in great part, the movable embellishments of the
seven chambers, upon occasion of this great *fête*; and it was his own guiding
taste which had given character to the masqueraders. Be sure they were
grotesque. There were much glare and glitter and piquancy and phantasm—
much of what has been since seen in "Hernani." There were arabesque

figures with unsuited limbs and appointments. There were delirious fancies such as the madman fashions. There was much of the beautiful, much of the wanton, much of the *bizarre*, something of the terrible, and not a little of that which might have excited disgust. To and fro in the seven chambers there stalked, in fact, a multitude of dreams. And these—the dreams— writhed in and about, taking hue from the rooms, and causing the wild music of the orchestra to seem as the echo of their steps. And, anon, there strikes the ebony clock which stands in the hall of the velvet. And then, for a moment, all is still, and all is silent save the voice of the clock. The dreams are stiff-frozen as they stand. But the echoes of the chime die away—they have endured but an instant—and a light, half-subdued laughter floats after them as they depart. And now again the music swells, and the dreams live, and writhe to and fro more merrily than ever, taking hue from the many tinted windows through which stream the rays from the tripods. But to the chamber which lies most westwardly of the seven, there are now none of the maskers who venture; for the night is waning away; and there flows a ruddier light through the blood-colored panes; and the blackness of the sable drapery appalls; and to him whose foot falls upon the sable carpet, there comes from the near clock of ebony a muffled peal more solemnly emphatic than any which reaches *their* ears who indulge in the more remote gayeties of the other apartments.

But these other apartments were densely crowded, and in them beat feverishly the heart of life. And the revel went whirlingly on, until at length there commenced the sounding of midnight upon the clock. And then the music ceased, as I have told; and the evolutions of the waltzers were quieted; and there was an uneasy cessation of all things as before. But now there were twelve strokes to be sounded by the bell of the clock; and thus it happened, perhaps, that more of thought crept, with more of time, into the meditations of the thoughtful among those who revelled. And thus, too, it happened, perhaps, that before the last echoes of the last chime had utterly sunk into silence, there were many individuals in the crowd who had found leisure to become aware of the presence of a masked figure which had arrested the attention of no single individual before. And the rumor of this new presence having spread itself whisperingly around, there arose at length from the whole company, a buzz, or murmur, expressive of disapprobation and surprise—then, finally, of terror, of horror, and of disgust.

In an assembly of phantasm such as I have painted, it may well be supposed that no ordinary appearance could have excited such sensation. In truth the masquerade license of the night was nearly unlimited; but the figure in question had out-Heroded Herod, and gone beyond the bounds of even the prince's indefinite decorum. There are chords in the hearts of the most reckless which cannot be touched without emotion. Even with the utterly lost, to whom life and death are equally jests, there are matters of which no jest can be made. The whole company, indeed, seemed now deeply to feel that in the costume and bearing of the stranger neither wit nor propriety existed. The figure was tall and gaunt, and shrouded from head to foot in the habiliments of the grave. The mask which concealed the visage was made so nearly to resemble the countenance of a stiffened corpse that the closest scrutiny must have had difficulty in detecting the cheat. And yet all this might have been endured, if not approved, by the mad revellers around. But the mummer had gone so far as to assume the type of the Red Death. His vesture was dabbled in *blood*—and his broad brow, with all the features of the face, was besprinkled with the scarlet horror.

When the eyes of Prince Prospero fell upon this spectral image (which with a slow and solemn movement, as if more fully to sustain its *rôle*, stalked to and fro among the waltzers) he was seen to be convulsed, in the first moment, with a strong shudder either of terror or distaste; but, in the next, his brow reddened with rage.

"Who dares?" he demanded hoarsely of the courtiers who stood near him—"who dares insult us with this blasphemous mockery? Seize him and unmask him—that we may know whom we have to hang at sunrise, from the battlements!"

It was in the eastern or blue chamber in which stood the Prince Prospero as he uttered these words. They rang throughout the seven rooms loudly and clearly—for the prince was a bold and robust man, and the music had become hushed at the waving of his hand.

It was in the blue room where stood the prince, with a group of pale courtiers by his side. At first, as he spoke, there was a slight rushing movement of this group in the direction of the intruder, who at the moment was also near at hand, and now, with deliberate and stately step, made closer approach to the speaker. But from a certain nameless awe with which the mad assumptions of the mummer had inspired the whole party, there were found none who put forth hand to seize him; so that, unimpeded, he passed within a yard of the prince's person; and, while the vast assembly, as if with one impulse, shrank from the centres of the rooms to the walls, he made his way uninterruptedly, but with the same solemn and measured step which had distinguished him from the first, through the blue chamber to the purple—through the purple to the green—through the green to the orange—through this again to the white—and even thence to the violet, ere a decided movement had been made to arrest him. It was then, however, that the Prince Prospero, maddening with rage and the shame of his own momentary cowardice, rushed hurriedly through the six chambers, while none followed him on account of a deadly terror that had seized upon all. He bore aloft a drawn dagger, and had approached, in rapid impetuosity, to within three or four feet of the retreating figure, when the latter, having attained the extremity of the velvet apartment, turned suddenly and confronted his pursuer. There was a sharp cry—and the dagger dropped gleaming upon the sable carpet, upon which, instantly afterwards, fell prostrate in death the Prince Prospero. Then, summoning the wild courage of despair, a throng of the revellers at once threw themselves into the black apartment, and, seizing the mummer, whose tall figure stood erect and motionless within the shadow of the ebony clock, gasped in unutterable horror at finding the grave-cerements and corpse-like mask which they handled with so violent a rudeness, untenanted by any tangible form.

And now was acknowledged the presence of the Red Death. He had come like a thief in the night. And one by one dropped the revellers in the blood-bedewed halls of their revel, and died each in the despairing posture of his fall. And the life of the ebony clock went out with that of the last of the gay. And the flames of the tripods expired. And Darkness and Decay and the Red Death held illimitable dominion over all.

A SUBALTERN'S LOVE-SONG[12]
—John Betjeman

Miss J. Hunter Dunn, Miss J. Hunter Dunn,
Furnish'd and burnish'd by Aldershot sun,
What strenuous singles we played after tea,
We in the tournament—you against me!

Love-thirty, love-forty, oh! weakness of joy,
The speed of a swallow, the grace of a boy,
With carefullest carelessness, gaily you won,
I am weak from your loveliness, Joan Hunter Dunn.

Miss Joan Hunter Dunn, Miss Joan Hunter Dunn,
How mad I am, sad I am, glad that you won.
The warm-handled racket is back in its press,
But my shock-headed victor, she loves me no less.

Her father's euonymus shines as we walk,
And swing past the summer-house, buried in talk,
And cool the verandah that welcomes us in
To the six-o'clock news and a lime-juice and gin.

The scent of the conifers, sound of the bath,
The view from my bedroom of moss-dappled path,
As I struggle with double-end evening tie,
For we dance at the Golf Club, my victor and I.

On the floor of her bedroom lie blazer and shorts
And the cream-coloured walls are be-trophied with sports,
And westering, questioning settles the sun
On your low-leaded window, Miss Joan Hunter Dunn.

The Hillman is waiting, the light's in the hall,
The pictures of Egypt are bright on the wall,
My sweet, I am standing beside the oak stair
And there on the landing's the light on your hair.

[12] From *Collected Poems by* John Betjeman. Reprinted by permission of John Murray (Publishers) Ltd. and Houghton Mifflin Co.

By roads "not adopted," by woodlanded ways,
She drove to the club in the late summer haze,
Into nine-o'clock Camberley, heavy with bells
And mushroomy, pine-woody, evergreen smells.

Miss Joan Hunter Dunn, Miss Joan Hunter Dunn,
I can hear from the car-park the dance has begun.
Oh! full Surrey twilight! important band!
Oh! strongly adorable tennis-girl's hand!

Around us are Rovers and Austins afar,
Above us, the intimate roof of the car,
And here on my right is the girl of my choice,
With the tilt of her nose and the chime of her voice,

And the scent of her wrap, and the words never said,
And the ominous, ominous dancing ahead.
We sat in the car park till twenty to one
And now I'm engaged to Miss Joan Hunter Dunn.

BUT HE WAS COOL

or: he even stopped for green lights[13]
—Don L. Lee

super-cool
ultrablack
a tan/purple
had a beautiful shade.

he had a double-natural
that wd put the sisters to shame.
his dashikis were tailor made
& his beads were imported sea shells
    (from some blk/country i never heard of)
he was triple-hip.

his tikis were hand carved
out of ivory
& came express from the motherland.
he would greet u in swahili
& say good-by in yoruba.
woooooooooooo-jim he bes so cool & ill tel li gent
              cool-cool is so cool he was un-cooled by
                    other niggers' cool

[13] From *Don't Cry Scream*, copyright 1969 by Don L. Lee. Reprinted by permission of Broadside Press.

cool-cool ultracool was bop-cool/ice box
      cool so cool cold cool
his wine didn't have to be cooled, him was
      air conditioned cool
cool-cool/real cool made me cool—now
      ain't that cool
cool-cool so cool him nick-named refrigerator.

cool-cool so cool
he didn't know,
after detroit, newark, chicago &c.,
we had to hip
          cool-cool/super-cool/real cool
      that
to be black
is
to be
very-hot.

FIRST LESSON[14]
—Phyllis McGinley

The thing to remember about fathers is, they're men.
A girl has to keep it in mind.
They are dragon-seekers, bent on improbable rescues.
Scratch any father, you find
Someone chock-full of qualms and romantic terrors,
Believing change is a threat—
Like your first shoes with heels on, like your first bicycle
It took such months to get.

Walk in strange woods, they warn you about the snakes there.
Climb, and they fear you'll fall.
Books, angular boys, or swimming in deep water—
Fathers mistrust them all.
Men are the worriers. It is difficult for them
To learn what they must learn:
How you have to journey to take and very likely,
For a while, will not return.

LOVE SONG[15]
—Dorothy Parker

My own dear love, he is strong and bold
   And he cares not what comes after.
His words ring sweet as a chime of gold,
   And his eyes are lit with laughter.
He is jubilant as a flag unfurled—
   Oh, a girl, she'd not forget him.
My own dear love, he is all my world—
   And I wish I'd never met him.

My love, he's mad, and my love, he's fleet,
   And a wild young wood-thing bore him!
The ways are fair to his roaming feet,
   And the skies are sunlit for him.
As sharply sweet to my heart he seems
   As the fragrance of acacia.
My own dear love, he is all my dreams—
   And I wish he was in Asia.

My love runs by like a day in June,
   And he makes no friends of sorrows.
He'll tread his galloping rigadoon
   In the pathway of the morrows.
He'll live his days where the sunbeams start,
   Nor could storm or wind uproot him.
My own dear love, he is all my heart—
   And I wish somebody'd shoot him.

FIFTEEN[16]
—William Stafford

South of the bridge on Seventeenth
I found back of the willows one summer
day a motorcycle with engine running
as it lay on its side, ticking over
slowly in the high grass. I was fifteen.

I admired all that pulsing gleam, the
shiny flanks, the demure headlights
fringed where it lay; I led it gently
to the road and stood with that
companion, ready and friendly. I was fifteen.

We could find the end of a road, meet
the sky on out Seventeenth. I thought about
hills, and patting the handle got back a
confident opinion. On that bridge we indulged
a forward feeling, a tremble. I was fifteen.

Thinking, back farther in the grass I found
the owner, just coming to, where he had flipped
over the rail. He had blood on his hand, was pale—
I helped him walk to his machine. He ran his hand
over it, called me good man, roared away.

I stood there, fifteen.

from SPOON RIVER ANTHOLOGY[17]
—*Edgar Lee Masters*

Knowlt Hoheimer

I was the first fruits of the battle of Missionary Ridge.
When I felt the bullet enter my heart
I wished I had staid at home and gone to jail
For stealing the hogs of Curl Trenary,
Instead of running away and joining the army.
Rather a thousand times the county jail
Than to lie under this marble figure with wings,
And this granite pedestal
Bearing the words, "*Pro Patria*."
What do they mean, anyway?

Minerva Jones

I am Minerva, the village poetess,
Hooted at, jeered at by the Yahoos of the street
For my heavy body, cock-eye, and rolling walk,
And all the more when "Butch" Weldy
Captured me after a brutal hunt.
He left me to my fate with Doctor Meyers;
And I sank into death, growing numb from the feet up,
Like one stepping deeper and deeper into a stream of ice.
Will some one go to the village newspaper,
And gather into a book the verses I wrote?—
I thirsted so for love!
I hungered so for life!

[17] Reprinted by permission of the Trustees of the Edgar Lee Masters Estate.

Doctor Meyers

No other man, unless it was Doc Hill,
Did more for people in this town than I.
And all the weak, the halt, the improvident
And those who could not pay flocked to me.
I was good-hearted, easy Doctor Meyers.
I was healthy, happy, in comfortable fortune,
Blest with a congenial mate, my children raised,
All wedded, doing well in the world.
And then one night, Minerva, the poetess,
Came to me in her trouble, crying.
I tried to help her out—she died—
They indicted me, the newspapers disgraced me,
My wife perished of a broken heart.
And pneumonia finished me.

Mrs. Meyers

He protested all his life long
The newspapers lied about him villainously;
That he was not at fault for Minerva's fall,
But only tried to help her.
Poor soul so sunk in sin he could not see
That even trying to help her, as he called it,
He had broken the law human and divine.
Passers-by, an ancient admonition to you:
If your ways would be ways of pleasantness,
And all your pathways peace,
Love God and keep his commandments.

Chapter 3

THE PRESENCE OF LITERATURE

In speaking of the *presential* quality of reality, philosopher Philip Wheelwright has said:

> A person's sense of presence is likely to be most strongly marked and most incontestably evident in his relationship, at certain heightened moments, with another human person. This is as it should be, for an individual sinks into a deadening egoism (however much he may gild it with idealistic verbiage or mitigate it by outward acts) unless he occasionally exercises and stretches his ability to realize another person as an independent presence to whom homage is due, rather than as merely an interruption of continuity in his environment. To know someone as a presence instead of as a lump of matter or a set of processes, is to meet him with an open, listening, responsive attitude; it is to become a *thou* in the presence of his *I*-hood.[1]

This sense of the reality of the other's *otherness* is the sense of presence;

[1] Philip Wheelwright, *Metaphor and Reality* (Bloomington: Indiana University Press, 1962), p. 154.

and, as Wheelwright recognizes, it can be felt toward inanimate as well as animate things. The Acropolis in Athens, which arrests one with its being; the cone of Mt. Fuji, which leads thousands in Japan to admire it; the Grand Canyon in Arizona, which amazes the sight—such inanimate objects all impress us with their presence. They *are,* and the aura of their *be*ing scarcely requires explanation. They increase our *own* awareness of the world. But lesser objects, too, can impress any one of us at any moment with a similar sense of their otherness: a flower in the garden, a sunset in the west, a redbird at the feeding station—our lives are filled with such momentary presences, which sometimes stay with us in memory for the remainder of our lives.

People often compel us in this way. It is common to speak of the great actor or actress as having "great stage presence." They compel our attention. There is about them a sense of the fullness with which they *are*, and we behave in their presence as if we were in a magnetic field, responding in a strongly *felt* way to their energies.

This response to presence is not really rare. All of us feel it from time to time. But it is scarcely the condition of our everyday lives; while it is not unique, neither is it ordinary. It is likely to be memorable beyond our memories of day-to-date routine.

Literature has presence. Its sense of presence may arise from any one, or a combination, of many qualities—striking figures of speech, rhythms, sounds, characterization, plot, passages of dialogue, descriptions; the list is almost endless. The reader giving rapt attention to the literary work is engaged with the sense of its otherness, as in the poem by Wallace Stevens at the beginning of this volume. For the interpreter, belief in the otherness of the text, full awareness of its state of being, is a major stage in mastering the art of performance.

In talking about the reality of prayer, the English poet and preacher John Donne confessed that often when he fell upon his knees to pray he was distracted by the rumbling of a passing cart, by the buzzing of a fly; such distractions interfered with the full reality of the communion he was trying to achieve with God. In a way, this is the problem of the oral reader: how to achieve full communion with the work of art when everything around him tempts him to lose contact with it. This is one of the dangers of an audience; it may distract the reader and lead him to play up to his listeners at the expense of the work of art. To say this is not to minimize the significance of the audience but to recognize an additional matter with which the performer must learn to cope. The field of energy created in an audience situation may—depending on the nature and degree of that energy—either serve or damage, inform or deform the performance. But when the interpreter achieves full communion with the work of art, and when the audience in turn joins him in full response, he has arrived.

The following diagram suggests a relationship between poem and interpreter that will be helpful:

It is possbile to think of the words on the page, the "thing seen," as the outer form of the poem. The words on the page are symbols pointing to the inner meaning, an experience or presence that *is* the poem. The outer form is a potential cause of that experience, an experience that is to be made real in different ways by different readers. What the interpreter does, through the arduous discipline that constitutes the art of interpretation, is to establish some congruence between the inner form of the poem and his own inner self (working backward and forward between the poem and himself), and then to embody the poem—literally giving body to experience—so that through his own outer form (his voice, his countenance, his body) he in a sense becomes the poem. The poem now becomes audible and visible—and if the interpreter succeeds in establishing congruence between the inner form of the poem and his own inner form, if he achieves a coalescence of the two things, the poem will be alive, will have presence, will be an organism.

It may be helpful to think of the poem-as-body in physiological terms. All living organisms are active—they participate in acts. The act is the basic unit of life forms.[2] Its characteristics are inception, acceleration, climax, and cadence (falling off). The life cycle itself is such an act—the total act that subsumes smaller acts. It takes place within a form, or structure, and has a rhythm. Form is the place-where-life-lives. Like a plant (the metaphor is traditional), a poem takes shape and develops first slowly, then more rapidly, until it is fully developed; after that it ends. Just as the plant must make contact with the external world to live, so must the poem, which in effect remains unconscious until it is brought to consciousness by a reader. The form itself is the boundary that both cuts the plant and the poem off from the outside world and is the point of contact with that world. Seen this way, the poem is a body, a life form, which means that it is active. The interpreter too is a body and is active. The process of interpreting is a process of matching the acts of the poem with the acts of the performer—the body of the poem

[2] This discussion of acts stems from Susanne Langer, *Mind: An Essay on Human Feeling* (Baltimore: Johns Hopkins Press, 1967).

with the body of the reader. Perfect congruence is not possible, not even to be hoped for, since there are in fact two different bodies involved. But it is best for the interpreter to seek to match his body with that of the poem, since the the interpreter exists (in terms of his art form) to perform the poem. Certain "personality readers" seek instead to turn all poems into their own bodies, and they make all poems sound pretty much alike. However profitable commercially such a personality reader may be, he is not the kind of performer we are interested in developing. Such readers do not grow, they stagnate; as artists they die.

MATCHING   Each matching of poem and reader will have its unique qualities. If five students read the same poem, there will be five somewhat different "bodies" perceptible to an audience. Twin performances may be possible, but they are rare. Nevertheless, something would surely be amiss if it were not possible to sense resemblance, blood relationships, among the bodies. While the body acts of the interpreter make the performance in some sense *that* interpreter's poem, the body of the poem itself must not disappear in the matching. While it is possible for an interpreter to kill off a poem in performance (happily, the poem's body is not permanently destroyed, since it can be revivified in another performance), no reader worthy of his salt will want to destroy or to damage it. The interpreter must not deny to the body of the poem its right to exist. It is perhaps not too much to suggest that ideally there is a love relationship between reader and poem.

RESPONSIVENESS   Love is an experience of the loved one as *another*—another whose being is somehow heightened in the recognition of its otherness. (As we have said, one may have this same sense of the otherness of objects, whether animate or inanimate.) This sense of the otherness of the other is a kind of miraculism, drawing us out of ourselves into a communion with the rest of the world. It is responsiveness. Responsible people are responsive people. All readers of literature ought to be responsive to literature, and the oral reader *must* be responsive. You may call this responding an "act of imagination," but that will not be a sufficient definition for the interpreter. He or she must finally respond in terms of voice, body, mind, heart, spirit—and must in the process learn to make each of these parts so flexible and sensitive that they can together encompass the experience of literature. The interpreter is like the dancer; the ideal situation, as seen by Yeats, is that in which the beholder cannot tell the dancer from the dance. But in the preparation of the dance, whenever there is a failure to achieve union with the form the dancer must look carefully to discover what has gone wrong.

If we return again to the diagram on page 37, we can doubtless say that the stage where the two inner forms are matched becomes the subtlest for the performer, and the stage at which teachers often find their greatest challenges. There are well-defined traditional methods of inquiry that move readers from the poem-in-print to cognitive apprehension of meaning. (Many of them are to be found in the second part of this textbook.) We know that some meanings are dictated by the structure of our language; syntax certainly controls directions in which we are free to move in interpretation. We can learn to examine structures such as meter, plot, and scene; we can follow certain kinds of directions for controlling tempos; we can learn to distinguish kinds of narrator, to assemble evidence of characterization, to establish crisis and climax in an action. These are all conscious, cognitive processes, and they are of considerable importance in coming to some sense of the body which is clothed in language. Nor is this cognitive process divorced from feeling responses. Study should lead to a sense of the life of the literature, but from the very beginning of our study in this book, we are concerned with the way thinking feels. We have begun with the poem itself. More detailed critical analysis, as a way of sharpening and deeping perceptions, will follow in Part Two. The best performance of a work of literature, as we see it, is the most complex reading the body of the text will bear. Ultimately, no form of analysis can be too subtle for the serious interpreter. This is not to say that there are not some readings too subtle for a text—more than the text can bear. (They are not usually the kind of reading a student performer comes to first!)

As the reader reads, silently or aloud—and if he or she *really* reads rather than simply looks at words—feeling responses accompany perception. They are not added on but are an integral part of the perceptual process, just as our perception of a sunset or a story or a flower or a dog or a child is accompanied by feeling responses. Pure intellectuality is not possible for the human being. Nor is pure sensationalism. Mind and body cohere, though all our history tells us that we are at certain times more simply concerned with either intellect or the senses than at others. Scientific discourse, for example, more often than not wishes to free us as much as possible from the way words feel, to throw the *concept* itself into highest relief. Certain kinds of oratory may seek to envelop us in sensation—some kinds of pulpit oratory or some kinds or political oratory, for example. Literature on the whole resides between these two poles, though it may tend to move toward one or the other in individual cases. Literature asks us to feel concepts, to feel the act of cognition in many ways—through rhythms, through sounds, through the interplay of characters, through narrative perspectives, and so on. In short, literature exists in tensive states, and one kind of tensiveness resides in the play between what words say and how words feel. They do not feel and say the same things to all readers. But as they say and feel to *you,* you begin to participate in the matching of inner forms,

RATIONAL AND
NONRATIONAL
PROCESSES
IN MATCHING

yours and the poem's. If you really listen, you respond. Some of your response is dictated by the structure that is the body of the poem; some of your response is dictated by the structure that is *you*. But in this matching of form with form, in the creation of presence, something new is always created. You and the poem participate in an act that is genuinely creative. The best kind of participation, in our view, is that which respects the body of the poem to begin with and to end with, which is capable of a certain humility in its relation with the poem. But humility is not timidity.

After the matching of inner forms is complete, there always remain certain choices (whether deliberate or intuitive) to be made in the *overt* act of performance. How does one convey to others the perceptions one has of the text? There are esthetic decisions to be made. But first of all, one must be as sensitively aligned with the text as possible. When you *realize* the poem, the poem alters you, just as it is itself always in some ways altered. It is important that the alteration be, as much as possible, to the advantage of both forms.

THE SENSE OF THE OTHER

What gives a work of literature its sense of presence? We can ask certain questions about a poem: Who wrote it, in what language is it written, what is its classification, what is its central idea or theme, what kinds of images does it contain? But these are all peripheral questions. The miracle of experiencing a tree or a flower does not require that we know how long it has taken to grow. It is not a matter of information; it is in some final way a mystery to which we pay homage, a mystery in which *tensiveness* and *coalescence* and *perspective* are involved, to borrow the terms employed by Philip Wheelwright. It is an acceptance of the otherness of the other.

We shall look at each of these terms. But first read the following passage from Eudora Welty's "A Visit of Charity." Read it attentively. Be responsive.

A VISIT OF CHARITY[3]
—*Eudora Welty*

It was mid-morning—a very cold, bright day. Holding a potted plant before her, a girl of fourteen jumped off the bus in front of the Old Ladies' Home, on the outskirts of town. She wore a red coat, and her straight yellow hair was hanging down loose from the pointed white cap all the little girls were wearing that year. She stopped for a moment beside one of the prickly dark shrubs with which the city had beautified the Home, and then proceeded slowly toward the building, which was of whitewashed brick and reflected the winter sunlight like a block of ice. As she walked vaguely up the steps she shifted the small pot from hand to hand; then she had to set it down and remove her mittens before she could open the heavy door.

"I'm a Campfire Girl. . . . I have to pay a visit to some old lady," she told the nurse at the desk. This was a woman in a white uniform who looked as if she were cold; she had close-cut hair which stood up on the very top of her head exactly like a sea wave. Marian, the little girl, did not tell her that this visit would give her a minimum of only three points in her score.

"Acquainted with any of our residents?" asked the nurse. She lifted one eyebrow and spoke like a man.

"With any old ladies? No—but—that is, any of them will do," Marian stammered. With her free hand she pushed her hair behind her ears, as she did when it was time to study Science.

The nurse shrugged and rose. "You have a nice *multiflora cineraria* there," she remarked as she walked ahead down the hall of closed doors to pick out an old lady.

There was loose, bulging linoleum on the floor. Marian felt as if she were walking on the waves, but the nurse paid no attention to it. There was a smell in the hall like the interior of a clock. Everything was silent until, behind one of the doors, an old lady of some kind cleared her throat like a sheep bleating. This decided the nurse. Stopping in her tracks, she first extended her arm, bent her elbow, and leaned forward from the hips—all to examine the watch strapped to her wrist; then she gave a loud double-rap on the door.

"There are two in each room," the nurse remarked over her shoulder.

"Two what?" asked Marian without thinking. The sound like a sheep's bleating almost made her turn around and run back.

One old woman was pulling the door open in short, gradual jerks, and when she saw the nurse a strange smile forced her old face dangerously awry. Marian, suddenly propelled by the strong, impatient arm of the nurse, saw next the sideface of another old woman, even older, who was lying flat in bed with a cap on and a counterpane drawn up to her chin.

"Visitor," said the nurse, and after one more shove she was off up the hall.

Marian stood tongue-tied; both hands held the potted plant. The old woman, still that terrible, square smile (which was a smile of welcome) stamped on her bony face, was waiting. . . .

This selection is filled with tensiveness.[4] It moves rhythmically between contrary pulls—between the ordinary and the unusual, between the

TENSIVENESS

---

[4] *Tensiveness* is here preferred to *tension,* since the latter word often has about it an aura of distress, a feeling of anxiety. The word *tensiveness* includes this notion of tension but is not limited to it.

warmth of a red coat and the cold of white bricks, between the freshness of a potted plant and the unfriendliness of prickly dark shrubs, between a "good deed" and a "duty." These oppositions create awareness in us if we attend to them without distraction. There are many other ways of creating tensiveness in language, and we shall look at them later: meter, rhyme, and tone color in poetry; conflict in drama; movements between summary and scene and description in fiction. But it is enough at present to look at the relationship between the young girl and the old ladies she has come to "visit." There is a constant ambivalence here, a looking two ways, a juxtaposition of two kinds of values, all of which Welty carefully controls. There is, finally, a tension between all the particular details the storywriter employs and the possible details she has omitted. What, for example, was Marian like at home?

Notice the contrast between the precision of purpose with which Marian comes (to gain points) and the vagueness with which she walks toward the Home. The day is cold but bright; the sunlight makes the Home look like a block of ice; the shrubs are dark and prickly. The nurse in her white uniform looks "as if she were cold." Her close-cut hair looks like a sea wave. (Notice that Marian wears a pointed white cap, but that her yellow hair hangs loose.) The linoleum bulges in waves, making Marian feel as if she were walking on water. The hallway smells like the interior of a clock, but the hall is silent—as if the clock had stopped. The old lady behind the closed door sounds like an animal. (Why a sheep?) Notice how the nurse first stops, then extends an arm, bends an elbow, and leans forward from the hips to examine her watch—like an automaton.

The door is opened in short, gradual jerks. What is the force of the strain between the words *smile* and *square* as the old woman stands waiting? And notice now how out-of-place that potted plant (named only with its Latin name, *multiflora cineraria*) has become. Marian held it in front of her as she jumped from the bus, shifted it from one mittened hand to another as she went up the steps, set it down to remove her mittens before opening the door—and now she stands tongue-tied at the door of the room, holding it in both hands. Can you sense the feeling in Marian's hands as she holds the flower pot? Try reading the passage aloud now, responding to these tensions but not forgetting that Marian, a fourteen-year-old, is not herself aware of all of them.

There are difficult matters here. As we shall see later on, in discussing the formal construction of fiction, *point of view* is operative in the selection of details. The writer, or the storyteller (they are not always simply to be identified in fiction), decides what we are to be given. But at what point does the control exercised by the teller begin to slacken? Does the dialogue sound like the teller, or like Marian and the nurse? To put it another way, does the voice of the teller disappear as we hear the actual words of Marian and the nurse, or do we get the teller's version, vocally, of these two characters? The tensive relationship between teller and character is a matter for finely tuned distinctions, and we shall return to it again.

COALESCENCE

We have been talking about ways in which elements of a literary work exist in states of tensiveness. We shall return to tensiveness in Chapter 6. Meanwhile, it is important to remember that ultimately tensive elements need to coalesce. *Coalescence* comes from the Latin word *coalescens,* meaning "growing up together," "growing together as the halves of a broken bone grow together." The fully effective literary work meshes its parts, so that none exists simply independently of others; instead, elements form a network that becomes the design and structure of the work. When a work fails to achieve coalescence, it leaves loose ends dangling; its body is in some sense incomplete, its bones not properly articulated.

Critics find in even the greatest works things to be criticized. The ideal body is simply that—an ideal rather than a reality. But some real bodies are better than others, and the best have parts that function well together. The interpreter, if he or she is to embody those works, needs in his or her turn to function as a unit.

When we come later to look at details in literary works, we must keep in mind the necessity of their coalescing. When we look at performance elements such as rate, pitch, diction, tone, volume we need to remember that they, too, must coalesce, and that performer and work ultimately must coalesce. The whole should not be lost in analysis of its parts. How, for example, will one manage (in terms, let us say, of tempo) the opening sentences of Eudora Welty's story? We begin with a very cold, bright day. The girl jumps off the bus. Then she stops for a moment. Then she proceeds slowly toward the Home. Note how the teller orchestrates these details so that they give us a unified sense of the movement of the sentences. Details affecting tempo coalesce—and the manner of coalescence is an intimate part of the story's line of direction. Look always for that line of direction.

PERSPECTIVE

One vital factor is *perspective,* which is the attitude, the angle of vision of the work. Every piece of literature has a perspective that is different from any other perspective and that makes it thus unique. The perspective determines the selection of details and directs the way in which the details are made to coalesce, producing and shaping particular kinds of tensions.

The perspective of "A Visit of Charity" keeps us from reading the story simply as if we were Marian. We feel things partly with Marian, partly from the perspective of the teller of the story. It is not necessary to believe that Marian sees the building as a block of ice, but it is necessary to sense the indefinite way in which she approaches the door. In the second paragraph, the phrase "some old lady" means to the storyteller (and hence to us) something a little different from what it means to Marian herself. In the third paragraph it is not Marian who is saying "as she did when it was time to study Science" but the storyteller—and the detail tells us something about Marian's visit to the Home. What?

We see the nurse and the old ladies partly through Marian's eyes, partly through the storyteller's. Neither the nurse nor the old ladies are as "close" to us as Marian. We move constantly, as we thread through details, between looking *at* Marian and looking *with* her, between feeling *with* her and feeling *about* her.

Point of view is a phrase used to describe perspective. The major point of view of a story is that of the teller of the story, the narrator, and usually the term is restricted to this single perspective. In "A Visit of Charity" the narrator is omniscient, unnamed, somewhat satirical in attitude, terse, rather colloquial; there is a vein of the comic in the language; there is certainly an eye for effective detail. There is nothing loose or really casual in the narrator; the language is economical though not quite spare. Do you see the speaker (or narrator) as a man or a woman? Or does the sex of the narrator not enter into the point of view at all?

Within this dominant perspective, or point of view, are the movements we have pointed to between the narrator and Marian, between the narrator and Marian and the nurse, and between these three and the old lady. Point of view controls these varying minor perspectives. Different readers will make different choices with respect to the performance of perspectives—one reader, for example, may move in closer to Marian (characterize her more fully and overtly at points) than another. But it is safe to say that an interpreter ought never to ignore or to blunt or warp the dominant perspective, the point of view, so that it gets lost in the shuffle. One must not lose sight of the woods by looking too singly at the trees.

Now read the passage again. See if you can keep the tensions in their proper place so that they coalesce, guided by the perspectives. The excellence of a first-rate oral interpreter consists in his being able, without radical displacement, to embody something closely resembling the original point of view of the work of art.

ANALYSIS OF A STORY: PRESENCE

It will now be worthwhile to look at a complete story in terms of our discussion. James Joyce's "Araby" is one of an integrated collection of stories called *Dubliners*. Read the story first to enjoy it; don't try to be critical. It has been said, with no little truth, that a reader, even a critical reader, must be receptive before he or she becomes critical.

ARABY[5]

—James Joyce

North Richmond Street, being blind, was a quiet street except at the hour when the Christian Brothers' School set the boys free. An uninhabited house of two storeys stood at the blind end, detached from its neighbours in a square ground. The other houses of the street, conscious of decent lives within them, gazed at one another with brown imperturbable faces.

The former tenant of our house, a priest, had died in the back drawing-room. Air, musty from having been long enclosed, hung in all the rooms, and the waste room behind the kitchen was littered with old useless papers. Among these I found a few paper-covered books, the pages of which were curled and damp: *The Abbot*, by Walter Scott, *The Devout Communicant* and *The Memoirs of Vidocq*. I liked the last best because its leaves were yellow. The wild garden behind the house contained a central apple-tree and a few straggling bushes under one of which I found the late tenant's rusty bicycle-pump. He had been a very charitable priest; in his will he had left all his money to institutions and the furniture of his house to his sister.

When the short days of winter came dusk fell before we had well eaten our dinners. When we met in the street the houses had grown sombre. The space of sky above us was the colour of ever-changing violet and towards it the lamps of the street lifted their feeble lanterns. The cold air stung us and we played till our bodies glowed. Our shouts echoed in the silent street. The career of our play brought us through the dark muddy lanes behind the houses where we ran the gauntlet of the rough tribes from the cottages, to the back doors of the dark dripping gardens where odours arose from the ashpits, to the dark odorous stables where a coachman smoothed and combed the horse or shook music from the buckled harness. When we returned to the street light from the kitchen windows had filled the areas. If my uncle was seen turning the corner we hid in the shadow until we had seen him safely housed. Or if Mangan's sister came out on the doorstep to call her brother in to his tea we watched her from our shadow peer up and down the street. We waited to see whether she would remain or go in and, if she remained, we left our shadow and walked up to Mangan's steps resignedly. She was waiting for us, her figure defined by the light from the half-opened door. Her brother always teased her before he obeyed and I stood by the railings looking at her. Her dress swung as she moved her body and the soft rope of her hair tossed from side to side.

Every morning I lay on the floor in the front parlour watching her door. The blind was pulled down to within an inch of the sash so that I could not be seen. When she came out on the doorstep my heart leaped. I ran to the hall, seized my books and followed her. I kept her brown figure always in my eye and, when we came near the point at which our ways diverged, I quickened my pace and passed her. This happened morning after morning. I had never spoken to her, except for a few casual words, and yet her name was like a summons to all my foolish blood.

Her image accompanied me even in places the most hostile to romance. On Saturday evenings when my aunt went marketing I had to carry some of the parcels. We walked through the flaring streets, jostled by drunken men and bargaining women, amid the curses of labourers, the shrill litanies of shopboys who stood on guard by the barrels of pigs' cheeks, the nasal chanting of street-singers, who sang a *come-all-you* about O'Donovan Rossa, or a ballad about the troubles in our native land. These noises converged in a single sensation of life for me: I imagined that I bore my chalice safely through a throng of foes. Her name sprang to my lips at moments in strange prayers and praises which I myself did not understand. My eyes were often full of tears (I could not tell why) and at times a flood from my heart seemed to pour itself out into my bosom. I thought little of the future. I did not know whether I would ever speak to her or not or, if I spoke to her, how I could tell her of my confused adoration. But my body was like a harp and her words and gestures were like fingers running upon the wires.

One evening I went into the back drawing-room in which the priest had died. It was a dark rainy evening and there was no sound in the house. Through one of the broken panes I heard the rain impinge upon the earth, the fine incessant needles of water playing in the sodden beds. Some distant lamp or lighted window gleamed below me. I was thankful that I could see so little. All my senses seemed to desire to veil themselves and, feeling that I was about to slip from them, I pressed the palms of my hands together until they trembled, murmuring: *"O love! O love!"* many times.

At last she spoke to me. When she addressed the first words to me I was so confused that I did not know what to answer. She asked me was I going to *Araby*. I forgot whether I answered yes or no. It would be a splendid bazaar, she said she would love to go.

"And why can't you?" I asked.

While she spoke she turned a silver bracelet round and round her wrist. She could not go, she said, because there would be a retreat that week in her convent. Her brother and two other boys were fighting for their caps and I was alone at the railings. She held one of the spikes, bowing her head towards me. The light from the lamp opposite our door caught the white curve of her neck, lit up her hair that rested there and, falling, lit up the hand upon the railing. It fell over one side of her dress and caught the white border of a petticoat, just visible as she stood at ease.

"It's well for you," she said.

"If I go," I said, "I will bring you something."

What innumerable follies laid waste my waking and sleeping thoughts after that evening! I wished to annihilate the tedious intervening days. I chafed against the work of school. At night in my bedroom and by day in the classroom her image came between me and the page I strove to read. The syllables of the word *Araby* were called to me through the silence in which my soul luxuriated and cast an Eastern enchantment over me. I asked for leave to go to the bazaar on Saturday night. My aunt was surprised and hoped it was not some Freemason affair. I answered few questions in class. I watched my master's face pass from amiability to sternness; he hoped I was not beginning to idle. I could not call my wandering thoughts together. I had hardly any patience with the serious work of life which, now that it stood between me and my desire, seemed to me child's play, ugly monotonous child's play.

On Saturday morning I reminded my uncle that I wished to go to the bazaar in the evening. He was fussing at the hallstand, looking for the hat-brush, and answered me curtly:

"Yes, boy, I know."

As he was in the hall I could not go into the front parlour and lie at the window. I left the house in bad humour and walked slowly towards the school. The air was pitilessly raw and already my heart misgave me.

When I came home to dinner my uncle had not yet been home. Still it was early. I sat staring at the clock for some time and, when its ticking began to irritate me, I left the room. I mounted the staircase and gained the upper part of the house. The high cold empty gloomy rooms liberated me and I went from room to room singing. From the front window I saw my companions playing below in the street. Their cries reached me weakened and indistinct and, leaning my forehead against the cool glass, I looked over at the dark house where she lived. I may have stood there for an hour, seeing nothing but the brown-clad figure cast by my imagination, touched discreetly by the lamplight at the curved neck, at the hand upon the railings and at the border below the dress.

When I came downstairs again I found Mrs. Mercer sitting at the fire. She was an old garrulous woman, a pawnbroker's widow, who collected used stamps for some pious purpose. I had to endure the gossip of the tea-table. The meal was prolonged beyond an hour and still my uncle did not come. Mrs. Mercer stood up to go: she was sorry she couldn't wait any longer, but it was after eight o'clock and she did not like to be out late, as the night air was bad for her. When she had gone I began to walk up and down the room, clenching my fists. My aunt said:

"I'm afraid you may put off your bazaar for this night of Our Lord."

At nine o'clock I heard my uncle's latchkey in the halldoor. I heard him talking to himself and heard the hallstand rocking when it had received the weight of his overcoat. I could interpret these signs. When he was midway through his dinner I asked him to give me the money to go to the bazaar. He had forgotten.

"The people are in bed and after their first sleep now," he said.

I did not smile. My aunt said to him energetically:

"Can't you give him the money and let him go? You've kept him late enough as it is."

My uncle said he was very sorry he had forgotten. He said he believed in the old saying: "All work and no play makes Jack a dull boy." He asked me where I was going and, when I told him a second time, he asked me did I know *The Arab's Farewell to his Steed*. When I left the kitchen he was about to recite the opening lines of the piece to my aunt.

I held a florin tightly in my hand as I strode down Buckingham Street towards the station. The sight of the streets thronged with buyers and glaring with gas recalled to me the purpose of my journey. I took my seat in a third-class carriage of a deserted train. After an intolerable delay the train moved out of the station slowly. It crept onward among ruinous houses and over the twinkling river. At Westland Row Station a crowd of people pressed to the carriage doors, but the porters moved them back, saying that it was a special train for the bazaar. I remained alone in the bare carriage. In a few minutes the train drew up beside an improvised wooden platform. I passed out on to the road and saw by the lighted dial of a clock that it was ten minutes to ten. In front of me was a large building which displayed the magical name.

I could not find any sixpenny entrance and, fearing that the bazaar would be closed, I passed in quickly through a turnstile, handing a shilling to a weary-looking man. I found myself in a big hall girdled at half its height by a gallery. Nearly all the stalls were closed and the greater part of the hall was in darkness. I recognised a silence like that which pervades a church after a service. I walked into the centre of the bazaar timidly. A few people were gathered about the stalls which were still open. Before a curtain over which the words *Café Chantant* were written in coloured lamps, two men were counting money on a salver. I listened to the fall of the coins.

Remembering with difficulty why I had come I went over to one of the stalls and examined porcelain vases and flowered tea-sets. At the door of the stall a young lady was talking and laughing with two young gentlemen. I remarked their English accents and listened vaguely to their conversation.

"O, I never said such a thing!"

"O, but you did!"

"O, but I didn't!"

"Didn't she say that?"

"Yes, I heard her."

"O, there's a . . . fib!"

Observing me the young lady came over and asked me did I wish to buy anything. The tone of her voice was not encouraging; she seemed to have spoken to me out of a sense of duty. I looked humbly at the great jars that stood like eastern guards at either side of the dark entrance to the stall and murmured:

"No, thank you."

The young lady changed the position of one of the vases and went back to the two young men. They began to talk of the same subject. Once or twice the young lady glanced at me over her shoulder.

I lingered before her stall, though I knew my stay was useless, to make my interest in her wares seem the more real. Then I turned away slowly and walked down the middle of the bazaar. I allowed the two pennies to fall against the sixpence in my pocket. I heard a voice call from one end of the gallery that the light was out. The upper part of the hall was now completely dark.

Gazing up into the darkness I saw myself as a creature driven and derided by vanity; and my eyes burned with anguish and anger.

The incidents in Joyce's story are, on the surface, slight. A sensitive and shy young boy, living on North Richmond Street in Dublin, falls in love with a girl and goes to a bazaar to buy her a present. After getting money from his uncle, he arrives at the bazaar late and is keenly disappointed to find that the greater part of the hall is already dark and that no one else shares the sense of excitement with which he had started out. His anticipated pleasure turns to anguish and anger.

But this is not really the story at all; the incidents in Joyce's story are simply the surfaces. The true story lies in the sharp sense we get of the inner experience of the boy through the tensiveness (the tensile strength) of the prose, the coalescence of elements, the perspective provided by Joyce. The real strength of "Araby" as a work of art is the success with which it *presents* the experience; "Araby" is not a thing, or a symbol of a thing, but a *presence*. It is the happy task of the oral interpreter to see that Joyce's prose is actualized; and the task can be achieved only through understanding (intuitive or not).

PERSPECTIVES

Examine the setting of the story. In a large sense, the setting is Dublin, Ireland, but in the opening paragraphs we are already on a single street in Dublin. The camera looks about broadly, but very quickly the locus shifts a little: in the first sentence of the second paragraph the word *our* is introduced. In the third sentence, Joyce uses the word *I*. By the third paragraph (at least), we realize that the point of view is first-person and that the story is a memory story: "When the short days of winter came dusk fell before we had well eaten our dinners." The "I" is now identified as a boy. The "I" is now not a single "I" but a man-boy, or a boy-man, remembering how it was when he was young. The reader does not, then, find himself trying to be a young boy while he reads aloud; he is a man looking backward. There is a vast difference in attitude between the two possibilities; there is a strong difference in the tensiveness of the two situations. It will be valuable to discuss in class the movement between the man and the boy throughout the story. When does the presence of the boy seem stronger? When does the presence of the man? How does Mangan's sister enter into the story? Does the reader see her (the reader as interpreter) simply through the eyes of the boy-man, or does she enter into the story in her own right? What about the young lady talking with the two young gentlemen at the bazaar? Do we hear their voices only through the ears of the narrator, or do they speak out in their own persons? These are not simple matters; they are of real concern to the interpreter. They are also aspects of tensiveness, contributing as they do to the play of forces within the body of the story, and they involve varying kinesthetic responses.

OTHER ASPECTS OF TENSIVENESS

Notice the way in which, from the beginning, Joyce creates tensiveness through the juxtaposition of opposites. The opening of the story is filled with opposite images. Words like *blind, quiet, uninhabited, imperturbable, musty, long-enclosed, waste, littered, useless, straggling, rusty, sombre, feeble, dark,* and *muddy* give us a strong sense, even a strong picture, of decay or paralysis or lifelessness. But along with these words, setting up a tension with them, come such words as *ever-changing, violet, stung, played, glowed, shouts, gauntlet, rough, odorous, horse, music, swung, tossed,* all of which suggest life or action or sound. There is a stretch and pull, a muscularity in the body of the story resulting from the juxtaposition.

There is a further complication: this dismal North Richmond Street itself has living, conscious qualities. The street is "blind," but blindness suggests life, since one must be alive to be blind. Each house has its "neighbours"; each has its "brown imperturbable face"; and one house, the one at the blind end, is "detached from its neighbours." In this mixture of light and shadow the figure of Mangan's sister is first introduced to us, standing in the light of the half-opened door. Against the darkness, the animal vitality of her figure is sharply apparent to the boy who watches her. The same detail opens the fourth paragraph, too: the boy, hidden behind the blind, watches the girl come out into the morning light. The sense of the boy's *life* in *darkness,* with which the story opens, thus intensifies the conclusion of the fourth paragraph: "her name was like a summons to all my foolish blood." Out of the dimness of this growth, the boy's blood responds to the call of *light,* in the person of the girl. All the details coalesce.

FOR FURTHER DISCUSSION

Point to other passages in the story in which a similar tensiveness is set up by such juxtaposition of details. Can you feel a kinesthetic response to such details? Do you see how, in their coalescing, in their becoming *one,* such details give a sense of life, of presence? And remember that we are not being given, at any time, an objective, uncolored view of North Richmond Street and of Dublin; we are looking constantly from a certain angle; there is always a perspective, though the locus keeps changing. It is because the point of view of the story is not limited to the perspective of the boy that we can understand the tears that fill the boy's eyes—tears that he himself is not able to understand.

To guide you in your search for other instances of tension, here are some questions: What examples do you find of oppositions between faith and denial? Between pagan and Christian? Between the routine and the exotic or romantic? Between priest and girl? What, indeed, is the significance of the title itself? Joyce makes such extended and intensive use of detail that it is customary to speak of the texture of his story as tight, or dense, as if the texture of prose were being compared with the texture of cloth. Writers vary greatly in the tightness of their textures. Look at the selections in earlier chapters and compare the textures with the texture of "Araby."

The bazaar, to which we finally come in "Araby," brings all the fine threads of the story together. It seems at first to be the fruit of all the ripening in the boy's hopes—he looks forward to it wholeheartedly. But it becomes a part of the darkness with which the story began: the hall is dark, delight is missing, the atmosphere is silent like *a church after a service.* The counting of money in front of the curtain lighted by colored lamps is like the clinking of coins in the counting of the church offering; it is the sound of something over and done with, being added up. A voice cries that the light is out. And the boy, torn brutally out of Araby, is again in the darkness of Dublin; the sense of the ridiculousness of his position and of his dreams burns into him.

COALESCENCE: EPIPHANY

The strong sense of revelation at the end of the story, the illuminating recognition on the part of the character, is what Joyce calls an *epiphany,* an almost miraculous manifestation of the inner core of life at a specific moment. The term is useful in describing a point at which the tensiveness of a story is made dramatically vivid by the coalescence of everything toward which the story has been moving; the whole point stands before us like a living presence, in a kind of utter nakedness of perspective. We are not *told,* we are *given.*

Try now to prepare at least a section of the story to read in class. Do not overlook any of the details, but remember that the details must merge. Watch for sensory responses to the language. Can you feel what Joyce is trying to achieve? (For example, when the boy presses the palms of his hands together, can you sense their trembling? Can you feel, not simply hear, his repeated "O love! O love!" and feel his confusion as he tries to answer the girl when she first speaks to him? Can you embody the attitudes you discover?) Remember that you are the man looking back on the boy, but looking on him as part of yourself; not being he, but feeling with him. When you practice reading, practice *aloud.* Walk about, if you wish, doing the things the characters do in the story, so that you can work the story into you physically. Then try to remember these organic sensations as you stand still and try to project the story out in front of you. The story is a presence in its own right, but you are a part of that presence. Watch. Listen. Remember where everything is going. Your responsibility is to be responsive.

PROJECTION

Always remember also that the story must not be buried in the book. Keep it out front; project it so that your audience is also involved. The energy flows from you into the body of the audience; the feeling should be that the story is propelled outward, not locked within the reader. Projection, seen this way, is not so much a technique as it is a state of mind. When you look at the book, try to look down at it in the person of the narrator; the movement should be part of the characterization, not primarily a technique of the reader for finding the words. It should not cut you off from the audience. Your energy (the embodiment of the story) must fill the whole space of the room. Accepting the challenge of space and filling it, living in the whole space available for the performance, is crucial to fine interpretation. That is one reason why stage fright blocks the sharing of a reading: it causes the reader to close in on himself, to hug the text to him (or to lose contact with it altogether), to turn himself off from the space available, the space which both the text-as-presence and the audience for the moment must exist.

MATERIALS FOR PRACTICE

Read one or part of one of the following selections in class. In your rehearsals, concentrate on achieving a sense of the selection's quality of presence. Try to feel it and to sense it outside yourself. Remember how to use your book. Watch the details, but remember that the details ought to coalesce, too. Try to state for yourself the perspective from which the selection is written.

MIDSUMMER[6]
—Manuel E. Arguilla[7]

He pulled down his hat until the wide brim touched his shoulders. He crouched lower under the cover of his cart and peered ahead. The road seemed to writhe under the lash of the noon-day heat; it swung from side to side, humped and bent itself like a fleeing serpent, and disappeared behind the spur of a low hill on which grew a scrawny thicket of bamboo.

There was not a house in sight. Along the left side of the road ran the deep, dry gorge of a stream, the banks sparsely covered by sun-burned *cogon* grass. In places, the rocky, waterless bed showed aridly. Farther, beyond the shimmer of quivering heat waves rose ancient hills not less blue than the cloud-palisaded sky. On the right stretched a sandy waste of low rolling dunes. Scattered clumps of hardy *ledda* relieved the otherwise barren monotony of the landscape. Far away he could discern a thin indigo line that was the sea.

The grating of the cartwheels on the pebbles of the road and the almost soundless shuffle of the weary bull but emphasized the stillness. Now

---

[6] Reprinted by permission of Lydia Arguilla Salas.

[7] Arguilla, a Filipino who achieved lasting recognition in his homeland with his collection *How My Brother Leon Brought Home a Wife,* was killed by the Japanese in 1944 because of his guerrilla activities.

and then came the dry rustling of falling earth as lumps from the cracked sides of the gorge rolled down to the bottom.

He struck at the bull with the slack of the rope. The animal broke into a heavy trot. The dust stirred slumbrously. The bull slowed down, threw up his head, and a glistening thread of saliva spun out into the dry air. The driving rays of the sun were reflected in points of light on the wet, heaving flanks.

The man in the cart did not notice the woman until she had rounded the spur of land and stood unmoving beside the road, watching the cart and its occupant come toward her. She was young, surprisingly sweet and fresh amidst her parched surroundings. A gayly striped kerchief covered her head, the ends tied at the nape of her neck. She wore a homespun bodice of light red cloth with small white checks. Her skirt was also homespun and showed a pattern of white checks with narrow stripes of yellow and red. With both hands she held by the mouth a large, apparently empty, water jug, the cool red of which blended well with her dress. She was barefoot.

She stood straight and still beside the road and regarded him with frank curiosity. Suddenly she turned and disappeared into the dry gorge. Coming to where she had stood a few moments before, he pulled up the bull and got out of the cart. He saw where a narow path had been cut into the bank and stood a while lost in thought, absently wiping the perspiration from his face. Then he unhitched his bull and for a few moments, with strong brown fingers, kneaded the hot neck of the beast. Driving the animal before him, he followed the path. It led up the dry bed of the stream; the sharp fragments of sun-heated rock were like burning coals under his feet. There was no sign of the young woman.

He came upon her beyond a bend in the gorge, where a big mango tree, which had partly fallen from the side of the ravine, cast its cool shade over a well.

She had filled her jar and was rolling the kerchief around her hand into a flat coil which she placed on her head. Without glancing at him, where he had stopped some distance off, she sat down on her heels, gathering the folds of her skirt between her wide-spread knees. She tilted the brimful jar to remove part of the water. One hand on the rim, the other supporting the bottom, she began to raise it to her head. She knelt on one knee—resting, for a moment, the jar on the other while she brushed away drops of water from the sides. In one lithe movement she brought the jar onto her head, getting to her feet at the same time. But she staggered a little and water splashed down on her breast. The single bodice instantly clung to her bosom, molding the twin hillocks of her breasts, warmly brown through the wet cloth. One arm remained uplifted, holding the jar, while the other shook the clinging cloth free of her drenched flesh. Then not once having raised her eyes, she passed by the young man, who stood mutely gazing beside his bull. The animal had found some grass along the path and was industriously grazing.

He turned to watch the graceful figure beneath the jar until it vanished around a bend in the path leading to the road. Then he led the bull to the well, and tethered it to a root of the mango tree.

"The underpart of her arm is white and smooth," he said to his blurred image on the waters of the well, as he leaned over before lowering the bucket made of half a petroleum can. "And her hair is thick and black." The bucket struck with a rattling impact. It filled with one long gurgle. He threw his hat on the grass and pulled the bucket up with both hands. The twisted bamboo rope bit into his hardened palms, and he thought how the same rope must have hurt *her*.

He placed the dripping bucket on a flat stone, and the bull drank. "Son of lightning!" he said, thumping the side of the bull after it had drunk the third bucketful, "you drink like the great Kabuntitiao!" A low, rich rumbling rolled through the cavernous body of the beast. He tied it again to the root, and the animal idly rubbed its horns against the wood. The sun had fallen from the perpendicular, and noticing that the bull stood partly exposed to the sun, he pushed it farther into the shade. He fanned himself with his hat. He wished to entice the wind from the sea, but not a breeze stirred.

After a while he put on his hat and hurriedly walked the short distance through the gorge up to the road where his cart stood. From inside he took a jute sack which he slung over one shoulder. With the other arm, he gathered part of the hay at the bottom of the cart. He returned to the well, slips of straw falling behind him as he picked his way from one tuft of grass to another, for the broken rocks of the path had grown exceedingly hot.

He gave the hay to the bull. Its rump was again in the sun, and he had to push it back. "Fool, do you want to broil yourself alive?" he said good-humoredly, slapping the thick haunches. It switched its long-haired tail and fell to eating. The dry, sweet-smelling hay made harsh gritting sounds in the mouth of the hungry animal. Saliva rolled out from the corners, clung to the stiff hairs that fringed the thick lower lip, fell and gleamed and evaporated in the heated air.

He took out of the jute sack a polished coconut shell. The top had been sawed off and holes bored at opposite sides, through which a string tied to the lower part of the shell passed in a loop. The smaller piece could thus be dipped up and down as a cover. The coconut shell contained cooked rice still a little warm. Buried on the top was an egg now boiled hard. He next brought out a bamboo tube of salt, a cake of brown sugar wrapped in banana leaf, and some dried shrimps. Then he spread the sack in what remained of the shade, placed his simple meal thereon, and prepared to eat his dinner. But first he drew a bucketful of water from the well, setting the bucket on a rock. He seated himself on another rock and ate with his fingers. From time to time he drank from the bucket.

He was half through with his meal when the girl came down the path once more. She had changed the wetted bodice. He watched her with lowered head as she approached, and felt a difficulty in continuing to eat, but went through the motions of filling his mouth nevertheless. He strained his eyes looking at the girl from beneath his eyebrows. How graceful she was! Her hips tapered smoothly down to rounded thighs and supple legs, showing against her skirt and moving straight and free. Her shoulders, small but firm, bore her shapely neck and head with shy pride.

When she was very near, he ate hurriedly, so that he almost choked. He did not look at her. She placed the jar between three stones. When she picked up the rope of the bucket, he came to himself. He looked up—straight into her face. He saw her eyes. They were brown and were regarding him gravely, without embarrassment; he forgot his own timidity.

"Won't you join me, *Ading?*"[8] he said simply. He remained seated.

Her lips parted in a half smile and a little dimple appeared high up on her right cheek. She shook her head and said: "God reward you, *Manong.*"[9]

"Perhaps the poor food I have is not fit for you?"

"No, no. It isn't that. How can you think of it? I should be ashamed. It is that I have just eaten myself. That is why I come to get water in the middle of the day—we ran out of it. I see you have eggs and shrimps and sugar. Why, we had nothing but rice and salt."

"Salt? Surely you joke."

"I would be ashamed . . ."

"But what is the matter with salt?

'Salt . . . salt . . .

Makes baby stout' "

he intoned. "My grandmother used to sing that to me when I complained of our food."

They laughed and felt more at ease and regarded each other more openly. He took a long time fingering his rice before raising it to his mouth, the while he gazed up at her and smiled for no reason. She smiled back in turn and gave the rope which she held an absent-minded tug. The bucket came down from its perch of rock in a miniature flood. He leaped to his feet with a surprised yell, and the next instant the jute sack on which lay his meal was drenched. Only the rice inside the coconut shell and the bamboo tube of salt were saved from the water.

She was distressed, but he only laughed.

"It is nothing," he said. "It was time I stopped eating. I am filled up to my neck."

"Forgive me, Manong," she insisted. "It was all my fault. Such a clumsy creature I am."

"It was not your fault," he assured her. "I am to blame for placing the bucket of water where I did."

"I will draw you another bucketful," she said, beginning to coil the rope.

"I will draw the water myself," he said. "I am stronger than you."

"No, you must let me do it."

But when he caught hold of the bucket and stretched forth a brawny arm for the coil of rope in her hands, she surrendered both to him quickly

[8] *Ading;* a term of endearment used to one younger than oneself.
[9] *Manong:* a term of affection and respect used to a male person older than oneself.

and drew back a step as though shy of his touch. He lowered the bucket with his back to her, and she had time to take in the tallness of him, the breadth of his shoulders, the sinewy length of his legs. Down below in the small of his back, two parallel ridges of rope-like muscles stuck out against the wet shirt. As he hauled up the bucket, muscles rippled all over his body. His hair, which was wavy, cut short behind but long in front, fell in a cluster over his forehead.

"Let me hold the bucket while you drink," she offered.

He flashed her a smile over his shoulders as he poured the water into her jar, and again lowered the bucket.

"No, no, you must not do that." She hurried to his side and held one of his arms. "I couldn't let you, a stranger . . ."

"Why not?" He smiled down at her, and noticed a slight film of moisture clinging to the down on her upper lip and experienced a sudden desire to wipe it away with his forefinger. He continued to lower the bucket while she had to stand by.

"Hadn't you better move over to the shade?" he suggested, as the bucket struck the water.

"What shall I do there?" she asked sharply, as though the idea of seeking protection from the heat were contemptible to her.

"You will get roasted standing here in the sun," he said, and began to haul up the bucket.

But she remained beside him, catching the rope as it fell from his hands, coiling it carefully. The jar was filled, with plenty to spare. Then he gave her the bucket and she held it up and told him to drink as she tilted the half-filled can until the water lapped the rim. He gulped a mouthful, gargled noisily, spewed it out, then commenced to drink in earnest. He took long, deep draughts of the sweetish water, for he was more thirsty than he had thought. A chuckling sound persisted in forming inside his throat at every swallow. It made him self-conscious. He was breathless when through, and red in the face.

"I don't know why it makes that sound," he said, fingering his throat and laughing shamefacedly.

"Father also makes that sound when he drinks, and mother always laughs at him," she said. She untied the headkerchief over her hair and started to roll it.

The sun had descended considerably and there was now hardly any shade under the tree. The bull was gathering with its tongue stray slips of straw. He untied the animal to lead it to the other side of the gorge, where the high bank was beginning to throw some shade, when the girl spoke: "Manong, why don't you come to our house and bring your animal with you? There is shade and you can sleep, though our house is very poor."

She had already placed the jar on her head and stood, half-turned toward him, waiting for his answer.

"It would be troubling you, Ading."

"No. You come. I have told mother about you." She turned and went down the path.

He sent the bull after her with a smart slap on its side. Then he quickly gathered the remains of his meal, put them inside the jute sack which had almost dried, and himself followed. Then seeing that the bull had stopped to nibble the tufts of grass that dotted the bottom of the gorge, he picked up the dragging rope and urged the animal on into a trot. They caught up with the girl near the cart. She had stopped to wait.

"Our house is just beyond that point," she said, indicating the spur of land topped by the sickly bamboo. "We have no neighbors."

He did not volunteer a word. He walked a step behind, the bull lumbering in front. More than ever he was conscious of her person. She carried the jar on her head without holding it. Her hands swung to her even steps. He threw back his square shoulders, lifted his chin, and sniffed the motionless air. There was a flourish in the way he flicked the rump of the bull with the rope in his hand. He felt strong. He felt that he could follow the slender, lithe figure ahead of him to the ends of the world.

THE WILD SWANS AT COOLE[10]
—*William Butler Yeats*

The trees are in their autumn beauty,
The woodland paths are dry,
Under the October twilight the water
Mirrors a still sky;
Upon the brimming water among the stones
Are nine-and-fifty swans.

The nineteenth autumn has come upon me
Since I first made my count;
I saw, before I had well finished,
All suddenly mount
And scatter wheeling in great broken rings
Upon their clamorous wings.

I have looked upon those brilliant creatures,
And now my heart is sore.
All's changed since I, hearing at twilight,
The first time on this shore,
The bell-beat of their wings above my head,
Trod with a lighter tread.

Unwearied still, lover by lover,
They paddle in the cold,

Companionable streams or climb the air;
Their hearts have not grown old;
Passion or conquest, wander where they will,
Attend upon them still.

But now they drift on the still water
Mysterious, beautiful;
Among what rushes will they build,
By what lake's edge or pool
Delight men's eyes when I awake some day
To find they have flown away?

THE SLOTH[11]
—Theodore Roethke

In moving-slow he has no Peer.
You ask him something in his Ear,
He thinks about it for a Year;

And, then, before he says a Word
There, upside down (unlike a Bird),
He will assume that you have Heard—

A most Ex-as-per-at-ing Lug.
But should you call his manner Smug,
He'll sigh and give his Branch a Hug;

Then off again to Sleep he goes,
Still swaying gently by his Toes,
And you just *know* he knows he knows.

IF I COULD ONLY LIVE AT THE PITCH THAT IS NEAR MADNESS[12]
—Richard Eberhart

If I could only live at the pitch that is near madness
When everything is as it was in my childhood
Violet, vivid, and of infinite possibility:
That the sun and the moon broke over my head.

Then I cast time out of the trees and fields,
Then I stood immaculate in the Ego;
Then I eyed the world with all delight,
Reality was the perfection of my sight.

And time has big handles on the hands,
Fields and trees a way of being themselves.
I saw battalions of the race of mankind
Standing stolid, demanding a moral answer.

I gave the moral answer and I died
And into a realm of complexity came
Where nothing is possible but necessity
And the truth wailing there like a red babe.

THE USE OF FORCE[13]
—*William Carlos Williams*

They were new patients to me, all I had was the name, Olson. Please come down as soon as you can, my daughter is very sick.

When I arrived I was met by the mother, a big startled looking woman, very clean and apologetic who merely said, Is this the doctor? and let me in. In the back, she added, You must excuse us, doctor, we have her in the kitchen where it is warm. It is very damp here sometimes.

The child was fully dressed and sitting on her father's lap near the kitchen table. He tried to get up, but I motioned for him not to bother, took off my overcoat and started to look things over. I could see that they were all very nervous, eyeing me up and down distrustfully. As often, in such cases, they weren't telling me more than they had to, it was up to me to tell them; that's why they were spending three dollars on me.

The child was fairly eating me up with her cold, steady eyes, and no expression to her face whatever. She did not move and seemed, inwardly, quiet; an unusually attractive little thing, and as strong as a heifer in appearance. But her face was flushed, she was breathing rapidly, and I realized that she had a high fever. She had magnificent blonde hair, in profusion. One of those picture children often reproduced in advertising leaflets and the photogravure sections of the Sunday papers.

She's had a fever for three days, began the father and we don't know what it comes from. My wife has given her things, you know, like people do,

---

[13] From William Carlos Williams, *The Farmers' Daughters*. Copyright 1933, 1938 by William Carlos Williams. Reprinted by permission of New Directions.

but it don't do no good. And there's been a lot of sickness around. So we tho't you'd better look her over and tell us what is the matter.

As doctors often do I took a trial shot at it as a point of departure. Had she had a sore throat?

Both parents answered me together, No . . . No, she says her throat don't hurt her.

Does your throat hurt you? added the mother to the child. But the little girl's expression didn't change nor did she move her eyes from my face.

Have you looked?

I tried to, said the mother, but I couldn't see.

As it happens we had been having a number of cases of diphtheria in the school to which this child went during that month and we were all, quite apparently, thinking of that, though no one had as yet spoken of the thing.

Well, I said, suppose we take a look at the throat first. I smiled in my best professional manner and asking for the child's first name I said, come on, Mathilda, open your mouth and let's take a look at your throat.

Nothing doing.

Aw, come on, I coaxed, just open your mouth wide and let me take a look. Look, I said opening both hands wide, I haven't anything in my hands. Just open up and let me see.

Such a nice man, put in the mother. Look how kind he is to you. Come on, do what he tells you to. He won't hurt you.

At that I ground my teeth in disgust. If only they wouldn't use the word "hurt" I might be able to get somewhere. But I did not allow myself to be hurried or disturbed but speaking quietly and slowly I approached the child again.

As I moved my chair a little nearer suddenly with one catlike movement both her hands clawed instinctively for my eyes and she almost reached them too. In fact she knocked my glasses flying and they fell, though unbroken, several feet away from me on the kitchen floor.

Both the mother and father almost turned themselves inside out in embarrassment and apology. You bad girl, said the mother, taking her and shaking her by one arm. Look what you've done. The nice man. . .

For heaven's sake, I broke in. Don't call me a nice man to her. I'm here to look at her throat on the chance that she might have diphtheria and possibly die of it. But that's nothing to her. Look here, I said to the child, we're going to look at your throat. You're old enough to understand what I'm saying. Will you open it now by yourself or shall we have to open it for you?

Not a move. Even her expression hadn't changed. Her breaths however were coming faster and faster. Then the battle began. I had to do it. I had to have a throat culture for her own protection. But first I told the parents that it was entirely up to them. I explained the danger but said that I would not insist on a throat examination so long as they would take the responsibility.

If you don't do what the doctor says you'll have to go to the hospital, the mother admonished her severely.

Oh yeah? I had to smile to myself. After all, I had already fallen in love with the savage brat, the parents were contemptible to me. In the ensuing struggle they grew more and more abject, crushed, exhausted while she surely rose to magnificent heights of insane fury of effort bred of her terror of me.

The father tried his best, and he was a big man but the fact that she was his daughter, his shame at her behavior and his dread of hurting her made him release her just at the critical moment several times when I had almost achieved success, till I wanted to kill him. But his dread also that she might have diphtheria made him tell me to go on, go on though he himself was almost fainting, while the mother moved back and forth behind us raising and lowering her hands in an agony of apprehension.

Put her in front of you on your lap, I ordered, and held both her wrists.

But as soon as he did the child let out a scream. Don't, you're hurting me. Let go of my hands. Let them go I tell you. Then she shrieked terrifyingly, hysterically. Stop it! Stop it! You're killing me!

Do you think she can stand it, doctor! said the mother.

You get out, said the husband to his wife. Do you want her to die of diphtheria?

Come on now, hold her, I said.

Then I grasped the child's head with my left hand and tried to get the wooden tongue depressor between her teeth. She fought, with clenched teeth, desperately! But now I also had grown furious—at a child. I tried to hold myself down but I couldn't. I know how to expose a throat for inspection. And I did my best. When finally I got the wooden spatula behind the last teeth and just the point of it into the mouth cavity, she opened up for an instant but before I could see anything she came down again and gripping the wooden blade between her molars she reduced it to splinters before I could get it out again.

Aren't you ashamed, the mother yelled at her. Aren't you ashamed to act like that in front of the doctor?

Get me a smooth-handled spoon of some sort, I told the mother. We're going through with this. The child's mouth was already bleeding. Her tongue was cut and she was screaming in wild hysterical shrieks. Perhaps I should have desisted and come back in an hour or more. No doubt it would have been better. But I have seen at least two children lying dead in bed of neglect in such cases, and feeling that I must get a diagnosis now or never I went at it again. But the worst of it was that I too had got beyond reason. I could have torn the child apart in my own fury and enjoyed it. It was a pleasure to attack her. My face was burning with it.

The damned little brat must be protected against her own idiocy, one says to one's self at such times. Others must be protected against her. It is a social necessity. And all these things are true. But a blind fury, a feeling of adult shame, bred of a longing for muscular release are the operatives. One goes on to the end.

In a final unreasoning assault I overpowered the child's neck and jaws. I forced the heavy silver spoon back of her teeth and down her throat till she gagged. And there it was—both tonsils covered with membrane. She had fought valiantly to keep me from knowing her secret. She had been hiding that sore throat for three days at least and lying to her parents in order to escape just such an outcome as this.

Now truly she *was* furious. She had been on the defensive before but now she attacked. Tried to get off her father's lap and fly at me while tears of defeat blinded her eyes.

SOW[14]

—Sylvia Plath

God knows how our neighbor managed to breed
His great sow:
Whatever his shrewd secret, he kept it hid

In the same way
He kept the sow—impounded from public stare,
Prize ribbon and pig show.

But one dusk our questions commended us to a tour
Through his lantern-lit
Maze of barns to the lintel of the sunk sty door

To gape at it:
This was no rose-and-larkspurred china suckling
With a penny slot

For thrifty children, nor dolt pig ripe for heckling,
About to be
Glorified for prime flesh and golden crackling

In a parsley halo;
Nor even one of the common barnyard sows,
Mire-smirched, blowzy,

Maunching thistle and knotweed on her snout-cruise—
Bloat tun of milk
On the move, hedged by a litter of feat-foot ninnies

Shrilling her hulk
To halt for a swig at the pink teats. No. This vast
Brobdingnag bulk

Of a sow lounged belly-bedded on that black compost,
Fat-rutted eyes
Dream-filmed. What a vision of ancient hoghood must

Thus wholly engross
The great grandam!—our marvel blazoned a knight,
Helmed, in cuirass,

Unhorsed and shredded in the grove of combat
By a grisly-bristled
Boar, fabulous enough to straddle that sow's heat.

But our farmer whistled,
Then, with a jocular fist thwacked the barrel nape,
And the green-copse-castled

Pig hove, letting legend like dried mud drop,
Slowly, grunt
On grunt, up in the flickering light to shape

A monument
Prodigious in gluttonies as that hog whose want
Made lean Lent

Of kitchen slops and, stomaching no constraint,
Proceeded to swill
The seven troughed seas and every earthquaking continent.

A TREE TELLING OF ORPHEUS [15]
—Denise Levertov

White dawn. Stillness.   When the rippling began
      I took it for sea-wind, coming to our valley with rumors
      of salt, of treeless horizons. But the white fog
didn't stir; the leaves of my brothers remained outstretched,
unmoving.
            Yet the rippling drew nearer—and then
my own outermost branches began to tingle, almost as if
fire had been lit below them, too close, and their twig-tips
were drying and curling.
                  Yet I was not afraid, only
                  deeply alert.

[15] From Denise Levertov, *Relearning the Alphabet*. Copyright © 1970 by Denise Levertov Goodman. Reprinted by permission of New Directions.

I was the first to see him, for I grew
        out on the pasture slope, beyond the forest.
He was a man, it seemed: the two
moving stems, the short trunk, the two
arm-branches, flexible, each with five leafless
                twigs at their ends,
and the head that's crowned by brown or gold grass,
bearing a face not like the beaked face of a bird,
      more like a flower's.
                He carried a burden made of
some cut branch bent while it was green,
strands of a vine tight-stretched across it. From this,
when he touched it, and from his voice
which unlike the wind's voice had no need of our
leaves and branches to complete its sound,
                came the ripple.
But it was now no longer a ripple (he had come near and
stopped in my first shadow) it was a wave that bathed me
    as if rain
          rose from below and around me
        instead of falling.
And what I felt was no longer a dry tingling:

        I seemed to be singing as he sang, I seemed to know
        what the lark knows; all my sap
          was mounting towards the sun that by now
            had risen, the mist was rising, the grass
was drying, yet my roots felt music moisten them
deep under earth.

        He came still closer, leaned on my trunk:
        the bark thrilled like a leaf still-folded.
Music! There was no twig of me not
          trembling with joy and fear.

Then as he sang
it was no longer sounds only that made the music:
he spoke, and as no tree listens I listened, and language
        came into my roots
            out of the earth,
      into my bark
           out of the air,
      into the pores of my greenest shoots
          gently as dew
and there was no word he sang but I knew its meaning.

He told of journeys,
          of where sun and moon go while we stand in dark,
     of an earth-journey he dreamed he would take some day
deeper than roots . . .
He told of the dreams of man, wars, passions, griefs,
          and I, a tree, understood words—ah, it seemed
my thick bark would split like a sapling's that
                              grew too fast in the spring
when a late frost wounds it.

                    Fire he sang,
that trees fear, and I, a tree, rejoiced in its flames.
New buds broke forth from me though it was full summer.
          As though his lyre (now I knew its name)
          were both frost and fire, its chords flamed
up to the crown of me.

               I was seed again.
                    I was fern in the swamp.
                         I was coal.

And at the heart of my wood
(so close I was to becoming man or a god)
     there was a kind of silence, a kind of sickness,
          something akin to what men call boredom,
                              something
(the poem descended a scale, a stream over stones)
          that gives to a candle a coldness
               in the midst of its burning, he said.

It was then,
          when in the blaze of his power that
                         reached me and changed me
          I thought I should fall my length,
that the singer began
                    to leave me.   Slowly
          moved from my noon shadow
                              to open light,
words leaping and dancing over his shoulders
back to me
          rivery sweep of lyre-tones becoming
slowly again
          ripple.

And I
     in terror
          but not in doubt of
                    what I must do

in anguish, in haste,
                    wrenched from the earth root after root,
the soil heaving and cracking, the moss tearing asunder—
and behind me the others: my brothers
forgotten since dawn. In the forest
they too had heard,
and were pulling their roots in pain
out of a thousand years' layers of dead leaves,
        rolling the rocks away,
                  breaking themselves
                        out of
                     their depths.
You would have thought we would lose the sound of the lyre,
            of the singing
so dreadful the storm-sounds were, where there was no storm,
            no wind but the rush of our
        branches moving, our trunks breasting the air.
        But the music!
                The music reached us.

Clumsily,
        stumbling over our own roots,
                rustling our leaves
                    in answer,
we moved, we followed.

All day we followed, up hill and down.
                We learned to dance,
for he would stop, where the ground was flat,
                and words he said
taught us to leap and to wind in and out
around one another   in figures   the lyre's measure designed.
The singer
        laughed till he wept to see us, he was so glad.
                  At sunset
we came to this place I stand in, this knoll
with its ancient grove that was bare grass then.
        In the last light of that day his song became
farewell.
        He stilled our longing.
        He sang our sun-dried roots back into earth,
watered them: all-night rain of music so quiet
                  we could almost
        not hear it in the
                moonless dark.
By dawn he was gone.
        We have stood here since,
in our new life.

We have waited.
                    He does not return.
It is said he made his earth-journey, and lost
what he sought.
                    It is said they felled him
and cut up his limbs for firewood.
                              And it is said
his head still sang and was swept out to sea singing.
Perhaps he will not return.
                         But what we have lived
comes back to us.
                 We see more.
                        We feel, as our rings increase,
something that lifts our branches, that stretches our furthest
                                              leaf tips
further.
         The wind, the birds,
                         do not sound poorer but clearer,
recalling our agony, and the way we danced.
The music!

THE SHEEP CHILD[16]
—*James Dickey*

Farm boys wild to couple
With anything   with soft-wooded trees
With mounds of earth   mounds
Of pinestraw   will keep themselves off
Animals by legends of their own:
In the hay-tunnel dark
And dung of barns, they will
Say   I have heard tell

That in a museum in Atlanta
Way back in a corner somewhere
There's this thing that's only half
Sheep   like a woolly baby
Pickled in alcohol   because
Those things can't live   his eyes
Are open   but you can't stand to look
I heard from somebody who . . .

But this is now almost all
Gone. The boys have taken

[16] Copyright © 1966 by James Dickey. Reprinted from *Poems 1957–1967*, by James Dickey, by permission of Wesleyan University Press.

Their own true wives in the city,
The sheep are safe in the west hill
Pasture   but we who were born there
Still are not sure. Are we,
Because we remember, remembered
In the terrible dust of museums?

Merely with his eyes, the sheep-child may

Be saying   saying

I am here, in my father's house.
I who am half of your world, came deeply
To my mother in the long grass
Of the west pasture, where she stood like moonlight
Listening for foxes. It was something like love
From another world that seized her
From behind, and she gave, not lifting her head
Out of dew, without ever looking, her best
Self to that great need. Turned loose, she dipped her face
Farther into the chill of the earth, and in a sound
Of sobbing   of something stumbling
Away, began, as she must do,
To carry me. I woke, dying,

In the summer sun of the hillside, with my eyes
Far more than human. I saw for a blazing moment
The great grassy world from both sides,
Man and beast in the round of their need,
And the hill wind stirred in my wool,
My hoof and my hand clasped each other,
I ate my one meal
Of milk, and died
Staring. From dark grass I came straight
To my father's house, whose dust
Whirls up in the halls for no reason
When no one comes   piling deep in a hellish mild corner,
And, through my immortal waters,
I meet the sun's grains eye
To eye, and they fail at my closet of glass.
Dead, I am most surely living
In the minds of farm boys: I am he who drives
Them like wolves from the hound bitch and calf
And from the chaste ewe in the wind.
They go into woods   into bean fields   they go
Deep into their known right hands. Dreaming of me,
They groan   they wait   they suffer
Themselves, they marry, they raise their kind.

FREDERICK DOUGLASS[17]
—*Robert Hayden*

When it is finally ours, this freedom, this liberty, this beautiful
and terrible thing, needful to man as air,
usable as earth; when it belongs at last to our children,
when it is truly instinct, brain matter, diastole, systole,
reflex action; when it is finally won; when it is more
than the gaudy mumbo jumbo of politicians:
this man, this Douglass, this former slave, this Negro
beaten to his knees, exiled, visioning a world
where none is lonely, none hunted, alien,
this man, superb in love and logic, this man
shall be remembered. Oh, not with statues' rhetoric,
not with legends and poems and wreaths of bronze alone,
but with the lives grown out of his life, the lives
fleshing his dream of the beautiful, needful thing.

Chapter 4

LOCUS
Relationships Between
Reader, Poem, and
Audience

In embodying the experience that is the poem (using the word *poem* broadly to cover all literary types), the interpreter is, as we have said, always reaching outward in what is essentially an act of homage to the poem. In this giving of self the interpreter extends and enriches the self, which is why it is possible to worry too soon about the audience for a reading. The performer who cares more about pleasing an audience than about enactment of the poem will endanger the whole poetic experience, both for the performer and for the audience. The interpreter needs always to remember that reader and audience must be brought together to the act of communion with the poem; if the reader communes with the audience but not with the poem, the audience is likely to come away with spirits unfed.

CREATIVITY IN INTERPRETATION

Some teachers of interpretation think of the interpreter as a middleman between poet and audience, speaking for the poet, but this is a view that we shall not adopt. It has the unhappy effect of making the interpreter sound like a funnel or megaphone through which the poet speaks, a middleman not responsible for the product but cashing in on the sale. If the view expressed in the preceding chapter is correct, any individual reading of a poem is a coalescence of the inner form of the poem with the inner form of the reader, and consequently the interpreter becomes a creative participant in the literary experience.

The performing arts seek to re-create an art object, but because human beings are doing the re-creating, there is necessarily a perspective introduced by the performer. Human beings cannot be simply highly polished mirrors reflecting a work of art; in some sense they must always be lamps illuminating the work of art from within themselves. These two analogies—the mirror and the lamp—have a long history in criticism, and they serve to make a point that must be made here: granting the creativity of interpreters—that they are lamps shedding light by their own perspective on the work of art—it is probably true that the best interpretation arises from the interpreters' deliberate minimizing of their own importance in the act and from their willingness to see themselves as mirrors reflecting, to the best of their ability, the view taken by the work itself. That is to say, art works best by indirection; the art of the interpreter is no exception to the rule.

What we are saying, then, is that the interpreter doubtless will do best to keep attention on the material and not on either the audience or the performer. *We need not deny the importance of both the audience and the individual interpreter.* We shall take account of both later, and ultimately the poem is of importance because of the way in which it gives satisfaction to both audience and interpreter. But the first consideration (*all others are secondary*) is the establishing of a living coalescence between inner poem and inner reader. This is a difficult task, and few readers achieve it constantly and fully; first-rate interpreters are every bit as rare as first-rate pianists or actors or dancers. Happily, however, that active participation in a literary text demanded by the art of interpretation will carry rewards even when the reading is less than perfect, and all readers can gain by reading aloud and by participating in the complex relationship between the poem, the audience, and themselves.

READER AND POEM: MIRROR AND LAMP

There is no way for the teacher and the class to test a reading except by listening to it and watching it, for the interpreter (unless performing on radio, on records, or on tape) is normally both audible and visible. What the class as audience watches for is congruence between the gestures of the reader and the gestures of the poem itself, for poems are made up of gestures, both verbal and nonverbal.

The primary appeal of interpretation is perhaps to the ear, but no performance can reach the ears of the audience without the careful participation of the performer's whole body. The interpreter's most expressive area is doubtless the area of the head and shoulders, the upper part of the body, which is what the audience usually watches during a solo performance, but the upper torso cannot act independently of the

READER AND AUDIENCE: ECONOMY

rest of the body. The reader reads from head to foot, and a slackness of tension in the lower part of the body (a slouch for King Lear) will betray inadequate responsiveness just as much as a meaningless gesture of the hand.

The whole reader is a gesturing agent. Thoughts, words, movements of the body, impulses in the mind, tensions and relaxations, attractions and repulsions—all are profitably thought of as gestures. If readers *overgesture*, they distract the attention of listeners from the poem and call attention to themselves. There is a necessary *economy* in the art of interpretation, a way of expending energy in which nothing is wasted. (*Economy* is a particularly useful term for discussions of performance, referring as it does to the management of resources, or, with reference to our particular interest, in the words of *Webster's Third New International Dictionary*, "the elimination of all unnecessary details so as to produce the maximum artistic effect." Interpreters at their best are thrifty; they avoid waste. In this respect they are like any creative artist. In a study of creativity, Harold Rugg suggests: "The significant act always tends to seek the simplest possible solution."[1] For the performer, it is not a question of how *much* the audience will take in order to participate fully in the experience of the reading. Economy in overt and covert behavior is a virtue, although this is not to say that there should be no behavior.

ACTING AND INTERPRETATION

The long argument about differences between acting and interpretation sometimes stems from this matter: when interpreters fail to observe economy, they are sometimes said to be acting—too much movement, too much attention to the craft of performance and not enough to the material. But such a distinction is clearly unfair to the art of acting. Actually, the economies of the two arts differ. The actor, housed within the play, must make us accept his or her visible body as the body of the character being performed. The interpreter is under no such injunction, though he or she must make us accept the body *act* as persuasive. It is not unusual for us to accept, say, a short, dark girl as being a tall, blonde girl in the interpretation situation; we do not so easily overlook explicit details of characterization in an actress. We know that the interpreter is not asking us to accept as theatrical *fact* the physical body of the performer, but the actor does ask that of us. A pianist may come in his own person as "interpreter" to play Bach, but the pianist who comes dressed as Bach to play Bach, and who asks us to accept him as Bach, is both interpreter and actor. The economies (since both means and ends differ) are different for the two arts.

We may make a broad distinction—one made often in the past—between actor, reader, and public speaker by saying that the public speaker normally speaks directly to the audience in order to persuade

[1] Harold Rugg, *Imagination* (New York: Harper & Row, 1963), p. 125.

them through some argument devised especially for them. The relationship is personal, direct, practical. The actor normally puts the scene onstage, faces other actors onstage, seems to perform as though living the lines quite apart from any awareness of the audience. The relationship is indirect, impersonal, not motivated by any practical aim to set forth an argument. (It is necessary to repeat the qualifier *normally,* for not all actors and not all speakers behave in the fashions described. Some speeches are much like poems; some plays are much like persuasive speeches, and the actor and speaker must modify their performance in terms of the nature of the thing being said.) The interpreter normally faces the audience but does not talk directly to them. Rather than making a speech, the interpreter is trying to let the audience see and hear beyond the performer to the work, but they can do that only through the performer. In a sense, the literary text is held out between audience and reader so that both can look at it. The interpreter takes more open cognizance of the audience than does the actor, in this way, and less than the public speaker. (This is obviously not to say that the actor cares less about the audience than the public speaker; it is simply that the actor recognizes it in a different way.)

Some poems are "public," almost like public speeches, and meant to be persuasive. The interpreter reading them will behave much as the public speaker behaves. Some poems are "private," highly subjective meditations that are simply "overheard" by an audience, and the interpreter reading such poems will be closer to the position of the actor speaking a soliloquy. Almost all literature is in some sense conversation. There is almost always a speaker and also a listener, whether clearly defined or not. Elizabeth Barrett Browning wrote the lines of this sonnet to Robert Browning:

> How do I love thee? Let me count the ways.
> I love thee to the depth and breadth and height
> My soul can reach, when feeling out of sight
> For the ends of Being and ideal Grace.
> I love thee to the level of everyday's
> Most quiet need, by sun and candle-light.
> I love thee freely, as men strive for Right;
> I love thee with the passion put to use
> In my old griefs, and with my childhood's faith.
> I love thee with a love I seemed to lose
> With my lost saints,—I love thee with the breath,
> Smiles, tears, of all my life—and, if God choose,
> I shall but love thee better after death.

No interpreter reading the sonnet would wish to look the audience directly in the eye and say "How do I love thee?" To do so would violate the relationship between speaker and listener built into the poem and would substitute for it a speaker-listener relationship that would be either embarrassing or laughable. Should the reader, then, pretend to be speaking directly to Robert Browning? That is a possible way, a way that would result in a "dramatic"reading involving two distinct and definite personalities. But there is another way that is perhaps happiest for most people: the poem may be taken simply as a lyrical expression of love between a man and a woman, not limited to Elizabeth Barrett and Robert Browning. In this case, one would not seem to be speaking to a certain definite person at all but speaking aloud in private. The audience *for* a poem and the audience *in* a poem are not by any necessity one and the same.

THE PROBLEMS OF LOCUS

Locus means "place," "site"; it has a mathematical meaning, too: "a line, plane, etc., every point of which satisfies a given condition and which contains no point that does not satisfy this condition." It is profitable to ask of every piece of literature that one reads: *What is its locus? Exactly where does it reside? Where does the speaker stand to see what he sees or say what he says?*

Locus is involved in the relationship we have been discussing between reader and poem and between reader and audience. When the speaker in a poem seems to talk directly to the audience, we may say that his or her locus with respect to them is eye-to-eye. Some teachers of interpretation refer to this as an *open situation.*[2] When the locus with respect to the audience is not direct, the situation is said to be a *closed situation.* Seen this way, the question of whether one reads "How do I love thee" directly to the listeners is a question of the speaker's locus or placement with respect to the audience.

But this is not the whole issue. One may speak directly to an audience *in* the poem rather than to the performer's immediate audience in the room. One may let Elizabeth Barrett speak to Robert Browning rather than simply speak aloud to herself. This is still, by our definition, a closed situation, even though the performer (as Elizabeth Barrett) might be speaking eye-to-eye with Robert Browning within the poem. Thus, in discussing locus, we must distinguish between possible loci for *audiences.*

Locus is also involved in the projection of a reading. We have argued that the reading is not to be thought of as "onstage" normally (though there are many exceptions), but rather as out in front, in the realm of the audience. When the situation is not open, or eye-to-eye with the audience, interpreters are sometimes advised to "place" the reading on the back wall of the room, but that seems to us inadvisable; a reading that is "really" on the back wall will make an audience want to turn to see it. The most efficient location is usually in the central area of the audience or just back of center, so that the front section of the audience will not feel overlooked and the back section will feel in-

---

[2] See Alethea Smith Mattingly and Wilma H. Grimes, *Interpretation: Writer, Reader, Audience,* 2d ed. (Belmont, Calif.: Wadsworth Publishing Co. Inc., 1970), pp. 18–19.

cluded. But the location is not simply fixed. It is distracting to have an interpreter look steadily at a single spot throughout a reading. The locus should be defined well enough so that the performer has a point of contact in the audience, a point to which energy must reach, but it should not be so narrowly confined that an audience begins to feel that the reader is mesmerized.

Another aspect of locus involves perspective. The angle of vision, the point of view of a work involves the location of the narrator with respect to the work. One of the tasks of the interpreter is to embody the narrator, of course, but it is not the narrator alone who contributes, as we shall make clear in a moment with a passage from Homer's *Odyssey* (see page 76). The concentration and attention of the interpreter follow a variety of leads in a narrative. Different readers will make different choices, and the choices will result in readings having different impacts—different in quality, though not necessarily in strength. This is an aspect of the creativity of the performer.

For this second aspect of locus, it may be helpful to think in terms of the movie or television camera, which sometimes stands far back to look at a scene, sometimes moves in very close to examine details, sometimes seems to look at a person or place or thing through the eyes of a character, sometimes juxtaposes two images, sometimes deliberately blurs images, sometimes fades. Literature (and hence the interpreter) is never static. Even long passages of description—which interpreters often read in a particularly ineffective, motionless way—have real vitality when they are well written, and to underestimate them is usually to kill a story or a novel.

These first aspects of locus involve location in space, whether real or imagined space. A third aspect of locus is situation in time: a shift in time is a shift of location. A fourth aspect is shift in attitude, but attitudinal changes are so constant and often so intimately related to one another that it becomes difficult to think of them in terms of locus. Doubtless we should restrict our term to the three major kinds of shift in location: relationships between reader and audience (involving placement), relationships among perspectives, relationships in time. In all three, essentially, physical space is involved, whether the real space in which the performer stands or the space in imagination where feeling is at work. If we think of the interpreter as embodying the poem—and we do—perhaps it is not very easy, after all, to separate the real and the imagined space. Not everything going on in the imagined space is audible or visible to the audience, but the effects of that inner activity certainly are. It is amazing how much is communicated when the interpreter concentrates on the felt sensing of the poem—and how little results when the interpreter only reads words. Interpreters are active; they are never passive.

Literary forms differ markedly in descriptions that may be given of their loci. The essay illustrates a number of positions: the personal essay is often indirect (closed) and suggestive; the formal essay may be directly expository or persuasive (open); the humorous essay is often a dramatic characterization of a speaker—a speaker whose locus may be either direct or indirect, depending on context. Letters have a direct writer-recipient relationship but not usually a direct performer-audience relationship. Drama is rather like letters, except that there is always a speaking "listener"—both the person speaking and the person spoken to normally take part in the dialogue, and the illusion of real life is usually the object of the dialogue.

Prose fiction is highly complex—perhaps the most complex of literary forms in this respect—as it moves through various loci: the writer may talk directly to the reader at times; at other times the writer disappears in a dramatic scene and we listen to his characters speak; the writer may employ a narrator who is at once a character and a director of other characters; or the narration may seem to come from no person at all, but from a concealed speaker who is nameless, formless, effaced. The possibilities are greater than we can indicate, but remember that when you choose a literary text to read you are faced at once, and sharply, with the problem of defining the position that you, as reader, must take. The inflexible reader is a failure.

We may illustrate the method with this passage:

HOMER'S ODYSSEY[3]
—Translation by *Robert Fitzgerald*

> Long before anyone else, the prince Telémakhos
> now caught signt of Athena—for he, too,
> was sitting there, unhappy among the suitors,
> a boy, daydreaming. What if his great father
> came from the unknown world and drove these men
> like dead leaves through the place, recovering
> honor and lordship in his own domains?
> Then he who dreamed in the crowd gazed out at Athena.
>
> Straight to the door he came, irked with himself
> to think a visitor had been kept there waiting,
> and took her right hand, grasping with his left
> her tall bronze-bladed spear. Then he said warmly:
> "Greetings, stranger! Welcome to our feast.
> There will be time to tell your errand later."
>
> He led the way, and Pallas Athena followed
> into the lofty hall. The boy reached up
> and thrust her spear high in a polished rack
> against a pillar, where tough spear on spear

[3] From *The Odyssey* by Homer, translated by Robert Fitzgerald. Copyright© 1961 by Robert Fitzgerald. Reprinted by permission of Doubleday & Company, Inc.

of the old soldier, his father, stood in order.
Then, shaking out a splendid coverlet,
he seated her on a throne with footrest—all
finely carved—and drew his painted armchair
near her, at a distance from the rest.
To be amid the din, the suitor's riot
would ruin his guest's appetite, he thought,
and he wished privacy to ask for news
about his father, gone for years.

                      A maid
brought them a silver finger bowl and filled it
out of a beautiful spouting golden jug,
then drew a polished table to their side.
The larder mistress with her tray came by
and served them generously. A carver lifted
cuts of each roast meat to put on trenchers
before the two. He gave them cups of gold,
and these the steward as he went his rounds
filled and filled again.

                      Now came the suitors,
young bloods trooping in to their own seats
on thrones or easy chairs. Attendants poured
water over their fingers, while the maids
piled baskets full of brown loaves near at hand,
and houseboys brimmed the bowls with wine.
Now they laid hands upon the ready feast
and thought of nothing more. Not till desire
for food and drink had left them were they mindful
of dance and song, that are the grace of feasting.
A herald gave a shapely cithern harp.
to Phemios, whom they compelled to sing—
and what a storm he plucked upon the strings
for prelude! High and clear the song arose.

Telémakhos now spoke to grey-eyed Athena,
his head bent close, so no one else might hear:
"Dear guest, will this offend you, if I speak?
It is easy for these men to like these things,
harping and song; they have an easy life,
scot free, eating the livestock of another—
a man whose bones are rotting somewhere now,
white in the rain on dark earth where they lie,
or tumbling in the groundswell of the sea.
If he returned, if these men ever saw him,
faster legs they'd pray for, to a man,
and not more wealth in handsome robes or gold.
But he is lost; he came to grief and perished,
and there's no help for us in someone's hoping
he still may come; that sun has long gone down.
But tell me now, and put it for me clearly—
who are you? Where do you come from? Where's your home

and family? What kind of ship is yours,
and what course brought you here? Who are your sailors?
I don't suppose you walked here on the sea.
Another thing—this too I ought to know—
is Ithaka new to you, or were you ever
a guest here in the old days? Far and near
friends knew this house; for he whose home it was
had much acquaintance in the world."
—*Book I, lines 135-175*

Notice that the point of view is that of the unnamed narrator. Our locus is with him; the angle of vision is his. But almost immediately we are concerned also with the perspective of Telémakhos, who catches sight of the goddess Athena as she appears disguised as a stranger. We move immediately inside Telémakhos, sharing his thoughts as he looks outward at the great hall. Now we go with him to the door, still through the eyes of the narrator, to greet Athena; the break in the stanza is also a sharp transition in the locus. One might summarize the steps in the first fourteen lines of the section as follows:

1. The narrator tells us that Telémakhos sees Athena.
2. Telémakhos sits dreaming unhappily among the suitors.
3. Telémakhos imagines his father returning and driving out the suitors and regaining his own place.
4. Telémakhos, aroused from his dreaming, sees Athena.
5. Telémakhos goes to greet her, berating himself for his negligence.
6. He greets her as a host, and speaks to her.
7. "Welcome to our feast," he says. "There will be time to tell your errand later."

Each of these steps is, in a sense, a shift in place, in locus; the attention turns from one point or place to another in a series of linked transitions. The interpreter keeps the poem alive by going through these transitions attentively, never losing sight of the total picture as conceived by the unnamed narrator.

Now go through the remainder of the section, marking out the various loci for yourself. Remember that the locus of any one character in a story is always in part defined by the general narrator's locus. The question is always: How, and to what extent, are the thoughts, actions, words of the character directed by, or limited by, the general narrator? (Even in a drama the writer, as general narrator, takes a position, has a locus, though he normally does not have a single line to speak, but speaks only through his characters. In reading any one character, the interpreter does not have complete freedom to interpret the lines of that character in any way seen fit; he or she is bound, in part, by the locus of the writer.) In lines 3 and 4, for example, should the interpreter read the lines with the feelings of Telémakhos, giving visible evidence of a behavior that suggests unhappy daydreaming, or should he read them matter-of-factly, simply as summary exposition from the narrator?

Is there a midposition? If one decides not to do the lines in the person and character of Telémakhos, is there nevertheless a point in later lines, prior to the dialogue, at which one must decide to characterize? If so, where would you place or locate this shift? (Variation in your answers is not only anticipated but inescapable.)

Here are the opening paragraphs from Stephen Crane's story "The Bride Comes to Yellow Sky." Read them, and then we shall examine together some of the questions of locus in the selection.

I

The great Pullman was whirling onward with such dignity of motion that a glance from the window seemed simply to prove that the plains of Texas were pouring eastward. Vast flats of green grass, dull-hued spaces of mesquit and cactus, little groups of frame houses, woods of light and tender trees, all were sweeping into the east, sweeping over the horizon, a precipice.

A newly married pair had boarded this coach at San Antonio. The man's face was reddened from many days in the wind and sun, and a direct result of his new black clothes was that his brick-coloured hands were constantly performing in a most conscious fashion. From time to time he looked down respectfully at his attire. He sat with a hand on each knee, like a man waiting in a barber's shop. The glances he devoted to other passengers were furtive and shy.

The bride was not pretty, nor was she very young. She wore a dress of blue cashmere, with small reservations of velvet here and there, and with steel buttons abounding. She continually twisted her head to regard her puff sleeves, very stiff, straight, and high. They embarrassed her. It was quite apparent that she had cooked, and that she expected to cook, dutifully. The blushes caused by the careless scrutiny of some passengers as she had entered the car were strange to see upon this plain, under-class countenance, which was drawn in placid, almost emotionless lines.

They were evidently very happy. "Ever been in a parlour-car before?" he asked, smiling with delight.

"No," she answered; "I never was. It's fine, ain't it?"

"Great! And then after a while we'll go forward to the diner, and get a big lay-out. Finest meal in the world. Charge a dollar."

"Oh, do they?" cried the bride. "Charge a dollar? Why, that's too much—for us—ain't it, Jack?"

"Not this trip, anyhow," he answered bravely. "We're going to go the whole thing."

Later he explained to her about the trains. "You see, it's a thousand miles from one end of Texas to the other, and this train runs right across it, and never stops but four times." He had the pride of an owner. He pointed out to her the dazzling fittings of the coach; and in truth her eyes opened wider as she contemplated the sea-green figured velvet, the shining brass, silver, and glass, the wood that gleamed as darkly brilliant as the surface of a pool of oil. At one end a bronze figure sturdily held a support for a separated chamber, and at convenient places on the ceiling were frescos in olive and silver.

To the minds of the pair, their surroundings reflected the glory of their marriage that morning in San Antonio; this was the environment of their new estate; and the man's face in particular beamed with an elation that made him appear ridiculous to the negro porter. This individual at times surveyed them from afar with an amused and superior grin. On other occasions he bullied them with skill in ways that did not make it exactly plain to them that they were being bullied. He subtly used all the manners of the most unconquerable kind of snobbery. He oppressed them; but of this oppression they had small knowledge, and they speedily forgot that infrequently a number of travellers covered them with stares of derisive enjoyment. Historically there was supposed to be something infinitely humorous in their situation.

"We are due in Yellow Sky at 3:42," he said, looking tenderly into her eyes.

We have given the entire text of the story at the end of this chapter so that you can explore it in full for yourself, but let's examine the initial paragraphs together. Here are some questions:

1. What is the point of view of the first paragraph? Do we look out the window with the narrator? With the man and woman? What evidence leads to your answer?

2. What happens, with respect to locus, as you move from the first to the second paragraph? As you move from the first sentence of paragraph two to the second sentence of the paragraph? Is there any change in the performer's relationship with the audience during these shifts? How much of the first twelve lines of the story is read directly to the audience? Indirectly to the audience? If any of the lines are in indirect relationship with the audience, how are they performed in relation to the man and woman in the Pullman? Describe the movements in terms of the eye of a camera.

3. Are any parts of paragraphs two and three read from the point of view of the man and woman being described? If so, which ones, and why? (There is not, probably, a *right* or *wrong* answer involved here.) Again, how much of paragraph three is directed specifically to the audience?

4. Once the dialogue begins, does the narrator disappear, or is he still present? What difference does it make? (Is there any difference between narration and dramatization?) Upon what evidence do you base your answers?

5. Would you employ the dialect of the speakers or the dialect of the narrator in performing the dialogue? Can you tell what the dialect of the narrator *is*?

6. When the story says "He pointed out to her the dazzling fittings of the coach," and so on, is the locus with the narrator (whose words these are) or with the man who is doing the pointing out?

7. How much does one characterize the porter in the Pullman? Do we survey the couple from the porter's point of view, or do we see both porter and couple from the narrator's position?

8. What happens in the movement of the story as we arrive at the line "We are due in Yellow Sky at 3:42 . . . ."?

All these ways of directing the attention are aspects of locus, and the choices one makes are part of the *creative* act of the reader in building a performance. The writer limits the performer sufficiently so that he says what he wants to say, but at the same times he leaves the performer open so that certain details of locus can be supplied. The reader is always in this sense a participant in the story.

One additional—and complex—matter is related to locus: the question of proximity in space of performer to audience, of character to character, of narrator to audience and to character. The anthropologist Edward Hall has written tellingly of what he calls *proxemics,* the study of ways in which men and women use space in their lives. Cultures vary in the use of space; in one culture, persons conversing may stand very close together—so close that persons from another culture would find the lack of distance disconcerting. As individuals, we differ in our feelings about such distances. Our public and our private selves may behave very differently with respect to use of space. Formal occasions and informal occasions provide us with different feelings about space. Conventions about our use of space mark our behavior as significantly as conventions of other kinds.

PROXEMICS

It is worthwhile, therefore, to consider carefully the distance one chooses to place between the performance and the audience. Sometimes, to be sure, the performer has no choice in the matter, but often there is opportunity to choose. What kinds of material would seem to you to thrive best on fairly intimate relationship with an audience? What kind would thrive best with greater distancing? Among the materials given at the close of this chapter, would you make distinctions, if you could, in terms of space between you and the audience for which you were performing?

Distances, since they affect us in our daily lives, also will affect characters in a story or a poem or a play and the narrator in fiction. The solo interpreter cannot always *literally* give us distances between two characters being performed; to try that would more often than not be fatal to the performance, since it would only underscore the performer's inability literally to inhabit two bodies at one time. But there are nevertheless ways of suggesting distance—volume, pitch, tempo, articulation, size of gestures, signals of retreat or aggression in the body: all these can be used in the service of suggesting locus in space.

In "The Bride Comes to Yellow Sky," for example, would the narrator, in performing the opening paragraph, seem to you to be close to the audience? Do you sense any feeling of intimacy in his relationship to his hearers? When he turns to tell us about the man (*turns*—why?), does he seem to you equidistant between audience and character? Does his degree of proximity to the man change at all during the paragraph? Notice that the man himself is highly conscious of his public self, in his unwonted attire; his glances toward other characters are "furtive and shy." Crane gives us, throughout these opening paragraphs, a continuous sense of movement in the language which carries the story's life.

We must remember the caution sounded in an earlier chapter: the space of the room in which one performs must be taken as the *real* locus of the work as a whole. Nevertheless, in filling that room, variations in the use of the *imagined* space are not only possible; they are almost always mandated by the work itself. They are in fact another aspect of tensiveness, of life.

In the pieces that follow, try to define the locus. Then, remembering all we have said thus far about use of the book, projection of the reading, attention to detail, tensiveness, the act of coalescing, and the matter of perspective, see whether you can succeed at least partially in giving the piece a sense of presence. Give in to it. Concentrate on it (not on yourself, not on the audience).

One further reminder: no reading can be prepared in a hurry. Practice diligently. It is wiser to spend a series of ten-minute periods on rehearsal than to try to accomplish everything in one rehearsal. A good reading is like any other performance: it grows and ripens with time. You are not prepared until you are secure with your text. It is not a matter simply of being acquainted with the words; that is only the first step to be taken in preparation. The words must be so effortless, finally, that (to paraphrase Yeats) one cannot tell the dancer from the dance, the reader from the poem. In a real sense, the poem must be worked into your muscles. And remember what we have said about economy in performance.

MATERIALS FOR PRACTICE

THE TRUE LOVER[4]
—*A. E. Housman*

> The lad came to the door at night,
> When lovers crown their vows,
> And whistled soft and out of sight
> In shadow of the boughs.
>
> I shall not vex you with my face
> Henceforth, my love, for aye;
> So take me in your arms a space
> Before the east is grey.

[4] From "A Shropshire Lad"—Authorised Edition—from *The Collected Poems of A. E. Housman*. Copyright 1939, 1940, © 1959 by Holt, Rinehart and Winston. Reprinted by permission of Holt, Rinehart and Winston and The Society of Authors as the literary representative of the Estate of the late A. E. Housman, and Messrs. Jonathan Cape Ltd., publishers of A. E. Housman's *Collected Poems*.

When I from hence away am past
   I shall not find a bride,
And you shall be the first and last
   I ever lay beside.

She heard and went and knew not why;
   Her heart to his she laid;
Light was the air beneath the sky
   But dark under the shade.

"Oh do you breathe, lad, that your breast
   Seems not to rise and fall,
And here upon my bosom prest
   There beats no heart at all?"

"O loud, my girl, it once would knock,
   You should have felt it then;
But since for you I stopped the clock
   It never goes again."

"Oh lad, what is it, lad, that drips
   Wet from your neck on mine?
What is it falling on my lips,
   My lad, that tastes of brine?"

"Oh like enough 'tis blood, my dear,
   For when the knife has slit
The throat across from ear to ear
   'Twill bleed because of it."

Under the stars the air was light
   But dark below the boughs,
The still air of the speechless night,
   When lovers crown their vows.

SONNET 94
—William Shakespeare

They that have power to hurt, and will do none,
That do not do the thing they most do show,
Who, moving others, are themselves as stone,
Unmovéd, cold, and to temptation slow,—
They rightly do inherit heaven's graces,
And husband nature's riches from expense;
They are the lords and owners of their faces,
Others, but stewards of their excellence.
The summer's flower is to the summer sweet
Though to itself it only live and die;

But if that flower with base infection meet,
The basest weed outbraves his dignity:
    For sweetest things turn sourest by their deeds;
    Lilies that fester smell far worse than weeds.

A WORN PATH[5]
—Eudora Welty

It was December—a bright frozen day in the early morning. Far out in the country there was an old Negro woman with her head tied in a red rag, coming along a path through the pinewoods. Her name was Phoenix Jackson. She was very old and small and she walked slowly in the dark pine shadows, moving a little from side to side in her steps, with the balanced heaviness and lightness of a pendulum in a grandfather clock. She carried a thin, small cane made from an umbrella, and with this she kept tapping the frozen earth in front of her. This made a grave and persistent noise in the air, that seemed meditative, like the chirping of a solitary little bird.

She wore a dark striped dress reaching down to her shoe-tops, and an equally long apron of bleached sugar sacks, with a full pocket; all neat and tidy, but every time she took a step she might have fallen over her shoe-laces, which dragged from her unlaced shoes. She looked straight ahead. Her eyes were blue with age. Her skin had a pattern all its own of numberless branching wrinkles and as though a whole little tree stood in the middle of her forehead, but a golden colour ran underneath, and the two knobs of her cheeks were illuminated by a yellow burning under the dark. Under the red rag her hair came down on her neck in the frailest of ringlets, still black, and with an odour like copper.

Now and then there was a quivering in the thicket. Old Phoenix said, "Out of my way, all you foxes, owls, beetles, jack rabbits, coons and wild animals! . . . Keep out from under these feet, little bob-whites. . . . Keep the big wild hogs out of my path. Don't let none of those come running my direction. I got a long way." Under her small black-freckled hand her cane, limber as a buggy whip, would switch at the brush as if to rouse up any hiding things.

On she went. The woods were deep and still. The sun made the pine needles almost too bright to look at, up where the wind rocked. The cones dropped as light as feathers. Down in the hollow was the mourning dove— it was not too late for him.

The path ran up a hill. "Seems like there is chains about my feet, time I get this far," she said, in the voice of argument old people keep to use with themselves. "Something always take a hold of me on this hill—pleads I should stay."

After she got to the top she turned and gave a full, severe look behind her where she had come. "Up through pines," she said at length. "Now down through oaks."

[5] Copyright 1941, 1969 by Eudora Welty. Reprinted from her volume *A Curtain of Green and Other Stories* by permission of Harcourt Brace Jovanovich, Inc. See further notice on copyright page.

Her eyes opened their widest, and she started down gently. But before she got to the bottom of the hill a bush caught her dress.

Her fingers were busy and intent, but her skirts were full and long, so that before she could pull them free in one place they were caught in another. It was not possible to allow the dress to tear. "I in the thorny bush," she said. "Thorns, you doing your appointed work. Never want to let folks pass, no sir. Old eyes thought you was a pretty little *green* bush."

Finally, trembling all over, she stood free, and after a moment dared to stoop for her cane.

"Sun so high!" she cried, leaning back and looking, while the thick tears went over her eyes. "The time getting all gone here."

At the foot of this hill was a place where a log was laid across the creek.

"Now come the trial," said Phoenix.

Putting her right foot out, she mounted the log and shut her eyes. Lifting her skirt, leveling her cane fiercely before her, like a festival figure in some parade, she began to march across. Then she opened her eyes and she was safe on the other side.

"I wasn't as old as I thought," she said.

But she sat down to rest. She spread her skirts on the bank around her and folded her hands over her knees. Up above her was a tree in a pearly cloud of mistletoe. She did not dare to close her eyes, and when a little boy brought her a little plate with a slice of marble-cake on it she spoke to him. "That would be acceptable," she said. But when she went to take it there was just her own hand in the air.

So she left that tree, and had to go through a barbed-wire fence. There she had to creep and crawl, spreading her knees and stretching her fingers like a baby trying to climb the steps. But she talked loudly to herself: she could not let her dress be torn now, so late in the day, and she could not pay for having her arm or her leg sawed off if she caught fast where she was.

At last she was safe through the fence and risen up out in the clearing. Big dead trees, like black men with one arm, were standing in the purple stalks of the withered cotton field. There sat a buzzard.

"Who you watching?"

In the furrow she made her way along.

"Glad this not the season for bulls," she said, looking sideways, "and the good Lord made his snakes to curl up and sleep in the winter. A pleasure I don't see no two-headed snake coming around that tree, where it come once. It took a while to get by him, back in the summer."

She passed through the old cotton and went into a field of dead corn. It whispered and shook and was taller than her head. "Through the maze now," she said, for there was no path.

Then there was something tall, black, and skinny there, moving before her.

At first she took it for a man. It could have been a man dancing in the field. But she stood still and listened, and it did not make a sound. It was as silent as a ghost.

"Ghost," she said sharply, "who be you the ghost of? For I have heard of nary death close by."

But there was no answer—only the ragged dancing in the wind.

She shut her eyes, reached out her hand, and touched a sleeve. She found a coat and inside that an emptiness, cold as ice.

"You scarecrow," she said. Her face lighted. "I ought to be shut up for good," she said with laughter. "My senses is gone. I too old. I the oldest people I ever know. Dance, old scarecrow," she said, "while I dancing with you."

She kicked her foot over the furrow, and with mouth drawn down, shook her head once or twice in a little strutting way. Some husks blew down and whirled in streamers about her skirts.

Then she went on, parting her way from side to side with the cane, through the whispering field. At last she came to the end, to a wagon track where the silver grass blew between the red ruts. The quail were walking around like pullets, seeming all dainty and unseen.

"Walk pretty," she said. "This is the easy place. This the easy going."

She followed the track, swaying through the quiet bare fields, through the little strings of trees silver in their dead leaves, past cabins silver from weather, with the doors and windows boarded shut, all like old women under a spell sitting there. "I walking in their sleep," she said, nodding her head vigorously.

In a ravine she went where a spring was silently flowing through a hollow log. Old Phoenix bent and drank. "Sweet-gum makes the water sweet," she said, and drank more. "Nobody knows who made this well, for it was here when I was born."

The track crossed a swampy part where the moss hung as white as lace from every climb. "Sleep on, alligators, and blow your bubbles." Then the track went into the road.

Deep, deep the road went down between the high green-coloured banks. Overhead the live-oaks met, and it was as dark as a cave.

A black dog with a lolling tongue came up out of the weeds by the ditch. She was meditating, and not ready, and when he came at her she only hit him a little with her cane. Over she went in the ditch, like a little puff of milk-weed.

Down there, her senses drifted away. A dream visited her, and she reached her hand up, but nothing reached down and gave her a pull. So she lay there and presently went to talking. "Old woman," she said to herself, "that black dog come up out of the weeds to stall you off, and now there he sitting on his fine tail, smiling at you."

A white man finally came along and found her—a hunter, a young man, with his dog on a chain.

"Well, Granny!" he laughed. "What are you doing there?"

"Lying on my back like a June-bug waiting to be turned over, mister," she said, reaching up her hand.

He lifted her up, gave her a swing in the air, and set her down. "Anything broken, Granny?"

"No, sir, them old dead weeds is springy enough," said Phoenix, when she had got her breath. "I thank you for your trouble."

"Where do you live, Granny?" he asked, while the two dogs were growling at each other.

"Away back yonder, sir, behind the ridge. You can't even see it from here."

"On your way home?"

"No, sir, I going to town."

"Why, that's too far! That's as far as I walk when I come out myself, and I get something for my trouble." He patted the stuffed bag he carried, and there hung down a little closed claw. It was one of the bob-whites, with its beak hooked bitterly to show it was dead. "Now you go on home, Granny!"

"I bound to go to town, mister," said Phoenix. "The time come round."

He gave another laugh, filling the whole landscape. "I know you old coloured people! Wouldn't miss going to town to see Santa Claus!"

But something held old Phoenix very still. The deep lines in her face went into a fierce and different radiation. Without warning, she had seen with her own eyes a flashing nickel fall out of the man's pocket on to the ground.

"How old are you, Granny?" he was saying.

"There is no telling, mister," she said, "no telling."

Then she gave gave a little cry and clapped her hands and said, "Git on away from here, dog! Look! Look at that dog!" she laughed as if in admiration. "He ain't scared of nobody. He a big black dog." She whispered, "Sic him!"

"Watch me get rid of that cur," said the man. "Sic him, Pete! Sic him!"

Phoenix heard the dogs fighting, and hear the man running and throwing sticks. She even heard a gunshot. But she was slowly bending forward by that time, further and further forward, the lids stretched down over her eyes, as if she were doing this in her sleep. Her chin was lowered almost to her knees. The yellow palm of her hand came out from the fold of her apron. Her fingers slid down and along the ground under the piece of money with the grace and care they would have in lifting an egg from under a sitting hen. Then she slowly straightened up, she stood erect, and the nickel was in her apron pocket. A bird flew by. Her lips moved. "God watching me the whole time. I come to stealing."

The man came back, and his own dog panted about them. "Well, I scared him off that time," he said, and then he laughed and lifted his gun and pointed it at Phoenix.

She stood straight and faced him.

"Doesn't the gun scare you?" he said, still pointing it.

"No, sir, I seen plenty go off closer by, in my day, and for less than what I done," she said, holding utterly still.

He smiled, and shouldered the gun. "Well, Granny," he said, "you must be a hundred years old, and scared of nothing. I'd give you a dime if I had any money with me. But you take my advice and stay home, and nothing will happen to you."

"I bound to go on my way, mister," said Phoenix. She inclined her head in the red rag. Then they went in different directions, but she could hear the gun shooting again and again over the hill.

She walked on. The shadows hung from the oak trees to the road like curtains. Then she smelled wood-smoke, and smelled the river, and she saw a steeple and the cabins on their steep steps. Dozens of little black children whirled around her. There ahead was Natchez shining. Bells were ringing. She walked on.

In the paved city it was Christmas time. There were red and green electric lights strong and criss-crossed everywhere, and all turned on in the daytime. Old Phoenix would have been lost if she had not distrusted her eyesight and depended on her feet to know where to take her.

She paused quietly on the sidewalk where people were passing by. A lady came along in the crowd, carrying an armful of red, green, and silver-wrapped presents; she gave off perfume like the red roses in hot summer, and Phoenix stopped her.

"Please, missy, will you lace my shoe?" she held up her foot.

"What do you want, Grandma?"

"See my shoe," said Phoenix. "Do all right for out in the country, but wouldn't look right to go in a big building."

"Stand still then, Grandma," said the lady. She put her packages down on the sidewalk beside her and laced and tied both shoes tightly.

"Can't lace 'em with a cane," said Phoenix. "Thank you, missy. I doesn't mind asking a nice lady to tie up my shoe, when I gets out on the street."

Moving slowly and from side to side, she went into the big building, and into a tower of steps, where she walked up and round and round until her feet knew to stop.

She entered a door, and there she saw nailed up on the wall the document that had been stamped with the gold seal and framed in the gold frame, which matched the dream that was hung up in her head.

"Here I be," she said. There was a fixed and ceremonial stiffness over her body.

"A charity case, I suppose," said an attendant who sat at the desk before her.

But Phoenix only looked above her head. There was sweat on her face, the wrinkles in her skin shone like a bright net.

"Speak up, Grandma," the woman said. "What's your name?" We must have your history, you know. Have you been here before? What seems to be the trouble with you?"

Old Phoenix only gave a twitch to her face as if a fly were bothering her.

"Are you dead?" cried the attendant.

But then the nurse came in.

"Oh, that's just old Aunt Phoenix," she said. "She doesn't come for herself—she has a little grandson. She makes these trips just as regular as clockwork. She lives away back off the Old Natchez Trace." She bent down. "Well, Aunt Phoenix, why don't you just take a seat? We won't keep you standing after your long trip." She pointed.

The old woman sat down, bolt upright in the chair.

"Now, how is the boy?" asked the nurse.

Old Phoenix did not speak.

"I said, how is the boy?"

But Phoenix only waited and stared straight ahead, her face very solemn and withdrawn into rigidity.

"Is his throat any better?" asked the nurse. "Aunt Phoenix, don't you hear me? Is your grandson's throat any better since the last time you came for the medicine?"

With her hands on her knees, the old woman waited, silent, erect and motionless, just as if she were in armour.

"You mustn't take up our time this way, Aunt Phoenix," the nurse said. "Tell us quickly about your grandson, and get it over. He isn't dead, is he?"

At last there came a flicker and then a flame of comprehension across her face and she spoke.

"My grandson. It was my memory had left me. There I sat and forgot why I made my long trip."

"Forgot?" The nurse frowned. "After you came so far?"

Then Phoenix was like an old woman begging a dignified forgiveness for waking up frightened in the night. "I never did go to school, I was too old at the Surrender," she said in a soft voice. "I'm an old woman without an education. It was my memory fail me. My little grandson he is just the same, and I forgot it in the coming."

"Throat never heals, does it?" said the nurse, speaking in a loud, sure voice to old Phoenix. By now she had a card with something written on it, a little list. "Yes. Swallowed lye. When was it?—January—two-three years ago—"

Phoenix spoke unasked now. "No, missy, he not dead, he just the same. Every little while his throat begin to close up again, and he not able to swallow. He not get his breath. He not able to help himself. So the time come round, and I go on another trip for the soothing medicine."

"All right. The doctor said as long as you came to get it, you could have it," said the nurse. "But it's an obstinate case."

"My little grandson, he sits up there in the house all wrapped up, waiting by himself," Phoenix went on. "We is the only two left in the world. He suffer and it don't seem to put him back at all. He got a sweet look. He going to last. He wear a little patch quilt and peep out holding his mouth open like a little bird. I remembers so plain now. I not going to forget him again, no, the whole enduring time. I could tell him from all the others in creation."

"All right.The nurse was trying to hush her now. She brought her a bottle of medicine. "Charity," she said, making a check mark in the book.

Old Phoenix held the bottle close to her eyes, and then carefully put it into her pocket.

"I thank you," she said.

"It's Christmas time, Grandma," said the attendant. "Could I give you a few pennies out of my purse?"

"Five pennies is a nickel," said Phoenix stiffly.

"Here's a nickel," said the attendant.

Phoenix rose carefully and held out her hand. She received the nickel and then fished the other nickel out of her pocket and laid it beside the new one. She stared at her palm closely, with her head on one side.

Then she gave a tap with her cane on the floor.

"This is what come to me to do," she said. "I going to the store and buy my child a little windmill they sells, made out of paper. He going to find it hard to believe there such a thing in the world. I'll march myself back where he waiting, holding it straight up in this hand."

She lifted her free hand, gave a little nod, turned around, and walked out of the doctor's office. Then her slow step began on the stairs, going down.

THIS IS JUST TO SAY[6]
—William Carlos Williams

I have eaten
the plums
that were in
the icebox

and which
you were probably
saving
for breakfast

Forgive me
they were delicious
so sweet
and so cold.

[6] From William Carlos Williams, *Collected Earlier Poems.* Copyright 1938 by William Carlos Williams. Reprinted by permission of New Directions Publishing Corporation.

THE IMPULSE[7]

—Robert Frost

It was too lonely for her there,
    And too wild,
And since there were but two of them,
    And no child,

And work was little in the house,
    She was free,
And followed where he furrowed field,
    Or felled tree.

She rested on a log and tossed
    The fresh chips,
With a song only to herself
    On her lips.

And once she went to break a bough
    Of black alder.
She strayed so far she scarcely heard
    When he called her—

And didn't answer—didn't speak—
    Or return.
She stood, and then she ran and hid
    In the fern.

He never found her, though he looked
    Everywhere,
And he asked at her mother's house
    Was she there.

Sudden and swift and light as that
    The ties gave,
And he learned of finalities
    Besides the grave.

MENDING WALL[8]
—Robert Frost

Something there is that doesn't love a wall,
That sends the frozen-ground-swell under it,
And spills the upper boulders in the sun;
And makes gaps even two can pass abreast.
The work of hunters is another thing:
I have come after them and made repair
Where they have left not one stone on a stone,
But they would have the rabbit out of hiding,
To please the yelping dogs. The gaps I mean,
No one has seen them made or heard them made,
But at spring mending-time we find them there.
I let my neighbor know beyond the hill;
And on a day we meet to walk the line
And set the wall between us once again.
We keep the wall between us as we go.
To each the boulders that have fallen to each.
And some are loaves and some so nearly balls
We have to use a spell to make them balance:
"Stay where you are until our backs are turned!"
We wear our fingers rough with handling them.
Oh, just another kind of out-door game,
One on a side. It comes to little more:
There where it is, we do not need the wall:
He is all pine and I am apple orchard.
My apple trees will never get across
And eat the cones under his pines, I tell him.
He only says, "Good fences make good neighbors."
Spring is the mischief in me, and I wonder
If I could put a notion in his head:
"*Why* do they make good neighbors? Isn't it
Where there are cows? But here there are no cows.
Before I built a wall I'd ask to know
What I was walling in or walling out,
And to whom I was like to give offence.
Something there is that doesn't love a wall,
That wants it down." I could say "Elves" to him,
But it's not elves exactly, and I'd rather
He said it for himself. I see him there
Bringing a stone grasped firmly by the top
In each hand, like an old-stone savage armed.
He moves in darkness as it seems to me,
Not of woods only and the shade of trees.

He will not go behind his father's saying,
And he likes having thought of it so well
He says again, "Good fences make good neighbors."

NEITHER OUT FAR NOR IN DEEP[9]
—*Robert Frost*

The people along the sand
All turn and look one way.
They turn their back on the land.
They look at the sea all day.

As long as it takes to pass
A ship keeps raising its hull;
The wetter ground like glass
Reflects a standing gull.

The land may vary more;
But wherever the truth may be—
The water comes ashore,
And the people look at the sea.

They cannot look out far.
They cannot look in deep.
But when was that ever a bar
To any watch they keep?

[9] From *Complete Poems of Robert Frost*. Copyright 1916, 1921, 1930, 1939, 1947 by Holt, Rinehart and Winston. Copyright 1936, 1942, 1944, © 1958 by Robert Frost. Copyright © 1964 by Lesley Frost Ballantine. Reprinted by permission of Holt, Rinehart and Winston.

from TOM JONES: A FOUNDLING
—*Henry Fielding*

BOOK VI. Containing about Three Weeks.

CHAPTER I. Of Love.

In our last book we have been obliged to deal pretty much with the passion of love; and in our succeeding book shall be forced to handle this subject still more largely. It may not therefore in this place be improper to apply ourselves to the examination of that modern doctrine, by which certain philosophers, among many other wonderful discoveries, pretend to have found out, that there is no such passion in the human breast.

Whether these philosophers be the same with that surprising sect, who are honorably mentioned by the late Dr. Swift, as having, by the mere force of genius alone, without the least assistance of any kind of learning, or even reading, discovered that profound and invaluable secret that there is no

God; or whether they are not rather the same with those who some years since very much alarmed the world, by showing that there were no such things as virtue or goodness really existing in human nature, and who deduced our best actions from pride, I will not here presume to determine. In reality, I am inclined to suspect, that all these several finders of truth, are the very identical men who are by others called the finders of gold. The method used in both these searches after truth and after gold, being indeed one and the same, viz. the searching, rummaging, and examining into a nasty place; indeed, in the former instances, into the nastiest of all places, A BAD MIND.

But though in this particular, and perhaps in their success, the truth-finder and the gold-finder may very properly be compared together; yet in modesty, surely, there can be no comparison between the two; for who ever heard of a gold-finder that had the impudence or folly to assert, from the ill success of his search, that there was no such thing as gold in the world? whereas the truth-finder, having raked out that jakes, his own mind, and being there capable of tracing no ray of divinity, nor anything virtuous or good, or lovely, or loving, very fairly, honestly, and logically concludes that no such things exist in the whole creation.

To avoid, however, all contention, if possible, with these philosophers, if they will be called so; and to show our own disposition to accommodate matters peaceably between us, we shall here make them some concessions, which may possibly put an end to the dispute.

First, we will grant that many minds, and perhaps those of the philosophers, are entirely free from the least traces of such a passion.

Secondly, that what is commonly called love, namely, the desire of satisfying a voracious appetite with a certain quantity of delicate white human flesh, is by no means that passion for which I here contend. This is indeed more properly hunger; and as no glutton is ashamed to apply the word love to his appetite, and to say he LOVES such and such dishes; so may the lover of this kind, with equal propriety, say he HUNGERS after such and such women.

Thirdly, I will grant, which I believe will be a most acceptable concession, that this love for which I am an advocate, though it satisfies itself in a much more delicate manner, doth nevertheless seek its own satisfaction as much as the grossest of all our appetites.

And, lastly, that this love, when it operates towards one of a different sex, is very apt, towards its complete gratification, to call in the aid of that hunger which I have mentioned above; and which it is so far from abating, that it heightens all its delights to a degree scarce imaginable by those who have never been susceptible of any other emotions than what have proceeded from appetite alone.

In return to all these concessions, I desire of the philosphers to grant, that there is in some (I believe in many) human breasts a kind and benevolent disposition, which is gratified by contributing to the happiness of others. That in this gratification alone, as in friendship, in parental and filial affection, as indeed in general philanthropy, there is a great and exquisite delight.

That if we will not call such disposition love, we have no name for it. That through the pleasures arising from such pure love may be heightened and sweetened by the assistance of amorous desires, yet the former can subsist alone, nor are they destroyed by the intervention of the latter. Lastly, that esteem and gratitude are the proper motives to love, as youth and beauty are to desire, and therefore, though such desire may naturally cease, when age or sickness overtakes its object; yet these can have no effect on love, nor ever shake or remove, from a good mind, that sensation or passion which hath gratitude and esteem for its basis.

To deny the existence of a passion of which we often see manifest instances, seems to be very strange and absurd; and can indeed proceed only from that self-admonition which we have mentioned above: but how unfair is this! Doth the man who recognizes in his own heart no traces of avarice or ambition, conclude, therefore, that there are no such passions in human nature? Why will we not modestly observe the same rule in judging of the good, as well as the evil of others? Or why, in any case, will we, as Shakespeare phrases it, "put the world in our own person"?

Predominant vanity is, I am afraid, too much concerned here. This is one instance of that adulation which we bestow on our own minds, and this almost universally. For there is scarce any man, how much soever he may despise the character of a flatterer, but will condescend in the meanest manner to flatter himself.

To those therefore I apply for the truth of the above observations, whose own minds can bear testimony to what I have advanced.

Examine your heart, my good reader, and resolve whether you do believe these matters with me. If you do, you may now proceed to their exemplification in the following pages: if you do not, you have, I assure you, already read more than you have understood: and it would be wiser to pursue your business, or your pleasures (such as they are), than to throw away any more of your time in reading what you can neither taste nor comprehend. To treat of the effects of love to you, must be as absurd as to discourse on colors to a man born blind; since possibly your idea of love may be as absurd as that which we are told such blind man once entertained of the color scarlet; that color seemed to him to be very much like the sound of a trumpet: and love probably may, in your opinion, very greatly resemble a dish of soup, or a sirloin of roast-beef.

THE BRIDE COMES TO YELLOW SKY
—Stephen Crane

I

The great Pullman was whirling onward with such dignity of motion that a glance from the window seemed simply to prove that the plains of Texas were pouring eastward. Vast flats of green grass, dull-hued spaces of mesquit and cactus, little groups of frame houses, woods of light and tender trees, all were sweeping into the east, sweeping over the horizon, a precipice.

A newly married pair had boarded this coach at San Antonio. The man's face was reddened from many days in the wind and sun, and a direct result of his new black clothes was that his brick-coloured hands were constantly performing in a most conscious fashion. From time to time he looked down respectfully at his attire. He sat with a hand on each knee, like a man waiting in a barber's shop. The glances he devoted to other passengers were furtive and shy.

The bride was not pretty, nor was she very young. She wore a dress of blue cashmere, with small reservations of velvet here and there, and with steel buttons abounding. She continually twisted her head to regard her puff sleeves, very stiff, straight, and high. They embarrassed her. It was quite apparent that she had cooked, and that she expected to cook, dutifully. The blushes caused by the careless scrutiny of some passengers as she had entered the car were strange to see upon this plain, under-class countenance, which was drawn in placid, almost emotionless lines.

They were evidently very happy. "Ever been in a parlour-car before?" he asked, smiling with delight.

"No," she answered; "I never was. It's fine, ain't it?"

"Great! And then after a while we'll go forward to the diner, and get a big lay-out. Finest meal in the world. Charge a dollar."

"Oh, do they?" cried the bride. "Charge a dollar? Why, that's too much—for us—ain't it, Jack?"

"Not this trip, anyhow," he answered bravely. "We're going to go the whole thing."

Later he explained to her about the trains. "You see, it's a thousand miles from one end of Texas to the other; and this train runs right across it, and never stops but four times." He had the pride of an owner. He pointed out to her the dazzling fittings of the coach; and in truth her eyes opened wider as she contemplated the sea-green figured velvet, the shining brass, silver, and glass, the wood that gleamed as darkly brilliant as the surface of a pool of oil. At one end a bronze figure sturdily held a support for a separated chamber, and at convenient places on the ceiling were frescos in olive and silver.

To the minds of the pair, their surroundings reflected the glory of their marriage that morning in San Antonio; this was the environment of their new estate; and the man's face in particular beamed with an elation that made him appear ridiculous to the negro porter. This individual at times surveyed them from afar with an amused and superior grin. On other occasions he bullied them with skill in ways that did not make it exactly plain to them that they were being bullied. He subtly used all the manners of the most unconquerable kind of snobbery. He oppressed them; but of this oppression they had small knowledge, and they speedily forgot that infrequently a number of travellers covered them with stares of derisive enjoyment. Historically there was supposed to be something infinitely humorous in their situation.

"We are due in Yellow Sky at 3:42," he said, looking tenderly into her eyes.

"Oh, are we?" she said, as if she had not been aware of it. To evince surprise at her husband's statement was part of her wifely amiability. She took from a pocket a little silver watch; and as she held it before her, and stared at it with a frown of attention, the new husband's face shone.

"I bought it in San Anton' from a friend of mine," he told her gleefully.

"It's seventeen minutes past twelve," she said, looking up at him with a kind of shy and clumsy coquetry. A passenger, noting this play, grew excessively sardonic, and winked at himself in one of the numerous mirrors.

At last they went to the dining-car. Two rows of negro waiters, in glowing white suits, surveyed their entrance with the interest, and also the equanimity, of men who had been forewarned. The pair fell to the lot of a waiter who happened to feel pleasure in steering them through their meal. He viewed them with the manner of a fatherly pilot, his countenance radiant with benevolence. The patronage, entwined with the ordinary deference, was not plain to them. And yet, as they returned to their coach, they showed in their faces a sense of escape.

To the left, miles down a long purple slope, was a little ribbon of mist where moved the keening Rio Grande. The train was approaching it at an angle, and the apex was Yellow Sky. Presently it was apparent that, as the distance from Yellow Sky grew shorter, the husband became commensurately restless. His brick-red hands were more insistent in their prominence. Occasionally he was even rather absent-minded and far-away when the bride leaned forward and addressed him.

As a matter of truth, Jack Potter was beginning to find the shadow of a deed weigh upon him like a leaden slab. He, the town marshal of Yellow Sky, a man known, liked, and feared in his corner, a prominent person, had gone to San Antonio to meet a girl he believed he loved, and there, after the usual prayers, had actually induced her to marry him, without consulting Yellow Sky for any part of the transaction. He was now bringing his bride before an innocent and unsuspecting community.

Of course people in Yellow Sky married as it pleased them, in accordance with a general custom; but such was Potter's thought of his duty to his friends, or of their idea of his duty, or of an unspoken form which does not control men in these matters, that he felt he was heinous. He had committed an extraordinary crime. Face to face with this girl in San Antonio, and spurred by his sharp impulse, he had gone headlong over all the social hedges. At San Antonio he was like a man hidden in the dark. A knife to sever any friendly duty, any form, was easy to his hand in that remote city. But the hour of Yellow Sky—the hour of daylight—was approaching.

He knew full well that his marriage was an important thing to his town. It could only be exceeded by the burning of the new hotel. His friends could not forgive him. Frequently he had reflected on the advisability of telling them by telegraph, but a new cowardice had been upon him. He feared to do it. And now the train was hurrying him toward a scene of amazement, glee, and reproach. He glanced out of the window at the line of haze swinging slowly in toward the train.

Yellow Sky had a kind of brass band, which played painfully, to the delight of the populace. He laughed without heart as he thought of it. If the citizens could dream of his prospective arrival with his bride, they would parade the band at the station and escort them, amid cheers and laughing congratulations, to his adobe home.

He resolved that he would use all the devices of speed and plainscraft in making the journey from the station to his house. Once within that safe citadel, he could issue some sort of vocal bulletin, and then not go among the citizens until they had time to wear off a little of their enthusiasm.

The bride looked anxiously at him. "What's worrying you, Jack?"

He laughed again. "I'm not worrying, girl; I'm only thinking of Yellow Sky."

She flushed in comprehension.

A sense of mutual guilt invaded their minds and developed a finer tenderness. They looked at each other with eyes softly aglow. But Potter often laughed the same nervous laugh; the flush upon the bride's face seemed quite permanent.

The traitor to the feelings of Yellow Sky narrowly watched the speeding landscape. "We're nearly there," he said.

Presently the porter came and announced the proximity of Potter's home. He held a brush in his hand, and, with all his airy superiority gone, he brushed Potter's new clothes as the latter slowly turned this way and that way. Potter fumbled out a coin and gave it to the porter, as he had seen others do. It was a heavy and muscle-bound business, as that of a man shoeing his first horse.

The porter took their bag, and as the train began to slow they moved forward to the hooded platform of the car. Presently the two engines and their long string of coaches rushed into the station of Yellow Sky.

"They have to take water here," said Potter, from a constricted throat and in mournful cadence, as one announcing death. Before the train stopped his eye had swept the length of the platform, and he was glad and astonished to see there was none upon it but the station-agent, who, with a slightly hurried and anxious air, was walking toward the water-tanks. When the train had halted, the porter alighted first, and placed in position a little temporary step.

"Come on, girl," said Potter, hoarsely. As he helped her down they each laughed on a false note. He took the bag from the negro, and bade his wife cling to his arm. As they slunk rapidly away, his hang-dog glance perceived that they were unloading the two trunks, and also that the station-agent, far ahead near the baggage-car, had turned and was running toward him, making gestures. He laughed, and groaned as he laughed, when he noted the first effect of his marital bliss upon Yellow Sky. He gripped his wife's arm firmly to his side, and they fled. Behind them the porter stood, chuckling fatuously.

II

The California express on the Southern Railway was due at Yellow Sky in twenty-one minutes. There were six men at the bar of the Weary Gentleman saloon. One was a drummer who talked a great deal and rapidly; three were Texans who did not care to talk at that time; and two were Mexican sheep-herders, who did not talk as a general practice in the Weary Gentleman saloon. The barkeeper's dog lay on the board walk that crossed in front of the door. His head was on his paws, and he glanced drowsily here and there with the constant vigilance of a dog that is kicked on occasion. Across the sandy street were some vivid green grass-plots, so wonderful in appearance, amid the sands that burned near them in a blazing sun, that they caused a doubt in the mind. They exactly resembled the grass mats used to represent lawns on the stage. At the cooler end of the railway station, a man without a coat sat in a tilted chair and smoked his pipe. The fresh-cut bank of the Rio Grande circled near the town, and there could be seen beyond it a great plum-coloured plain of mesquit.

Save for the busy drummer and his companions in the saloon, Yellow Sky was dozing. The new-comer leaned gracefully upon the bar, and recited many tales with the confidence of a bard who has come upon a new field.

"—and at the moment that the old man fell downstairs with the bureau in his arms, the old woman was coming up with two scuttles of coal, and of course—"

The drummer's tale was interrupted by a young man who suddenly appeared in the open door. He cried: "Scratchy Wilson's drunk, and has turned loose with both hands." The two Mexicans at once set down their glasses and faded out of the rear entrance of the saloon.

The drummer, innocent and jocular, answered: "All right, old man. S'pose he has? Come in and have a drink, anyhow."

But the information had made such an obvious cleft in every skull in the room that the drummer was obliged to see its importance. All had become instantly solemn. "Say," said he, mystified, "what is this?" His three companions made the introductory gesture of eloquent speech; but the young man at the door forestalled them.

"It means, my friend," he answered, as he came into the saloon, "that for the next two hours this town won't be a health resort."

The barkeeper went to the door, and locked and barred it; reaching out of the window, he pulled in heavy wooden shutters, and barred them. Immediately a solemn, chapel-like gloom was upon the place. The drummer was looking from one to another.

"But say," he cried, "what is this, anyhow? You don't mean there is going to be a gun-fight?"

"Don't know whether there'll be a fight or not," answered one man, grimly: "but there'll be some shootin'—some good shootin'."

The young man who had warned them waved his hand. "Oh, there'll be a fight fast enough, if any one wants it. Anybody can get a fight out there in the street. There's a fight just waiting."

The drummer seemed to be swayed between the interest of a foreigner and a perception of personal danger.

"What did you say his name was?" he asked.

"Scratchy Wilson," they answered in chorus.

"And will he kill anybody? What are you going to do? Does this happen often? Does he rampage around like this once a week or so? Can he break in that door?"

"No; he can't break down that door," replied the barkeeper. "He's tried it three times. But when he comes you'd better lay down on the floor, stranger. He's dead sure to shoot at it, and a bullet may come through."

Thereafter the drummer kept a strict eye upon the door. The time had not yet been called for him to hug the floor, but, as a minor precaution, he sidled near to the wall. "Will he kill anybody?" he said again.

The men laughed low and scornfully at the question.

"He's out to shoot, and he's out for trouble. Don't see any good in experimentin' with him."

"But what do you do in a case like this? What do you do?"

A man responded: "Why, he and Jack Potter—"

"But," in chorus the other men interrupted, "Jack Potter's in San Anton'."

"Well, who is he? What's he got to do with it?"

"Oh, he's the town marshal. He goes out and fights Scratchy when he gets on one of these tears."

"Wow!" said the drummer, mopping his brow. "Nice job he's got."

The voices had toned away to mere whisperings. The drummer wished to ask further questions, which were born of an increasing anxiety and bewilderment; but when he attempted them, the men merely looked at him in irritation and motioned him to remain silent. A tense waiting hush was upon them. In the deep shadows of the room their eyes shone as they listened for sounds from the street. One man made three gestures at the barkeeper; and the latter, moving like a ghost, handed him a glass and a bottle. The man poured a full glass of whisky, and set down the bottle noiselessly. He gulped the whisky in a swallow, and turned again toward the door in immovable silence. The drummer saw that the barkeeper, without a sound, had taken a Winchester from beneath the bar. Later he saw this individual beckoning to him, so he tiptoed across the room.

"You better come with me back of the bar."

"No, thanks," said the drummer, perspiring; "I'd rather be where I can make a break for the back door."

Whereupon the man of bottles made a kindly but peremptory gesture. The drummer obeyed it, and, finding himself seated on a box with his head below the level of the bar, balm was laid upon his soul at sight of various zinc and copper fittings that bore a resemblance to armour-plate. The barkeeper took a seat comfortably upon an adjacent box.

"You see," he whispered, "this here Scratchy Wilson is a wonder with a gun—a perfect wonder; and when he goes on the war-trail, we hunt our holes—naturally. He's about the last one of the old gang that used to hang out along the river here. He's a terror when he's drunk. When he's sober he's all right—kind of simple—wouldn't hurt a fly—nicest fellow in town. But when he's drunk—whoo!"

There were periods of stillness. "I wish Jack Potter was back from San Anton'," said the barkeeper. "He shot Wilson up once—in the leg—and he would sail in and pull out the kinks in this thing."

Presently they heard from a distance the sound of a shot, followed by three wild yowls. It instantly removed a bond from the men in the darkened saloon. There was a shuffling of feet. They looked at each other. "Here he comes," they said.

III

A man in a maroon-coloured flannel shirt, which had been purchased for purposes of decoration, and made principally by some Jewish women on the East Side of New York, rounded a corner and walked into the middle of the main street of Yellow Sky. In either hand the man held a long, heavy, blue-black revolver. Often he yelled, and these cries rang through a semblance of a deserted village, shrilly flying over the roofs in a volume that seemed to have no relation to the ordinary vocal strength of a man. It was as if the surrounding stillness formed the arch of a tomb over him. These cries of ferocious challenge rang against walls of silence. And his boots had red tops with gilded imprints, of the kind beloved in winter by little sledding boys on the hillsides of New England.

The man's face flamed in a rage begot of whisky. His eyes, rolling, and yet keen for ambush, hunted the still doorways and windows. He walked with the creeping movement of the midnight cat. As it occurred to him, he roared menacing information. The long revolvers in his hands were as easy as straws; they were moved with an electric swiftness. The little fingers of each hand played sometimes in a musician's way. Plain from the low collar of the shirt, the cords of his neck straightened and sank, straightened and sank, as passion moved him. The only sounds were his terrible invitations. The calm adobes preserved their demeanour at the passing of this small thing in the middle of the street.

There was no offer of fight—no offer of fight. The man called to the sky. There were no attractions. He bellowed and fumed and swayed his revolvers here and everywhere.

The dog of the barkeeper of the Weary Gentleman saloon had not appreciated the advance of events. He yet lay dozing in front of his master's door. At sight of the dog, the man paused and raised his revolver humorously. At sight of the man, the dog sprang up and walked diagonally away, with a sullen head, and growling. The man yelled, and the dog broke into a gallop. As it was about to enter an alley, there was a loud noise, a whistling, and something spat the ground directly before it. The dog screamed, and, wheeling in terror, galloped headlong in a new direction. Again there was a noise, a whistling, and sand was kicked viciously before it. Fear-stricken, the dog turned and flurried like an animal in a pen. The man stood laughing, his weapons at his hips.

Ultimately the man was attracted by the closed door of the Weary

Gentleman saloon. He went to it and, hammering with a revolver, demanded drink.

The door remaining imperturbable, he picked a bit of paper from the walk, and nailed it to the framework with a knife. He then turned his back contemptuously upon this popular resort and, walking to the opposite side of the street and spinning there on his heel quickly and lithely, fired at the bit of paper. He missed it by a half-inch. He swore at himself, and went away. Later he comfortably fusilladed the windows of his most intimate friend. The man was playing with this town; it was a toy for him.

But still there was no offer to fight. The name of Jack Potter, his ancient antagonist, entered his mind, and he concluded that it would be a glad thing if he should go to Potter's house, and by bombardment induce him to come out and fight. He moved in the direction of his desire, chanting Apache scalp-music.

When he arrived at it, Potter's house presented the same still front as had the other adobes. Taking up a strategic position, the man howled a challenge. But this house regarded him as might a great stone god. It gave no sign. After a decent wait, the man howled further challenges, mingling with them wonderful epithets.

Presently there came the spectacle of a man churning himself into deepest rage over the immobility of a house. He fumed at it as the winter wind attacks a prairie cabin in the North. To the distance there should have gone the sound of a tumult like the fighting of two hundred Mexicans. As necessity bade him, he paused for breath or to reload his revolvers.

IV

Potter and his bride walked sheepishly and with speed. Sometimes they laughed together shamefacedly and low.

"Next corner, dear," he said finally.

They put forth the efforts of a pair walking bowed against a strong wind. Potter was about to raise a finger to point the first appearance of the new home when, as they circled the corner, they came face to face with a man in a maroon-coloured shirt, who was feverishly pushing cartridges into a large revolver. Upon the instant the man dropped his revolver to the ground and, like lightning, whipped another from its holster. The second weapon was aimed at the bridegroom's chest.

There was a silence. Potter's mouth seemed to be merely a grave for his tongue. He exhibited an instinct to at once loosen his arm from the woman's grip, and he dropped the bag to the sand. As for the bride, her face had gone as yellow as old cloth. She was a slave to hideous rites, gazing at the apparitional snake.

The two men faced each other at a distance of three paces. He of the revolver smiled with a new and quiet ferocity.

"Tried to sneak up on me," he said. "Tried to sneak up on me!" His eyes grew more baleful. As Potter made a slight movement, the man thrust his revolver venomously forward "No; don't you do it, Jack Potter. Don't you move a finger toward a gun just yet. Don't you move an eyelash. The time has come for me to settle with you, and I'm goin' to do it my own way, and loaf along with no interferin'. So if you don't want a gun bent on you, just mind what I tell you."

Potter looked at his enemy. "I ain't got a gun on me Scratchy," he said. "Honest, I ain't." He was stiffening and steadying, but yet somewhere at the back of his mind a vision of the Pullman floated: the sea-green figured velvet, the shining brass, silver, and glass, the wood that gleamed as darkly brilliant as the surface of a pool of oil—all the glory of the marriage, the environment of the new estate. "You know I fight when it comes to fighting, Scratchy Wilson; but I ain't got a gun on me. You'll have to do all the shootin' yourself."

His enemy's face went livid. He stepped forward, and lashed his weapon to and fro before Potter's chest. "Don't you tell me you ain't got no gun on you, you whelp. Don't tell me no lie like that. There ain't a man in Texas ever seen you without no gun. Don't take me for no kid." His eyes blazed with light, and his throat worked like a pump.

"I ain't takin' you for no kid," answered Potter. His heels had not moved an inch backward. "I'm takin' you for a damn fool. I tell you I ain't got a gun, and I ain't. If you're goin' to shoot me up, you better begin now; you'll never get a chance like this again."

So much enforced reasoning had told on Wilson's rage; he was calmer. "If you ain't got a gun, why ain't you got a gun?" he sneered. "Been to Sunday-school?"

"I ain't got a gun because I've just come from San Anton' with my wife. I'm married," said Potter. "And if I'd thought there was going to be any galoots like you prowling around when I brought my wife home, I'd had a gun, and don't you forget it."

"Married!" said Scratchy, not at all comprehending.

"Yes, married. I'm married," said Jack Potter, distinctly.

"Married?" said Scratchy. Seemingly for the first time, he saw the drooping, drowning woman at the other man's side. "No!" he said. He was like a creature allowed a glimpse of another world. He moved a pace backward, and his arm, with the revolver, dropped to his side. "Is this the lady?" he asked.

"Yes; this is the lady," answered Potter.

There was another period of silence.

"Well," said Wilson at last, slowly, "I s'pose it's all off now."

"It's all off if you say so, Scratchy. You know I didn't make the trouble." Potter lifted his valise.

"Well, I 'low it's off, Jack," said Wilson. He was looking at the ground. "Married!" He was not a student of chivalry; it was merely that in the presence of this foreign condition he was a simple child of the earlier plains. He picked up his starboard revolver, and, placing both weapons in their holsters, he went away. His feet made funnel-shaped tracks in the heavy sand.

ETHAN FROME (from Chapter I)[10]
—*Edith Wharton*

Frome was in the habit of walking into Starkfield to fetch home his wife's cousin, Mattie Silver, on the rare evenings when some chance of amusement drew her to the village. It was his wife who had suggested, when the girl came to live them, that such opportunities should be put in her way. Mattie Silver came from Stanford, and when she entered the Fromes' household to act as her cousin Zeena's aid it was thought best, as she came without pay, not to let her feel too sharp a contrast between the life she had left and the isolation of a Starkfield farm. But for this—as Frome sardonically reflected—it would hardly have occurred to Zeena to take any thought for the girl's amusement.

When his wife first proposed that they should give Mattie an occasional evening out he had inwardly demurred at having to do the extra two miles to the village and back after his hard day on the farm; but not long afterward he had reached the point of wishing that Starkfield might give all its nights to revelry.

Mattie Silver had lived under his roof for a year, and from early morning till they met at supper he had frequent chances of seeing her; but no moments in her company were comparable to those when, her arm in his, and her light step flying to keep time with his long stride, they walked back through the night to the farm. He had taken to the girl from the first day, when he had driven over to the Flats to meet her, and she had smiled and waved to him from the train, crying out, "You must be Ethan!" as she jumped down with her bundles, while he reflected, looking over her slight person: "She don't look much on housework, but she ain't a fretter, anyhow." But it was not only that the coming to his house of a bit of hopeful young life was like the lighting of a fire on a cold hearth. The girl was more than the bright serviceable creature he had thought her. She had an eye to see and and ear to hear: he could show her things and tell her things, and taste the bliss of feeling that all he imparted left long reverberations and echoes he could wake at will.

It was during their night walks back to the farm that he felt most intensely the sweetness of this communion. He had always been more sensitive than the people about him to the appeal of natural beauty. His unfinished studies had given form to this sensibility and even in his unhappiest moments field and sky spoke to him with a deep and powerful persuasion. But hitherto the emotion had remained in him as a silent ache, veiling with sadness the beauty that evoked it. He did not even know whether any one else in the world felt as he did, or whether he was the sole victim of this mournful privilege. Then he learned that one other spirit had trembled with the same touch of wonder: that at his side, living under his roof and eating his bread, was a creature to whom he could say: "That's Orion down yonder;

[10] Reprinted with the permission of Charles Scribner's Sons from *Ethan Frome*, pages 31-34, by Edith Wharton. Copyright 1911 Charles Scribner's Sons; renewal copyright 1939 William R. Tyler.

the big fellow to the right is Aldebaran, and the bunch of little ones—like bees swarming—they're the Pleiades . . ." or whom he could hold entranced before a ledge of granite thrusting up through the fern while he unrolled the huge panorama of the ice age, and the long dim stretches of succeeding time. The fact that admiration for his learning mingled with Mattie's wonder at what he taught was not the least part of his pleasure. And there were other sensations, less definable but more exquisite, which drew them together with a shock of silent joy: the cold red of sunset behind winter hills, the flight of cloud-flocks over slopes of golden stubble, or the intensely blue shadows of hemlocks on sunlit snow. When she said to him once: "It looks as if it was painted!" it seemed to Ethan that the art of definition could go no farther, and that words had at last been found to utter his secret soul. . . .

PASSING REMARK[11]
—*William Stafford*

> In scenery I like flat country.
> In life I don't like much to happen.
>
> In personalities I like mild colorless people.
> And in colors I prefer gray and brown.
>
> My wife, a vivid girl from the mountains,
> says, "Then why did you choose me?"
>
> Mildly I lower my brown eyes—
> there are so many things admirable people
>   do not understand.

MUSHROOMS[12]
—*Sylvia Plath*

> Overnight, very
> Whitely, discreetly,
> Very quietly
>
> Our toes, our noses
> Take hold on the loam,
> Acquire the air.
>
> Nobody sees us,
> Stops us, betrays us;
> The small grains make room.

Soft fists insist on
Heaving the needles,
The leafy bedding,

Even the paving.
Our hammers, our rams,
Earless and eyeless,

Perfectly voiceless,
Widen the crannies,
Shoulder through holes. We

Diet on water,
On crumbs of shadow,
Bland-mannered, asking

Little or nothing.
So many of us!
So many of us!

We are shelves, we are
Tables, we are meek,
We are edible,

Nudgers and shovers
In spite of ourselves.
Our kind multiplies:

We shall by morning
Inherit the earth.
Our foot's in the door.

AS I WALKED OUT ONE EVENING[13]
—W. H. Auden

As I walked out one evening,
    Walking down Bristol Street,
The crowds upon the pavement
    Were fields of harvest wheat.

And down by the brimming river
    I heard a lover sing
Under an arch of the railway:
    "Love has no ending.

"I'll love you, dear, I'll love you
    Till China and Africa meet

[13] Copyright 1940 and renewed 1968 by W. H. Auden. Reprinted from *Collected Poems*, by W. H. Auden, edited by Edward Mendelson, by permission of Random House, Inc.

And the river jumps over the mountain
    And the salmon sing in the street.

"I'll love you till the ocean
    Is folded and hung up to dry
And the seven stars go squawking
    Like geese about the sky.

"The years shall run like rabbits
    For in my arms I hold
The Flower of the Ages
    And the first love of the world."

But all the clocks in the city
    Began to whirr and chime:
"O let not Time deceive you,
    You cannot conquer Time.

"In the burrows of the Nightmare
    Where Justice naked is,
Time watches from the shadow
    And coughs when you would kiss.

"In headaches and in worry
    Vaguely life leaks away,
And Time will have his fancy
    To-morrow or to-day.

"Into many a green valley
    Drifts the appalling snow;
Time breaks the threaded dances
    And the diver's brilliant bow.

"O plunge your hands in water,
    Plunge them in up to the wrist;
Stare, stare in the basin
    And wonder what you've missed.

"The glacier knocks in the cupboard,
    The desert sighs in the bed,
And the crack in the tea-cup opens
    A lane to the land of the dead.

"Where the beggars raffle the banknotes
    And the Giant is enchanting to Jack,
And the Lily-white Boy is a Roarer
    And Jill goes down on her back.

"O look, look in the mirror,
    O look in your distress;
Life remains a blessing
    Although you cannot bless.

"O stand, stand at the window
    As the tears scald and start;
You shall love your crooked neighbour
    With your crooked heart."

It was late, late in the evening,
    The lovers they were gone;
The clocks had ceased their chiming
    And the deep river ran on.

from **MEN WITHOUT CHESTS**[14]
—*C. S. Lewis*

So he sent the word to slay
And slew the little childer.
                        Carol

I doubt whether we are sufficiently attentive to the importance of elementary text-books. That is why I have chosen as the starting-point for these lectures a little book on English intended for "boys and girls in the upper-forms of schools." I do not think the authors of this book (there were two of them) intended any harm, and I owe them, or their publisher, good language for sending me a complimentary copy. At the same time I shall have nothing good to say of them. Here is a pretty predicament. I do not want to pillory two modest practising school-masters who were doing the best they knew: but I cannot be silent about what I think the actual tendency of their work. I therefore propose to conceal their names. I shall refer to these gentlemen as Gaius and Titius and to their book as *The Green Book*. But I promise you there is such a book and I have it on my shelves.

In their second chapter Gaius and Titius quote the well-known story of Coleridge at the waterfall. You remember that there were two tourists present: that one called it "sublime" and the other "pretty": and that Coleridge mentally endorsed the first judgement and rejected the second with disgust. Gaius and Titius comment as follows: "When the man said *That is sublime,* he appeared to be making a remark about the waterfall. . . . Actually . . . he was not making a remark about the waterfall, but a remark about his own feelings. What he was saying was really *I have feelings associated in my mind with the word "Sublime,"*or shortly, *I have sublime feelings.*" Here are a good many deep questions settled in a pretty summary fashion. But the authors are not yet finished. They add: "This confusion is continually present in language as we use it. We appear to be saying something very important about something: and actually we are only saying something about our own feelings.*

[14] From C. S. Lewis, *The Abolition of Man.* Copyright 1944, 1947 by Macmillan Publishing Co., Inc.; renewed 1972, 1975 by Alfred Cecil Harwood and Arthur Owen Barfield. Reprinted by permission of Macmillan Publishing Co., and Collins, Publishers, London.
* *The Green Book,* pp. 19,20.

Before considering the issues really raised by this momentous little paragraph (designed, you will remember, for "the upper forms in schools") we must eliminate one mere confusion into which Gaius and Titius have fallen. Even on their own view—on any conceivable view—the man who says *This is sublime* cannot mean *I have sublime feelings*. Even if it were granted that such qualities as sublimity were simply and solely projected into things from our own emotions, yet the emotions which prompt the projection are the correlatives, and therefore almost the opposites, of the qualities projected. The feelings which make a man call an object sublime are not sublime feelings but feelings of veneration. If *This is sublime* is to be reduced at all to a statement about the speaker's feelings, the proper translation would be *I have humble feelings*. If the view held by Gaius and Titius were consistently applied it would lead to obvious absurdities. It would force them to maintain that *You are contemptible* means *I have contemptible feelings:* in fact that *Your feelings are contemptible* means *My feelings are contemptible*. But we need not delay over this which is the very *pons asinorum* of our subject. It would be unjust to Gaius and Titius themselves to emphasize what was doubtless a mere inadvertence.

The schoolboy who reads this passage in *The Green Book* will believe two propositions: firstly, that all sentences containing a predicate of value are statements about the emotional state of the speaker, and, secondly, that all such statements are unimportant. It it true that Gaius and Titius have said neither of these things in so many words. They have treated only one particular predicate of value (*sublime*) as a word descriptive of the speaker's emotions. The pupils are left to do for themselves the work of extending the same treatment to all predicates of value: and no slightest obstacle to such extension is placed in their way. The authors may or may not desire the extension: they may never have given the question five minutes' serious thought in their lives. I am not concerned with what they desired but with the effect their book will certainly have on the schoolboy's mind. In the same way, they have not said that judgements of value are unimportant. Their words are that we "*appear* to be saying something very important" when in reality we are "*only* saying something about our own feelings." No schoolboy will be able to resist the suggestion brought to bear upon him by that word *only*. I do not mean, of course, that he will make any conscious inference from what he reads to a general philosophical theory that all values are subjective and trivial. The very power of Gaius and Titius depends on the fact that they are dealing with a boy: a boy who thinks he is "doing" his "English prep" and has no notion that ethics, theology, and politics are all at stake. It is not a theory they put into his mind, but an assumption, which ten years hence, its origin forgotten and its presence unconscious, will condition him to take one side in a controversy which he had never recognized as a controversy at all. The authors themselves, I suspect, hardly know what they are doing to the boy, and he cannot know what is being done to him.

Chapter 5

CHARACTERIZATION AND PLACEMENT

Thus far we have said little about characterization. What happens when the interpreter, in reading a poem or a work of fiction, moves from description or summary or the comments of a narrator who is not specifically characterized to a definitely defined character?

In *Vanity Fair,* Thackeray describes the young Becky Sharp thus:

> She was small and slight in person; pale, sandy-haired, and with eyes habitually cast down; when they looked up they were very large, odd, and attractive: so attractive that the Reverend Mr. Crisp, fresh from Oxford and curate to the Vicar of Chiswick, the Reverend Mr. Flowerdew, fell in love with Miss Sharp, being shot dead by a glance of her eyes which was fired all the way across the Chiswick Church from the school-pew to the reading desk. . . .

> By the side of many tall and bouncing young ladies in the establishment, Rebecca Sharp looked like a child. But she had the dismal precocity of poverty. Many a dun had she talked to, and turned away from her father's door; many a tradesman had she coaxed and wheedled into good-humor, and into the granting of one meal more. . . .But she never had been a girl, she said; she had been a woman since she was eight years old. Oh, why did Miss Pinkerton let such a dangerous bird into her cage?

Thackeray later lets Becky describe Rawdon Crawley, in a letter to Amelia Sedley:

> "Well, he is a very large young dandy. He is six feet high, and speaks with a great voice; and swears a great deal; and orders about the servants, who all adore him nevertheless; for he is very generous of his money, and the domestics will do anything for him . . .

> "The captain has a hearty contempt for his father, I can see, and calls him an old *put,* an old *snob,* an old *chaw-bacon,* and numberless other pretty names. He has a *dreadful reputation* among the ladies. He brings his hunters home with him, lives with the squires of the county, asks whom he pleases to dinner, and Sir Pitt dares not say no, for fear of offending Miss Crawley, and missing his legacy when she dies of her apoplexy. Shall I tell you a compliment the captain paid me? I must, it is so pretty. One evening we actually had a dance; there was Sir Huddleston Fuddleston and his family, Sir Giles Wapshot and his young ladies, and I don't know how many more. Well, I heard him say, "By Jove, she's a neat little filly!" meaning your humble servant; and he did me the honor to dance two country-dances with me. He gets on pretty gayly with the young squires, with whom he drinks, bets, rides, and talks about hunting and shooting; but he says the country girls are *bores;* indeed, I don't think he is far wrong. You should see the contempt with which they look down on poor me! When they dance I sit and play the piano very demurely; but the other night, coming rather flushed from the dining-room, and seeing me employed in this way, he swore out loud that I was the best dancer in the rooms, and took a great oath that he would have the fiddlers from Mudbury."

This second passage, in telling about Captain Crawley, also tells us more about Becky Sharp, who is describing him.

Later, Becky marries Rawdon Crawley. Their marriage, as might be expected from the cues Thackeray gives in these passages, is less than happy. Rawdon is imprisoned for debt; released suddenly and unexpectedly, he returns home to find Becky entertaining another man, Lord Steyne:

> Rawdon . . . walked home rapidly. It was nine o'clock at night. He ran across the streets, and the great squares of Vanity Fair, and at length came up breathless opposite his own house. He started and fell against the railings, trembling as he looked up. The drawing-room windows were blazing with light. She had said that she was in bed and ill. He stood there for some time, the light from the rooms on his pale face.

> He took out his door-key and let himself into the house. He could hear laughter in the upper rooms. He was in the ball-dress in which he had been captured the night before. He went silently up the stairs; leaning against the banisters at the stairhead.—Nobody was stirring in the house besides—all the servants had been sent away.

Rawdon heard laughter within—laughter and singing. Becky was singing a snatch of the song of the night before; a hoarse voice shouted "Brava! Brava!"—it was Lord Steyne's.

Rawdon opened the door and went in. A little table with a dinner was laid out—and wine and plate. Steyne was hanging over the sofa on which Becky sat. The wretched woman was in a brilliant full toilet, her arms and all her fingers sparkling with bracelets and rings: and the brilliants on her breast which Steyne had given her. He had her hand in his, and was bowing over to kiss it, when Becky started up with a faint scream as she caught sight of Rawdon's white face. At the next instant she tried to smile, a horrid smile, as if to welcome her husband: and Steyne rose up, grinding his teeth, pale, and with fury in his looks.

He, too, attempted a laugh—and came forward holding out his hand. "What, come back! How d'ye do, Crawley?" he said, the nerves of his mouth twitching as he tried to grin at the intruder.

There was that in Rawdon's face which caused Becky to fling herself before him. "I am innocent, Rawdon," she said; "before God, I am innocent." She clung hold of his coat, of his hands; her own were all covered with serpents, and rings, and baubles. "I am innocent—Say I am innocent," she said to Lord Steyne.

He thought a trap had been laid for him, and was as furious with the wife as with the husband. "You innocent! Damn you," he screamed out. "You innocent! Why, every trinket you have on your body is paid for by me. I have given you thousands of pounds which this fellow has spent, and for which he has sold you. Innocent, by—! You're as innocent as your mother, the ballet-girl, and your husband, the bully. Don't think to frighten me as you have done others. Make way, sir, and let me pass;" and Lord Steyne seized up his hat, and, with flame in his eyes, and looking his enemy fiercely in the face, marched upon him, never for a moment doubting that the other would give way.

But Rawdon Crawley, springing out, seized him by the neck-cloth, until Steyne, almost strangled, writhed, and bent under his arm. "You lie, you dog!" said Rawdon. "You lie, you coward and villain!" And he struck the peer twice over the face with his open hand, and flung him bleeding to the ground. It was all done before Rebecca could interpose. She stood there trembling before him. She admired her husband, strong, brave, and victorious.

"Come here," he said.—She came up at once.

"Take off those things."—She began, trembling, pulling the jewels from her arms, and the rings from her shaking fingers, and held them all in a heap, quivering and looking up at him. "Throw them down," he said, and she dropped them. He tore the diamond ornament out of her breast, and flung it at Lord Steyne. It cut him on his bald forehead. Steyne wore the scar to his dying day.

"Come up stairs," Rawdon said to his wife. "Don't kill me, Rawdon," she said. He laughed savagely.—"I want to see if that man lies about the money as he has about me. Has he give you any?"

"No," said Rebecca, "that is—"

"Give me your keys," Rawdon answered, and they went out together. Rebecca gave him all the keys but one; and she was in hopes that he would not have remarked the absence of that. It belonged to the little desk which Amelia had given her in early days, and which she kept in a secret place. But Rawdon flung open boxes and wardrobes, throwing the multifarious trumpery of their contents here and there, and at last he found the desk. The woman was forced to open it. It contained papers, love-letters many years old-all sorts of small trinkets and woman's memoranda. And it contained a pocketbook with bank notes. Some of these were dated ten years back, too, and one was quite a fresh one—a note for a thousand pounds which Lord Steyne had given her.

"Did he give you this?" Rawdon said.

"Yes," Rebecca answered.

"I'll send it to him today," Rawdon said. . . . "You might have spared me a hundred pounds, Becky, out of all this—I have always shared with you."

"I am innocent," said Becky. And he left her without another word.

What were her thoughts when he left her? She remained for hours after he was gone, the sunshine pouring into the room, and Rebecca sitting alone on the bed's edge. The drawers were all opened and their contents scattered about,—dresses and feathers, scarfs and trinkets, a heap of tumbled vanities lying in a wreck. Her hair was falling over her shoulders; her gown was torn where Rawdon had wrenched the brilliants out of it. She heard him go down stairs a few minutes after he left her, and the door slamming and closing on him. She knew he would never come back. He was gone forever.

If this were a drama, the director might cast these two characters (Rawdon and Becky) as Thackeray describes them, helping out the physical features of his actors with makeup and costume. Becky might well be in "brilliant full toilet, her arms and all her fingers sparkling with bracelets and rings." But what does the interpreter do, faced with the problem of reading both these characters (as well as Lord Steyne)? He cannot (and it would be ridiculous if he tried to) change costume as he moves from character to character. He cannot literally look like either of the two, probably. Furthermore, the single reader is either male or female, and is faced with reading a character of each sex.

Some readers overexaggerate. Sometimes a girl will try to adopt a deep bass voice for a male character, or a boy will try to read in a high-

CHARACTERIZATION

pitched tone. If the pitch is unnatural for the interpreter, this kind of mechanical distinction between male and female will not work, for it will make the character sound like a caricature; the audience will not be able to see or hear the character the author intended because the read-er's distorted product will be in the way. (One caution: There are times when caricature and gross exaggeration are what the author wants, but we are not talking here about such a situation.) It is perfectly true that a flexible voice ought to permit a good range in pitch without appearing to be forced; students who need to extend their range should be en-couraged to exercise to do so. Any serviceable voice will accommodate itself to changes.

Thackeray helps us by giving us limited descriptions, and the audi-ence will, therefore, already have Thackeray's distinctions in mind when the characters speak. Still, the interpreter never reads simply in his or her own person but is always, in the literary experience, a coalescence of self and other. When Rawdon Crawley speaks or when Becky Sharp speaks, we want to listen to them, not simply to the interpreter. Even in the narration (as distinct from the dialogue), we do not want to hear the interpreter in his or her own person. What can the reader do to give us the illusion that Rawdon and Becky themselves are present?

What the reader does, by making use of the cues given by the author, is embody the tensive qualities written into the language. Try, without saying a word, to respond physically to the differences in weight and tone between Rawdon and Becky. Rawdon is six feet tall, heavy, big-voiced; in the scene he is middle-aged; he has gained weight, we learn elsewhere. Becky is small, vivacious, "dangerous." How do these differences in weight and size affect the kind of move-ment of each character? Their buoyance or lack of it? The carriage of their shoulders? Their rate of response? When you, as interpreter, shift from Becky to Rawdon, do you feel any difference in the weight on your feet? Any difference in the carriage of heads? Look for a moment at the line "Steyne was hanging over the sofa on which Becky sat." If you were acting the line, and it said "Becky was hanging over the sofa on which Steyne sat," what differences would the change of line make in your behavior and your feeling of that behavior? Be as specific as possible in pointing to the changes.

At the beginning of the scene, Rawdon has been walking rapidly, is breathless and trembling. Imagine you are Rawdon leaning against the railings, looking up at the lighted windows of the drawing room—try actually leaning against something and see whether you can feel what Rawdon feels. Breathe rapidly. If necessary, jump up and down several times to stimulate the feeling that you have walked some distance. Now sit down and try to imagine yourself in Becky's situation at the sofa when Rawdon walks in and surprises her. Read the paragraph beginning "There was that in Rawdon's face which caused Becky to fling herself before him." If you have responded with your body to the situation as you have acted it out (remember that body response involves mental response as well), you will find that your voice too is affected. Take up your hat as Lord Steyne and try to make your way past Rawdon. Speak his lines. (These are all preparatory exercises for your reading, *not* what you will do when you read the scene.) If your rehearsal is effective, you will find vocal changes accompanying changes in character. Look at them carefully. How ought these voices to sound? You may need to make additional modifications to sharpen vocal characteristics.

Since you will probably not scream where the text says "Becky started up with a faint scream," what will you do to respond to her scream? Since you will not literally be hanging on Rawdon's coat, what will you do to embody the tensions described? What will you do when Rawdon flings the diamond ornament at Lord Steyne? All these actions involve body responses, empathic behavior, though literal copying of all the actions will render the reader ludicrous. It is the simulation of the muscle tensions that creates characterization in interpretation—the feel of Becky differs from the feel of Rawdon and the feel of Lord Steyne. All the clues the author gives enter into this simulation of tensions—sex, age, size, costume, situation, attitude, temperament. One must strive to visualize the characters; one must also try to embody them within the limits of the interpreter's medium. Gestures cannot always be as full and overt as in acted drama, but they must be clear and forceful even while they are minimal and often covert. Try saying Rawdon's line "You lie, you dog!" to suggest his springing at Lord Steyne, but without more than minimal movement. All the changes in Thackeray's scene involve changes in body tension.

SPOTS OF INDETERMINACY

As we have said elsewhere (see page 12), writers depend upon readers to fill in what Roman Ingarden has called "spots of indeterminacy" in the text.[1] In the real world, objects are complete: a tulip in bloom, for example, has a specific shape and color, a specific location, specific surroundings. In a poem, a tulip may be dislodged from such specificity. In "Up at a Villa—Down in the City," for example, Browning writes,

> The wild tulip, at end of its tube, blows out
>   its great red bell
> Like a thin clear bubble of blood, for the children
>   to pick and sell.

We get the color, a sense of the fragility of the petals, a suggestion of shape—but Browning's tulip is not really quite like any tulip we have known in life. It exists only here, and Browning is at pains to give us only so much of the tulip as fits his need in the poem. We may— probably do—fill in at least enough detail to keep the tulip alive and

---

[1] The translation by George C. Grabowicz of Ingarden's *The Literary Work of Art* (Evanston, Ill.: Northwestern University Press, 1973) explores the matter in some detail.

growing in the earth; it is not a painting of a red tulip. But provided that we keep what Browning needs for *his* tulip, he will not mind our filling in the "spots" the poem, as distinct from the real tulip in the phenomenal world, leaves open.

So it is with people in literature, too. We create our own pictures of them from details in the text, but pictures differ from reader to reader. If the differences result from readers' ignoring of things specified in the text, we may say that the differences are not defensible; if, however, the text *is* taken carefully into account, two readers may still fill in the "spots of indeterminacy" in rather different ways. Both pictures will be valid. That is one reason why novelists nowadays do not have illustrations in their books. Novels reprinted after they have been filmed sometimes have pictures from the film included in the text; such pictures may in an unfortunate way tie the reader to the specific details with which the film has filled in the "open" spaces. Our sense of a character in reading may be very different from the film personality who has created the character in the film.

But the interpreter, standing before an audience, *does* have a specific body—he or she does not literally have "open places," but behaves as a fully defined body. The task is to match that body, within the limits of one's capacity, with the character in the text. Knowledge of general human behavior must be called upon to fill in what the author leaves unspoken. For example, Thackeray tells us how Rawdon springs at Steyne and seizes him, but he does not specifically give us a picture of Rawdon's face as he says "You lie, you dog!" Nevertheless, any reader will know that *some* ways of matching that face at this moment would be wrong and some would be "right." Some tones of voice will accommodate that speech; others will not. Some behaviors of the speaker's eyes will match the text; others will not. It would be wrong, for instance, if Rawdon were to open his eyes wide as if in amazement. Why, in the context of the novel? If a reader's behavior seems to the audience incongruous in view of the intention of the text, the passage will cease to be persuasive. Hence the details one supplies to fill in the "open spaces" in the text—spaces that *must* be filled in performance—are as much a part of the performer's concern as the details supplied by the writer. Emotional states of characters can be revealed only when the performer is willing to assume the appropriate adaptive behaviors. (We are not talking now of passages where the narrator simply *tells* us of characters' emotional states, but rather of *scenes,* where we are given characters in action.)

KINDS OF BEHAVIOR

Some behavior patterns are largely conventional, and are often dependent upon historical considerations of dress, manners, taste. One cannot sit in a farthingale the same way one would sit in jeans—or move in the same way. A cardinal's gown will move differently than armor. These are crude examples, but they point to an important truth: the performer has many kinds of movement at his call—and can learn more! The carriage of one's head under the pressure of a towering hairpiece is not that of crew-cut head. Bare feet do not move as high heels move. Bodies make adaptations to places, times, manners, dress; the broader the interpreter's lexicon of behaviors, the better equipped he or she is to match the range of characters to be found in the world's literature. Personality is often *inferred* from such behavior. We may say of someone "He moves like a dancer," and we may attach values of one sort or another to that movement. Or we watch someone sitting slumped in a chair, eyes tightly closed, brow wrinkled, shoulders lifted and tense, and we know that something is wrong. The *whole* body participates, whether or not overtly, in the emotional state of the individual—but it is from the overt behavior that we as audience get some sense of the inner state. The outer form must lead us to the inner form.

Just as the writer leaves "open spaces" in the creation of character, so will the performer. The solo reader cannot do everything with every character, nor should he try. The performer, like the writer, fills in what is useful; his task differs from the writer's primarily by virtue of the fact that the performer is a visible and audible body. There is economy in both arts.

One may give a simple list of ways in which to study behaviors:

Physical Qualities of a Character: male, female; young, old; light, dark; strong, weak; short, tall; quick, slow; tenor, bass; soprano, alto—endless variations of these. Some of these are under the control of the performer: It *is* possible, for example, for a male performer to create for us a strong sense of a female character. Others are not: A dark female performer cannot, from visual clues alone, suggest a blonde female character. The best advice, perhaps, is not to decide too soon that you cannot give a sufficient formulation of physical qualities different from your own. A short performer can grow taller in the eyes of an audience; a performer in fine physical health can persuade us of a state of ill health. But it seems true that readers have more to gain by giving us "just enough," by keeping the performance sufficiently subtle, than by trying to give *all*. (Certain comic effects are always an exception.) Even with flat (as opposed to round) characters, economies dictate choices.

Life Roles: child, parent; son, daughter; banker, clerk; teacher, student; peasant, king; nun, friar; Muslim, Buddhist; salesman, singer—again with endless variations. Some of these role distinctions spring from cultural considerations and are related to conventional "masks" which the roles often assume. A king, we are told, shouldn't behave like a beggar. Or differences may arise from environmental and national differences: A Fijian neither looks, dresses, nor behaves like a Norwegian, though at certain levels of society differences may tend to be reduced as the world gets smaller. As large cities look more and more alike no matter where on the globe they are found, so individuals of a certain class—"big businessmen," perhaps—may dress and behave more alike. Too bad, one may think; the world is more interesting when there *are* distinctions, though one may understand why the distinctions may go.

Situations: married, divorced; well, ill; happy, miserable; just getting started, retired; under pressure, relaxed; dominated, dominating; free, imprisoned—and again, endless variations.

With respect to literary texts, in addition to the specific evidence supplied by the writer, such as we examined in the Thackeray passage, there are additional sources of study:

Criticism: Critics will often discuss characterization (as well as any other literary element, to be sure) in detail. While one must watch for critical bias, it is clear enough that critics can be helpful companions to interpreters.

Biography and History: Historical characters can be studied outside literary texts. Again, there is a caveat: The historical character in a work of literature may be very unlike the real person. Shakespeare's Richard III is not an accurate treatment of the historical king, and there is no way to make him so. But so-called "historical novels," which often have a historical setting without being literally "true to life," may well gain in performance if the interpreter is willing to study the historical period out of which the life of the novel may spring. We have already suggested that knowledge of historical costume and manners will be profitable as study.

Paintings and Photographs: These may give you the fully-detailed body which in the text has "open spots." They may well help you select the kind of detail most useful to your purpose.

Ultimately one comes back to the text, to one's own knowledge of how people behave. It is not a matter of thinking that there is only *one* formulation that will serve; it is, however, a matter of knowing that some kinds of formulation will serve better than others, and that it is possible for a formulation to be "wrong."

Now, standing on your feet and with your book in your hand, visualize the scene in *Vanity Fair* out in front of you. Read what Thackeray has written, taking time to fill in the emotions of the characters. Remember that the narrator too is empathically involved in the scene, though his degree of involvement is different from that of Becky and Rawdon. In fixing locus in the first passage (the initial description of Becky), where will you move from the narrator to Becky? While you cannot literally do everything Thackeray says the characters are doing in the scene, you must nevertheless know what they are doing and respond to it in terms of muscle tone, empathy, tensiveness. Decide as specifically as possible on the motivations of each character: What does he or she want? What drives them? To what are they driven? (Thackeray will tell your listeners what he wants them to know. It is your task not simply to tell them but to let them feel what Thackeray wants them to feel. They cannot do this if you stand in the way.)

The interpreter in such a scene faces the problem of *locus.* We begin outside the home of the Crawleys, and then go inside it. But notice the relationships of the characters within the room. First Rawdon hears voices. Then he sees Becky and Steyne before they see him. Meanwhile, we, with the narrator, are watching Rawdon. Becky sees Rawdon; then Steyne sees him. It is the narrator who lets us see Becky and Steyne at the sofa, but we see them as if we were standing with Rawdon. With Rawdon and the narrator, we watch Steyne bow over Becky's hand; but we share empathically in Steyne's action, also. Then with Becky we catch sight of Rawdon's white face. The locus does not remain static with the narrator; for the interpreter, it shifts from narrator to character and from one character to another as we participate in their tensions. Though the eye of the narrator may be the camera taking in the scene, the narration can be read effectively only when the interpreter actively takes part in the tensions that he "sees" through that eye. One feels what one sees. One does not say "What, come back! How d'ye do, Crawley?" with Lord Steyne, *as* Lord Steyne, and then relax to say objectively, as the narrator, "he said, the nerves of his mouth twitching as he tried to grin at the intruder." No, the narration is read from the point of view, the locus, of Steyne himself, so that the interpreter feels the twitching mouth of Lord Steyne as he says the lines of Lord Steyne. Otherwise the effect is ludicrous as the reader drops the character and reads the narration as if it were stage directions. You can illustrate this by reading the following passage in two ways: " 'You lie, you dog!' said Rawdon. 'You lie, you coward and villain!' " Read it first saying "said Rawdon" as if it were part of the dialogue itself, sharing the same tensions. Now read it as if "said Rawdon" were objective narration, quite apart from Rawdon's feelings. There is a difference in locus in the two readings; the first reading is the proper one.

Follow through the remainder of the scene, observing how frequently the locus keeps shifting as Thackeray tells his story. Don't let the narrator become a character in the scene. In *Vanity Fair* he is not a character.

All these complex movements and tensions the interpreter must keep alive. While you practice your oral reading, go slowly enough so that you will have time to manage everything. Most interpreters read much too quickly; it takes time to embody all these details, though ultimately this scene will move in quick tempo. Why?

Another scene involving characterization may be illustrated in a poem. Matthew Arnold's "Dover Beach" has two characters in it, though one of them is silent.

SHIFTING OF LOCUS

DOVER BEACH
—Matthew Arnold

The sea is calm to-night.
The tide is full, the moon lies fair
Upon the straits; on the French coast the light
Gleams and is gone; the cliffs of England stand,
Glimmering and vast, out in the tranquil bay.
Come to the window, sweet is the night-air!
Only, from the long line of spray
Where the sea meets the moon-blanched land,
Listen! You hear the grating roar
Of pebbles which the waves draw back, and fling,
At their return, up the high strand,
Begin, and cease, and then again begin,
With tremulous cadence slow, and bring
The eternal note of sadness in.

Sophocles long ago
Heard it on the Aegean, and it brought
Into his mind the turbid ebb and flow
Of human misery; we
Find also in the sound a thought,
Hearing it by this distant northern sea.

The Sea of Faith
Was once, too, at the full, and round earth's shore
Lay like the folds of a bright girdle furled.
But now I only hear
Its melancholy, long, withdrawing roar,
Retreating, to the breath
Of the night-wind, down the vast edges drear
And naked shingles of the world.

Ah, love, let us be true
To one another! for the world, which seems
To lie before us like a land of dreams,
So various, so beautiful, so new,
Hath really neither joy, nor love, nor light,
Nor certitude, nor peace, nor help for pain;
And we are here as on a darkling plain
Swept with confused alarms of struggle and flight,
Where ignorant armies clash by night.

Who is the speaker? Who is being spoken to? Where is the scene placed? What do you know about the personal qualities of the two characters?

To begin with, it is at least theoretically true that the speaker might be a woman; but because the poem is by Arnold, and because the notions in the poem are like notions elsewhere held by Arnold, it is natural to assume that the speaker is masculine, whether or not we wish to identify him with the poet himself. Automatically, then, the other character (the one not speaking) seems to be a woman. The two are in a room—a room in England, on the Dover coast overlooking the beach and the bay and the sea. Light gleams from the French coast. It is night; the tide is full; the air is sweet. The constant washing of pebbles on the sand in a slow, tremulous cadence can be heard on the night air, and the long, slow cadence is somehow sad. We assume that the speaker is English (the poem does not say so), just as we assume that he is masculine. We know nothing about his height, his coloring, his age—although he does not sound adolescent, certainly. We know a good deal about his temperament: he is philosophical, aware of sadness, filled with a poignant sympathy for the turbid ebb and flow of human misery. Whatever his chronological age, he is mature. He has a keen eye and ear. He is in love, but his love is scarcely tempestuous; he looks for an anchor in love, for truth that will be a light (not one that gleams and is gone) on this "darkling plain" of life.

Only a single detail persuades us that another person is present: the direct statement "Come to the window." Otherwise the poem might be a soliloquy, the poet simply speaking aloud. We know nothing concrete, really, about the second person, except that the speaker calls her "love." Is she his wife? Perhaps. That isn't important; indeed, the importance of the poem does not reside in the fact that the speaker is speaking to someone. What matters primarily is the speaker's state of mind; the tensiveness is strong and complex. Nevertheless, there is a dramatic effect achieved by the direct address to another person, and the sense of another presence is of great importance in an interpretation of the poem. Read the poem aloud with this in mind. Visualize the scene; hear the sounds—but remember that they do not exist independently; they must coalesce from the point of view of the speaker. You will find that the word *shingles,* incidentally, has an interesting meaning here.

The poem moves in cadences: the first stanza is a portrait of the night and the sea: its second section brings in the second person and the note of sadness; the second stanza enlarges the theme by relating it to the whole history of western man; the third stanza introduces the revolutions in faith; the last stanza, in a kind of great sigh, turns from this melancholy view of human history to the role of love, and to the silent witness to the scene—but notice that the closing tone is scarcely a happy one, and the view of man's lot is full of sorrow. The interpreter should mark these cadences or movements in the poem. How? What happens within you when you change from one thought to another in your own daily conversation? Make up an exercise in which you talk for a few moments about one subject and then shift to another—see how you manage the change. Do not, however, let Arnold's poem fall into unrelated pieces while you separate the cadences through which it moves.

Although Thackeray characterizes his speakers with specific details about their appearance and Arnold does not, the interpreter in both cases must characterize. The processes are about the same, though in one case we have physical traits to work with and in the other case only mental qualities. In both instances we want to get at the inner sense of the person speaking.

How does the speaker's mood affect the general tonicity of his body? Does he move quickly? Is he sitting or standing? (In reading the poem, would you sit if the speaker seemed to be sitting or not? What difference would your choice make in your effect?) What if the period at the end of line 1 were a comma? How would this affect the tensiveness of the opening lines? What differences are there between the pause at the end of line 1 and the pause at the end of line 5? What is the effect of the exclamation mark in line 9? These matters are not separate from characterization but parts of it, since they affect the "feel" of the passage. They are aspects of the felt sensing of the speaker, and hence of the interpreter.

Now let us look at another kind of scene—this time from a play.

from **STRIFE**[2]
—*John Galsworthy*

[*Galsworthy's play concerns a dispute between capital and labor at a tin works. Mr. Anthony is chairman of the board of the works; Enid Underwood is his daughter, married to Underwood, who is an officer at the works. Roberts is the leader of the opposing labor group; Annie Roberts is his wife. In the scene given here, Enid has come to the Roberts home to intercede with Roberts in the bitter dispute which centers around him and Anthony, because she is worried about her father's condition.—Ed.*]

ENID. (*Earnestly, to Roberts*) I've come on purpose to speak to you; will you come outside a minute?
(*She looks at Mrs. Roberts.*)
ROBERTS. (*Hanging up his hat*) I have nothing to say, ma'am.
ENID. But I *must* speak to you, please.
(*She moves towards the door.*)
ROBERTS. (*With sudden venom*) I have not the time to listen!
MRS. ROBERTS. David!
ENID. Mr. Roberts, *please!*
ROBERTS. (*Taking off his overcoat*) I am sorry to disoblige a lady—Mr. Anthony's daughter.
ENID. (*Wavering, then with sudden decision*) Mr. Roberts, I know you've another meeting of the men. (*Roberts bows*) I came to appeal to you. Please, please try to come to some compromise; give way a little, if it's only for your own sakes!

---

2 Reprinted by permission of G. P. Putnam's Sons.

ROBERTS. (*Speaking to himself*) The daughter of Mr. Anthony begs me to give way a little, if it's only for our own sakes.

ENID. For everybody's sake; for your wife's sake.

ROBERTS. For my wife's sake, for everybody's sake—for the sake of Mr. Anthony.

ENID. Why are you so bitter against my father? He has never done anything to you.

ROBERTS. Has he not?

ENID. He can't help his views, any more than you can help yours.

ROBERTS. I really didn't know that I had a right to views!

ENID. He's an old man, and you—
> (*Seeing his eyes fixed on her, she stops.*)

ROBERTS. (*Without raising his voice*) If I saw Mr. Anthony going to die, and I could save him by lifting my hand, I would not lift the little finger of it.

ENID. You—you—
> (*She stops again, biting her lips.*)

ROBERTS. I would not, and that's flat!

ENID. (*Coldly*) You don't mean what you say, and you know it!

ROBERTS. I mean every word of it.

ENID. But why?

ROBERTS. (*With a flash*) Mr. Anthony stands for tyranny! That's why!

ENID. Nonsense!
> (*Mrs. Roberts make a movement as if to rise, but sinks back in her chair.*)

ENID. (*With an impetuous movement*) Annie!

ROBERTS. Please not to touch my wife!

ENID. (*Recoiling with a sort of horror*) I believe—you are mad.

ROBERTS. The house of a madman then is not the fit place for a lady.

ENID. I'm not afraid of you.

ROBERTS. (*Bowing*) I would not expect the daughter of Mr. Anthony to be afraid. Mr. Anthony is not a coward like the rest of them.

ENID. (*Suddenly*) I suppose you think it brave, then, to go on with this struggle.

ROBERTS. Does Mr. Anthony think it brave to fight against women and children? Mr. Anthony is a rich man, I believe; does he think it brave to fight against those who haven't a penny? Does he think it brave to set children crying with hunger, an' women shivering with cold?

ENID. (*Putting up her hand, as though warding off a blow*) My father is acting on his principles, and you know it!

ROBERTS. And so am I!

ENID. You hate us; and you can't bear to be beaten.

ROBERTS. Neither can Mr. Anthony, for all that he may say.

ENID. At any rate, you might have pity on your wife.

(Mrs. Roberts who has her hand pressed to her heart, takes it away, and tries to calm her breathing.)

ROBERTS. Madam, I have no more to say.

(There is a knock at the door, and Underwood comes in. He stands looking at them, Enid turns to him, then seems undecided.)

UNDERWOOD. Enid!

ROBERTS. *(Ironically)* Ye were not needing to come for your wife, Mr. Underwood. We are not rowdies.

UNDERWOOD. I know that, Roberts. I hope Mrs. Roberts is better. *(Roberts turns away without answering.)* Come, Enid!

ENID. I make one more appeal to you, Mr. Roberts, for the sake of your wife.

ROBERTS. *(With polite malice)* If I might advise ye, ma'am—make it for the sake of your husband and your father.

This scene from Act 2 of *Strife* takes place in the kitchen of the Roberts' cottage near the works. The kitchen is tidy but bare, with a brick floor and whitewashed walls, smoke stained. A meager fire burns; there is a kettle on, and on a table are a cup, saucer, teapot, knife, and a plate of bread and cheese. Mrs. Roberts is thin and dark, about thirty-five, her hair down but tied with a ribbon. Enid Underwood is tall, twenty-eight, with a "small, decided face." Roberts is lean, middle height, somewhat stooped, with a "little rat-gnawn, brown-grey beard, moustaches, high cheek-bones, hollow cheeks, small fiery eyes." Underwood, manager of the works, is a quiet man "with a long, stiff jaw and steady eyes." There is snow on the streets outside the house. The time of year is February; the place, the borders of England and Wales.

In your rehearsal of such a scene, try walking through the stage business as if you were acting each character separately in a fully staged production. Don't try to achieve everything in a single rehearsal. Don't be satisfied until you are sure that you have developed a "feel" for each character. How does it affect your feeling for the scene and the characters when you know that Annie is Roberts' wife, and that Underwood is Enid's husband? How does the knowledge that the setting is Roberts' house affect the behavior of Mr. and Mrs. Roberts on the one hand and Enid on the other?

In performance, you will not wish to have Annie Roberts seated, since you certainly will not want to get up and down out of a chair as you move from character to character. But notice that, in the discussion that follows, we indicate her somewhat recessive position by placing her to the side of the scene.

Other movements (Enid's biting of the lip, Annie's impulse to move, Enid's recoiling, Roberts' bowing, and so on) should be made a part of the scene, since they are a real part of its tensiveness. Underwood's entrance poses a problem. Ordinarily the interpreter ought not to read stage directions, but should try instead to make entrances and

exits clear in his performance. Here, one might wish to say in the introduction that Underwood enters late in the scene. The knock provides a
special problem. It is usually unwise for the interpreter to knock on the
lectern, since it emphasizes the artificiality of the reader's position,
though it is true enough that a fine interpreter can violate almost any
convention on occasion. In this particular scene, since Roberts' last line
before the knock is so conclusive, there is less danger than usual in
interrupting the flow of the scene by reading the directions. Perhaps the
best compromise is to read them and omit a knock.

Now, working with the book, remember all that you have done to
establish the physical qualities of the characters and to respond to the
setting. Even though you are no longer going through all the stage business literally, remember all of it. Take time, as you read the lines, to
respond to that memory. Don't rush. Prepare a short introduction to
help you open the reading, so that when you say "Why are you so bitter
against my father?" the effect for the audience and for you will be that
the curtain has just gone up and the play is about to begin—though this
is not the beginning of the play.

How does reading the scene from a play differ from reading the
scene from the novel or from the poem? In some ways there is no
difference at all, but at the same time the people in a play are fully
dramatized; the playwright intends us to see and hear them as flesh-
and-blood people living in front of us, speaking always for themselves.
In the novel or in poetry the writer does not always wish his people to
have this same degree of actuality, and the interpreter must be wary of
overcharacterizing (though not many beginning readers do overcharac-
terize!). In a play, the interpreter always runs the risk of undercharacter-
izing. A good interpretation of a play, like a good performance of a play,
must engage the audience; the interpreter must not seem simply to be
summarizing the dramatic action. As nearly as possible, he or she will *be*
the character speaking, though the interpreter faces special problems
and must seek somewhat different solutions than the actor. The body
fact is that the interpreter stands visible before the audience, but the
body *act* is the act of the characters in the play. Dullness will defeat the
whole purpose of a play reading—indeed, of any reading at all.

This distinction between *act* and *fact* has been pointed to by philosophers on more than one occasion. It provides us with a way of
obviating a difficulty often found in discussions of interpretation—the
problem of distinguishing between *being* on the one hand and *acting*
(or interpreting) on the other. Does the interpreter or actor *become* the
character? Do acting and interpretation differ in that the actor *does*
become the character while the interpreter simply *suggests* the character? The word *suggestion* has always been problematic, for it seems to
say that the interpreter doesn't really *do* anything, but simply *suggests*
something. But of course suggestion is a way of doing, and the interpreter is like the actor in needing to persuade us of the truth of the
character's being during the performance. It seems helpful to adopt the
phenomenological distinction between act and fact: The actor or interpreter is in *fact* the performer seeking to persuade us of his existence;

but the *act* in which the performer engages is the act of the character. Laurence Olivier in *Hamlet* is in fact Olivier but in act Hamlet. Otherwise there is no effective coalescence of performer and character at all.

True enough, the actor, with his larger freedom by virtue of the fact that other actors appear on the stage with him, can afford a wider range of movement, gesture, physical locus than is *normally* granted to the interpreter. (Notice that once more we say *normally,* for this is a generalization, not a rule.) But with his stricter economy—stricter by virtue of the fact that the solo interpreter does not have the support of a full cast of actors—the interpreter, too, must give us the body *act* of the character. Indeed, he must give us the body acts of all the characters in the scene, to be successful. The demands upon the performer are thus very great indeed; in addition to being actor or actress, he or she must be director and in some sense costumer and designer. The challenge is great, but so are the rewards when the performance succeeds.

PLACEMENT OF CHARACTERS

How does the interpreter achieve the illusion of movement onstage when he is reading four characters and placing the scene not onstage at all but out in the audience? Conventions have been established in interpretation to aid the illusion. For the sake of illustration, suppose that we imagine the opening of the scene from the interpreter's point of view. (All directions in the discussion will be stage directions, given from the point of view of the reader, not of the audience.) Here is a diagram representing an effective placement of the characters:

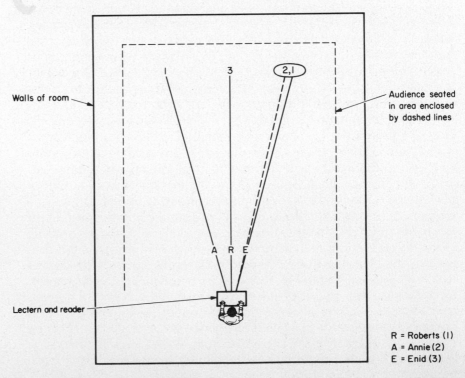

Walls of room

Audience seated in area enclosed by dashed lines

Lectern and reader

R = Roberts (1)
A = Annie (2)
E = Enid (3)

Since the scene belongs largely to Roberts and Enid, we have given them center stage, with Enid on Roberts' right. Whenever Roberts talks—*no matter to how many other characters,* his location is always along the line labelled *R.* When the interpreter speaks from that position, he is *Roberts* and no one else. As Roberts speaks, he is looking at Enid (whom we have numbered 3 on the diagram). When Annie speaks (she has only one line in the scene, to her husband), she speaks along the line labeled *A,* and she is looking at Roberts (whom we have numbered 1.) When Enid speaks, usually to Roberts, she looks along the line labeled *E,* and to Roberts (whom we have numbered 1). But Enid speaks also to Annie. When she does, she may make a slight movement from the position in which she addresses Roberts, so that she seems to speak along the dotted line to Annie (whom we have numbered 2 on the diagram). This is the stage picture for the interpreter: Annie, far left; Roberts, centered but to the left of Enid; Enid, centered but to the right of Roberts. Whenever a character speaks, *to whomever he speaks,* he keeps virtually the location we have assigned to him. Thus the audience knows, when a reader takes a location (even if he doesn't say a word), what character they are watching. As a character, in his essential location, moves from one to another of the characters onstage, he may make slight adjustments left and right, depending on the location of those characters to his left or right, but he will not essentially change the location we have indicated. Thus, while Enid speaks to both Roberts and Mrs. Roberts, her general stage position remains unchanged. Whatever she sees, she sees within the oval we have indicated on the chart. (A similar oval might be inscribed for each of the other characters if they addressed more than one person.) Remember: the interpreter, speaking as the character, sees out front the character to whom he is speaking. While the scene is projected out front (offstage), the interpreter is nevertheless a part of that scene, not cut off from it. The energy of the speaker goes from his position at the lectern to the point in the audience where the addressee is imaginarily located.

The more strongly the illusion of placement is established, the more wary the reader must be of accidentally shifting the positions of the characters, for then the audience will be confused as to the speaker's identity. Keep the essential locations clear.

When Underwood appears in the scene, let's decide to put him at Enid's right, as if he were entering from that side of the stage. (In a staged production, he might well enter someplace else. The interpreter should not try to reproduce stage pictures; since he is only one person and his movement is minimal, he cannot hope to do all that a group of actors with a full stage could achieve. Nevertheless, he must within the conventions of his art attempt to involve the audience actively and fully in the play.) The diagram now looks as it appears on page 128.

Notice that each character still has an essential locus and that his focus shifts only slightly as he moves from one addressee to another. Roberts maintains 3 as his line to Enid, but shifts slightly to 4 as he addresses Underwood; Enid speaks to Roberts along 1 but looks at her husband along 4; Underwood speaks to Enid along 3 but to Roberts along 1. Annie, of course, has no further lines to speak.

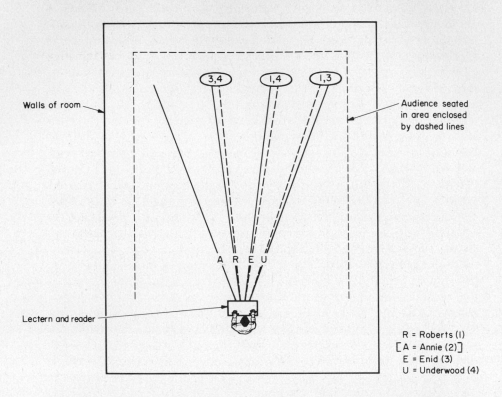

Walls of room

Audience seated in area enclosed by dashed lines

Lectern and reader

R = Roberts (I)
[A = Annie (2)]
E = Enid (3)
U = Underwood (4)

This kind of placement of characters is an aid to the illusion of stage movement. It helps the audience keep the characters separated; even more importantly, it gives the interpreter himself a point of focus out in the audience, a place where he can imagine the characters whom he addresses, with the kind of scenic background he envisions for the play. In rehearsing, you may even want to place chairs in front of you so that you can get used to fixing the scene in a specific place. But be careful! Remember that you do not have to stare at the point once you have fixed it, any more than you stare steadily into the eyes of someone with whom you are carrying on a conversation in life. Keep the point clearly defined, but feel free to look down, look away, look up as the scene permits, so long as you keep the general location of the character firm (left, right, center). This combination of a fixed location for speech directed sharply to another character and freedom to behave physically as you do in natural dialogue situations will help amazingly to persuade the audience that a real scene is in progress.

If placement, movement of the eyes from one position to another, and assumption of differences in posture for different characters remain simply mechanical, with no belief at all on your part, this advice about stage illusion is useless. Remember that you are not in a vacuum but involved in a scene, and your relations with other characters in that scene are continuous and tensive. Some teachers and some performers are impatient with conventions of this sort. Conventions are, of course, simply that—agreements arrived at which help both performer and audience. Any convention *can* be successfully violated, and at any rate conventions ought not become straitjackets that hamper imaginative activity. But nothing is to be gained by pretending that the conventions do not exist. It is a matter of practical fact that they do; hence performers need to be aware of them even if they ignore them in practice. Expectations of the audience cannot be wholly overlooked.

Other precautions: As soon as one character finishes speaking or reacting in a play reading, the next character must be present (although not necessarily speaking). There must be no "dead space" between speeches, no feeling that for a moment the reader himself comes between the characters and the audience. Cues must be picked up quickly; reactions must be instantaneous. After Enid first addresses Roberts and looks at Mrs. Roberts, there must be no dead space *after* Enid's pause to look at Annie. As soon as her look is completed (and it must be completed), Roberts must be present. Try completing Enid's look; then, *as* you move to Roberts' line for speaking, do it in Roberts' character, not in your own. Roberts' reaction to Enid's speech is included in the movement from Enid's position. There is no moment when neither character is present.

It is not a good idea to look down into your book to find Roberts' line before you read it. This is the worst place to use the book, because it interferes with the projection of reactions out into the audience. Once into the speech, then you may look down at the book—but do so *in character,* and do not forget to keep your mind fixed on the position out front where you have located the addressee. Your eyes may drop to the page but your attention must not. As soon as attention focuses wholly on the pages of the book, the imagined scene collapses. It is as if the stage curtain has fallen in front of the reader. And what reader wants to be caught in that distressing position?

Remember, then, that the propulsion from reader to scene is always forward, out into the audience; energy must never be permitted to sag, to drop into the book. Keep the scene far enough back in the room so that the whole audience is involved in the flow of energy from you, as reader, to the imagined scene.

Don't look into the eyes of members of your audience; keep your eyes for the character to whom you are speaking. And remember that when you look out into the audience, you *are* looking at the character to whom you are speaking—and not simply looking into space. The character who is *not* speaking is often the one the interpreter needs to work hardest with, since the audience must be given the illusion that he is present. How the silent character responds to what is being said must

PROJECTION AND FOCUS

show in the character speaking. For example, can you imagine how the silent person addressed in the following speech must be responding?

> You mean to tell me that you aren't going to go with me after all? Don't just stand there—say something. Do you hear me? Come back here! Now I'll ask you once more—are you going with me or not?

Try delivering the speech as if it were a speech from a play, so that the audience will know exactly what the addressee is doing. Take time to permit the addressee to do what he must be doing. Watch him. What gestures do you find yourself making? What feelings do you have? Do you find yourself wanting to move forward at times, and to pull back at others? What specific vocal changes (in pitch, volume, force, rate) accompany the body changes? Describe your responses as accurately as you can in a short paper to see whether you can verbalize them.

We turn now to another aspect of the problem of locus. We have said that the interpreter, in characterizing, must try to embody the tensions of characters. You must never forget, however, that even in the dramatic form there is always a controlling point of view that modifies handling of characterization. While the problem is not restricted to the reading of drama, it may be illustrated in plays with a sharp comic or satiric touch. Hence we will look at a scene from Oscar Wilde's *The Importance of Being Earnest*. In this scene, the eminently "proper" Lady Bracknell confronts Jack Worthing, who is in love with her daughter Gwendolen.

THE IMPORTANCE OF BEING EARNEST
—*Oscar Wilde*

[*Gwendolen, the daughter of the very proper Lady Bracknell, is in love with Jack Worthing. In the present scene, Lady Bracknell is confronting her would-be son-in-law.*—Ed.]

LADY BRACKNELL. (*Sitting down*) You can take a seat, Mr. Worthing. (*Looks in her pocket for note-book and pencil.*)

JACK. Thank you, Lady Bracknell, I prefer standing.

LADY BRACKNELL. (*Pencil and note-book in hand*) I feel bound to tell you that you are not down on my list of eligible young men, although I have the same list as the dear Duchess of Bolton has. We work together, in fact. However, I am quite ready to enter your name, should your answers be what a really affectionate mother requires. Do you smoke?

JACK. Well, yes, I must admit I smoke.

LADY BRACKNELL. I am glad to hear it. A man should always have an occupation of some kind. There are far too many idle men in London as it is. How old are you?

JACK. Twenty-nine.

LADY BRACKNELL. A very good age to be married at . I have always been of the opinion that a man who desires to get married should know either everything or nothing. Which do you know?

JACK. *(After some hesitation)* I know nothing, Lady Bracknell.

LADY BRACKNELL. I am pleased to hear it. I do not approve of anything that tampers with natural ignorance. Ignorance is like a delicate exotic fruit; touch it and the bloom is gone. The whole theory of modern education is radically unsound. Fortunately in England, at any rate, education produces no effect whatsoever. If it did, it would prove a serious danger to the upper classes, and probably lead to acts of violence in Grosvenor Square. What is your income?

JACK. Between seven and eight thousand a year.

LADY BRACKNELL. *(Makes a note in her book)* In land, or in investments?

JACK. In investments, chiefly.

LADY BRACKNELL. That is satisfactory. What between the duties expected of one during one's lifetime, and the duties exacted from one after one's death, land has ceased to be either a profit or a pleasure. It gives one position, and prevents one from keeping it up. That's all that can be said about land.

JACK. I have a country house with some land, of course, attached to it, about fifteen hundred acres, I believe; but I don't depend on that for my real income. In fact, as far as I can make out, the poachers are the only people who make anything out of it.

LADY BRACKNELL. A country house! How many bedrooms? Well, that point can be cleared up afterwards. You have a town house, I hope? A girl with a simple, unspoiled nature, like Gwendolen, could hardly be expected to reside in the country.

JACK. Well, I own a house in Belgrave Square, but it is let by the year to Lady Bloxham. Of course, I can get it back whenever I like, at six months' notice.

LADY BRACKNELL. Lady Bloxham? I don't know her.

JACK. Oh, she goes about very little. She is a lady considerably advanced in years.

LADY BRACKNELL. Ah, now-a-days that is no guarantee of respectability of character. What number in Belgrave Square?

JACK. 149.

LADY BRACKNELL. *(Shaking her head)* The unfashionable side. I thought there was something. However, that could easily be altered.

JACK. Do you mean the fashion, or the side?

LADY BRACKNELL. *(Sternly)* Both, if necessary, I presume. What are your politics?

JACK. Well, I am afraid I really have none. I am a Liberal Unionist.

LADY BRACKNELL. Oh, they count as Tories. They dine with us. Or come in the evening, at any rate. Now to minor matters. Are your parents living?

JACK. I have lost both my parents.

LADY BRACKNELL. Both? . . . That seems like carelessness. Who was your father? He was evidently a man of some wealth. Was he born in what the Radical papers call the purple of commerce, or did he rise from the ranks of aristocracy?

JACK. I am afraid I really don't know. The fact is, Lady Bracknell, I said I had lost my parents. It would be nearer the truth to say that my parents seem to have lost me.. . . I don't actually know who I am by birth. I was . . . Well, I was found.

LADY BRACKNELL. Found!

JACK. The late Mr. Thomas Cardew, an old gentleman of a very charitable and kindly disposition, found me, and gave me the name of Worthing, because he happened to have a first-class ticket for Worthing in his pocket at the time. Worthing is a place in Sussex. It is a seaside resort.

LADY BRACKNELL. Where did the charitable gentleman who had a first-class ticket for this seaside resort find you?

JACK. (*Gravely*) In a hand-bag.

LADY BRACKNELL. A hand-bag?

JACK. (*Very seriously*) Yes, Lady Bracknell. I was in a hand-bag—a somewhat large, black leather hand-bag, with handles to it—an ordinary hand-bag in fact.

LADY BRACKNELL. In what locality did this Mr. James, or Thomas, Cardew come across this ordinary hand-bag?

JACK. In the cloak-room at Victoria Station. It was given to him in mistake for his own.

LADY BRACKNELL. The cloak-room at Victoria Station?

JACK. Yes. The Brighton line.

LADY BRACKNELL. The line is immaterial. Mr. Worthing, I confess I feel somewhat bewildered by what you have just told me. To be born, or at any rate, bred in a hand-bag, whether it had handles or not, seems to me to display a contempt for the ordinary decencies of family life that reminds one of the worst excesses of the French Revolution. And I presume you know what that unfortunate movement led to? As for the particular locality in which the hand-bag was found, a cloak-room at a railway station might serve to conceal a social indiscretion—has probably, indeed, been used for that purpose before now—but it could hardly be regarded as an assured basis for a recognized position in good society.

JACK. May I ask you then what you would advise me to do? I need hardly say I would do anything in the world to insure Gwendolen's happiness.

LADY BRACKNELL. I would strongly advise you, Mr. Worthing, to try and acquire some relations as soon as possible, and to make a definite effort to produce at any rate one parent, of either sex, before the season is quite over.

JACK. Well I don't see how I could possibly manage to do that. I can produce the hand-bag at any moment. It is in my dressing-room at home. I really think that should satisfy you, Lady Bracknell.

LADY BRACKNELL. Me, sir! What has it to do with me? You can hardly imagine that I and Lord Bracknell would dream of allowing our only daughter—a girl brought up with the utmost care—to marry into a cloak-room, and form an alliance with a parcel? Good morning, Mr. Worthing!

It is clear that the scene is a serious one from the point of view of both Lady Bracknell and Jack Worthing. But in the eyes of the playwright and the audience the scene is highly comic. The selection of details, juxtaposition of attitudes, degree of empathy with characters is so carefully controlled by the camera's eye that we are able to laugh. Empathy is the central matter in determining the correct locus for the interpreter.

Perhaps an example from life may help: suppose you see a too self-consciously proper matron slip on the ice and sit down with a great flailing of arms and a general disarray. If no harm is done except to her vanity, you may find the episode laughable. If, on the other hand, she is hurt in the fall, your laughter is likely to fade away, to be replaced by practical concern for her welfare. In the first instance, you are not empathizing with the victim but enjoying your own point of view; in the second instance, your feeling with her forbids your divorcing your attitude from hers. The first illustrates the comic point of view; the second, the tragic. (The two points of view are seldom this distinct.) The locus of the viewer is not the same in the two cases.

Thus, in the scene from Wilde's play, the detachment with which the viewer listens to Lady Bracknell and Jack Worthing is an aspect of locus. The interpreter does not simply identify with the two speakers; he embodies only those aspects of the characters that Wilde wishes to emphasize and adds an awareness of the ridiculousness of the scene, which is in the play but not in either of the characters. (Rather, there is no awareness of it in Lady Bracknell, but there is a certain amount of it in Jack.) If the interpreter plays the characters "straight," identifying with them, embodying only their view of the scene, the humor is likely to disappear and the whole purpose of Wilde will be lost. On the other hand, if he does not embody the characters sufficiently, he will produce only gross caricature—and while such caricature may make the injudicious howl, it will only offend the judicious. Such comedy as Wilde's succeeds best when the interpreter persuades us that Lady Bracknell and Jack are *real* without losing sight of the fact that the camera taking their pictures is laughing.

ASPECTS
OF LOCUS

The interpreter must follow Wilde in elaborating details. The notebook and pencil are not usual in such an interrogation as this! Lady Bracknell is rather larger than life (though real) in her inquiries and in her responses to Jack's answers. The solemnity with which both characters invest the scene is larger than life—how hilarious, for example, is Lady Bracknell's stately pronouncement that "ignorance is like a delicate exotic fruit; touch it and the bloom is gone." Her deportment and her syntax are impeccable, but she has no sense of humor at all. The interpreter, however, must have a sense of humor or the humorlessness of Lady Bracknell will turn simply to dullness. Incongruity and exaggeration fill the scene from beginning to end, but they must be touched deftly. Probably the interpreter should delight in both persons even while mocking them. A person who hates Lady Bracknell is not likely to be a persuasive reader of her lines.

LOCUS AND COMEDY

This particular aspect of locus is found in texts that are comic and satiric. This double location of things is difficult to master; it explains why many readers and actors feel that they can perform comedy but not tragedy, or vice versa. The detachment of comedy may ruin a reading of tragedy; simple empathy with characters may ruin certain kinds of comedy. Perhaps here lies the key to the dilemma that often confronts the satirist: if his satire is too heavy-handed, he will seem to lack sophistication; if his satire is too deft and light in touch, it may be lost on an audience altogether and what he intends for satire will be taken for "truth." Audiences differ in their ability to sense complications in locus. A reader may need to be a little more blunt with some audiences than with others in pointing to the double placement. But being too blunt with an audience that does not require it will cause the reader to fail with that audience, just as too little bluntness will cause failure with the less sensitive audience. The challenge is great; faced with it, the interpreter can either sit down in confusion and defeat or can rise to meet it.

You will find it worthwhile to work with the various scenes at the end of this chapter. The reading of drama is extraordinarily complicated, and only long, hard practice will enable you to succeed in it. You may find that you do not enjoy reading from a play as much as reading from a novel or short story or poem—or you may find that you enjoy it *more*. In any event, the lessons to be learned are necessary to all good interpreters, because the problems you face in the interpretation of drama you will also face in handling scenes and characters in other literary forms. Whenever the writer chooses to use a fully developed scene (whether it be a dramatic monologue by Robert Browning or a scene in a story by Henry James), the interpreter will find useful the techniques described here.

Remember, once again, that the placement of characters in a scene must never be simply mechanical. And don't place characters too far apart. The distance of characters *onstage* is not to be confused with the distance *offstage*. The reader can speak intimately to a character he has "placed" well back in the audience, though one would not try to speak intimately to a character twenty feet away on a stage. Do not confuse the two conventions. Furthermore, the reader must be wary of too much movement of the head. Characters can be separated by movement of the eyes in rooms the size of most classrooms. It is distressing to follow broad movements of the head back and forth between characters, as if one were watching a tennis match. It is wise to keep your scenes placed well back in the audience (so that everyone is included in the span of your attention) and well in the middle section of the room. Don't believe that you can't get as many as six or seven characters easily into such an area—you can, with no crowding.

Here is a list of things to remember:

1. Establish a physical *feel* for the characters, including their vocal qualities.

2. Define your imagined scene sharply: know how the characters look, how the setting looks; place the characters.

3. Keep the energy moving forward to the imagined scene. (This is what is meant by *projection of scene*.)

4. Keep the scene far enough into the audience to involve the whole audience in the flow of energy.

5. Do not permit any dead space between speeches; all pauses must be *filled*.

6. Do not focus on the pages of your book at moments of transition from one character to another. (You may need to memorize quick transitions.)

7. Don't stare at the spot where you have placed a character. Move easily to and from the spot with your eyes.

8. Remember to keep the silent character alive.

9. Keep the whole scene within the limits defined by the audience seating arrangement—but don't look directly into the faces of the audience.[3]

10. Rehearse, rehearse, rehearse. Don't try to do it all in a single rehearsal; many short rehearsal periods will give your scene a chance to grow with you, or rather will give you a chance to grow into your scene.

MATERIALS FOR PRACTICE

We begin with a group of poems, each of which is in some sense dramatic—that is, each involves a character other than the speaker, some particular person whom the speaker is addressing (who may or may not be actually present with the speaker). How shall the interpreter distinguish between the nature and degree of characterization involved in

[3] There are exceptions. Some soliloquies, for example, are meant to be spoken directly to members of the audience.

each of these poems? What determines the degree to which the poem becomes dramatic rather than lyric or epic in mode? How does this involve the question of locus?

From the poems we move to scenes from plays and a novel.

WHEN I HAVE FEARS THAT I MAY CEASE TO BE
—John Keats

When I have fears that I may cease to be
Before my pen has gleaned my teeming brain,
Before high-piléd books, in charact'ry,
Hold like rich garners the full-ripened grain;
When I behold, upon the night's starred face,
Huge cloudy symbols of a high romance,
And think that I may never live to trace
Their shadows, with the magic hand of chance;
And when I feel, fair creature of an hour!
That I shall never look upon thee more,
Never have relish in the faery power
Of unreflecting love;—then on the shore
Of the wide world I stand alone, and think,
Till Love and Fame to nothingness do sink.

IT IS A BEAUTEOUS EVENING
—William Wordsworth

It is a beauteous evening, calm and free,
The holy time is quiet as a Nun
Breathless with adoration: the broad sun
Is sinking down in its tranquillity;
The gentleness of heaven broods o'er the Sea:
Listen! the mighty Being is awake,
And doth with his eternal motion make
A sound like thunder—everlastingly.

Dear Child! dear Girl! that walkest with me here,
If thou appear untouched by solemn thought,
Thy nature is not therefore less divine:
Thou liest in Abraham's bosom all the year,
And worship'st at the Temple's inner shrine,
God being with thee when we know it not.

PORPHYRIA'S LOVER
—Robert Browning

The rain set early in tonight,
    The sullen wind was soon awake,

It tore the elm-tops down for spite,
   And did its worst to vex the lake:
I listened with heart fit to break.
When glided in Porphyria; straight
   She shut the cold out and the storm,
And kneeled and made the cheerless grate
   Blaze up, and all the cottage warm;
Which done, she rose, and from her form
Withdrew the dripping cloak and shawl,
   And laid her soiled gloves by, untied
Her hat, and let the damp hair fall,
   And, last, she sat down by my side
And called me. When no voice replied,
She put my arm about her waist,
   And made her smooth white shoulder bare
And all her yellow hair displaced,
   And, stooping, made my cheek lie there,
And spread, o'er all, her yellow hair,
Murmuring how she loved me—she
   Too weak, for all her heart's endeavor,
To set its struggling passion free
   From pride, and vainer ties dissever,
And give herself to me forever.
But passion sometimes would prevail,
   Nor could tonight's gay feast restrain
A sudden thought of one so pale
   For love of her, and all in vain:
So, she was come through wind and rain.
Be sure I looked up at her eyes
   Happy and proud; at last I knew
Porphyria worshipped me; surprise
   Made my heart swell, and still it grew
While I debated what to do.
That moment she was mine, mine, fair,
   Perfectly pure and good: I found
A thing to do, and all her hair
   In one long yellow string I wound
Three times her little throat around,
And strangled her. No pain felt she;
   I am quite sure she felt no pain.
As a shut bud that holds a bee,
   I warily oped her lids; again
Laughed the blue eyes without a stain.
And I untightened next the tress
   About her neck; her cheek once more
Blushed bright beneath my burning kiss:
   I propped her head up as before,
Only, this time my shoulder bore
Her head, which droops upon it still:
   The smiling rosy little head,
So glad it has its utmost will,
   That all it scorned at once is fled.

And I, its love, am gained instead!
Porphyria's love: she guessed not how
   Her darling one wish would be heard.
And thus we sit together now,
   And all night long we have not stirred,
And yet God has not said a word!

from GHOSTS[4]
—*Henrik Ibsen*

[*In this scene from Act I of Ibsen's play, Pastor Manders has come to speak with Mrs. Alving, a widow, about her plans for building an orphanage.*—Ed.]

MANDERS. Now first of all, here is—(*Breaks off*) Tell me, Mrs. Alving, what are these books doing here?

MRS. ALVING. These books? I am reading them.

MANDERS. Do you read this sort of thing?

MRS. ALVING. Certainly I do.

MANDERS. Do you feel any the better or the happier for reading books of this kind?

MRS. ALVING. I think it makes me, as it were, more self-reliant.

MANDERS. That is remarkable. But why?

MRS. ALVING. Well, they give me an explanation or a confirmation of lots of different ideas that have come into my own mind. But what surprises me, Mr. Manders, is that, properly speaking, there is nothing at all new in these books. There is nothing more in them than what most people think and believe. The only thing is, that most people either take no account of it or won't admit it to themselves.

MANDERS. But, good heavens, do you seriously think that most people—?

MRS. ALVING. Yes, indeed, I do.

MANDERS. But not here in the country at any rate? Not here amongst people like ourselves?

MRS. ALVING. Yes, amongst people like ourselves too.

MANDERS. Well, really, I must say—!

MRS. ALVING. But what is the particular objection that you have to these books?

MANDERS. What objection? You surely don't suppose that I take any particular interest in such productions?

MRS. ALVING. In fact, you don't know anything about what you are denouncing?

4 From *Plays by Henrik Ibsen.* Reprinted by permission of Random House, Inc.

MANDERS. I have read quite enough about these books to disapprove of them.

MRS. ALVING. Yes, but your own opinion—

MANDERS. My dear Mrs. Alving, there are many occasions in life when one has to rely on the opinion of others. That is the way in this world, and it is quite right that it should be so. What would become of society, otherwise?

MRS. ALVING. Well, you may be right.

MANDERS. Apart from that, naturally, I don't deny that literature of this kind may have a considerable attraction. And I cannot blame you, either, for wishing to make yourself acquainted with the intellectual tendencies which I am told are at work in the wider world in which you have allowed your son to wander for so long. But—

MRS. ALVING. But—?

MANDERS. (*Lowering his voice*) But one doesn't talk about it, Mrs. Alving. One certainly is not called upon to account to every one for what one reads or thinks in the privacy of one's own room.

MRS. ALVING. Certainly not. I quite agree with you.

MANDERS. Just think of the consideration you owe to this Orphanage, which you decided to build at a time when your thoughts on such subjects were very different from what they are now—as far as I am able to judge.

MRS. ALVING. Yes, I freely admit that. But it was about the Orphanage—

MANDERS. It was about the Orphanage we were going talk; quite so. Well—walk warily, dear Mrs. Alving! And now let us turn to the business in hand. . . .

HUCKLEBERRY FINN (from Chapter III)
   —Mark Twain

Well, I got a good going-over in the morning from old Miss Watson on account of my clothes; but the widow she didn't scold, but only cleaned off the grease and clay, and looked so sorry that I thought I would behave awhile if I could. Then Miss Watson she took me in the closet and prayed, but nothing come of it. She told me to pray every day, and whatever I asked for I would get it. But it warn't so. I tried it. Once I got a fish-line, but no hooks. It warn't any good to me without hooks. I tried for the hooks three or four times, but somehow I couldn't make it work. By and by, one day, I asked Miss Watson to try for me, but she said I was a fool. She never told me why, and I couldn't make it out no way.

I set down one time back in the woods, and had a long think about it. I said to myself, if a body can get anything they pray for why don't Deacon Winn get back the money he lost on pork? Why can't the widow get back her silver snuff-box that was stole? Why can't Miss Watson fat up? No, says

I to myself, there ain't nothing in it. I went and told the widow about it, and she said the thing a body could get by praying for it was "spiritual gifts." This was too many for me, but she told me what she meant—I must help other people, and do everything I could for other people, and look out for them all the time, and never think about myself. This was including Miss Watson, as I took it. I went out in the woods and turned it over in my mind a long time, but I couldn't see no advantage about it—except for the other people; so at last I reckoned I wouldn't worry about it any more, but just let it go. Sometimes the widow would take me one side and talk about Providence in a way to make a body's mouth water; but maybe next day Miss Watson would take hold and knock it all down again. I judged I could see that there was two Providences, and a poor chap would stand considerable show with the widow's Providence, but if Miss Watson's got him there warn't no help for him any more. I thought it all out, and reckoned I would belong to the widow's if he wanted me, though I couldn't make out how he was a-going to be any better off then than what he was before, seeing I was so ignorant, and so kind of low-down and ornery.

HUCKLEBERRY FINN (from Chapter XI)

[*Huck has disguised himself as a girl in a calico gown and bonnet and has come to seek information in a little shanty where he finds "a woman about forty year old. . . ."*—Ed.]

The woman kept looking at me pretty curious, and I didn't feel a bit comfortable. Pretty soon she says:

"What did you say your name was, honey?"

"M—Mary Williams."

Somehow it didn't seem to me that I said it was Mary before, so I didn't look up—seemed to me I said it was Sarah; so I felt sort of cornered, and was afeard maybe I was looking it, too. I wished the woman would say something more; the longer she set still the uneasier I was. But now she says:

"Honey, I thought you said it was Sarah when you first come in?"

"Oh, yes'm, I did. Sarah Mary Williams. Sarah's my first name. Some calls me Sarah, some calls me Mary."

"Oh, that's the way of it?"

"Yes'm."

I was feeling better then, but I wished I was out of there, anyway. I couldn't look up yet.

Well, the woman fell to talking about how hard times was, and how poor they had to live, and how the rats was as free as if they owned the place, and so forth and so on, and then I got easy again. She was right about the rats. You'd see one stick his nose out of a hole in the corner every little while. She said she had to have things handy to throw at them when she was alone, or they wouldn't give her no peace. She showed me a bar of lead twisted up into a knot, and said she was a good shot with it generly, but she'd wrenched her arm a day or two ago, and didn't know whether she could throw true now. But she watched for a chance, and directly banged away at a rat; but she missed him wide, and said, "Ouch!" it hurt her arm so. Then she told me to try for the next one. I wanted to be getting away before the old man got back, but of course I didn't let on. I got the thing, and the first rat that showed his nose I let drive, and if he'd 'a' stayed where he was he'd 'a' been 'a' tolerable sick rat. She said that was first rate, and she reckoned I would hive the next one. She went and got the lump of lead and fetched it back, and brought along a hank of yarn which she wanted me to help her with. I held up my two hands and she put the hank over them, and went on talking about her arm and her husband's matters. But she broke off to say:

"Keep your eye on the rats. You better have the lead in your lap, handy."

So she dropped the lump into my lap just at that moment, and I clapped my legs together on it and she went on talking. But only about a minute. Then she took off the hank and looked me straight in the face, and very pleasant, and says:

"Come, now, what's your real name?"

"Wh-hat, mum?"

"What's your real name? Is it Bill, or Tom, or Bob?—or what is it?"

I reckon I shook like a leaf, and I didn't know hardly what to do. But I says:

"Please to don't poke fun at a poor girl like me, mum. If I'm in the way here, I'll—"

"No, you won't. Set down and stay where you are. I ain't going to hurt you, and I ain't going to tell on you, nuther. You just tell me your secret, and trust me. I'll keep it; and, what's more, I'll help you. So'll my old man if you want him to. You see, you're a runaway 'prentice, that's all. It ain't anything. There ain't no harm in it. You've been treated bad, and you made up your mind to cut. Bless you, child, I wouldn't tell on you. Tell me all about it now, that's a good boy."

So I said it wouldn't be no use to try to play it any longer, and I would just make a clean breast and tell her everything, but she mustn't go back on her promise. Then I told her my father and mother was dead, and the law had bound me out to a mean old farmer in the country thirty mile back from the river, and he treated me so bad I couldn't stand it no longer; he went away to be gone a couple of days, and so I took my chance and stole some of his daughter's old clothes and cleared out, and I had been three nights coming the thirty miles. I traveled nights, and hid daytimes and slept, and the bag of bread and meat I carried from home lasted me all the way, and I had a-plenty. I said I believed my uncle Abner Moore would take care of me, and so that was why I struck out for this town of Goshen.

"Goshen, child? This ain't Goshen. This is St. Petersburg. Goshen's ten mile further up the river. Who told you this was Goshen?"

"Why a man I met at daybreak this morning, just as I was going to turn into the woods for my regular sleep. He told me when the roads forked I must take the right hand, and five mile would fetch me to Goshen."

"He was drunk, I reckon. He told you just exactly wrong."

"Well, he did act like he was drunk, but it ain't no matter now. I got to be moving along. I'll fetch Goshen before daylight."

"Hold on a minute. I'll put you up a snack to eat. You might want it."

So she put me up a snack, and says:

"Say, when a cow's laying down, which end of her gets up first? Answer up prompt now—don't stop to study over it. Which ends gets up first?"

"The hind end, mum."

"Well, then a horse?"

"The for-rard end, mum."

"Which side of a tree does the moss grow on?"

"North side."

"If fifteen cows is browsing on a hillside, how many of them eats with their heads pointed the same direction?"

"The whole fifteen, mum."

"Well, I reckon you *have* lived in the country. I thought maybe you was trying to hocus me again. What's your real name, now?"

"George Peters, mum."

"Well, try to remember it, George. Don't forget and tell me it's Elexander before you go, and then get out by saying it's George Elexander when I catch you. And don't go about women in that old calico. You do a girl tolerable poor, but you might fool men, maybe. Bless you, child, when you set out to thread a needle don't hold the thread still and fetch the needle up to it; hold the needle still and poke the thread at it; that's the way a woman most always does, but a man always does t'other way. And when you throw at a rat or anything, hitch yourself up a-tiptoe and fetch your hand up over your head as awkward as you can, and miss your rat about six or seven foot. Throw stiff-armed from the shoulder, like there was a pivot there for it to turn on, like a girl; not from the wrist and elbow, with your arm out to one side, like a boy. And, mind you, when a girl tries to catch anything in her lap she throws her knees apart; she don't clap them together, the way you did when you catched the lump of lead. Why, I spotted you for a boy when you was threading the needle; and I contrived the other things just to make certain. Now trot along to your uncle, Sarah Mary Williams George Elexander Peters, and if you get into trouble you send word to Mrs. Judith Loftus, which is me, and I'll do what I can to get you out of it."

THE GLASS MENAGERIE (from Scene 4)[5]
—*Tennessee Williams*

[*Amanda Wingfield, "a little woman of great but confused vitality clinging frantically to another time and place," is talking with her son, Tom ("a poet with a job in a warehouse") about her daughter Laura, who is crippled in one leg and has gradually withdrawn from reality. The setting of the play is a rear apartment in St. Louis.*—Ed.]

AMANDA. *(Touching his sleeve)* You know how Laura is. So quiet but—still water runs deep! She notices things and I think she—broods about them. *(Tom look us)* A few days ago I came in and she was crying.

TOM. What about?

AMANDA. You.

TOM. Me?

AMANDA. She has an idea that you're not happy here.

TOM. What gave her that idea?

AMANDA. What gives her any idea? However, you do act strangely. I—I'm not criticizing, understand that! I know your ambitions do not lie in the warehouse, that like everybody in the whole wide world—you've had to—make sacrifices, but—Tom—Tom—life's not easy, it calls for—Spartan endurance! There's so many things in my heart that I cannot describe to you! I've never told you but I—loved your father. . . .

TOM. *(Gently)* I know that, Mother.

AMANDA. And you—when I see you taking after his ways! Staying out late—and—well, you had been drinking the night you were in that—terrifying condition! Laura says that you hate the apartment and that you go out nights to get away from it! Is that true, Tom?

TOM. No. You say there's so much in your heart that you can't describe to me. That's true of me, too. There's so much in my heart that I can't describe to you! So let's respect each other's—

TOM. But why—why, Tom—are you always so restless? Where do you go to, nights?

TOM. I—go to the movies.

AMANDA. Why do you go to the movies so much, Tom?

TOM. I go to the movies because—I like adventure. Adventure is something I don't have much of at work, so I go to the movies.

AMANDA. But, Tom, you go to the movies entirely too much!

TOM. I like a lot of adventure.

AMANDA. *(Looks baffled, then hurt. As the familiar inquisition resumes he becomes hard and impatient again. Amanda slips back into her querulous attitude toward him.)* Most young men find adventure in their careers.

TOM. Then most young men are not employed in a warehouse.

AMANDA. The world is full of young men employed in warehouses and offices and factories.

TOM. Do all of them find adventure in their careers?

AMANDA. They do or they do without it! Not everybody has a craze for adventure.

TOM. Man is by instinct a lover, a hunter, a fighter, and none of those instincts are given much play at the warehouse!

AMANDA. Man is by instinct! Don't quote instinct to me! Instinct is something that people have got away from! It belongs to animals! Christian adults don't want it!

TOM. What do Christian adults want, then, Mother?

AMANDA. Superior things! Things of the mind and the spirit! Only animals have to satisfy instincts! Surely your aims are somewhat higher than theirs! Than monkeys—pigs—

TOM. I reckon they're not.

AMANDA. You're joking. However, that isn't what I wanted to discuss.

TOM. *(Rising)* I haven't much time.

AMANDA. *(Pushing his shoulders)* Sit down.

TOM. You want me to punch in red at the warehouse, Mother?

AMANDA. You have five minutes. I want to talk about Laura.

TOM. All right! What about Laura?

AMANDA. We have to be making some plans and provisions for her. She's older than you, two years, and nothing has happened. She just drifts along doing nothing. It frightens me terribly how she just drifts along.

TOM. I guess she's the type that people call home girls.

AMANDA. There's no such type, and if there is, it's a pity! That is unless the home is hers, with a husband!

TOM. What?

AMANDA. Oh, I can see the handwriting on the wall as plain as I see the nose in front of my face! It's terrifying!

More and more you remind me of your father! He was out all hours without explanation!—Then left! Good-bye!

And me with the bag to hold. I saw that letter you got from the Merchant Marine. I know what you're dreaming of. I'm not standing here blindfolded.

Very well, then. Then do it!

But not till there's somebody to take your place.

TOM. What do you mean?

AMANDA. I mean that as soon as Laura has got somebody to take care of her, married, a home of her own, independent—why, then you'll be free to go wherever you please, on land, on sea, whichever way the wind blows you!

But until that time you've got to look out for your sister. I don't say me because I'm old and don't matter! I say for your sister because she's young and dependent.

I put her in business college—a dismal failure! Frightened her so it made her sick at the stomach.

I took her over to the Young People's League at the church. Another fiasco. She spoke to nobody, nobody spoke to her. Now all she does is fool with those pieces of glass and play those worn-out records. What kind of a life is that for a girl to lead?

TOM. What can I do about it?

AMANDA. Overcome selfishness! Self, self, self is all that you ever think of!

(Tom springs up and crosses to get his coat. It is ugly and bulky. He pulls on a cap with earmuffs.)

Where is your muffler? Put your wool muffler on! *(He snatches it angrily from the closet and tosses it around his neck and pulls both ends tight.)*

Tom! I haven't said what I had in mind to ask you.

TOM. I'm too late to—

AMANDA. *(Catching his arm—very importunately. Then shyly)* Down at the warehouse, aren't there some—nice young men?

TOM. No!

AMANDA. There must be—some . . .

TOM. Mother—*(Gesture)*

AMANDA. Find out one that's clean-living—doesn't drink and—ask him out for Sister!

TOM. What?

AMANDA. For Sister! To meet! Get acquainted!

TOM. *(Stamping to door)* On, my go-osh!

AMANDA. Will you? *(He opens door. Imploringly)* Will you? *(He starts down)* Will you? Will you, dear?

TOM. *(calling back)* Yes!

AMANDA. *(Closes the door hesitantly and with a troubled but faintly hopeful expression.)*

AS I WALKED OUT IN THE STREETS OF LAREDO

—*(Anonymous)*

As I walked out in the streets of Laredo,
As I walked out in Laredo one day,
I spied a poor cowboy wrapped up in white linen,
Wrapped up in white linen as cold as the clay.

"I see by your outfit that you are a cowboy,"
These words he did say as I boldly stepped by.
"Come, sit down beside me and hear my sad story;
I was shot in the breast and I know I must die.

Once in my saddle I used to look handsome,
Once in my saddle I used to look gay.
I first went to drinkin' and then to card playin',
Got shot in the breast, which ended my day.

Let sixteen gamblers come handle my coffin,
Let sixteen girls come carry my pall;
Put bunches of roses all over my coffin,
Put roses to deaden the clods as they fall.

And beat the drums slowly and play the fife lowly,
And play the dead march as you carry me along;
Take me to the prairie and lay the sod o'er me,
For I'm a young cowboy and I know I've done wrong."

We beat the drums slowly and played the fife lowly,
And bitterly wept as we bore him along;
For we all loved our comrade so brave, young and handsome,
We loved the young cowboy although he'd done wrong.

THE MOTHER[6]
—Gwendolyn Brooks

Abortions will not let you forget.
You remember the children you got that you did not get,
The damp small pulps with a little or with no hair,
The singers and workers that never handled the air.
You will never neglect or beat
Them, or silence or buy with a sweet.
You will never wind up the sucking-thumb
Or scuttle off ghosts that come.
You will never leave them, controlling your luscious sigh,
Return for a snack of them, with gobbling mother eye.

I have heard in the voices of the wind the voices of my dim killed
    children.
I have contracted. I have eased
My dim dears at the breast they could never suck.
I have said, Sweets, if I sinned, if I seized
Your luck
And your lives from your unfinished reach,
If I stole your births and your names,
Your straight baby tears and your games,
Your stilted or lovely loves, your tumults, your marriages, aches, and
    your deaths,
If I poisoned the beginnings of your breaths,
Believe that even in my deliberateness I was not deliberate.
Though why should I whine,
Whine that the crime was other than mine?—
Since anyhow you are dead.
Or rather, or instead,
You were never made.
But that too, I am afraid,
Is faulty: oh, what shall I say, how is the truth to be said?
You were born, you had body, you died.
It is just that you never giggled or planned or cried.

Believe me, I loved you all.
Believe me, I knew you, though faintly, and I loved, I loved you
All.

GWENDOLYN BROOKS[7]
—Don L. Lee

she doesn't wear
costume jewelry
& she knew that walt disney
was/is making a fortune off
false-eyelashes and that time magazine is the
authority on the knee/grow.
her makeup is total-real.

a negro english instructor called her:
    "a fine negro poet."
a whi-te critic said:
    "she's a credit to the negro race."
somebody else called her:
    "a pure negro writer."
johnnie mae, who's a senior in high school said:
    "she & langston are the only negro poets we've
    read in school and i understand her."
pee wee used to carry one of her poems around in his back pocket;
    the one about being cool. that was befo pee wee
    was cooled by a cop's warning shot.

into the sixties
a word was born. . . . . BLACK
& with black came poets
& from the poet's ball points came:
black doubleblack purpleblack blueblack beenblack was
black daybeforeyesterday blackerthan ultrablack super
black blackblack yellowblack niggerblack blackwhi-te-man
blackerthanyoueverbes ¼ black unblack coldblack clear
black my momma's blackerthanyourmomma pimpleblack
    fall
black so black we can't even see you black on black in
black by black technically black mantanblack winter
black coolblack 360degreesblack coalblack midnight
black black when it's convenient rustyblack moonblack
black starblack summerblack electronblack spaceman
black shoeshineblack jimshoeblack underwearblack ugly
black auntjimammablack, uncleben'srice black
    williebest
black blackisbeautifulblack i justdiscoveredblack negro
black unsubstanceblack.

[7] From *Don't Cry Scream,* copyright 1969 by Don L. Lee. Reprinted by permission of Broadside Press.

and everywhere the
lady "negro poet"
appeared the poets were there.
they listened & questioned
& went home feeling uncomfortable/unsound & so-untogether
they read/re-read/wrote & re-wrote
& came back the next time to tell the
lady "negro poet"
how beautiful she was/is & how she had helped them
& she came back with:
    how necessary they were and how they've helped her.
the poets walked & as spaced filled the vacuum between
    them & the
lady "negro poet"
u could hear one of the blackpoets say:
    "bro, they been callin that sister by the wrong name."

from WHITE LIES[8]
—Peter Shaffer

[*Sophie, Baroness Lemberg, is a fortune teller in an English seaside resort. The scene is in her seedy living room occupied by dusty Victorian furniture. Sophie is about forty-eight; her appearance is "rather neglected." Frank, who comes as a client, is about twenty-five—"cold, watchful, ambiguous." He wears a leather jacket.—Ed.*]

SOPHIE. (*Very winningly*) Good afternoon. I am the Baroness Lemberg. Welcome and please sit down.

    (*Frank sits, examining her.*)

SOPHIE. Let me give you my scale of charges, mister. One pound for cards alone. Thirty shillings for cards and palms. Two pounds for the crystal ball. The ball of course is by far the most profound. It costs just a little more, it's true—but in this world if one wants the best one has to pay for it, doesn't one? (*She gives him a ravishing smile.*)

    (*He returns it, thinly, nodding Yes.*)

SOPHIE. Good: You agree. So—you'll take the ball—ja?

    (*He shakes his head: No.*)

SOPHIE. Oh . . . Which do you want then, please?

FRANK. None.

SOPHIE. I don't understand.

FRANK. I like your slogan outside. "Lemberg never lies."

SOPHIE. Thank you.

FRANK. Is it true?

SOPHIE. Of course.

FRANK. Pity.

SOPHIE. I beg your pardon.

FRANK. White lies never harm you. (*He examines the cage.*) Who's this? Your familiar?

SOPHIE. Please?

FRANK. All witches have familiars, don't they? Creepy little animals they share confidences with . . . ! I suppose you'd lose all your mystic powers without him, wouldn't you?

SOPHIE. (*Still sitting*) Stand away from there, mister, if you please. He's a very sensitive bird. . . .

FRANK. That's alright. I'm an expert on sensitive birds.

SOPHIE. (*Controlling herself*) Stand away, please, I asked you.

FRANK. (*Lightly*) Alright . . . Alright . . . !

SOPHIE. Now, mister, what do you want from me?

FRANK. A giggle, Baroness. (*He smiles at her, unexpectedly.*)

SOPHIE. A giggle? What is that?

FRANK. A laugh. A little fun. You look like you enjoy fun yourself. I hope you do.

SOPHIE. If the situation is amusing, sir, I imagine I can manage a—what?—a giggle.

FRANK. I'm glad to hear that, Baroness. Because that's what I want to consult you about. That's what I want to create right here in this room—an amusing situation.

SOPHIE. Create?

FRANK. Exactly. For him—the boy who's come here with me. You see, him and me, we have this crazy relationship going, like, well, we kid all the time—have the laugh on each other: you know. What they call practical jokes. Some people think it's adolescent. I hope you don't.

SOPHIE. That depends.

FRANK. He's a clever kid—very impressionable. I got him here to see you by telling him you were one of the most famous fortune-tellers in the Western world. Doing a summer season for her health's sake. (*She lowers her eyes and makes modest noises.*) His name's Tom, and he's lead singer with our group. We're called The White Lies. I don't suppose you've ever heard of us.

SOPHIE. On the contrary, you are singing tonight . . . at the Holiday Camp.

FRANK. (*Impressed*) How d'you know that?

SOPHIE. (*Laughing*) I saw it on the poster! You're on the same bill with the Lettuce Leaves. That's a pity: they're lousy. However, you have the Serial Numbers to top the bill, and they're excellent.

FANK. Well, well, a fan!

SOPHIE. A vulgar word, but true. Are you any good?

FRANK. He's good. A real talent. The girls go mad for him. . . .

SOPHIE. And you? Do you sing also?

FRANK. Me? No. I'm their manager.

SOPHIE. Well!

FRANK. (*Staring at her*) That's my scene, really. I manage.

SOPHIE. (*Nervous*) How interesting.

FRANK. It can be. It's why I'm here now—to manage this little scene.
. . . (*He smiles at her again.*) When we drove into Grinmouth this afternoon
and I saw your sign, I thought to myself immediately: Baroness Lemberg,
you're the lady for me. In your mysterious parlour I could stage the best
joke ever played. I could get him so brilliantly he'd never forget it.

SOPHIE. Really?

FRANK. With your help, of course. And with someone of your fame—
consultant to royalty and all that—I wouldn't expect you to do it for nothing. I'm prepared to offer quite a large fee. I'll do anything for a giggle. I
really will. (*He gives his smile.*)

SOPHIE. (*Interested despite herself*) What kind of giggle would this be
exactly, mister?

FRANK. Well, it's sort of a game, really. I'd want you to tell him his
past, present and future.

SOPHIE. Well, that's my profession, after all.

FRANK. I mean precisely. I don't mean to be rude—I'm sure you're fine
on your own—but with me you'd be perfect, you see? No, you don't! In this
envelope are the main facts of Tom's life—the things he's told me over the
past year. No one else knows them but me. Some of it's pretty lurid stuff.
Unhappy childhood. Coal-mining background. Drunken father who beat
him and threw his guitar on the fire. It's all there.

SOPHIE. And are you suggesting I use it?

FRANK. Well now, listen. Tom's a bit dim but he's not an idiot. You'll
have your work cut out for you to convince him you're genuine. That's
where the fun comes in. By the time you've finished telling back to him
what's in here, he'll be fish-mouthed, I tell you!

SOPHIE. Mister, I see no joke in this. It's not funny at all.

(*Pause.*)

FRANK. To be honest, Baroness, this game isn't entirely for laughs.
Mainly, but not entirely. I see it as a sort of warning game. Like I'm using it
to say something to him. Do you understand? I mean, if you can get Tom to
the point when he really believes you have the power to see his whole life,
he'll really believe you when you see something a bit nasty in his future. It'll
sort of scare him off a bit. Do you see?

SOPHIE. Scare him off what?

FRANK. A girl. I told you I was interested in sensitive birds. What are
they? (*Staring at her necklace, which she is fingering.*)

SOPHIE. Greek worry beads.

FRANK. Are you worried?

SOPHIE. Why should I be?

FRANK. Her name's Helen, and she's the girl in our group. She's got a nice voice—nothing special, but it can carry a tune and won't sour the cream. I've known her for a couple of years, on and off. Mostly *on*, if you follow me. In fact, these last eighteen months we've had what I'd call a perfect working relationship.

SOPHIE. It sounds very romantic.

FRANK. *(Lightly)* It isn't romantic: it works, or did till he came along. Tom the Talent, then things began to change. Mostly with her. She found she couldn't resist all that shy working-class charm. The downcast look . . . Yorkshire murmur, very trendy. . . . And when she looked . . . he looked. I don't exactly know what's been going on between them: nothing much I should think at the moment. She's too timid and he's too hung up on his loyalty to me, which he damn well should be by the way. I gave that boy a marvelous bloody chance. And this is his way of repaying me. He thinks I don't know, you know. Well, it's time we undeceived him, isn't it?

SOPHIE. You are in love with this girl?

FRANK. That word's rather got rigor mortis round the edges, hasn't it? *(He laughs)* Look: the way we are is the way I like it. Cool . . . easy . . . not strenuous. . . . Anyway, if there's any leaving ever done in my life I do it: do you see? *(Quietly)* Can't you leave them alone? *(She stops fiddling with the beads. He smiles.)* I suppose that's why they're called worry beads. Because they worry other people. . . . *(She returns his smile even more uncertainly. A pause)* Well, let's get back to my little game, shall we? By this time you've done his past and present, and as far as he's concerned you're the hottest thing since the Witch of Endor. Right. Now you move in for the grand finale. I want you to have a vision, Baroness. A strange, symbolic vision. Let's see it right. . . .*(Slowly)* You look a little deeper into your crystal ball and you see pink. Shocking pink. Helen's dressing gown. Yeh, that's a good touch—very intimate. You see her wearing it, a pretty blonde girl lying on a bed. Describe the bed. Brass rails top and bottom, and above it, a picture on the wall: some droopy tart holding a lily and flopping her tresses over a stone balcony. It's called *Art Nouveau*, which is French for Sentimental Rubbish. Helen loves it, of course! Anyway—use it. Establish the room. *My* room. You'll have him goggling! Now look deeper. "Good heavens, there's someone else on the bed! Why, it's you, Tom! And what are you doing, my dear? Gracious me, what a passionate creature you are. You're kissing her neck, running your fingers through her blonde hair. . . . *(Mockingly)* Inside that thin frame of yours is a raging animal, isn't there? . . ." *(He laughs.)* I'd love to be here during that bit. They've never even held hands, I shouldn't think.

SOPHIE. Go on, please.

FRANK. *(Carefully)* Well now, you'll have to darken it a bit, won't you? . . . Change the mood. I'd thought of something like this. I hope you like it.

. . .The door opens. A man stands there. You can't see his face but he's wearing a green corduroy jacket, with black piping round the lapels. That'll get him best, a detail like that. The lovers look up, eyes wide and guilty! Corduroy begins to move towards them. They try to rise, but they're like glued on the bed. Slow motion. Him coming on—them tangled in the sheets—trying to escape. He arrives at the foot of the bed and suddenly—his hand shoots out—like an order!—and what? Why, the girl's whole manner alters at once. She smiles—takes the hand—allows herself to be lifted up, light as a pink feather—high over the brass rails to safety. Our Tom is left alone. . . . And now you see scare in the ball! Tom staring at them both. Them staring back, laughing. Yeh. And what's that now in her hands? Something—it looks like a metal can. Yes, a large metal can. She raises it—upends it—begins to pour from it over the sheets. And then, slowly, Corduroy raises his hands too—a matchbox in the air—strikes it—drops a match onto the bed. (*Very quietly*) Oh, look, the orange! Soft fire like orange squirrels running over the bed, over his arms, up onto his head . . . his head bursts into flowers! (*Gesturing dreamily*) The whole ball becomes orange—flame whirling, raging inside the crystal, obliterating everything. Then slowly it sinks in. Glass pales from orange to pink to grey, it clears. And then you see him. Tom the Talent. Still sitting upright on my bed—mouth open, one arm raised—like a salute to death. The only difference is—the whole figure is made of ash. (*Pause*) Interpret that vision, Baroness. Question it. "Who is the corduroy jacket?" "That's Frank," he'll say. "Well, know something, Tom. Frank and that girl are right together. Leave them alone."

SOPHIE. (*Softly*) Right together?

FRANK. If you come between them, it'll mean disaster for you. Maybe even death.

SOPHIE. "Right together."

FRANK. "Right together." "Belong together." What's it matter? Just so long as you scare him out of his wits.

JULIUS CAESAR, Act IV, Scene 3[9]
—William Shakespeare

[*The two conspirators, Brutus and Cassius, begin to quarrel in front of their armies; in some embarrassment, Brutus asks Cassius to settle differences in Brutus' tent, and Cassius agrees. They enter the tent and the scene begins as follows.*—Ed.]

CASSIUS. That you have wronged me doth appear in this:
You have condemned and noted Lucius Pella
For taking bribes here of the Sardians;
Wherein my letters, praying on his side,
Because I knew the man, was slighted off.

[9] From *The New Shakespeare,* edited by John Dover Wilson.

BRUTUS. You wronged yourself to write in such a case.

CASSIUS. In such a time as this it is not meet
That every nice offence should bear his comment.

BRUTUS. Let me tell you, Cassius, you yourself
Are much condemned to have an itching palm,
To sell and mart your offices for gold
To undeservers.

CASSIUS.   I an itching palm!
You know that you are Brutus that speaks this,
Or, by the gods, this speech were else your last.

BRUTUS. The name of Cassius honours this corruption,
And chastisement doth therefore hide his head.

CASSIUS. Chastisement!

BRUTUS. Remember March, the ides of March remember!
Did not great Julius bleed for justice' sake?
What villain touched his body, that did stab,
And not for justice? What, shall one of us,
That struck the foremost man of all this world
But for supporting robbers, shall we now
Contaminate our fingers with base bribes,
And sell the mighty space of our large honours
For so much trash as may be graspéd thus?
I had rather be a dog, and bay the moon,
Than such a Roman.

CASSIUS.   Brutus, bay not me,
I'll not endure it: you forget yourself,
To hedge me in; I am a soldier, I,
Older in practice, abler than yourself
To make conditions.

BRUTUS.   Go to; you are not, Cassius.

CASSIUS. I am.

BRUTUS. I say you are not.

CASSIUS. Urge me no more, I shall forget myself;
Have mind upon your health; tempt me no farther.

BRUTUS. Away, slight man!

CASSIUS. Is't possible?

BRUTUS.   Hear me, for I will speak.
Must I give way and room to your rash choler?
Shall I be frighted when a madman stares?

CASSIUS. O ye gods, ye gods! must I endure all this?

BRUTUS. All this! ay, more: fret till your proud heart break;
Go show your slaves how choleric you are,
And make your bondmen tremble. Must I budge?

Must I observe you? must I stand and crouch
Under your testy humour? By the gods,
You shall digest the venom of your spleen,
Though it do split you; for, from this day forth,
I'll use you for my mirth, yea, for my laughter,
When you are waspish.

CASSIUS.   Is it come to this?

BRUTUS. You say you are a better soldier:
Let it appear so; make your vaunting true,
And it shall please me well: for mine own part,
I shall be glad to learn of noble men.

CASSIUS. You wrong me every way; you wrong me, Brutus.
I said, an elder soldier, not a better:
Did I say, better?

BRUTUS.   If you did, I care not.

CASSIUS. When Caesar lived, he durst not thus have moved me.

BRUTUS. Peace, peace! you durst not so have tempted him.

CASSIUS. I durst not?

BRUTUS. No.

CASSIUS. What, durst not tempt him?

BRUTUS.   For your life you durst not.

CASSIUS. Do not presume too much upon my love,
I may do that I shall be sorry for.

BRUTUS. You have done that you should be sorry for.
There is no terror, Cassius, in your threats;
For I am armed so strong in honesty
That they pass by me as the idle wind
Which I respect not. I did send to you
For certains sums of gold, which you denied me:
For I can raise no money by vile means:
By heaven, I had rather coin my heart,
And drop my blood for drachmas, than to wring
From the hard hands of peasants their vile trash
By any indirection. I did send
To you for gold to pay my legions,
Which you denied me: was that done like Cassius?
Should I have answered Caius Cassius so?
When Marcus Brutus grows so covetous,
To lock such rascal counters from his friends,
Be ready, gods, with all your thunderbolts,
Dash him to pieces!

CASSIUS.   I denied you not.

BRUTUS. You did.

CASSIUS.   I did not: he was but a fool

That brought my answer back. Brutus hath rived my heart:
A friend should bear his friend's infirmities,
But Brutus makes mine greater than they are.

    BRUTUS. I do not, till you practise them on me.

    CASSIUS. You love me not.

    BRUTUS.   I do not like your faults.

    CASSIUS. A friendly eye could never see such faults.

    BRUTUS. A flatterer's would not, though they do appear
As huge as high Olympus.

    CASSIUS. Come, Antony, and young Octavius, come,
Revenge yourselves alone on Cassius,
For Cassius is aweary of the world;
Hated by one he loves; braved by his brother;
Checked like a bondman; all his faults observed,
Set in a note-book, learned and conned by rote,
To cast into my teeth. O, I could weep
My spirit from mine eyes! there is my dagger,
And here my naked breast; within, a heart
Dearer than Pluto's mine, richer than gold:
If that thou be'st a Roman, take it forth;
I, that denied thee gold, will give my heart:
Strike, as thou didst at Caesar; for I know,
When thou didst hate him worst, thou lovedst him better
Than ever thou lovedst Cassius.

    BRUTUS.   Sheathe your dagger:
Be angry when you will, it shall have scope;
Do what you will, dishonour shall be humour.
O, Cassius, you are yokéd with a lamb,
That carries anger as the flint bears fire,
Who, much enforcéd, shows a hasty spark
And straight is cold again.

    CASSIUS.   Hath Cassius lived
To be but "mirth" and "laughter" to his Brutus,
When grief and blood ill-tempered vexeth him?

    BRUTUS. When I spoke that, I was ill-tempered too.

    CASSIUS. Do you confess so much? Give me your hand.

    BRUTUS. And my heart too.

    CASSIUS.   O Brutus!

    BRUTUS.   What's the matter?

    CASSIUS. Have not you love enough to bear with me,
When that rash humour which my mother gave me
Makes me forgetful?

    BRUTUS.   Yes, Cassius, and from henceforth,
When you are over-earnest with your Brutus,
He'll think your mother chides, and leave you so.

Chapter **6**

TENSIVENESS

. . . The right frame of mind for the artist is only reached when the preparing and the creating, the technical and the artistic, the material and the spiritual, the project and the object, flow together without a break. . . . He is now required to exercise perfect control over the various ways of concentration and self-effacement. . . .

—Eugen Herrigel, in *Zen in the Art of Archery*

Communion exists for us as creatures. Because we as living, corporeal beings find ourselves opposite to the world and yet encompassed by the world as creatures and parts, we can meet other beings which, in a meaningful synkinesis, prove themselves partners. The encompassing *other* which becomes visible to us in seeing, makes possible the communion between us; it mediates between Me and You.

—Erwin Straus, in *The Primary World of Senses*

RECAPITULATION[1] We have been looking at interpretation as a way of bringing together, in the fullest experiential sense, of two *life forms:* the whole body of the reader (and, later, of the audience member) and the whole body of the literary text. *Body* here, when used in reference to the reader, is taken to mean not simply the physical body but the total human being—that

---

[1] This brief section is revised from the author's *Oral Interpretation and the Teaching of Literature in Secondary Schools* (Urbana, Ill.: ERIC Clearinghouse on Reading and Communication Skills, 1974), pp. 2–4.

feeling, sentient individual who ought always to be the central concern in humanistic studies. Used with reference to the literary, text, *body is a metaphor for the literary structure itself, that structure which takes the form of an act* (or of an act subsuming acts) paralleling the acts of all life forms and consisting of stages identified as inception, acceleration, climax, and cadence or falling-off. The literary text is a manmade form, but it duplicates in many ways the forms of nature. It has an outer form, or "skin," that separates it from its environment and makes it definable but also serves as its point of contact with the environment. By first observing (reading) that outer form, the reader seeks to get inside the skin of the work to the inner form, and comes to know it in much the same way as one comes to know another human being—by observing and listening, by relating what is learned to one's total experience, by talking *about* it with others, by "talking" *with* it. The whole experience is a process of matching, and the point is to understand through the process of matching. The understanding that results is an understanding of *both* forms.

In the study of literature in any class, a process of performance is involved—silent readers as well as oral readers perform, though often at a minimal level. But in the class in interpretation, there is a particular result that makes the interpretative performance distinct from other kinds of performance: the interpreter attempts to make the matching complete—metaphorically, to *become* the work of literature, since when interpreters perform they embody the work; insofar as possible, they seek to be what they speak. The whole process of study is to make that matching as full as possible within the limitations arising from the individual's bodily understanding and the economies observed by the medium. The definition of the two bodies demands an understanding of both and a sympathetic interaction between them.

It is an exciting prospect to see the poem as a life form—and to know that, like other life forms, it can be injured! At a recent college festival in interpretation, a black student performed a poem by Don L. Lee to an audience he took (perhaps mistakenly) to be unfriendly. Since he felt that the audience was turning him off, he responded by doing the like to them. The whole life went out of his performance; what was left of the poem was simply its bone structure—in a sense too often intended in the study of literature, its "meaning." In a discussion of the performance later, the critic asked the student whether in fact he *really* cared about that poem by Don L. Lee. The student said that indeed he did, that it was "too good" for the audience.

"But if you really care about it," said the critic, "why did you hurt it that way?"

"What do you mean?"

"If you think of the poem as having a life, and if you respect that life, you are being completely irresponsible when you kill it off in performance as you did. It has nothing to do with the audience. They may like it or they may not—you hope that they will. But even if they don't, you have a responsibility to the life of the poem—and to Don L. Lee, if you will—and your job is to meet that responsibility."

He had never thought of it that way. It hadn't been, for him, "the two of us," the poem and himself, matched; it had been himself only, and the audience. But what had been suggested to him, the notion of the poem as a thing alive, responsive to him when he was responsive to it, excited him. It excites many a reader. It is good for readers; it is good for poems.

Seen this way, the act of interpreting is a kind of love relationship between reader and text in which a sense of the "otherness" of the other is a vital consideration.

Self and other exist in tensive balance. A responsive and responsible reader shares the movement of the poem through empathy, kinesthesis, full sensory participation. In this sense a reader learns from literature, shares in the experience of its life. When the reader performs for an audience, the audience in turn participates and shares, even while it remains part of the external environment affecting the poem. Between poem, reader, and audience there is communion. This communion is in effect the pleasure of literature.

THE NATURE OF TENSIVE RELATIONSHIPS

Tensiveness is a key word in the view of interpretation with which we have been concerned. The word *tension,* which it may suggest, carries with it as part of its movement a sense of strain; tensiveness is meant to eliminate the emphasis upon strain but to retain the sense of stretch, which implies the possibility of movement from one position to another, with a capacity for return. The human body is tensive; muscle systems are tensive; life, whether it be animal or plant, is tensive. Ambiguities in language exist on tensiveness, the balancing of meaning against meaning, import against import; the movement from subject to verb, from verb to object is tensive. Juxtaposition of poetic feet is tensive, with stress or accent or pitch rising and falling from syllable to syllable. Relationships bewtween dramatic characters are tensive. Relationships between feelings are tensive. A sixteenth-century Hamlet has a tensive relationship with a twentieth-century Hamlet.

It is possible, of course, to feel that a word with so much stretch begins to lose significance. But if it remains squarely attached to the notion of incipient movement, *tensiveness* serves a very useful purpose to the interpreter because it keeps him or her aware of the motility of all life, including the life in literature. Between where the reader has been and where the reader is going, tensiveness exists. Between where a poem has been and where a poem is going, tensiveness exists. The performer's problem (and it is a large one) is how to get the two acts together.

DEGREES OF MATCHING: RELATING BODY FACT AND BODY ACT

It is always interesting, and very often highly profitable, to hear more than a single performance of a poem; since readers differ (and bodies differ and qualities of acts in different bodies differ), performances will in the very nature of things differ. It would be idle, even if it were desirable, to seek complete congruity from reading to reading. This is not to say, of course, that there are no resemblances among readings; if there are none, one is faced either with a very bad poem or with some bad readers. All readers must observe the "organized arrangement" they seek to embody, and that organized arrangement has some consistency from reader to reader.

What is said of man in the following statement by Gellhorn and Loofbourrow may be said, by comparison, of a poem:

> Man not only acts, he also feels. But he is not two beings: one feeling, the other acting. He is one. His actions, his thoughts and his emotions are but different aspects of the single complex of processes in the interacting organs which comprise the individual and which interact in turn with the environment.[2]

As the poem acts (moving from beginning through middle to end), it feels and thinks: meaning (understanding) for the interpreter involves all three things in coalescence. The interpreter cannot demonstrate understanding without showing how thinking feels as it organizes. That is the total challenge faced by the interpreter. The more complicated the body of the poem is, the more difficult the problem of matching. But it is the nature of skilled performers (however alarmed they may be by the force of challenges) to take pleasure in the match, which consists of both conflict and confluence.

Just as physical growth takes time, so the growth of a reading takes time. One element here is common to most forms of creativity. Harold Rugg speaks of the "off-conscious" functioning of the mind-body relationship in creative work as a process, a technique, for "inducing transliminal states." He sees creativity as involving a conscious preparatory period of struggle, an interlude of "giving up," a subsequent flash of insight and statement, and a period of verification or reconstruction.[3] In essence, this is what occurs too in the matching process of the interpreter: there is a period of coping with the outer form (reaching toward inner form) of the text, a plateau in which the reading seems not to be going anywhere, a fresh gathering of forces involved in the act, and a final "putting it together." Unless the interpreter takes the time in his preparation to allow for the plateau period, he or she does not usually get all the way.

In the process of perceiving the poem, the reader goes through the usual processes of perception, which involve "more than a response to sensory stimulation."[4] In Bryant Cratty's words, perception

> is a holistic term referring to meanings attached to an object, event, or situation occurring within spatial and temporal proximity of the

[2] Ernst Gellhoen and G. N. Loofbourrow, *Emotions and Emotional Disorders: A Neurophysiological Study* (New York: Harper & Row, 1963), p. 4.

[3] Harold Rugg, *Imagination* (New York: Harper & Row, 1963), pp. 6–7. See also Brewster Ghiselin's *The Creative Process* (Berkeley: University of California Press, 1952), pp. 4–5.

[4] Bryant J. Cratty, *Movement Behavior and Motor Learning,* 2nd ed. (Philadelphia: Lea & Febiger, 1967), p. 23.

individual. Perception is an ever continuing, as well as an immediate, phenomenon, dependent not only upon a situation's momentary core, but also upon the context in which the event occurs and upon past experience. The process involves organizing, feeling change, and selecting from among the complexity of events to which humans are continually exposed, so that order may be attached to experience.[5]

As the reader reads, whether silently or aloud, he or she brings to the poem past experience, conscious and subconscious; and there is thus an environment in which the poem is placed, and from which it must draw the energies that give it life. But the poem has its own context and its own experience, too. In "ingesting it," the reader is fed and grows by it. Going through the total act (made up of smaller acts) of the poem, the reader has an ongoing experience of felt sensing. Each thing perceived conditions the next thing perceived in the poem. Organizing as he or she goes along, the reader selects from among the responses those that match the poem—but each reader's own responses will differ in some respects from those of other readers going through a similar process of perception. Hence, for each reader the poem and the experience of the poem (they are ultimately the same thing) constitute a *becoming*. The sense of "ongoingness" is essential. When the poem stops, it dies, though it may live on in the memory of the reader. One virtue that the poem possesses and that human beings do not is that the poem has more than one life. It is born anew—really *anew,* with changes—every time it is read. Shakespeare's *Hamlet* in the seventeenth century is not the *Hamlet* of the twentieth century, though surely there are resemblances between the two.

In creativity and in the process of perceiving a poem, absolute concentration is a prerequisite. *There is no substitute for concentration.* Unless one keeps uppermost the body *act* (i.e., the act of matching the literary work), the body fact intrudes and the work in some part dies.

IDEA AND MOVEMENT

"Experimental evidence," says H. J. Eysenck, "is overwhelmingly in support of the contention that an idea, or image, of a movement tends to produce the precise movement imagined, or a modified form of it."[6] The school of elocution in Boston under S. S. Curry was in this respect not nearly so old-fashioned as some modern critics have suggested when it urged students to "think the thought." While thinking the thought is not enough—and Curry never thought that it was—it is the basis from which all else springs. If Eysenck is right, incipient movement (kinesthetic, empathic response) accompanies, or is indeed the same as, the imagined idea.[7] What the interpreter does in preparing the poem is, by going over and over the movement, to augment and strengthen it, to

[5] Ibid.
[6] *Dimensions of Personality* (London: K. Paul, Trench, Trubner, 1947), p. 195.
[7] See also Rugg, p. 147.

make it shareable. Relation with the poem is tensive. The reader expresses this relationship through gesture—*total* gesture, as we have earlier described it.

Try some exercises involving tensiveness. Say *thin* and make what seem to you appropriate movements (vocal, bodily—both). Say *huge,* with appropriate responses. Try *heavy, feathery, bitter, airy.* Now try some phrases: *a warm sky, a spreading tree, a distant sound, a shrill cry.* Say the phrase *a spreading tree* again, and imagine first a small, young tree and then a huge, old tree.

Say "He shoved the drawer in hard," and *mean* it. Then say, equally meaningfully, "He drew the drawer out very, very slowly." Now combine them: "He drew the drawer out very, very slowly; but when he heard his father coming, he shoved it in hard."

Imagine that you are watching a balloon swelling as it fills with gas. Gradually it becomes enormous and you are certain that it will burst. Show us this as you say of it, "It grew bigger, and bigger—and bigger—and BIGGER!" (By the way you say it, we should know whether you are dreading its bursting or looking forward to the bang!)

Imagine that you are watching two cars moving in opposite directions on an expressway. Something has happened to the driver of one of the cars and he has lost control of his vehicle, which is headed straight for the other one. Your heart pounds, your breath grows short, a cry catches in your throat—and then, just in time, the driver recovers and gets back safely to his lane. Describe, in physical terms, what happens in the ebb and flow that characterize your tension.

As you try these exercises, describe your movements, internal and external, vocal and body. How do the words and phrases feel while they mean? Repeat the words often enough so that you can pin down these responses, duplicate them. Project them as you would project a reading, but into the room in which you are rehearsing. The tonicity, or tonus, of your body keeps you always "in tune," so that you may "tune in" to the words, but it is up to you to respond with movements large enough to be shared with an audience. For the interpreter, meaning is shareable as gesture. Projection is the extension of tension.

Try another kind of exercise, this time without words. Act as if you were going to strike out at a table with your fist, in anger. What happens to sensations in your chest, for example? In your throat or neck? In your elbow? In your feet? (And so on.) Now repeat the act, this time with an audible sound that seems appropriate as an accompaniment to the act. Now, without actually doing the full act, say "He struck out with his fist," holding in your memory (and your muscles) a covert "feel" of the act. How does this saying compare with the doing? How does the remembered action affect your vocal utterance of the sentence? If you were reading a story containing this sentence, doubtless this latter way is the way you would do it, rather than indulging in the full act, though we must be careful not to suggest that interpreters cannot move. It is

EXERCISES IN TENSIVENESS

again a question of economy; save the movements for the moments when they *tell.* If you do every movement overtly, broadly, the audience will not be able to see the woods for the trees. They will receive vivid images, but the point of the image may be swallowed up in the image itself. But remember that economy should not result in a weakening or watering down of the tension.

TENSIVENESS AND IMAGERY

There are various kinds of images. We will come to one way of classifying them later, in Chapter 8, in the section on devices of language. But here we may follow Rugg's classification, which is rather different.[8] There are memory images (something seen before), imagination images (something one has only read about but can imagine), and autistic images (dream images, hypnoidal images, images of distortion). Images are involved, of course, in the tensive relationships we have been discussing. If, when you said the phrase *a spreading tree,* you were thinking of a kind of tree you have seen (a chestnut, an elm, perhaps), your image would be a memory image. If you were thinking of a tree you had never seen (a pomegranate, a banyan, a flame tree, perhaps), your image would be an imagination image. One may be every bit as vivid as the other, but an imagination image is not necessarily as true to fact as the remembered image. One student who had never seen a pomegranate confessed to his great disappointment when he finally did see one—the reality was far less for him than the imaginary experience of the tree and the fruit.

Both the memory image and the imagination image (as Rugg describes them) are "reality images," since both can be verified by direct experience. Autistic images, on the other hand, derive from earlier experience modified by the unconscious, fusing and dissolving and distorting memory images to produce new creations not verifiable by direct experience. In *Biographia Literaria,* Coleridge speaks of this magical power of the "secondary imagination" in yoking together disparate images; essentially this is the operation of metaphor in language, and for Coleridge it has a magical power.

Between the direct experience, the imagined experience, or the distorted or modified experience and the current context (the poem, for the reader) there exists a tensive relationship. For example, if you have a very vivid memory image of a chestnut tree and you are reading the Longfellow line "Under a spreading chestnut tree," there may be an elastic, alive relationship between that memory and Longfellow's line. Doubtless no one in your audience will be able to describe your memory image, but it is sure to condition the Longfellow line—and the audience *can* describe its response to your reading of that line. This is one sense in which each reader's reading of a poem differs from that of other readers. What the reader does in his imagined space is not identi-

[8] Rugg, chap. 4.

cal with what he does in his real space. There is a tensive relation between these two loci.

Let's look together at a short poem, examining aspects of its tensiveness. Looking back at our discussion of "A Visit of Charity" and "Araby," you will see that some of the tensive states in those prose pieces resemble things we are pointing out here. We choose a poem at this point because it can be treated in a relatively brief space; a story, novel, or play would take a great many pages.

TENSIVE
RELATIONS
IN A SPECIFIC
FORM

Let's begin by reading the poem through:

EARTH DWELLER[9]
—*William Stafford*

It was all the clods at once become
precious; it was the barn, and the shed,
and the windmill, my hands, the crack
Arlie made in the axehandle: oh, let me stay
here humbly, forgotten, to rejoice in it all;
let the sun casually rise and set.
If I have not found the right place,
teach me, for, somewhere inside, the clods are
vaulted mansions, lines through the barn sing
for the saints forever, the shed and windmill
rear so glorious the sun shudders like a gong.

Now I know why people worship, carry around
magic emblems, wake up talking dreams
they teach to their children: the world speaks.
The world speaks everything to us.
It is our only friend.

If we look first at the total "act," we can establish, at least roughly, a sense in which the poem begins (inception), then quickens (acceleration), grows to a crescendo (climax), and finally drops away (cadence). Let us think of the first part of the first sentence (down through "precious") as the inception. Taking this line in conjunction with the title, we see that the clods are clods of earth, and that the speaker is an "earth dweller." Notice the activity in the lines: not just "All the clods are precious" but *all* of them at *one and the same time* and they *become*. Notice how the isolation of the word *precious* from the other words, at the beginning of line 2, augments its value. We rise to it from line 1. The degree of tensivity is high from the outset.

Now the poem accelerates. Notice the cataloging of clods and the indiscrimate lumping together of objects and people (hands, Arlie). No-

---

tice the heightening of response in the exclamatory *oh,* and the filling out of the meaning of *precious* in the clause "let me stay/here humbly, forgotten, to rejoice in it all." Do you think that the line "let the sun casually rise and set" should be read at the same tempo as the four preceding lines? What difference will it make in meaning (felt sensing) whether you say yes or no to that question? Certainly the quality of tension will depend on your choice.

While the middle section of the poem may all be called acceleration, the tempo is not unvaried—it hastens, slows, hastens in an ebb and flow of tension and release. It is alive. It is also more extensive than the inception. Notice the renewed sweep in "vaulted mansions," "lines . . . sing for the saints forever," "rear so glorious the sun shudders like a gong." The extravagance of the feeling is all part of the sensing of *precious,* with which we began.

After the "statement" in the first eleven lines, there is a break. The poem gathers like a wave for a final movement toward shore. This too is part of its tensiveness. The exuberance and passion of the first eleven lines, as the speaker responds to "all the clods at once," leads to an epiphany that is the climax of the poem: "the world speaks. The world speaks everything to us." Surely there is a very full pause after that line. The significance of earth dwelling resides there: "the world speaks. The world speaks everything to us." Then, after the full silence (not empty silence—for an empty silence is a vain silence): "It is our only friend." Cadence.

There are tensions operating between meanings and kinds of meanings. *Clods* is ordinarily a very dumpy word in its connotation, but these clods are "vaulted mansions." Barn and shed and perhaps even windmill are not ordinarily thought of as taking part in glory, but here they do. Even so humdrum a thing as a crack in the axehandle becomes an occasion for rejoicing. Notice the tension between *forgotten* and *rejoice,* between the notion of *casually,* suggested for sunrise and sunset, and the normal notion that there is really nothing casual in the rising and setting of the sun. *Casual* is a strange word for the event—but the sun is indeed a casual thing in light of the speaker's feeling about the earth.

What does *somewhere inside* mean? Is it inside the earth? Inside the speaker? Inside the clods? All three?

Notice how *vaulted mansions,* like *precious* in line 2, is augmented in value by its initial placement in the line. It's as if one holds his breath for a moment in saying "the clods are" and then rises into the statement "vaulted mansions," lifting both pitch and energy level and coupling this with a kinesthetic response to *vaulted* that makes it lift and soar. The tension between *clod* and *mansion* is also great, as between *lines through the barn* and *saints.* How do you describe your kinesthetic response to "the sun shudders like a gong"? Be as specific as you can in locating your response.

The typographical arrangement suggests a strong break after this phrase before the speaker begins again. In the initial sections of the poem, we develop some sense of the religious aspects of the speaker's experience—preciousness, rejoicing, mansions, songs for saints, glory, gong. The experience is really mystical, one in which the body and spirit of the celebrant merge with the world around him in a sense of oneness with it. This is indeed the very thing that Japanese poets are said to attempt in their haiku: to objectify emotion by the presentation of objects, to submerge self in objects, to create oneness. There is nothing "relaxed" about the attempt, however simply the lines may be drawn.

After the break, the sense of worship is increased and made explicit. The worship involves magic and dreams, too. The images of the poem are (in Rugg's term) autistic, refashioned from past experience. Clods and mansions exist in the world, but clods *as* mansions, and vaulted mansions at that, are created experience.

In the last section there are tensions among the verbs *worship, carry around, wake up talking,* and *teach.* Their degrees of activity vary, their kinds of activity vary, their qualities vary. Notice too the movement from parents to children; this sense of glory is transmitted from generation to generation. All this floods in upon the speaker in his epiphany.

Then the "reason why": the world speaks. The force of *speaks* is very great because it is augmented by all the activity that has preceded it and which is a part of the language of the world. The world speaks: the poet repeats this and adds, "speaks everything to us." The word *everything* is about as full in its degree of tensiveness as one can imagine. Try saying that one word aloud, believing in it. What sensations do you feel in your body as you say it? Once again, be specific in pointing to your feelings. Then notice the simplicity of the last line, and the word *only,* which contrasts vividly with everything. We have *one* friend; but that friend is *everything.*

The sense of exaltation achieved by Stafford is admirable, and it is all an aspect of tensiveness, aliveness in the act. Connotations, denotations, images, line lengths, contrasts, yoking of opposites, coupling of the usual and the unusual, personification (shed, barn, windmill, sun), variations in tempo, placement of pauses, shifts in pitch, transitions from point to point, lumping of disparate objects—all are involved in the ebb and flow, the tension and release, which constitute the elasticity and muscularity of the poem. The interpreter seeks these out in his preparation, responds to them empathically and kinesthetically as he thinks—that is, he *feels* the poem; he adjusts pitch patterns, inflections, volume, and rate of utterance to maximize the values he finds; he rehearses frequently enough so that he can count on his physical congruence with the text; he projects it in performance.

It would be possible to discuss here a further aspect of tensiveness, the poem's prosody, but we shall reserve that for a later chapter on poetry. Meanwhile, we have at least touched on the matter in talking about the divisions between lines 1 and 2 and between lines 8 and 9.

The life of a good poem (or story or play, if we wish to use *poem* in its narrow sense for a moment) is exciting.[10] Writers create life. Interpreters, fitting their bodies to the bodies of the created literary life, in turn renew that life and change it because they are in a metaphorical relationship with it; from the yoking of poem and reader, a new creation results. The interpreter is a mirror, reflecting; he is a lamp, shedding light from within. There is nothing passive or subservient or simply intermediate about the position of the interpreter. Hence, he must be just as careful, just as precise, just as accurate as the writer in sharing that life with others through the medium of his performance. This, in sum, is his challenge and his privilege. It is the source of his pleasure. It is his reason, for the moment, for being.

MATERIALS FOR PRACTICE

RANDOLF'S PARTY[11]
—John Lennon[12]

It was Chrisbus time but Randolph was alone. Where were all his good pals. Bernie, Dave, Nicky, Alice, Beddy, Freba, Viggy, Nigel, Alfred, Clive, Stan, Frenk, Tom, Harry, George, Harold? Where were they on this day? Randolf looged saggly at his only Chrispbut cart from his dad who did not live there.

"I can't understan this being so aloneley on the one day of the year when one would surely spect a pal or two?" thought Rangolf. Hanyway he carried on putting ub the desicrations and muzzle toe. All of a surgeon there was amerry timble on the door. Who but who could be a knocking on my door? He opened it and there standing there who? but only his pals. Bernie, Dave, Nicky, Alice, Beddy, Freba, Viggy, Nigel, Alfred, Clive, Stan, Frenk, Tom, Harry, George, Harolb weren't they?

Come on in old pals buddys and mates. With a big griff on his face Randoff welcombed them. In they came jorking and labbing shoubing "Haddy Grimmble, Randoob." and other hearty, and then they all jumbed on him and did smite him with mighty blows about his head crying, "We never liked you all the years we've known you. You were never raelly one of us you know, soft head."

They killed him you know, at least he didn't *die* alone did he? Merry Chrustchove, Randolf old pal buddy.

---

[10] A word of caution: An excessive degree of tension (as in stage fright)—excessive with respect to optimal performance—leads to a breakdown or disorganization of the performance. See Paul Thomas Young, *Emotion in Man and Animal* (New York: John Wiley & Sons, 1943), p. 98.

[11] From *In His Own Write,* by John Lennon; reprinted with permission.

[12] John Lennon is sometimes identified as author, actor, and Beatle.

I GIVE YOU THANKS MY GOD[12]
—*Bernard Dadié (Ivory Coast)*

I give you thanks my God for having created me black,
For having made me
The total of all sorrows,
and set upon my head
the World.
I wear the livery of the Centaur
And I carry the World since the first morning.

White is a colour improvised for an occasion
Black, the colour of all days
And I carry the World since the first night.

I am happy
with the shape of my head
fashioned to carry the World,
satisfied with the shape of my nose,
Which should breathe all the air of the World,
happy
with the form of my legs
prepared to run through all the stages of the World.

I give you thanks my God, for having created me black,
for having made me
the total of all sorrows.
Thirty-six swords have pierced my heart.
Thirty-six brands have burned my body,
And my blood on all the calvaries has reddened the snow,
And my blood from all the east has reddened nature.
And yet I am
Happy to carry the World,
Content with my short arms,
with my long legs,
with the thickness of my lips.

I give you thanks my God, for having created me black,
White is a colour for an occasion,
Black the colour of all days
And I carry the World since the morning of time.
And my laughter in the night brought forth day over the World.
I give you thanks my God for having created me black.

[12] From *La Ronde des Jours* (1956) by Bernard B. Dadié. Reprinted by permission of Editions Seghers, Paris.

THE BEAUTY OF IT[13]
—Don L. Lee

I have often wondered
    about the beauty of its

                darkness

tall,
short,
at ninety degree angles,
      to my right,

              left,
              at my rear,
              (keeping watch)
              in front,
              (running away)

with the sun as its lover,
I have often wondered
    about the beauty of its

                darkness,

my Shadow.

COLLECTOR'S ITEMS[14]
—Phyllis McGinley

Some lives are filled with sorrow and woe
  And some with joys ethereal.
But the days may come and the weeks may go,
  My life is filled with cereal.
My cupboards bulge and my shelves are bunchy
With morsels crispy or cracked or crunchy,
With rice things, corn things,
  Barley things, wheaten—
All top-of-the-morn things
  And all uneaten.
Ignored they sparkle, unheard they pop
When once they've yielded the Premium Top.

For Cheerios may be just the fare
  To energize whippersnappers,
But mine consider they've had their share
  As soon as they've filched the wrappers.
Breathes there a child with hopes so dim
That Kix are innocent Kix to him,

[13] From *Black Pride,* copyright 1968 by Don L. Lee. Reprinted by permission of Broadside Press.
[14] From *Times Three* by Phyllis McGinley. Copyright 1950 by Phyllis McGinley. Originally appeared in *The New Yorker.* Reprinted by permission of The Viking Press, Inc.

Not loot for filling
   His crowded coffers
With Big New Thrilling
   Premium Offers?
If such (as I fervently doubt) there be,
He is no kin to my progeny.

As a gardener lusts for a marigold
   As a miser loves what he mises,
So dotes the heart of a nine-year-old
   On sending away for prizes.
The postman rings and the mail flies hence
With Premium Tops and fifteen cents.
The postman knocks and the gifts roll in:
Guaranteed cardboard, genuine tin,
Paper gadgets and gadgets plastic,
Things that work till you lose the elastic,
Things to molder in drawers and pockets,
Magnets, parachutes, pistols, rockets,
Weapons good for cop's assistant,
Whistles for dogs that are nonexistent,
Toys designed
   To make mothers tremble,
That fathers find
   They have to assemble,
Things Tom Mixish or Supermanish.
How gadgets come and the box tops vanish!
Then hippity-hop
To the grocer's shop
For a brand-new brand with a Premium Top.

Oh, some lives read like an open book
   And some like a legend hoary.
But life to me, wherever I look,
   Seems one long cereal story.

from ALL CREATURES GREAT AND SMALL[15]
Chapter 45
—James Herriot

As I sat at breakfast I looked out at the autumn mist dissolving in the early
sunshine. It was going to be another fine day but there was a chill in the old
house this morning, a shiveriness as though a cold hand had reached out to
remind us that summer had gone and the hard months lay just ahead.

---

[15] Reprinted by permission of St. Martin's Press, Inc. and Michael Joseph Ltd.
from *All Creatures Great and Small* by James Herriot.

"It says here," Siegfried said, adjusting his copy of the *Darrowby and Houlton Times* with care against the coffee-pot, "that farmers have no feeling for their animals."

I buttered a piece of toast and looked across at him.

"Cruel, you mean?"

"Well, it wouldn't do if they were all like poor Kit Bilton, would it? They'd all go mad."

Kit was a lorry driver who, like so many of the working men of Darrowby, kept a pig at the bottom of his garden for family consumption. The snag was that when killing time came, Kit wept for three days. I happened to go into his house on one of these occasions and found his wife and daughter hard at it cutting up the meat for pies and brawn while Kit huddled miserably by the kitchen fire, his eyes swimming with tears. He was a huge man who could throw a twelve stone sack of meal on to his wagon with a jerk of his arms, but he seized my hand in his and sobbed at me "I can't bear it, Mr. Herriot. He was like a Christian was that pig, just like a Christian."

"No, I agree," Siegfried leaned over and sawed off a slice of Mrs. Hall's home-baked bread. "But Kit isn't a real farmer. This article is about people who own large numbers of animals. The question is, is it possible for such men to become emotionally involved? Can the dairy farmer milking maybe fifty cows become really fond of any of them or are they just milk producing units?"

"It's an interesting point," I said, "And I think you've put your finger on it with the numbers. You know there are a lot of our farmers up in the high country who have only a few stock. They always have names for their cows—Daisy, Mabel, I even came across one called Kipperlugs the other day. I do think these small farmers have an affection for their animals but I don't see how the big men can possibly have."

Siegfried rose from the table and stretched luxuriously. "You're probably right. Anyway, I'm sending you to see a really big man this morning. John Skipton of Dennaby Close—he's got some tooth rasping to do. Couple of old horses losing condition. You'd better take all the instruments, it might be anything."

I went through to the little room down the passage and surveyed the tooth instruments. I always felt at my most mediaeval when I was caught up in large animal dentistry and in the days of the draught horse it was a regular task. One of the commonest jobs was knocking the wolf teeth out of young horses. I have no idea how it got its name but you found the little wolf tooth just in front of the molars and if a young horse was doing badly it always got the blame.

It was no good the vets protesting that such a minute, vestigial object couldn't possibly have any effect on the horse's health and that the trouble was probably due to worms. The farmers were adamant; the tooth had to be removed.

We did this by having the horse backed into a corner, placing the forked end of a metal rod against the tooth, and giving a sharp tap with an absurdly large wooden mallet. Since the tooth had no proper root the operation was not particularly painful, but the horse still didn't like it. We usually had a couple of fore-feet waving around our ears at each tap.

And the annoying part was that after we had done the job and pointed out to the farmer that we had only performed this bit of black magic to humour him, the horse would take an immediate turn for the better and thrive consistently from then on. Farmers are normally reticent about our successful efforts for fear we might put a bit more on the bill but in these cases they cast aside all caution. They would shout at us across the market place: "Hey, remember that 'oss you knocked wolf teeth out of? Well he never looked back. It capped him."

I looked again with distaste at the tooth instruments; the vicious forceps with two-feet-long arms, sharp-jawed shears, mouth gags, hammers and chisels, files and rasps; it was rather like a quiet corner in the Spanish Inquisition. We kept a long wooden box with a handle for carrying the things and I staggered out to the car with a fair selection.

Dennaby Close was not just a substantial farm, it was a monument to a man's endurance and skill. The fine old house, the extensive buildings, the great sweep of lush grass land along the lower slopes of the fell were all proof that old John Skipton had achieved the impossible; he had started as an uneducated farm labourer and he was now a wealthy landowner.

The miracle hadn't happened easily; old John had a lifetime of grinding toil behind him that would have killed most men, a lifetime with no room for a wife or family or creature comforts, but there was more to it than that; there was a brilliant acumen in agricultural matters that had made the old man a legend in the district. "When all t'world goes one road, I go t'other" was one of his quoted sayings and it is true that the Skipton farms had made money in the hard times when others were going bankrupt. Dennaby was only one of John's farms; he had two large arable places of about four hundred acres each lower down the Dale.

He had conquered, but to some people it seemed that he had himself been conquered in the process. He had battled against the odds for so many years and driven himself so fiercely that he couldn't stop. He could be enjoying all kinds of luxuries now but he just hadn't the time; they said that the poorest of his workers lived in better style than he did.

I paused as I got out of the car and stood gazing at the house as though I had never seen it before; and I marvelled again at the elegance which had withstood over three hundred years of the harsh climate. People came a long way to see Dennaby Close and take photographs of the graceful manor with its tall, leaded windows, the massive chimneys towering over the old moss-grown tiles; or to wander through the neglected garden and climb up the sweep of steps to the entrance with its wide stone arch over the great studded door.

There should have been a beautiful woman in one of those pointed hats peeping out from that mullioned casement or a cavalier in ruffles and hose pacing beneath the high wall with its pointed copings. But there was just old John stumping impatiently towards me, his tattered, buttonless coat secured only by a length of binder twine round his middle.

"Come in a minute, young man," he cried. "I've got a little bill to pay you." He led the way round to the back of the house and I followed, pondering on the odd fact that it was always a "little bill" in Yorkshire. We went in through a flagged kitchen to a room which was graceful and spacious but furnished only with a table, a few wooden chairs and a collapsed sofa.

The old man bustled over to the mantelpiece and fished out a bundle of papers from behind the clock. He leafed through them, threw an envelope on to the table then produced a cheque book and slapped it down in front of me. I did the usual—took out the bill, made out the amount on the cheque and pushed it over for him to sign. He wrote with a careful concentration, the small-featured, weathered face bent low, the peak of the old cloth cap almost touching the pen. His trousers had ridden up his legs as he sat down showing the skinny calves and bare ankles. There were no socks underneath the heavy boots.

When I had pocketed the cheque, John jumped to his feet. "We'll have to walk down to t'river; 'osses are down there." He left the house almost at a trot.

I eased my box of instruments from the car boot. It was a funny thing but whenever I had heavy equipment to lug about, my patients were always a long way away. This box seemed to be filled with lead and it wasn't going to get any lighter on the journey down through the walled pastures.

The old man seized a pitch fork, stabbed it into a bale of hay and hoisted it effortlessly over his shoulder. He set off again at the same brisk pace. We made our way down from one gateway to another, often walking diagonally across the fields. John didn't reduce speed and I stumbled after him, puffing a little and trying to put away the thought that he was at least fifty years older than me.

About half way down we came across a group of men at the age-old task of "walling"—repairing a gap in one of the dry stone walls which trace their patterns everywhere on the green slopes of the Dales. One of the men looked up. "Nice mornin', Mr. Skipton," he sang out cheerfully.

"Bugger t'mornin'. Get on wi' some work," grunted old John in reply and the man smiled contentedly as though he had received a compliment.

I was glad when we reached the flat land at the bottom. My arms seemed to have been stretched by several inches and I could feel a trickle of sweat on my brow. Old John appeared unaffected; he flicked the fork from his shoulder and the bale thudded on to the grass.

The two horses turned towards us at the sound. They were standing fetlock deep in the pebbly shallows just beyond a little beach which merged into the green carpet of turf; nose to tail, they had been rubbing their chins gently along each other's backs, unconscious of our approach. A high cliff overhanging the far bank made a perfect wind break while on either side of us clumps of oak and beech blazed in the autumn sunshine.

"They're in a nice spot, Mr. Skipton," I said.

"Aye, they can keep cool in the hot weather and they've got the barn when winter comes." John pointed to a low, thick-walled building with a single door. "They can come and go as they please."

The sound of his voice brought the horses out of the river at a stiff trot and as they came near you could see they really were old. The mare was a chestnut and the gelding was a light bay but their coats were so flecked with grey that they almost looked like roans. This was most pronounced on their faces where the sprinkling of white hairs, the sunken eyes and the deep cavity above the eyes gave them a truly venerable appearance.

For all that, they capered around John with a fair attempt at skittishness, stamping their feet, throwing their heads about, pushing his cap over his eyes with their muzzles.

"Get by, leave off!" he shouted. "Daft awd beggars." But he tugged absently at the mare's forelock and ran his hand briefly along the neck of the gelding.

"When did they last do any work?" I asked.

"Oh, about twelve years ago, I reckon."

I stared at John. "Twelve years! And have they been down here all that time?"

"Aye, just lakin' about down here, retired like. They've earned it an' all." For a few moments he stood silent, shoulders hunched, hands deep in the pockets of his coat, then he spoke quietly as if to himself. "They were two slaves when I was a slave." He turned and looked at me and for a revealing moment I read in the pale blue eyes something of the agony and struggle he had shared with the animals.

"But twelve years! How old are they, anyway?"

John's mouth twisted up at one corner. "Well you're t'vet. You tell me."

I stepped forward confidently, my mind buzzing with Galvayne's groove, shape of marks, degree of slope and the rest; I grasped the unprotesting upper lip of the mare and looked at her teeth.

"Good God!" I gasped, "I've never seen anything like this." The incisors were immensely long and projecting forward till they met at an angle of about forty-five degrees. There were no marks at all—they had long since gone.

I laughed and turned back to the old man. "It's no good. I'd only be guessing. You'll have to tell me."

"Well she's about thirty and gelding's a year or two younger. She's had fifteen grand foals and never ailed owt except a bit of teeth trouble. We've had them rasped a time or two and it's time they were done again, I reckon. They're both losing ground and dropping bits of half chewed hay from their mouths. Gelding's the worst—has a right job champin' his grub."

I put my hand into the mare's mouth, grasped her tongue and pulled it out to one side. A quick exploration of the molars with my other hand revealed what I suspected; the outside edges of the upper teeth were overgrown and jagged and were irritating the cheeks while the inside edges of the lower molars were in a similar state and were slightly excoriating the tongue.

"I'll soon make her more comfortable, Mr. Skipton. With those sharp edges rubbed off she'll be as good as new." I got the rasp out of my vast box, held the tongue in one hand and worked the rough surface along the teeth, checking occasionally with my fingers till the points had been sufficiently reduced.

"That's about right," I said after a few minutes. "I don't want to make them too smooth or she won't be able to grind her food."

John grunted. "Good enough. Now have a look at t'other. There's summat far wrong with him."

I had a feel at the gelding teeth. "Just the same as the mare. Soon put him right, too."

But pushing at the rasp, I had an uncomfortable feeling that something was not quite right. The thing wouldn't go fully to the back of the mouth; something was stopping it. I stopped rasping and explored again, reaching with my fingers as far as I could. And I came upon something very strange, something which shouldn't have been there at all. It was like a great chunk of bone projecting down from the roof of the mouth.

It was time I had a proper look. I got out my pocket torch and shone it over the back of the tongue. It was easy to see the trouble now; the last upper molar was overlapping the lower one resulting in a gross overgrowth of the posterior border. The result was a sabre-like barb about three inches long stabbing down into the tender tissue of the gum.

That would have to come off—right now. My jauntiness vanished and I suppressed a shudder; it meant using the horrible shears—those great long-handled things with the screw operated by a cross bar. They gave me the willies because I am one of those people who can't bear to watch anybody blowing up a balloon and this was the same sort of thing only worse. You fastened the sharp blades of the shears on to the tooth and began to turn the bar slowly, slowly. Soon the tooth began to groan and creak under the tremendous leverage and when it did it was like somebody letting off a rifle in your ear. That was when all hell usually broke loose but mercifully this was a quiet old horse and I wouldn't expect him to start dancing around on his hind legs. There was no pain for the horse because the overgrown part had no nerve supply—it was the noise that caused the trouble.

Returning to my crate I produced the dreadful instrument and with it a Haussman's gag which I inserted on the incisors and opened on its ratchet till the mouth gaped wide. Everything was easy to see then and, of course, there it was—a great prong at the other side of the mouth exactly like the first. Great, great, now I had two to chop off.

The old horse stood patiently, eyes almost closed, as though he had seen it all and nothing in the world was going to bother him. I went through the motions with my toes curling and when the sharp crack came, the white-bordered eyes opened wide, but only in mild surprise. He never even moved. When I did the other side he paid no attention at all; in fact, with the gag prising his jaws apart he looked exactly as though he was yawning with boredom.

As I bundled the tools away, John picked up the bony spicules from the grass and studied them with interest. "Well, poor awd beggar. Good job I got you along, young man. Reckon he'll feel a lot better now."

On the way back, old John, relieved of his bale, was able to go twice as fast and he stumped his way up the hill at a furious pace, using the fork as a staff. I panted along in the rear, changing the box from hand to hand every few minutes.

About half way up, the thing slipped out of my grasp and it gave me a chance to stop for a breather. As the old man muttered impatiently I looked back and could just see the two horses; they had returned to the shallows and were playing together, chasing each other jerkily, their feet splashing in the water. The cliff made a dark backcloth to the picture—the shining river, the trees glowing bronze and gold and the sweet green of the grass.

Back in the farm yard, John paused awkwardly. He nodded once or twice, said "Thank ye, young man," then turned abruptly and walked away.

I was dumping the box thankfully into the boot when I saw the man who had spoken to us on the way down. He was sitting, cheerful as ever, in a sunny corner, back against a pile of sacks, pulling his dinner packet from an old army satchel.

"You've been down to see t'pensioners, then? By gaw, awd John should know the way."

"Regular visitor, is he?"

"Regular? Every day God sends you'll see t'awd feller ploddin' down there. Rain, snow or blow, never misses. And allus has summat with him— bag o' corn, straw for their bedding."

"And he's done that for twelve years?"

The man unscrewed his thermos flask and poured himself a cup of black tea. "Aye, them 'osses haven't done a stroke o' work all that time and he could've got good money for them from the horse flesh merchants. Rum 'un, isn't it?"

"You're right," I said, "it is a rum 'un."

Just how rum it was occupied my thoughts on the way back to the surgery. I went back to my conversation with Siegfried that morning; we had just about decided that the man with a lot of animals couldn't be expected to feel affection for individuals among them. But those buildings back there were full of John Skipton's animals—he must have hundreds.

Yet what made him trail down that hillside every day in all weathers? Why had he filled the last years of those two old horses with peace and beauty? Why had he given them a final ease and comfort which he had withheld from himself?

It could only be love.

A SONG IN THE FRONT YARD [16]
—Gwendolyn Brooks

I've stayed in the front yard all my life.
I want a peek at the back
Where it's rough and untended and hungry weed grows.
A girl gets sick of a rose.

[16] From *Selected Poems* by Gwendolyn Brooks. Copyright © 1945 by Gwendolyn Brooks Blakely. Reprinted by permission of Harper & Row, Publishers, Inc.

I want to go in the back yard now
And maybe down the alley,
To where the charity children play.
I want a good time today.

They do some wonderful things.
They have some wonderful fun.
My mother sneers, but I say it's fine
How they don't have to go in at quarter to nine.
My mother, she tells me that Johnnie Mae
Will grow up to be a bad woman.
That George'll be taken to Jail soon or late
(On account of last winter he sold our back gate).

But I say it's fine. Honest, I do.
And I'd like to be a bad woman, too,
And wear the brave stockings of night-black lace
And strut down the streets with paint on my face.

IN WESTMINSTER ABBEY[17]
—John Betjeman

Let me take this other glove off
    As the *vox humana* swells
And the beauteous fields of Eden
    Bask beneath the Abbey bells.
Here, where England's statesmen lie,
Listen to a lady's cry.

Gracious Lord, oh bomb the Germans.
    Spare their women for Thy Sake,
And if that is not too easy
    We will pardon Thy Mistake.
But, gracious Lord, whate'er shall be,
Don't let anyone bomb me.

Keep our Empire undismembered
    Guide our Forces by Thy Hand,
Gallant blacks from far Jamaica,
    Honduras and Togoland;
Protect them Lord in all their fights,
And, even more, protect the whites.

Think of what our Nation stands for,
    Books from Boots' and country lanes,
Free speech, free passes, class distinction,
    Democracy and proper drains.
Lord, put beneath Thy special care
One-eight-nine Cadogan Square.

[17] From *Collected Poems* by John Betjeman. Reprinted by permission of John Murray (Publishers) Ltd. and Houghton Mifflin Co.

Although dear Lord I am a sinner,
   I have done no major crime;
Now I'll come to Evening Service
   Whensoever I have the time.
So, Lord, reserve for me a crown,
And do not let my shares go down.

I will labour for Thy Kingdom,
   Help our lads to win the war,
Send white feathers to the cowards
   Join the Women's Army Corps,
Then wash the Steps around Thy Throne
In the Eternal Safety Zone.

Now I feel a little better,
   What a treat to hear Thy Word,
Where the bones of leading statesmen,
   Have so often been interr'd.
And now, dear Lord, I cannot wait
Because I have a luncheon date.

DEATH OF A SON[18]

(who died in a mental hospital aged one)
   —Jon Silkin

Something has ceased to come along with me.
Something like a person: something very like one.
   And there was no nobility in it
     Or anything like that.

Something was there like a one year
Old house, dumb as stone. While the near buildings
   Sang like birds and laughed
     Understanding the pact

They were to have with silence. But he
Neither sang nor laughed. He did not bless silence
   Like bread, with words.
     He did not forsake silence.

But rather, like a house in mourning
Kept the eye turned in to watch the silence while
   The other houses like birds
     Sang around him.

And the breathing silence neither
Moved nor was still.

[18] Copyright ©1954 by Jon Silkin. Reprinted from *Poems New and Selected,* by Jon Silkin, by permission of Wesleyan University Press and Chatto and Windus Ltd.

I have seen stones: I have seen brick
But this house was made up of neither bricks nor stone
But a house of flesh and blood
With flesh of stone

And bricks for blood. A house
Of stones and blood in breathing silence with the other
Birds singing crazy on its chimneys.
But this was silence,

This was something else, this was
Hearing and speaking though he was a house drawn
Into silence, this was
Something religious in his silence,

Something shining in his quiet,
This was different this was altogether something else:
Though he never spoke, this
Was something to do with death.

And then slowly the eye stopped looking
Inward. The silence rose and became still.
The look turned to the outer place and stopped,
With the birds still shrilling around him.
And as if he could speak

He turned over on his side with his one year
Red as a wound
He turned over as if he could be sorry for this
And out of his eyes two great tears rolled, like stones,
and he died.

YOUNG SOUL [19]
—LeRoi Jones

First, feel, then feel, then
read, or read, then feel, then
fall, or stand, where you
already are. Think
of your self, and the other
selves . . . think
of your parents, your mothers
and sisters, your bentslick
father, then feel, or
fall, on your knees
if nothing else will move you,

[19] From *Black Magic Poetry 1961-1967*, copyright © 1969 by LeRoi Jones (Im-amu Amiri Baraka). Reprinted by permission of The Sterling Lord Agency.

then read
and look deeply
into all matters
come close to you
city boys—
country men

Make some muscle
in your head, but
use the muscle
in yr heart

CONSTANTLY RISKING ABSURDITY . . .[20]
—Lawrence Ferlinghetti

Constantly risking absurdity
                                and death
          whenever he performs
                          above the heads
                                    of his audience
      the poet like an acrobat
                      climbs on rime
                        to a high wire of his own making
  and balancing on eyebeams
                          above a sea of faces
              paces his way
                      to the other side of day
          performing entrechats
                        and sleight-of-foot tricks
      and other high theatrics
                        and all without mistaking
              any thing
                        for what it may not be

      For he's the super realist
                            who must perforce perceive
              taut truth
                        before the taking of each stance or step
      in his supposed advance
                        toward that still higher perch
    where Beauty stands and waits
                        with gravity
                              to start her death-defying leap

[20] Lawrence Ferlinghetti, *A Coney Island of the Mind.* Copyright © 1958 by Lawrence Ferlinghetti. Reprinted by permission of New Directions Publishing Corporation.

And he
a little charleychaplin man
who may or may not catch
her fair eternal form
spreadeagled in the empty air
of existence

Chapter 7

SOME TECHNICAL CONSIDERATIONS

A good interpreter should know how to use a lectern, just as he or she needs to know how to use a book. The question of whether either book or lectern should be used is complicated, involving matters of convention, taste, and prejudice. Often there are considerations in the poem being read that will lead you to a specific choice. The decision to use or not use a book may be a matter of locus and perspective, of the relationship between speaker-in-the-poem, performer, and audience. For example, the use of a book may give to the reading of an intimate lyric a certain distance (and hence perspective) that would be lost without the book. The lyric tends to become more dramatic, more "a speech by a character," when the book is absent. Scenes from a play may be kept too distant if the reader tries to use a book within short exchanges of dialogue. We shall not take a stand for or against the use of either book or lectern—both are negotiable matters. But one thing is clear: as we suggested at the opening of the discussion, the interpreter should know how to use both. Not knowing how to use a book or lectern is probably the poorest reason for not using them.

The approach to the platform and, if one is used, the lectern is a kind of entrance to the reading. It ought to be suitable in tone to the occasion. In a day of class readings it may be useful to spend time discussing the ways in which readers begin, examining what seems effective, what seems ineffective. Generalizations are not very useful here.

If you find that you are frightened (as you surely will be from time to time) just remember that stage fright is useful so long as it can be controlled. Your body is making certain preparations for activity; energies are being aroused. Keep your mind on what you are going to read, not on yourself and your fright. Think about the text. One reason for having the book is that it frees you from having to remember, though not from the need to be fully familiar with the text, and this can be a matter of major importance.

Open the book or the manuscript, if you are using one, and place it on the lectern. If the print in the book is too small, if the book will not lie open of itself, if the pages of the book include so much type that easy location of your place is difficult, or if for any of a variety of reasons you find the printed book hard to use, type your manuscript neatly, using double or triple spacing. (You may wish to put the pages, if there are more than one, in a folder.) If you are tall and the lectern seems far down, push the book up toward the top of the lectern. Some readers even use a blackboard eraser or a small block to keep the book from sliding down again. The object in this placement is to make it easier for you to get to and from the printed page, so that you need not look too far down, thus making the audience uneasily aware of your use of the book. If this happens, the manuscript will obstruct your reading.

THE INTRODUCTION

It is almost always helpful to have an introduction. It might be worthwhile to spend a class period exclusively on the details involved in getting up from your seat, going to the lectern, placing your book, and giving an introduction to one of the selections included in earlier chapters. Introductions should usually not be fully written out, read, or memorized. Know what you want to say in your introduction and practice it several times before your reading performance, but keep it extemporaneous. Speak directly to your audience. This is an important moment in the performance and is helpful in establishing a comfortable relationship between you and your listeners. You need not stand behind the lectern; stand beside it, if you wish, or stand in front of it, or rest your hand or arm on it. The lectern may give a focal point for your performance even if you do not choose to use it for your book or manuscript. It may, indeed, by used as a prop for something or some place significant in your reading. Its presence, after all, helps *define* space, if you wish to use it that way. (Space must always be defined in a reading, whether one uses a lectern or not.)

Don't try to say too much in the introduction. If you are reading a story, don't summarize the whole plot. If you are reading from a play, don't tell the audience in advance how they ought to feel about the characters. If you are reading a poem, don't call attention to specific details within the poem; if you do, the audience will wait for those details and will single them out from the text, interfering with the wholeness of the experience. It is probably unwise to provide the audience with specific goals before the performance. You may want to tell something about the writer or relate something about the circumstances surrounding the writing of the text or make some reference to the general subject of the piece.

Remember that the introduction should look ahead to the reading and should set a tone that will prepare for it. Defensive, apologetic, condescending, didactic, dogmatic introductions may alienate an audience and deny the writer any chance to be heard. A good introduction will put you and the work you are reading in proper position with the audience and make you both eager to begin.

Sample Introductions

An introduction to a nonsense story by Archibald Marshall, for example, went like this:

> "The Ancient Roman" is a story by Archibald Marshall, whose name is nowadays rather unfamiliar. It comes from a book entitled *Simple Stories for Children and Grownups*— a title I have always liked because it leaves one perfectly free to choose which he will be, and no one will be the wiser. One may be a grownup today and a child tomorrow, for that matter.
>
> Marshall's stories are nonsense. Nonsense is like ladies' stockings: the best kind are *sheer*. "The Ancient Roman" is sheer nonsense.

Here is an introduction to a long and serious work, a story from the Roman poet Ovid's *Metamorphoses:*

> The *Metamorphoses,* by the Roman writer Ovid, is surely one of the world's great collections of tales. It has been rifled by countless writers since Ovid's time. Indeed, one of the stories—the one I wish to read to you this evening—is a source of Shakespeare's bloodiest tragedy, *Titus Andronicus.* It is possible to believe that in this instance Ovid himself is the better storyteller.
>
> This is the tale of Tereus, Procne, and Philomela. It is taken from the sixth book of Ovid's work, and the translation is by the American poet Rolfe Humphries. We begin midway in the story. Ovid has told us that Pandion, the King of Athens, has been besieged by his enemies. Tereus, the great King of Thrace, has come to his aid, and the two have won the final battle. In gratitude, Pandion has given to Tereus in marriage the hand of his daughter Procne, sister of Philomela. As we begin, the marriage has just been celebrated—but Ovid says, "The omens, though, were baleful."

When you have finished with the introduction, you are at your place behind the lectern (if you are using one). Take a moment before you begin the reading. A pause—not too long—is useful. If you wish, you may repeat the name of the selection you are going to read and the name of the author just before the pause.

THE READING   Then begin the reading *not* by looking at the book (though you will perhaps wish to look at it just before you begin) but by establishing the locus out in the audience and looking there. Don't begin before you have achieved this. Be sure that your attention is focused, not left vague and generalized (unless vagueness is what the script calls for), but don't fix a point and stare at it through a reading; it is more a matter of the mind's being attentive than of the eye's fixation.

If you have rehearsed your reading sufficiently, you will not have to keep looking down at your book (if you are using one) to refresh your memory. Try to make your use of the book part of your rehearsal periods. Use it as part of the whole performance; it should not be a crutch. For example, if you are reading a scene from a play, build your use of the book into your characterization, so that when your eyes drop to the page they drop *in character,* and it seems to be the character rather than the interpreter who looks down. Don't let your use of the book become mechanical. Nothing is more distracting to an audience than watching a reader look down at the end of every line of poetry or at the end of every phrase of a story or at the beginning of every speech of a play. A good exercise is to take up any book at hand, one you do not know well, and try to read aloud from it without keeping your eyes on the pages. When you look down, be easy about it; take in enough of the text so that you can go on when you are looking out into the audience. You will develop a facility in using the pages.

If the location of your reading is right, and if the proper tension exists between your position at the lectern and the existing focus in the audience, you will feel a forward impulse, as if your whole energy is going into lifting the text from the book to the audience. There will be a strong kinesthesis, a propulsion toward the audience, and the audience will be drawn toward the text and you. The miracle of a good reading resides almost entirely in this polarization of audience and reader, both caught up in the living presence of the piece. The sense of the reader as an individual apart from the literature is lost in the experience of the literature itself. You are not seen as yourself—you become the poem. You can never achieve this new identity if you draw the literature into yourself; you must reach out to it. You grow by reaching.

AUDIENCE   We have said comparatively little of the audience, since our primary
FEEDBACK   interest is the activity of the interpreter. But it is important now to locate the audience in the total act that is the goal of interpretation.

Just as the reader may be said to match his or her body to the body of the text, so the members of the audience, responding kinesthetically and sharing in the act of the poem, may be said to match their bodies to the matched poem-interpreter. The tensive relationship between the three acts involved is highly complex, varying form person to person, with many kinds of overtones. There is no single poem for the whole roomful of people, but neither should there be totally separate poems for each of the persons listening.

The interpreter is a listener too, of course. Every performer is his or her own monitor. Indeed, evidence suggests that if speakers *cannot* hear their own words as they speak, the whole speech process becomes disorganized and breaks down. Rate may slow down, intensity may increase, pitch may rise, stuttering may occur, and so on.[1] While audiences sometimes say of an ineffective reading that the reader "seems to be in love with the sound of his own voice" and hence pays inadequate attention to the voice of the poem, it is worth remembering that the immediate feedback readers get from the process of sounding words aloud is a necessary part of performance. When something goes wrong, the performer may compensate by adjusting what follows. But working too hard to make up for what has been lost may make an audience feel instinctively that the reader is belaboring the poem. If a sense of distress leads the reader to back too far from the poem, the audience begins to lose interest. In either case, the failure is an inadequate matching of poem and reader; there is a noticeable gap between them. Often, however, adjustments are managed subtly and effectively, and the general audience may be completely unaware of the reader's own criticism of the performance. Such management as this is, of course, the ideal. In any event, it is almost always a bad thing for an interpreter who makes a mistake to interrupt the poem entirely and say to the audience, "Excuse me." The whole act of the poem is shattered; the curtain comes down and the audience's sympathies go out empathically to the interpreter, or the audience becomes impatient or angry.

Just as performers get feedback from their own bodies and vocal movements, so they get feedback from the audience. Often one can see effects on the listeners' faces. Sometimes one senses it in their concentration or in their quietness (hopefully) or in their noisiness (alas). When the feedback suggests that things are not going well, the reader may become uneasy, angry, distressed, or frightened. The failure may indeed be a failure on the part of the audience itself—is is not true that a good performer with a good poem can automatically hold any audience; but while audiences (like interpreters) have a responsibility to be responsive, it doesn't help the interpreter to be able to blame the audience. During the performance the interpreter must assume to the limits of his or her power the responsibility for matching self with poem, for projecting it so that the audience can share in it, and for making adjustments (when necessary) that do not distort or weaken the poem's act.

When the reader likes the selected text, has prepared it properly and rehearsed it fully, and if the audience in turn likes and responds to it, the event of the oral performance is a delight for everyone. Such events are not uncommon and are what the reader always hopes will happen. Such an event is a communion—a movement of all concerned into the act of the poem. It is not a matter of the reader's "telling" the audience and having them say "Oh, I get it" or "I don't get it," but

---

[1] Karl Smith and William Smith, *Perception and Motion* (Philadelphia: W. B. Saunders Company, 1962), pp. 34, 251–252.

rather a matter of bringing them bodily into the experience which the reader is embodying. This is the act and the art of interpretation; it is the *felt sensing* of a work of literature. It is what the poem, and the poet, most wants. It is the poem being loved for itself. It is the poem made incarnate.

FINISHING   When you have finished the reading, do not close your book and rush to your seat without giving the audience time to digest the experience. Just as you need a moment before you begin to read, so you need a moment at the end of the reading. So does the audience. The precise timing of that moment depends both on the piece and on your sensitiveness to the audience's reaction. The pause can be too long or too short. When it is over, take up your book and return to your seat. This may be done in your own person, for the experience is over. If the audience applauds, recognize the applause, though not too elaborately. You should remember that while they are in part applauding your performance, they are also applauding the work of the writer. Be modest!

THE VOICE   Some textbooks in interpretation might include in this chapter rules for pausing, inflection, and phrasing during a reading. But these matters are too flexible, too varying, to permit rules and set techniques. This is not to suggest that the problems are unimportant, but they are problems you have faced all your lives, problems inherent in the use of language at any time. Often pauses, inflections, and groupings of words may be somewhat formalized, heightened, and emphasized, but the norms for conventional speech govern departures made from such speech. Gestures in a performance are useful only when based on gestures recognizable from other situations, though gestures in a performance may be heightened or stylized. So too with modulations of the voice. The voice is no separate or special concern of interpretation—all speech work involves the training of an adequate vocal mechanism, and there are excellent books devoted to the specific training of this instrument. Nevertheless, there can never be complete coalescence of poem and reader unless the reader's voice is capable of embodying the nuances of the poem. Hence, the student of interpretation must work for ease and flexibility in the production of sound.

Indeed, in all that we have been saying throughout this book, the total body of the reader, *including* his voice, has been our concern. Movement is vocal as well as physical, and tensiveness is reflected in the voice as well as in the visible—and invisible—movements of the performer. It is all one, though in preparatory periods the parts may be separated for attention and discussion.

We have suggested that *projection* is in large measure the active desire to reach out, to share, to empathize with an experience outside oneself. It is also in part a matter of voice. It is not to be confused with loudness; one may be loud without achieving projection. Projection involves proper articulation, support of tone, and resonance; these elements can be worked on in isolation, but they must also be worked on in the context of your reading.

Stand in front of the class, concentrate on a spot on the lectern, and say firmly to the spot, *No!* Now, still standing in front of the class, concentrate on a spot in the back of the room and again say firmly, *No!* What differences between the two situations can you feel? Ask the class what differences they can describe.

Read the following passage to the class:

> . . . Some time after that I, not being very well, stayed at home on a Lord's Day. And on the afternoon of said day, the doors being shut, I did see a black pig in the room coming towards me. So I went towards it to kick it and it vanished away. Immediately after I sat down . . . and did see a black thing jump into the window. And [it] came and stood just before my face. . . . The body of it looked like a monkey, only the feet were like a cock's feet with claws, and the face somewhat more like a man's than a monkey's.[2]

Now pick up your book, turn your back to the class, and remembering where the instructor is standing in the classroom, read to him or her even though you are facing in the opposite direction. Concentrate hard on the place in the room where the instructor is standing. Persuade the class that you are reading to that person. When you convince the class that even with your back turned you feel as though you are reading directly to the instructor, try to describe for the class and for yourself what sensations and movements this effort aroused in you. Be as precise as possible. Did you become aware, for example, of the muscles in your neck? The muscles that move your ears? Ask the class to describe any difference they may have noticed in your vocal response. When your back is turned thus, and you are still trying to project a reading to an audience, you are likely to make a greater effort than is normal. This exercise is often useful for a reader who is having difficulty making a reading seem direct, frequently because the reader is not exerting sufficient effort to make contact with a *real* location in the audience.

Now try another exercise. Read the following line from e. e. cummings' poem "anyone lived in a pretty how town":

with up so floating many bells down

On the word *up,* lift the tone, as if you were suddenly but easily batting a balloon into the air, and then let the rest of the line float gently downward like a balloon (or the sound of musical notes falling like petals through the air). The lift on the word *up* is a matter of touch. Notice

---

[2] From Chadwick Hansen, *Witchcraft at Salem* (New York: G. Braziller, 1969), p. 69.

how it involves pitch, force, tonal support, visual memory—all part of the process by which you feel your way into the poem and ultimately project your feeling so that others can behold it. Try the line again; keep sending the balloon farther and farther and notice what it does to your management of your voice. There is a point in what you are doing. You are not trying to create sound for the sake of sound; you are rather trying to manage the production of sound so that you can let the poem say what it wants to say. If your audience is aware only of your manipulation of sound, you have failed.

Say *No!* tightening the muscles in your neck and keeping your teeth clenched. Now say it with normal opening of the mouth and with support from your diaphragm. (Your teacher will illustrate the difference if you are not sure of it.) How do you describe the differences between the two actions? Be as specific as you can in locating different areas of tension. Meaning involves movement, and different meanings involve different movements, whether of voice or of body.

Some students habitually prolong vowels; others do not give enough attention to the holding of vowels. Some students do not give sufficient attention to the bite, crispness, and force of certain consonant sounds; other students habitually make use of too sharp an attack on consonants. Some chop off final *g, d, t,* and so on; occasionally a student will make too much of final consonant sounds, and pronunciation will seem affected, stiff, or unnatural.

On the other hand, any of these aspects of vocal production may be extremely useful as aspects of characterization in a reading. Cutting off final consonants may effectively make a speaker seem careless of speech, very colloquial, or slangy. Minute attention to final sounds and an excessively conscious modulation of vowels may make a character seem arty, affected, or cautious. Public speeches demand more care in articulation than intimate conversation—though perhaps some few people are more careful even in intimate conversation than others are in public speaking. The differences among individuals are very great. The point is that the interpreter should have as flexible a vocal instrument as possible so as to be able to match these differences in others.

These matters are more than matters of characterization. They affect tone color in poetry (which we shall discuss in a later chapter). The attack, or touch, given to a word affects strongly the value of the word. Say "The sun was bright," with no particular force on the *b* and *t* of *bright.* Now repeat the sentence, making both consonants as crisp and forceful as possible. How does this change affect the vowel *i*? How does it (if it does) affect the quality of the day described? Why?

Try another exercise. (We could go on with them forever, but we shall not!) Say "They drank coffee." Do you find that you tend to drop the *k* in drank? If not, try doing so. Then say the sentence, being very careful to articulate the *k*. What happens to the rate of utterance when you pay particular attention to that juncture between *drank* and *coffee*? In terms of the placement of the sounds in your vocal apparatus, what

happens as you shift from the *k* to the initial sounds of the next word—
co? Describe the movement as specifically as you can. Sensation is involved in articulation. While it would be folly to pay conscious attention to every movement of the vocal apparatus (just as it would be folly
to think consciously of every movement one makes during the course of
a day) it is nevertheless true that in works of literature (and particularly
in poetry) one is often more than usually conscious of the sensation of
sounds. At any rate, during exercises it is necessary to be conscious of
them.

The voice is the oral reader's primary tool, and it must permit one
to give body to many subtleties in expression; but the voice alone, no
matter how flexible and wondrous it may be, will not of itself make a
good interpreter. A lesson should be gained from the student who suffered from a voice so beautiful that his listeners always said to him after
he had finished reading, "What a beautiful voice you have!" The student finally said one day in class, in considerable exasperation, "I hate
my voice. I wish someone would just say to me sometime, 'That was a
fine reading.'"

Like all living things, a fine reading is made up of a series of vital
parts; each has its function, each has its place, and any one that develops at an improper pace throws the whole organism off balance. How
hard it is—how very hard—to keep the right balance. No interpreter, no
matter how expert, achieves such balance all the time.

Throughout our discussion in this book, we have taken *movement* to be
a central concern since literature, as an act, *moves*. Readers, too, *move*,
whether or not the movement is visible to a listening audience. The
tensive state that signals life is a felt state; we are aware of shifts and
changes within us as the mind and body co-relate. Our language—and
the language of the writers we read—signals movements (thoughts, feelings, incipient behaviors) and hence symbolizes those activities which
reflect our being alive (sometimes in processes that seem vague, fleet-
ing, nebulous—but tensiveness is not tied to definiteness!). Literature is
*un*like many of the forms of our daily movements in having a more-or-
less conscious direction of flow, a structure that has a beginning, a
middle, and an end which can be discovered and described by any
literate reader.

We have talked, most of the time, about use of book and lectern.
Until relatively lately, interpretation classrooms assumed the use of
both, and many teachers still feel that the presence of the book or
manuscript serves as a visual reminder of the presence of the writer with
whom the performer joins in the act of performing.

MOVEMENT IN INTERPRETATION: PHYSICAL ACTION

As a matter of convention, as well as in fact, the presence of the book
during the performance signals to the audience that they are sharing
with the performer the act of *reading*. It is within the literary act created

The Book

initially by an author that ideas, feelings, characters, narrators—in effect, a world—exist. The presence of the book, then, signals the presence of the author. The performer is present in body. The book, the world of the text, and the body of the performer bring together the three elements with which we begin. (The audience makes a fourth, in the toal process.) This is a simple fact.

What happens when the performer begins the performance? How do the three elements interact? When the reader looks at the book, the audience will have a strong sense of the presence of the *writer*; when the reader speaks to the audience without reference to the book, even though he or she speaks in the voice of the storyteller or the work's persona, a subtle change takes place: the awareness of the author tends to recede as attention centers upon the body fact of the performer. *Both* presences remain, but foreground and background alter somewhat.

As the world of the story or poem or play begins to take shape, meanwhile, our attention shifts to *that*. It is this phenomenon to which some critics point in saying that in a good performance the performer tends to disappear. Literally, of course, the performer is always present—just as, literally, the fact of the author's book remains present, but the center of attention shades off from author and performer to the world of the work, and to the language in which it in part inheres. Hidden, as it often is, on a lectern, the physical book recedes; it becomes background. Author is thus subsumed in the world he has created. The performer, too, as a distinct personality, in some sense recedes as he or she foregrounds the world of the work and accommodates the *fact* of the body to the *act* of the text.

There is a wonderfully complex pattern of acts which the body undergoes through its accommodations in pitch, stress, articulation, vocal quality, use of dialect, volume, pause, tempo, touch; through its accommodations in gesture, movement, posture—the repertoire of behavioral expressions it has acquired; through its bringing into coalescence, whether consciously or not, the linguistic and kinetic processes through which it daily ranges. And in the process we have been describing, writer, reader, and textual world participate, in varying degrees of emphasis, in this pattern of acts. In its turn, the audience participates and often affects the performance.

The presence of the book and the body fact of the reader create an esthetic condition for the performance. It is within this condition that the fictive world is created and exists. We say of it that the work "seems to have come alive." It *has* in fact come to life in the body of the performer.

But the book may appear in many forms—as a printed volume, as a manuscript, as a prop (a letter, a menu, a diary, for example); and it may be more noticeably present at one time than another, or employed more obviously in one performance than another. Indeed, it is possible to dispense with the literal book entirely and to create in other ways the sense of the author's presence—in an introduction, by using a slide or a photograph. But when the illusion of the author's presence is gone, when the esthetic condition becomes that of the performer's *being* the author, we are in a different realm—often, as we shall see later (pages 417–418), the realm of the actor rather than the interpreter. This is not a matter of worth, but a matter of fact. The conventions differ; each has its place.

The lectern has certain obvious uses: it frees the reader's arms from holding the book, so that they may be used for gestures; it minimizes the symbolic presence of the author; it may usefully deemphasize the body *fact* of the performer in given instances and strengthen focus upon the body *act* of the persona in the work. But it may also be employed to define changes in locus during a performance—to separate one area from another, to suggest either restriction or release in a speaker's psychological states, to augment or to diminish distance between speaker and audience. Movement from behind a lectern, return to a lectern, retreat from a lectern can suggest a variety of tensions operative within characters and scenes. Furthermore, the lectern need not be the conventional pedestal with raked top to which we usually give the name. It may be a stool or a bench or a chair; it may be of so free a form that it can be used symbolically as a physical detail within the work being performed. In sum, it ought not to be something behind which a reader hides. Better to have no lectern than to have one which weakens rather than aids the performance. Both book and lectern can be positive, contributing forces in interpretation, but they ought not be there simply because some definition of interpretation says they ought to be there.

The Lectern

Without book or lectern, the solo interpreter provides us with a rather different esthetic condition. When he or she adds costume, lights, and setting, we have moved into still another condition. At some point, the medium we call *interpretation* has shaded off into another medium—monodrama, impersonation, or something loosely called a "one-man" or "one-woman show." Tastes certainly differ, and these hybrid forms are at one time popular and at another time disliked. The question that concerns us here is when the foregrounding of text leaves off and the foregrounding of the performer begins. Interpretation, in the view of this book, emphasizes the foregrounding of text, of body *act* rather than of body *fact*. Within that foregrounding of text, it is certainly possible to minimize or even to eliminate both book and lectern. But the performer must accept the new definition of space that results from eliminating the lectern, which can now no longer serve as a focal point. The solo performer in a large empty space can look very lonely. In certain works, that sense of isolation, alienation, distance can be very useful. In other works, it will not. Space can be used by being filled; it can be used by

Movement without Book or Lectern

keeping it empty—negative space, we call such empty space. Negative space may function visually much as silence functions with respect to speech. Absence exists in tension with presence.

Granted the enjoyment of a performing space not marked by a lectern, the performer must decide whether the piece to be performed will accept such space. It is also important to ask whether what is to be done in the way of visible movement is consistent with asking an audience to accept a *single* person as performer. One performer cannot do what three can do; if he or she tries, the result may be disastrous. Some performers feel restricted by a lectern; others find that it frees them. Extensive overt movement may help; it does not *necessarily* improve; it may attentuate and weaken. We are not prepared to take a final stand on the question, but only to remind ourselves that these various performing situations are not identical, and that it is always useful to ask oneself, Why do I want to eliminate book and lectern? before giving them up. The tradition and the convention have been that both are present—but conventions change.

THE ANALYSIS OF LITERATURE FOR PERFORMANCE

Part **II**

Chapter 8

LANGUAGE AND EMBODIMENT

We have discussed qualities shared by a variety of literary forms and also the basic problems in establishing a relationship between work and reader. Once such a tensive relationship has been established, there is no end to the study of the delicate, sensitive ways in which both poet and reader contribute to the fullest exploration of experience in language. The more passionately a reader *cares* about literature, the more devoted will be the search into its nature. The caring must come first; no amount of cold critical analysis will itself lead to genuine literary life. Nevertheless, such critical analysis can stimulate the reader who already feels the life of literature. The capable reader draws on reservoirs of knowledge and feeling. One cannot simply wait until there is a specific need for knowledge; one must seek it constantly, ingest it, be nourished by it. We do not suddenly develop strength; we grow to it.

In so short a space as this single volume, directions for analytical study can only be pointed to; we shall not go beyond primary problems. The material in Part Two is meant to underscore and illustrate the issues raised in Part One. It is not to be thought of as existing separately and independently. Analysis is viewed in this book as an aspect of interpretation, not a separate concern. Analysis provides tools and names useful in the careful preparation of a reading—we look at the forest differently when we know the names of the trees.

Not all classes will use Part Two in the same way. That is as it should be. Parts of the discussion may be a repetition for some, or perhaps there is more here than you need at the moment, but it seemed wise to provide a reasonably full discussion of language and structure so that you could at least touch on some of the complications involved in the language of literature.

It may be profitable to discuss certain inadequate relationships between people and poems first. It is not true that one reading of a poem is necessarily as good as another. Readers (like poems) vary in their success.

THE AFFECTIVE FALLACY

W. K. Wimsatt and Monroe C. Beardsley describe one danger in judgment as "a confusion between the poem and its *results* (what it *is* and what it *does* . . .)."[1] Suppose, for example (the example is ours and not Wimsatt's or Beardsley's), that a mother who has recently lost a child sees on television a play in which a mother loses a child under similar circumstances. She may be so reminded of her own loss that the experience is not in the least esthetic; she may simply dissolve again into the agonies of her own sorrows. Under such conditions, she might be much better off not seeing the play at all. But let us assume that she is able to be objective enough about herself to realize that the play is a play and that the mother in the play is not herself. She may still be moved by the closeness of the literary experience to her own experience—much more moved than she would be, let us say, by Shakespeare's *King Lear.* Let us say that the television play is not so good a play as *King Lear*—that it is a fairly sentimental, stereotyped performance. The real mother need not make the mistake of thinking that the degree of her response proves a high degree of merit in the television play itself. If she does make this mistake, and if she judges the worth of the play simply by the intensity of its appeal to her own emotions, she is guilty of the *affective fallacy.* She is guilty, say Wimsatt and Beardsley, of impressionism in judgment, and the play itself disappears as the proper object of criticism.

The point is a telling one, for each of us is at times in danger of falling into the trap they have described. In making literary judgments, we must distinguish between the grounds of emotion and the emotion itself. Someone other than the real-life mother, watching the television play we have described, might respond quite differently, but the play itself has not changed. The objective thing must be the source of judgment, and this must not be lost in a welling up of emotion.

We do not suggest that emotions are irrelevant to a consideration of literature, which includes the experiencing of emotion. The poem is a form for objectifying, fixing, and making permanent emotions and attitudes that are otherwise transient. However, when you find that a poem makes you cry but the student next to you disclaims such a re-

[1] *The Verbal Icon* (University of Kentucky Press, 1954), p. 21.

sponse, you and he are not necessarily differing in your value judgments of the poem. One must distinguish between relevant and irrelevant emotions in the experience of literature. Watching a performance of Shakespeare's *Othello* or reading the play silently, we must certainly feel in part as Othello feels—that is, we must share his state of mind so far as is consistent with sharing also the state of mind of Desdemona at, let us say, the moment of the murder. Unless we are compelled by Othello's state, assuming that Shakespeare has succeeded in his intention, we have failed properly to understand the scene. The emotional response is obligatory; probably the more sensitive the reader, the sharper the emotional response—always within the limits proper to the esthetic experience.

But the response must arise from, must be governed by, and must be directed toward the experience within Shakespeare's scene. You would experience an irrelevant emotion if Othello, holding a light close to Desdemona's face, should make you feel terror lest the hair of the actress playing Desdemona should catch fire from the flame. This is not part of Shakespeare's scene, though it would be part of the performance onstage. Great though your emotion on such an occasion might be, you must not confuse it with the emotional power of *Othello*. You must remain free to feel as the characters in the play feel and, if Shakespeare has been generally successful over the centuries in controlling the feelings of a large proportion of his audiences, we can surely say that those feelings are not only obligatory but are a responsible measure of the worth of the play itself.

The specific problem for the interpreter is that the performance may fail to distinguish between the emotion aroused in the speaker-in-the-poem (the persona) and the emotion aroused in the interpreter *by* the persona. This problem is essentially a matter of locus. In some cases the two emotions are very nearly alike; in other cases there are wide variations. For example, in *Othello* Iago is clearly villainous; we know from the outset that he is two-faced and that he will go to almost any lengths to get even with the Moor. But it would be a mistake to play him simply that way, since within the action of the drama almost everyone takes him at first to be open and honest. The emotions of the audience (and the interpreter who comes to the play first as audience) are not to be played as the emotions of Iago.

THE INTENTIONAL FALLACY

Probably no fallacy has provoked such widespread discussion among contemporary students of literature as the *intentional fallacy,* by which Wimsatt and Beardsley mean the error of confusing the psychological causes of a poem with the poem itself. That is, the naïve intentionalist might argue that a poem is successful if it does what its writer set out to do. But once created, a poem has a life of its own; what matters is what it says, not what its creator intended it to say. We usually have no exact way of knowing what the author intended it to say outside the testimony of the poem itself, and it is a common experience among writers to find that the intention and the created poem differ. A poet may intend to shock a reader, but if the reader likes and values the poem without being shocked, the poet's intention is irrelevant to the judgment.

There is nothing wrong, of course, in being interested in a writer's intentions. They may be of interest simply in themselves. But they are not the central interest of *literary* criticism, though they may be of profound interest to psychological or biographical criticism. One does not, for example, need to know who *the* Dark Lady was (if she ever existed) to enjoy a sonnet by Shakespeare that seems to be addressed to a dark lady, though many critics have spent many years trying to track down Shakespeare's particular inspiration. The poet may have had a particular lady in mind, but that is his concern and not ours, unless he makes allusions that *require* our knowing who the original lady was if we are to understand fully what he says. In the latter event, we must indeed go to external evidence, if it exists. If it doesn't, part of the poem may remain forever a mystery to anyone.

Wimsatt and Beardsley are not suggesting that knowledge of a poet's intention may not be helpful; they are arguing that if the poet has done his work, it is the poem's rather than the poet's intent that is our object of study. If one is *required* to go outside the poem for evidence by which to understand it, then the poem itself has in some degree not succeeded.

If one is required to outside, then of course one goes outside.

DEVICES TO CREATE TENSIVENESS IN LANGUAGE

Granted that our interest lies in the work of literature; and that we are interested in the intent of the author only insofar as that intention manifests itself within the work (though as students of psychology, history, or biography we might take a perfectly proper interest in the writer apart from his work), we will find it no easy matter to be always sure what the intention is. Literature makes use of language that is often a strong departure from the language of everyday life. It is often more figurative, connotative, tight, dense, sharply patterned. The locus is often startlingly subtle and complex. The language may range from a very open, loose texture to a close, tight texture. Ambiguities in language are often functional, and two meanings are sometimes better than one. (This is not an argument for simple confusion; ambiguity may function to increase clarity when a deliberate ambivalence is required as the perspective of the work.) A literary piece may gain in effectiveness by the deliberate employment of vaguely defined views and sensations, provided always that the point is itself clear.

Suppose we look at some of the ways in which language works for the creation of *presence* in a poem, since it is the presence that we are after. Your sense of "being aware" will help to make it possible for your listeners to believe in you as a reader and to feel assured that you and the poem are indeed in communion with one another.

Suggestion

Look at this translation of a Japanese *haiku* (a poem which in the original language is made up of three lines consisting respectively of 5, 7, and 5 syllables:

> On the jutting rock
> Another man also is
> A guest of the moon.

> *(Iwa-bana ya*
> *koko ni mo hitori*
> *tsuki no kyaku.)*

This haiku, by the poet Kyorai, was intended to express the pleasure the poet experienced in coming unexpectedly upon another man, like himself enjoying the harvest moon. The poem says nothing specifically about the pleasure. It is as simple as a Japanese painting—a few brushstrokes showing the rock, the nameless man, the moon. The effect is gained, indeed, because the poet does *not* specifically say how he feels. Japanese poets often submerge themselves in the object in this way and hence symbolize the emotion by the presentation of the object, drawing forth a sense of the oneness of things. It is the very awareness of the solitary man beneath the moon which we are after, and which is the tensive presence of the poem. What do you make of the suggestion made to Kyorai by the great master of the haiku, the poet Bashō, that the poem would be even subtler (hence better) if the "other man" were interpreted to mean the poet himself?

Literary language is often oblique, indirect, blurred at the edges—not *less* but rather *more* effective for this reason. Japanese esthetics makes much of what it calls *sabi* ("color," "melancholy," "tone"), *shiori* (pathos residing in the quality of bending before strong forces), *hosomi* ("slenderness," "fragility," "tenderness"). These elements combine to produce depth of response in the Japanese reader. One of the primary requisites of great poetry in traditional Japanese literature is the quality called *yūgen* ("mystery," "suggestiveness"). It is this sense of hovering between possibilities that gives such literature much of its life, its tensiveness. It is possible for such slight forms as the haiku to degenerate into mere syllable counting—and there are doubtless thousands of bad haiku to be found—but one does not judge the form by its lowest manifestations.

Can you name pieces of literature in English that depend on suggestiveness in this sense? What problems do they pose for the interpreter? To answer this latter question, read aloud the haiku by Kyorai.

What particular difficulties do you face in reading it? Of what use do you find the division into lines?

Here is another Japanese poem in translation:

Can this world
From of old,
Always have been so sad?
Or did it become so for the sake
Of me alone?

How does one establish the mood and perspective of the poem? Is it angry? Bitter? Sarcastic? Sad? Amused? Probably the best reading is the most complex reading, the one richest in possibilities. The best reading always explores the utmost in the text, though one must not stuff the text with things it will not hold. Can you read this particular haiku in a way that makes it seem both sad and amused, with a sense of the irony of fate—a wry reading rather than one filled with self-pity? The poem is full of suggestion.

Denotation and Connotation

Another way of creating overtones, suggestiveness, and echoes in language is through the use of words having both denotative and connotative value. A difficulty is that the poet may not sufficiently control the meanings of his words and hence may allow confusions to enter into the experience of the reader. Or the poet may use a word that has for some readers a meaning of which he is totoally unaware, and the result may be hilarious (often bawdy) laughter on the part of the readers. Ideally, the poet controls meaning within limits and permits some freedom to readers in supplying connotations beyond those limits. Thus, no two readings are exactly alike. Each performer lends to the poem something of himself, but the differences between readings ought not to wipe out the poem itself. Every oral performance of a poem is in this sense a kind of metaphor, a union of the poet's poem with the reader's poem. *But no reader should seek to impose a poem on the poet's poem.* The reader's task is to keep eye—and mind, spirit, and body—on the poem in its own right, seeking to fit his or her body to the body of the poem. But when the two have become congruent, or as nearly congruent as possible, some adjustment on the part of both the poem and the reader has taken place. We cannot, then, tell the "dancer from the dance."

Awareness of both denotation and connotation is part of this process of fitting. For example, in a passage from "Intimations of Immortality" Wordsworth writes:

—But there's a Tree, of many, one,
A single Field which I have looked upon,
Both of them speak of something that is gone.

His point is that in each of these aspects of nature something is missing;

the world no longer looks as it once looked to him. While he says *one* tree, he does not say what kind of tree it is. While he says a *single* field, he does not say what grows in the field. He makes his point on the denotative level—tree, field. But it is difficult (for one reader, it is impossible) to think of "treeness" in Wordsworth's line without seeing a tree, so sharp is the sensation of the *oneness* (the presence) of this tree, partly because the poet capitalizes the word. From the point of view of Wordsworth's meaning, it does not really matter whether the tree is seen as an oak or an elm or a maple, though Wordsworth would doubtless be startled to have the reader see a banana tree or a banyan. It does not really matter whether the field is a field of heather or grain or grass— though it would be surprising to see a field of rice or of cogon-grass or of *camotes.* (Why would some of these be surprising? Would they also be wrong?) *Tree* may well call up for a particular reader a certain tree he is especially aware of, and his tree will be, perhaps, different from the tree that Wordsworth may have had in mind; but *so long as his addition to the poem does not interfere with any details within the poem,* the reader's connotation will not interfere with the denotation Wordsworth has in mind. The reader tries to rule out as irrelevant any connotative meanings that will not fit the poem—if he does not we will certainly be able to tell the dancer from the dance when he reads! But a sense of his knowing a very special tree will contribute to the poem's tensiveness.

In the poem by William Carlos Williams on page 90, "This is just to say," the plums are a crucial concern. But notice that Williams does not say whether they are purple plums or green plums or red plums or yellow plums. Nor does he say anything about their size. But doubtless you, as reader, have filled in some of these details for yourself. You may see large purple plums. Does anyone see wild plums or beach plums? Again, the poem makes its point on the denotative level, and readers may (without harming the poem at all) supply plums of a specific kind. Or one may see a certain kind of icebox, though Williams says only "icebox."

A writer may choose, on the other hand, to deal specifically with connotations. When Joyce writes in "Araby" of North Richmond Street as being *blind,* he begins with the denotative meaning (the street is a dead-end street), but he soon adds the connotative meaning: the street is sightless, a dead end for its inhabitants. The movement from the one kind of meaning to the other is almost habitual with Joyce, and it is the source of many of his richest and most startling effects.

Another writer may move more immediately to connotative qualities. When Wordsworth writes "It is a beauteous evening" (page 136), he has clearly made a choice between *beauteous* and what would seem to us the commoner *beautiful.* When he says the "mighty Being . . . doth with his eternal motion make a sound like thunder," rather than "*does* with his eternal motion make a sound like thunder," he has made another choice. Notice also *walkest, thou, thy, liest, worship'st,* and *thee.* What differences do these choices make? Why not *walk, you, our,* and so on? (Some of the substitutions would involve metrical changes, but others do not; that does not seem to be the reason behind the choices.) The qualities of the old forms are not the qualities of the current forms of these words. Why not?

In the next poem on the same page, by Browning, why does Porphyria *glide* into the room rather than *walk* or *hasten* or *slip*? To be sure, there are denotative differences among these words, but connotation is also involved. It is not easy, in many cases, to separate the differences between denotation and connotation. The dictionary may say, for example, that *soiled* (in line 12 of Browning's poem) is denotatively synonymous with *dirty,* but *is* it? At what point do the connotative differences become (or cease to be) also denotative differences? Since we made a good deal in Part One of this volume of the "feel" of words, these degrees of difference in meaning become a matter of considerable importance to the interpreter. They affect the "taste" of language.

Figures of Sense: Comparison

Thus far we have argued that literature thrives on overtones. The thing beyond definition is often, perhaps always, the object of literature—life which dissection always in a sense kills. A poem may be dissected, may in a sense die in the process of being anatomized, but it can be restored. Definition sometimes kills. Suppose you try to "define" your brother or sister or mother or father. "John is twenty years old; he is five feet ten inches tall; he has brown hair and brown eyes; he is muscular; his teeth are exceptionally good." This is not so much John as it is a report of John. The presence is lacking.

We may say of a man "He is very strong." Does that tell us more or less than if we say of him "He is as strong as an oak" or "He is as tough as a steel bar"? What if we say "He is an oak" or "He is a steel bar"?

These ways of describing the man are figurative—not literal, not "everyday." They are figures of comparison. Many poets have suggested that a kind of miracle occurs when figures of comparison operate effectively; two things that are in some respects dissimilar are made suddenly to coalesce, and the coalescence (though made up of two things) is different from either of them. When the writer says "He is *as* tough *as* an oak" or "He is *like* an oak" or "He is stronger *than* an oak," he is expressing a comparison. When he says "He is an oak," he is *implying* but not expressing the comparison. Expressed comparisons are called *similies* and implied comparisons are called *metaphors,* but because both are figures of comparison, critics often refer to both as metaphors.

Figures of comparison may be more successful than simple statements of fact; they may say *more* because of their indirection. The poet may consider "She is pretty" less expressive than "She is a jasmine blossom." There are ineffective metaphors and dead metaphors. "He is an ass" no longer calls up for most readers a comparison with a beast—though when Bottom, in *A Midsummer-Night's Dream,* wearing an ass head, suggests that his friends are simply trying to "make an ass" of him, the metaphor takes on real life and becomes hilarious. Metaphors always hope to be more effective than literal speech; when they are not, they seem ornamental, excessive. Metaphors should not seek to avoid being specific; at their best, they are more specific in terms of their purpose than everyday speech.

Metaphor functions centrally in the development of our capacity to use language. Through *metaphoring*[2] the child who first associates the word *dog* with a single *particular* animal possessed of four legs and a tail comes to realize that *dog* cannot be used for *all* such animals (a cat, a horse, a cow, for example), though in the early stages the child thinks so and may call a pony a doggy. The process of associating things similar in some respect but unlike in others (essentially the process of metaphor) is a necessary step in learning to make distinctions, and children live in a world made vivid by the *reality* of the presence pointed to by words. In growing up, we abstract and generalize, and the strong sense of the initial presence begins to weaken. What was once "real" becomes "only a metaphor." The fact is, of course, that the word *only* is out of place here. The philosopher may and does use language to reflect upon the world; the poet, who is also often interested in reflection, is nevertheless most often primarily concerned with the perceptual *body* on which reflection is based. The poet and the philosopher, the poet and the man of science, however alike in some ways, differ fundamentally in their relation to the phenomenal world. We are talking, of course, about them in their professional roles, not necessarily about them as men and women.

The good metaphor is hence not a fancy, loose way of approximating something, but a way of grasping the reality of something. In a way, the poet seeks to recapture some of the immediacy felt by the child—but the poet is not a child, and possesses linguistic capabilities no very young child *can* possess. The poet tries, thus, to have the best of both worlds, not simply to recover his or her youth. Metaphor creates a *new* presence, but does so through a process inherent in human linguistic development.

All figures of sense share this desire to say more or to speak more significantly. A limited list of such figures is given in Appendix B, though you may wish to go to handbooks of literature for additions to the list; you will find dozens of such figures if you do. We will mention here only one other class of figures: figures of contiguity.

Imagine that a man standing on the shore looks out over the water and sees five ships. He may say simply "I see five ships." Or he may say "I see five sails." In the second instance, he is substituting for the whole object

**Figures
of Sense:
Contiguity**

[2] We are touching here upon a complex subject. For a survey of the reading, I refer you to Kristina Minister, *The Perception of Literature by Silent Readers and Oral Interpreters: A Theory and an Exploratory Experimental Study,* an unpublished doctoral dissertation, Northwestern University, 1977. The use of the gerundive *metaphoring* is hers.

ship a part of that object—in this case, the part he most clearly sees from the shore, the *sails.* The relationship between the ship and the sails is not the relationship between the man and the oak described in metaphors, in which the two objects are essentially distinct; it is rather one of *contiguity,* of part to whole. Such a figure is called a *synecdoche.* The relationship may be expressed either by referring to a part (as in *sails* for ship) or by referring to a whole: "I locked the house" instead of "I locked the door" or "I locked the lock." The point is that the thing referred to (whether part or whole) is never the thing really being pointed to—if one says "I see five ships," he is not being figurative at all.

Another type of contiguity may be expressed figuratively. Suppose a man says "I drank five bottles." Everyone understands that he did not literally drink bottles at all; he drank what was in the bottles. This is not the part-whole relationship expressed by the figure *synecdoche;* nevertheless the bottle and the drink contained in the bottle are contiguous, and this is a figure of contiguity. Its name is *metonymy.* (In Appendix B you will find further refinements of metonymy.) Just as simile and metaphor are both often referred to jointly as metaphor, so the figures of contiguity are both often referred to jointly as *synecdoche.* Robert Frost once referred to himself as a "synecdochist." What do you think he meant?

The point in discussing these (or other) figures is that literary language often takes an indirect path in order to be more sharply expressive, to give a stronger sense of the presence of the thing being expressed. Figures aim at greater tensiveness and hence at a sharper perspective; they seek to create through coalescence of things. The oral reader who reads the line "He is very strong" may well behave quite differently from the reader who reads "He is a giant oak." Why? How are the differences likely to express themselves through the body? Remember what we have said: to be a responsible reader, one must be responsive. Also, response to any single image must be kept in proper proportion within the piece as a whole. No one image should kill off the others around it. Not all responses are full and overt; the degree always depends on the context.

Imagery

We have just referred to images. What is an image? Is it the same as a figure? Does it have the same purpose as a figure?

As used here, imaging refers to the reconstitution of previous experience, in the absence of the original stimulating object or situation. The image itself is the response produced by this activity. For example, once you have seen a tree, you can *imagine* (make an image of) a tree thereafter simply as a result of seeing the word *tree.* You do not need the real tree as a stimulus. It is this imitating of the original experience rather than the original experience itself to which the term *imagery* refers. Image making is a vital part of experience; without image making the literary experience is impossible. Indeed, language itself cannot function without it.

When one reads in the line from Wordsworth, "There is a tree—of many, one," one forms an image of a tree. The stimulus is always, to begin with, mental—a word, that is, a symbol. The image produced may (as here, perhaps) be visual—or it may derive from any of the other senses ("It tastes hot," for example). The senses may actually be combined, translated into one another ("It smells hot," when the senses of smell and taste or touch are coalescent or "He has a brown taste in his mouth," when sight and taste, and perhaps another sense are combined), a phenomenon known as *synesthesia*. Literature often asks for keenness on the part of the reader's image-making capacity. The oral reader who is a fat and flabby image maker will fail. (Again, remember that no single image should be allowed to kill off the images around it—though writers sometimes do the deed of murder themselves with respect to imaging.)

It is clear by now that we must be careful about our original definition of *image*. Images do not simply reproduce previous experience but reconstitute it. (See the earlier discussion of images in Chapter 6, drawn from Rugg.)

Images may be figurative or literal. "There is a tree" is a literal image, but "She is a peach" is figurative, though it is not particularly alive as an image. "She is a peach" is both an image and a figure of comparison (a metaphor), but the term *image* and the term *figure* do not point to precisely the same thing in the sentence. The interpreter responds to both image and figure. That is the whole point in discussing these matters: to bring to the level of consciousness the various parts of the literary experience so that the reader can become responsive to all of them. This is the process of dissecting. In the actual process of reading it would be fatal for the interpreter to respond separately to these parts.

Images are often classified in terms of the sense to which they appeal; visual, auditory, gustatory, tactile, olfactory are usual classes, but surely one must add others: thermal, kinesthetic, the sense of pain, and so on—the possible list is not fixed. Such classifications have some point, since they help to bring to life the images imbedded in language. The act of naming is a cognitive act, but if the interpreter is using analysis properly, he or she relates this cognitive act to noncognitive internal states—becomes aware of the *feel* of the image, since this is part of the tensiveness the performer is seeking to embody in performance. One warning: *one must try not, in concentrating on one sensory area, to neglect or overlook others.* Furthermore, we must recognize that sensory responses vary a great deal from individual to individual. What is for one reader a visual image may be for another reader auditory or thermal or tactile. That is the difficulty of classifying images according to sense appeal alone; such classification tends to neglect differences in the personalities and environmental backgrounds of readers. To what sense, for example, does the following image point? *The waves were massive.* How might context change the nature of the sense appeal?

Images must usually be considered in terms of their meaning, not simply in terms of their appeal to the senses. Studies have been made of the function of particular image groups in the structure of meaning in the plays of Shakespeare, for example. *Macbeth* uses clothing and garment images, apparently to underscore the notion that Macbeth's crown sits uneasily upon him, does not suit him well; *Romeo and Juliet* uses images of light and darkness to suggest the opposite forces at work in the actionn; *King Lear* uses images of sight to underscore the blindness-vision paradoxes in the play. There are also studies of image *groups* in poetry and in prose fiction; on close study, one frequently finds amazing density in the image texture of literature. Imagery thus becomes a central element of literary structure, a vital component in the experience literature embodies. Notice in the following sonnet by Shakespeare, for example, how sharply the figurative images derived from law condition the experience expressed within the sonnet. (How would you compare the sensory content of these images with the sensory content of the images in a poem such as "Dover Beach"?)

SONNET 134
—*William Shakespeare*

So, now I have confess'd that he is thine
And I myself am mortgag'd to thy will,
Myself I'll forfeit, so that other mine
Thou wilt restore, to be my comfort still.
But thou wilt not, nor he will not be free,
For thou art covetous and he is kind;
He learn'd but surety-like to write for me
Under that bond that him as fast doth bind.
The statute of thy beauty thou wilt take,
Thou usurer, that put'st forth all to use,
And sue a friend came debtor for my sake;
So him I lose through my unkind abuse.
    Him have I lost; thou hast both him and me:
    He pays the whole, and yet am I not free.

Figures of Sound

Literature combines a high degree of tensiveness in meaning with a high degree of tensiveness in sound. The two do not ordinarily exist independently in literature of high order. The imbalance of elements in some of the poems of Swinburne, for example, leads to the sacrificing of sense for sound; or in a writer like Theodore Dreiser, the ear may seem to function badly—though this is debatable. At any rate, the interpreter needs to be responsive not only to nuances of meaning but also to nuances of sound—and, indeed, to the capacity of sounds to be molded to fit meaning. Ultimately, sound and sense ought to coalesce in the total presence of the poem.

Just as figures of speech are means by which language seeks to extend the normal capacities for expression, so figures of sound are a means by which language tries to promote (heighten) certain aural effects normally subdued.

A limited list of figures of sound will be found in the Glossary (Appendix B), each figure briefly defined. Here we are concerned rather with the general nature of such figures. Sometimes a word or phrase will try to duplicate a sound heard in life: bang! whoosh! bzzz! Such duplications are not really very accurate, but by convention we have learned to accept them as representing the sounds. Different nationalities accept different sounds as representations of one thing; the Frenchman, the Korean, and the American have different words for the sound of a rooster, for instance. Still, in each language the symbol is accepted as a relatively effective way of embodying the real thing. The oral reader is not limited by the sound in print. The story may say "Cock-a-doodle-do," but if the reader can make a more effective rooster sound he is usually free to improve on print. Spelling is sadly lacking for many sounds the vocal apparatus is able to make. While no reader wants to be simply a sound-effects man, any capable reader must be able to fill out significant cues the writer sets down. Any reader who reads *"Bang!* went the gun as the hunter fired" and "The balloon floated lazily into the air" with the same degree of tension and energy is irresponsible, unless some comic effect is intended.

The writer may increase the frequency of sounds by arranging them in a condensed pattern: "She sells sea shells down by the seashore," in which rhyme in a transverse arrangement (*she/sea* and *sells/shells*) combines with alliteration in an inverse arrangement (*sh/s* and *s/sh*). Sheer fun seems to be the point in this example, but the effects may be much more subtle, as in Gerard Manley Hopkins' phrase "dapple dawn-drawn falcon," in which the succession of *d*s is joined by repetitions of vowel sounds, liquids, and nasals, and the inclusion of the rhyme in *dawn-drawn*.

What patterns do you find in the following more elaborate series of sounds employed by Milton?

PARADISE LOST (from Book VI)
—*John Milton*

Hell heard th' unsufferable noise, Hell saw
Heav'n ruining from Heav'n and would have fled
Affrighted; but strict Fate had cast too deep
Her dark foundations, and too fast had bound.

> Nine days they fell; confounded Chaos roar'd,
> And felt tenfold confusion in their fall
> Through his wild Anarchy, so huge a rout
> Incumber'd him with ruin: Hell at last
> Yawning recev'd them whole, and on them clos'd,
> Hell their fit habitation fraught with fire
> Unquenchable, the house of woe and pain.

For a discussion of the whole range of ways in which sounds may be combined we would need a vastly larger space than we have in this chapter. The Glossary provides names for certain arrangements of sounds, including devices of rhyme; meanwhile, it is important to remember that readers must be wary of manipulating sound for the sake of sound itself. *Tone color,* or *timbre,* is a name often applied to the resonance quality of voiced sounds, and every good interpreter must be responsive to tone coloring in literature—but it is better not to employ tone coloring at all than to turn every poem into sound alone. Remember too that tone color is not simply a matter of "beautiful" sounds. It may be used to arouse feelings of buoyancy, vigor, motion, and so forth. No reader is more irritating than one who has fallen in love with his own tone colors. Follow the clues in the poem, but do not try to double what the poet has already achieved in the management of sound.

LIFE IN LANGUAGE

Language that is drab and limp is almost useless for any purpose other than the display of drabness and limpness. Even expository prose requires starch if it is to stand up to its task. But the liveliness of literary language is different from the liveliness of nonliterary language, if we may make for the moment a too simple distinction between what is literary and what is nonliterary. Nonliterary language, whatever the degree of its vitality, seeks primarily to denote, to point to. There is a difference in intention between "The oak is a tree" and "The oak is a giant." While the sensory impression may be strong in the first sentence, it is urged on us in the second. The liveliness of the first sentence (if it is lively) is the liveliness of things-as-they-really-are; the liveliness of the second sentence is the liveliness of things-as-they-feel. Both sentences may be "true," but the first sentence is interested in fact and the second is interested in the reality of the fictive. We need not ask of literature that it give us the truth—otherwise what do we do with *Alice in Wonderland,* in which rabbits are like no rabbits under the sun? It isn't even psychological truth that we are after; we may not know enough to judge whether a particular act in literature is, in fact, psychologically true. It is belief that we ask—a belief in the existence of the world the literature creates, whether or not that world is much like the world we know through our own senses. Strangely enough, we can believe in literary worlds we would not accept at all as real worlds—a world in which crime, for example, suddenly becomes a joke to be enjoyed. There is a kind of miracle in the "making" which is literature; a poem is a life to be sensed and known, and the language that participates in the making is a language that has a life of its own to be savored for its own sake and not primarily for its being able to point, transparently, to things in "real" life.

This is not an ivory-tower view of literature. Literature has a relationship to life and often enriches it, but we should not ask that it make statements for life. Because literature *is* a form of life, it becomes a part of our whole process of making sense of the forms of life we know; I fit literature into my scheme of presences just as I fit my dog, my garden, my mother and father, and my friends into the scheme. And just as I learn things about my own life by being a careful observer of my dog, my garden, my mother and father, and my friends, so I learn things about my life by being a careful observer of literature. It is only when I assume that it has no life of its own that literature fails me—when I eat it simply to satisfy appetites or treat it as a guidebook to morals or refer to it as a repository of facts.

The wonderful thing about literature as a form of life is that it manages to give us both individual forms of life (Othello, Little Miss Muffet, Mrs. Malaprop) and the worlds in which they exist. We know perfectly well that Othello and Little Miss Muffet and Mrs. Malaprop are not real people, and we do not ask that they behave exactly as real people behave; nevertheless, while I am in the world in which they live, I believe in them (which is not the same as saying I sympathize with them). By suggesting, by working through indirection, by miraculous creating through metaphor, by promoting sounds and qualities and colors in language, even by the most astonishing denial of the claims of common sense—by all these and other devices, language *embodies;* and that is why, in a textbook on the art of interpretation, it seems profitable to suggest an interest in the devices of language since the interpreter, in turn, will seek to embody the "body" of the poem. One must learn the dance before he can become submerged in it, before he can make it an indistinguishable part of himself and himself an indistinguishable part of it. It is a difficult dance to learn. It requires the most intense application of the whole interpreter, head to foot and all the way through! Despite its difficulty, and even though it brings with it periods of despair, it is essentially a joy.

MATERIALS FOR PRACTICE

In the following selections look for the various devices the writer uses to establish tensiveness in his work. Consider both sound and sense, since it is the relationship between the two that concerns us.[3] Try to describe the way in which these devices affect your oral performance of

[3] Consult the Glossary under FIGURES OF SOUND and FIGURES OF SENSE for the definitions of these general classes, and see what examples you can find of the particular figures listed there and defined under other entries in the Glossary.

the work. Do not overlook such matters as sentence length and structure, levels of difficulty in diction, and departures from normal syntax.

THE EAGLE
—Alfred, Lord Tennyson

He clasps the crag with crooked hands;
Close to the sun in lonely lands,
Ringed with the azure world, he stands.

The wrinkled sea beneath him crawls;
He watches from his mountain walls,
And like a thunderbolt he falls.

THE DESTRUCTION OF SENNACHERIB
—George Gordon, Lord Byron

The Assyrian came down like a wolf on the fold,
And his cohorts were gleaming in purple and gold;
And the sheen of their spears was like stars on the sea,
When the blue wave rolls nightly on deep Galilee.

Like the leaves of the forest when Summer is green,
That host with their banners at sunset were seen;
Like the leaves of the forest when Autumn hath blown,
That host on the morrow lay withered and strown.

For the Angel of Death spread his wings on the blast,
And breathed in the face of the foe as he passed;
And the eyes of the sleepers waxed deadly and chill,
And their hearts but once heaved, and for ever grew still!

And there lay the steed with his nostril all wide,
But through it there rolled not the breath of his pride;
And the foam of his gasping lay white on the turf,
And cold as the spray of the rock-beating surf.

And there lay the rider distorted and pale,
With the dew on his brow, and the rust on his mail;
And the tents were all silent, the banners alone,
The lances uplifted, the trumpet unblown.

And the widows of Ashur are loud in their wail,
And the idols are broke in the temple of Baal;
And the might of the Gentile, unsmote by the sword,
Hath melted like snow in the glance of the Lord!

SILVER[4]
—Walter de la Mare

Slowly, silently, now the moon
Walks the night in her silver shoon;
This way, and that, she peers, and sees
Silver fruit upon silver trees;
One by one the casements catch
Her beams beneath the silvery thatch;
Couched in his kennel, like a log,
With paws of silver sleeps the dog;
From their shadowy cote the white breasts peep
Of doves in a silver-feathered sleep;
A harvest mouse goes scampering by,
With silver claws and a silver eye;
And moveless fish in the water gleam,
By silver reeds in a silver stream.

VERY LIKE A WHALE[5]
—Ogden Nash

One thing that literature would be greatly the better for
Would be a more restricted employment by authors of simile and
    metaphor.
Authors of all races, be they Greeks, Roman, Teutons or Celts,
Can't seem just to say that anything is the thing it is but have to go
    out of their way to say that it is like something else.
What does it mean when we are told
That the Assyrian came down like a wolf on the fold?
In the first place, George Gordon Byron had had enough experience
To know that it probably wasn't just one Assyrian, it was a lot of
    Assyrians.
However, as too many arguments are apt to induce apoplexy and thus
    hinder longevity,
We'll let it pass as one Assyrian for the sake of brevity.
Now then, this particular Assyrian, the one whose cohorts were
    gleaming in purple and gold,
Just what does the poet mean when he says he came down like a wolf
    on the fold?

In heaven and earth more than is dreamed of in our philosophy there
are a great many things,
But I don't imagine that among them there is a wolf with purple and
gold cohorts or purple and gold anythings.
No, no, Lord Byron, before I'll believe that this Assyrian was actually
like a wolf I must have some kind of proof;
Did he run on all fours and did he have a hairy tail and a big red
mouth and big white teeth and did he say Woof woof woof?
Frankly I think it very unlikely, and all you were entitled to say at the
very most,
Was that the Assyrian cohorts came down like a lot of Assyrian
cohorts about to destroy the Hebrew host.
But that wasn't fancy enough for Lord Byron, oh dear me no, he had
to invent a lot of figures of speech and then interpolate them,
With the result that whenever you mention Old Testament soldiers to
people they say Oh yes, they're the ones that a lot of wolves
dressed up in gold and purple ate them.
That's the kind of thing that's being done all the time by poets, from
Homer to Tennyson;
They're always comparing ladies to lilies and veal to venison.
How about the man who wrote,
Her little feet stole in and out like mice beneath her petticoat?
Wouldn't anybody but a poet think twice
Before stating that his girl's feet were mice?
Then they always say things like that after a snow storm
The snow is a white blanket. Oh it is, is it, all right then, you sleep
under a six-inch blanket of snow and I'll sleep under a half-inch
blanket of unpoetical blanket material and we'll see which one
keeps warm,
And after that maybe you'll begin to comprehend dimly
What I mean by too much metaphor and simile.

POEM WRITTEN AT MORNING[6]
—*Wallace Stevens*

A sunny day's complete Poussiniana
Divide it from itself. It is this or that
And it is not.
         By metaphor you paint
A thing. Thus, the pineapple was a leather fruit,
A fruit for pewter, thorned and palmed and blue,
To be served by men of ice.
               The senses paint
By metaphor. The juice was fragranter
Than wettest cinnamon. It was cribled pears
Dripping a morning sap.

               The truth must be
That you do not see, you experience, you feel,
That the buxom eye brings merely its element
To the total thing, a shapeless giant forced
Upward.
               Green were the curls upon that head.

THE HOLLOW MEN[7]
—T. S. Eliot
A penny for the Old Guy

I
We are the hollow men
We are the stuffed men
Leaning together
Headpiece filled with straw. Alas!
Our dried voices, when
We whisper together
Are quiet and meaningless
As wind in dry grass
Or rats' feet over broken glass
In our dry cellar.

Shape without form, shade without color,
Paralyzed force, gesture without motion;

Those who have crossed
With direct eyes, to death's other Kingdom
Remember us—if at all—not as lost
Violent souls, but only
As the hollow men
The stuffed men.

II
Eyes I dare not meet in dreams
In death's dream kingdom
These do not appear:
There, the eyes are
Sunlight on a broken column
There, is a tree swinging
And voices are
In the wind's singing
More distant and more solemn
Than a fading star.

---

[7] From *Collected Poems 1909–1962* by T. S. Eliot, copyright 1936, by Harcourt Brace Jovanovich, Inc.; copyright, © 1963, 1964 by T. S. Eliot. Reprinted by permission of Harcourt Brace Jovanovich, Inc. Reprinted by permission of Faber and Faber Ltd from *Collected Poems 1909–1962* by T. S. Eliot. See further notice on the copyright page.

Let me be no nearer
In death's dream kingdom
Let me also wear
Such deliberate disguises
Rat's coat, crowskin, crossed staves
In a field
Behaving as the wind behaves
No nearer—

Not that final meeting
In the twilight kingdom.

III
This is the dead land
This is cactus land
Here the stone images
Are raised, here they receive
The supplication of a dead man's hand
Under the twinkle of a fading star.

Is it like this
In death's other kingdom
Waking alone
At the hour when we are
Trembling with tenderness
Lips that would kiss
Form prayers to broken stone.

IV
The eyes are not here
There are no eyes here
In this valley of dying stars
In this hollow valley
This broken jaw of our lost kingdoms

In this last of meeting places
We grope together
And avoid speech
Gathered on this beach of the tumid river

Sightless, unless
The eyes reappear
As the perpetual star
Multifoliate rose
Of death's twilight kingdom
The hope only
Of empty men.

V
Here we go round the prickly pear
Prickly pear prickly pear
Here we go round the prickly pear
At five o'clock in the morning.

Between the idea
And the reality
Between the motion
And the act
Falls the Shadow
            For Thine is the Kingdom

Between the conception
And the creation
Between the emotion
And the response
Falls the Shadow
                Life is very long

Between the desire
And the spasm
Between the potency
And the existence
Between the essence
And the descent
Falls the Shadow
            For Thine is the Kingdom

For Thine is
Life is
For Thine is the

This is the way the world ends
This is the way the world ends
This is the way the world ends
Not with a bang but a whimper.

from **THE BLUE HOTEL**[8]
—Stephen Crane

The Swede, tightly gripping his valise, tacked across the face of the storm as
if he carried sails. He was following a line of little naked, gasping trees
which, he knew, must mark the way of the road. His face, fresh from the
pounding of Johnnie's fists, felt more pleasure than pain in the wind and the

---

[8] From *Stephen Crane: An Omnibus,* edited by Robert Wooster Stallman.
Published 1952 by Alfred A. Knopf, Inc. Reprinted by permission of the publisher.

driving snow. A number of square shapes loomed upon him finally, and he knew them as the houses of the main body of the town. He found a street and made travel along it, leaning heavily upon the wind whenever, at a corner, a terrific blast caught him.

He might have been in a deserted village. We picture the world as thick with conquering and elate humanity, but here, with the bugles of the tempest pealing, it was hard to imagine a peopled earth. One viewed the existence of man then as a marvel, and conceded a glamour of wonder to these lice which were caused to cling to a whirling, fire-smitten, ice-locked, disease-stricken, space-lost bulb. The conceit of man was explained by this storm to be the very engine of life. One was a coxcomb not to die in it. However, the Swede found a saloon.

In front of it an indomitable red light was burning, and the snowflakes were made blood-color as they flew through the circumscribed territory of the lamp's shining. The Swede pushed open the door of the saloon and entered. A sanded expanse was before him, and at the end of it four men sat about a table drinking. Down one side of the room extended a radiant bar, and its guardian was leaning upon his elbows listening to the talk of the men at the table. The Swede dropped his valise upon the floor and, smiling fraternally upon the barkeeper, said, "Gimme some whisky, will you?" The man placed a bottle, a whisky-glass, and a glass of ice-thick water upon the bar. The Swede poured himself an abnormal portion of whisky and drank it in three gulps. "Pretty bad night," remarked the bartender, indifferently. He was making the pretension of blindness which is usually a distinction of his class; but it could have been seen that he was furtively studying the half-erased bloodstains on the face of the Swede. "Bad night," he said again.

"Oh, it's good enough for me," replied the Swede, hardily, as he poured himself some more whisky. The barkeeper took his coin and maneuvered it through its reception by the highly nickeled cash-machine. A bell rang; a card labeled "20 cts." had appeared.

part of the Choric Song
from THE LOTOS-EATERS
—Alfred, Lord Tennyson

[*Notice the effect achieved through the use of vowels which can be manipulated to underscore the sense. Observe also the "gesture" involved in the lengthening lines at the close of the stanza.*—Ed.]

There is a sweet music here that softer falls
Than petals from blown roses on the grass,
Or night-dews on still waters between walls
Of shadowy granite, in a gleaming pass;
Music that gentlier on the spirit lies,
Than tired eyelids upon tired eyes;
Music that brings sweet sleep down from the blissful skies.

Here are cool mosses deep,
And thro' the moss the ivies creep,
And in the stream the long-leaved flowers weep,
And from the craggy ledge the poppy hangs in sleep.

LOVE SONG[9]
—*Anonymous*

My loved one is unique, without a peer,
More beautiful than any other.
See, she is like the star that rises on the horizon
At the dawn of an auspicious year.
She moves in a shimmer of perfection, her complexion
                                        superb,

Her eyes are marvellously seductive,
On her lips linger persuasive words.
Never does she speak one word too many!
Her neck is slender, ample her breast,
Her hair is lapis lazuli;
Her arms more splendid than gold
And her fingers like lotus-petals.
Her robe is tightly caught in around her waist,
Revealing the most beautiful legs in all the world . . .
You cannot help following her with your eyes wherever
                                        she goes,

She is such an unrivalled goddess in appearance.

JAMAICA MARKET
—*Agnes Maxwell-Hall (Jamaica)*

Honey, pepper, leaf-green limes,
Pagan fruit whose names are rhymes,
Mangoes, breadfruit, ginger-roots,
Granadillas, bamboo-shoots,
Cho-cho, ackees, tangerines,
Lemons, purple Congo-beans,
Sugar, okras, kola-nuts,
Citrons, hairy coconuts,
Fish, tobacco, native hats,
Gold bananas, woven mats,
Plantains, wild-thyme, pallid leeks,
Pigeons with their scarlet beaks,
Oranges and saffron yams,
Baskets, ruby guava jams,

---

[9] An Egyptian poem from the fourteenth century B.C.

Turtles, goat-skins, cinnamon,
Allspice, conch-shells, golden rum.
Black skins, babel—and the sun
That burns all colours into one.

THE PEASANT DECLARES HIS LOVE
—Émile Roumer (Haiti)

High-yellow of my heart, with breasts like tangerines,
you taste better to me than eggplant stuffed with crab,
you are the tripe in my pepper-pot,
the dumpling of my peas, my tea of aromatic herbs.
You are the corned beef whose customhouse is my heart,
my mush with syrup that trickles down the throat.
You are a steaming dish, mushroom cooked with rice,
crisp potato fries, and little fish fried brown. . . .
My hankering for love follows you wherever you go.
Your bum is a gorgeous basket brimming with fruits and meat.

MUSÉE DES BEAUX ARTS[12]
—W. H. Auden

About suffering they were never wrong,
The Old Masters: how well they understood
Its human position; how it takes place
While someone else is eating or opening a window or just walking
                                        dully along;
How, when the aged are reverently, passionately waiting
For the miraculous birth, there always must be
Children who did not specially want it to happen, skating
On a pond at the edge of the wood:
They never forgot
That even the dreadful martyrdom must run its course
Anyhow in a corner, some untidy spot
Where the dogs go on with their doggy life and the torturer's horse
Scratches its innocent behind on a tree.

In Brueghel's *Icarus*, for instance: how everything turns away
Quite leisurely from the disaster; the ploughman may
Have heard the splash, the forsaken cry,
But for him it was not an important failure; the sun shone
As it had to on the white legs disappearing into the green
Water; and the expensive delicate ship that must have seen
Something amazing, a boy falling out of the sky,
Had somewhere to get to and sailed calmly on.

Chapter 9

STRUCTURE AS ACT: POETRY

We have been discussing qualities of literary *structure,* the inclusive term that designates the whole architecture through and in which the poet embodies meaning. In their *Theory of Literature*[1] Wellek and Warren suggest that it may be profitable to think of all the elements the poet uses as *materials,* and the esthetic shape created from them as *structure.* In this sense, sounds, words, ideas, even isolated images may be thought of as materials. As soon as the poet begins to build with them, to arrange and modify and organize them, he is structuring.

Everyone knows that sound is a part of the substance of language, and that the way a work feels arises in part from the way it sounds. Milton and Keats not only think and feel differently, they sound different from one another. Literary language is likely to have distinctive tune or melody or rhythm. One way of capturing these tunes and rhythms in oral performance is through conscious recognition of their existence and of the elements of which they are composed.

Suppose we discuss, to begin with, certain aspects of poetic (as distinguished from prose) structure. Poetry creates its presence in language that is based on *return.* Perhaps the Latin *versus* (from which is

---

[1] René Wellek and Austin Warren, *Theory of Literature,* 3d ed. (New York: Harcourt Brace Jovanovich, Inc., 1962).

derived the English word *verse,* although verse, strictly speaking, means a single line of poetry) will help indicate what return means. *Versus* means "a turning back," the opposite of *prorsus (from which we derive the word prose*), which means "forward" or "straight ahead." Poetry is written in repeated sections, and within these sections some form of patterning is taking place. *Prosody* is the word that designates the art or science of patterning in poetry.[2]

PROSODY   Sometimes we are introduced to prosody as if it were simply a mechanical matter, something of interest (possibly) to the poet himself but of only peripheral concern to the reader. However, the effects of poetry are tied to words, sounds, and rhythms in such a way that one cannot separate the feel of a poem from its prosody. Stanley Kunitz, a contemporary poet, questioned about the matter in an interview, responded:

> When I first began to teach, in the late 40's, it seemed quite obvious that instruction in prosody was part of the workshop discipline. Today the young are mostly indifferent to such matters, not only indifferent but strongly antipathetic. They praise novelty, spontaneity, and ease, and they resist the very concept of form, which they relate to mechanism and chains. Few understand that, for a poet, even breathing comes under the heading of prosody.[3]

In addition, as Kunitz remarks later in the same interview, metrics is an aspect of tensiveness, a part of the ebb and flow, which now restrains and now lets go the sense of momentum. Prosody is thus as much a matter of biology as it is of mechanics for Kunitz: "It involves everything that has to do with the making of a poem, the way it moves, the way it sounds, the way it lives from word to word, the way it breathes." It is the "variable pulse" of the poem, which is a sign of its being alive: "Even before it is ready to change into language a poem may begin to assert its buried life in the mind with wordless surges of rhythm and counter-rhythm." Hence, we must study prosody if we are to grasp those wordless surges with which the poet in part comes to what is finally the poem. One aspect of prosody is rhyme.

RHYME   Rhyme is the repetition of identical or similar accented vowel sounds in combination with identical *succeeding* sounds but different *preceding* sounds. (*Ring* and *sing* rhyme, but *ring* and *caring* do not; *paring* and

---

[2] Despite the fact that the word *prosody* itself looks as if it were allied to the word *prose,* it is not. We do not speak of the prosody of prose, though we shall talk later about prose rhythms; the term *prosody* is restricted to patterns in verse.

[3] From "Craft Interview with Stanley Kunitz," *New York Quarterly* (Fall 1970), 9–22. Reprinted by permission of the *New York Quarterly.*

caring rhyme, *preparing* and *repairing* rhyme, but *paring* and *preparing* do not.) Not all poetry rhymes, of course, but blank verse is the only major nonrhyming form with a continuous history in English verse. Rhyme creates tensiveness by binding groups of words together, heightening the appeal to the ear. While it can be largely ornamental, in the best poetry it is not, but serves to underscore and heighten meaning. In a good poem, rhymes must not be allowed to dominate other aspects of structure. An ear (and a mind) can be put to sleep by too fat a feast of sound. But to seek to *avoid* rhyming sounds is to weaken the structure of a poem which rhymes. As one writer puts it, "The incorporation of rhyme in a poem is part of the poet's struggle with language. It should be no less for the oral interpreter."[4]

Rhyme is used by poets at line ends and within lines (*terminal rhyme* and *internal rhyme*). Yeats uses terminal rhyme in this passage from "The Lake Isle of Innisfree":

> I will arise and go now, and go to Innis*free,*
>   And a small cabin build there, of clay and wattles *made,*
> Nine bean rows will I have there, a hive for the honey *bee,*
>   And live alone in the bee-loud *glade.*[5]

Assigning the letter *a* to the first rhyme and *b* to the second, we say that the rhyme scheme of the stanza is *abab*. A passage from Shelley's "The Cloud" illustrates the use of internal rhyme:

> I bring fresh *showers,* for the thirsting *flowers,*
>   From the seas and the streams;
> I bear light *shade* for the leaves when *laid*
>   In their noonday dreams.

The first and third lines do not have terminal rhyme; the second and fourth lines do. The rhyme scheme here is *abcb*. The designation of rhyme schemes does not ordinarily include internal rhymes, though perhaps it should. (We might describe the scheme for these four lines as *aa b cc b*.)

The kind of rhyme we have been describing is *exact* or *full rhyme*. When the vowel sounds involved in the rhymes are similar but not identical, the effect is called *half rhyme* or *slant rhyme*. The following poem by Yeats indicates the poet's fondness for combining full and half rhymes. Notice that *right* and *night* rhyme exactly. How would you describe the effect Yeats achieves by combining the two kinds of rhyme?

[4] William E. Rickert, "Structural Functions of Rhyme and the Performance of Poetry," *Quarterly Journal of Speech*, 62 (1976), 250.

[5] Reprinted with permission of The Macmillan Company, Miss Anne Yeats, M. B. Yeats, and The Macmillan Co. of London and Basingstoke from *Collected Poems* by W. B. Yeats. Copyright 1906 by The Macmillan Company, renewed 1934 by William Butler Yeats.

AFTER LONG SILENCE[6]
—*William Butler Yeats*

Speech after long silence; it is right,	a
All other lovers being estranged or dead,	b
Unfriendly lamplight hid under its shade,	b
The curtains drawn upon unfriendly night,	a
That we descant and yet again descant	c
Upon the supreme theme of Art and Song:	d
Bodily decrepitude is wisdom; young	d
We loved each other and were ignorant.	c

Rhymes may be classified as either *masculine* or *feminine* (strong or weak). Masculine rhymes are those in which the rhyming syllables are the final and stressed syllables of the line:

> . . . right,
> . . . night.

Feminine rhymes are those in which the rhyming stressed syllables precede the final syllables of the line:

> . . . *never*
> . . . *sever*

Such rhyme may also be called *double rhyme. Triple rhyme* carries the rhyming back still another syllable:

> . . . *rosier*
> . . . *cosier*

Triple rhyme begins to seem ingenious, however, and more often than not produces a comic effect. It may be used deliberately for such an effect:

> THE DENTIST
> (*an epitaph*)
> Stranger! Approach this spot with gravity!
> John Brown is filling his last cavity.

RHYME
AND
MEANING

It is important to repeat that rhyme is an aspect of meaning, not simply a pattern of sounds divorced from meaning. Rhyme is part of structure, part of the poem's body. Relations of sound and sense are another aspect of tensiveness. We have defined poems as being, among other things, language structured in repeated sections. Rhyme is one aspect of

[6] Reprinted with permission of The Macmillan Company, Miss Anne Yeats, M. B. Yeats, and The Macmillan Co. of London and Basingstoke from *Collected Poems* by W. B. Yeats. Copyright 1933 The Macmillan Company, renewed 1961 by Bertha Georgie Yeats.

repetition. It may be used to urge a reader forward; it may be used to bring a reader to a sense of stoppage.

The purely euphonic function of rhyme is restricted to limited kinds of verse—nonsense poems, nursery rhymes, for example, where the conceptual content is minimal. Such use of rhyme is surely fun, even for adults, from time to time. But in most poetry, while the euphonic function continues, the conceptual content increases. W. K. Wimsatt (in *The Verbal Icon*) has pointed out how the poet will rhyme one part of speech with a different part of speech, how the syntax of one line may vary from the syntax of another, so that a constant tensive relationship, rather than a simple pattern of repetition, is set up between lines. In the following lines from Byron's *Don Juan,* for example, observe the variations in syntax accompanying the rhyme scheme:

> His mother was a learned lady, famed
>   For every branch of every science known—
> In every Christian language ever named,
>   With virtues equaled by her wit alone:
> She made the cleverest people quite ashamed,
>   And even the good with inward envy groan,
> Finding themselves so very much exceeded
> In their own way by all the things that she did.

Note, also, how the alternate rhymes lead one onward (one expects a rhyme-fellow for *famed, known,* particularly after one has read one stanza setting up the pattern); but see how the concluding two lines *stop* that movement by interrupting the alternation. Here, too, as often, Byron punctuates the comic effects he intends in the poem by the ingenuity of the rhyme—*exceeded, she did.* (Other such rhymes in *Don Juan* are frequent: *intellectual–hen-pecked you all; gunnery–nunnery; maxim–tax 'em.*) Often they are triple rhymes. The comic effect is not *added* to meaning but *is* meaning. Rhyme is an integral aspect of the poem's body.

METER

Rhyme, as we have said, is not a necessary part of poetry. Meter is not always necessary, though T. S. Eliot has suggested that the ghost of a simple meter probably lurks behind even the freest of free verse. Nevertheless, the bulk of traditional poetry in English has a metrical base.

Meter is the patterning of two elements in poetry. It is common practice to define these elements as stressed sounds and unstressed sounds, or accented and unaccented sounds. A better way to describe the pattern is to say that it is based on a varied alternation of conspicuous and less conspicuous elements, because not only stress and accent (which are two different things) but also such elements as pitch, inflection, and time enter into the patterning.

Stress is the *ictus,* or beat, employed to distinguish one syllable from another by the application of greater force or loudness of utterance. In the sentence "The rain has stopped," there are two stresses, one on *rain* and one on *stopped,* both one-syllable words. Except in particular cases, nouns and verbs are stressed in English sentences; articles and auxiliary verbs normally are not stressed. In the sentence "The tornado struck," the subject is a word of three syllables, only the second being stressed. In words of more than one syllable, the syllable that receives the stress is called the accented syllable. *Accent,* in other words, is the habitual stress placed in pronouncing on a particular syllable or syllables of a word containing more than a single syllable. Monosyllables may have stress; they cannot, by definition, have accent. Some words have two accents, primary and secondary: *multiplication,* for example, has a secondary accent on the first syllable and a primary accent on the fourth syllable. Actually, linguists find at least four degrees of stress operating in the English language, and there are doubtless more than four; our usual practice of describing only two in meter is for certain poems a dangerous oversimplification.[7]

Here are some lines from "Annabel Lee," by Edgar Allan Poe:

> It was many and many a year ago
>   In a kingdom by the sea,
> That a maiden there lived whom you may know
>   By the name of Annabel Lee;
> And this maiden she lived with no other thought
>   Than to love and be loved by me.

These verses together make up a six-line stanza. Stanzas are another means of patterning, another aspect of prosody.

Suppose we begin an analysis of the verses by pointing out the accented syllables:

>   /   /   /
> It was *ma*ny and *ma*ny a year a*go*
>   /
>   In a *king*dom by the sea,
>   /
> That a *mai*den there lived whom you may know
>   /
>   By the name of *An*nabel Lee;
>   /   /
> And this *mai*den she lived with no *o*ther thought
>
>   Than to love and be loved by me.

[7] See the symposium on metrics in *The Kenyon Review* (Summer 1956), which reviews the theory behind the Trager–Smith analysis of stress, pitch, and juncture.

Now to these accents let us add stresses suggested by the sense in addition to those dictated by the accent:

```
         /         /      /     /
It was many and many a year ago
         /               /
  In a kingdom by the sea,
         /               /                    /
That a maiden there lived whom you may know
         /        /       /
  By the name of Annabel Lee;
         /           /           /        /
And this maiden she lived with no other thought
         /           /         /
  Than to love and be loved by me.
```

Notice that most of these sense stresses are on nouns and verbs, key words in the sentence. Personal pronouns are not normally stressed in English sentences, but you will see that a stress has been placed over the word *me* in the last line of the stanza—for two reasons: (1) the word *me* here rhymes with *sea* and *Lee,* and is thus made conspicuous by the rhyme position, and (2) it has a particular emphasis in the syntax, since the maiden is not simply to love and be loved, but to love and be loved by *me.*

Observe the pattern of stresses per line:

> 4 stresses
> 2 stresses
> 3 stresses
> 3 stresses
> 4 stresses
> 3 stresses

Now try using the *temporal* pattern of line 1 as a measuring stick for determining the temporal pattern of succeeding lines, with four beats to each line. You will find that the punctuation at the end of lines 2, 4, and 6 gives you a break or pause that may be counted as one beat. You will also find that the word *by* in line 2 and the word *you* in line 3 now get stresses, and that the total stress pattern becomes this:

> 4 stresses
> 3 stresses (plus a pause)
> 4 stresses
> 3 stresses (plus a pause)
> 4 stresses
> 3 stresses (plus a pause)

What we are saying is that the temporal pattern *promotes* stresses, and lifts to a stressed position words that might not normally receive stress. Verse in which this occurs can be called *isochronous;* it is structured in such a way that normal stress patterns either fit naturally into approximately equal time units or are pressured into fitting.

Some poetry is patterned solely by the number of stresses per line. The number may remain constant from line to line (as in Anglo-Saxon poetry, in which the stresses number four per line), or it may be arranged in a pattern (4-3-4-3-4-3). The system in which the number of stresses constitutes the prosodic principle is called *stress prosody.*

But in Poe's poem there is something besides a simple stress system. Poe himself, as we know from his own treatise on prosody, would talk about additional matters. Suppose that we break the lines up into *measures* or *feet,* by putting a bar after each stress:

```
x  x   /   x  x   /  x x /    x /
It was ma | ny and ma | ny a year | ago
  x x /     x   / x /
 In a king | dom by | the sea,
  x x /     x   x   /      x    /   x   /
That a mai | den there lived | whom you | may know
   x  x   /    x  /   x x   /
 By the name | of An | nabel Lee;
 x   x   /    x  x /    x  x / x   /
And this mai | den she lived | with no o | ther thought
   x  x /    x  x /    x  /
 Than to love | and be loved | by me.
```

Observe how we have added to the description of the pattern. The first, third, and fifth lines each contain four feet. Lines containing four feet are called *tetrameter* lines (*tetra-,* meaning "four," and *meter*). The second, fourth, and sixth lines each contain three feet. Lines containing three feet are called *trimeter* lines (*tri,* meaning "three," and *meter*). Here are some other terms:

> dimeter—two feet per line
> pentameter—five feet per line
> hexameter—six feet per line
> heptameter—seven feet per line
> octameter—eight feet per line

You are not likely to get monometer (one foot per line), nor to have lines of more than eight feet, although longer lines are not unknown.

We have, then, in "Annabel Lee" (at least the stanza we have quoted), alternating tetrameter and trimeter lines, with the trimeter lines all rhyming with each other. Now notice the feet within each line: they are of two kinds only, xx/ and x/. The first of these kinds of feet is called an *anapest*. An anapest is a metrical foot made up of two unstressed or less conspicuous syllables and one stressed or conspicuous syllable. The other foot is called an *iambus,* or an *iamb.* An iamb is a metrical foot consisting of a single unstressed or less conspicuous syllable and a single stressed or conspicuous syllable. The iambus and the anapest are two of the commonest feet in English verse. Other common feet are the *trochee* (a reversed iambus), the *dactyl* (a reversed anapest), the *pyrrhic* (two unstressed syllables), and the *spondee* (two stressed syllables). Here are examples of each:

> /   x   /   x   /   x   /   x   **Trochee**
> Bacchus' | blessings | are a | treasure,
> Drinking is the soldier's pleasure;
>   Rich the treasure,
>   Sweet the pleasure
> Sweet is pleasure after pain.
> —John Dryden
>   from *Alexander's Feast*

> /   x   x   /   x   x   / x   x   /   **Dactyl**
> Black were her | eyes as the | berry that | grows
> x   x   /   x   x   / /
> on the | thorn by the | wayside
> —Henry Wadsworth Longfellow
>   from *Evangeline*

The last foot in the line from *Evangeline* above is a spondee. Both spon-   **Spondee** daic and pyrrhic feet are found only in mixed meters—that is, they are not used alone.

> x   /   x /   x   /   x   x   x   /   **Pyrrhic**
> This med | iae | val mir | acle | of song
> —Henry Wadsworth Longfellow
>   from Sonnet II, *Divina Commedia*

The fourth foot is a pyrrhic foot. Or there, as frequently, the pyrrhic can be regarded as an iambus if one takes the third syllable of *miracle* to have a secondary stress.

Notice that the question of where the division between feet comes is decided by looking for an overall pattern. If one were to divide the line from Dryden (under *Trochee* above) this way

```
/    x    /    x   /    x  /    x
Bac | chus' bless | ings are | a trea | sure
```

one would have three iambs and two half feet. The line would seem highly irregular. If one were to divide the second line this way

```
/ x    x x  /   x    /    x
Drinking | is the sol | dier's pleas | ure
```

one would have a trochee, an anapest, an iamb, and a half foot. These divisions do not conceal the fact that we have an alternation of greater and lesser stress, but they do fail to show the regularity of the pattern. The stanza can be scanned regularly: four trochees (tetrameter) in the first and second lines, two trochees (dimeter) in the third and fourth lines. The single variation is the last line, which contains only seven syllables, so that it cannot be divided neatly into two-syllable feet. Probably the line should be read as three trochees followed by a half foot that consists of a single stress. Notice how the single stress at the end of the last line serves musically to punctuate and terminate the stanza.

Poems written in iambs and anapests are said to be in *rising rhythm* (the foot rises toward the stress); the trochee and the dactyl are employed to produce *falling rhythm* (the foot falling from the stress). It is sometimes said that the English language is essentially a language based on rising rhythm and that it is difficult to keep dactyls and trochees from being inverted. Iambs and anapests frequently substitute for one another in poetry; dactyls and trochees substitute for one another. This does not preclude mixed measures, and both pyrrhic and spondaic feet are found in either rising or falling rhythm. Prosodists who talk about meter in terms of feet are called *foot prosodists*. We are so accustomed to talking about poetry in terms of feet that we sometimes forget the possibility of poetry's being written in simple stress patterns or in simple syllabic groups. Observe the second stanza from John Donne's "Song":

> If thou be'st born to strange sights,
>   Things invisible to see,
> Ride ten thousand days and nights,
>   Till Age snow white hairs on thee;
> Thou, when thou return'st, wilt tell me
>   All strange wonders that befell thee,
>   And swear
>   No where
> Lives a woman true, and fair.

If you try to divide Donne's lines into feet, you will find some difficulty in discovering a regular, clear pattern in certain lines. Donne employs a freely shifting stress that gives both weight and energy to his verse. More "regular" writers have sometimes deplored what seemed to them the erratic behavior of Donne's stresses; in a famous comment, Ben Jonson said that for not keeping of accent Donne deserved hanging! But Donne is not writing verse that is completely free. If you count the syllables per line, you will find a pattern in the count: 7, 7, 7, 7, 8, 8, 2, 2, 7. This pattern is repeated throughout the three stanzas of the poem. (Certain lines in stanzas 1 and 3 that appear to have an extra syllable actually lose that syllable by a conventional species of elision.) Donne's poems are often described as *syllabic prosody* (based on a count of syllables). Far more poems have been written by syllable count than writers of prosodic treatises have imagined. We should remember not to impose systems on poems by forcing them into the prosodic designs we happen to champion; always look for the descriptive term that best points to the design within the poem itself. A poem written in an absolutely regular meter may be described in several ways. For example, the lines

> When I have fears that I may cease to be
> Before my pen has gleaned my teeming brain

may be described as syllabic prosody (10 syllables per line), as foot prosody (iambic pentameter), or as stress prosody (five stresses per line), but in this case the phrase *foot prosody*, with the descriptive identification *iambic pentameter*, tells us more than either *syllabic prosody* or *stress prosody*.

Another kind of prosody is today comparatively rare, though you will easily find examples of it in the work of e. e. cummings and of Dylan Thomas; it is *visual prosody*, in which poems are arranged typographically on the page to form pictures or symbols—a cross, a lozenge, angel wings, steam rising from a locomotive. The oral reader is sometimes helpless with this kind of prosody, though visual clues may, on the other hand, serve as kinesthetic and aural cues.

THE FUNCTION OF RHYTHM IN POETRY

Rhythm is the tension in the prosodic surface of a poem produced by the recurrence of a pattern of sound interrupted or varied by substitutions in the meter, by pauses, by inflections—indeed, by any aspect of sound other than the simple recurrence of the basic metrical unit. Rhythm in poetry is a kind of *counterpoint*. You will observe in the stanza of "Annabel Lee" that the rhythm involves not only the mixing of anapests and iambs but the recurrence of a rise and fall in pitch and in emphasis, the latter based in turn on an alternation of rhetorically conspicuous and rhetorically less conspicuous words.

Cutting across word boundaries and foot divisions are phrases and clauses. They too have rhythms—looser than the metrical pattern but working in counterpoint with and against it. The give-and-take between meter and sentence patterns (for the English language has normal inflection patterns within sentences) is an aspect of tensiveness, of the poem's muscularity. In Keats's line "When I have fears that I may cease to be," one does not beat out five iambs in absolute temporal regularity, breaking the line into artificial phrases: "When I—have fears—that I—may cease—to be." The abstract form of the meter must not be permitted to drown out the feel and sense of the line. Just as our personal acts and movements vary in tempo, so the phrases and lines and parts of poems vary in tempo. Absolute regularity is death, though one must except certain very short poems—some nonsense verse, for example—in which absolute regularity of meter may simply be fun:

> I put my hat upon my head
> And walked into the Strand,
> And there I met another man
> Whose hat was in his hand.

The movement of language is not apart from but a part of its meaning and feel.

A poet quickens, alters, slows down his lines as part of what his poem is trying to become. Ebb and flow, tension and release, movement and countermovement—these qualities, measured against an abstract metrical base, account for the phenomenon of rhythm in poetry. These movements may be underscored by rhyme, by figures of sound (see the Glossary), and even by waves and clusters of images that act as intensifiers.

It is usual to say that three-syllable feet are more lilting than two-syllable feet and quicker in time. There was a time when very conservative prosodists thought that the trisyllabic foot lacked dignity. We tend now to like mixtures of feet for the sake of variety in the poetic line, though not all mixtures are acceptable to the ear.

Now let us take a passage of poetry by an English poet who is a great master of rhythmic effects, to see how we can best explain its prosodic structure. The stanza is from Shelley's "The Cloud":

```
      /    (/)   /              /          /
I bring fresh showers for the thirsting flowers,          1
             /               /
   From the seas and the streams;                          2
   /    (/)    /           /           /
I bear light shade for the leaves when laid                3
           /          /
   In their noonday dreams.                                4
          /           /          /          /
From my wings are shaken the dews that waken               5
```

```
       /    (/)   /     /
The sweet buds every one,                          6
     /        /          /        /
When rocked to rest on their mother's breast,      7
         /        /        /
As she dances about the sun.                       8
     /        /        /        /
I wield the flail of the lashing hail,             9
        /        /    (/)   /
And whiten the green plains under                  10
 (/)    /        /        /
And then again I dissolve it in rain,              11
      /        /        /
And laugh as I pass in thunder.                    12
```

The stresses have been marked with a diagonal line; in addition, the accents have been italicized. Notice that the stresses are largely on verbs, nouns, and adjectives—all normally stressed in English. The adverb *again* is stressed partly because it is dissyllabic and hence has accent, partly because it rhymes with *rain* and hence has promoted stress. The adverb-prepositions *about* and *under* receive stress because they are dissyllabic and because *under* rhymes with *thunder*. The indefinite pronoun *one* is stressed (though personal pronouns, we have already said, are not). Such pronouns are really nominal (nounlike) in function. Also, *one* rhymes with *sun*. The pattern we have found so far looks like this:

> 5 stresses
> 2 stresses
> 5 stresses
> 2 stresses
> 4 stresses
> 4 stresses
> 4 stresses
> 3 stresses
> 4 stresses
> 4 stresses
> 4 stresses
> 3 stresses

THE NATURE OF STRESS

Clearly there is a pattern of fives, twos, fours, and threes, but it is possible to raise a series of questions about the pattern, and we shall do so. First of all, stress is not a fixed thing; there are not simply two degrees of it—some writers speak of at least four.[8] Indeed, linguists have shown that speakers often cannot wholly distinguish between matters of stress

---

[8] Usually indicated thus: primary /; secondary ∧; tertiary ╲ ; weak ∪.

and matters of pitch and chest pulsation. While words of more than a single syllable have one inherent (habitual) stress—i.e., accent—secondary stresses in polysyllables are often optional and may be either suppressed or promoted in poetry. Special stresses for particular rhetorical emphases may occur on any word or syllable—for example, the preposition *in,* not normally stressed, may be stressed in such a sentence as this: "It is *in* the desk, not *on* it."

Furthermore, what apparently happens in poetry is that while several degrees of stress may be involved, what we actually respond to in an overall way is the contrasts. When one syllable is different (lighter, let us say) from the two surrounding it, we tend to mark the sequence as / x /, even though the two marked stresses may vary considerably in degree. Hence, the foot patterns that indicate two degrees (light and heavy) are simply a way of recognizing contrasting values, and the values may involve (along with actual stress) contrasts in pitch, pulsation, and duration. That is why we said earlier that a foot is made up of more conspicuous and less conspicuous elements.

UNRESOLVED VALUES: TENSIVENESS

Now look at lines 1 and 3 of Shelley's stanza. It is possible to argue that *fresh* in line 1 and *light* in line 3 are unstressed. That is, each adjective comes between two other stresses (*bring* and *show-* in line 1, *bear* and *shade* in line 3), and a pattern of alternation would suggest lighter stresses on the two adjectives, and on *buds* in line 6 and *plains* in line 10. Notice that this is not a question of lexical meaning—the lexical meaning is essentially unchanged whether one does or does not stress these words, though the emphases differ. In performing, one may choose to keep the stress or not to keep it. Indeed, we should probably say of the lines that the rhythmic effect actually involves the hovering of two values in the adjectives, so that lines 1 and 3 are quite different rhythmically from lines 5 and 7, in which the stresses are undeniably only four. One may also argue that the alliteration of *f*resh and *f*lowers and of *l*ight, *l*eaves, and *l*aid further promotes stress on the two adjectives. Hence, it is very difficult to say in any final way whether lines 1 and 3 are actually five-stress or four-stress lines, and readings of them will vary. It is an aspect of the tensiveness of Shelley's prosody that he leaves many such issues open. Unvarying meter is deadly—a completed and fixed pattern has rigor mortis. Live prosody moves toward completion and is always a becoming; organisms tend to complete acts, but when the act is completed it is over and done with. Life itself is literally unstable. As Rugg says, "Life is possible only through the basic continuity of the tension-release-tension cycle, each phase passing from imbalance to balance, but always with enough surplus energy to carry the organism over dead center to imbalance."[9]

[9] Harold Rugg, *Imagination* (New York: Harper & Row, 1963), pp. 242–243.

Our pattern, if we omit the second stress in lines 1, 3, and 6, and the third stress in line 10, now becomes this:

                    4 stresses
                    2 stresses
                    4 stresses
                    2 stresses
                    4 stresses
                    3 stresses
                    4 stresses
                    3 stresses
                    4 stresses
                    3 stresses
                    4 stresses
                    3 stresses

So far we have said nothing about time, but English is essentially a stress-timed language, whether in prose or in verse. Notice the following:

        /   /
    the nick of time
            /   /
    in the summer of his youth

The first phrase has four syllables, the second has seven. Yet temporally they are equal. Read them with a metronome ticking, with the *tick* coming at the point indicated as a stress, and they take the same length of time to pronounce.

With the metronome still ticking (not too fast!) read the stanza from "The Cloud," letting the *tick* fall on the stresses. You will find that the poem easily reads this way:

TIME IN
"THE CLOUD"

    x /   x   / x x x / x / x
    I bring fresh showers for the thirsting flowers,
        x   x /   x x   /   /   /
        From the seas and the streams;
    x /   x   /   x x /   x /
    I bear light shade for the leaves when laid
       x   x   /   x /   /   /
       In their noonday dreams.
      x   x   /   x / x x /   x / x
    From my wings are shaken the dews that waken
        x   /   x / x /   /
        The sweet buds every one,

```
  x    /     x  /  x   x   /  x      /
When rocked to rest on their mother's breast,
    x  x   /  x  x /   x   /          /
    As she dances about the sun.
 x   /   x   /  x  x  /  x    /
I wield the flail of the lashing hail,
      x    /x  x    /    x  /  x      /
      And whiten the green plains under
  x    /  x /  x x   /   x x  /
And then again I dissolve it in rain,
        x   /    x x /  x   /   x    /
        And laugh as I pass in thunder.
```

All the lines, seen temporally, are four-beat lines, with the pauses at the ends of the even-numbered lines functioning to fill up the measures. Notice now that we have eliminated the stresses on *fresh, light, buds,* and *plains,* as we suggested earlier we might do.

The lines are *isochronous* (equal in time), but there are varying degrees of stress within the time units. Internal rhyme in the odd-numbered lines further contributes to the variety. There is alliteration, and there are other figures of sound (see the Glossary for a listing of some of these figures). Because of the pauses at the ends of the even-numbered lines, the stanza seems to exist in parcels of two lines each, and you will notice that the punctuation and syntax support such division.

How shall we describe the feet in the poem? Clearly we find combinations of two-syllable and three-syllable feet, usually iambs and anapests. But there are certain problems. Is the second foot in the first line, for example, an iambus (x /) or an amphibrach (x / x)?[10] The answer depends in part on your view of the word *showers.* Is it one syllable or two? What about *flowers* at the end of the line? (Do you distinguish, in pronunciation, between *flowers* and *flours*?) If you think of the words as having one syllable, the problem disappears: you have two iambs in the feet involving them. But if you allow two syllables, you have the question of deciding whether to break the line this way

```
  x  /  |  x  /  |  x  x  x  /  |  x  /  |  x
```

or this way

```
  x  /  |  x  /  x  |  xx  /  |  x  /  x
```

If you think of feet as being divided by stresses, then clearly the first scansion is the one to use. The extra syllable at the end of the line may be thought of as combining with the beginning of the next line to produce x x x /, which duplicates the foot involved in "-ers for the thirst" in line 1, since there is no necessary pause at the end of line 1.

---

[10] Feet are independent of word boundaries. A foot may begin or end either at the beginning or end of a word or within a word.

If you are not bound by the notion that stresses alone divide lines into feet, it is possible to employ the amphibrach (x / x), a so-called "rocking foot," for the second and fourth feet. The point is that while time is involved, time is not to be thought of as moving along in unbroken sequence. One may hasten syllables or draw them out, employing syncopation, or making up for lost time by quickening what follows a slowed-down syllable. There is one good rule to remember: when you scan, scan as you read; let your scansion show as accurately as you can the way in which you respond to the actual feel of the line. When your instructor asks you for the scansion of a poem, he is really asking for your objective analysis of the way in which the poem moves. There is no great virtue in arguing about the issue raised in the first line of Shelley's poem.

In this stanza by Shelley, lines 2 and 4 have two feet each, whereas all the other even-numbered lines have three feet. The "missing" foot in these lines is accounted for only in the temporal scheme. The rhyme scheme is

aa
b
cc
b
dd
e
ff
e
gg
h
ii
h

A caesura (from the Latin word *caedo,* to cut) is a clearly discernible pause in the middle of a line, often marked with punctuation. The caesura is an aspect of rhythm, another means of counterpointing the movement of the poem. In the following line by Browning, notice how the caesuras at the close of the first anapest and after the initial syllable of the fourth foot affect the movement of the line:

CAESURA

```
x  x  /   || x   x  /   x  x   / x   ||x   / x   x /
And I paused, held my breath in such silence, and listened apart.
```

We have marked the caesuras with double bars. They are not part of the *meter,* but they are part of the *rhythm* of the line. Notice how different the effect of these other lines by the same poet, where we have no caesuras but do have strong stoppage at the *ends* of lines each made up of five syllables:

> The year's at the spring;
> And day's at the morn;
> Morning's at seven;
> The hillside's dew-pearled;
> The lark's on the wing;
> The snail's on the thorn:
> God's in his heaven—
> All's right with the world!

What is the effect of the absolutely regular syllable count conjoined with the strong end stoppage of lines? In the two instances from Browning, what relationship do you find between sound/time and sense?

Some prosodists would say that the pause must be *clearly marked* (either by punctuation or rhetorically, or both) before it is to be called a caesura. For example, while one might pause briefly after the word *consider* in the following line

> When I consider how my light is spent

such a pause is more or less arbitrary; it is far from clear that the poet himself would have wished it, and it is unclear also that the poem requires it. Probably the word *caesura* should be kept for those pauses which are clearly marked, but there is no hard-and-fast rule.

SCANSION AND THE INTERPRETER

Scansion is significant for the performer not as a mechanical aspect of poetic structure but as a method for exploring tensiveness, the living musculature of form. The language of a poem flows in carefully orchestrated ways; the performer, too, tends to have a personal tempo or rhythm. In interpretation, we bring the two sets of tempi together. Here, as in all other aspects of the art we have been exploring, the performer's body in part conditions the appearance and sound of the poem's body in performance; but here, as always, the better part of discretion is to give primacy to the poem. This is not to say, of course, that *either* poem or performer moves to an unvaried beat! The poetic line differs from usual prose lines in being more tightly patterned, more controlled in sound; sound and sense become so closely knit that one cannot easily distinguish between them.

The basic movement of the line should not be obscured. Notice the difference in the march of the following words from Shakespeare's *Henry V* printed first as prose and then as verse:

> And what art thou, thou idol Ceremony? What kind of god art thou,
> that suffer'st more of mortal griefs than do thy worshippers?

And what art thou, thou idol Ceremony?
What kind of god art thou, that suffer'st more
Of mortal griefs than do thy worshippers?

To read the speech as if it were prose would be, we think, wrong. If one observes the iambic pentameter (i.e., blank verse) in which Shakespeare wrote, one promotes certain stresses (*what,* probably the first and third *thou, do*); observes line breaks; senses the regular rise and fall in stress to which the shorter units (i.e., lines rather than the full sentence) invite attention. Attention to sense *alone* will not lead one to such a reading; attention to sense in combination with an understanding (whether intuitive or not) of the ways in which poetic lines flow *will* yield such a reading. Here, as in all instances where we are talking about the techniques of literature, our vocabulary and the study in which we employ it are meant to serve the life of the literary work itself. Criticism is not identical with the creative act, but criticism is a useful guide to an understanding of it. Understanding—full understanding of the whole body of the work—is essential to the creation of presence.

You will notice that in the long lines in the Shelley stanza the feet tend to fall into pairs:

DIPODIC STRUCTURES

I bring fresh showers   for the thirsting flowers
I bear light shade   for the leaves when laid
From my wings are shaken   the dews that waken
When rocked to rest   on their mother's breast
I wield the flail   of the lashing hail
and then again   I dissolve it in rain

This is partly a function of the internal rhyme, of course, which does in part what a caesura, a definitely marked pause, might do in other poems (see, for example, the passage quoted under DIPODY in the Glossary). Such functioning of feet in pairs gives these lines a dipodic structure. While our description of the poem's rhythm may seem already unduly complicated, one may add a further complication arising from the dipodic structure. Read the poem once more to a metronome, letting the beats come on *bring, thirst-, bear, leaves, wings, dews, rocked, moth-, wield, lash-, then, -solve.* You will find that it reads easily (though quickly) that way, and that within the pairs of feet in each half line there is a contrast in values. There is, in effect, a two-beat scheme operating concurrently with the four-beat scheme.

This analysis is a way of getting at the sound of the poem— whether it is read aloud or heard only by the mind's ear. Different readers will read the poem in slightly different ways, and the variations will reside in the answers the readers provide to the problems we have raised. These problems are real; the variations they result in when the poem is read aloud are significant. The best readings will accept Shelley's variations without permitting them to obscure the regularities. The mixture of rising and falling effects (reversals in expected patterns) is a part of the tension in the prosodic surface of the poem. *It is important not to let an arbitrary pattern of analysis override the variations which so clearly characterize Shelley's rhythm.*

From this discussion we may conclude that poetry is that literary art in which the words conveying the experience are arranged in a repeating pattern of units that are more or less equal to one another. The arrangement of elements determining the equalities may vary from poem to poem, from poet to poet, from period to period; but within any given poem it is likely to be constant. The elements themselves are essentially stress, accent, pitch, and time (including pause). In the poetry we have looked at thus far, the units tend to be equal either in time or in stress-accent patterning, or in some combination of these.

FREE VERSE

Free verse, however, complicates our analysis. No brief account can take cognizance of all the varieties of free verse (any more than it can examine all kinds of regular verse). Some kinds are so free as no longer to constitute verse at all, but only prose set down in broken lines on the page—bad free verse, and usually bad prose, too.

At its freest, free verse does not employ rhyme, nor does it employ regular meter. It does, however, have rhythm. Free verse may, on the other hand, employ rhyme and move fairly close to regular metrical effects. Suppose we look at a few passages of free verse to single out at least the most obvious elements of patterning.

T. S. Eliot's *The Waste Land* begins thus[11]

> April is the cruellest month, breeding
> Lilacs out of the dead land, mixing
> Memory and desire, stirring
> Dull roots with spring rain.
> Winter kept us warm, covering
> Earth in forgetful snow, feeding
> A little life with dried tubers.

It is difficult to see any precise patterning in syllable count, in stressing, or in kinds of feet employed. There is a clear syntactical patterning, however:

[11] From *Collected Poems 1909-1962* by T. S. Eliot, copyright, 1936, by Harcourt Brace Jovanovich, Inc.; copyright, © 1963, 1964 by T. S. Eliot. Reprinted by permission of Harcourt Brace Jovanovich, Inc. and Faber and Faber Ltd. See further notice on copyright page.

April is the cruellest month, / breeding
Lilacs out of the dead land, / mixing
Memory and desire, / stirring
Dull roots with spring rain.
Winter kept us warm, / covering
Earth in forgetful snow, / feeding
A little life with dried tubers.

This patterning may be described thus:

subject phrase	participle
object phrase	participle
object phrase	participle
object phrase	
subject phrase	participle
object phrase	participle
object phrase	

While the syllabic count of the lines is certainly not even, the lines are not strikingly uneven in length. The syntactical patterns (the isosyntactical units) are not lost sight of simply because the number of syllables per line varies. Notice that there is considerable patterning of assonance and alliteration, too, with augmentation and diminution and with acrostic scrambling.[12] It is difficult to think of verse so richly patterned being in any sense "free" verse!

The patterning in free verse, then, may be syntactical. The lines immediately following these in *The Waste Land* are even more complex in their syntactical pattern:

Summer surprised us, coming over the Starnbergersee
With a shower of rain; we stopped in the colonnade,
And went on in sunlight, into the Hofgarten,
And drank coffee, and talked for an hour.

The lines are again broken (as are many of the subsequent lines of the poem), but the break is not based on repetition of so obvious a syntactical pattern. Still, there *is* a pattern: "[verbal] over . . . Starnbergersee, with . . . shower of rain, [verb] in . . . colonnade, [verb] in sunlight, into . . . Hofgarten, [verb] for . . . hour." Furthermore, the verb-preposition-object pattern is accompanied by a sound pattern:

s . . . s . . . z . . . s . . . St . . . z
sh . . . st
s

[12] For definitions of these terms, with examples, see the Glossary (Appendix B).

One might go on, but it is dangerous to push the notion of sound repetition too far as an argument for distinguishing verse from prose, since prose too has repetitions of sounds. After all, there are only a certain number of sounds in the language, and they are bound to repeat. It is only when clear patterns are discernible that comment is particularly helpful.

But there is another aspect of patterning in the four lines from Eliot's poem: each line is made up of two speech phrases, or cadences. A *cadence,* literally, is a fall; it takes its name from the fall of the voice at the end of syntactical units, though, to be sure, the voice does not always fall at such points. The cadences in the four lines of *The Waste Land* are:

> Summer surprised us
> coming over the Starnbergersee
> with a shower of rain;
> we stopped in the colonnade,
> and went on in sunlight,
> into the Hofgarten,
> and drank coffee,
> and talked for an hour.

Strictly speaking, the second and third phrases constitute as single unit rather than two units, and you will notice that Eliot does not punctuate the line ending with Starnbergersee. All these phrases are roughly the same length, with the short ("and drank coffee") probably making up for its shortness by taking longer to pronounce because of the juncture in *nk c* ("drank coffee"). Notice that the effect of the lines when the speech phrases are written in separate lines is not at all the effect of the lines when two cadences are written in a single line. Eliot's own arrangement is less monotonous (because more varied in flow) than the simple use of a line for each cadence.

Much of the free verse in *The Waste Land* approaches blank verse—a kind of "as-if" iambic pentameter, which is itself a rhythmic effect. References to Shakespeare, and even quotation from Shakespeare in the text, heighten this illusion of blank verse (unrhymed iambic pentameter). Tags from ragtime music and from other poetry also set up rhythmic echoes:

> O O O O that Shakespeherian Rag
> It's so elegant
> So intelligent

Or:

> Sweet Thames, run softly, till I end my song

Again, in the same poem, still another kind of patterning by repetition of words:

> Here is no *water* but only *rock*
> *Rock* and no *water* and the sandy *road*
> The *road* winding above among the *mountains*
> Which are *mountains* of *rock* without *water*
> If there were *water* we should *stop* and *drink*
> Amongst the *rock* one cannot *stop* or *think*

The pattern here is elaborate and balanced:

water	rock						
	rock	water	road				
			road	mountains			
				mountains	rock	water	
						water	stop and drink
					rock		stop or think

This is complicated, in the last two lines, by the combination of repetition and rhyme in "stop and drink" and "stop or think." Such echoing, balance, hesitation, and allusion are characteristic of the poetic voice of T. S. Eliot. Examine the remainder of this section of *The Waste Land*,[13] and see how the pattern continues:

> Here is no water but only rock
> Rock and no water and the sandy road
> The road winding above among the mountains
> Which are mountains of rock without water
> If there were water we should stop and drink
> Amongst the rock one cannot stop or think
> Sweat is dry and feet are in the sand
> If there were only water amongst the rock
> Dead mountain mouth of carious teeth that cannot spit
> Here one can neither stand nor lie nor sit
> There is not even silence in the mountains
> But dry sterile thunder without rain
> There is not even solitude in the mountains
> But red sullen faces sneer and snarl
> From doors of mudcracked houses
>   If there were water
> And no rock
> If there were rock
> And also water

[13] From "The Waste Land" in *Collected Poems 1909–1962* by T. S. Eliot, copyright 1936, by Harcourt Brace Jovanovich, Inc.; copyright © 1963, 1964 by T. S. Eliot. Reprinted by permission of the publishers and Faber and Faber Ltd. See further notice on copyright page.

> And water
> A spring
> A pool among the rock
> If there were the sound of water only
> Not the cicada
> And dry grass singing
> But sound of water over a rock
> Where the hermit-thrush sings in the pine trees
> Drip drop drip drop drop drop drop
> But there is no water

Free verse may be patterned very closely in terms of temporal units. Look again at the poem by William Carlos Williams on page 90 of this book. "This is just to say" would not really be a poem at all if it were printed thus:

> I have eaten the plums that were in the
> icebox, and which you were probably saving for
> breakfast. Forgive me. They were delicious—
> so sweet and so cold.

One might break the passage up this way, and move closer to a discernible pattern:

> I have eaten the plums
> That were in the icebox
> And which you were probably saving for breakfast.
>
> Forgive me,
> They were delicious.
> So sweet and so cold.

This would give us two stanzas, the first two lines in each stanza constituting a speech phrase and the third line consisting of two speech phrases. Each of the shorter lines might be heightened by employing a slight pause at the end of it.

But notice that Williams heightens the *tensiveness* of the lines by shortening them still further, giving us three sections of four lines each. Now try reading the poem to the beat of a metronome, letting the *tick* come on the syllables *eat-, plums, in, ice-, which, prob-, sav-, break-, -give, -li-, sweet, cold.* Now try once more, letting the *tick* of the metronome fall on these same words, but allowing an *extra tick* between, so that we get *eat-* extra tick *plums* extra tick, and so on. This magnifies the attention to each of the single lines. Notice now that the extra tick added at the end of each line makes possible an interesting effect. Imagine a husband writing the poem as a note to his wife after he has raided the icebox. Allow him a wry sense of humor mingled with his apology. As you read the poem aloud with this kind of temporal movement in mind, imagine yourself to be writing as you speak. It takes longer to write than to speak; the extra *tick* you allow at the end of each line will give you time to finish the writing. Tensiveness now exists between the spoken and the written line, whether or not you are *literally* writing. It is the strong promotion of temporality which makes "This is just to say" a poem and not a prose note. The pattern of repetition is not that of meter, nor of rhyme, nor of pairing of sounds, but a pattern clearly exists. It is a pattern of temporal cadences.

Examine the poem "But he was cool," by Don L. Lee, on pages 30–31 of this text. What reason do you find for the arrangement of the poem on the page? And to what extent is it possible to carry the print-arrangement over into performance?

Look at the William Stafford poem, "Fifteen," on pages 32–33. Do you find in the lines a fairly even pattern of stresses per line (i.e., a count of *stresses,* not of *feet*)? How does the repeated "I was fifteen," with the variation in its placement in the last stanza, function in the structure? The five-line stanzas also lend pattern.

Free verse may be a highly modified variant of a traditional metrical pattern or a mixture of patterns. It is clear, too, that our print-orientation (as contrasted with an aural/oral orientation) affects patterns of poems on the page. Of some of these poems we shall speak later.

Perhaps enough has been said to show that free verse can be described as patterned. It is probably safe to say that unless verse is patterned, it is not verse at all, since by definition verse is based on return. Poetry, whether regular or free, comes in waves of sound and sense, rising and falling and falling over its own rising, and mixing and mingling its parts in its rising and falling, from boundary to boundary. But the figure will not express all: a poem, like a story or a play, tends to reach the peak of its movement somewhere not too far from its close, but not at its close. All the temporal arts—music, song, dance—follow this pattern, which is again an alternating of tensions and a return. Essentially, this is what we have called the form of the *act*.

In describing patterns in free verse, one must be wary of attributing too much to the mere fact of cadence. After all, prose too has cadence; cadence is inherent in language. One does not make poetry by chopping prose up into lines of about the same number of syllables.

Here is a list of the most frequently encountered stanzaic arrangements:

STANZAIC PATTERNS

couplet	two lines of verse, usually rhymed[14]
heroic couplet	a couplet in iambic pentameter lines, or decasyllabic lines; the couplet is said to be *closed* when it contains a complete thought

[14] While the couplet may be a stanzaic form, in its rhymed form it often functions as an element in more complicated stanza patterns. See, for example, the concluding couplet in the passage quoted earlier from Byron's *Don Juan.* Couplets may be *open* or *closed.* Open couplets are run-on (see the Glossary for a definition of this term.)

tercet or triplet	three rhyming lines of verse
terza rima	tercets in a pattern rhyming as follows: *aba bcb cdc ded* (etc.)
quatrain	four-line stanza; a special form is the ballad stanza (alternating iambic tetrameter and trimeter rhyming *abcd*)
quintet	five-line stanza
sestet	six-line stanza
sestina	a special kind of sestet arrangement: six six-line stanzas, the last word in each of the six lines repeated in a different order in each stanza, and a three-line envoy using all six of these six words
septet	seven-line stanza; a special form is called *rime royal* because King James I of Scotland used it: it is seven lines of iambic pentameter rhyming *ababbcc*
octave	eight-line stanza; *ottava rima* is rhyme in eight-line stanzas arranged *abababcc*
Spenserian stanza	a nine-line stanza made up of eight lines of iambic pentameter followed by a hexameter line (an Alexandrine) rhyming *ababbcbcc*
sonnet	originally any short, song-like lyric, the term now refers specifically to lyrics in fourteen lines (normally but not necessarily iambic pentameter); the Shakespearean (English) sonnet rhymes *ababcdcdefefgg* and is particularly characterized by the concluding couplet; the Petrarchan (Italian) sonnet has an octave rhyming *abbaabba* and a sestet with a varying rhyme scheme; the Petrarchan sonnet normally has a marked transition between octave and sestet.

Other highly specialized forms from the French are the rondeau, rondel, villanelle, and triolet, all of which appear occasionally in English verse. (See the Glossary.)

LITERARY MODES AND TYPES

Another kind of poetic classification cuts across such divisions by stanzaic arrangements and attempts to get at matters of perspective, locus, and presence. James Joyce's extensions of Aristotle's terms *lyric, epic,* and *dramatic* are useful here, though they refer to both poetry and prose. *Lyric* is that mode in which the writer stands in most immediate relation to the audience (seeming to speak directly to us in his own person); *epic* is that mode in which the writer (or a narrator speaking as if he were the author) speaks in part directly to us and in part through characters who appear to speak for themselves; *dramatic* is that mode in which the writer is entirely submerged and speaks to us only through characters. Some critics prefer the term *narrative mode* to *epic mode,* since *epic* as a term also applies to a particular *kind* of narratives—those telling the story of large-scale, heroic individuals (Ulysses, Aeneas, God, Satan, for example). But *narrative* has difficulties as a term for the mode, too, since it is sometimes used simply to mean *stories* as distinguished from *plays* or *poems*. Whichever term is used (and we are using *epic*), it is important to remember that *modality* cuts across literary *genres*.

Remember that we are talking not about the performer, but about the writer. A performer reading one of Hamlet's soliloquies may choose to address the soliloquy directly to the audience, but the mode is still dramatic, not lyric, since the writer is submerged in the character. Thus a poem like Tennyson's *Ulysses*, in which the speaker is the Homeric hero Ulysses, is in the dramatic mode; Keats's sonnet "When I Have Fears that I May Cease to Be" is in the lyric mode; the following stanza from "Sir Patrick Spens" is in the epic mode:

> The king sits in Dumferling town,
>   Drinking the blood-red wine:
> "O where will I get a good sailor
>   To sail this ship of mine?"

because the first two lines are the words of the narrator while the last two lines are the words of a character, the king. These are matters of the greatest importance to the oral interpreter, involving both the source of the words and the angle of vision.

Nevertheless, these modal terms provide difficulties for the critic. Is it necessary, for example, to assume that the "I" of a sonnet is the writer of the sonnet? Keats himself said that it was not. What about Arnold's "Dover Beach"? Must one assume that Arnold himself is the speaker, or that the second person in the poem is Mrs. Arnold? (See pp. 416–419 in connection with the discussion of the persona in personal documents.) It is clear that the terms must be employed with caution, but they are of use to the performer in deciding questions of locus and in exploring the question of characterization.

Another set of terms may be used to define kinds of subject matter. The *elegy* is today thought of as a poem employing a particular kind of subject matter—eulogy of the dead—though originally it was simply a poem written in elegiac meter. The *ode* is thought of as a poem of praise. The *epic* is thought of as a poem about wars and heroes.

Still another kind of classification cuts across divisions by mode and subject matter. The *popular ballad* is written in the ballad stanza (see the definition under the stanza form *quatrain*) and is normally either epic or dramatic in mode and frequently tragic in theme, with strong supernatural elements. The *metrical romance* or *metical tale* is a story in verse form. The *literary ballad* is rather like the popular ballad but it has a single known author. The *lyric* (not now in Aristotle's sense) is frequently classified according to subject matter (ode, for example), perspective (descriptive lyric, dramatic lyric, song, dramatic monologue) or form (ballad, rondeau, rondel, triolet, villanelle); in this sense, lyric refers to poetry that is subjective in attitude, usually short in form, and musical in feeling.

There was a time, prior to our print orientation, when *lyric* referred specifically to poems meant to be sung or chanted; hence our association of "musical" with the modern term. But with the advent of print and the habit of reading rather than listening to poetry, few or no distinctions were made between the song-lyric and the print-lyric, despite the fact that melodic accompaniment now was normally lacking. The basic consideration seems to be that *lyric* points to something essentially musical in the structure even in the absence of musical accompaniment—subtle weaving of consonantal and assonantal patterns, rise and fall of cadences, and so on. Lyrics more often than not explore subjective emotional states. Lyrical elements can, however, be found in other genres and not simply in poems which can be designated as lyrics.

These terms (inadequate though many of them seem at times), are useful in attempts to separate poems from one another and to separate kinds from kinds. They are useful in helping to determine the nature of the body that oral readers must seek to reembody. We cannot fit ourselves to something we do not understand. In some respects, we naturally assume the shape of the literature we read, but in other respects the art of assuming literary shapes must be consciously studied. Remember that critical terms have functions; they are not the masters but the helpers of the interpreter. Do not be surprised when such terms overlap; not all sets of terms attempt to define the same things. While it is helpful to say of a poem that it is a descriptive lyric or a reflective lyric, it is naïve to assume that the terms will answer all questions about perspective, locus, and tensions; they will distinguish a descriptive or reflective lyric from a dramatic monologue, but will not distinguish one descriptive lyric from another—hence such terms are *generally* useful to the interpreter, but not quite *specifically* helpful. As a presence, each poem is individual.

CONCRETE POETRY

Finally, we must recognize the existence of a kind of poetry that has drawn new attention since the 1950s. Though what we have to say about it here may seem tangential to the views we have been examining, the popularity of the form is clear.

Concrete poets vary greatly in their aims and views; it is difficult to say succinctly (even for the poets themselves) what the movement embraces in its entirety. On the whole, however, the terse statement made in 1952 by the founders of *Noigandres,* a Brazilian review devoted to concretism, seems useful: "Concrete poetry: tension of object-words in the time-space continuum; dynamic structures; multiplicity of concomitant movements."[15]

Concrete poetry juxtaposes words and optical signs to produce what frequently amount to ideograms—calligraphic signs with both visual and symbolic values, as in Japanese and Chinese writing. But these ideograms, or visual structures, are largely free from the traditional re-

[15] One of the most comprehensive and beautiful books on concrete poetry is Mary Ellen Solt's *Concrete Poetry: A World View* (Bloomington: Indiana University Press, 1968). The comments on Mike Weaver may be found on p. 7 of Solt's introduction. See also Eugene Wildman, *The Chicago Review Anthology of Concretism* (Chicago: Swallow Press, 1967), and Emmet Williams, *An Anthology of Concrete Poetry* (New York: Something Else Press, Inc., 1967).

strictions of language and syntax, and they are meant to produce an immediate sensing in the perceiver. They are unparaphrasable. Words, where whole words appear (often they do not, only fragments appear), are used like building blocks. It is usual to respond to the structures in the spirit of a game. While there is some overlapping between the terms *concrete poetry* and *visual prosody* (i.e., poems with visual prosody are also visual structures), concrete poetry frees itself from linear organization in a way often not achieved by traditional visual prosodic structures. In the materials to be found at the end of this chapter, for example, "Easter Wings" presents us with a visual form which underscores the linguistic "argument" of the poem. But the argument could be understood very well without the prosodic (print) arrangement. In contemporary concrete poems, more is at stake than pictures which reflect argument. The concretion in print, for concrete poetry, is the thing itself.

When isolated words are employed (sometimes in almost endless repetition), the words themselves are meant to create a field of force, a field of meaning in which the reader often must contribute as much as the writer. It is important for the reader of concrete poetry to feel free to *help* the poet create; his participation is necessary.

Concrete poets (though some of them do not like the name) are engaged in a process that recurs, historically, among writers: the attempt to free words, language, from old bondages placed on words by meter, syntax, and associations of many kinds. The material of concrete poetry is *language,* but language thought of as not tied to emotions or to ideas. Concrete poetry emphasizes the physical material—language—which constitutes the building material of the poet and attempts to reinstitute or reconstitute the force of words and letters in themselves.

The critic Mike Weaver speaks of three general types of concrete poems: visual or optic; phonetic or sound-based; kinetic or movement-based. Cutting across these, he sees two other classifications: constructivist and expressionistic, the first type arising from a self-dictating scheme of arrangement set up by the poet, the second an intuitive structure.

In an essay discussing concrete poems as material for interpretation, Francine Merritt gives another set of kinds, pointing additionally to codes, anagrams, directions of reading, and happenings or chances. She quotes Eugen Gomringer as urging the reader's cooperation with the poet in bringing the concrete poem to fulfillment and suggests that much concrete poetry is intended to be voiced, despite some disclaimers, She speaks eloquently of the poem "Temor," by Mario da Silva Brito, in which *temor* ("fear") is repeated ten times in a vertical column, followed by a single *morte* ("death") in an adjacent column, saying, "Given the voiced repetitions even as auditory imagery, there follows for some readers a strange verbal magic—an auditory transposition of syllables comparable to reversible perspective—so that one hears now and again a shadowy ironic joining of the second syllable of one line to the first of the next, producing 'mor-te' even before the finality of the

"Talk Walk Talk Walk" by Kriwet

second column is reached. Either an oral reading or a silent reading slowed sufficiently to permit the mind's ear to operate can convert columns of repetitious print into a profound statement with haunting ambiguities."[16] All this, she points out, disappears if the poem is translated into English with *fear* and *death* as the two terms.

Another teacher of interpretation, Janet Larsen McHughes, explores *presence* in concrete poetry as in part a function of *absence*. Filled time and space are juxtaposed with empty or still time and space. Repetition becomes a prosodic device of major importance (as in the poem *silencio* on the next page.) Word length and line length often exist in a tensive relationship. Visual patterns may provide analogues for natural phenomena (the poem may assume the shape of a flower, the shifting form of the wind); or sound patterns may point to significant semantic intentions in the poem, producing what McHughes calls "sound-drama."[17] She concludes that "in concrete poetry, space is charged with experiential qualities; space, not time, is the dimensional axis from which the poem emerges, and is indeed a new *poesis*." She is doubtless correct in arguing that prosody, in addition to analyzing felt *time* in poetry, must learn to take into account felt *space*.

With some concrete poetry the oral performer is relatively helpless: the quality of the print itself is often an essential part of the effect, so that the poems are a poetry of print rather than a poetry of utterance. But the gestures of the printed, optical signs may be given a correspondence in oral performance (which, after all, also employs visual signs), and interpreters may indeed enjoy the game of trying to find such correspondence. What, for example, might you do with this? (*Silencio* means "silence.")

silencio   silencio   silencio

silencio   silencio   silencio

silencio   silencio

silencio   silencio   silencio

silencio   silencio   silencio

[16] From "Concrete Poetry—*Verbivocovisual*," *Speech Teacher*, 18 (March 1969), 109–14. Reprinted by permission of the *Speech Teacher*. See also her article "eyear: Shape/Sound Concrete Poetry" (*Southern Speech Journal* 34 [Spring 1969, 213–224), in which she gives a brief background of the movement.

[17] Janet Larsen McHughes, "The Poesis of Space: Prosodic Structures in Concrete Poetry," *Quarterly Journal of Speech*, 63 (1977), 168–79. The statement quoted below is on p. 178.

The poem is by Eugen Gomringer,[18] a Swiss writer (..lled by Emmet Williams the "acknowledged father of concrete poetry") who has been one of the major informers of concretism. Notice that the word *silencio,* while it means "silence," has sound value for you. It is almost impossible not to say it as you read. But the void in the center of the poem *is* silence, and the empty space serves to underscore and to give life to the "sound" which surrounds it. Can you achieve this effect with a group of readers, using them as "sounding building blocks" to create a form? (Would it be easier if the readers were to be seen from overhead?) Might you use recorded sounds in conjunction with silent readers? (Concrete poetry in such forms overlaps matters discussed in the later chapter on group performances.)

Now look at the next poem by Haroldo de Campos,[19] of Brazil.

speech
silver

    silence
    gold

        heads
        silver

            tails
            gold

                speech
                silence

            stop

    silver   **golden**
    silence   **speech**

                        clarity

What do you make of the order in which the words are arranged, with both gold and silver coupled with speech and with silence? Why *golden* rather than *gold* at the "end" of the poem? Why does the word *stop* appear where it does? And how is *clarity* related to the other words? Finally, why the startling insertion of the words *heads* and *tails?*

---

[18] Reprinted by permission of the author, whose complete constellations 1951–1968 were published in 1969 by the Rowohlt Verlag Reinbek Bei, Hamburg, Germany.

[19] From *Concrete Poetry: A World View,* edited and translated by Mary Ellen Solt. Copyright © 1968 by Hispanic Arts, Indiana University. Reprinted by permission of Indiana University Press.

Do you get something of the effect of two sides of the same coin, a coin consisting of both gold and silver, a coin both silent and speaking? Seen as an *act,* can you perform the poem so that the climax comes with *stop,* followed by a cadence that issues in *clarity?* Does it help—or get in the way—if you employ a group of readers, perhaps using one reader for each word? Would you use a single reader for *stop* and for *clarity,* or would you use groups for those words? What is involved in your answer?

Immediately below is another form, by Décio Pignatari,[20] a fellow Brazilian who with de Campos was a founder of *Noigandres.* It employs the type found in a cover-page heading of the magazine *Life.* Notice

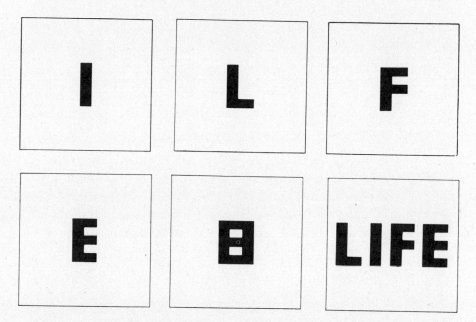

that the visual element now becomes even more difficult for the oral performer. Has it become *too* difficult to make the poem useful for the interpreter? Are we, perhaps, at a point where we must move from considerations of the capacities of the solo performer and consider the function of groups, with visual and auditory accompaniments beyond the voice and body of the performer? Things can be accomplished by groups of performers that the solo interpreter can never achieve. The minimal movement that often serves the single reader well may require radical alteration in group interpretation. Consider, for these poems and the additional concrete poems at the end of the practice materials, the contributions that can be made by several performers working together.

Emmet Williams speaks of concrete poetry in the 1950s as "a poetry of direct presentation—the *word, not words, words, words* or ex-

[20] From *Antologia Noigandres.* Printed in *Lugano Review* 1 (1966), 5–6. Reprinted by permission of the *Lugano Review.*

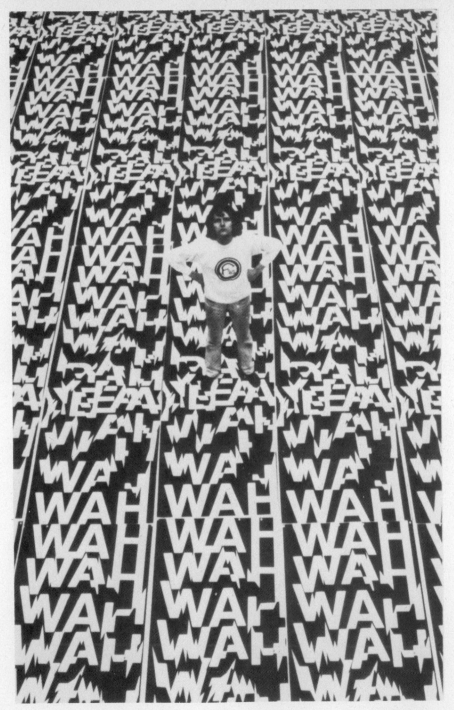

"WAH" BY Kriwet

pressionistic squiggles—using the semantic, visual, and phonetic elements of language as raw materials in a way seldom used by the poets of the past. It was a kind of game, perhaps, but so is life,"[21] and he speaks of the diversity of aims and kinds that have come to flourish since those beginnings.

Perhaps one of the most useful views for the interpreter is that of Gomringer himself: "thus the new poem will be simple and perceivable both as a whole & in its parts. It will be something to be seen & used but also something to be thought of: object of thought in a play of ideas. it will work through brevity & compression. it will be memorable & (as image) easy-to-remember. it will serve man through its objective play elements, as the poet will serve him through his special knack for just this kind of play: for the poet is an expert in the principles of play & language, the inventor of their future formulations."[22] Concrete poetry, in short, shares with other literature—and with life itself—radical (root) interests in tension, movement, environment.

MATERIALS FOR PRACTICE

Consider prosodic effects in the poems that follow, relating them where you can to problems of meaning. Try to classify the poems by kinds. Consult the Glossary (Appendix B) for terms.

I KNEW A WOMAN[23]
—Theodore Roethke

I knew a woman, lovely in her bones,
When small birds sighed, she would sigh back at them;
Ah, when she moved, she moved more ways than one:
The shapes a bright container can contain!
Of her choice virtues only gods should speak,
Or English poets who grew up on Greek
(I'd have them sing in chorus, cheek to cheek.)

How well her wishes went! She stroked my chin,
She taught me Turn, and Counter-turn, and Stand;
She taught me Touch, that undulant white skin;
I nibbled meekly from her proffered hand;
She was the sickle; I, poor I, the rake,
Coming behind her for her pretty sake
(But what prodigious mowing we did make).

[21] *Anthology of Concrete Poetry* (New York: Something Else Press, Inc., 1967), p. vi.

[22] From the preface to *The Book of Hours and Constellations* (New York: Something Else Press, Inc., 1968). Reprinted by permission of the author.

[23] Copyright 1954 by Theodore Roethke, *The Collected Poems of Theodore Roethke*. Reprinted by permission of Doubleday & Company, Inc.

Love likes a gander, and adores a goose:
Her full lips pursed, the errant note to seize;
She played it quick, she played it light and loose;
My eyes, they dazzled at her flowing knees;
Her several parts could keep a pure repose,
Or one hip quiver with a mobile nose
(She moved in circles, and those circles moved).

Let seed be grass, and grass turn into hay:
I'm martyr to a motion not my own;
What's freedom for? To know eternity.
I swear she cast a shadow white as stone.
But who would count eternity in days?
These old bones live to learn her wanton ways:
(I measure time by how a body sways).

THE SERPENT[24]
—Theodore Roethke

There was a Serpent who had to sing.
There was. There was.
He simply gave up Serpenting.
Because. Because.

He didn't like his Kind of Life;
He couldn't find a proper Wife;
He was a Serpent with a soul;
He got no Pleasure down his Hole.
And so, of course, he had to Sing,
And Sing he did, like Anything!
The Birds, they were, they were Astounded;
And various Measures Propounded
To stop the Serpent's Awful Racket:
They bought a Drum. He wouldn't Whack it.
They sent,—you always send,—to Cuba
And got a Most Commodious Tuba;
They got a Horn, they got a Flute,
But Nothing would suit.
He said, "Look, Birds, all this is futile:
I do *not* like to Bang or Tootle."
And then he cut loose with a Horrible Note
That practically split the Top of his Throat.
"You see," he said, with a Serpent's Leer,
"I'm Serious about my Singing Career!"
And the Woods Resounded with many a Shriek
As the Birds flew off to the End of Next Week.

THE ROUNDEL
—Algernon Charles Swinburne

A roundel is wrought as a ring or a star-bright sphere,
With craft of delight and with cunning of sound unsought,
That the heart of the hearer may smile if to pleasure his ear
    A roundel is wrought.

Its jewel of music is carven of all or of aught—
Love, laughter, or mourning—remembrance of rapture or fear—
That fancy may fashion to hang in the ear of thought.

As a bird's quick song runs round, and the hearts in us hear
Pause answer to pause, and again the same strain caught,
So moves the device whence, round as a pearl or tear,
    A roundel is wrought.

TRIOLET[25]
—Robert Bridges

When first we met we did not guess
That Love would prove so hard a master;
Of more than common friendliness
When first we met we did not guess.
Who could foretell this sore distress,
This irretrievable disaster
When first we met?—We did not guess
That Love would prove so hard a master.

PAYSAGE MORALISÉ[26]
—W. H. Auden

Hearing of harvests rotting in the valleys,
Seeing at end of street the barren mountains,
Round corners coming suddenly on water,
Knowing them shipwrecked who were launched for islands,
We honour founders of these starving cities
Whose honour is the image of our sorrow,

Which cannot see its likeness in their sorrow,
That brought them desperate to the brink of valleys;
Dreaming of evening walks through learned cities

[25] Reprinted by permission of the Oxford University Press
[26] Copyright 1937 and renewed 1965 by W. H. Auden. Reprinted from *Collected Poems* by W. H. Auden, edited by Edward Mendelson, by permission of Random House, Inc., and Faber and Faber Ltd.

They reined their violent horses on the mountains,
Those fields like ships to castaways on islands,
Visions of green to them who craved for water.

They built by rivers and at night the water
Running past windows comforted their sorrow;
Each in his little bed conceived of islands
Where every day was dancing in the valleys
And all the green trees blossomed on the mountains
Where love was innocent, being far from cities.

But dawn came back and they were still in cities;
No marvelous creature rose up from the water;
There was still gold and silver in the mountains
But hunger was a more immediate sorrow,
Although to moping villagers in valleys
Some waving pilgrims were describing islands . . .

"The gods," they promise, "visit us from islands,
Are stalking, head-up, lovely, through our cities;
Now is the time to leave your wretched valleys
And sail with them across the lime-green water,
Sitting at their white sides, forget your sorrow,
The shadow cast across your lives by mountains."

So many, doubtful, perished in the mountains,
Climbing up crags to get a view of islands,
So many, fearful, took with them their sorrow
Which stayed them when they reached unhappy cities,
So many, careless, dived and drowned in water,
So many, wretched, would not leave their valleys.

It is our sorrow. Shall it melt? Ah, water
Would gush, flush, green these mountains and these valleys,
And we rebuild our cities, not dream of islands.

THE FLEA
—John Donne

Mark but this flea, and mark in this
How little that which thou deny'st me is;
It suck'd me first, and now sucks thee,
And in this flea our two bloods mingled be;
Thou know'st that this cannot be said
A sin, nor shame, nor loss of maidenhead,
    Yet this enjoys before it woo,
    And pamper'd swells with one blood made of two,
    And this, alas, is more than we would do.

Oh stay, three lives in one flea spare,
Where we almost, yea more than married are;

This flea is you and I, and this
Our marriage bed and marriage temple is.
Though parents grudge, and you, we'are met
And cloistered in these living walls of jet.
    Though use make you apt to kill me,
    Let not to that, self murder added be,
    And sacrilege, three sins in killing three.

Cruel and sudden, hast thou since
Purpled thy nail in blood of innocence?
Wherein could this flea guilty be,
Except in that drop which it sucked from thee?
Yet thou triumph'st, and say'st that thou
Find'st not thyself nor me the weaker now.
    'Tis true; then learn how false fears be;
    Just so much honor, when thou yield'st to me,
    Will waste, as this flea's death took life from thee.

LUCIFER IN STARLIGHT
—George Meredith

On a starred night Prince Lucifer uprose.
Tired of his dark dominion, swung the fiend
Above the rolling ball, in cloud part screened,
Where sinners hugged their specter of repose.
Poor prey to his hot fit of pride were those.
And now upon his western wing he leaned,
Now his huge bulk o'er Afric's sands careened,
Now the black planet shadowed Arctic snows.
Soaring through wider zones that pricked his scars
With memory of the old revolt from Awe,
He reached a middle height, and at the stars,
Which are the brain of heaven, he looked, and sank.
Around the ancient track marched, rank on rank,
The army of unalterable law.

VIRTUE
—George Herbert

Sweet day, so cool, so calm, so bright,
The bridal of the earth and sky:
The dew shall weep thy fall tonight,
        For thou must die.

Sweet rose, whose hue angry and brave
Bids the rash gazer wipe his eye:
Thy root is ever in its grave,
        And thou must die.

Sweet spring, full of sweet days, and roses,
A box where sweets compacted lie;
My music shows ye have your closes,
      And all must die.

Only a sweet and virtuous soul,
Like season'd timber, never gives;
But though the whole world turn to coal,
      Then chiefly lives.

SONNET 73
—William Shakespeare

That time of year thou mayst in me behold
When yellow leaves, or none, or few, do hang
Upon those boughs which shake against the cold,
Bare, ruin'd choirs, where late the sweet birds sang.
In me thou seest the twilight of such day
As after sunset fadeth in the west,
Which by and by black night doth take away,
Death's second self, that seals up all in rest.
In me thou seest the glowing of such fire
That on the ashes of his youth doth lie,
As the death-bed whereon it must expire,
Consum'd with that which it was nourish'd by.
  This thou perceiv'st, which makes thy love more strong,
  To love that well, which thou must leave ere long.

SONNET 129
—William Shakespeare

Th'expense of spirit in a waste of shame
Is lust in action, and till action, lust
Is perjur'd, murd'rous, bloody, full of blame,
Savage, extreme, rude, cruel, not to trust,
Enjoy'd no sooner but despised straight,
Past reason hunted, and no sooner had,
Past reason hated as a swallowed bait
On purpose laid to make the taker mad:
Mad in pursuit, and in possession so;
Had, having, and in quest to have, extreme,
A bliss in proof, and prov'd, a very woe;
Before, a joy propos'd; behind, a dream.
  All this the world well knows, yet none knows well
  To shun the heaven that leads men to this hell.

MY LAST DUCHESS
Ferrara

—*Robert Browning*

That's my last Duchess painted on the wall,
Looking as if she were alive. I call
That piece a wonder, now: Frá Pandolf's hands
Worked busily a day, and there she stands.
Will't please you sit and look at her? I said
"Frá Pandolf" by design, for never read
Strangers like you that pictured countenance,
The depth and passion of its earnest glance,
But to myself they turned (since none puts by
The curtain I have drawn for you, but I)
And seemed as they would ask me, if they durst,
How such a glance came there; so, not the first
Are you to turn and ask thus. Sir, 'twas not
Her husband's presence only, called that spot
Of joy into the Duchess' cheek: perhaps
Frá Pandolf chanced to say "Her mantle laps
Over my lady's wrist too much," or "Paint
Must never hope to reproduce the faint
Half-flush that dies along her throat"; such stuff
Was courtesy, she thought, and cause enough
For calling up that spot of joy. She had
A heart—how shall I say?—too soon made glad,
Too easily impressed; she liked whate'er
She looked on, and her looks went everywhere.
Sir, 'twas all one! My favor at her breast,
The dropping of the daylight in the West,
The bough of cherries some officious fool
Broke in the orchard for her, the white mule
She rode with round the terrace—all and each
Would draw from her alike the approving speech,
Or blush, at least. She thanked men—good! but thanked
Somehow—I know not how— as if she ranked
My gift of a nine-hundred-years-old name
With anybody's gift. Who'd stoop to blame
This sort of trifling? Even had you skill
In speech—(which I have not)—to make your will
Quite clear to such an one, and say, "Just this
Or that in you disgusts me; here you miss,
Or there exceed the mark"—and if she let
Herself be lessoned so, nor plainly set
Her wits to yours, forsooth, and made excuse
—E'en then would be some stooping; and I choose
Never to stoop. Oh sir, she smiled, no doubt,
Whene'er I passed her; but who passed without
Much the same smile? This grew; I gave commands;

Then all smiles stopped together. There she stands
As if alive. Will't please you rise? We'll meet
The company below, then. I repeat,
The Count your master's known munificence
Is ample warrant that no just pretense
Of mine for dowry will be disallowed;
Though his fair daughter's self, as I avowed
At starting, is my object. Nay, we'll go
Together down, sir. Notice Neptune, though,
Taming a sea horse, thought a rarity,
Which Claus of Innsbruck cast in bronze for me!

PSALM 19
—The Holy Bible (King James Version)

The heavens declare the glory of God; and the firmament sheweth his
    handywork.
Day unto day uttereth speech, and night unto night sheweth
    knowledge.
There is no speech nor language, where their voice is not heard.
Their line is gone out through all the earth, and their words to the
    end of the world. In them hath he set a tabernacle for the sun.
Which is as a bridegroom coming out of his chamber, and rejoiceth as
    a strong man to run a race.
His going forth is from the end of the heaven, and his circuit unto the
    ends of it: and there is nothing hid from the heat thereof.
The law of the Lord is perfect, converting the soul; the testimony of
    the Lord is sure, making wise the simple.
The statutes of the Lord are right, rejoicing the heart; the
    commandment of the Lord is pure, enlightening the eyes.
The fear of the Lord is clean, enduring for ever; the judgments of the
    Lord are true and righteous altogether.
More to be desired are they than gold, yea, than much fine gold:
    sweeter also than honey and the honeycomb.
Moreover by them is thy servant warned: and in keeping of them
    there is great reward.
Who can understand his errors? cleanse thou me from secret faults.
Keep back thy servant also from presumptuous sins; let them not have
    dominion over me: then shall I be upright, and I shall be
    innocent from the great transgression.
Let the words of my mouth, and the meditation of my heart, be
    acceptable in thy sight, O Lord, my strength, and my redeemer.

from SONG OF MYSELF
—Walt Whitman

I have said that the soul is not more than the body,
And I have said that the body is not more than the soul,
And nothing, not God, is greater to one than one's self is,

And whoever walks a furlong without sympathy walks to his own
      funeral drest in his shroud,
And I or you pocketless of a dime may purchase the pick of the earth,
And to glance with an eye or show a bean in its pod confounds the
      learning of all times,
And there is no trade or employment but the young man following it
      may become a hero,
And there is no object so soft but it makes a hub for the wheel'd
      universe,
And I say to any man or woman, Let your soul stand cool and
      composed before a million universes.

And I say to mankind, Be not curious about God,
For I who am curious about each am not curious about God,
(No array of terms can say how much I am at peace about God and
      about death.)
I hear and behold God in every object, yet understand God not in the
      least,
Nor do I understand who there can be more wonderful than myself.
Why should I wish to see God better than this day?
I see something of God each hour of the twenty-four, and each
      moment then,
In the faces of men and women I see God, and in my own face in the
      glass,
I find letters from God dropt in the street, and every one is signed by
      God's name,
And I leave them where they are, for I know that wheresoe'er I go,
Others will punctually come for ever and ever.

A POSTCARD FROM THE VOLCANO[27]
—Wallace Stevens

Children picking up our bones
Will never know that these were once
As quick as foxes on the hill;

And that in autumn, when the grapes
Made sharp air sharper by their smell
These had a being, breathing frost;

And least will guess that with our bones
We left much more, left what still is
The look of things, left what we felt

At what we saw. The spring clouds blow
Above the shuttered mansion-house,
Beyond our gate and the windy sky

Cries out a literate despair.
We knew for long the mansion's look
And what we said of it became

A part of what it is . . . Children,
Still weaving budded aureoles,
Will speak our speech and never know,

Will say of the mansion that it seems
As if he that lived there left behind
A spirit storming in blank walls,

A dirty house in a gutted world,
A tatter of shadows peaked to white,
Smeared with the gold of the opulent sun.

THE GIFT OUTRIGHT[28]
—Robert Frost

The land was ours before we were the land's.
She was our land more than a hundred years
Before we were her people. She was ours
In Massachusetts, in Virginia,
But we were England's still colonials,
Possessing what we still were unpossessed by,
Possessed by what we now no more possessed.
Something we were withholding made us weak
Until we found out that it was ourselves
We were withholding from our land of living,
And forthwith found salvation in surrender.
Such as we were we gave ourselves outright
(The deed of gift was many deeds of war)
To the land vaguely realizing westward,
But still unstoried, artless, unenhanced,
Such as she was, such as she would become.

ANYONE LIVED IN A PRETTY HOW TOWN[29]

—e.e. cummings

anyone lived in a pretty how town
(with up so floating many bells down)
spring summer autumn winter
he sang his didn't he danced his did.

Women and men(both little and small)
cared for anyone not at all
they sowed their isn't they reaped their same
sun moon stars rain

children guessed(but only a few
and down they forgot as up they grew
autumn winter spring summer)
that noone loved him more by more

when by now and tree by leaf
she laughed his joy she cried his grief
bird by snow and stir by still
anyone's any was all to her

someones married their everyones
laughed their cryings and did their dance
(sleep wake hope and then)they
said their nevers they slept their dream

stars rain sun moon
(and only the snow can begin to explain
how children are apt to forget to remember
with up so floating many bells down)

one day anyone died i guess
(and noone stooped to kiss his face)
busy folk buried them side by side
little by little and was by was

all by all and deep by deep
and more by more they dream their sleep
noone and anyone earth by april
wish by spirit and if by yes.

Women and men(both dong and ding)
summer autumn winter spring
reaped their sowing and went their came
sun moon stars rain

SOPHOCLES SAYS[30]
—William Stafford

History is a story God is telling,
by means of hidden meanings written closely
inside the skins of things. Far over the sun
lonesome curves are meeting, and in the clouds
birds bend the wind. Hunting a rendezvous,
soft as snowflakes ride through a storm their pattern down,
men hesitate a step, touched by home.

A man passes among strangers; he never smiles;
the way a flame goes begging among the trees
he goes, and he suffers, himself, the kind of dark
that anything sent from God experiences,
until he finds through trees the lights of a town—
a street, the houses blinded in the rain—
and he hesitates a step, shocked—at home.

For God will take a man, no matter where,
and make some scene a part of what goes on:
there will be a flame; there will be a snowflake form;
and riding with the birds, wherever they are,
bending the wind, finding a rendezvous
beyond the sun or under the earth—that man
will hesitate a step—and meet his home.

from A SHROPSHIRE LAD[31]
—A. E. Housman

VIII
"Farewell to barn and stack and tree,
    Farewell to Severn shore.
Terence, look your last at me,
    For I come home no more.

"The sun burns on the half-mown hill,
    By now the blood is dried;
And Maurice amongst the hay lies still
    And my knife is in his side.

"My mother thinks us long away;
   'Tis time the field were mown.
She had two sons at rising day,
   To-night she'll be alone.

"And here's a bloody hand to shake,
   And oh, man, here's good-bye;
We'll sweat no more on scythe and rake,
   My bloody hands and I.

"I wish you strength to bring you pride
   And a love to keep you clean,
And I wish you luck, come Lammastide,
   At racing on the green.

"Long for me the rick will wait,
   And long will wait the fold,
And long will stand the empty plate,
   And dinner will be cold."

FIVE POEMS
—Eugen Gomringer

you blue
you red
you yellow
you black
you white
you

baum
baum kind

kind
kind hund

hund
hund haus

haus
haus baum

baum kind hund haus

Reprinted by permission of the author. [*baum,* tree; *kind,* child; *hund,* dog.]

hang and swinging hang and swinging
hang and grow and swinging hang
and grow downwards and swinging hang and
grow downwards and touch the ground and
swinging hang and grow downwards and
touch the ground and then off and search
and swinging hang and grow downwards
and touch the ground and then off and
search and not find a place and swinging
hang and grow downwards and touch
the ground and then off and search and not
find a place and grow and swinging
hang and grow downwards and touch
the ground and then off and search and not
find a place and grow upwards and swinging
hang and grow downwards and touch
the ground and then off and search and not
find a place and grow upwards and force
a new growth and swinging hang and
grow downwards and touch the ground and
then off and search and not find a place
and grow upwards and force a new growth
and hang and swinging hang and
grow downwards and touch the ground and
then off and search and not find a place
and grow upwards and force a new growth and
swinging hang

comes along and
looks around

calls aside and
straightens out

pulls together and
oversees

goes away and
leaves behind

words are shadows
shadows become words

words are games
games become words

are shadows words
do words become games

are games words
do words become shadows

are words shadows
do games become words

are words games
do shadows become words

THE MURDER OF TWO MEN BY A YOUNG KID WEARING LEMON-COLORED GLOVES
—Kenneth Patchen

Wait.

Wait.

Wait.

Wait. Wait.

Wait.

Wait.

W a i t .

Wait.

Wait.

Wait.

Wait.

Wait.

Wait.

NOW.

EASTER-WINGS
—George Herbert

Lord, who createdſt man in wealth and ſtore,
Though fooliſhly he loſt the ſame,
Decaying more and more,
Till he became
Moſt poore :
With thee
O let me riſe
As larks, harmoniouſly,
And ſing this day thy victories:
Then ſhall the fall further the flight in me.

Eaſter wings.

My tender age in ſorrow did beginne
And ſtill with ſickneſſes and ſhame
Thou didſt ſo puniſh ſinne,
That I became
Moſt thinne.
With thee
Let me combine,
And feel this day thy victorie :
For, if I imp my wing on thine,
Affliction ſhall advance the flight in me.

Eaſter wings.

ACROSTIC
(17th century, anonymous)

These may be read two or three wayes.

Your face	Your tongue	your wit
so faire	so smooth	so sharp
first drew	then mov'd	then knit
mine eye	mine eare	my heart
Mine eye	Mine eare	My heart
thus drawn	thus mov'd	thus knit
affects	hangs on	yeelds to
Your face	Your tongue	your wit

The third way, incidentally, goes from right to left and from left to right in alternate lines, in imitation of the ancient Greek manner of writing called *boustrophedon*, "as the ox turns in plowing."

THE FACE
—Stevie Smith

There is a face I know too well,
A face I dread to see,
So vain it is, so eloquent
Of all futility.

It is a human face that hides
A monkey soul within,
That bangs about, that beats a gong,
That makes a horrid din.

Sometimes the monkey soul will sprawl
Athwart the human eyes,
And peering forth, will flesh its pads,
And utter social lies.

So wretched is this face, so vain,
So empty and forlorn,
You well may say that better far
This face had not been born.

—*Emmett Williams*

like   attracts   like

like   attracts   like

like   attracts   like

like   attracts   like

like   attracts   like

like attracts like

like attracts like

likeattractslike

likeattractlike

likattraclike

lihttradike

litteralike

liiteiikts

from **THE SONGS OF THE EARTH**
—*Ronald Johnson*

W   A   N   E

W a n e w E
   a N e w
   A n e N

W a n e w E
   A n e w
   a N e N

W   A   N   E

A N E W
A N E W
A N E W
A N E W

Chapter 10

STRUCTURE AS ACT: PROSE FICTION, DRAMA

THE
STRUCTURE
OF PROSE
FICTION

Like poetry, prose employs both literal and figurative language, and it may make use of all the devices of language described in Chapter 8. It is possible to feel that the more richly figurative prose is, the nearer it approaches poetry, in which language tends to have a greater density, a closer texture. It has been said that poetry is the language of the emotions, but in most senses this distinction between poetry and prose will not really hold. Like poetry, prose may be highly charged in its emotional tone.

Nevertheless, it is true that prose is less regularly patterned than poetry. Its rhythms are not based on so apparent a return. Coleridge has said (in Chapter 18 of *Biographia Literaria*) that meter in poetry owes its existence to a state of increased excitement in the poet, apparently as if in a feeling of excitement one should burst into song. This state of excitement calls for language appropriate to it, in the interests of decorum. The poet willfully and designedly arranges the language into meter "for the purpose of blending delight with emotion." Meter increases "the vivacity and susceptibility both of the general feelings and of the attention." If the language employed does not live up to the expectations aroused by the metrical arrangement, the poem suffers.

On the other hand, we tend not to want prose to approach metrical regularity too closely. If the prose that approaches such regularity carries with it density in its use of language and a strong degree of emotionality, we say it is really poetry. If it lacks these elements, we say it is self-conscious or monotonous. If it has richly figurative language but seems sentimental (without a proper balance of emotionality), we say it is "purple" or flowery. Underneath all such judgments lies a feeling that prose is prose and poetry is poetry, though some prose is very poetic and some poetry is very prosaic. Probably the best we can do to make a distinction is to say again that poetry is more closely patterned, normally more figurative and condensed, and higher in its degree of emotionality. It seems likely that this greater emotional freight is kept at proper distance in the esthetic experience by the high degree of pattern or formality in the structure of poetry. In life too it can be observed that increase in emotion can lead to more rhythmic behavior—jumping up and down, beating with one's fist, pronounced pounding of the heart, tapping with the foot, repetition of words such as "no no no." Apparently this patterning of behavior helps avoid the disruptive effects that might otherwise accompany the emotion.

Space forbids our analyzing a novel in the same way in which we analyzed poetry in the last chapter. And since a short story is to be analyzed in detail in the next chapter, perhaps it will not be necessary here to examine even a story, though generalizations must be tested against the actual example. But remember that this chapter cannot simply be divorced from many of the materials discussed in the preceding chapter. Our attempt throughout this book has been to recognize parallels between literary structures as well as distinctions between them, and we have already discussed many elements common to all forms. We turn now to elements that bulk large or in some special sense in prose fiction and in drama.

Prose fiction is the presentation of experience in language so arranged through scene, summary, and description as to narrate a complete action in a unique world, the world of the story or novel.[1] Traditional terms for describing elements in the narrative are *plot* (made up of actions so articulated as to yield a beginning, a middle, and an end), *setting* (environment, in its broadest sense), and *character*. Prose fiction, like poetry and like all acts, whether in literature or in life, ordinarily reaches the peak of its movement somewhere near—but not at—the close, though the position will vary from story to story. There may or may not be (since a narrative takes place in *time*) a precise moment that marks a crucial limitation in the direction the plot may thereafter take; when such a moment exists, it may be called the *crisis* of the story. The moment at which the major action reaches its peak (the point to which it has been moving throughout) may be called the *climax* of the story. Neither the crisis nor the climax *need* be (as their names may suggest)

---

[1] The terms *scene, summary,* and *description* as used here are taken from Phyllis Bentley's *Some Observations on the Art of Narrative* (New York: The Macmillan Company, 1947).

the emotional high points for a reader, nor need they be the most interesting points in the narrative. The terms are tools for describing points in the progress of the action in which the story is engaged.

An Illustration of Terms

Now let us illustrate certain of these terms with an example furnished by one of the greatest masters of fiction, Henry James. On Thursday evening, January 10, 1895, James attended a dinner. (It is fascinating to observe how frequently James received food for the artist as well as food for the man when he went out to dine.) At this particular dinner, the Archbishop of Canterbury repeated to James a story told to him by "a lady who had no art of relation, and no clearness." An undisclosed number of children of undisclosed age had been left in the care of wicked and depraved servants in an old country house after their parents had died. The servants corrupted the children and made them evil to a "sinister degree." Then the servants died. Afterward, the servants' apparitions returned to haunt the house and children and to tempt them to their deaths. They try and try and try, says James in his report, to get hold of the children. "It is all obscure and imperfect, the picture, the story," writes James in his *Notebooks,* "but there is a suggestion of strangely gruesome effect in it. The story to be told—tolerably obviously—by an outside spectator, observer."

Here, then, are incidents to be articulated into a plot that will constitute an action. A setting is suggested (the old country house), and characters (the children and servants). The tone, or atmosphere, of the setting, which will be a strong element in the particular world to be created, is also here: evil, depravity, wickedness, temptation. This suggests too a strong element of suspense leading to a climax: the success or lack of success of the servants. The action of the story will be the union of plot, setting, and characterization arranged in a sequence that is temporal. No piece of prose fiction lacks an *action* (a progression from one position or one point of awareness to another). Someone must undergo a change in awareness because a story *cannot be* (though a poem *may be* and a pure lyric poem *is*) in this sense static. The change in awareness may or may not be in a character or characters within the story; it may be produced within the reader alone while the characters remain unaware. But this revelation is basic to the life of the story and constitutes its design, its action.

Point of View

Observe that James, even this early in his work on the story, seizes upon the point of view from which the story is to be told. It is for James a crucial matter. The particular quality a story takes on, the nature and tone of its action, is strongly influenced by the angle or position from which the events and characters are seen. James says that an outside spectator must tell his story. Why? Presumably because neither the children nor the servants could give us an impartial picture of the matter, or a complete picture of it. James counted heavily, in his best work, on the presence of a sensitive, intelligent spectator who could function as a kind of thinking camera to let us see what was happening; and to this spectator he gave the name *central intelligence*. But this particular kind of spectator is not the narrator but a character presented to us through the narrator.

In writing this story, which he called "The Turn of the Screw," James chose to use the first-person point of view, but not quite that of an outside spectator. (His first impulse has been altered.) The story begins: "I remember the whole beginning as a succession of flights and drops, a little see-saw of the right throbs and the wrong." The first-person character (the "I") is a young governess. The children are put under her charge—a little girl named Flora and her brother Miles, about ten years old. Also in the country house is a housekeeper, Mrs. Grose. You must read for yourself what happened, for no summary can do justice to the action James manages to evolve.

It must be pointed out that while what may be called the story proper begins with the sentence we have cited, there is a kind of prologue in which James's narrator is a different "I," a surrogate for the author. The prologue begins: "The story had held us, round the fire, sufficiently breathless, but except for the obvious remark that it was gruesome, as on Christmas Eve in an old house a strange tale should essentially be, I remember no comment uttered till somebody happened to note it as the only case he had met in which such a visitation had fallen on a child." James goes on to introduce a specific member of that group referred to as "us," a man named Douglas, who tells the narrator that he has a manuscript written by a woman dead "these twenty years" which tells a story also about "a visitation on a child" (two children). He sends for that manuscript, and after giving some information about the people involved begins to read the manuscript aloud to the others. That manuscript begins: "I remember the whole beginning as a succession of flights and drops. . . ." James's treatment illustrates the fact that point of view need not remain single, that more than a single narrator may function in a story. The effect, here, is of a shift of locus as well as perspective. *This* time and *this* place melt into *that* time and *that* place, an earlier time. But *that* time and *that* place become in turn, as we read and listen, *this* time and *this* place. The narrative tense is past, but the past is nevertheless a fictive present for us as we participate in the story. James's surrogate, the initial "I" who speaks in the prologue, listens to a story read by Douglas (whose *voice* is thus the one we hear initially as we begin the story proper), but in the story which is read still another "I" is speaking. The interpreter is faced with a fascinating performance question: At which point does the audience begin to hear the voice of the governess?

It is clear that the first-person point of view limits what is seen to the particular person seeing it. James's choice of the governess has led to endless argument about interpretations of this story, since it is not entirely clear how reliable her report seems. She is *subjective* in her views, since she is responsible for the children and is thus involved in the action. She cannot be detached. One may also, however, employ a first-person point of view with an *objective* position when the story permits detached observation.

There is a sense in which *all* narrators must be thought of properly as first-person, whether or not the pronoun "I" is being used. For example, Stephen Crane's "Maggie: A Girl of the Streets" begins in this fashion:

> A very little boy stood upon a heap of gravel for the honour of Rum Alley. He was throwing stones at howling urchins from Devil's Row, who were circling madly about the heap and pelting him. His infantile countenance was livid with the fury of battle. His small body was writhing in the delivery of oaths.

No "I" is here to signal a first person point of view, but clearly someone is telling the story to us—and it must be in his or her person, since language does not come out of a vacuum. Such an unnamed narrator is often *omniscient,* having it in his power to know what is going on in the minds of all the characters of a story. He may be of *limited omniscience,* fully cognizant of some thoughts and actions and only partly aware of others. He may seem fully reliable, or only partly reliable.

Narrators may or may not, as we have seen, themselves be participants in the action of the story. They may or may not be named.

Another perspective makes use of a character in the story (not in the first person) as the central reflecting surface, as in this opening from Booth Tarkington's "Penrod's Busy Day":

> Although the pressure had thus been relieved and Penrod found peace with himself, nevertheless there were times during the rest of that week when he felt a strong distaste for Margaret. His schoolmates frequently reminded him of such phrases in her letter as they seemed least able to forget, and for hours after each of these experiences he was unable to comport himself with human courtesy when constrained (as at dinner) to remain for any length of time in the same room with her. But by Sunday these moods had seemed to pass; he attended church in her close company, and had no thought of the troubles brought upon him by her correspondence with a person who throughout remained unknown to him.

Such a narrator is sometimes called *third-person,* but that is a confusing term. It refers to the fact that it is a third person ("he," in this case) who is our usual source of information in the story, but the true teller of the story is *not* Penrod but a narrator standing in for the author. (There are times in Tarkington's story where we learn things not easily knowable by Penrod; here the omniscient author shows through.) It may be profitable to discard the term *third-person narrator* altogether, since it is not at all parallel with the term *first-person,* which refers specifically to the *teller* speaking of himself or herself as "I." We are really talking here about degrees of immediacy in the relationship between teller and auditor (audience). Strictly speaking, one could use the term *third-person* narrator only for stories in which the teller referred to himself as *he.* In use, however, the term is loosely applied.

The term *second-person* is sometimes used to describe the narrator who employs the pronoun *you* in such a fashion as this: "You look at her and you say, 'I hate you.'" The *you* in such use may indeed seem to relate directly to the speaker (who is using *you* to involve the reader or listener in the activity); on the other hand, it may not be tied in any clear sense to the speaker, but may be pointed at the auditor alone. It is more helpful to distinguish between such positions than simply to reduce both to *second-person* situations. (It is clear enough, of course, that whatever the person—first, second, or third—the narrator hopes to involve the auditor!)

The second person is rarely used, though amateur writers frequently experiment with it. It tends to place a needlessly intimate burden upon the reader, who may object to being told how to think and feel. This is not to say that the second-person narrator *cannot* be used effectively. "Aura," a story by Carlos Fuentes, begins thus:

> You're reading the advertisement: an offer like this isn't made every day. You read it and reread it. It seems to be addressed to you and nobody else. You don't even notice when the ash from your cigarette falls into the cup of tea you ordered in this cheap, dirty café. You read it again. "Wanted, young historian, conscientious, neat. Perfect knowledge of colloquial French. Youth . . . knowledge of French, preferably after living in France for a while. . . . Four thousand pesos a month, all meals, comfortable bedroom-study." All that's missing is your name. The advertisement should have two more words, in bigger, blacker type: Felipe Montero. Wanted. Felipe Montero, formerly on scholarship at the Sorbonne, historian full of useless facts, accustomed to digging among yellowed documents, part-time teacher in private schools, nine hundred pesos a month. But if you read that, you'd be suspicious, and take it as a joke. "Address, Donceles 815." No telephone; come in person.[2]

Thus Fuentes lets us know that Felipe Montero (who seems to be talking to himself as "you") is the real narrator of the story, and gives us necessary exposition about Montero from Montero's own mouth. What happens when Montero answers the advertisement constitutes the story which is told. Only a full reading of the story will serve to demonstrate the effect which the second-person narration achieves. It is in part hypnotic.

[2] A selection from *Aura* by Carlos Fuentes, translated by Lysander Kemp. Copyright © 1965 by Carlos Fuentes. Reprinted with the permission of Farrar, Straus & Giroux, Inc.

Perspective and Point of View

So crucial is point of view that the same events told from two different points of view become two quite different plots. Point of view is far more complex than such terms as *first-person, second-person, third-person* will serve to indicate. James's term *central intelligence* is a more perceptive one, since it relates to a particular *quality* of narrating consciousness, in a particular relationship with us. But *central intelligence* is useful only for that particular kind of consciousness.

The significant fact is that perspective shifts, as we said in Chapter 4, and it is the task of the interpreter to follow these shifts of locus. Points of view may indeed be multiple. And while the narrator selects the details we are to hear, the degree of our awareness of his hold on details changes. In the passage from *Vanity Fair* on pages 111–113, for example, we saw how it is possible to read certain passages either from the perspective of the narrator or from the perspective of the character. It is true enough, of course, that the narrator controls what we know of the character. But there is a real difference between reading a character's thoughts in the person of the character and reading them as if the narrator were talking. Interpreters must make many choices of this kind, and the choices clearly affect the tone of the performance.

The questions to ask are such questions as Who is talking, What is the speaker seeing or hearing or thinking or feeling, What kind of person or consciousness is at work? It is from the answers to such questions as this that the *presence* of the narrator can be defined, that the separate revelations can be made to *coalesce*. They are questions of tensiveness. In sum, they constitute *perspective*. But the interpreter must always remember that the most interesting writing makes the answers to these questions highly complex because perspective interacts with all other parts of structure. The question "Who speaks?" is not necessarily the most interesting question to ask of a piece of fiction. Indeed, there are works of literature where it may not be profitable at all to think of a "speaker," in the sense of a speaker's being a specific identity. Some literature asks us to accept its vision as *real,* without the mediation of a carefully defined intelligence—as if a camera were itself to speak. This is not to say that there is no perspective; it *is* to say that there is not always clearly "a speaker."

Rhythm of Action

When the story incidents have been arranged, the setting chosen, the characters assembled, and the position of authority (the point of view—on whose authority is the story told?) determined, the rhythm of the action is determined in part by the manner in which the writer uses *scene, summary,* and *description.* This is not to say that a writer must sit down and arrange the parts of his story as he might arrange the pieces of a puzzle; he may work largely without conscious deliberation, he may begin with anything in the story that appeals to his imagination first; he may do anything in any order he chooses. But all these elements are involved in the process.

Suppose the story ("The Siege of London," by Henry James) begins:

> That solemn piece of unholstery, the curtain of the Comédie Française, had fallen upon the first act of the piece, and our two Americans had taken advantage of the interval to pass out of the huge, hot theatre, in company with the other occupants of the stalls.

This is *summary,* which is useful for hurrying over information that the reader must know but that does not require a great deal of his time. Summary is frequently used for *exposition* or for cementing together tenser moments in the action.

Now suppose that the writer wishes to give a picture of something important to the story (in this case, a character):

> She turned . . . and presented her face to the public—a fair, well-drawn face, with smiling eyes, smiling lips, ornamented over the brow with delicate rings of black hair and, in each ear, with the sparkle of a diamond sufficiently large to be seen across the Théâtre Français.

This is *description*. It looks more closely and hence more slowly at things than does summary.

Now suppose that the writer wishes us to see and hear the characters of the story as if they were dramatized on the stage before our eyes. We watch and listen very closely:

> Littlemore looked at her; then, abruptly, he gave an exclamation. "Give me the glass!"
>
> "Do you know her?" his companion asked, as he directed the little instrument.
>
> Littlemore made no answer; he only looked in silence; then he handed back the glass. "No, she's not respectable," he said. And he dropped into his seat again. As Waterville remained standing, he added, "Please sit down: I think she saw me."

This is *scene.* It usually involves dialogue, although it may simply present single specific actions, "stage" business. Scene may be interior scene, where we are given a character's thoughts—in effect, soliloquy, though this term is usually restricted to the utterance of thought by a character speaking aloud to himself (and to us) in a play. For example,

> I am already neurasthemic. Even the slightest noise is irritating to me. My hands shake. My ears buzz. My head is tightened as if

bound with hoops. I have lost my appetite and cannot sleep all night long. As I look in the mirror I see in front of me a pale mask with features distorted by suffering.[3]

As Phyllis Bentley puts it, scene, summary, and description involve the tempo, or rate, at which a writer unfolds the world he is creating. Summary moves rapidly; scene moves in normal time; description is cessation of movement. Or, to use the analogy of the motion-picture camera, summary is panorama, description is close-up, scene is close-up with an audible sound track of voices. Scene, summary, and description normally appear mixed rather than pure in writing, but the nature of the mixture has a pervasive effect on the rhythm of the story; tempo is part of a writer's style. The point of view also affects the tempo because it affects what can be seen and heard.

Suppose a passage reads this way:

She is asleep. She is a little changed, I think. I have thought so more than once lately. I cannot decide how she is changed, but something in the familiar beauty of her face looks different to me. She has been anxious about him. I wonder how that love will end.

This is interior scene. Note now, as we shift to the text Dickens actually provides for us in *Bleak House*,[4] how time and space change, how scene blends with summary. The effect is very different from that in the scene above:

She was asleep, and I thought as I looked at her that she was a little changed. I had thought so more than once lately. I could not decide, even looking at her while she was unconscious, how she was changed, but something in the familiar beauty of her face looked different to me . . . and I said to myself, "She has been anxious about him," and I wondered how that love would end.

What would be the difference in effect (in tensiveness, specifically) if Dickens were to have written "and I said to myself that she had been anxious about him, and I wondered how that love would end."

Characterization

Just as the nature of the action affects the choice of setting, the arrangement of episodes, the tempo, the point of view, the quality of language, and the number of characters (for unity demands that all these elements coalesce in the presence which is the story), so it affects the nature of

---

[3] From "The Man Who Came from America," by Svetoslav Minkov, translated by Victor Sharenkoff. From *The Best of Modern European Literature*, ed. Klaus Mann and Hermann Kesten (Philadelphia: The Blakiston Company, 1945), p. 337.

[4] From the close of Chapter 50.

the characterization. Characters may be *static* or *dynamic, flat* or *round.* The flat or static character seems to possess a single dominant and unchanging trait; he may or may not be so sharply outlined as to be a caricature, but frequently flat characterization moves in the direction of caricature. The rounder a character is, the more dynamic he is; we watch him changing, exhibiting aspect after aspect of personality. One must be careful not to insist that flat characters are inadequate; a story often makes excellent use of flat characters. One need object only when a flat character is used where a round character is needed, or vice versa, since sometimes a round character is needlessly complex; if the villain in a melodrama were made a round character, for example, the melodrama would probably disappear. Flat characters are usually identified with *types* or *stock characters,* though doubtless both round characters and all living people are made up of mixtures of type and stock traits. In his sonnets Shakespeare takes delight in making his lady dark and brunette when blonde, blue-eyed beauty is conventionally regarded as the ideal in poetry.

A writer may present his characters in set descriptions—a few sentences or a paragraph or more devoted to the character as he appears. Thackeray does this with Becky Sharp (page 110) in the selection we examined from *Vanity Fair.* Many earlier writers introduce characters in this way. The *character* of characters is often fixed at the outset of such stories, though it may change.

Contemporary writers more frequently let us come to know characters gradually, unfolding them as the story progresses. According to Macauley and Lanning, such a method is more lifelike, since in life we come to know people only gradually—and "the way of life," they say, "is the way of modern fiction, which places its emphasis more on organic form than on plot."[5] Our attitudes toward such characters shift, change, grow; we may not fully know them (if we ever do) until the end of the story. Emphasis on the plot (seen narrowly as the arrangement of incidents) is often minimal in such pieces of fiction; in Virginia Woolf, for example, the interior life of the characters is often almost everything. But in the richer sense of plot, which involves the articulation of character with event, it is still true, as James said in "The Art of Fiction," that character and incident are inseparable.

Fiction may describe (as Thackeray does Becky Sharp) the physical appearance of characters, the mannerisms of characters—particular ways in which they move and speak and behave, and the way in which they respond to other characters and to the environment. It may characterize through interior monologues, letting us know how and in what kind of language the characters think and feel. Or an author may, himself (as the "author in the poem") or through his narrator, tell us directly about a character or have other characters address themselves to that subject. A character's name may have value as an indication of qualities. (The notebooks of Henry James are filled with possible names for characters, many of them suggesting types of characters.) These cues are evidence for the interpreter who seeks to embody the character—and all set limits on the nature of the characterization. The questions are: How clearly defined are the external qualities of the character? How can I indicate internal qualities through external manners? At what point will my specific physical manifestations begin to hamper the character and scene I am creating? Remember that embodiment involves both visible physical body and all interior states. *Never think of characterization in terms of the visible body alone.* Sometimes, indeed, the visible body of a character is of minimal concern to a writer, but the *total* body is always a concern for the interpreter.

Modality and Fiction

In Aristotle's terms, fiction exists in the epic mode (sometimes called the narrative mode), in which the writer sometimes employs a specifically identified narrator for the story and sometimes is submerged in characters who seem to speak for themselves. But there are short stories in which the mode seems lyrical, in which the teller seems to be the author himself; and there are stories and novels (see, for example, the Hemingway story in the next chapter) that are largely dramatic. Modality certainly conditions the interpreter's performance; the question Who is speaking? is for the oral reader a primary question.

As Wayne Booth has shown,[6] the narrator may or may not be dramatized. The narrator may be the "implicit second self" of the writer, the "implied author," as distinct from the actual living author—the author-in-the-work, we may call him. There may be no pronoun ("I") to remind us that the narrator exists, but the effect of what happens on the consciousness of the narrator is always of the greatest importance, since we depend on this narrator for everything we learn, though we sometimes learn from him things of which he is himself unaware. There may be a clearly defined quality of mind in the narrator even when his person and his personality remain shadowy to us.

The narrator may, on the other hand, be dramatized, be a definable person and character. In such a case, the narrative mode moves close to the dramatic mode, and the words of the narrator often become a kind of exposition and commentary, as in the speeches of a character in a play. Indeed, fiction may run the full gamut from fully dramatized to undramatized narrators. The narrator may be a mirror, reflecting the experience he reports; he may be a lamp, shedding light on it from within his own mind and spirit. In either case, he affects and effects the

[6] See "Distance and Point of View," *Essays in Criticism* 11 (1961), 60–79 and *The Rhetoric of Fiction* (Chicago: University of Chicago Press, 1961), pp. 151–159.

quality of the experience that is given to us. A reader may identify with a narrator or may be in direct opposition to him. The narrator may in turn be very close to the characters, may even identify with them, or may be very remote from them. He may be close at one time and distant at another. None of these positions is necessarily fixed, and each presents problems of characterization.

Reliability of the Narrator

Do we always take for granted that the "facts" reported by the narrator are true? Hardly—it depends on the narrator. When the narrator is a character in the story, we judge him as we judge the other characters in the story and believe him, half believe him, or disbelieve him, depending on our judgments of him. When the narrator is effaced, when we seem to be hearing the author-in-the-work, we are perhaps more likely to think that we are listening to "the truth," though we may ultimately change our minds. But remember that "the truth" here means the truth in the story, not necessarily the truth in life.

Again, the amount the narrator can know depends on the nature of the narrator and his relationship to events; and our knowledge of the nature of the narrator may come even from such indirect sources as summary and exposition, since the way in which he gives us such information may be a clue to his nature. The range of comments about the reliability of James's governess in "The Turn of the Screw" suggests to readers of the commentaries that one must be wary of too simple acceptance of the narrator's reliability as witness.[7] In satire too one must be careful not to miss the satire. Author and reader may often know more than the narrator does.

Novel and Short Story

It is difficult at best to distinguish sharply between the novel and the short story. A short story ("The Turn of the Screw") may run as long as 35,000 words; a novel may be relatively short, a "novelette" or novella. In general, the short story aims at singleness of effect; the novel, while it must have an overall unity of effect, is usually more comprehensive in range. Just as the short lyric poem is usually more demanding of the reader than a long narrative poem in the degree of concentration required of him; so the short story is usually more demanding than the novel. *This is not a value judgment*—a reader often willingly spends a week or two on a novel, but he would probably weary of a short story that required such a length of time for reading, since psychologically one's single-minded attention will not endure that long. Novels permit greater variety in rhythms. They alternate close and open textures, scene, summary, and description, perspective and tensions more freely than

---

[7] See Robert Heilman, "The Turn of the Screw as Poem," in *Forms of Modern Fiction,* ed. W. V. O'Connor (Minneapolis: University of Minnesota Press, 1948), pp. 211–228. The essay originally appeared in the summer 1948 issue of the *University of Kansas City Review.*

does the short story. A novel may, in its greater comprehensiveness, nevertheless have a tight structure of its own.

Other
Ways of
Classifying

There are various other ways of classifying fiction. (See the Glossary entry under NOVEL, for example.) One classification (by Thomas Uzzell) is concerned with the nature of the conflict presented: it may be psychological (a clash between character and society) or it may be between man and nature (an adventure story).[8] Obviously these divisions are not fixed; crossovers are endless.

Northrop Frye offers another method of classification; he finds the four chief strands of fiction to be novel, romance, confession, and anatomy.[9] The novelist "deals with personality, with characters wearing their *personae* or social masks. He needs the framework of a stable society. . . ." The romancer "does not attempt to create 'real people' so much as stylized figures which expand into psychological archetypes," and he "deals with individuality, with characters *in vacuo* idealized by revery. . . ."

The confession is a form in which autobiography and novel seem to merge. The anatomy is more concerned with mental attitudes than it is with people—it "resembles the confession in its ability to handle abstract ideas and theories, and differs from the novel in its characterization, which is stylized rather than naturalistic, and presents people as mouthpieces of the ideas they represent." The anatomy, says Frye, springs from an early form of satire.

Gulliver's Travels is, in Frye's terms, an anatomy. *The Pilgrim's Progress* is a romance, as is *Wuthering Heights. Tom Jones* is a novel. A work such as Defoe's *Moll Flanders,* a dramatic confession, combines elements of confession and novel, since the confession is not that of the novelist himself. Here, as with Uzzell's classification, we must admit many mixed types.

Time and
Fiction

Fiction normally exists in the past tense. The epic situation is in the past—the story has already happened and is being recounted—but from the point of view of the reader the sensation is usually that of a story existing in the present. The more nearly scenic the telling, the more present the account seems; the more nearly summary it is, the more past in tense. The shifts in tensiveness in time shifts are of great importance to the performer; it is not only tempo that is affected but the nature of the tensions involved in the sense of *now*. Notice the difference between "He was dying of suffocation" and "I am suffocating to death," if

[8] See Thomas H. Uzzell, *The Technique of the Novel* (New York: Citadel Press, 1964), pp. 136–140.

[9] From Northrop Frye, *Anatomy of Criticism* (Princeton, N.J.: Princeton University Press, 1957), reprinted in Philip Stevick, *The Theory of the Novel* (New York: The Free Press, 1967), pp. 31–43.

the latter is taken to mean that the speaker literally is suffocating. The difference exists even when the text of the fiction reads, for example, "Jeremy stepped back from the fumes, his face terrible with effort, and cried, 'I am suffocating to death.'"

Modern authors deal freely—often very closely—with time; they juxtapose times, give interior monologues, create circles and cycles of time. They may create two or more selves for the narrator by having him recount at a later time an action or event in his own past, giving both his earlier and later feelings. ("Araby" does this, as we have seen.)

Time and Language

A particular problem is posed in the reading of fiction written in an older era (though it exists for poetry and drama as well as for fiction, to be sure). A modern reader who reads a historical novel by a modern writer already has the writer's help in recovering past time, but a reader who reads a fourteenth-century story will have a problem forced on him by the fact that the far-off events are seen through a language that is in some respects foreign to him. The interpreter is faced with the problem of embodying the text. He must make the old text exert as much as possible of its original force, although he cannot escape the fact that the language itself has probably lost force. In drama, readers of Shakespeare often have difficulty feeling comfortable with the age of the language, but so long as the language seems to the performer strange and unreal, the characters speaking in that language will not be sufficiently alive. It is helpful to paraphrase, to try putting the older language in one's own words—but it is also dangerous. The life of the language resides in the language, not in a paraphrase of it. Do not avoid the language, do not try simply to "see through it," but work for the life of the words as they are. As A. A. Mendilow says, "The later the reader, the more knowledge is demanded of him and the greater is the imaginative effort required fully to savour the novel and to do justice to the reactions of the characters and the significance of the theme."[10]

Direct and Indirect Discourse

Differing degrees of pastness are frequent in fiction. We have already mentioned the relationships between scene and summary in terms of verb tense. Exposition, a summary of things already past when the story begins, will seem more past than the happenings within the story—for example: "He had finished college in June. Now he was looking for a job." While the verb is still past tense (was looking), the *now* effectively establishes a shift in time from the pluperfect *had finished*. If we put this into dialogue—"I finished college in June. Now I am looking for a job," he said—we have a still different situation with respect to tensiveness. The degree to which the reader makes the dialogue *present* or

[10] "The Position of the Present in Fiction," from *Time and the Novel* (London: P. Nevill, 1965), reprinted in Philip Stevick, *The Theory of the Novel* (New York: The Free Press, 1967), pp. 255–280.

allows it to remain *past* (as if he were simply reporting the dialogue) will greatly affect the performance. Choices must be made, and they are not always wholly established by the writer himself. Consider how one may read this simple statement: "'It hurts,' he said." A reader may overdramatize dialogue in fiction or may underdramatize it. Everything depends on the total context one wishes (as one sees the literature) to establish. Obviously some choices are better than others.

We are talking, among other things, about differences between direct and indirect discourse in fiction (or in poetry or drama, though they are less typically found there). Suppose a story says "John said, 'I am vitally interested in this matter.'" If we take John to mean what he says, the word *vitally* takes on a high degree of tensiveness in the reading. But what if the story says "John said that he was vitally interested in the matter." We have moved from direct to indirect discourse (see the Glossary) and have modified the quality of the tension in the words. If we move still farther away ("John expressed interest in the matter"), the tensions lessen even more; we have moved along a continuum from more to less dramatic, from dramatic to narrative mode (though we do not mean to imply that the narrative mode is typically without dramatic qualities, for it is not).

Read the series of sentences which follows:

"What is the use of it all?"

"What is the use of it all?" he asked himself.

What is the use of it all, he asked himself. [Why is it difficult to decide whether or not to use a question mark at the end of that sentence?]

What was the use of it all, he asked himself.

While it sometimes has been argued that sentences two and three are direct discourse of precisely the same degree of fullness, we do not quite share that view. It is true enough that if one were to speak both sentences aloud, each might be made to say the same thing, since the quotation marks function most clearly to the eye. But given the difference between the use and the nonuse of the quotation marks, would one necessarily *want* to make the two sentences yield precisely the same meaning and effect? At what point does the dialogue begin to turn inward, and how far inward does it turn? To put it another way, at what point does the speaker's voice begin to merge with the narrator's voice, and at what point does the narrative voice become the dominant voice? When do the direct words of the speaker become the narrator's interpretation of the thoughts those words are meant to convey? The question is not simply one of a distinction *between* direct and indirect discourse, but of shifting degrees of immediacy *within* each of the two categories.

Macauley and Lanning say of stories: "Somewhere in that flow of time must be drawn the visible line dividing past from present. All novels have a past; all novels should live in a present of their own. Only that part of *then* that is important to, that has a bearing on, *now* is worth being told. The fictional past lives only insofar as it is embodied in the fictional present."[11] But the fictional present varies in its pastness-presentness locus. It is really an extraordinarily complex (but happily apparently simple) question of loci, involving the position in time of the reader, of the writer, and of the narrator or narrators.

The interpreter will want to examine the setting of the novel or story he is to perform. Setting influences character in many ways; indeed, it may in some pieces be an aspect of character, so interwoven with the feelings of an individual that the two seem inseparable. It may give rise to action, causing a character to act as he does. It may alter events—a gray, rainy day may turn what was to have been a happy occasion into a sad one. It may act in opposition to a character. The world created by a writer of fiction, while it need not be true to the actual world around us, must be true to itself. Things can happen in a fictional world, in a particular fictional setting, that would happen no place else. Hence the qualities of the setting affect the tensions of an interpreter's performance—as in the story by Eudora Welty we examined in Chapter 3.

> **Setting in Fiction**

In conclusion, prose fiction, though it varies from poetry in some of the structural elements with which it works, and though it has its own complexities and values, shares with poetry the fact of being tensive, coalescent, and presential. It too is an act which the interpreter must seek to embody.

It is often said that all literature is dramatic in nature, involving a speaker, a situation, and a listener. There is a strong element of truth in the view—though like all generalizations it can be carried too far. Some narrators in fiction do, as we have seen, speak to us as specific men and women; others are only dimly perceptible to us as describable persons. There are occasional poems where *no* "speaker" can be said to exist, though there are words, of course. In such poems, language is like pigments in painting; it is employed by the artist to create a work of art but without the sense that *a* human being must be speaking the words. (This is not to deny that words come from men and women.) One of the difficulties posed for some listeners in hearing poems performed by professional actors is that the sense of the speaker's literal person may be too strong for the poem to bear.

> **THE STRUCTURE OF DRAMA**

But aside from this word of caution, it is helpful to think of works of literature as having speakers. In a purely lyrical poem, the speaker is one person speaking aloud. The situation may be a single moment of subjective reflection. The listener may be simply the reader who is

[11] Macauley and Lanning, p. 2l.

"overhearing." Narrative poetry and prose fiction move closer to the realm of the drama by giving us a more extended action, a group of characters, and (usually) dialogue: they are in that middle, mixed mode that Aristotle called *epic.* But drama in its pure form does not make use of a narrator to mediate between action and reader (as do fiction and narrative poetry); it makes its presentation solely through the use of characters speaking lines and engaging in actions that advance an articulated plot.

There are, of course, plays that employ narrators—Thornton Wilder's *Our Town,* for example; such plays are, however, narrative (epic in mode) rather than dramatic, though with a dramatized narrator. Also, there are elements in a play that may be called lyrical—a soliloquy, for example, where the character speaks directly to us rather than to other characters; but this is still the dramatic rather than the lyric mode, for it is not the author or his surrogate who speaks directly to us but the character he has created. We must always remember that literary forms are fluid and mobile; modern fiction often resembles the lyric poem, as in the work of Virginia Woolf, and attempts to avoid the "tyranny" of temporal arrangement. A play such as Arthur Miller's *Death of a Salesman* is a complex structure that is only in part dramatic in mode.

Like a poem, a story, or a novel, a play has a beginning, a middle, and an end. It has a necessary form, which the plot shapes; it is more or less self-contained; it begins at a point that permits all else to develop from it, moves through a crisis, and reaches a climax at or near its close. It may be written in either poetry or prose; when it is written in poetic form, it makes use of the principle of pattern or return characteristic of all poetic rhythms. It is commonly felt that poetic drama has a greater emotionality than drama written in prose, but this generalization is only a generalization and must include a full recognition of the varieties of emotionality possible in prose.

Overt Behavior

Since the drama ordinarily makes use of visible, audible characters it is likely to make far greater demands on the oral reader with respect to characterization than does poetry or fiction. The playwright is free to describe in stage directions what audiences are to see, whereas the writer of fiction and poetry leaves nothing solely to the eye. Overt responses are therefore frequently necessary in an interpreter's reading of drama if the audience is not to be confused. Gesture without words becomes a necessary tool for the expression of meaning. The more the interpreter knows about personality and behavior, the more finely discriminating will be his reading of drama. In drama, at least, actions frequently speak louder than words.

This characteristic of drama—that part of its impact resides in business and movement rather than in language alone—sometimes leads critics to say that the drama is the least literary of literary forms. As interpreters of literature we quarrel with this view, for if all language is gesture, the drama may be said to use stage directions as an addition to language much as a composer adds words to a musical score; the result is not less but more. Furthermore, the argument in this book is that the oral performance of a poem or a story likewise gains because it involves gesture.

The difficulty lies in the amount and kind of gesture. Too much is too much—no doubt about that. A ludicrous aspect of much drama reading is that the reader may try to do everything that a whole cast of actors might manage onstage—run up on a platform to read the words of Juliet in the balcony scene, and then run down to read the words of Romeo below. The reader can do only as much in the way of overt action as will not strain our awareness that he is one reader pretending to be many. This often calls for the most careful economy in gesture, but surely it is nonsense to say, as the rules for contests in interpretation sometimes do, that "gestures of the arms and body will be counted against contestants." Some readers of drama need and use effectively more gestures than other readers; some plays clearly call for more overt gesture than others. Many plays lean so heavily on overt action that they are not suitable choices for oral readers, because they make requirements that a single oral reader cannot—without making his performance either burlesque or tour de force—fulfill.

Scene and Tempo

A play exists entirely in scene. Summary may appear, but only in terms of scene. In the opening act, one of the characters may narrate information needed for further development of the plot: his summary (called exposition in the drama) exists within the scene we are watching. Or a character may employ description, but again it exists within the scene we are watching. This is what we mean when we say that drama is the most vital of the arts: it *lives* before our eyes and ears.

Tempo in drama is regulated partly by the use of exposition and description, but it is regulated more sharply by the degree of emotional tension within scenes. A scene in which the excitement is high will have a quicker tempo for the viewer than a scene in which characters are relaxed and quiet.

Characterization

Characters in a play, as in fiction, may be flat (stock) or round (three-dimensional), but the effect of drama resides almost entirely in the success with which the playwright gives clarity and intensity to his presentation of a social situation involving conflict between two or more human beings. All that we said about characterization in Chapter 5 and most of what we said about it in connection with prose fiction will be of use to the interpreter of drama. The cues given by the dramatist are often extremely complex and subtle; it is not unusual for a performer to find that a central element in characterization becomes clear only after two or three weeks of rehearsal.

There are specific questions to which an interpreter seeks answers in trying to set characterization: How old are the characters? In what settings do they move? How do they dress? What specific information is given about size and weight? About mannerisms? About behavior? About modes of thought? How are characters seen by other characters? How do they see themselves? What are their temperaments? At what tempo do they seem to move and speak? What things change their behavior? Most important of all, what do they want—what drives them to do what they do?

In period plays the sense of costume is important even though the interpreter may be wearing his or her own clothes. The imagined effect of the costume worn by the character can be made visible to the audience by the posture, carriage, and movement of the interpreter—for an interpreter does move, even when standing behind a lectern. The interpreter tries, within the limits of the art and within its economies, to be the character—not just to suggest it, but to be it, as fully as the art form permits (though almost never will it permit all that the fully staged performance will permit).

Point of View in Drama

Does point of view enter at all into the experience of drama? We have already said that drama does not ordinarily make use of a narrator. Point of view is nevertheless present, though frequently we are not aware that our angle of vision is being carefully controlled. The playwright may be highly objective, as Shakespeare usually is; his own personal feelings about the characters may be submerged in the life of the characters, so that we are not aware of the personality of the writer. Such a playwright lets the characters speak for themselves, pointing the way only through the arrangement of incidents and the attitudes expressed through characters in the action. Or he may employ a character in the play as a commentator, letting us see how that single character *as a character* sees the action of the play, letting us adopt his opinions. He may employ a character as a mouthpiece for his own point of view, subordinating interest in the life of the character to interest in the point of view. In the so-called propaganda play, the playwright may subordinate the life of all the characters to the thesis or argument, but this unwillingness to free the characters from his own predilections seems to most critics a weakness in the playwright, a denial of literature in the interests of propaganda. In this sense even so distinguished a playwright as Bernard Shaw may at times seem less playwright than critic.

Forms of Drama

Plays are normally divided into acts, partly for the convenience of audiences but more for structural considerations. The acts of a play are like the waves of return gathered into stanzas in poetry, or into sections, episodes, or chapters in fiction. The modern short story frequently seems to have a dramatic structure: the sections mount and grow as acts grow within the play.

There are, of course, many one-act plays. Indeed, the one-act form has had a renaissance of late, and many first-rate dramatists are employing the form. Television has created a market for short plays, though it also makes use of longer forms. Until recently, the professional theater rarely used the short play—though O'Neill was a marked exception—feeling, apparently, that it was too brief to permit full development of significant action. But the short form can accomplish many things—concentrate on an incident, explore a state of mind, illustrate a concept, present a memory, for example—and we are doubtless better off for its rebirth. At its *traditional* best (probably Synge's *Riders to the Sea* has become the classic example), the one-act play is high compressed, beginning at a moment close to its climax and resulting in what is called an epiphany. The modern short play, however, often eschews compression, minimizes characterization, avoids a sharp sense of ending. Indeed, Samuel Beckett has even given us plays without words, and he often emphasizes the fact that we are always beginning, never ending. Doubtless there is truth in the statement of Edward Albee, who has had marked success with the form: "They're *all* full-length plays. A play can be full-length be it three minutes or twelve hours long. It has its own duration and an audience should be able to receive gratification within any time limits."[12]

Of longer forms, the three-act and the five-act form are best known, though there have been many four-act plays. Two acts are rare, though in contemporary production many plays are performed with a single intermission. The traditional action may be reduced to a pattern: the play begins with necessary exposition, singles out in the lives of its characters a particular conflict pointed to by this exposition, introduces complications into the conflict, reaches a moment of crisis after which the line of action is limited in direction, faces these limitations, and comes to a climax, after which the action is quickly brought to a close. The crisis is usually found in the third act of a five-act play, and late in the second or early in the third act in a three-act play. But a warning is in order: Let the crisis be where it is, rather than where some rule suggests it ought to be. One way of getting at the structure (and hence the meaning) of a play is to ask oneself what in the action constitutes the climax toward which the whole play has moved; then, what is the critical moment that functions as a turn in direction in the action. (Remember that this kind of analysis can come only after one has read the play receptively; don't torture the play by dissecting it as you give it a preliminary reading or viewing.) In *Romeo and Juliet*, the death of the lovers (with the resulting cessation of the feud) is the climax (followed by its resolution); Romeo's slaying of Tybalt is the crisis. The crisis is a result of Romeo's attempt, because of his marriage to Juliet, to treat Tybalt as a kinsman dear to him. The attempt fails because of Mercutio's and Tybalt's passion, and Romeo's killing of Tybalt is the particular inci-

[12] Quoted in Stanley Richards (ed.), *Best Short Plays of the World Theatre, 1958-1967* (New York: Crown Publishers, Inc., 1968), p. xiv.

dent that produces the remainder of the action—Romeo's banishment, Juliet's engagement to Paris, the use of the potion, and death. The crisis, incidentally, need not be an external action; it may be some decision of the play's leading character or even a failure to act.

The recent theater has greatly complicated the long forms. Movement in modern drama often seems circular rather than linear (though there is a sense in which movement around the perimeter of a circle is linear, of course). Relationships between characters are sometimes hard to define, and one often has a "feeling" rather than a definable view of such relationships. Vagueness, uncertainty, insecurity, a sense of loss may be pervasive, may be a central point of the play's intention. One must know how to create a sense, then, of vagueness, uncertainty, insecurity, loss. The performer must not make clear or simple things which the playwright wishes left unclear and complex. In the older drama, playwrights tended to put most of the action into the language; in contemporary drama, much of the greatest significance is left to silence, pointed to only mutely. While we have repeatedly emphasized the importance to the interpreter of covert behavior, we must remember that the interpreter as well as the actor also uses overt behavior. For much modern drama it is essential.

Tensiveness in Drama

We have said that tempo in a play is regulated in part by the degree of emotional tension in its scenes. Tensiveness in drama may be found everywhere—as in poetry and prose fiction. If the play is in verse, the poetry has tensions of its own, as we discovered in the last chapter. If it is in prose, the degree of tensiveness shifts as we move from simple exposition to the action and interaction of characters. Unlike prose fiction, drama almost always exists in the present tense—it is something we are watching here and now.

Within a given scene there is usually a beginning, middle, and end. Changes in attitude, emotion, or idea, the introduction of new characters and events, the physical states of characters, conflicts (or lack of conflict) between characters, the effects of setting and weather, the impact of memories and of images—all affect tensiveness within scenes and help move scenes along. No good scene is static. It is almost always fatal for the interpreter to settle for a generalized feeling for a scene and seek simply to project that; the feelings must be particularized, made sequential, allowed to run the course of all acts, though the total act is never really over until the play is ended.

Dramatic Genres

Just as poetry may be divided into types, or genres (epic, elegy, sonnet, ode, dramatic monologue, and so forth), and just as prose fiction may be divided into types (short story, novel, novella, exemplum, fable, and so on), so drama falls into types: comedy, tragedy, history, farce, melodrama, tragicomedy, pastoral. These categories (and even types of types) involve judgments of subject and attitude as parts of structure. These are in many ways the most fascinating of all literary judgments, but no book such as this can hope to explore such matters more than briefly. The complexities of the literary art are enough to provide any individual, no matter how brilliant, with a lifetime of study, though it must be said that the experience of literature is available within limits to any of us.

It is sometimes argued that since the drama is meant to be performed onstage by a group of actors it is not proper material for the solo interpreter. But clearly there are many readers who enjoy reading plays, and in the silent reading of plays the reader must perform as he participates in the life of the drama. He must envision each of the characters, must hear their voices, must see what they do, must come to understand their feelings. He must know the setting in which they act and will benefit from understanding the way in which they dress and move.

Drama and Interpretation

The solo interpreter is a reader who shares this single realization of the dramatic text. He or she is actor, director, designer, costumer; all the actors come under the control of the single vision. It used to be said of the great Charlotte Cushman, when she read to audiences Shakespeare's *Macbeth,* that it was wonderful to hear a performance in which all the actors were as good as Charlotte Cushman. There is no doubt about the fact that the solo performer of drama faces formidable tasks, and it is clear that some audiences do not care for interpreted plays. But it is also clear that solo performance, like silent reading, can be a pleasurable experience. It is not the same as the fully acted play, but it has its own rewards. In the study of interpretation, it has much to teach the interpreter. It engages the reader with the text of the play in a way silent reading often does not. In interpretation, we may have the opportunity to hear fine plays that are rarely seen or heard in full theatrical performance.

MATERIALS FOR PRACTICE

from **THE AMERICAN DREAM**[13]
   —*Edward Albee*

[*Albee says that the play is a picture of our time as he sees it. It was part of his intention, he says, to offend, as well as amuse and entertain. Mommy and Daddy and Grandma have been talking—not really commu-*

nicating, however. Grandma is Mommy's mother; there has been talk of sending her to a nursing home—Mommy's idea. Love seems to be no part of this family. At the point where we begin, Mrs. Barker, who is up to her ears in activities, arrives—she isn't quite sure which activity has brought her here. —Ed.]

DADDY. Come in. You're late. But, of course, we expected you to be late; we were saying that we expected you to be late.

MOMMY. Daddy, don't be rude! We were saying that you just can't get satisfaction these days, and were talking about you, of course. Won't you come in?

MRS. BARKER. Thank you. I don't mind if I do.

MOMMY. We're very glad that you're here, late as you are. You do remember us, don't you? You were here once before. I'm Mommy, and this is Daddy, and that's Grandma, doddering there in the corner.

MRS. BARKER. Hello, Mommy; hello, Daddy; and hello there, Grandma.

DADDY. Now that you're here, I don't suppose you could go away and maybe come back some other time.

MRS. BARKER. Oh no; we're much too efficient for that. I said, hello there, Grandma.

MOMMY. Speak to them, Grandma.

GRANDMA. I don't see them.

DADDY. For shame, Grandma; they're here.

MRS. BARKER. Yes, we're here, Grandma. I'm Mrs. Barker. I remember you; don't you remember me?

GRANDMA. I don't recall. Maybe you were younger, or something.

MOMMY. Grandma! What a terrible thing to say!

MRS. BARKER. Oh now, don't scold her, Mommy; for all she knows she may be right.

DADDY. Uh . . . Mrs. Barker, is it? Won't you sit down?

MRS. BARKER. I don't mind if I do.

MOMMY. Would you like a cigarette, and a drink, and would you like to cross your legs?

MRS. BARKER. You forget yourself, Mommy; I'm a professional woman. But I will cross my legs.

DADDY. Yes, make yourself comfortable.

MRS. BARKER. I don't mind if I do.

GRANDMA. Are they still here?

MOMMY. Be quiet, Grandma.

MRS. BARKER. Oh, we're still here. My, what an unattractive apartment you have!

MOMMY. Yes, but you don't know what a trouble it is. Let me tell you . . .

DADDY. I was saying to Mommy . . .

MRS. BARKER. Yes, I know. I was listening outside.

DADDY. About the icebox, and . . . the doorbell . . . and the . . .

MRS. BARKER. . . . and the johnny. Yes, we're very efficient; we have to know everything in our work.

DADDY. Exactly what do you do?

MOMMY. Yes, what is your work?

MRS. BARKER. Well, my dear, for one thing, I'm chairman of your woman's club.

MOMMY. Don't be ridiculous. I was talking to the chairman of my woman's club just yester—Why, so you are. You remember, Daddy, the lady I was telling you about? The lady with the husband who sits in the *swing?* Don't you remember?

DADDY. No . . . no . . .

MOMMY. Of course you do. I'm so sorry, Mrs. Barker. I would have known you anywhere, except in this artificial light. And look! You have a hat just like the one I bought yesterday.

MRS. BARKER. *(With a little laugh)* No, not really; this hat is cream.

MOMMY. Well, my dear, that may look like a cream hat to you, but I can . . .

MRS. BARKER. Now, now; you seem to forget who I am.

MOMMY. Yes, I do, don't I? Are you sure you're comfortable? Won't you take off your dress?

MRS. BARKER. I don't mind if I do.

(She removes her dress.)

MOMMY. There. You must feel a great deal more comfortable.

MRS. BARKER. Well, I certainly *look* a great deal more comfortable.

DADDY. I'm going to blush and giggle.

MOMMY. Daddy's going to blush and giggle.

MRS. BARKER. *(Pulling the hem of her slip above her knees)* You're lucky to have such a man for a husband.

MOMMY. Oh, don't I know it!

DADDY. I just blushed and giggled and went sticky wet.

MOMMY. Isn't Daddy a caution, Mrs. Barker?

MRS. BARKER. Maybe if I smoked . . . ?

MOMMY. Oh, that isn't necessary.

MRS. BARKER. I don't mind if I do.

MOMMY. No; no, don't. Really.

MRS. BARKER. I don't mind . . .

MOMMY. I won't have you smoking in my house, and that's that! You're a professional woman.

DADDY. Grandma drinks AND smokes; don't you, Grandma?

GRANDMA. No.

MOMMY. Well, now, Mrs. Barker; suppose you tell us why you're here.

A RAISIN IN THE SUN (from Act I, Scene 2)[14]
—*Lorraine Hansberry*

MAMA. *(Still quietly)* Walter, what is the matter with you?

WALTER. Matter with me? Ain't nothing the matter with *me*!

MAMA. Yes there is. Something eating you up like a crazy man. Something more than me not giving you this money. The past few years I been watching it happen to you. You get all nervous acting and kind of wild in the eyes—*(Walter jumps up impatiently at her words.)* I said sit there now, I'm talking to you!

WALTER. Mama—I don't need no nagging at me today.

MAMA. Seem like you getting to a place where you always tied up in some kind of knot about something. But if anybody ask you 'bout it you just yell at 'em and bust out of the house and go out and drink somewheres. Walter Lee, people can't live with that. Ruth's a good, patient girl in her way—but you getting to be too much. Boy, don't make the mistake of driving that girl away from you.

WALTER. Why—what she do for me?

MAMA. She loves you.

WALTER. Mama—I'm going out. I want to go off somewhere and be by myself for a while.

MAMA. I'm sorry 'bout your liquor store, son. It just wasn't the thing for us to do. That's what I want to tell you about—

WALTER. I got to go out, Mama—
   (He rises.)

MAMA. It's dangerous, son.

WALTER. What's dangerous?

MAMA. When a man goes outside his home to look for peace.

WALTER. *(Beseechingly)* Then why can't there never be no peace in this house then?

MAMA. You done found it in some other house?

WALTER. No—there ain't no woman! Why do women always think there's a woman somewhere when a man gets restless. *(Coming to her)* Mama—Mama—I want so many things . . .

MAMA. Yes, son—

WALTER. I want so many things that they are driving me kind of crazy . . . Mama—look at me.

MAMA. I'm looking at you. You a good-looking boy. You got a job, a nice wife, a fine boy and—

WALTER. A job. (*Looks at her*) Mama, a job? I open and close car doors all day long. I drive a man around in his limousine and I say, "Yes, sir; no, sir; very good, sir; shall I take the Drive, sir?" Mama, that ain't no kind of job . . . that ain't nothing at all. (*Very quietly*) Mama, I don't know if I can make you understand.

MAMA. Understand what, baby?

WALTER. (*Quietly*) Sometimes it's like I can see the future stretched out in front of me—just plain as day. The future, Mama. Hanging over there at the edge of my days. Just waiting for me—a big, looming blank space—full of *nothing*. Just waiting for *me*. (*Pause*) Mama—sometimes when I'm downtown and I pass them cool, quiet-looking restaurants where them white boys are sitting back and talking 'bout things . . . sitting there turning deals worth millions of dollars . . . sometimes I see guys don't look much older than me—

MAMA. Son—how come you talk so much 'bout money?

WALTER. (*With immense passion*) Because it is life, Mama!

MAMA. (*Quietly*) Oh—(*Very quietly*) So now it's life. Money is life. Once upon a time freedom used to be life—now it's money. I guess the world really do change . . .

WALTER. No—it was always money, Mama. We just didn't know about it.

MAMA. No . . . something has changed. (*She looks at him.*) You something new, boy. In my time we was worried about not being lynched and getting to the North if we could and how to stay alive and still have a pinch of dignity too . . . Now here come you and Beneatha—talking 'bout things we ain't never even thought about hardly, me and your daddy. You ain't satisfied or proud of nothing we done. I mean that you had a home; that we kept you out of trouble till you was grown; that you don't have to ride to work on the back of nobody's streetcar—You my children—but how different we done become.

WALTER. You just don't understand, Mama, you just don't understand.

MAMA. Son—do you know your wife is expecting another baby? (*Walter stands, stunned, and absorbs what his mother has said.*) That's what she wanted to talk to you about. (*Walter sinks down into a chair.*) This ain't for me to be telling—but you ought to know. (*She waits.*) I think Ruth is thinking 'bout getting rid of that child.

WALTER. (*Slowly understanding*) No—no—Ruth wouldn't do that.

MAMA. When the world gets ugly enough—a woman will do anything for her family. *The part that's already living.*

WALTER. You don't know Ruth, Mama, if you think she would do that.

(*Ruth opens the bedroom door and stands there a little limp.*)

RUTH. *(Beaten)* Yes I would too, Walter. *(Pause)* I gave her a five-dollar down payment.

> *(There is total silence as the man stares at his wife and the mother stares at her son.)*

MAMA. *(Presently)* Well— *(Tightly)* Well—son, I'm waiting to hear you say something . . . I'm waiting to hear how you be your father's son. Be the man he was . . . *(Pause)* Your wife say she going to destroy your child. And I'm waiting to hear you talk like him and say we a people who give children life, not who destroys them— *(She rises.)* I'm waiting to see you stand up and look like your daddy and say we done give up one baby to poverty and that we ain't going to give up nary another one . . . I'm waiting.

WALTER. Ruth—

MAMA. If you a son of mine, tell her! *(Walter turns, look at her and can say nothing. She continues, bitterly.)* You . . . you are a disgrace to your father's memory. Somebody get me my hat.

CURTAIN

SAINT JOAN (from Scene 2)[15]
—Bernard Shaw

JOAN. *(To the Dauphin)* Who be old Gruff-and-Grum?

CHARLES. He is the Duke de la Trémouille.

JOAN. What be his job?

CHARLES. He pretends to command the army. And whenever I find a friend I can care for, he kills him.

JOAN. Why dost let him?

CHARLES. *(Petulantly moving to the throne side of the room to escape from her magnetic field)* How can I prevent him? He bullies me. They all bully me.

JOAN. Art afraid?

CHARLES. Yes: I am afraid. It's no use preaching to me about it. It's all very well for these big men with their armor that is too heavy for me, and their swords that I can hardly lift, and their muscle and their shouting and their bad tempers. They like fighting: most of them are making fools of themselves all the time they are not fighting: but I am quiet and sensible; and I don't want to kill people: I only want to be left alone to enjoy myself in my own way. I never asked to be king: it was pushed on me. So if you are going to say "Son of St. Louis: gird on the sword of your ancestors, and lead us to victory," you may spare your breath to cool your porridge; for I cannot do it. I am not built that way; and there is an end of it.

JOAN. *(Trenchant and masterful)* Blethers! We are all like that to begin with. I shall put courage into thee.

CHARLES. But I don't want to have courage put into me. I want to

[15] Reprinted by permission of The Society of Authors, for the Bernard Shaw Estate.

sleep in a comfortable bed, and not live in continual terror of being killed or wounded. Put courage into the others, and let them have their bellyful of fighting; but let me alone.

JOAN. It's no use, Charlie: thou must face what God puts on thee. If thou fail to make thyself king, thou'lt be a beggar: what else art fit for? Come! Let me see thee sitting on the throne. I have looked forward to that.

CHARLES. What is the good of sitting on the throne when the other fellows give all the orders? However! (*He sits enthroned, a piteous figure.*) here is the king for you! Look your fill at the poor devil.

JOAN. Thou'rt not king yet, lad: thou'rt Dauphin. Be not led away by them around thee. Dressing up don't fill empty noddle. I know the people: the real people that make thy bread for thee; and I tell thee they count no man king of France until the holy oil has been poured on his hair and himself consecrated and crowned in Rheims Cathedral. And thou needs new clothes, Charlie. Why does not Queen look after thee properly?

CHARLES. We're too poor. She wants all the money we can spare to put on her own back. Besides, I like to see her beautifully dressed; and I don't care what I wear myself; I should look ugly anyhow.

JOAN. There is some good in thee, Charlie; but it is not yet a king's good.

CHARLES. We shall see. I am not such a fool as I look. I have my eyes open; and I can tell you that one good treaty is worth ten good fights. These fighting fellows lose all on the treaties that they gain on the fights. If we can only have a treaty, the English are sure to have the worst of it, because they are better at fighting than at thinking.

JOAN. If the English win, it is they that will make the treaty; and then God help poor France! Thou must fight, Charlie, whether thou will or no. I will go first to hearten thee. We must take our courage in both hands: aye, and pray for it with both hands too.

CHARLES. (*Descending from his throne and again crossing the room to escape from her dominating urgency*) Oh, do stop talking about God and praying. I can't bear people who are always praying. Isn't it bad enough to have to do it at the proper times?

JOAN. (*Pitying him*) Thou poor child, thou hast never prayed in thy life. I must teach thee from the beginning.

CHARLES. I am not a child: I am a grown man and a father; and I will not be taught any more.

JOAN. Aye, you have a little son. He that will be Louis the Eleventh when you die. Would you not fight for him?

CHARLES. No: a horrid boy. He hates me. He hates everybody, selfish little beast! I don't want to be bothered with children. I don't want to be a father; and I don't want to be a son: especially a son of St. Louis. I don't want to be any of these fine things you all have your heads full of: I want to be just what I am. Why can't you mind your own business, and let me mind mine?

JOAN. (*Again contemptuous*) Minding your own business is like minding your own body: it's the shortest way to make yourself sick. What is my business? Helping mother at home. What is thine? Petting lapdogs and sucking sugarsticks. I call that muck. I tell thee it is God's business we are here to do: not our own. I have a message to thee from God; and thou must listen to it, though thy heart break with the terror of it.

CHARLES. I don't want a message; but can you tell me any secrets? Can you do any cures? Can you turn lead into gold, or anything of that sort?

JOAN. I can turn thee into a king, in Rheims Cathedral; and that is a miracle that will take some doing, it seems.

CHARLES. If we go to Rheims, and have a coronation, Anne will want new dresses. We can't afford them. I am all right as I am.

JOAN. As you are! And what is that? Less than my father's poorest shepherd. Thou'rt not lawful owner of thy own land of France till thou be consecrated.

CHARLES. But I shall not be lawful owner of my own land anyhow. Will the consecration pay off the mortgages? I have pledged my last acre to the Archbishop and that fat bully. I owe money even to Bluebeard.

JOAN. (Earnestly) Charlie: I come from the land, and have gotten my strength working on the land; and I tell thee that the land is thine to rule righteously and keep God's peace in, and not to pledge at the pawnshop as a drunken woman pledges her children's clothes. And I come from God to tell thee to kneel in the cathedral and solemnly give thy kingdom to Him for ever and ever, and become the greatest king in the world as His steward and His bailiff, His soldier and His servant. The very clay of France will become holy; her soldiers will be the soldiers of God: the rebel dukes will be rebels against God: the English will fall on their knees and beg thee let them return to their lawful homes in peace. Wilt be a poor little Judas, and betray me and Him that sent me?

CHARLES. (Tempted at last) Oh, if I only dare!

JOAN. I shall dare, dare, and dare again, in God's name! Art for or against me?

CHARLES. (Excited) I'll risk it. I warn you I shan't be able to keep it up; but I'll risk it. You shall see. (Running to the main door and shouting.) Hallo! Come back, everybody (To Joan, as he runs back to the arch opposite.) Mind you stand by and don't let me be bullied. (Through the arch.) Come along, will you: the whole Court. (He sits down in the royal chair as they all hurry in to their former places, chattering and wondering.) Now I'm in for it; but no matter: here goes.

A MAN FOR ALL SEASONS (from Act 1) [16]
—*Robert Bolt*

HENRY. Thomas. You *are* my friend, are you not?

MORE. Your Majesty.

HENRY. And thank God I have a friend for my Chancellor. (*Laughs.*)

Readier to be friends, I trust, than he was to be Chancellor. Thomas . . . Did you know that Wolsey named you for Chancellor?

MORE. Wolsey!

HENRY. Aye; before he died. Wolsey named you and Wolsey was no fool.

MORE. He was a statesman of incomparable ability, Your Grace.

HENRY. Was he so? Then why did he fail me. It was villainy then. I was right to break him; he was all pride. And he failed me in the one thing that matters, then or now. And why? He wanted to be Pope! I'll tell you something, Thomas—it was never merry in England while we had Cardinals amongst us. (*More lowers his eyes. Henry pauses and then resumes in a calculatedly offhand manner.*) Touching this matter of my divorce, Thomas; have you thought of it since we last talked?

MORE. Of little else.

HENRY. Then you see your way clear to me?

MORE. That you should put away Queen Catherine, Sire? Oh, alas—as I think of it I see so clearly that I can *not* come with Your Grace, that my endeavor is not to think of it at all.

HENRY. Then you have not thought enough! (*With real appeal.*) Great God, Thomas, why do you hold out against me in the desire of my heart?

MORE. (*Drawing up sleeve and baring his arm*)—There is my right arm. Take your dagger and saw it from my shoulder, and I will laugh and be thankful, if by that means I can come with Your Grace with a clear conscience.

HENRY. Ha! So I break my word, Master More! (*Reconsiders.*)No, no, I'm joking . . . I joke roughly. (*Wandering away.*) I often think I'm a rough young fellow. (*Becoming more reasonable and pleasant.*) You must consider, Thomas, that I stand in peril of my soul. It was no marriage; she was my brother's widow. Leviticus: Chapter 18: "Thou shalt not uncover the nakedness of thy brother's wife."

MORE. Yes, Your Grace. But Deuteronomy—

HENRY. (*Triumphant*)—But Deuteronomy's ambiguous!

MORE. (*Bursting out*)—Your Grace, I'm not fit to meddle in these matters—to me it seems a matter for the Holy See—

HENRY. (*Reprovingly*)—Thomas, Thomas, does a man need a Pope to tell him when he's sinned? It was a sin. I admit it; I repent. And God has punished me. . . . Son after son she's borne me, Thomas, all dead at birth, or within a month; I never saw the hand of God so clear in anything. It is my bounded *duty* to put away the Queen, and all the Popes back to St. Peter shall not come between me and my duty! How is it that you cannot see? Everyone else does.

MORE. Then why does Your Grace need my poor support?

HENRY. Because you are honest. What's more to the purpose, you're known to be honest. . . . There are those like Norfolk who follow me because I wear the crown, and there are those like Master Cromwell who follow me because they are jackals with sharp teeth and I am their lion, and there is a mass that follows me because it follows anything that moves—and there is you.

MORE. I am sick to think how much I must displease Your Grace.

HENRY. No, Thomas, I respect your sincerity. Respect? Oh, man, it's water in the desert. *(Pauses briefly.)* How did you like our music?

MORE. Could it have been Your Grace's own?

HENRY. *(Smiling)*—Discovered!

MORE. To me it seemed—delightful.

HENRY. Thomas—I chose the right man for Chancellor.

MORE. I must in fairness add that my taste in music is reputedly deplorable.

HENRY. Your taste in music is excellent. It exactly coincides with my own. *(Turns to More, his face set.)* Touching this other business mark you, Thomas, I'll have no opposition. Your conscience is your own affair; but you are my Chancellor. There, you have my word—I'll leave you out of it. But I don't take it kindly, Thomas, and I'll have no opposition! Am I to burn in Hell because the Bishop of Rome, with the Spanish King's knife to his throat, mouths me Deuteronomy? Hypocrites! *(More rises.)* Lie low if you will, but—no words, no signs, no letters, no pamphlets—mark it, Thomas—no writings against me!

MORE. Your Grace is unjust. I am Your Grace's loyal minister.

MORE. You are stubborn. *(Attempting to woo More.)* If you could come with me, you are the man I would soonest raise—yes, with my own hand.

MORE. *(Sitting and covering his face)*—Oh, Your Grace overwhelms me!

HENRY. *(Uneasily eyeing More)*—Oh, lift yourself up, man—have I not promised? *(More braces.)* Shall we eat? *(The chimes strike eight.)*

MORE. If Your Grace pleases. *(Recovering as Lady Alice re-enters.)*

HENRY. Eight o'clock? Thomas, the tide will be changing. I was forgetting the tide. I'd better go. Lady Alice, I had forgotten in your haven here how time flows past outside. Affairs call me to court and so I give you my thanks and say good night. *(He leaves.)*

ALICE. *(To More)*—You crossed him—

MORE. Well, Alice—what would you *want* me to do?

ALICE. Be ruled! If you won't rule him, be ruled!

MORE. I neither could nor would rule my King. But there's a little . . . little, area . . . where I must rule myself. It's very little—less to him than a tennis court.

ALICE. I wish he'd eaten here . . .

MORE. Yes—we shall be living on that "simple supper" of yours for a fortnight. (*Alice will not laugh.*) Alice, set your mind at rest—this (*Tapping himself*) is not the stuff of which martyrs are made.

THREE GENERATIONS[17]
—Nick Joaquin[18]

The elder Monzon was waiting for his wife to speak. He had finished breakfast and had just laid down the newspaper through which he had been glancing. Across the table, his wife played absently with a spoon. Her brows were knitted, but a half-smile kept twitching on her lips. She was a handsome, well-preserved woman and, her husband was thinking, a great deal more clever than she allowed herself to appear.

"It is about Chitong," she said at last. "He does not want to continue the law-course he is taking. The boy has a vocation, Celo. He wants to study for the priesthood."

"When did he speak to you?"

"About a month ago, the first time. But I told him to make sure. Last night, he said he was sure. Of course, you have noticed how devout he has been lately?"

Monzon rose. "Well, I would never have expected it of him," he said, but his wife shook her head.

"Has he not always been quiet and reserved, even as a boy?"

"Yes, but not noticeably of a religious temper."

"Only because he did not understand then. He has taken a long time maturing, Celo, but I think it is for the best. Now he knows what really calls him, but he is really very sincere. Are you glad?"

"It is a career, like all the others. Did he say what seminary?"

"We can talk that over later. He feared you would refuse."

"What does he take me for? A heretic?"

The servant-girl came in to clear the table, and the señora rose and followed her husband to the sala. "Celo, when are you going to see your father? Nena called up last night. She was crying. She says she can do nothing with the old man. Your cousin Paulo is not there any more to help her. It seems the old man broke a plate on his head. . . ."

Monzon paused, his hand on the door-knob. He had put on his hat already. Suddenly, he looked very old and tired. His wife came nearer and placed a hand on his shoulder. "Why will you not let him have his woman again, Celo? He does not have very long to live."

He stared at her fiercely. "Please do not be vulgar, Sofía," he growled, but his wife only smiled.

For all the years they had lived together, he was still startled by a

---

[17] Reprinted by permission of the author.

[18] Nick Joaquin is widely regarded as the foremost contemporary author of the Philippines. Although he has written poetry, he is best known for his prose fiction and for his single long play, *Portrait of the Artist as Filipino.*

certain nakedness in his wife's mind; in the mind of all women, for that matter. You took them for what they appeared: shy, reticent, bred by nuns, but after marriage, though they continued to look demure, there was always in their attitude toward sex, an amused irony, even a deliberate coarseness; such as he could never allow himself, even in his own mind, or with other men.

"Well," said Doña Sofía, withdrawing her hand, "he has certainly become wild since you drove that woman away. Nena says he refuses to eat. He takes what is served to him and throws it to the floor, plates and everything. He lies awake the whole night roaring like a lion. Yesterday, Nena said, he tried to get up. She was outside and did not hear him. When she came in, there he lay on the floor, all tangled up in his blankets, out of breath, and crying to the heavens. She called in Paulo to get him in bed again, and he grabbed a plate and broke it on poor Paulo's head."

Monzon did not look at his wife's face: he knew very well what he would see. He stared instead at his hands, huge, calloused, and ugly, and suddenly they were his father's hands he was seeing, and he was a little boy that cowered beneath them and the whip they held: "Lie down, you little beast! Lie down, beast!" "Not in the face, father! Do not hit me in the face, father!" "I will hit you where the thunder I want to. I will teach my sons to answer back. Lie down, you beast!"

"Your father never could live without women," Doña Sofía was saying. "And now you have driven that one away. It is death by torture."

"You certainly can choose your words," Monzon retorted. "You know very well what the doctor said."

"But what does it matter since he is going to die anyway? Why not let him have what he wants?"

"You do not sound like a decent woman, Sofía." He turned his back on her and opened the door. "Tell Chitong to have the car ready this afternoon. He and I will go there together."

It was still early, only half-past seven; and when he came to the Dominican church, he went in. He knew he would find Chitong there. He did not know why he wanted to. But he went in and there were few people inside. From the high windows a many-colored light filtered in, drenching the floor violet, but in the side-chapel of the Virgin it was dark, with only the gold glow of candles: he saw his son kneeling there, near the altar, saying his rosary.

Monzon knelt down himself, and tried to compose his mind to prayer, but there was suddenly, painfully, out of his very heart, a sharp, hot, rushing, jealous bitterness towards that devout young man praying so earnestly over there.

He did not understand the feeling. He did not want to understand it. Enough that this thing was clear: that he hated his son for being able to kneel there, submitted utterly to his God. Yet why should he resent that so bitterly?

His own youth had been very unhappy, yes; but whose fault was it that he had suffered so much? The old man had really been no more heavy of hand and temper than most fathers of that time. He knew that. Those times gave to the head of a family absolute dominion over his women and children. He could not remember that any of his brothers had found the system particularly oppressive. They bowed to the paternal whip as long as they had to; then broke away to marry and breed and establish families over whom they had in turn set themselves up as lords almighty.

As for the women, he had suspected that they even took a certain delight in the barbaric cruelties of their lords. His father was never without two or three concubines whom he had whipped as regularly as he did his sons; but none of them, once fallen into his power, had bothered to strive for a more honorable status. If they went away, it was because the old man wearied of them; though at his bidding, they would return as meekly, to work in his house or in his fields, to cook his food, to wash his clothes, to attend to his children, and to bare their flesh to the blows of his anger or to the blows of his love.

Monzon had wept as a boy for his mother; but later on he had found out that she was only too thankful, worn out as she was with toil and childbearing, for the company and assistance of these other women. If she fought the old man at all, it was in defense of her children, and especially of himself (for she had been quick to notice that he would not be so easy to break).

She had singled him out from among all her sons to bear and fulfill her few childish dreams and ambitions, and in her last, long, lingering illness, this faith in him had shone in her eyes and trembled in her hands whenever he came near her, and it had frightened and terrified him. For, even then, he was beginning to realize that, though he might set himself against all those things for which his father stood as symbol, he, himself, would never quite completely escape them. Go where he might, he would still be carrying the old man's flesh along; and that flesh smouldered darkly with fires that all a lifetime was too short to quench.

Monzon buried his face in his hands. He felt strangely exhausted. Peace, he thought, peace of mind, of body: he had been praying for that all his life. Just a little peace. It was not possible that he was to go on forever and ever, divided against himself. But there was that little voice, as usual, that voice at his ears, mocking him: Your father could find peace in the simple delights of the body; but you thought yourself too good for that.

His bitterness leapt into active anger: Is this then what I get for having tried to be clean? But the voice laughed at him: When were you ever a lover of purity? All that solemn virtuousness of yours began as a gesture of rebellion against your father. And so it still is. If he had been a chaste man your defiance would have taken a more perverse form.

And suppose I give up now, stop fighting, submit; would I be at peace? No, said the voice. You would be as miserable in your surrender to your body as you have been in your struggle against it. Besides, it is too late. Men like your father find their brief escapes in the whip, the table, and the bed. That rapt young man over there—your son!—is now groping for a more complete release. For him also there shall be peace. But for you . . .

Monzon rose. And just then his son looked around. Their eyes met. The young man stood up and came towards his father. He was still holding his beads, and his hands began to tremble. Why does the old man look so fierce? Has mother told him? He looks as if he hated me. As if he would do me a violence.

But as the boy approached, the older Monzon turned away and walked rapidly out of the church.

"He was not angry at all," Doña Sofía said. "He was very pleased. You do not understand your father, Chitong. He does not speak much, but he is really concerned over what your are going to make of your life."

"But the way he looked at me . . ." Chitong began. He was having his breakfast and Doña Sofía sat across the table watching him.

"That, you probably imagined only."

"Oh, no," insisted her son. "And suddenly, he turned away, without even speaking to me." He pushed the plates away and propped his elbows on the table. "I could not pray anymore afterwards. I felt empty and ridiculous. Mother, I said last night I was sure about this thing, and I still am. But have I any right . . . I mean . . . But how shall I say it!" He paused and considered for a moment, drumming his fingers on the table. "You know, mother, he did have a hard time of it. It shows in his face. I often feel sorry for him. He has made it possible that I should not go through whatever he had to go through. But is such a thing right? And anyway, is it good for me?"

"Whatever are you talking about, Chitong?"

Her son sighed and shrugged his shoulders. "Nothing," he replied, and got up.

"You are to accompany him this afternoon to your grandfather. The old man is getting worse. You are to take the car."

Chitong was standing by the window. She had never seen his face look so grave. She was worried and, rising, approached him.

"Son," she said, "if you are going to dedicate yourself to God, then nothing else should matter to you."

"But that is it, that is it precisely!" cried the boy "I do wish there was something else that did matter. Something big and fierce and powerful. That I would have to fight down because I loved God more. But there is nothing." He made a gesture with his hand. "Nothing. And father knows it. And that is why he despises me. And he is right."

"Your father does not despise you. How you talk."

Suddenly the boy crumpled up on his knees, his face in his hands.

"I am not sincere, mother! I am a coward! I try to run away! I am nothing! And father knows it! Father knows it! He knows everything!"

She stopped and gathered him to her breast. She was terribly frightened. She was suddenly only a woman. Men were entirely different and alien creatures. Yes, even this one, whom she had borne in her own body. This one, also.

It was a good afternoon for a drive. The wind that met their faces smelled of rain and earth, and in the twilight became vaguely fragrant. They were silent most of the way for, usually, when they were alone together, they felt embarrassed and shy, as though they were lovers.

Chitong was at the wheel. The elder Monzon sat beside him, smoking a cigar. From time to time, he found himself glancing at his son's profile. There was a difference there, he felt. They boy looked tense, tight-strung, even ill. When the darkness fell about them, they both felt easier and the older man began to talk.

"Your mother tells me that you want to give up law."

"Did she tell you why?"

"And I could hardly believe my ears."

"I know I am quite unworthy."

"Oh, as for that, I should say that no one can ever be worthy enough. I was merely wondering at the sudden conversion."

"It was not sudden, father. I had been coming to this for a long time without knowing it."

"Well, how did you know?"

"I simply woke up one night and said to myself: I belong there. And all at once I knew why I had been finding everything so unsatisfactory."

"We all have such moments—when everything clicks into place."

"And becomes beautiful."

"It was through the appeal of beautiful things that you found God?"

"With the senses, yes. Certainly not with the mind: I am no thinker. Nor yet with the heart: I am not a saint. I guess that's why it took me so long to realize where I was heading."

"You should have come to me for information. I could have shared my experience with you."

"Your experience, father?"

"—of a vocation. I could have—But why do you look so shocked? I was young once myself, you know."

"But what happened, father?"

"Nothing. My mother wanted me to be a priest. I was quite willing. But when she died, I abandoned the idea."

"I never knew!"

"I never told anyone—not even your mother. Shall we keep it a secret between us?"

For a moment, the wall that stood always between them disappeared, and they could touch each other. I am an unclean man, the elder Monzon was thinking, but what was depravity in me and my fathers becomes, in my son, a way to God.

And the young man thought: I am something after all, I am this old man's desire that he has fleshed alive. It sprang from him, began in him; that which now I will myself to be. . . .

The evening flowed turgid with the fragrance of the night-flowers and of their thoughts; but the moment passed and they were suddenly cold and tired. They fell silent again, and shy, as though they had loved.

The house stood at the edge of the town. Monzon always thought of it as something tremendous and eternal. Each time he went back to it, he was surprised afresh to find that it was not very big really and that it would not last much longer; the foundations were rotting, the roof leaked, white ants were disintegrating the whole structure.

Here, at the foot of the stairs, always he must pause and gather himself together. A shrunken, rotting house. But here it was that he had been a little boy, and the roof seemed to expand above his head till it was as high and wide as the heavens.

At the sound of their coming up, a little harassed-looking woman came to the door to meet them. Monzon felt sorry for her. She was his youngest sister. All of them had managed to get away except this one. And she would never get away at all, he thought, as he took her fluttering hands in his. "How is he?" he asked. She merely shook her head and turned to Chitong, who bowed and kissed her hand.

It was dark in that sala; an oil lamp on a table gave the only light. As they moved, the three of them cast huge, nervous shadows. The old man lay in the next room and they could hear his heavy, angry breathing, punctuated with coughs and oaths.

"He is like that all the time," Nena complained, wringing her thin hands. "He has not eaten for days. He shouts at me whenever I enter. He tries to get up all the time and he falls, of course, and I have to call in someone to put him back." There was a pathetic pleading in the eyes she turned shyly on her brother. "He keeps asking for the girl, Celo. Maybe it would be much better. . . ."

But Monzon refused to meet her eyes. "Go and prepare something, Nena. I am going to make him eat," he said. She sighed and went off to the kitchen.

The door of the old man's room stood open. When the two of them entered, the sick man, sprawled in the big four-posted bed upon a mountain of pillows became silent. As in the sala, a single oil-lamp illuminated the room. The bed stood in the shadow but they were aware of the old man's eyes, watching them intently.

Before those eyes, Monzon felt himself stripped, one by one, of all his defenses: maturity, social position, wealth, success. He was a little boy again and he bent down and lifted his father's enormous, damp hand to his lips, and at the contact, a million pins seemed to prick his whole body.

But Chitong came forward and kissed the old man on the brow. The boy felt himself fascinated by those intensely hating eyes. He, also, was rather afraid of this old man; but with a difference. Even as a boy, he had felt the force of those eyes, lips, hands; but his grandfather had still been, then, in the plenitude of strength. But now, when he lay helpless, his legs paralyzed, the flesh gone loose about the bones, the face grown pale and shriveled, did he communicate all the more unbearably that pride, that exultation in simple brute power.

The boy felt himself becoming a single wave of obedience towards the old man. His lips lingered upon that moist brow as though they would drink in the old man's very brains. The feel of the wet flesh was an almost sensual delight, something new and terrifying to him and, at the same time, painful; almost as if the kiss were also a kind of death. It was a multitudinous moment for the boy. When he straightened up, he found himself trembling. And at the same time, he wanted to run away—to some quiet corner, to pray.

"Well, father, why have you sent Paulo away?" Monzon asked, speaking very loudly. The old man continued to stare at them in silence. He seemed to be checking even his breath. His thick lips were pressed tightly shut. Only his eyes spoke. His eyes hated them. His eyes sprang at their throats and wrung lifeless their voices. His eyes challenged this unafraid-pretending solid man that was his son; at that challenge, Monzon stepped nearer and abruptly stripped the blankets from the old man. For a moment they stared at each other.

Monzon had collected himself. Of you, I am not going to be afraid, his eyes told the old man. Not anymore. . . . Often had he said that in his mind; now, he wanted to say it aloud because, almost, he believed it to be true. But he spoke to Chitong instead: "Your Tía Nena may want you to help her. If the food for your grandfather is ready, bring it in here."

When Chitong came back with the tray of food, he found that his father had taken off his coat and rolled up his shirtsleeves. He had propped the sick man up to a sitting position and had changed his clothes.

The sick man's face had altered. He sat among the pillows, his face turned away, the eyes closed, the beautiful lips parted, as if in anguish. His hands lay clenched on his lap. He would not look at his son. He would not look at the food.

"You are going to eat, father," Monzon told him. He had taken the tray from Chitong. He did not speak loudly now. He knew he had won. This old man of whom all his life he had been afraid: had he not just dressed him like any baby? And now, like a mere baby again, he would be fed. "You are going to eat, father," he said again in his quiet voice.

The old man turned around and opened his eyes. They were fierce no longer. The were full of tiredness and the desire for death.

Chitong felt the old man's agony as his own. He could not stand it. He had an impulse to approach his father and knock the tray from his hands. He could not trust himself to speak.

The elder Monzon must have sensed this fury, for suddenly he turned to his son. "Chitong, you must be hungry. Better go and find something to eat."

Chitong swallowed the words in his mouth and turned away. At the door he paused and looked back. His father had laid a hand against the old man's breast; with the other he tried to push a spoonful of food into the tightly closed mouth. The old man tried to evade it, but now he could not turn his face away; his son had him pinned against the bed. At last he gave up, opened his mouth, and received the food. His eyes closed and tears ran down his cheeks.

Chitong glanced at his father. The elder Monzon was smiling. . . .

In the kitchen, he found his Tía Nena, sitting motionless in a corner. She looked as if she had been struck down. Her eyes were full of fear and suffering. Chitong realized that what he had felt for a moment when he kissed the old man's brow, this woman had known all her life. That was why she could not leave the old man; why, of all his children, she had remained faithful. She was in his power; and like himself, Chitong thought bitterly, she was the kind for whom life is possible only in the immolation of self to something mightier outside it.

"Did he eat?" she asked and, when he nodded, began to cry. He stooped and took her in his arms and tried to still her sobbing, but he remembered how, this morning, he, himself, had cried in his mother's arms and was not able to find, nor in her bosom, nor in her words, the answering strength he sought. . . .

Monzon, when he came out, found them sharing a scanty supper. For once, he looked quite happy. He kept rubbing his hands and smiling absently. He shook his head at Nena's offer of food.

"No, I am not hungry. And I have to go now." He took out his watch. "Is there still a bus I can take, Nena? Chitong, you are to remain with the car. Tomorrow I will come back with the doctor."

Chitong rose and accompanied his father to the door. The single lamp in the sala had gone out and they walked in darkness.

"Your grandfather is sleeping. If he wakes up, you can tell him I have gone."

They had reached the stairs. The elder Monzon paused and laid a hand on his son's shoulder. "Your mother has told you I am willing that you should follow your vocation, no?"

"Yes, father." Chitong could feel how in the dark his father's face had changed again. Even his voice had lost its momentary confidence.

"Yes. That is a good life," Monzon went on, "and it is, perhaps, the best for you."

He descended the stairs, opened the street-door below, and stepped out into the night. Chitong remained for some time at the head of the stairs, wondering just what those last words had meant.

In his grandfather's room, he spread a mat on the floor, undressed, and lay down. He had placed the lamp on a chair beside him and, now, he took out his breviary and began to read. The words that opened out to him were like cool arms into which he surrendered his troubled body. That had been a strange day, full of unrest and uncertainties; but as he read, an earlier sureness and peace came back to him.

". . . *my soul had relied on His word. My soul had hoped in the Lord. From the morning watch even until night, let Israel hope in the Lord. For with the Lord, there is mercy and with Him plentiful redemption. And he shall redeem Israel from all his iniquities. . . .*"

In his bed, on the other side of the room, the old man was awake and restless. Chitong could hear him turning, now to one side, now to the other. His breath came in short gasps, as if in difficulty. He reached out with his hands. He clutched at the pillows. He tried to rise.

The boy rose from time to time to cover him up again or to pick up the pillows. The old man's hands sought and clung to the boy's arms but his eyes, Chitong saw, were closed.

Names poured from the old man's lips. He called on every woman he had ever loved. He wanted his women. He became angry and shouted for them as in the days of his strength. He commanded them to come near. He cursed and shook his fists at them. No one came. He tried to rise and fell back, moaning and beating on the bed with his hands.

Afterwards, he became quiet. He must have realized that he was powerful no longer. Then he began to call on his women again, but softly, tenderly. He wooed them as a shy boy might; his lips shaped broken and beautiful phrases of adoration. But still no one came.

He fell into despair. He became furious again. He raged in his bed. He howled with all his might. He tore at the pillows. He tried to get up. The bed shook with his anger.

Chitong, lying on the floor, tried to deafen his ears to the old man's cries. He tried to read, but the words would not stand still. He closed the book and tried to sleep but, even in the intervals when the old man lay silent, he could feel him suffering, desiring, despairing, there in his bed in the darkness.

He got up and thought: I will pray for him. I will pray that he be delivered from temptation. I will pray that God quiet the fever of his flesh.

He approached and knelt beside the old man's bed, but a glance at that tortured face shot hollow all the prayers in his mouth. He felt again, as at Santo Domingo that morning, empty and ridiculous.

The sick man stared at him, yet did not see him. Those eyes saw only women and the bodies of women. Pain and desire had made him blind to all else. He stretched out his shriveled hands for the women that were not there. He had exhausted his voice; now he could only moan. Chitong could bear it no longer.

He rose and left the room. He was thinking of that woman—no, only a girl really—whom his grandfather had kept before his legs collapsed. The older Monzon had driven the girl away, but she might still be living somewhere in the town. His Tía Nena was still up, ironing clothes in the kitchen; he could ask her.

But she was frightened when she learned what he proposed to do. Yes, the girl was living in the town. "But your father will surely find out, Chitong, if she comes here. Oh, no do not ask me how. He will. He knows everything."

The words cut through the boy, "Then, let him!" he cried. "But I am going to bring the girl back. The old man needs her. Now, tell me where she lives."

It took him almost an hour to find the house, but only a few words to make the girl come. Chitong had seen her many times before, but when she came running down the stairs and stood beside him in the moonlight, he knew that he was seeing her really for the first time.

She was not very pretty, and still very young; but her body, her eyes, the way she moved, hinted that attractive maturity which only physical love develops. She had wrapped an old shawl around her head and shoulders, and as they hurried through the empty streets, Chitong could feel her thoughts running ahead towards the old man.But his mind, sensitive in such things, was not repelled.

There was in her, he knew, as in his grandfather, that simple unity which he, himself, had been denied. It was not strange that two such people should desire each other, or that so young a girl, when she might have more youthful lovers, should prefer the sexagenarian in whose arms she had become a woman. They had had to drive her away when he fell sick.

Chitong had been there when it happened and he recalled his father's exquisite brutality and how this girl had seemed to him, at the time, incapable of either fear or shame. She had refused to leave the house; had stood before the elder Monzon, thrusting her defiant face into his; and Chitong remembered how his father's hand had trembled though not a nerve in his face had twitched.

Monzon had released his belt on the sly, pushed the girl away suddenly, and given her a full stroke across the shoulders with the belt. And with the belt, he had pursued her out of the room and down the stairs, slamming the door in her face. She had remained down there, screaming and kicking at the door till the police came and dragged her away.

But she was not thinking at all of these things, Chitong saw, as he hurried beside her, glancing into her passionate face. She was going to her first lover. He had called her. He needed her. Young men were only young men: they could offer nothing in love to make her wiser than she had been in such things from the very beginning. And her nervous fingers, clutching the shawl across her breasts, spoke almost aloud the violence of her need.

A few steps from the house, a woman abruptly emerged from shadow. Chitong recognized his Tía Nena. She had been running; she could hardly speak.

"Chitong," she gasped, "your father has come back. He could not find a bus." She turned to the girl: "You must not come. Go back at once!"

The girl stepped back, but Chitong grasped her hand. "Do not be afraid," he said. "You are coming."

His aunt stared at him. "Chitong, you know how it is when your father gets angry. . . ."

"I am not afraid."

"I think he suspects where you went. . . ."

"So much the better then. Come on."

It was the first time in his life he had made a decision. He felt released.

The elder Monzon was standing in the sala when they entered. He had lighted the lamp and now stood watching it thoughtfully, his hands locked behind him. He glanced up as they filed in. When he saw the girl, he flushed darkly and he felt again the multitude of pins pricking his flesh. He dropped his eyes at once, but the girl's image persisted before him: the fierce eyes, the small, round mouth, the long, thin, girlish neck. She had drawn her shawl away, and he had seen where her breasts began and how they rose and fell with her breath.

He had a sudden, delirious craving to unloose his belt and whip her again, to make her suffer, to tear her flesh into shreds, to mutilate that supple, defiant, sweet, animal body of hers. His hands shook and his desire became an anger towards his son who had brought this voluptuous being so near.

"Who told you to bring this woman here, Chitong?" He tried in vain to make his voice calm. He doubled his fists: the nails dug into his flesh.

Chitong stared, open-mouthed. He realized now that what he had done was an action for which his soul would later demand reasons. It was not his father before whom he stood. It was God.

The girl was standing beside him and he felt her moving away. He sprang to life. "No, no," he cried. "You are not to go! He needs you! You must not go!" He held her back.

"A fine priest you will make!" snapped the elder Monzon.

Chitong came nearer. His eyes entreated the older man to understand. He stretched out a hand; with the other, he detained the girl. He had never found it so hard to make himself articulate.

"Father," he said at last, "if it is a sin to allow him his woman, then I will take the sin on my shoulders. I will pray that it . . ."

"Release that woman!" cried the elder man. "Let her go away!"

The boy's face hardened. "No, father. She is not going."

They were standing almost face to face. Suddenly, the father lifted his clenched fist and struck the boy in the face.

"Not in the face, father!" the boy cried out, lifting his hands too late to shield himself; the blow had already fallen.

Monzon, horrified, heard the boy's cry through every inch of his body. He had never before laid hands on the boy. The impulse to strike had come so suddenly. He tortured his mind for an explanation. He had not wanted to hurt the boy, no. He had, the moment before, desired the girl evil, but it was not she, either, who had prompted his fist. Was it the old man, then? Was it his father he had struck?

No. No, it was himself: that self of his, inherited, long fought, which had, the moment before, looked on the girl with strange fury. It was that self of his, which perpetuated the old man, against whom he had lifted his fist, but it was his son who had received the blow—and the blow was a confession of his whole life.

Now he stood silent, watching they boy's flesh darken where his fist had fallen, and the gradual blood defining the wound.

They stood staring at each other, as if petrified, and the girl, forgotten, slipped swiftly away from them and into the old man's room, locking the door behind her.

A clock somewhere began striking ten. Nena sat in a corner, crying. A late cock could be heard crowing. And from the next room came the voices of the lovers: the old man's voice, tired and broken; the girl's sharp and taut and passionate.

"No," she was saying, "I shall never leave you again. I am not going away again. No one shall take me away from you again."

THE SECOND TREE FROM THE CORNER[19]
—E. B. White

"Ever have any bizarre thoughts?" asked the doctor.

Mr. Trexler failed to catch the word. "What kind?" he said.

"Bizarre," repeated the doctor, his voice steady. He watched his patient for any slight change of expression, any wince. It seemed to Trexler that the doctor was not only watching him closely but was creeping slowly toward him, like a lizard toward a bug. Trexler shoved his chair back an inch and gathered himself for a reply. He was about to say "Yes" when he realized that if he said yes the next question would be unanswerable. Bizarre thoughts, bizarre thoughts? Ever have any bizarre thoughts? What kind of thoughts *except* bizarre had he had since the age of two?

Trexler felt the time passing, the necessity for an answer. These psychiatrists were busy men, overloaded, not to be kept waiting. The next patient was probably already perched out there in the waiting room, lonely, worried, shifting around on the sofa, his mind stuffed with bizarre thoughts and amorphous fears. Poor bastard, thought Trexler. Out there all alone in that misshapen ante-chamber, staring at the filing cabinet and wondering whether to tell the doctor about that day on the Madison Avenue bus.

Let's see, bizarre thoughts. Trexler dodged back along the dreadful corridor of the years to see what he could find. He felt the doctor's eyes upon him and knew that time was running out. Don't be so conscientious, he said to himself. If a bizarre thought is indicated here, just reach into the bag and pick anything at all. A man as well supplied with bizarre thoughts as you are should have no difficulty producing one for the record. Trexler darted into the bag, hung for a moment before one of his thoughts, as a hummingbird pauses in the delphinium. No, he said, not that one. He darted to another (the one about the rhesus monkey), paused, considered. No, he said, not that.

Trexler knew he must hurry. He had already used up pretty nearly four seconds since the question had been put. But it was an impossible situation—just one more lousy, impossible situation such as he was always getting himself into. When, he asked himself, are you going to quit maneuvering yourself into a pocket? He made one more effort. This time he stopped at the asylum, only the bars were lucite—fluted, retractable. Not here, he said. Not this one.

He looked straight at the doctor. "No," he said quietly. "I never have any bizarre thoughts."

The doctor sucked in on his pipe, blew a plume of smoke toward the rows of medical books. Trexler's gaze followed the smoke. He managed to make out one of the titles, "The Genito-Urinary System." A bright wave of fear swept cleanly over him, and he winced under the first pain of kidney stones. He remembered when he was a child, the first time he ever entered a doctor's office, sneaking a look at the titles of the books—and the flush of fear, the shirt wet under the arms, the book on t.b., the sudden knowledge that he was in the advanced stages of consumption, the quick vision of the hemorrhage. Trexler sighed wearily. Forty years, he thought, and I still get thrown by the title of a medical book. Forty years and I still can't stay on life's little bucky horse. No wonder I'm sitting here in this dreary joint at the end of this woebegone afternoon, lying about my bizarre thoughts to a doctor who looks, come to think of it, rather tired.

The session dragged on. After about twenty minutes, the doctor rose and knocked his pipe out. Trexler got up, knocked the ashes out of his brain, and waited. The doctor smiled warmly and stuck out his hand. "There's nothing the matter with you—you're just scared. Want to know how I know you're scared?"

"How?" asked Trexler.

"Look at the chair you've been sitting in! See how it has moved back away from my desk. You kept inching away from me while I asked you questions. That means you're scared."

"Does it?" said Trexler, faking a grin. "Yeah, I suppose it does."

They finished shaking hands. Trexler turned and walked out uncertainly along the passage, then into the waiting room and out past the next patient, a ruddy pin-striped man who was seated on the sofa twirling his hat nervously and staring straight ahead at the files. Poor, frightened guy, thought Trexler, he's probably read in the *Times* that one American male out of every two is going to die of heart disease by twelve o'clock next Thursday. It says that in the paper almost every morning. And he's also probably thinking about that day on the Madison Avenue Bus.

A week later, Trexler was back in the patient's chair. And for several weeks thereafter he continued to visit the doctor, always toward the end of the afternoon, when the vapors hung thick above the pool of the mind and darkened the whole region of the East Seventies. He felt no better as time went on, and he found it impossible to work. He discovered that the visits were becoming routine and that although the routine was one to which he certainly did not look forward, at least he could accept it with cool resignation, as once, years ago, he had accepted a long spell with a dentist who had settled down to a steady fooling with a couple of dead teeth. The visits, moreover, were now assuming a pattern recognizable to the patient.

Each session would begin with a résumé of symptoms—dizziness in the streets, the constricting pain in the back of the neck, the apprehensions, the tightness of the scalp, the inability to concentrate, the despondency and the melancholy times, the feeling of pressure and tension, the anger at not being able to work, the anxiety over work not done, the gas on the stomach. Dullest set of neurotic symptoms in the world, Trexler would think, as he obediently trudged back over them for the doctor's benefit. And then, having listened attentively to the recital, the doctor would spring his question: "Have you ever found anything that gives you relief?" And Trexler would answer, "Yes. A drink." And the doctor would nod his head knowingly.

As he became familiar with the pattern Trexler found that he increasingly tended to identify himself with the doctor, transferring himself into the doctor's seat—probably (he thought) some rather slick form of escapism. At any rate, it was nothing new for Trexler to identify himself with other people. Whenever he got into a cab, he instantly became the driver, saw everything from the hackman's angle (and the reaching over with the right hand, the nudging of the flag, the pushing it down, all the way down along the side of the meter), saw everything—traffic, fare, everything—through the eyes of Anthony Rocco, or Isidore Freedman, or Matthew Scott. In a barbershop, Trexler was the barber, his fingers curled around the comb, his hand on the tonic. Perfectly natural, then, that Trexler should soon be occupying the doctor's chair, asking the questions, waiting for the answers. He got quite interested in the doctor, in this way. He liked him, and he found him a not too difficult patient.

It was on the fifth visit, about halfway through, that the doctor turned to Trexler and said, suddenly, "What do you want?" He gave the word "want" special emphasis.

"I d'know," replied Trexler uneasily. "I guess nobody knows the answer to that one."

"Sure they do," replied the doctor.

"Do *you* know what *you* want?" asked Trexler narrowly.

"Certainly," said the doctor. Trexler noticed that at this point the doctor's chair slid slightly backward, away from him. Trexler stifled a small, internal smile. Scared as a rabbit, he said to himself. Look at him scoot!

"What *do* you want?" continued Trexler, pressing his advantage, pressing it hard.

The doctor glided back another inch away from his inquisitor. "I want a wing on the small house I own in Westport. I want more money, and more leisure to do the things I want to do."

Trexler was just about to say, "And what are those things you want to do, Doctor?" when he caught himself. Better not go too far, he mused. Better not lose possession of the ball. And besides, he thought, what the hell goes on here, anyway—me paying fifteen bucks a throw for these séances and then doing the work myself, asking the questions, weighing the answers. So he wants a new wing! There's a fine piece of theatrical gauze for you! A new wing.

Trexler settled down again and resumed the role of patient for the rest of the visit. It ended on a kindly, friendly note. The doctor reassured him that his fears were the cause of his sickness, and that his fears were unsubstantial. They shook hands, smiling.

Trexler walked dizzily through the empty waiting room and the doctor followed along to let him out. It was late: the secretary had shut up shop and gone home. Another day over the dam. "Good-bye," said Trexler. He stepped into the street, turned west toward Madison, and thought of the doctor all alone there, after hours, in that desolate hole—a man who worked longer hours than his secretary. Poor, scared, overworked bastard, thought Trexler. And that new wing!

It was an evening of clearing weather, the Park showing green and desirable in the distance, the last daylight applying a high lacquer to the brick and brownstone walls and giving the street scene a luminous and intoxicating splendor. Trexler meditated, as he walked, on what he wanted. "What do you want?" he heard again. Trexler knew what he wanted, and what, in general, all men wanted; and he was glad, in a way, that it was both inexpressible and unattainable, and that it wasn't a wing. He was satisfied to remember that it was deep, formless, enduring, and impossible of fulfillment, and that it made men sick, and that when you sauntered along Third Avenue and looked through the doorways into the dim saloons, you could sometimes pick out from the unregenerate ranks the ones who had not forgotten, gazing steadily into the bottoms of the glasses on the long chance that they could get another little peek at it. Trexler found himself renewed by the remembrance that what he wanted was at once great and microscopic, and that although it borrowed from the nature of large deeds and of youthful love and of old songs and early intimations, it was not any one of these things, and that it had not been isolated or pinned down, and that a man who attempted to define it in the privacy of a doctor's office would fall flat on his face.

Trexler felt invigorated. Suddenly his sickness seemed health, his dizziness stability. A small tree, rising between him and the light, stood there saturated with the evening, each gilt-edged leaf perfectly drunk with excellence and delicacy. Trexler's spine registered an ever so slight tremor as it picked up this natural disturbance in the lovely scene. "I want the second tree from the corner, just as it stands," he said, answering an imaginary question from an imaginary physician. And he felt a slow pride in realizing that what he wanted none could bestow, and that what he had none could take away. He felt content to be sick, unembarrassed at being afraid; and in the jungle of his fear he glimpsed (as he had so often glimpsed them before) the flashy tail feathers of the bird courage.

Then he thought once again of the doctor, and of his being left there all alone, tired, frightened. (The poor, scared guy, thought Trexler.) Trexler began humming "Moonshine Lullaby," his spirit reacting instantly to the hypodermic of Merman's healthy voice. He crossed Madison, boarded a downtown bus, and rode all the way to Fifty-second Street before he had a thought that could rightly have been called bizarre.

from HARD TIMES
—Charles Dickens

Book I · I: The One Thing Needful
"Now, what I want is, facts. Teach these boys and girls nothing but Facts.

Facts alone are wanted in life. Plant nothing else, and root out everything else. You can only form the minds of reasoning animals upon Facts: nothing else will ever be of any service to them. This is the principle on which I bring up my own children, and this is the principle on which I bring up these children. Stick to Facts, sir!"

The scene was a plain, bare, monotonous vault of a schoolroom, and the speaker's square forefinger emphasised his observations by underscoring every sentence with a line on the schoolmaster's sleeve. The emphasis was helped by the speaker's square wall of a forehead, which had his eyebrows for its base, while his eyes found commodious cellarage in two dark caves, overshadowed by the wall. The emphasis was helped by the speaker's mouth, which was wide, thin, and hard set. The emphasis was helped by the speaker's voice, which was inflexible, dry, and dictatorial. The emphasis was helped by the speaker's hair, which bristled on the skirts of his bald head, a plantation of firs to keep the wind from its shining surface, all covered with knobs, like the crust of a plum pie, as if the head had scarcely warehouse-room for the hard facts stored inside. The speaker's obstinate carriage, square coat, square legs, square shoulders,—nay, his very neckcloth, trained to take him by the throat with an unaccommodating grasp, like a stubborn fact, as it was,—all helped the emphasis.

"In this life, we want nothing but Facts, sir; nothing but Facts!"

The speaker, and the schoolmaster, and the third grown person present, all backed a little, and swept with their eyes the inclined plane of little vessels then and there arranged in order, ready to have imperial gallons of facts poured into them until they were full to the brim.

Book I · II: Murdering the Innocents

Thomas Gradgrind, sir. A man of realities. A man of facts and calculations. A man who proceeds upon the principle that two and two are four, and nothing over, and who is not to be talked into allowing for anything over. Thomas Gradgrind, sir—peremptorily Thomas—Thomas Gradgrind. With a rule and a pair of scales, and the multiplication table always in his pocket, sir, ready to weigh and measure any parcel of human nature, and tell you exactly what it comes to. It is a mere question of figures, a case of simple arithmetic. You might hope to get some other nonsensical belief into the head of George Gradgrind, or Augustus Gradgrind, or John Gradgrind, or Joseph Gradgrind (all supposititious, nonexistent persons), but into the head of Thomas Gradgrind—no, sir!

In such terms Mr. Gradgrind always mentally introduced himself, whether to his private circle of acquaintance, or to the public in general. In such terms, no doubt, substituting the words "boys and girls," for "sir," Thomas Gradgrind now presented Thomas Gradgrind to the little pitchers before him, who were to be filled so full of facts.

Indeed, as he eagerly sparkled at them from the cellarage before mentioned, he seemed a kind of cannon loaded to the muzzle with facts, and prepared to blow them clean out of the regions of childhood at one discharge. He seemed a galvanising apparatus, too, charged with a grim mechanical substitute for the tender young imaginations that were to be stormed away.

"Girl number twenty," said Mr. Gradgrind, squarely pointing with his square forefinger, "I don't know that girl. Who is that girl?"

"Sissy Jupe, sir," explained number twenty, blushing, standing up, and curtseying.

"Sissy is not a name," said Mr. Gradgrind. "Don't call yourself Sissy. Call yourself Cecilia."

"It's father as calls me Sissy, sir," returned the young girl in a trembling voice, and with another curtsey.

"Then he has no business to do it," said Mr. Gradgrind. "Tell him he mustn't. Cecilia Jupe. Let me see. What is your father?"

"He belongs to the horse-riding, if you please, sir."

Mr. Gradgrind frowned, and waved off the objectionable calling with his hand.

"We don't want to know anything about that, here. You mustn't tell us about that, here. Your father breaks horses, don't he?"

"If you please, sir, when they can get any to break, they do break horses in the ring, sir."

"You mustn't tell us about the ring, here. Very well, then. Describe your father as a horsebreaker. He doctors sick horses, I dare say?"

"Oh yes, sir."

"Very well, then. He is a veterinary surgion, a farrier, and horsebreaker. Give me your definition of a horse."

(Sissy Jupe thrown into the greatest alarm by this demand.)

"Girl number twenty unable to define a horse!" said Mr. Gradgrind, for the general behoof of all the little pitchers. "Girl number twenty possessed of no facts, in reference to one of the commonest of animals! Some boy's definition of a horse. Bitzer, yours."

The square finger, moving here and there, lighted suddenly on Bitzer, perhaps because he chanced to sit in the same ray of sunlight which, darting in at one of the bare windows of the intensely whitewashed room, irradiated Sissy. For, the boys and girls sat on the face of the inclined plane in two compact bodies, divided up the centre by a narrow interval; and Sissy, being at the corner of a row on the sunny side, came in for the beginning of a sunbeam, of which Bitzer, being at the corner of a row on the other side, a few rows in advance, caught the end. But, whereas the girl was so dark-eyed and dark-haired, that she seemed to receive a deeper and more lustrous colour from the sun, when it shone upon her, the boy was so light-eyed and light-haired that the self-same rays appeared to draw out of him what little colour he ever possessed. His cold eyes would hardly have been eyes, but for the short ends of lashes which, by bringing them into immediate contrast with something paler than themselves, expressed their form. His short-cropped hair might have been a mere continuation of the sandy freckles on his forehead and face. His skin was so unwholesomely deficient in the natural tinge, that he looked as though, if he were cut, he would bleed white.

"Bitzer," said Thomas Gradgrind. "Your definition of a horse."

"Quadruped. Graminivorous. Forty teeth, namely twenty-four grinders, four eye-teeth, and twelve incisive. Sheds coat in the spring; in marshy countries, sheds hoofs, too. Hoofs hard, but requiring to be shod with iron. Age known by marks in mouth." Thus (and much more) Bitzer.

"Now girl number twenty," said Mr. Gradgrind. "You know what a horse is."

She curtseyed again, and would have blushed deeper, if she could have blushed deeper than she had blushed at this time. Bitzer, after rapidly blinking at Thomas Gradgrind with both eyes at once, and so catching the light upon his quivering ends of lashes that they looked like the antennae of busy insects, put his knuckles to his freckled forehead, and sat down again.

The third gentleman now stepped forth. A mighty man at cutting and drying, he was; a government officer; in his way (and in most other people's too), a professed pugilist; always in training, always with a system to force down the general throat like a bolus, always to be heard of at the bar of his little Public-office, ready to fight all England. To continue in fistic phraseology, he had a genius for coming up to the scratch, wherever and whatever it was, and proving himself an ugly customer. He would go in and damage any subject whatever with his right, follow up with his left, stop, exchange, counter, bore his opponent (he always fought All England) to the ropes, and fall upon him neatly. He was certain to knock the wind out of common sense, and render that unlucky adversary deaf to the call of time. And he had it in charge from high authority to bring about the great public-office Millennium, when Commissioners should reign upon earth.

"Very well," said this gentleman, briskly smiling, and folding his arms. That's a horse. Now, let me ask you girls and boys, Would you paper a room with representations of horses?"

After a pause, one half of the children cried in chorus, "Yes, sir!" Upon which the other half, seeing in the gentleman's face that Yes was wrong, cried out in chorus, "No, sir!"—as the custom is, in these examinations.

"Of course, No. Why wouldn't you?"

A pause. One corpulent slow boy, with a wheezy manner of breathing, ventured the answer, Because he wouldn't paper a room at all, but would paint it.

"You *must* paper it," said the gentleman, rather warmly.

"You must paper it," said Thomas Gradgrind, "whether you like it or not. Don't tell *us* you wouldn't paper it. What do you mean, boy?"

"I'll explain to you, then," said the gentleman, after another and a dismal pause, "why you wouldn't paper a room with representations of horses. Do you ever see horses walking up and down the sides of rooms in reality—in fact? Do you?"

"Yes sir!" from one half. "No, sir!" from the other.

"Of course, No," said the gentleman, with an indignant look at the wrong half. "Why, then, you are not to see anywhere, what you don't see in fact; you are not to have anywhere, what you don't have in fact. What is called Taste, is only another name for Fact."

Thomas Gradgrind nodded his approbation.

"This is a new principle, a discovery, a great discovery," said the gentleman. "Now, I'll try you again. Suppose you were going to carpet a room. Would you use a carpet having a representation of flowers upon it?"

There being a general conviction by this time that "No, sir!" was always the right answer to this gentleman, the chorus of No was very strong. Only a few feeble stragglers said Yes; among them Sissy Jupe.

"Girl number twenty," said the gentleman, smiling in the calm strength of knowledge.

Sissy blushed, and stood up.

"So you would carpet your room—or your husband's room, if you were a grown woman, and had a husband—with representations of flowers, would you," said the gentleman. "Why would you?"

"If you please, sir, I am very fond of flowers," returned the girl.

"And is that why you would put tables and chairs upon them, and have people walking over them with heavy boots?"

"It wouldn't hurt them, sir. They wouldn't crush and wither, if you please, sir. They would be the pictures of what was very pretty and pleasant, and I would fancy—"

"Ay, ay, ay! But you mustn't fancy," cried the gentleman, quite elated by coming so happily to his point. "That's it! You are never to fancy."

"You are not, Cecilia Jupe," Thomas Gradgrind solemnly repeated, "to do anything of that kind."

"Fact, fact, fact!" said the gentleman. And "Fact, fact, fact!" repeated Thomas Gradgrind.

"You are to be in all things regulated and governed," said the gentleman, "by fact. We hope to have, before long, a board of fact, composed of commissioners of fact, who will force the people to be a people of fact, and of nothing but fact. You must discard the word Fancy altogether. You have nothing to do with it. You are not to have, in any object of use or ornament, what would be a contradiction in fact. You don't walk upon flowers in fact; you cannot be allowed to walk upon flowers in carpets. You don't find that foreign birds and butterflies come and perch upon your crockery; you cannot be permitted to paint foreign birds and butterflies upon your crockery. You never meet with quadrupeds going up and down walls; you must not have quadrupeds represented upon walls. You must use," said the gentleman "for all these purposes, combinations and modifications (in primary colours) of mathematical figures which are susceptible of proof and demonstration. This is the new discovery. This is fact. This is taste."

The girl curtseyed, and sat down. She was very young, and she looked as if she were frightened by the matter of fact prospect the world afforded.

"Now, if Mr. M'Choakumchild," said the gentleman, "will proceed to give his first lesson here, Mr. Gradgrind, I shall be happy, at your request, to observe his mode of procedure."

Mr. Gradgrind was much obliged. "Mr. M'Choakumchild, we only wait for you."

So, Mr. M'Choakumchild began in his best manner. He and some one hundred and forty other schoolmasters, had been lately turned at the same time, in the same factory, on the same principles, like so many pianoforte legs. He had been put through an immense variety of paces, and had answered volumes of head-breaking questions. Orthography, etymology, syntax, and prosody, biography, astronomy, geography, and general cosmography, the sciences of compound proportion, algebra, land-surveying and levelling, vocal music, and drawing from models, were all at the ends of his ten chilled fingers. He had worked his stony way into Her Majesty's most Honourable Privy Council's Schedule B, and had taken the bloom off the higher branches of mathematics and physical science, French, German, Latin, and Greek. He knew all about all the Water Sheds of all the world (whatever they are), and all the histories of all the peoples, and all the names of all the rivers and mountains, and all the productions, manners, and customs of all the countries, and all their boundaries and bearings on the two and thirty points of the compass. Ah, rather overdone, M'Choakumchild. If he had only learnt a little less, how infinitely better he might have taught much more!

He went to work in this preparatory lesson, not unlike Morgiana in the Forty Thieves: looking into all the vessels ranged before him, one after another, to see what they contained. Say, good M'Choakumchild. When from thy boiling store, thou shalt fill each jar brim full by-and-by, dost thou think that thou wilt always kill outright the robber Fancy lurking within—or sometimes only maim him and distort him!

PARKER'S BACK[20]
—Flannery O'Connor

Parker's wife was sitting on the front porch floor, snapping beans. Parker was sitting on the step, some distance away, watching her sullenly. She was plain, plain. The skin on her face was thin and drawn as tight as the skin on an onion and her eyes were gray and sharp like the points of two icepicks. Parker understood why he had married her—he couldn't have got her any other way—but he couldn't understand why he stayed with her now. She was pregnant and pregnant women were not his favorite kind. Nevertheless, he stayed as if she had him conjured. He was puzzled and ashamed of himself.

The house they rented sat alone save for a single tall pecan tree on a high embankment overlooking a highway. At intervals a car would shoot past below and his wife's eyes would swerve suspiciously after the sound of it and then come back to rest on the newspaper full of beans in her lap. One of the things she did not approve of was automobiles. In addition to her other bad qualities, she was forever sniffing up sin. She did not smoke or dip, drink whiskey, use bad language or paint her face, and God knew some paint would have improved it, Parker thought. Her being against color, it was the more remarkable she had married him. Sometimes he supposed that she had married him because she meant to save him. At other times he had a suspicion that she actually liked everything she said she didn't. He could account for her one way or another; it was himself he could not understand.

She turned her head in his direction and said, "It's no reason you can't work for a man. It don't have to be a woman."

"Aw shut your mouth for a change," Parker muttered.

If he had been certain she was jealous of the woman he worked for he would have been pleased but more likely she was concerned with the sin that would result if he and the woman took a liking to each other. He had told her that the woman was a hefty young blonde; in fact she was nearly seventy years old and too dried up to have an interest in anything except getting as much work out of him as she could. Not that an old woman didn't sometimes get an interest in a young man, particularly if he was as attractive as Parker felt he was, but this old woman looked at him the same way she looked at her old tractor—as if she had to put up with it because it was all she had. The tractor had broken down the second day Parker was on it and she had set him at once to cutting bushes, saying out of the side of her mouth to the nigger, "Everything he touches, he breaks." She also asked him to wear his shirt when he worked; Parker had removed it even though the day was not sultry; he put it back on reluctantly.

This ugly woman Parker married was his first wife. He had had other women but he had planned never to get himself tied up legally. He had first seen her one morning when his truck broke down on the highway. He had managed to pull it off the road into a neatly swept yard on which sat a peeling two-room house. He got out and opened the hood of the truck and began to study the motor. Parker had an extra sense that told him when there was a woman nearby watching him. After he had leaned over the motor a few minutes, his neck began to prickle. He cast his eye over the empty yard and porch of the house. A woman he could not see was either nearby beyond a clump of honeysuckle or in the house, watching him out the window.

Suddenly Parker began to jump up and down and fling his hand about as if he had mashed it in the machinery. He doubled over and held his hand close to his chest. "God dammit!" he hollered, "Jesus Christ in hell! Jesus God Almighty damm! God dammit to hell!" he went on, flinging out the same few oaths over and over as loud as he could.

Without warning a terrible bristly claw slammed the side of his face and he fell backwards on the hood of the truck. "You don't talk no filth here!" a voice close to him shrilled.

Parker's vision was so blurred that for an instant he thought he had been attacked by some creature from above, a giant hawk-eyed angel wielding a hoary weapon. As his sight cleared, he saw before him a tall raw-boned girl with a broom.

"I hurt my hand," he said. "I HURT my hand." He was so incensed that he forgot that he hadn't hurt his hand. "My hand may be broke," he growled although his voice was still unsteady.

"Lemme see it," the girl demanded.

Parker stuck out his hand and she came closer and looked at it. There was no mark on the palm and she took the hand and turned it over. Her own hand was dry and hot and rough and Parker felt himself jolted back to life by her touch. He looked more closely at her. I don't want nothing to do with this one, he thought.

The girl's sharp eyes peered at the back of the stubby reddish hand she held. There emblazoned in red and blue was a tattooed eagle perched on a cannon. Parker's sleeve was rolled to the elbow. Above the eagle a serpent was coiled about a shield and in the spaces between the eagle and the serpent there were hearts, some with arrows through them. Above the serpent there was a spread hand of cards. Every space on the skin of Parker's arm, from wrist to elbow, was covered in some loud design. The girl gazed at this with an almost stupefied smile of shock, as if she had accidentally grasped a poisonous snake; she dropped the hand.

"I got most of my other ones in foreign parts," Parker said. "These here I mostly got in the United States. I got my first one when I was only fifteen year old."

"Don't tell me," the girl said. "I don't like it. I ain't got any use for it."

"You ought to see the ones you can't see," Parker said and winked.

Two circles of red appeared like apples on the girl's cheeks and softened her appearance. Parker was intrigued. He did not for a minute think that she didn't like the tattoos. He had never yet met a woman who was not attracted to them.

Parker was fourteen when he saw a man in a fair, tattooed from head to foot. Except for his loins which were girded with a panther hide, the man's skin was patterned in what seemed from Parker's distance—he was near the back of the tent, standing on a bench—a single intricate design of brilliant color. The man, who was small and sturdy, moved about on the platform, flexing his muscles so that the arabesque of men and beasts and flowers on his skin appeared to have a subtle motion of its own. Parker was filled with emotion, lifted up as some people are when the flag passes. He was a boy whose mouth habitually hung open. He was heavy and earnest, as ordinary as a loaf of bread. When the show was over, he had remained standing on the bench, staring where the tattooed man had been, until the tent was almost empty.

Parker had never before felt the least motion of wonder in himself. Until he saw the man at the fair, it did not enter his head that there was anything out of the ordinary about the fact that he existed. Even then it did not enter his head, but a peculiar unease settled in him. It was as if a blind boy had been turned so gently in a different direction that he did not know his destination had been changed.

He had his first tattoo some time after—the eagle perched on the cannon. It was done by a local artist. It hurt very little, just enough to make it appear to Parker to be worth doing. This was peculiar too for before he had thought that only what did not hurt was worth doing. The next year he quit school because he was sixteen and could. He went to the trade school for a while, then he quit the trade school and worked for six months in a garage. The only reason he worked at all was to pay for more tattoos. His mother worked in a laundry and could support him, but she would not pay for any tattoo except her name on a heart, which he had put on, grumbling. However, her name was Betty Jean and nobody had to know it was his mother. He found out that the tattoos were attractive to the kind of girls he liked but who had never liked him before. He began to drink beer and get in fights. His mother wept over what was becoming of him. One night she dragged him off to a revival with her, not telling him where they were going. When he saw the big lighted church, he jerked out of her grasp and ran. The next day he lied about his age and joined the navy.

Parker was large for the tight sailor's pants but the silly white cap, sitting low on his forehead, made his face by contrast look thoughtful and almost intense. After a month or two in the navy, his mouth ceased to hang open. His features hardened into the features of a man. He stayed in the navy five years and seemed a natural part of the gray mechanical ship, except for his eyes, which were the same pale slate-color as the ocean and reflected the immense spaces around him as if they were a microcosm of the mysterious sea. In port Parker wandered about comparing the run-down places he was in to Birmingham, Alabama. Everywhere he went he picked up more tattoos.

He had stopped having lifeless ones like anchors and crossed rifles. He had a tiger and a panther on each shoulder, a cobra coiled about a torch on his chest, hawks on his thighs, Elizabeth II and Philip over where his stomach and liver were respectively. He did not care much what the subject was so long as it was colorful; on his abdomen he had a few obscenities but only because that seemed the proper place for them. Parker would be satisfied with each tattoo about a month, then something about it that had attracted him would wear off. Whenever a decent-sized mirror was available, he would get in front of it and study his overall look. The effect was not of one intricate arabesque of colors but of something haphazard and botched. A huge dissatisfaction would come over him and he would go off and find another tattooist and have another space filled up. The front of Parker was almost completely covered but there were no tattoos on his back. He had no desire for one anywhere he could not readily see it himself. As the space on the front of him for tattoos decreased, his dissatisfaction grew and became general.

After one of his furloughs, he didn't go back to the navy but remained away without official leave, drunk, in a rooming house in a city he did not know. His dissatisfaction, from being chronic and latent, had suddenly become acute and raged in him. It was as if the panther and the lion and the serpents and the eagles and the hawks had penetrated his skin and lived inside him in a raging warfare. The navy caught up with him, put him in the brig for nine months and then gave him a dishonorable discharge.

After that Parker decided that country air was the only kind fit to breathe. He rented the shack on the embankment and bought the old truck and took various jobs which he kept as long as it suited him. At the time he met his future wife, he was buying apples by the bushel and selling them for the same price by the pound to isolated homesteaders on back country roads.

"All that there," the woman said, pointing to his arm, "is no better than what a fool Indian would do. It's a heap of vanity." She seemed to have found the word she wanted. "Vanity of vanities," she said.

Well what the hell do I care what she thinks of it? Parker asked himself, but he was plainly bewildered. "I reckon you like one of these better than another anyway," he said, dallying until he thought of something that would impress her. He thrust the arm back at her. "Which you like best?"

"None of them," she said, "but the chicken is not as bad as the rest."

"What chicken?" Parker almost yelled.

She pointed to the eagle.

"That's an eagle," Parker said. "What fool would waste their time having a chicken put on themself?"

"What fool would have any of it?" the girl said and turned away. She went slowly back to the house and left him there to get going. Parker remained for almost five minutes, looking agape at the dark door she had entered.

The next day he returned with a bushel of apples. He was not one to be outdone by anything that looked like her. He liked women with meat on them, so you didn't feel their muscles, much less their old bones. When he arrived, she was sitting on the top step and the yard was full of children, all as thin and poor as herself; Parker remembered it was Saturday. He hated to be making up to a woman when there were children around, but it was fortunate he had brought the bushel of apples off the truck. As the children approached him to see what he carried, he gave each child an apple and told it to get lost; in that way he cleared out the whole crowd.

The girl did nothing to acknowledge his presence. He might have been a stray pig or goat that had wandered into the yard and she too tired to take up the broom and send it off. He set the bushel of apples down next to her on the step. He sat down on a lower step.

"Hep yourself," he said, nodding at the basket; then he lapsed into silence.

She took an apple quickly as if the basket might disappear if she didn't make haste. Hungry people made Parker nervous. He had always had plenty to eat himself. He grew very uncomfortable. He reasoned he had nothing to say so why should he say it? He could not think now why he had come or why he didn't go before he wasted another bushel of apples on the crowd of children. He supposed they were her brothers and sisters.

She chewed the apple slowly but with a kind of relish of concentration, bent slightly but looking out ahead. The view from the porch stretched off across a long incline studded with iron weed and across the highway to a vast vista of hills and one small mountain. Long views depressed Parker. You look out into space like that and you begin to feel as if someone were after you, the navy or the government or religion.

"Who them children belong to, you?" he said at length.

"I ain't married yet," she said. "They belong to momma." She said it as if it were only a matter of time before she would be married.

Who in God's name would marry her? Parker thought.

A large barefooted woman with a wide gap-toothed face appeared in the door behind Parker. She had apparently been there for several minutes.

"Good evening," Parker said.

The woman crossed the porch and picked up what was left of the bushel of apples. "We thank you," she said and returned with it into the house.

"That your old woman?" Parker muttered.

The girl nodded. Parker knew a lot of sharp things he could have said like "You got my sympathy," but he was gloomily silent. He just sat there, looking at the view. He thought he must be coming down with something.

"If I pick up some peaches tomorrow I'll bring you some," he said.

"I'll be much obliged to you," the girl said.

Parker had no intention of taking any basket of peaches back there but the next day he found himself doing it. He and the girl had almost nothing to say to each other. One thing he did say was, "I ain't got any tattoo on my back."

"What you got on it?" the girl asked.

"My shirt," Parker said. "Haw."

"Haw, haw," the girl said politely.

Parker thought he was losing his mind. He could not believe for a minute that he was attracted to a woman like this. She showed not the least interest in anything but what he brought until he appeared the third time with two cantaloups. "What's your name?" she asked.

"O. E. Parker," he said.

"What does the O. E. stand for?"

"You can just call me O. E.," Parker said. "Or Parker. Don't nobody call me by my name."

"What's it stand for?" she persisted.

"Never mind," Parker said. "What's yours?"

"I'll tell you when you tell me what them letters are the short of," she said. There was just a hint of flirtatiousness in her tone and it went rapidly to Parker's head. He had never revealed the name to any man or woman, only to the files of the navy and the government, and it was on his baptismal record which he got at the age of a month; his mother was a Methodist. When the name leaked out of the navy files, Parker narrowly missed killing the man who used it.

"You'll go blab it around," he said.

"I'll swear I'll never tell nobody," she said. "On God's holy word I swear it."

Parker sat a few minutes in silence. Then he reached for the girl's neck, drew her ear close to his mouth and revealed the name in low voice.

"Obadiah," she whispered. Her face slowly brightened as if the name came as a sign to her. "Obadiah," she said.

The name still stank in Parker's estimation.

"Obadiah Elihue," she said in a reverent voice.

"If you call me that aloud, I'll bust your head open," Parker said. "What's yours?"

"Sarah Ruth Cates," she said.

"Glad to meet you, Sarah Ruth," Parker said.

Sarah Ruth's father was a Straight Gospel preacher but he was away, spreading it in Florida. Her mother did not seem to mind his attention to the girl so long as he brought a basket of something with him when he came. As for Sarah Ruth herself, it was plain to Parker after he had visited three times that she was crazy about him. She liked him even though she insisted that pictures on the skin were vanity of vanities and even after hearing him curse, and even after she had asked him if he was saved and he had replied that he didn't see it was anything in particular to save him from. After that, inspired, Parker had said, "I'd be saved enough if you was to kiss me."

She scowled. "That ain't being saved," she said.

Not long after that she agreed to take a ride in his truck. Parker parked it on a deserted road and suggested to her that they lie down together in the back of it.

"Not until after we're married," she said—just like that.

"Oh that ain't necessary," Parker said and as he reached for her, she thrust him away with such force that the door of the truck came off and he found himself flat on his back on the ground. He made up his mind then and there to have nothing further to do with her.

They were married in the County Ordinary's office because Sarah Ruth thought churches were idolatrous. Parker had no opinion about that one way or the other. The Ordinary's office was lined with cardboard file boxes and record books with dusty yellow slips of paper hanging on out of them. The Ordinary was an old woman with red hair who had held office for forty years and looked as dusty as her books. She married them from behind the iron-grill of a stand-up desk and when she finished, she said with a flourish, "Three dollars and fifty cents and till death do you part!" and yanked some forms out of a machine.

Marriage did not change Sarah Ruth a jot and it made Parker gloomier than ever. Every morning he decided he had had enough and would not return that night; every night he returned. Whenever Parker couldn't stand the way he felt, he would have another tattoo, but the only surface left on him now was his back. To see a tattoo on his own back he would have to get two mirrors and stand between them in just the correct position and this seemed to Parker a good way to make an idiot of himself. Sarah Ruth who, if she had had better sense, could have enjoyed a tattoo on his back, would not even look at the ones he had elsewhere. When he attempted to point out special details of them, she would shut her eyes tight and turn her back as well. Except in total darkness, she preferred Parker dressed and with his sleeves rolled down.

"At the judgement seat of God, Jesus is going to say to you, 'What you been doing all your life besides have pictures drawn all over you?'" she said.

"You don't fool me none," Parker said, "you're just afraid that hefty girl I work for'll like me so much she'll say, 'Come on Mr. Parker, let's you and me . . .'"

"You're tempting sin," she said, "and at the judgement seat of God you'll have to answer for that too. You ought to go back to selling the fruits of the earth."

Parker did nothing much when he was at home but listen to what the judgement seat of God would be like for him if he didn't change his ways. When he could, he broke in with tales of the hefty girl he worked for. "'Mr. Parker,'" he said she said, 'I hired you for your brains.'" (She had added, "So why don't you use them?")

"And you should have seen her face the first time she saw me without my shirt," he said. "'Mr. Parker,'" she said, 'you're a walking panner-rammer!'" This had, in fact, been her remark but it had been delivered out of one side of her mouth.

Dissatisfaction began to grow so great in Parker that there was no containing it outside of a tattoo. It had to be his back. There was no help for it. A dim half-formed inspiration began to work in his mind. He visualized having a tattoo put there that Sarah Ruth would not be able to resist— a religious subject. He thought of an open book with HOLY BIBLE tattooed under it and an actual verse printed on the page. This seemed just the thing for a while; then he began to hear her say, "Ain't I already got a real Bible? What you think I want to read the same verse over and over for when I can read it all?" He needed something better even than the Bible! He thought about it so much that he began to lose sleep. He was already losing flesh— Sarah Ruth just threw food in the pot and let it boil. Not knowing for certain why he continued to stay with a woman who was both ugly and pregnant and no cook made him generally nervous and irritable, and he developed a little tic in the side of his face.

Once or twice he found himself turning around abruptly as if someone were trailing him. He had had a granddaddy who had ended in the state mental hospital, although not until he was seventy-five, but as urgent as it might be for him to get a tattoo, it was just as urgent that he get exactly the right one to bring Sarah Ruth to heel. As he continued to worry over it, his eyes took on a hollow preoccupied expression. The old woman he worked for told him that if he couldn't keep his mind on what he was doing, she knew where she could find a fourteen-year-old colored boy who could. Parker was too preoccupied even to be offended. At any time previous, he would have left her then and there, saying drily, "Well, you go ahead on and get him then."

Two or three mornings later he was baling hay with the old woman's sorry baler and her broken down tractor in a large field, cleared save for one enormous old tree standing in the middle of it. The old woman was the kind who would not cut down a large old tree because it was a large old tree. She had pointed it out to Parker as if he didn't have eyes and told him to be careful not to hit it as the machine picked up hay near it. Parker began at the outside of the field and made circles inward toward it. He had to get off the tractor every now and then and untangle the baling cord or kick a rock out of the way. The old woman had told him to carry the rocks to the edge of the field, which he did when she was there watching. When he thought he could make it, he ran over them. As he circled the field his mind was on a suitable design for his back. The sun, the size of a golf ball, began to switch regularly from in front to behind him, but he appeared to see it both places as if he had eyes in the back of his head. All at once he saw the tree reaching out to grasp him. A ferocious thud propelled him into the air, and he heard himself yelling in an unbelievably loud voice "GOD ABOVE!"

He landed on his back while the tractor crashed upside down into the tree and burst into flame. The first thing Parker saw were his shoes, quickly being eaten by the fire; one was caught under the tractor, the other was some distance away, burning by itself. He was not in them. He could feel the hot breath of the burning tree on his face. He scrambled backwards, still sitting, his eyes cavernous, and if he had known how to cross himself he would have done it.

His truck was on a dirt road at the edge of the field. He moved toward it, still sitting, still backwards, but faster and faster; halfway to it he got up and began a kind of forward-bent run from which he collapsed on his knees twice. His legs felt like two old rusted rain gutters. He reached the truck finally and took off in it, zigzagging up the road. He drove past his house on the embankment and straight for the city, fifty miles distant.

Parker did not allow himself to think on the way to the city. He only knew that there had been a great change in his life, a leap forward into a worse unknown, and that there was nothing he could do about it. It was for all intents accomplished.

The artist had two large cluttered rooms over a chiropodist's office on a back street. Parker, still barefooted, burst silently in on him at a little after three in the afternoon. The artist, who was about Parker's own age—twenty-eight—but thin and bald, was behind a small drawing table, tracing a design in green ink. He looked up with an annoyed glance and did not seem to recognize Parker in the hollow-eyed creature before him.

"Let me see the book you got with all the pictures of God in it," Parker said breathlessly. "The religious one."

The artist continued to look at him with his intellectual, superior stare. "I don't put tattoos on drunks," he said.

"You know me!" Parker cried indignantly. "I'm O. E. Parker! You done work for me before and I always paid!"

The artist looked at him another moment as if he were not altogether sure. "You've fallen off some," he said. "You must have been in jail."

"Married," Parker said.

"Oh," said the artist. With the aid of mirrors the artist had tattooed on the top of his head a miniature owl, perfect in every detail. It was about the size of a half-dollar and served him as a show piece. There were cheaper artists in town but Parker had never wanted anything but the best. The artist went over to a cabinet at the back of the room and began to look over some art books. "Who are you interested in?" he said, "saints, angels, Christs or what?"

"God," Parker said.

"Father, Son or Spirit?"

"Just God," Parker said impatiently. "Christ. I don't care. Just so it's God."

The artist returned with a book. He moved some papers off another table and put the book down on it and told Parker to sit down and see what he liked. "The up-t-date ones are in the back," he said.

Parker sat down with the book and wet his thumb. He began to go through it, beginning at the back where the up-to-date pictures were. Some of them he recognized—The Good Shepherd, Forbid Them Not, The Smiling Jesus, Jesus the Physician's Friend, but he kept turning rapidly backwards and the pictures became less and less reassuring. One showed a gaunt green dead face streaked with blood. One was yellow with sagging purple eyes. Parker's heart began to beat faster and faster until it appeared to be roaring inside him like a great generator. He flipped the pages quickly, feeling that when he reached the one ordained, a sign would come. He continued to flip through until he had almost reached the front of the book. On one of the pages a pair of eyes glanced at him swiftly. Parker sped on, then stopped. His heart too appeared to cut off; there was absolute silence. It said as plainly as if silence were a language itself, Go BACK.

Parker returned to the picture—the haloed head of a flat stern Byzantine Christ with all-demanding eyes. He sat there trembling; his heart began slowly to beat again as if it were being brought to life by a subtle power.

"You found what you want?" the artist asked.

Parker's throat was too dry to speak. He got up and thrust the book at the artist, opened at the picture.

"That'll cost you plenty," the artist said. "You don't want all those little blocks though, just the outline and some better features."

"Just like it is," Parker said, "just like it is or nothing."

"It's your funeral," the artist said, "but I don't do that kind of work for nothing."

"How much?" Parker asked.

"It'll take maybe two days work."

"How much?" Parker said.

"On time or cash?" the artist asked. Parker's other jobs had been on time, but he had paid.

"Ten down and ten for every day it takes," the artist said.

Parker drew ten dollar bills out of his wallet; he had three left in.

"You come back in the morning," the artist said, putting the money in his own pocket. "First I'll have to trace that out of the book."

"No no!" Parker said. "Trace it now or gimme my money back," and his eyes blared as if he were ready for a fight.

The artist agreed. Any one stupid enough to want a Christ on his back, he reasoned, would be just as likely as not to change his mind the next minute, but once the work was begun he could hardly do so.

While he worked on the tracing, he told Parker to go wash his back at the sink with the special soap he used there. Parker did it and returned to pace back and forth across the room, nervously flexing his shoulders. He wanted to go look at the picure again but at the same time he did not want to. The artist got up finally and had Parker lie down on the table. He swabbed his back with ethyl chloride and then began to outline the head on it with his iodine pencil. Another hour passed before he took up his electric instrument. Parker felt no particular pain. In Japan he had had a tattoo of the Buddha done on his upper arm with ivory needles; in Burma, a little brown root of a man had made a peacock on each of his knees using thin pointed sticks, two feet long; amateurs had worked on him with pins and soot. Parker was usually so relaxed and easy under the hand of the artist that he often went to sleep, but this time he remained awake, every muscle taut.

At midnight the artist said he was ready to quit. He propped one mirror, four feet square, on a table by the wall and took a smaller mirror off the lavatory wall and put it in Parker's hands. Parker stood with his back to the one on the table and moved the other until he saw a flashing burst of color reflected from his back. It was almost completely covered with little red and blue and ivory and saffron squares; from them he made out the lineaments of the face—a mouth, the beginning of heavy brows, a straight nose, but the face was empty; the eyes had not yet been put in. The impression for the moment was almost as if the artist had tricked him and done the Physician's Friend.

"It don't have eyes," Parker cried out.

"That'll come," the artist said, "in due time. We have another day to go on it yet."

Parker spent the night on a cot at the Haven of Light Christian Mission. He found these the best places to stay in the city because they were free and included a meal of sorts. He got the last available cot and because he was still barefooted, he accepted a pair of second-hand shoes which, in his confusion, he put on to go to bed; he was still shocked from all that had happened to him. All night he lay awake in the long dormitory of cots with lumpy figures on them. The only light was from a phosphorescent cross glowing at the end of the room. The tree reached out to grasp him again, then burst into flame; the shoe burned quietly by itself; the eyes in the book said to him distinctly Go BACK and at the same time did not utter a sound. He wished that he were not in this city, not in this Haven of Light Mission, not in a bed by himself. He longed miserably for Sarah Ruth. Her sharp tongue and icepick eyes were the only comfort he could bring to mind. He decided he was losing it. Her eyes appeared soft and dilatory compared with the eyes in the book, for even though he could not summon up the exact look of those eyes, he could still feel their penetration. He felt as though, under their gaze, he was as transparent as the wing of a fly.

The tattooist had told him not to come until ten in the morning, but when he arrived at that hour, Parker was sitting in the dark hallway on the floor, waiting for him. He had decided upon getting up that, once the tattoo was on him, he would not look at it, that all his sensations of the day and night before were those of a crazy man and that he would return to doing things according to his own sound judgement.

The artist began where he left off. "One thing I want to know," he said presently as he worked over Parker's back, "why do you want this on you? Have you gone and got religion? Are you saved?" he asked in a mocking voice.

Parker's throat felt salty and dry. "Naw," he said, "I ain't got no use for none of that. A man can't save his self from whatever it is he don't deserve none of my sympathy." These words seemed to leave his mouth like wraiths and to evaporate at once as if he had never uttered them.

"Then why . . ."

"I married this woman that's saved," Parker said. "'I never should have done it. I ought to leave her. She's done gone and got pregnant."

"That's too bad," the artist said. "Then it's her making you have this tattoo."

"Naw," Parker said, "she don't know nothing about it. It's a surprise for her."

"You think she'll like it and lay off you a while?"

"She can't hep herself," Parker said. "She can't say she don't like the looks of God." He decided he had told the artist enough of his business. Artists were all right in their place but he didn't like them poking their noses into the affairs of regular people. "I didn't get no sleep last night," he said. "I think I'll get some now."

That closed the mouth of the artist but it did not bring him any sleep. He lay there, imagining how Sarah Ruth would be struck speechless by the face on his back and every now and then this would be interrupted by a vision of the tree of fire and his empty shoe burning beneath it.

The artist worked steadily until nearly four o'clock, not stopping to have lunch, hardly pausing with the electric instrument except to wipe the dripping dye off Parker's back as he went along. Finally he finished. "You can get up and look at it now," he said.

Parker sat up but he remained on the edge of the table.

The artist was pleased with his work and wanted Parker to look at it at once. Instead Parker continued to sit on the edge of the table, bent forward slightly but with a vacant look. "What ails you?" the artist said. "Go look at it."

"Ain't nothing ail me," Parker said in a sudden belligerent voice. "That tattoo ain't going nowhere. It'll be there when I get there." He reached for his shirt and began gingerly to put it on.

The artist took him roughly by the arm and propelled him between the two mirrors. "Now *look*," he said, angry at having his work ignored.

Parker looked, turned white and moved away. The eyes in the reflected face continued to look at him—still, straight, all-demanding, enclosed in silence.

"It was your idea, remember," the artist said. "I would have advised something else."

Parker said nothing. He put on his shirt and went out the door while the artist shouted, "I'll expect all of my money!"

Parker headed toward a package shop on the corner. He bought a pint of whiskey and took it into a nearby alley and drank it all in five minutes. Then he moved on to a pool hall nearby which he frequented when he came to the city. It was a well-lighted barn-like place with a bar up one side and gambling machines on the other and pool tables in the back. As soon as Parker entered, a large man in a red and black checkered shirt hailed him by slapping him on the back and yelling, "Yeyyyyyy boy! O. E. Parker!"

Parker was not yet ready to be struck on the back. "Lay off," he said, "I got a fresh tattoo there."

"What you got this time?" the man asked and then yelled to a few at the machines. "O. E.'s got him another tattoo."

"Nothing special this time," Parker said and slunk over to a machine that was not being used.

"Come on," the big man said. "let's have a look at O. E.'s tattoo," and while Parker squirmed in their hands, they pulled up his shirt. Parker felt all the hands drop away instantly and his shirt fell again like a veil over the face. There was a silence in the pool room which seemed to Parker to grow from the circle around him until it extended to the foundations under the building and upward through the beams in the roof.

Finally some one said, "Christ!" Then they all broke into noise at once. Parker turned around, an uncertain grin on his face.

"Leave it to O.E.!" the man in the checkered shirt said. "That boy's a real card!"

"Maybe he's gone and got religion," some one yelled.

"Not on your life," Parker said.

"O. E.'s got religion and is witnessing for Jesus, ain't you, O.E.?" a little man with a piece of cigar in his mouth said wryly. "An o-riginal way to do it if I ever saw one."

"Leave it to Parker to think of a new one!" the fat man said.

"Yyeeeeeeyyyyyyy boy!" someone yelled and they all began to whistle and curse in compliment until Parker said, "Aaa shut up."

"What'd you do it for?" somebody asked.

"For laughs," Parker said. "What's it to you?"

"Why ain't you laughing then?" somebody yelled. Parker lunged into the midst of them and like a whirlwind on a summer's day there began a fight that raged amid overturned tables and swinging fists until two of them grabbed him and ran to the door with him and threw him out. Then a calm descended on the pool hall as nerve shattering as if the long barnlike room were the ship from which Jonah had been cast into the sea.

Parker sat for a long time on the ground in the alley behind the pool hall, examining his soul. He saw it as a spider web of facts and lies that was not at all important to him but which appeared to be necessary in spite of his opinion. The eyes that were now forever on his back were eyes to be obeyed. He was as certain of it as he had ever been of anything. Throughout his life, grumbling and sometimes cursing, often afraid, once in rapture,

Parker had obeyed whatever instinct of this kind had come to him—in rapture when his spirit had lifted at the sight of the tattooed man at the fair, afraid when had had joined the navy, grumbling when he had married Sarah Ruth.

The thought of her brought him slowly to his feet. She would know what he had to do. She would clear up the rest of it, and she would at least be pleased. It seemed to him that, all along, that was what he wanted, to please her. His truck was still parked in front of the building where the artist had his place, but it was not far away. He got in it and drove out of the city and into the country night. His head was almost clear of liquor and he observed that his dissatisfaction was gone, but he felt not quite like himself. It was as if he were himself but a stranger to himself, driving into a new country though everything he saw was familiar to him, even at night.

He arrived finally at the house on the embankment, pulled the truck under the pecan tree and got out. He made as much noise as possible to assert that he was still in charge here, that his leaving her for a night without word meant nothing except it was the way he did things. He slammed the car door, stamped up the two steps and across the porch and rattled the door knob. It did not respond to his touch. "Sarah Ruth!" he yelled, "let me in."

There was no lock on the door and she had evidently placed the back of a chair against the knob. He began to beat on the door and rattle the knob at the same time.

He heard the bed springs screak and bent down and put his head to the keyhole, but it was stopped up with paper. "Let me in!" he hollered, bamming on the door again. "What you got me locked out for?"

A sharp voice close to the door said, "Who's there?"

"Me," Parker said, "O.E."

He waited a moment.

"Me," he said impatiently, "O.E."

Still no sound from inside.

He tried once more. "O.E.," he said, bamming the door two or three more times. "O. E. Parker. You know me."

There was a silence. Then the voice said slowly, "I don't know no O.E."

"Quit fooling," Parker pleaded. "You ain't got any business doing me this way. It's me, old O.E., I'm back. You ain't afraid of me."

"Who's there?" the same unfeeling voice said.

Parker turned his head as if he expected someone behind him to give him the answer. The sky had lightened slightly and there were two or three streaks of yellow floating above the horizon. Then as he stood there, a tree of light burst over the skyline.

Parker fell back against the door as if he had been pinned there by a lance.

"Who's there?" the voice from inside said and there was a quality about it now that seemed final. The knob rattled and the voice said peremptorily, "Who's there, I ast you?"

Parker bent down and put his mouth near the stuffed keyhole. "Obadiah," he whispered and all at once he felt the light pouring through him, turning his spider web soul into a perfect arabesque of colors, a garden of trees and birds and beasts.

"Obadiah Elihue!" he whispered.

The door opened and he stumbled in. Sarah Ruth loomed there, hands on her hips. She began at once, "That was no hefty blonde woman you was working for and you'll have to pay her every penny on her tractor you busted up. She don't keep insurance on it. She came here and her and me had us a long talk and I . . ."

Trembling, Parker set about lighting the kerosene lamp.

"What's the matter with you, wasting that kerosene this near daylight?" she demanded. "I ain't got to look at you."

A yellow glow enveloped them. Parker put the match down and began to unbutton his shirt.

"And you ain't going to have none of me this near morning," she said.

"Shut your mouth," he said quietly. "Look at this and then I don't want to hear no more out of you." He removed the shirt and turned his back to her.

"Another picture," Sarah Ruth growled. "I might have known you was off after putting some more trash on yourself."

Parker's knees went hollow under him. He wheeled around and cried, "Look at it! Don't just say that! *Look* at it!"

"I done looked," she said.

"Don't you know who it is?" he cried in anguish.

"No, who is it?" Sarah Ruth said. "It ain't anybody I know."

"It's him," Parker said.

"Him who?"

"God!" Parker cried.

"God? God don't look like that!"

"What do you know how he looks?" Parker moaned. "You ain't seen him."

"He don't *look*," Sarah Ruth said. "He's a spirit. No man shall see his face."

"Aw, listen," Parker groaned, "this is just a picture of him."

"Idolatry!" Sarah Ruth screamed. "Idolatry! Enflaming yourself with idols under every green tree! I can put up with lies and vanity but I don't want no idolator in this house!" and she grabbed up the broom and began to thrash him across the shoulders with it.

Parker was too stunned to resist. He sat there and let her beat him until she nearly knocked him senseless and large welts had formed on the face of the tattooed Christ. Then he staggered up and made for the door.

She stamped the broom two or three times on the floor and went to the window and shook it out to get the taint of him off it. Still gripping it, she looked toward the pecan tree and her eyes hardened still more. There he was—who called himself Obadiah Elihue—leaning against the tree, crying like a baby.

THE WITCH[21]
—Shirley Jackson

The coach was so nearly empty that the little boy had a seat all to himself, and his mother sat across the aisle on the seat next to the little boy's sister, a baby with a piece of toast in one hand and a rattle in the other. She was strapped securely to the seat so she could sit up and look around, and whenever she began to slip slowly sideways the strap caught her and held her halfway until her mother turned around and straightened her again. The little boy was looking out the window and eating a cookie, and the mother was reading quietly, answering the little boy's questions without looking up.

"We're on a river," the little boy said. "This is a river and we're on it."

"Fine," his mother said.

"We're on a bridge over a river," the little boy said to himself.

The few other people in the coach were sitting at the other end of the car; if any of them had occasion to come down the aisle the little boy would look around and say, "Hi," and the stranger would usually say, "Hi," back and sometimes ask the little boy if he were enjoying the train ride, or even tell him he was a fine big fellow. These comments annoyed the little boy and he would turn irritably back to the window.

"There's a cow," he would say, or, sighing, "How far do we have to go?"

"Not much longer now," his mother said, each time.

Once the baby, who was very quiet and busy with her rattle and her toast, which the mother would renew constantly, fell over too far sideways and banged her head. She began to cry, and for a minute there was noise and movement around the mother's seat. The little boy slid down from his own seat and ran across the aisle to pet his sister's feet and beg her not to cry, and finally the baby laughed and went back to her toast, and the little boy received a lollipop from his mother and went back to the window.

"I saw a witch," he said to his mother after a minute. "There was a big old ugly old bad old witch outside."

"Fine," his mother said.

"A big old ugly witch and I told her to go away and she went away," the little boy went on, in a quiet narrative to himself, "she came and said, 'I'm going to eat you up,' and I said, 'no, you're not,' and I chased her away, the bad old mean witch."

He stopped talking and looked up as the outside door of the coach opened and a man came in. He was an elderly man, with a pleasant face under white hair; his blue suit was only faintly touched by the disarray that comes from a long train trip. He was carrying a cigar, and when the little boy said, "Hi," the man gestured at him with the cigar and said, "Hello yourself, son." He stopped just beside the little boy's seat, and leaned against the back, looking down at the little boy, who craned his neck to look upward. "What you looking for out that window?" the man asked.

"Witches," the little boy said promptly. "Bad old mean witches."

"I see," the man said. "Find many?"

"My father smokes cigars," the little boy said.

"All men smoke cigars," the man said. "Someday you'll smoke a cigar, too."

"I'm a man already," the little boy said.

"How old are you?" the man asked.

The little boy, at the eternal question, looked at the man suspiciously for a minute and then said, "Twenty-six. Eight hunnerd and forty eighty."

His mother lifted her head from the book. "Four," she said, smiling fondly at the little boy.

"Is that so?" the man said politely to the little boy. "Twenty-six." He nodded his head at the mother across the aisle. "Is that your mother?"

The little boy leaned forward to look and then said, "Yes, that's her."

"What's your name?" the man asked.

The little boy looked suspicious again. "Mr. Jesus," he said.

"*Johnny*," the little boy's mother said. She caught the little boy's eye and frowned deeply.

"That's my sister over there," the little boy said to the man. "She's twelve-and-a-half."

"Do you love your sister?" the man asked. The little boy stared, and the man came around the side of the seat and sat down next to the little boy. "Listen," the man said. "shall I tell you about my little sister?"

The mother, who had looked up anxiously when the man sat down next to her little boy, went peacefully back to her book.

"Tell me about your sister," the little boy said. "Was she a witch?"

"Maybe," the man said.

The little boy laughed excitedly, and the man leaned back and puffed at his cigar. "Once upon a time," he began, "I had a little sister, just like yours." The little boy looked up at the man, nodding at every word. "My little sister," the man went on, "was so pretty and so nice that I loved her more than anything else in the world. So shall I tell you what I did?"

The little boy nodded more vehemently, and the mother lifted her eyes from her book and smiled, listening.

"I bought her a rocking-horse and a doll and a million lollipops," the man said, "and then I took her and I put my hands around her neck and I pinched her and I pinched her until she was dead."

The little boy gasped and the mother turned around, her smile fading. She opened her mouth, and then closed it again as the man went on, "And then I took and I cut her head off and I took her head—"

"Did you cut her all in pieces?" the little boy asked breathlessly.

"I cut off her head and her hands and her feet and her hair and her nose," the man said, "and I hit her with a stick and I killed her."

"Wait a minute," the mother said, but the baby fell over sideways just at that minute and by the time the mother had set her up again the man was going on.

"And I took her head and I pulled out all her hair and—"

"Your little *sister?*" the little boy prompted eagerly.

"My little sister," the man said firmly. "And I put her head in a cage with a bear and the bear ate it all up."

"Ate her *head* all up?" the little boy asked.

The mother put her book down and came across the aisle. She stood next to the man and said, "Just what do you think you're doing?" The man looked up courteously and she said "Get out of here."

"Did I frighten you?" the man said. He looked down at the little boy and nudged him with an elbow and he and the little boy laughed.

"This man cut up his little sister," the little boy said to his mother.

"I can very easily call the conductor," the mother said to the man.

"The conductor will *eat* my mommy," the little boy said. "We'll chop her head off."

"And little sister's head, too," the man said. He stood up, and the mother stood back to let him get out of the seat. "Don't ever come back in this car," she said.

"My mommy will eat *you,*" the little boy said to the man.

The man laughed, and the little boy laughed, and then the man said, "Excuse me," to the mother and went past her out of the car. When the door had closed behind him the little boy said, "How much longer do we have to stay on this old train?"

"Not much longer," the mother said. She stood looking at the little boy, wanting to say something, and finally she said, "You sit still and be a good boy. You may have another lollipop."

The little boy climbed down eagerly and followed his mother back to her seat. She took a lollipop from a bag in her pocketbook and gave it to him. "What do you say?" she asked.

"Thank you," the little boy said. "Did that man really cut his little sister up in pieces?"

"He was just teasing," the mother said, and added urgently, "Just *teasing.*"

"Prob'ly," the little boy said. With his lollipop he went back to his own seat, and settled himself to look out the window again. "Prob'ly he was a witch."

ADDIE[22]

—*William Faulkner*

[*Addie Bundren, the "I" of the title of William Faulkner's novel* As I Lay Dying, *is the wife of Anse Bundren, the mother of five children, and the very keystone of her family. She sets the story of the novel in motion by her insistence on being buried with her kinfolk in the cemetery at Jefferson, Mississippi. When Addie dies, the keystone is removed and the psychological dissolution of the family becomes evident, but their allegiance to her is*

[22] From *As I lay Dying,* by William Faulkner. Copyright 1930 and renewed 1958 by William Faulkner. Reprinted by permission of Random House, Inc.

sufficiently strong to make them cooperate in the task of moving Addie's remains from their farm to Jefferson, the county seat.

The section that follows is a soliloquy by Addie, about midway in the novel. Faulkner has already given us an account of Addie's death.—Ed.]

In the afternoon when school was out and the last one had left with his little dirty snuffling nose instead of going home I would go down the hill to the spring where I could be quiet and hate them. It would be quiet there then, with the water bubbling up and away and the sun slanting quiet in the tree and the quiet smelling of damp and rotting leaves and new earth; especially in the early spring, for it was worst then.

I could just remember how my father used to say that the reason for living was to get ready to stay dead a long time. And when I would have to look at them day after day, each with his and her secret and selfish thought, and blood strange to each other blood and strange to mine, and think that this seemed to be the only way I could get ready to stay dead, I would hate my father for having ever planted me. I would look forward to the times when they faulted, so I could whip them. When the switch fell I could feel it upon my flesh; when it welted and ridged it was my blood that ran, and I would think with each blow of the switch: Now you are aware of me! Now I am something in your secret and selfish life, who have marked your blood with my own for ever and ever.

And so I took Anse. I saw him pass the school house three or four times before I learned that he was driving four miles out of his way to do it. I noticed then how he was beginning to hump—a tall man and young—so that he looked already like a tall bird hunched in the cold weather, on the wagon seat. He would pass the school house, the wagon creaking slow, his head turning slow to watch the door of the school house as the wagon passed, until he went on around the curve and out of sight. One day I went to the door and stood there when he passed. When he saw me he looked quickly away and did not look back again.

In the early spring it was worst. Sometimes I thought that I could not bear it, lying in bed at night, with the wild geese going north and their honking coming faint and high and wild out of the wild darkness, and during the day it would seem as though I couldn't wait for the last one to go so I could go down to the spring. And so when I looked up that day and saw Anse standing there in his Sunday clothes, turning his hat round and round in his hands, I said:

"If you've got any womenfolks, why in the world dont they make you get your hair cut?"

"I aint got none," he said. Then he said suddenly, driving his eyes at me like two hounds in a strange yard: "That's what I come to see you about."

"And make you hold your shoulders up," I said. "You haven't got any?" But you've got a house. They tell me you've got a house and a good farm. And you live there alone, doing for yourself, do you?" He just looked at me, turning the hat in his hands. "A new house," I said. "Are you going to get married?"

And he said again, holding his eyes to mine: "That's what I come to see you about."

Later he told me, "I aint got no people. So that wont be no worry to you. I dont reckon you can say the same."

"No. I have people. In Jefferson."

His face fell a little. "Well, I got a little property. I'm forehanded; I got a good honest name. I know how town folks are, but maybe when they talk to me . . ."

"They might listen," I said. "But they'll be hard to talk to." He was watching my face. "They're in the cemetery."

"But your living kin," he said. "They'll be different."

"Will they?" I said. "I dont know. I never had any other kind."

So I took Anse. And when I knew that I had Cash, I knew that living was terrible and that this was the answer to it. That was when I learned that words are no good; that words dont ever fit even what they are trying to say at. When he was born I knew that motherhood was invented by someone who had to have a word for it because the ones that had the children didn't care whether there was a word for it or not. I knew that fear was invented by someone that had never had the fear; pride, who never had the pride. I knew that it had been, not that they had dirty noses, but that we had had to use one another by words like spiders dangling by their mouths from a beam, swinging and twisting and never touching, and that only through the blows of the switch could my blood and their blood flow as one stream. I knew that it had been, not that my aloneness had to be violated over and over each day, but that it had never been violated until Cash came. Not even by Anse in the nights.

He had a word, too. Love, he called it. But I had been used to words for a long time. I knew that that word was like the others: just a shape to fill a lack; that when the right time came, you wouldn't need a word for that anymore than for pride or fear. Cash did not need to say it to me nor I to him, and I would say, Let Anse use it, if he wants to. So that it was Anse or love, love or Anse: it didn't matter.

I would think that even while I lay with him in the dark and Cash asleep in the cradle within the swing of my hand. I would think that if he were to wake and cry, I would suckle him, too. Anse or love: it didn't matter. My aloneness had been violated and then made whole again by the violation: time, Anse, love, what you will, outside the circle.

Then I found that I had Darl. At first I would not believe it. Then I believed that I would kill Anse. It was as though he had tricked me, hidden within a word like within a paper screen and struck me in the back through it. But then I realized that I had been tricked by words older than Anse or love, and that the same word had tricked Anse too, and that my revenge would be that he would never know I was taking revenge. And when Darl was born I asked Anse to promise to take me back to Jefferson when I died, because I knew that father had been right, even when he couldn't have known he was right anymore than I could have known I was wrong.

"Nonsense," Anse said; "you and me aint nigh done chapping yet, with just two."

He did not know that he was dead, then. Sometimes I would lie by him in the dark, hearing the land that was now of my blood and flesh, and I would think: Anse. Why Anse. Why are you Anse. I would think about his name until after a while I could see the word as a shape, a vessel, and I would watch him liquefy and flow into it like cold molasses flowing out of the darkness into the vessel, until the jar stood full and motionless: a significant shape profoundly without life like an empty door frame; and then I would find that I had forgotten the name of the jar. I would think: The shape of my body where I used to be a virgin is in the shape of a _____ and I couldn't think *Anse*, couldn't remember *Anse*. It was not that I could think of myself as no longer unvirgin, because I was three now. And when I would think *Cash* and *Darl* that way until their names would die and solidify into a shape and then fade away, I would say, All right. It doesn't matter. It doesn't matter what they call them.

And so when Cora Tull would tell me I was not a true mother, I would think how words go straight up in a thin line, quick and harmless, and how terribly doing goes along the earth, clinging to it, so that after a while the two lines are too far apart for the same person to straddle from one to the other; and that sin and love and fear are just sounds that people who never sinned nor loved nor feared have for what they never had and cannot have until they forget the words. Like Cora, who could never even cook.

She would tell me what I owed to my children and to Anse and to God. I gave Anse the children. I did not ask for them. I did not even ask him for what he could have given me: not-Anse. That was my duty to him, to not ask that, and that duty I fulfilled. I would be I; I would let him be the shape and echo of his word. That was more than he asked, because he could not have asked for that and been Anse, using himself so with a word.

And then he died. He did not know he was dead. I would lie by him in the dark, hearing the dark land talking of God's love and His beauty and His sin; hearing the dark voicelessness in which the words are the deeds, and the other words that are not deeds, that are just the gaps in peoples' lacks, coming down like the cries of the geese out of the wild darkness in the old terrible nights, fumbling at the deeds like orphans to whom are pointed out in a crowd two faces and told, That is your father, your mother.

I believed that I had found it. I believed that the reason was the duty to the alive, to the terrible blood, the red bitter flood boiling through the land. I would think of sin as I would think of the clothes we both wore in the world's face, of the circumspection necessary because he was he and I was I; the sin the more utter and terrible since he was the instrument ordained by God who created the sin, to sanctify that sin He had created. While I waited for him in the woods, waiting for him before he saw me, I would think of him as dressed also in sin, he the more beautiful since the garment which he had exchanged for sin was sanctified. I would think of the sin as garments which we would remove in order to shape and coerce the terrible blood to the forlorn echo of the dead word high in the air. Then I would lay with Anse again—I did not lie to him: I just refused, just as I refused my breast to Cash and Darl after their time was up—hearing the dark land talking the voiceless speech.

I hid nothing. I tried to deceive no one. I would not have cared. I merely took the precautions that he thought necessary for his sake, not for my safety, but just as I wore clothes in the world's face. And I would think then when Cora talked to me, of how the high dead words in time seemed to lose even the significance of their dead sound.

Then it was over. Over in the sense that he was gone and I knew that, see him again though I would, I would never again see him coming swift and secret to me in the woods dressed in sin like a gallant garment already blowing aside with the speed of his secret coming.

But for me it was not over. I mean, over in the sense of beginning and ending, because to me there was no beginning nor ending to anything then. I even held Anse refraining still, not that I was holding him recessional, but as though nothing else had ever been. My children were of me alone, of the wild blood boiling along the earth, of me and of all that lived; of none and of all. Then I found that I had Jewel. When I waked to remember to discover it, he was two months gone.

My father said that the reason for living is getting ready to stay dead. I knew at last what he meant and that he could not have known what he meant himself, because a man cannot know anything about cleaning up the house afterward. And so I have cleaned my house. With Jewel—I lay by the lamp, holding up my own head, watching him cap and suture it before he breathed—the wild blood boiled away and the sound of it ceased. Then there was only the milk, warm and calm, and I lying calm in the slow silence, getting ready to clean my house.

I gave Anse Dewey Dell to negative Jewel. Then I gave him Vardaman to replace the child I robbed him of. And now he has three children that are his and not mine. And then I could get ready to die.

from THE GOVERNOR'S LADY[23]
—David Mercer

SCENE ONE [*The opening of the play is in a bungalow in Africa. Harriet is Lady Harriet Boscoe.—Ed.*]

AFTERNOON BEFORE TEA
   (African music.)
   ((HARRIET *is seated at the tea-table. She is writing in her diary.*)

HARRIET. May 15th . . . I cannot resist the temptation to anticipate Charmian's visit this afternoon, for the pleasure of writing my insights now and feeling them vindicated when she has gone. *(Pause)* Some women should not live in Africa, and Charmian is one of them. The heat withers her skin and the boredom withers her spirit . . . yet she still inspires in me that weary affection which passes for a bond between old women. *(Pause)* I wonder . . . I have no doubt she and John consider it eccentric of us to take this house on the plateau . . . what was it John said? Practically the jungle. *(Pause)* She will drive herself here in that ghastly what is it? Jeep? *(Pause)* And harass me with her inanities for two hours or more . . .

AMOLO. Mrs. Maudsley, Madam—

HARRIET. Surely not! What time is it?

CHARMIAN. Harriet, darling . . . I know I'm too early—

HARRIET. Of course not. How nice to see you. Such a wretched drive out here in the middle of the afternoon. Let's have tea at once, shall we? Amolo—tea. And you're just the person to help me, Charmian.

CHARMIAN. Help you?

HARRIET. I can't find Gilbert's gun.

CHARMIAN. I can't think why you should want Gilbert's gun. Are you going to attack somebody or are you expecting to *be* attacked? Anyway, how should I know where it is? *(Pause)* I came for tea, darling, since you invited me for tea.

HARRIET. You know you've always had a flair for finding Gilbert's things when he loses them—

CHARMIAN. That is true, but it is a flair of no practical value in the circumstances.

HARRIET. Circumstances?

CHARMIAN. Harriet, how could Gilbert lose *anything*, when Gilbert is dead?

(Pause.)

HARRIET. Did I ask Amolo to bring in the tea? I am a good shot, you know, Charmian. And I feel safer when I have the means to protect myself. There *was* a time when a white woman in this colony could dispense with such vulgarities. Now, however—

CHARMIAN. One doesn't say "this colony" any longer, Harriet. Times have changed, my dear. Since they won their precious freedom you have to be careful what you say.

HARRIET. I have always thought . . . and I always shall think . . . that the natives are children. I know I am an old-fashioned woman, a stubborn old woman—

CHARMIAN. But you want to die in full possession of all your prejudices?

HARRIET. What's that, Charmian?

CHARMIAN. I said—

HARRIET. But I fail to see why they should wish to exchange their simplicity and innocence for *our* vices and machines. *(Pause)* Leave the trolley, Amolo . . . I shall not need you.

AMOLO. Yes, Madam.

HARRIET. I agree with Gilbert. Independence at this stage would mean anarchy. *(Pause)* Lemon?

CHARMIAN. Please. *(Pause)* Dear Harriet!

HARRIET. Why, Charmian . . . you are almost in tears!

CHARMIAN. Listen darling. You're quite sure you know when and where you are?

HARRIET. But why on on earth shouldn't I?

CHARMIAN. Harriet, it is one year since this colony became independent. And six months since Gilbert died. Harriet, you are not the Governor's wife . . . You are the ex-Governor's widow. *(Pause)* I've . . . I can't go on pretending I don't notice that your mind . . . is wandering. There, I've said it. I've tried and tried to think of a kinder way of putting it. But there isn't one. Harriet, John and I think . . . we think you should consider going home. Have you seen a doctor?

HARRIET. My dear Charmian, I *am* at home. And I am perfectly well, thank you. *(Pause)* I think the drive must have tired you out. *(Pause)* And yet, it is so lovely up here. It has its compensations. Gilbert says that it is always five degrees cooler up here than anywhere else in the colony.

> *(Pause.)*

CHARMIAN. I meant—London, Harriet.

HARRIET. You don't know what you are saying, my dear. Leave Karalinga now? *(Pause)* You know Charmian, Gilbert feels—and I couldn't agree with him more—that it is precisely now when they need us most. When they have to choose between *us* and those awful little demagogues of theirs with a degree from Manchester or wherever it is.

CHARMIAN. You can quote Gilbert till you're blue in the face, darling, but it won't do me a bit of good. And it makes *them* fractious. *(Pause)* Peter says they've got us by the short and curlies—

HARRIET. By the *what?*

CHARMIAN. It does sound ghastly, doesn't it? Children are so mature nowadays. John says when he was Peter's age he spent all his time reading Shelley and worrying about self-abuse. Thank God we only have one grandchild. I'd be prostrate by now if Tim and Mary had any more like Peter.

HARRIET. Short and curly indeed! A boy of sixteen—

CHARMIAN. Curlies, Harriet.

HARRIET. Well, I ask you!

CHARMIAN. It has a certain crude vigour, as dormitory language goes—

HARRIET. My dear Charmian, a boy who can be as facetious as that at sixteen can be a Socialist at twenty-one!

CHARMIAN. I don't *quite* see the connection—

HARRIET. From the moment they came to power in 1945, Gilbert noticed the prevailing tone in their dealings with him was one of disrespect . . . a, a want of feeling and discretion.

CHARMIAN. Well, darling, you remember what the Permanent Under Secretary said at the time—

HARRIET. I don't believe I do.

CHARMIAN. Uneasy lies the Red that wears a crown! (*Laughs*) No, Harriet, it won't do. Gilbert failed to adapt, and people who fail to adapt—especially in colonial matters—are, as I have no doubt Peter would say, sitting ducks.

HARRIET. I shall never understand you. You talk as though it is all over and done with.

CHARMIAN. But isn't it?

(*Pause.*)

HARRIET. So long as Gilbert is Governor of Karalinga, it is the *colony* that must learn to adapt.

CHARMIAN. Harriet—

HARRIET. Will you have some more tea?

CHARMIAN. Harriet—

HARRIET. (*Petulantly*) Now what is it?

CHARMIAN. Gilbert is dead.

HARRIET. Then I have nothing more to say on the subject. We all have our, our indiosyncrasies, Charmian. You must cling to yours, and I must cling to mine.

CHARMIAN. I would hardly call it an idiosyncrasy, to ignore the fact that Gilbert caught pneumonia, and died, and has been buried nearly six months.

(*Pause.*)

HARRIET. *I* was speaking of the subtleties of colonial administration, Charmian.

(*Pause.*)

CHARMIAN. Look, darling, why not let John and me come and help you to pack? Have everything sent off by sea, and book you an air passage to London? (*Pause*) This house is too lonely, Harriet. Anything could happen to you out here, and none of us would know. (*Pause*) Living out here with two or three native servants . . . not even a telephone . . . must you, Harriet? At least, come and stay with us for a while—

HARRIET. (*Sharply*) Do *not* insist on treating me as if I were mentally infirm, Charmian. (*Pause*) Amolo can reach the town on his bicycle in forty minutes. Should I need you in any way during Gilbert's absence, I am grateful to think you would come if I sent for you.

(*Pause.*)

CHARMIAN. Well, if you will insist on being indomitable—

(*Pause.*)

HARRIET. Not indomitable, Charmian. Independent.

CHARMIAN. (*Jungle noises start*) Well, it's nice to know you're not entirely without faith in independence! (*Pause*) I think I'd better be going. Come out and see what I did, to the jeep thing on the way up here—

(*Exit both. Blackout.*)

from **THE ORCHESTRA**[24]

—*Jean Anouilh, translated by Miriam John*

The orchestra is an all-female orchestra except for the male pianist; the scene, the platform of a spa town brasserie. All the women are dressed in bespangled black gowns with single pink roses as ornaments. Suzanne plays the cello; Patricia, the first violin; Pamela, the second violin. They are talking about Madame Hortense, double bass player and leader of the orchestra.—Ed.]

SUZANNE D. She never stops, does she?

PIANIST. We were just chatting.

SUZANNE D. If you don't shut her up, I will.

PIANIST. It's difficult to stop her while the customers are here. After all, she's the leader, isn't she?

SUZANNE D. Coward! Coward! (*She sits down again.*)

PATRICIA. (*Continuing a conversation with Pamela of which we have not heard the beginning*) Then I rub it with a bit of Kleenall and a really dry, soft rag.

PAMELA. I prefer a drop of ammonia.

PATRICIA. (*Acidly*) Ammonia removes the varnish, not the mark.

PAMELA. (*Also aggressive*) Each to her own method.

PATRICIA. Yes, but some methods are bad. Certain women have no pride in their homes.

PAMELA. My home looks just as good as yours. (*With a laugh*) Maybe there aren't so many little mats and table runners and things.

PATRICIA. Well, not everyone has artistic taste, I mean, have they? I like my little soft, warm nest, with all my souvenirs around me. The mats and things make it cosy.

PAMELA. Dust traps. My little place is modern, I'm proud to say. Tubular furniture and formica surfaces. Everything neat and bright. No ornaments.

PATRICIA. (*With a nervous little sneer*) Oh, I can just see it—a clinic! I'm not an invalid.

PAMELA. And I *am*, I suppose?

PATRICIA. Well, with those eyes . . .

PAMELA. My eyes may be a little haggard, my dear, but that's because I have a lover who adores me, and that's more than you can say. At least both *my* eyes look in the same direction.

PATRICIA. (*Squinting nervously*) Oh! What a thing to say about a phys-

[24] From *Jean Anouilh: Seven Plays* (vol. 3). Reprinted by permission of Hill & Wang, Inc.

ical handicap. Anyway, it's hardly noticeable. How low can you sink? And as for your lover, there's no need to boast about him. A bottle washer!

PAMELA. *(Laughing quite good-naturedly)* One does what one can. The great thing is to make a good job of it. I like a job well done. *(She is cooing insolently.)*

PATRICIA. You're unspeakable. I wonder women like you are tolerated in a respectable orchestra.

from **MACBETH** (Act I, Scene vii) [25]
—*William Shakespeare*

A court in Macbeth's castle, open to the sky, with doors to the rear, one on the left the main gate or south entry, one on the right leading to rooms within, and between them a covered recess running back, beneath a gallery, to a third door, through the which when ajar may be seen a flight of stairs to an upper chamber. A bench with a table before it against a side wall.

Hautboys. Torches. Enter a sewer directing divers servants who pass with dishes and service across the court. As they come through the door on the right a sound of feasting is heard within. Then enter MACBETH from the same door.]

MACBETH. If it were done, when 'tis done, then 'twere well
It were done quickly: if th'assassination
Could trammel up the consequence, and catch,
With his surcease, success; that but this blow
Might be the be-all and the end-all. . . . here,
But here, upon this bank and shoal of time,
We'ld jump the life to come. But in these cases
We still have judgement here—that we but teach
Bloody instructions, which being taught return
To plague th'inventor: this even-handed justice
Commends th'ingredience of our poisoned chalice
To our own lips. He's here in double trust:
First, as I am his kinsman and his subject,
Strong both against the deed; then, as his host,
Who should against his murderer shut the door,
Not bear the knife myself. Besides, this Duncan
Hath borne his faculties so meek, hath been
So clear in his great office, that his virtues
Will plead like angels, trumpet-tongued, against
The deep damnation of his taking-off:
And pity, like a naked new-born babe,

[25] From *The New Shakespeare*, edited by John Dover Wilson.

Striding the blast, or Heaven's cherubin, horsed
Upon the sightless couriers of the air,
Shall blow the horrid deed in every eye,
That tears shall drown the wind. I have no spur
To prick the sides of my intent, but only
Vaulting ambition, which o'erleaps itself,
And falls on th'other—
      How now, what news?

LADY M. He has almost supped: why have you left the chamber?

MACBETH. Hath he asked for me?

LADY M.   Know you not he has?

MACBETH. We will proceed no further in this business:
He hath honoured me of late, and I have bought
Golden opinions from all sorts of people,
Which would be worn now in their newest gloss,
Not cast aside so soon.

LADY M.   Was the hope drunk
Wherein you dressed yourself? hath it slept since?
And wakes it now, to look so green and pale
At what it did so freely? From this time
Such I account thy love. Art thou afeard
To be the same in thine own act and valour
As thou art in desire? Wouldst thou have that
Which thou esteem'st the ornament of life,
And live a coward in thine own esteem,
Letting "I dare not" wait upon "I would,"
Like the poor cat i'th'adage?

MACBETH.   Prithee, peace:
I dare do all that may become a man;
Who dares do more, is none.

LADY M.   What beast was't then
That made you break this enterprise to me?
When you durst do it, then you were a man;
And, to be more than what you were, you would
Be so much more the man. Nor time nor place
Did then adhere, and yet you would make both:
They have made themselves, and that their fitness now
Does unmake you. I have given suck, and know
How tender 'tis to love the babe that milks me—
I would, while it was smiling in my face,
Have plucked my nipple from his boneless gums,
And dashed the brains out, had I so sworn as you
Have done to this.

MACBETH.   If we should fail?

LADY M.   We fail?

But screw your courage to the sticking place,
And we'll not fail. When Duncan is asleep
(Whereto the rather shall his day's hard journey
Soundly invite him) his two chamberlains
Will I with wine and wassail so convince,
That memory, the warder of the brain,
Shall be a fume, and the receipt of reason
A limbec only: when in swinish sleep
Their drenchéd natures lie as in a death,
What cannot you and I perform upon
Th'unguarded Duncan? what not put upon
His spongy officers, who shall bear the guilt
Of our great quell?

      MACBETH.   Bring forth men-children only!
For thy undaunted mettle should compose
Nothing but males. Will it not be received,
When we have marked with blood those sleepy two
Of his own chamber, and used their very daggers,
That they have done't?

      LADY M.   Who dares receive it other,
As we shall make our griefs and clamour roar
Upon his death?

      MACBETH.   I am settled, and bend up
Each corporal agent to this terrible feat.
Away, and mock the time with fairest show:
False face must hide what the false heart doth know.
      [they return to the chamber]

from **BELLAVITA**[26]

Luigi Pirandello, translated by William Murray

[*The scene is a sitting-room in the home of Contento, a lawyer. Denora is a notary. Bellavita is the owner of a café and pastry shop in a small
southern Italian town. Denora is fat, forty, with thinning reddish hair and
a large, purplish, pimply face; Mrs. Contento is 30, pretty, bright-eyed.
Denora has come to consult Contento about a matter which exasperates
him and makes him feel ridiculous; it involves another person, as yet unnamed, and something about "the best school in Naples." At this point
Denora is left alone with Mrs. Contento, who tries to keep him calm. —
Ed.*]

MRS. CONTENTO. I don't think you ought to admit right away that the boy is your son. I'd at least express a few doubts. That's what I told my husband.

DENORA. No, no! It doesn't matter! Even if he weren't, it makes no difference! I admit everything! I accept everything!

MRS. CONTENTO. But why? If you could prove he wasn't yours—

DENORA. How can I prove it? It's not only the father, my dear lady, who can never know for sure. Not even the mother herself could say with any certainty whether her own son was fathered by her husband or her lover. It's all guesswork.

MRS. CONTENTO. Does the boy resemble you?

DENORA. So they say. Sometimes I think he does, sometimes I think he doesn't. You can't put trust in resemblances. Anyway, as I said, I don't want to argue the point. I'm ready to do everything: adopt him, change my will in his favor, anything! I don't have anyone else. And I don't care any more about anything! I want to get rid of him—*the father*, I mean—at any cost! But the sound of money falls on deaf ears with that man, and it won't do any good to try that tack. He's never acted for profit. That's why I'm so desperate.

MRS. CONTENTO. It's really unheard of!

DENORA. *(Leaping to his feet)* Unheard of! Unheard of! And it had to be just my luck to have to deal with a husband like him!

MRS. CONTENTO. Why do they call him Bellavita? It must be some kind of nickname, isn't it?

DENORA. Yes, given him out of envy. People used to pass in front of his shop and see it always full of clients, his wife sitting behind the counter like a great lady, and they'd say, "Eh, *bella vita! The good life!*" They've been calling him that ever since.

MRS. CONTENTO. I was by the shop only yesterday. It was pitiful. Those beautiful white counters and the coffee machine that used to be so bright and shiny, why you wouldn't recognize the place! Everything's yellow and dirty. And the sad, faded curtains, one pink, the other blue, stretched across those dried-up cakes and moldy pies! No one goes there any more. Was it you who kept the shop going for him?

DENORA. Me? Certainly not! Not a word of truth in it, if that's what you heard! He wouldn't even let his wife accept the time of day from me. He'd let me pay for an occasional coffee, when I'd show up there with my friends, because it would have been unnatural for him not to. But I'm sure he hated it.

MRS. CONTENTO. It seems hard to explain.

DENORA. What is there to explain, Mrs. Contento? Some things just can't be explained.

MRS. CONTENTO. How can anyone be like that?

DENORA. When we don't want to know something—it's easy—we pretend we don't know it. And if we're more concerned with fooling ourselves than others, believe me, it's exactly, exactly as if we don't really know. . . . He's even overflowing with gratitude for me.

MRS. CONTENTO. Gratitude?

DENORA. Oh, yes. For the way I stood up for him, from the beginning of the marriage.

MRS. CONTENTO. Yes, he was sickly-looking, always in poor health. . . . I don't know why she married him. She came from a good family.

DENORA. Fallen on hard times.

MRS. CONTENTO. I can't imagine what she saw in him.

DENORA. She used to accuse him of poor judgment, of being tactless with their customers, even of stupidity.

MRS. CONTENTO. Well, he really is stupid. . . .

DENORA. You're telling me?—The scenes they'd have!—Well, you understand, I was in the habit of dropping in with my friends for a coffee. . . . I'm a peaceful type—it used to upset me. . . . It began with my trying to make peace between them and . . .

MRS. CONTENTO. . . . peace today, a friend the next, and eventually . . .

DENORA. Unfortunately, these things do happen.

MRS. CONTENTO. Unfortunately. She was so pretty! I can still see her, sitting behind the counter, smiling and so full of life, with her pert little nose all powdered white and that red-silk shawl with the yellow moons on it around her neck, those big golden hoops in her ears and the dimples she had when she smiled! She was adorable! (*At this description of her, Denora begins to sob with his stomach, then, all choked up with emotion, to wheeze through his nose. He raises a hand to his eyes.*) Poor Denora, you really did love her!

DENORA. Yes, yes, I did! and I hate this man because it wasn't enough for him to poison my life; now he has to poison my grief at losing her! And you know how? By reveling in it! Yes. As if he were providing it for me to feed on, to suck on, like a mother offering her breast to her baby! That's why I hate him! Because he won't let me do what I want, to mourn her by myself! You can understand, can't you, the disgust I feel in having to share even her death with him? He came to see me before the funeral, with the boy, to tell me that he'd ordered *two* wreaths, one for him and one for me, and that he'd arranged for them to be placed next to each other on the hearse. He said they talked.

MRS. CONTENTO. (*Bewildered*) Who talked?

DENORA. Those two wreaths. Next to each other like that. He said they talked louder than words. He must have seen the hate in my eyes. He threw himself on my neck, crying and wailing at the top of his lungs, and he began shouting and begging me not to abandon him, for heaven's sake, and to have consideration and pity for him, because only I could understand him, because only I had had the same loss to bear. I swear to you, Mrs. Contento that his eyes, as he spoke, were those of a madman, or I'd have been tempted to push him away and boot him out of my sight.

MRS. CONTENTO. I can't believe it! I just can't believe it!

DENORA. I can still feel the horror of touching him. I had to take him by the arms—they were sticks under the furry cloth of that black-dyed suit of his—and free myself of that desperate grip he had around my neck! Funny, isn't it, how at certain times you notice little things that stay with you forever? There he was, crying on my neck like that. I turned toward the window, as if looking for a way out, I suppose, and somebody had traced a cross in the dust on the windowpanes. The whole sad business of this ruined bachelor life of mine, it was summed up for me in that cross, on the panes of that window, on that cloudy sky beyond. Ah, Mrs. Contento, that cross, those dirty windowpanes, I'll *never* get them out of my sight!

from CRAWLING ARNOLD[27]
—Jules Feiffer

[*The Enterprise home. As the play opens, Mr. and Mrs. Enterprise, in their 70's, are talking with Miss Sympathy, a pretty young social worker, largely about their child LittleWill, two years old, though there are references to another child, Arnold, who suffers by comparision; Arnold is 35. When Arnold enters, he enters crawling. He crawls into a corner with a coloring book. Finally the Enterprises maneuver so that they can leave Miss Sympathy alone with Arnold.—Ed.*]

MISS SYMPATHY. (*There is an awkward silence. She decides to get right to it.*) Don't you know how to walk?

ARNOLD. That's a funny question. Why do you ask?

MISS SYMPATHY. Well, you're not walking.

ARNOLD. I'm not smoking, either. Why don't you ask me if I know how to smoke?

MISS SYMPATHY. (*Containing herself*) That's very good. (*Arnold shrugs.*) Do you mind if I crawl with you?

ARNOLD. (*Hotly*) Yes, I do!

MISS SYMPATHY. But *you* do it!

ARNOLD. I do it because I believe in it. You do it because you think you're being therapeutic. You're not. You're only being patronizing. I realize that in your field it's sometimes difficult to tell the difference.

MISS SYMPATHY. (*With difficulty*) That's very good.

ARNOLD. If you really feel the urge to crawl with me—*really* feel it, I mean—then you'll be most welcome. Not any more welcome or unwelcome than you are now by the way. I am by no means a missionary. Did you see my coloring book?

MISS SYMPATHY. When anyone says anything you don't like, you retreat into that coloring book.

[27] Reprinted by permission of the author.

ARNOLD. I admit it's rude. I shouldn't do it unless I have a coloring book for you too. (*He studies her.*) Do you wear glasses?

MISS SYMPATHY. Contact lenses.

ARNOLD. (*Suddenly shy*) You'd be prettier with glasses. Or rather *I* think you'd be prettier with glasses. I like the way a girl looks with glasses. It makes her face look—less undressed.

MISS SYMPATHY. You think contact lenses make me look naked?

ARNOLD. I think the more people have on, the better they get along with each other. If everybody in the world wore big hats, thick glasses, and dark overcoats they'd all pass each other by thinking, "What an interesting person must be inside all that." And they'd be curious, but they wouldn't ask questions. Who'd dare ask questions like "What are you really like?" to a person in a big hat, thick glasses, and a dark overcoat? The desire to invade privacy rises in direct proportion to the amount of clothing a person takes off. It's what we call "communication." Take off the big hat, and they say, "Good morning, sir!" Take off the thick glasses, and they say, "My, don't you have *haunted* eyes!" Take off the overcoat, and they say, "Tell me *everything!*" So there you have intimacy, followed by understanding, followed by disillusion, followed by—(*Shrugs*). If only everybody wore more clothing, we wouldn't have wars.

MISS SYMPATHY. You're saying you'd like to wear an overcoat with me. Is that it?

ARNOLD. I'd feel better if one of us at least wore a big hat. Do you ever have fantasies?

MISS SYMPATHY. Aren't you getting intimate?

ARNOLD. *You* decided to wear the contact lenses.

MISS SYMPATHY. Everybody has fantasies.

ARNOLD. What are yours about?

MISS SYMPATHY. Being a better social worker.

ARNOLD. Dear God.

MISS SYMPATHY. (*Sadly*) I used to have fantasies about Adlai Stevenson. But that's all over now.

ARNOLD. I have fantasies all the time. When I'm awake, when I'm asleep, I *live* with them. I embellish them. Polish them day after day. You cultivate a good fantasy long enough, and soon it can seep out into the real world. Do you know how old my parents are?

MISS SYMPATHY. I hadn't thought of it. Middle fifties?

ARNOLD. They're both over seventy.

MISS SYMPATHY. And they had a *baby?*

ARNOLD. (*Shrugs, reaches for the coloring book, changes his mind*) My father doesn't look very much older than me, does he?

MISS SYMPATHY. (*Evasive*) I don't know if I noticed.

ARNOLD. You're kind. But that's how it's been always. They're both alert, involved, aggressive people. So while I'm out trying, unsuccessfully, to make it with a girl and I come home, mixed up and angry and feeling like not much of anything, what are they waiting up proudly to tell me? *They're* having a baby. I'll try to say this in as uninvolved and unneurotic a way as I know how—it's hard to face a daily series of piddling, eroding defeats and, in addition, have the fact thrown in your face that your *father* at *age seventy* can still do better than you can.

THE STRONGER[28]
—*August Strindberg*
(*translated by Elizabeth Sprigge*)

Scene: A corner of a ladies' café (in Stockholm in the eighteen eighties). Two small wrought-iron tables, a red plush settee and a few chairs. Miss Y. is sitting with a half-empty bottle of beer on the table before her, reading an illustrated weekly which from time to time she exchanges for another.

Mrs. X. enters, wearing a winter hat and coat and carrying a decorative Japanese basket.

Mrs. X. Why, Millie, my dear, how are you? Sitting here all alone on Christmas Eve like some poor bachelor.

(*Miss Y. looks up from her magazine, nods, and continues to read.*)

Mrs. X. You know it makes me feel really sad to see you. Alone. Alone in a café and on Christmas Eve of all times. It makes me feel as sad as when once in Paris I saw a wedding party at a restaurant. The bride was reading a comic paper and the bridegroom playing billiards with the witnesses. Ah me, I said to myself, with such a beginning how will it go, and how will it end? He was playing billiards on his wedding day! And she, you were going to say, was reading a comic paper on hers. But that's not quite the same.

(*A waitress brings a cup of chocolate to Mrs. X. and goes out.*)

Mrs. X. Do you know, Amelia, I really believe now you would have done better to stick to him. Don't forget I was the first who told you to forgive him. Do you remember? Then you would be married now and have a home. Think how happy you were that Christmas when you stayed with your fiancé's people in the country. How warmly you spoke of domestic happiness! You really quite longed to be out of the theatre. Yes, Amelia dear, home is best—next best to the stage, and as for children—but you couldn't know anything about that.

(*Miss Y.'s expression is disdainful. Mrs. X. sips a few spoonfuls of chocolate, then opens her basket and displays some Christmas presents.*)

Mrs. X. Now you must see what I have bought for my little chicks. (*Takes out a doll.*) Look at this. That's for Lisa. Do you see how she can roll her eyes and turn her head. Isn't she lovely? And here's a toy pistol for Maja.*

---

[28] Portion of "The Stronger" from the book *Six Plays of Strindberg* by August Strindberg, new translations by Elizabeth Sprigge. Copyright © 1955 by Elizabeth Sprigge. Reprinted by permission of Doubleday & Company, Inc.

* Pronounced Maya.

(*She loads the pistol and shoots it at* MISS Y. *who appears frightened.*)

MRS. X. Were you scared? Did you think I was going to shoot you? Really, I didn't think you'd believe that of me. Now if *you* were to shoot *me* it wouldn't be so surprising, for after all I did get in your way, and I know you never forget it—although I was entirely innocent. You still think I intrigued to get you out of the Grand Theatre, but I didn't. I didn't, however much you think I did. Well, it's no good talking, you will believe it was me. . . . (*Takes out a pair of embroidered slippers.*) And these are for my old man, with tulips on them that I embroidered myself. As a matter of fact I hate tulips, but he has to have tulips on everything.

(MISS Y. *looks up, irony and curiosity in her face.*)

MRS. X. (*Putting one hand in each slipper*) Look what small feet Bob has, hasn't he? And you ought to see the charming way he walks—you've never seen him in slippers, have you?

(MISS Y. *laughs.*)

MRS. X. Look, I'll show you. (*She makes the slippers walk across the table, and* MISS Y. *laughs again.*)

MRS. X. But when he gets angry, look, he stamps his foot like this. "Those damn girls who can never learn how to make coffee! Blast! That silly idiot hasn't trimmed the lamp properly!" Then there's a draught under the door and his feet get cold. "Hell, it's freezing, and the damn fools can't even keep the stove going!" (*She rubs the sole of one slipper against the instep of the other.* MISS Y. *roars with laughter.*)

MRS. X. And then he comes home and has to hunt for his slippers, which Mary has pushed under the bureau. . . . Well, perhaps it's not right to make fun of one's husband like this. He's sweet anyhow, and a good, dear husband. You ought to have had a husband like him, Amelia. What are you laughing at? What is it? Eh? And, you see, I know he is faithful to me. Yes, I know it. He told me himself—what *are* you giggling at?—that while I was on tour in Norway that horrible Frederica came and tried to seduce him. Can you imagine anything more abominable? (*Pause*) I'd have scratched her eyes out if she had come around while I was at home. (*Pause*) I'm glad Bob told me about it himself, so I didn't just hear it from gossip. (*Pause*) And, as a matter of fact, Frederica wasn't the only one. I can't think why, but all the women in the company* seem to be crazy about my husband. They must think his position gives him some say in who is engaged at the Theatre. Perhaps you have run after him yourself? I don't trust you very far, but I know he has never been attracted by you, and you always seemed to have some sort of grudge against him, or so I felt. (*Pause. They look at one another guardedly.*)

MRS. X. Do come and spend Christmas Eve with us tonight, Amelia— just to show that you're not offended with us, or anyhow not with me. I

---

* "In the company": translator's addition.

don't know why, but it seems specially unpleasant not to be friends with you. Perhaps it's because I did get in your way that time . . . (*slowly*) or—I don't know—really, I don't know at all why it is.

(*Pause.* Miss Y. *gazes curiously at* Mrs. X.)

Mrs. X. (*thoughtfully*) It was so strange when we were getting to know one another. Do you know, when we first met, I was frightened of you, so frightened I didn't dare let you out of my sight. I arranged all my goings and comings to be near you. I dared not be your enemy, so I became your friend. But when you came to our home, I always had an uneasy feeling, because I saw my husband didn't like you, and that irritated me—like when a dress doesn't fit. I did all I could to make him be nice to you, but it was no good—until you went and got engaged. Then you became such tremendous friends that at first it looked as if you only dared show your real feelings then—when you were safe. And then, let me see, how was it after that? I wasn't jealous—that's queer. And I remember at the christening, when you were the godmother, I told him to kiss you. He did, and you were so upset. . . . As a matter of fact I didn't notice that then . . . I didn't think about it afterwards either . . . I've never thought about it—until *now!* (*Rises abruptly*) Why don't you say something? You haven't said a word all this time. You've just let me go in talking. You have sat there with your eyes drawing all these thoughts out of me—they were there in me like silk in a cocoon—thoughts. . . . Mistaken thoughts? Let me think. Why did you break off your engagement? Why did you never come to our house after that? Why don't you want to come to us tonight?

(Miss Y. *makes a motion, as if about to speak.*)

Mrs X. No. You don't need to say anything, for now I see it all. That was why—and why—and why. Yes. Yes, that's why it was. Yes, yes, all the pieces fit together now. That's it. I won't sit at the same table as you. (*Moves her things to the other table.*) That's why I have to embroider tulips, which I loathe, on his slippers—because you liked tulips. (*Throws the slippers on the floor.*) That's why we have to spend the summer on the lake—because you couldn't bear the seaside. That's why my son had to be called Eskil—because it was your father's name. That's why I had to wear your colours, read your books, eat the dishes you liked, drink your drinks—your chocolate, for instance. That's why—oh my God, it's terrible to think of, terrible! Everything, everything came to me from you—even your passions. Your soul bored into mine like a worm into an apple, and ate and ate and ate and burrowed and burrowed, till nothing was left but the skin and a little black mould. I wanted to fly from you, but I couldn't. You were there like a snake, your black eyes fascinating me. When I spread my wings, they only dragged me down. I lay in the water with my feet tied together, and the harder I worked my arms, the deeper I sank—down, down, till I reached the bottom, where you lay in waiting like a giant crab to catch me in your claws—and now here I am. Oh how I hate you! I hate you, I hate you! And you just go on sitting there, silent, calm, indifferent, not caring whether the moon is new or full, if it's Christmas or New Year, if other people are happy or unhappy. You don't know how to hate or to love. You just sit there without moving—like a cat* at a mouse-hole. You can't drag your prey out, you can't chase it, but you can outstay it. Here you sit in your corner—you know they call it the rat-trap after you—reading the papers to see if anyone's ruined or wretched or been thrown out of the company. Here you sit sizing up your victims and weighing your chances—like a pilot his shipwrecks for the salvage. *(Pause)* Poor Amelia! Do you know, I couldn't be more sorry for you. I know you are miserable, miserable like some wounded creature, and vicious because you are wounded. I can't be angry with you. I should like to be, but after all you are the small one—and as for your affair with Bob, that doesn't worry me in the least. Why should it matter to me? And if you or somebody else taught me to drink chocolate, what's the difference? *(Drinks a spoonful. Smugly.)* Chocolate is very wholesome anyhow. And if I learnt from you how to dress, *tant mieux!*—that only gave me a stronger hold over my husband, and you have lost what I gained. Yes, to judge from various signs, I think you have now lost him. Of course, you meant me to walk out, as you once did, and which you're now regretting. But I won't do that, you may be sure. One shouldn't be narrow-minded, you know. And why should nobody else want what I have? *(Pause)* Perhaps, my dear, taking everything into consideration, at this moment it is I who am the stronger. You never got anything from me, you just gave away—from yourself. And now, like the thief in the night, when you woke up I had what you had lost. Why was it then that everything you touched became worthless and sterile? You couldn't keep a man's love—for all your tulips and your passions—but I could. You couldn't learn the art of living from your books—but I learnt it. You bore no little Eskil, although that was your father's name. *(Pause)* And why is it you are silent—everywhere, always silent? Yes, I used to think this was strength, but perhaps it was because you hadn't anything to say, because you couldn't think of anything. *(Rises and picks up the slippers.)* Now I am going home, taking the tulips with me—*your* tulips. You couldn't learn from others, you couldn't bend, and so you broke like a dry stick. I did not. Thank you, Amelia, for all your good lessons. Thank you for teaching my husband how to love. Now I am going home—to love him.

    (Exit.)

* In Swedish, "stork."

Chapter **11**
ANALYSIS OF A POEM, A STORY, AND A PLAY

Literary study, for the interpreter at least, ought to result in a vital comprehension of the work itself. Unless it does this, critical analysis is useless and literary study is deprived of its reason for being. Hence it seems proper to look now at three separate literary kinds in some detail. It is hoped that the stages of analysis will seem fairly natural, but remember that there is no fixed procedure for the analysis of a work of literature; the point at which you begin is determined in part by your own capacities and in part by the purpose of your analysis. Furthermore, the task of analysis is almost unending ; you are in no way limited to the analyses set down here—you may be able to add to them.

In these analyses we try to make use of the principles enunciated in the first part of the volume—to point to various kinds and degrees of tensions residing in the works, to examine locus and perspective, to discover how in coalescing the elements of the piece create a distinctive presence. We must seek to reveal the complicated life of each piece by looking for the springs of meaning.

ANALYSIS OF A POEM

We have chosen, first of all, a poem by a writer significant enough to merit the attention of any student of modern literature: D. H. Lawrence. Read the poem receptively. Read it simply for the experience it embodies. During the initial reading, don't worry about anything except your own enjoyment of the poem.

SNAKE[1]
—D. H. Lawrence

A snake came to my water-trough
On a hot, hot day, and I in pyjamas for the heat,
To drink there.

In the deep, strange-scented shade of the great dark carob-tree
I came down the steps with my pitcher
And must wait, must stand and wait, for there he was at the trough
    before me.

He reached down from a fissure in the earth-wall in the gloom
And trailed his yellow-brown slackness soft-bellied down, over the edge
  of the stone trough
And rested his throat upon the stone bottom,
And where the water had dripped from the tap, in a small clearness,
He sipped with his straight mouth,
Softly drank through his straight gums, into his slack long body
Silently.

Someone was before me at my water-trough,
And I, like a second-comer, waiting.

He lifted his head from his drinking, as cattle do,
And looked at me vaguely, as drinking cattle do,
And flickered his two-forked tongue from his lips, and mused a
    moment,
And stooped and drank a little more,
Being earth-brown, earth-golden from the burning bowels of the earth
On the day of Sicilian July, with Etna smoking.

The voice of my education said to me
He must be killed,
For in Sicily the black, black snakes are innocent, the gold are
    venomous.

And voices in me said, if you were a man
You would take a stick and break him now, and finish him off.
But must I confess how I liked him,
How glad I was he had come like a guest in quiet, to drink at my
    water-trough
And depart peaceful, pacified, and thankless,
Into the burning bowels of this earth?

Was it cowardice, that I dared not kill him?
Was it perversity, that I longed to talk to him?
Was it humility, to feel so honoured?
I felt so honoured.

And yet those voices:
If you were not afraid, you would kill him!

And truly I was afraid, I was most afraid,
But even so, honoured still more
That he should seek my hospitality
From out the dark door of the secret earth.

He drank enough
And lifted his head, dreamily, as one who has drunken,
And flickered his tongue like a forked night on the air, so black,
Seeming to lick his lips,
And looked around like a god, unseeing, into the air,
And slowly turned his head,
And slowly, very slowly, as if thrice adream,
Proceeded to draw his slow length curving round
And climb again the broken bank of my wall-face.

And as he put his head into that dreadful hole,
And as he slowly drew up, snake-easing his shoulders, and entered
        farther,
A sort of horror, a sort of protest against his withdrawing into that
        horrid black hole,
Deliberately going into the blackness, and slowly drawing himself
        after,
Overcame me now his back was turned.

I looked round, I put down my pitcher,
I picked up a clumsy log
And threw it at the water trough with a clatter.

I think it did not hit him,
But suddenly that part of him that was left behind convulsed in
        undignified haste,
Writhed like lightning, and was gone
Into the black hole, the earth-lipped fissure in the wall-front,
At which, in the intense still noon, I stared with fascination.

And immediately I regretted it.
I thought how paltry, how vulgar, what a mean act!
I despised myself and the voices of my accursed human education.

And I thought of the albatross,
And I wished he would come back, my snake.

For he seemed to me again like a king,
Like a king in exile, uncrowned in the underworld,
Now due to be crowned again.

And so, I missed my chance with one of the lords
Of life.
And I have something to expiate;
A pettiness.

It is probably safe to say that a snake is for most people an object of both horror and fascination. All literature bears witness to the ambivalence in our attitudes toward snakes. The biblical function of the snake as (paradoxically) persuader to both evil and knowledge, counseling Eve in the Garden of Eden, embodying Satan himself; the idea of the snake as a hidden danger lurking in the grass ("snake in the grass," or Shakespeare's "Look like the innocent flower, but be the serpent under it"); the hypnotic picture of the deadly cobra swaying to the pipe of a snakecharmer; the knowledge of the tremendous muscular strength of the boa constrictor, with its ability to expand or to contract his length; the dreadful *silence* with which the serpent moves—such notions are buried somewhere in the consciousness of most readers, together with feelings of revulsion taught us from childhood. Some of these notions, and the emotions attached to them, are called up even by the title of Lawrence's poem and are with us as we begin reading.

But the poem itself begins matter-of-factly: a snake comes to drink on a hot, hot day, a day so hot that the "I" of the poem (the point of view is selected at once) is wearing "pyjamas." The visual and thermal images are primary in the opening three lines.

The second section (in addition to setting up sound patterns, to which we shall return, and perhaps yielding additional sensory responses for certain readers) introduces notions of *depth* and *strangeness* and *darkness*. Doubtless the word *carob,* which will send most readers to the dictionary, also creates a sense of the strange or exotic. Otherwise the section is again rather matter-of-fact: the speaker must come down to the water trough—he too for water against the heat—and must wait. Why? Because *he* (not *it,* but *he:* why?) is already there. The second section is weightier in content than the first; it is also longer, though both sections have only three lines. The effect in these first sections is that of moving from summary to scene in narrative. And now the tempo becomes very slow as we move in close to watch.

The speaker is no longer the center of the picture; the snake, "he," is what we watch—we and the narrator, who establishes the point of view for us.

Now the darkness and the strangeness and the sensation of depth barely suggested in the second section begin to take shape as direct sensory responses; the snake reaches down in the gloom; he trails his slackness down into the stone trough; then, so quietly that one must only *imagine* he hears it, the snake drinks. The sense of movement, of

reaching, of trailing, of resting, of sipping, of drinking is sharply underscored by the narrator; but everything is in the silence. The snake has
dignity; like the human being who observes him, he needs water against
the heat. And he is here first. The snake is invested with a life of his
own, needs of his own, before the poem presents other considerations.

The fourth section sharply restores the speaker to our sight. It is
brief, simple; it punctuates the vision, sums up the fact; at the same
time, it arouses a certain amount of apprehension. What will happen
now? The poem gathers itself for a forward movement.

In the fifth section, we return to the snake himself. Again we
watch. The reference to cattle (which is not figurative, but literal) again
underscores the snake's likeness to other creatures. Only the reference
to his "two-forked tongue" reminds us that he *is* a snake. He takes his
time, muses, drinks. Then, with a reference again to the heat, we return
to the speaker, who sees this golden creature as a snake from the bowels
of the earth—and we are again aware of the snake as snake, for (paradoxically, again) the goldness (rather than the blackness) of the serpent
is a sign of venomousness: this is the subject of section 6, which says
that here in Sicily (where the poem takes place) educated sense tells the
speaker that poisonous snakes ought to be put to death.

The seventh section repeats this notion, but more compellingly.
The compulsion to kill is urged on by the voices. Self-preservation is a
basic consideration. The poem gathers again. But the snake is no longer
for the speaker (nor is he for us) simply a snake. The eighth section
makes this explicit: the speaker, almost despite himself, "likes" the
snake, feels a kinship with him in his need to drink—though, not being
human, the snake will depart "thankless" again into the burning bowels
of the earth.

Now the poem, midway in its course, poses the questions: Is the
speaker afraid? Is it some perversity in him that makes him feel kinship
with the snake? Is it even some sense of personal abasement or lowli
ness that makes him feel honored in the presence of this strange guest?
The fact remains that he *does* feel honored; that is the truth behind the
question. And yet—

The short tenth section repeats the voices, italicizing their words:
"If you were not afraid, you would kill him!" The strong sense of hatred
and fear that most of us feel out of a long history of responses the
speaker very much shares—at least, fear.

Fear—but even more, honor. Honor that the snake has visited him,
partaken of his hospitality, "from out the dark door of the secret earth."
We are back again to the darkness and the strangeness, and it is almost
as if, with the speaker, we were leaving the world of men (with its
obligation to kill golden snakes) and entering some world where all
creatures minister to the needs of one another: the secret earth, which
keeps its secrets by concealing them from our sight.

But what of the snake now? In the next section, the twelfth, we
again observe him: something has to be decided, one way or another;

he finishes his drink, looks about, flickers his tongue, godlike looks about him, and slowly, deep in a kind of trance, proceeds to leave.

The spell cast by the snake's quiet drinking is broken as he departs. Again the sensation of movement is strong in the lines—the drawing, curving, easing, withdrawing, going, drawing of the snake becomes hideous as the snake does that frightful thing—puts his head into the black hole in the earth and begins to enter. This voluntary, deliberate, purposeful return to the condition of *snake* (the evilness of *snake*) violates the awareness of kinship the speaker of the poem has created; for the speaker, as for us, this going into the earth is a kind of dying, a return to the subhuman, the nameless blackness. And the speaker retaliates by hurling a log, clumsily, instinctively, hatefully.

The snake, in his snake fashion, responds: no longer godlike, no longer human, no longer a guest, he "convulsed in undignified haste, writhed like lightning, and was gone into the black hole."

The poem has now reached the height of its movement. The snake is gone, the spell is broken. The "story" is finished. In a short resolution, covering the last four sections, the speaker draws his own thoughts together: he regrets his act, recognizes that the "voices of his education" have misled him into trying to kill something meaningful and good, suggests kinship between himself and Coleridge's ancient mariner (who killed the albatross and thereby brought a curse upon himself), repeats his sense of the dignity of the snake (king in exile, king of the underworld), and knows that he must do penance for his pettiness.

These last four sections have lost their intensity, their tension—like a spring that has uncoiled or a snake that has struck—but here it is the man, not the snake, who has struck. It is possible to feel that the tension has been too greatly relaxed in these sections, that Lawrence has said too much—or rather that he has, by saying more than he needed to, said too little. The comment in the last four sections is for some readers less significant than the preceding experience.

Thus far we have been paraphrasing Lawrence's poem. No paraphrase can take the place of the poem, but on the other hand, the paraphrase is one of the simplest ways of "getting at" the poem; perhaps it is ultimately the only way in which we can verbalize our responses. We must only be careful that our paraphrase does not violate or replace the poem.

We began by saying that we tend to open our reading with a "feeling" about snakes. It is important that our own feelings initially be kept distinct from those of the poet, who may not share them. Lawrence's poem, however, not only permits us to use these feelings; it depends to begin with on our having them. Writers almost always rely, although carefully, on some experience or some aspects of experience that they share with their readers. It would be impossible for any work of art to attempt to provide the whole of an experience: a reader has some responsibility in preparing himself to be a reader.

Anything we can say about the poem from this point on ought, if our paraphrase has been accurate, to serve the meaning of the poem as we have described it. Lawrence has given us, within a specific environment, the sensations and thoughts of a specific speaker as he observes the coming, the drinking, and the departure of the snake. The poem is both lyrical and narrative. It is free verse, written in stanzas or "batches." It is in the first person; it is a scene that contains tempos varying from summary to description. Lawrence also skillfully combines aspects of the lyrical with aspects of the epic and dramatic. Can you show how?

Our paraphrase has sought to underscore the degree of sensation, or feeling, in the poem; no full reading can result from a totally dispassionate response to "Snake," because the tensions in the speaker of the poem result from the strength of his feelings, which we must therefore share to some degree. The heat, the depth, the strangeness, the shadow, the movement, the suspension of movement, the colors, the sounds, the horror—all these (the list is not exhaustive) the words of the poem explicitly underscore, and the reader who feels no muscular responses to them must surely be too remote from the poem. How many kinds of images do *you* find in your reading of "Snake?"

The reader who has such a horror of snakes that he cannot subordinate his own feelings to those explicitly directed in the poem is guilty of projection; he too is too remote from the poem. We read "Snake" not to confirm our own attitudes but to experience the attitudes of the poem—presumably, the attitudes of Lawrence himself. What we learn from Lawrence makes his poem a form of knowledge, though what we learn need not be set down in a topic sentence. The snake we are talking about is *this* snake. The feelings we are talking about are feelings connected with *this* snake on *this* occasion. But it is equally true that as the sharpness of the immediate sensory experience of this poem begins to wear away, reflection leads us both to a consideration of the form of the poem and to some awareness of the poem's universality.

"Snake" owes a great measure of its power to the fact that the experience it embodies, symbolically, is related to primitive, fundamental drives in each of us. The snake seems immediately to be an enemy, an object potentially destructive of the self. The "voices" speaking to the "I" of the poem are all the educated voices that counsel the self to guard its life—educated but primitive, since education has here spelled out and underscored the necessity of self-protection. Education has made defense against such an enemy "manly," too; both instinct and education tell this man to kill.

But something equally instinctive, equally primitive (one might say, equally educated—though this is not the poet's point of view and hence is irrelevant here) is at work. A Freudian analyst would notice the sexuality that the images suggest (the heat, the snake itself, the fissure in the earth, the recess within the earth, the softness and hardness) and would speak of the Oedipus myth, but surely this would limit the poem too sharply. Furthermore, we are primarily interested in literature and not in psychoanalysis, though the psychoanalysts have had a field day with Lawrence. No, the poem is not specifically sexual in its meaning, though its sexuality is a part of its meaning. But surely the role of the serpent in myth has something to do with the tension the speaker of the poem feels. Why is the serpent's being an *underground* creature of such weight? The snake comes out of the burning bowels of the earth; so long as it remains above ground it seems like a guest, and welcome, but once it begins to withdraw, to go into blackness, the speaker is revolted and the instinctive motions toward self-protection are no longer suppressed. Why is the snake given this double character? And why is the snake's *goldness* (beauty, value), his kingliness, his godliness underscored? Why the speaker's reverence, awe, humility in the face of this creature come out of the dark door of the secret earth? We have already said in our initial paraphrase that the snake is *one* creature, and that it reminds the speaker of other living creatures with whom he shares life.

This is a literal explanation; but there is a figurative, symbolic, or metaphorical level from which we may look, too; the snake is not simply a living creature but is "one of the lords of life," a king uncrowned in the underworld but now "due to be crowned again." Something about the snake speaks to deep, instinctive things in this man. Some part of life that has been unrecognized, buried, even legislated against by education proves to be valuable and necessary in this "recognition scene" which the act of the poem presents. Jung, the psychoanalyst whose findings have been particularly fruitful for the student of literature, might say that the snake symbolizes those things in the unconscious that have been repressed, and that the recognition of the snake is a recognition of part of the individual that has been buried, a governing part of the self that has been consigned (or has involuntarily consigned itself) to darkness, where it lies uncrowned. The throwing of the log is an attempt at destruction of the newly acknowledged part of the self, in protest against the split in consciousness that its retreat involves. The poem tells us more about the speaker than it does about the snake, and the snake's function in the poem's meaning is first of all to be a snake and second to be a symbol that helps us evaluate the meaning of the poem.

To repeat, it is possible to feel that the poem expresses these meanings so sharply and so fully in the picturing of the experience that the explicit comments contained in the last four sections are too reductive of the experience and hence weaken the poem as a poem. Do the last two lines of the poem really underscore (as they seem intended to) the heart of the poem's experience, or do they reduce it? Is *pettiness* a good word for the speaker's act? You may argue (though the argument seems somehow not good enough) that *pettiness* is an example of understatement and that understatement is an effective positive device here.

We have talked about the poem's movement, about its alternation of tensions and tempos, about its varying lengths of batches; suppose we look at the devices of language that enter into the experience of the poem and certain of the devices of form.

We have said that the first section is matter-of-fact, but that is a relative judgment. Actually, the ordering of the words in the first sentence differs considerably from the usual prose statement. Can you show how? And notice the patterning of sounds: "*snake came*" (acrostic scrambling, with the nasal sound varying); "*water-trough*" (repetition); "*hot, hot . . . heat*" (alliteration and consonance). Even "*day*" and "*drink*" may not be too far apart to have echo value in the sound patterning. Observe also that the *d* is picked up in the first line of the next section. (Remember that such patterns exist in prose as well as in verse, but that the patterning is less noticeable in prose, less frequent, and usually less deliberate.) Can you justify the line divisions in this section? (They seem to us rather arbitrary.)

Suppose we list a few of the patterns that follow:

strange-scented *shade*	alliteration (or para-alliteration)
scente*d* sha*de*	hidden alliteration
great *d*ark *c*arob-*t*ree	a kind of alliteration: *g* and c are cognate sounds, the first voiced and the second voiceless; *d* and *t* are similar in relationship; the cognates alternate to produce what is called *transverse alliteration.* Notice in addition the effect of the final stops, *t, k, b* preceding three of these cognates.
deep, strange . . . shade . . . great . . . tree	assonance
*f*rom a *f*issure	alliteration
*f*rom a *f*issure	augmentation
yellow-*brown* . . . soft-bellied *down*	internal rhyme

Or in the fifth section:

*H*e lifte*d* *h*is *h*ead from *h*is *d*rin*k*ing, as cattle *d*o	alliteration and hidden alliteration
*f*lickered . . . *t*wo-*f*orked *t*ongue	transverse alliteration (*f t f t*) acrostic scrambling (*f k r d, f r k d*)
*m*used a *m*o*m*ent	alliteration and hidden alliteration
*ear*th-br*ow*n, *ear*th-g*o*lden from the b*ur*ning b*ow*els of the *ear*th	assonance (*er-ow, er-o, er-ow, er*)

Continue the list if you like. You will find that the poem is heavily and skillfully patterned in sound, but you will find that the patterning is heaviest in the long sections, where the tempo is slowest.

The snake is personified. Why? You will find examples of tone color and onomatopoeia early in the poem. Can you identify the figure involved in "bowels of the earth"? And in "voice of my education"? In the ninth section can you find an example of consonance? What is the figure involved in "the dark door of the secret earth"? In "flickered his tongue like a forked night"? Why "clumsy log," when it is not the log that is clumsy? What other figures do you find in the poem?

The significant thing is not that there are patterns and figures here (although you don't know that unless you know what patterns and figures are), but that the patterns and figures all operate to give the poem tensiveness—to call constant attention, by varying the language from its usual nonfigurative nature or from its looser arrangement of figures, to the experience the language embodies. What the poet cares about is not some meaning to be derived from the words (as is the case in expository writing) but the meaning *in* the words themselves. We are meant to savor the sounds of these signs.

We have already suggested that "Snake" is patterned most heavily in the long sections, in which description operates significantly. Because of the closeness of texture apparent in part in the sound patterning, it is probably true too that these sections are likely to be the "best" sections for the reader. It may be true that the patterning is richest here because the poet himself was most sharply caught up in response to the experience. It is also of interest to observe that "Snake" is figured more richly in sound than in sense. (We employ here the distinction between figures of sound and figures of sense made in Chapter 8.)

Check the division of the sections into lines. Do you find that line endings seem in some sections more arbitrarily placed than in other sections? Which sections are these? How are they related to passages in which the figurative or symbolical freight of the poem is greatest?

In studying this analysis of "Snake," as well as in reading the analyses of the story and play to follow, you will find it helpful to consult the definitions in the Glossary, Appendix B.

ANALYSIS OF A STORY

We have chosen next to look at a short story and again we have selected a work by a writer of recognized merit. "A Clean, Well-Lighted Place" is taken from the third of Ernest Hemingway's books of stories, *Winner Take Nothing*. Remember that your first reading of the piece should be receptive rather than critical. Read the story for enjoyment.

A CLEAN, WELL-LIGHTED PLACE[2]
—*Ernest Hemingway*

It was late and every one had left the café except an old man who sat in the shadow the leaves of the tree made against the electric light. In the day time the street was dusty, but at night the dew settled the dust and the old man liked to sit late because he was deaf and now at night it was quiet and he felt

[2] Reprinted with permission of Charles Scribner's Sons from *Winner Take Nothing* by Ernest Hemingway. Copyright 1933 Charles Scribner's Sons; renewal copyright © 1961 Ernest Hemingway.
Caution: Oral reading of "A Clean, Well-Lighted Place" is restricted to classroom use only and in conjunction with use of *The Art of Interpretation.* The story may not be dramatized or otherwise performed without written permission from Alfred Rice, Trustee of the Estate of Ernest Hemingway, 8 West 40th Street, New York, New York.

the difference. The two waiters inside the café knew that the old man was a
little drunk, and while he was a good client they knew that if he became too
drunk he would leave without paying so they kept watch on him.

"Last week he tried to commit suicide," one waiter said.

"Why?"

"He was in despair."

"What about?"

"Nothing."

"How do you know it was nothing?"

"He has plenty of money."

They sat together at a table that was close against the wall near the
door of the café and looked at the terrace where the tables were all empty
except where the old man sat in the shadow of the leaves of the tree that
moved slightly in the wind. A girl and a soldier went by in the street. The
street light shone on the brass number on his collar. The girl wore no head
covering and hurried beside him.

"The guard will pick him up," one waiter said.

"What does it matter if he gets what he's after?"

"He had better get off the street now. The guard will get him. They
went by five minutes ago."

The old man sitting in the shadow rapped on his saucer with his glass.
The younger waiter went over to him.

"What do you want?"

The old man looked at him. "Another brandy," he said.

"You'll be drunk," the waiter said. The old man looked at him. The
waiter went away.

"He'll stay all night," he said to his colleague. "I'm sleepy now. I never
get into bed before three o'clock. He should have killed himself last week."

The waiter took the brandy bottle and another saucer from the
counter inside the café and marched out to the old man's table. He put
down the saucer and poured the glass full of brandy.

"You should have killed yourself last week," he said to the deaf man.
The old man motioned with his finger. "A little more," he said. The waiter
poured on into the glass so that the brandy slopped over and ran down the
stem into the top saucer of the pile. "Thank you," the old man said. The
waiter took the bottle back inside the café. He sat down at the table with his
colleague again.

"He's drunk now," he said.

"He's drunk every night."

"What did he want to kill himself for?"

"How should I know?"

"How did he do it?"

"He hung himself with a rope."

"Who cut him down?"

"His niece."

"Why did they do it?"

"Fear for his soul."

"How much money has he got?"

"He's got plenty."

"He must be eighty years old."

"Anyway I should say he was eighty."

"I wish he would go home. I never get to bed before three o'clock. What kind of hour is that to go to bed?"

"He stays up because he likes it."

"He's lonely, I'm not lonely. I have a wife waiting in bed for me."

"He had a wife once too."

"A wife would be no good to him now."

"You can't tell. He might be better with a wife."

"His niece looks after him."

"I know. You said she cut him down."

"I wouldn't want to be that old. An old man is a nasty thing."

"Not always. This old man is clean. He drinks without spilling. Even now, drunk. Look at him."

"I don't want to look at him. I wish he would go home. He has no regard for those who must work."

The old man looked from his glass across the square, then over at the waiters.

"Another brandy," he said, pointing to his glass. The waiter who was in a hurry came over.

"Finished," he said, speaking with that omission of syntax stupid people employ when talking to drunken people or foreigners. "No more tonight. Close now."

"Another," said the old man.

"No. Finished." The waiter wiped the edge of the table with a towel and shook his head.

The old man stood up, slowly counted the saucers, took a leather coin purse from his pocket and paid for the drinks, leaving half a peseta tip.

The waiter watched him go down the street, a very old man walking unsteadily but with dignity.

"Why didn't you let him stay and drink?" the unhurried waiter asked. They were putting up the shutters. "It is not half-past two."

"I want to go home to bed."

"What is an hour?"

"More to me than to him."

"An hour is the same."

"You talk like an old man yourself. He can buy a bottle and drink at home."

"It's not the same."

"No, it is not," agreed the waiter with a wife. He did not wish to be unjust. He was only in a hurry.

"And you? You have no fear of going home before your usual hour?"

"Are you trying to insult me?"

"No, hombre, only to make a joke."

"No," the waiter who was in a hurry said, rising from pulling down the metal shutters. "I have confidence. I am all confidence."

"You have youth, confidence, and a job," the older waiter said. "You have everything."

"And what do you lack?"

"Everything but work."

"You have everything I have."

"No. I have never had confidence and I am not young."

"Come on. Stop talking nonsense and lock up."

"I am one of those who like to stay late at the café," the older waiter said. "With all those who do not want to go to bed. With all those who need a light for the night."

"I want to go home and into bed."

"We are of two different kinds," the older waiter said. He was now dressed to go home. "It is not only a question of youth and confidence although those things are very beautiful. Each night I am reluctant to close up because there may be some one who needs the café."

"Hombre, there are bodegas open all night long."

"You do not understand. This is a clean and pleasant café. It is well lighted. The light is very good and also, now, there are shadows of the leaves."

"Good night," said the younger waiter.

"Good night," the other said. Turning off the electric light he continued the conversation with himself. It is the light of course but it is necessary that the place be clean and pleasant. You do not want music. Certainly you do not want music. Nor can you stand before a bar with dignity although that is all that is provided for these hours. What did he fear? It was not fear or dread. It was nothing that he knew too well. It was all a nothing and a man was nothing too. It was only that and light was all it needed and a certain cleanness and order. Some lived in it and never felt it but he knew it all was a nada y pues nada y nada y pues nada. Our nada who art in nada, nada be thy name thy kingdom nada thy will be nada in nada as it is in nada. Give us this nada our daily nada and nada us our nada as we nada our nadas and nada us not into nada but deliver us from nada; pues nada. Hail nothing full of nothing, nothing is with thee. He smiled and stood before a bar with a shining steam pressure coffee machine.

"What's yours?" asked the barman.

"Nada."

"Otro loco mas," said the barman and turned away.

"A little cup," said the waiter.

The barman poured it for him.

"The light is very bright and pleasant but the bar is unpolished," the waiter said.

The barman looked at him but did not answer. It was too late at night for conversation.

"You want another copita?" the barman asked.

"No, thank you," said the waiter and went out. He disliked bars and bodegas. A clean, well-lighted café was a very different thing. Now, without thinking further, he would go home to his room. He would lie in the bed and finally, with daylight, he would go to sleep. After all, he said to himself, it is probably only insomnia. Many must have it.

Hemingway's story is a study in empathy, of the impingement of one life upon another in such a way that the second character's humanity leads him to a compassionate awareness of his own loneliness. The action of the story moves toward this awareness by shifting the focus of the writer's "camera" from the old man in the café to the older of the two waiters, about whom the eventual truth is to be told. The younger waiter, without whom Hemingway could not manage the action of the story, is essentially a flat character, which is all the action requires him to be.

After the opening paragraph, it is convenient to divide the story into three sections—metaphorically, the three acts of the little drama. The first section will take us to the old man's departure from the café; the second, to the younger waiter's departure from the story; the third, to the story's end. The first paragraph is a kind of prologue, a setting of the scene, an adjusting of the camera—time, place, characters, opening situation. The paragraph is an excellent combination of elements of summary, of scene, and of description. It is clear at once that the point of view is that of the omniscient narrator. The mode is epic, though much of the narrative becomes dramatic.

The dialogue begins. Notice that, with his customary economy, Hemingway does not bother to identify the speakers once the first line has been assigned; it is not necessary to do so,[3] and the effect of a conversation overheard is better achieved by giving only the dialogue. The old man is the subject of the conversation, and his predicament is immediately made the object of our curiosity; he has tried to commit suicide, he has been in despair, but he has no reason for despair because he has plenty of money. Hemingway does not yet tell us which of the waiters says what, because we are not yet interested in the waiters. Some feeling of cynicism (or some obtuseness, we do not yet know which) in the waiter who makes the final speech is already suggested to us, since we know that lack of money is not the only cause for despair. Any awareness we have of this added interest in character, however, is subordinate to our interest in the old man.

Hemingway gives us another paragraph of narrative: a sharp picture of the setting, with the two waiters sitting just inside the door of the café, the old man in the shadow cast by the leaves against the light. A hint of another, more active world of youth and the pursuit of pleasure flashes through the paragraph as the girl and soldier pass along the street. The dialogue following in the next three speeches gives us some further notion of the story's setting in time and suggests again either a

---

[3] But Hemingway seems to have made one slip; the two speeches "His niece looks after him" and "I know. You said she cut him down" will not work in the alternating pattern. The second seems to belong to the older waiter, but obviously cannot.

slight cynicism or a bluntly pragmatic quality about one of the two waiters: "What does it matter if he gets what he's after?" (By the time the story is finished you will find it possible to go back and assign both these deliberately ambiguous passages to the older waiter. Why?)

Now that the waiters have moved a little more into the center of our consciousness, now that two additional perspectives are added to the point of view, we return to the old man, and the rest of this section remains carefully centered on him, though with enough interest in the two waiters so that we take an interest in them, too. It is the loneliness, the isolation of the old man on which we focus our attention. His sitting in the window is a literal image, but the application is metaphorical, as eventually the clean, well-lighted café will take on metaphorical value for us—but first of all the shadow is a shadow, the café is a café. The reality of these images is not to be discounted once the symbolical values have been uncovered.

The old man is not only in shadow, he is also deaf. And he is drunk. The isolation is almost but not entirely complete, or perhaps the need for the brandy would disappear. He is not without relatives; he has a niece. He has money. But he is very old, he has lost his wife, he has nothing better to do with his time. The younger waiter is impatient with him. "An old man is a nasty thing," he says. It is not hard for any of us to think of very old people who by their very age seem isolated from those around them, but the word *nasty,* while we may feel pangs of conscience as we recognize precisely what the younger waiter means, seems to us harsh and unfeeling. The younger waiter has a wife, a world to which he belongs, interests beyond his job. He is not isolated, no matter how limited his interests may be, though his being "in life" does not move him to any sympathy with the old man. He even dares say to the old man, who cannot hear him, "You should have killed yourself last week." He is either very young or very limited in vision or both. Hemingway tips his hand, as author, when he uses the word *stupid* in remarking on the younger man's speech.

But the second waiter, older, is compassionate without being voluble. He seems to speak quietly as he speaks simply. It is not he but the younger man who brings this section to a close by dismissing the old man.

Notice how carefully Hemingway has written the dialogue to let us come to our own conclusions about the characters. Except for the word *stupid,* he has not taken sides—in his own person, that is, since in another sense he has been responsible for the attitudes we have taken toward the characters. This is the dramatic method. The tempo of the first section is managed by the movement from scene (which is predominant) to summary-description. The scene itself moves quickly because the dialogue is clipped, brief. As the section ends, we (and the waiter) watch the old man go down the street, "a very old man walking unsteadily but with dignity," Both the unsteadiness and the dignity matter very much to this story, for they underscore the uncertainty and the essential humanity of the old man, which make possible the action to follow.

Now that the two waiters occupy our interest, Hemingway sharpens the distinctions between them. The one becomes "the unhurried waiter," the other the "waiter with a wife." The younger waiter is hurried because he *has* a wife; the other is without a wife, without youth—without confidence and unsteady, though surely we would not say without dignity. The young man is young enough (perhaps newly married enough) to be offended by the older waiter's joke. The two are "of two different kinds."

The older waiter now moves some of the details of the story toward metaphor. He speaks of those who need "a light for the night," who need the café and its clean, pleasant air. Cleanliness, light, air, companionship—these are values that the old man wants and lacks, that the older waiter wants and lacks; they are the "life" that the darkness negates. The old do not want simply the light, but good light and the shadows of the leaves make a tempting combination.

The younger waiter now disappears imperceptibly. He says "Good night," the older waiter begins speaking to himself, and soon we realize that the older man has left the café and is standing before a bar. He has begun the old man's search. It is really *his* need, *his* loneliness, *his* uncertainty the story has been moving toward, and not that of the deaf old man. The reasons for his compassion become moving to us, and we suddenly see how deep is his sense of the nothingness (the *nada*) of his life. He smiles as he stands before the bar, and outwardly there is in him a kind of tolerance and a gentleness toward the nothingness, but the interior dialogue (lyrical in its impact) tells us how bleak his despair really is. Exterior dialogue, conversation with the younger waiter could never give us this, because the older waiter would never speak so to his colleague. And now the symbolic values of the bar, the light, the shadow, the café, the cleanliness and pleasantness become sharply outlined. Now we know far more than the barman knows, and the little joke the waiter makes to him ("The light is very bright and pleasant but the bar is unpolished") has for us a grimness where it has for the barman only irrelevance. And no attempt, in the last two sentences of the story, to shrug off the night's events as being "probably only insomnia" will persuade us—nor, indeed, is it meant to persuade us—that the next night will be any better. But the final line ("Many must have it") drives home the picture of despair that this waiter shares with many others in his world.

Remember that the story is not saying that the world is a dreadful place. It is saying that for some people life is empty; it is empty for a deaf old man and a no-longer-young waiter whom we are permitted to see and to hear. Awareness of such experience, compassion for it, understanding of it—these things rather than an acceptance of despair are what "A Clean, Well-Lighted Place" asks of a reader.

The sense of the characters is so sharp that it may come to you as a shock that Hemingway has told us nothing of the way these people look. We know their hearts, we feel that we know them—but of the color of their eyes, their hair, their clothes (aside from their uniforms) we know nothing at all. They do not even have names. In this respect, all three characters are flat characters. The details are selected to give us the quality rather than the appearance of the characters. And yet it is safe to say that most readers will feel that they "saw" the story. The dramatic form and the emphasis on visual and audible detail create a strongly visual image that permits us to fill in such other details as we need to give us the illusion of full scene. But Hemingway rules out all detail not strictly necessary to the development of the action on which he centers. The oral reader must be likewise economical.

The shifts from summary to scene, from exterior to interior, from character to character; the repetition of details, the incremental use of detail; the terseness of the speeches and the sense of things unspoken— these factors give the story its rhythm. The closer kind of patterning in poetry is not to be found here, though the second sentence of the story, for example, will yield several instances of alliteration and scrambling of sounds. The metaphors are not set down openly, as in poetry; they uncover for us gradually, they are not explicitly introduced. The rhythms of prose are hidden under the complexities that the greater freedom of prose permits. Nevertheless, it would be a mistake to overlook the fact that prose has rhythm. The peculiar rhythm of any work is a fundamental aspect of the style of the work. This aspect of Hemingway's style is so marked for most readers that a whole generation of young writers fell into the error of imitating it, hoping thereby to achieve a quality the equal of Hemingway's.

In our analysis we have spoken constantly of Hemingway. We ought, perhaps, to say "narrator" instead, distinguishing between the author and the author-in-the-work. Notice that while the method of the story is largely dramatic, there is clearly a point of view that is controlled by the narrator, who decides what we are to see, to hear, to feel. The very spareness of the narration is part of the quality of the mind that is the perceiving and recording agent. The fact that the mode is very close to the mode of the drama should not minimize the significance of the point of view. It is because the quality of this particular narrator so closely resembles a characteristic manner of Hemingway that we tend to think of the narrator himself as Hemingway, though perhaps we should not.

The third of the forms to be discussed is the play. We have chosen a one-act play to show how much can be accomplished when the writer is as skillful as Giraudoux.

ANALYSIS OF A PLAY

THE APOLLO OF BELLAC⁴
—*Jean Giraudoux, translated by Maurice Valency*

CAST OF CHARACTERS

Agnes
Therese
The Clerk
The Man
The Vice-President
Mr. Cracheton
Mr. Lepédura
Mr. Rasemutte
Mr. Schultz
The President
Chevredent
The Chairman of the Board

TIME: Autumn in Paris. The present or shortly before.

     The Man from Bellac is not Apollo. The Man from Bellac is a little shabby fellow who doesn't know where his next meal is coming from. He is a vagabond and a poet, therefore an inventor. He dreams things up, but he does nothing and he has nothing. He was cast very sensibly on the Ford Omnibus television program, when Claude Dauphin played the role—a fine character-actor, not a matinee idol. The Man from Bellac must evoke Apollo, but visually he must remain the shabby little figure throughout the play. The moment he is cast as a big beautiful man with curly ringlets, the play is spoiled.

MAURICE VALENCY

     SCENE: *The reception room of The International Bureau of Inventions, S.A.*

     This is a large, well-appointed room on the second floor of a magnificent office building in Paris. The French windows are open and afford us a view of treetops. There is an elaborate crystal chandelier hanging from the ceiling. The morning sun plays upon it. On a pedestal large enough to conceal a man a bust of Archimedes is set. Four doors open off the room. Three of them are marked Private. These lead into the office of the President, right, and the First Vice-President rear right, and the Directors' Conference Room rear left. The effect is French and very elegant, perhaps a trifle oppressive in its opulence.

     Behind a period desk sits the Reception Clerk. The desk has an ivory telephone and a row of signal lights. It has also a period blotter on which the clerk is writing something in an appointment book. The Clerk is well on in years and his face makes one think of a caricature by Daumier.

AT RISE: *The Clerk is writing with a meticulous air. The outer door opens. Agnes comes in timidly from outer door, and stands in front of the desk. The Clerk does not look up.*

AGNES. Er—

CLERK. Yes?

AGNES. Is this the International Bureau of Inventions, Incorporated?

CLERK. Yes.

AGNES. Could I please see the Chairman of the Board?

CLERK. (*Looks up*) The Chairman of the Board? No one sees the Chairman of the Board.

AGNES. Oh.

> (*The outer door opens again. Therese sweeps into the room. She is blonde, shapely, thirty-five, dressed in expensive mink. Clerk rises respectfully.*)

CLERK. Good morning, Madame.

THERESE. Is the President in?

CLERK. Yes, Madame. Of course. (*Therese walks haughtily to President's door. Clerk opens it for her and closes it behind her. He goes back to his desk where Agnes is waiting.*)

AGNES. Could I see the President?

CLERK. No one sees the President.

AGNES. But I have—

CLERK. What type of invention? Major? Intermediate? Minor?

AGNES. I beg pardon?

CLERK. Assistant Secretary to the Third Vice-President. Come back Tuesday. Name?

AGNES. My name?

CLERK. You have a name, I presume?

> (*The Man from Bellac appears suddenly from outer door. He is nondescript, mercurial, shabby.*)

MAN. Yes. The young lady has a name. But what permits you to conclude that the young lady's invention is as minor as all that?

CLERK. Who are you?

MAN. What chiefly distinguishes the inventor is modesty. You should know that by now. Pride is the invention of noninventors. (*A Street Singer, accompanied by violin and accordion, begins "La Seine" outside the windows. Clerk crosses to close them.*)

AGNES. (*To the Man*) Thanks very much, but—

MAN. To the characteristic modesty of the inventor, the young lady adds the charming modesty of her sex—(*He smiles at Agnes.*) But—(*Clerk closes one of the windows.*) how can you be sure, you, that she has not brought us at last the invention which is destined to transform the modern world?

CLERK. (*Closes the other window*) For world transformations it's the Second Vice-President. Mondays ten to twelve.

MAN. Today is Tuesday.

CLERK. Now how can I help that?

MAN. So! While all humanity awaits with anguish the discovery which will at last utilize the moon's gravitation for the removal of corns, and when we have every reason to believe that in all likelihood Mademoiselle—Mademoiselle?

AGNES. Agnes.

MAN. Mademoiselle Agnes has this discovery in her handbag— You tell her to come back Monday.

CLERK. (*Nervously*) There is going to be a Directors' meeting in just a few minutes. The Chairman of the Board is coming. I must beg you to be quiet.

MAN. I will not be quiet. I am quiet Mondays.

CLERK. Now, please. I don't want any trouble.

MAN. And the Universal Vegetable? Five continents are languishing in the hope of the Universal Vegetable which will once and for all put an end to the ridiculous specialization of the turnip, the leek, and the string bean, which will be at one and the same time bread, meat, wine, and coffee, and yield with equal facility cotton, potassium, ivory and wool. The Universal Vegetable which Paracelsus could not, and Burbank dared not, imagine! Yes, my friend. And while in this handbag, which with understandable concern she clutches to her charming bosom, the seeds of the Universal Vegetable await only the signal of your President to burst upon an expectant world, you say—come back Monday.

AGNES. Really, sir—

CLERK. If you wish an appointment for Monday, Mademoiselle—

MAN. She does not wish an appointment for Monday.

CLERK. (*Shrugs*) Then she can go jump in the lake.

MAN. What did you say?

CLERK. I said: She can go jump in the lake. Is that clear?

MAN. That's clear. Perfectly clear. As clear as it was to Columbus when—(*The buzzer sounds on the Clerk's desk. A light flashes on.*)

CLERK. Excuse me. (*He crosses to the Vice-President's door, knocks and enters. Man smiles. Agnes smiles back wanly.*)

AGNES. But I'm not the inventor of the Universal Vegetable.

MAN. I know. I am.

AGNES. I'm just looking for a job.

MAN. Typist?

AGNES. Not really.

MAN. Stenographer?

AGNES. Not at all.

MAN. Copyreader, translator, bookkeeper, editor, file clerk—stop me when I come to it.

AGNES. You could go on like that for years before I could stop you.

MAN. Well then—your specialty? Charm? Coquetry, devotion, seduction, flirtation, passion, romance?

AGNES. That's getting warmer.

MAN. Splendid. The best career for a female is to be a woman.

AGNES. Yes, but—men frighten me.

MAN. Men frighten you?

AGNES. They make me feel weak all over.

MAN. That clerk frightens you?

AGNES. Clerks, presidents, janitors, soldiers. All a man has to do is to look at me, and I feel like a shoplifter caught in the act.

MAN. Caught in what act?

AGNES. I don't know.

MAN. Perhaps it's their clothes that frighten you. Their vests? Their trousers?

AGNES. (*Shakes her head*) I feel the same panic on the beach when they don't wear their trousers.

MAN. Perhaps you don't like men.

AGNES. Oh, no, I like them. I like their doglike eyes, their hairiness, their big feet. And they have special organs which inspire tenderness in a woman—Their Adam's apple, for instance, when they eat dinner or make speeches. But the moment they speak to me, I begin to tremble—

MAN. (*He looks appraisingly at her a moment.*) You would like to stop trembling?

AGNES. Oh, yes. But— (*She shrugs hopelessly.*)

MAN. Would you like me to teach you the secret?

AGNES. Secret?

MAN. Of trembling before men. Of getting whatever you want out of them. Of making the directors jump, the presidents kneel and offer you diamonds?

AGNES. Are there such secrets?

MAN. One only. It is infallible.

AGNES. Will you really tell it to me?

MAN. Without this secret a girl has a bad time of it on this earth. With it, she becomes Empress of the World.

AGNES. Oh tell it to me quickly.

MAN. (*Peering about the room*) No one is listening?

AGNES. (*Whispers*) No one.

MAN. Tell them they're handsome.

AGNES. You mean, flatter them? Tell them they're handsome, intelligent, kind?

MAN. No. As for the intelligence and the kindness, they can shift for themselves. Tell them they're handsome.

AGNES. All?

MAN. All. The foolish, the wise, the modest, the vain, the young, the old. Say it to the professor of philosophy and he will give you a diploma. Say it to the butcher and he will give you a steak. Say it to the president here, and he will give you a job.

AGNES. But to say a thing like that, one has to know a person well—

MAN. Not at all. Say it right off. Say it before he has a chance even to open his mouth.

AGNES. But one doesn't say a thing like that before people.

MAN. Before people. Before all the world. The more witnesses, the better.

AGNES. But if they're not handsome—and for the most part they're not, you know—how can I tell them that they are?

MAN. Surely you're not narrow-minded, Agnes? (*She shrugs, not quite sure.*) The ugly, the pimply, the crippled, the fat. Do you wish to get on in this world? Tell them they're handsome.

AGNES. Will they believe it?

MAN. They will believe it because they've always known it. Every man, even the ugliest, feels in his heart a secret alliance with beauty. When you tell him he's handsome, he will simply hear outwardly the voice he has been listening to inwardly all his life. And those who believe it the least will be the most grateful. No matter how ugly they may have thought themselves, the moment they find a woman who thinks them handsome, they grapple her to their hearts with hooks of steel. For them, she is the magic glass of truth, the princess of an enchanted world. When you see a woman who can go nowhere without a staff of admirers, it is not so much because they think she is beautiful, it is because she has told them they are handsome.

AGNES. There are women then who already know this secret?

MAN. Yes. But they know it without really knowing it. And usually they evade the issue, they go beside the point. They tell the hunchback he is generous, the walleyed that he's strong. There's no profit in that. I've seen a woman throw away a cool million in diamonds and emeralds because she told a clubfooted lover that he walked swiftly, when all he wanted to hear was—you know what. And now—to work. The President is in every day to those who come to tell him he's handsome.

AGNES. I'd better come back another day. I have to have training. I have a cousin who's not at all bad-looking—I'll practice on him tomorrow, and then the next day I'll—

MAN. You can practice right now. On the receptionist.

AGNES. That monster?

MAN. The monster is perfect for your purpose. After that, the Vice-President. I know him. He's even better. Then the President.

(*The Vice-President's door opens. The Clerk comes in.*)

CLERK. (*Into the doorway*) Very good sir.

VOICE. And another thing—

CLERK. (*Turns*) Yes sir?

VOICE. When the Chairman of the Board— (*Clerk goes back in and closes the door.*)

AGNES. No, I can't!

MAN. (*Indicating the bust of Archimedes at rear*) Begin with this bust then.

AGNES. Whose is it?

MAN. What does it matter? It's the bust of a man. It's all ears. Speak!

AGNES. (*Shuddering*) It has a beard.

MAN. Begin with what you like. With this chair. With this clock.

AGNES. They're not listening.

MAN. This fly, then. See? He's on your glove. He's listening.

AGNES. Is he a male?

MAN. Yes. Speak. Tell him.

AGNES. (*With an effort*) How handsome he is!

MAN. No, no, no. Say it to him.

AGNES. How handsome you are!

MAN. You see? He's twirling his mustache. Go on. More. More. What is a fly especially vain of?

AGNES. His wings? His eyes?

MAN. That's it. Tell him.

AGNES. How beautiful your wings are, beautiful fly! They sparkle in the sun like jewels. And your eyes—so large, so sad, so sensitive!

MAN. Splendid. Shoo him away now. Here comes the clerk.

AGNES. He won't go. He's clinging to me.

MAN. Naturally.

AGNES. (*To the fly*) You're bowlegged. (*She smiles*) He's gone.

MAN. You see? And now— (*The Vice-President's door opens slowly.*) Here he comes.

AGNES. (*In panic*) What must I say?

(*Clerk comes in and walks to his desk. Man disappears behind the bust of Archimedes.*)

AGNES. (*After an agony of indecision*) How handsome you are!

CLERK. (*Stops dead*) What?

AGNES. I said, how handsome you are!

CLERK. Do you get this way often?

AGNES. It's the first time in my life that I've ever—

CLERK. (*Finishing the sentence for her*) Called a chimpanzee handsome? Thanks for the compliment. But—why?

AGNES. You're right. Handsome is not the word. I should have said beautiful. Because, mind you, I never judge a face by the shape of the nose or the arch of the brow. To me, what counts is the ensemble.

CLERK. So what you're telling me is: your features are ugly, but they go beautifully together. Is that it?

AGNES. It serves me right. Very well—It's the first time I've ever told a man he was handsome. And it's going to be the last.

CLERK. Now don't get excited, please. I know girls. At your age a girl doesn't calculate; she says whatever comes into her head. I know you meant it. Only—why did you say it so badly? (*Man sticks his head out and makes a face at Agnes behind the Clerk's back.*)

AGNES. (*To the Man*) Did I say it badly? (*To the Clerk, who thinks it is said to him*) I thought you were handsome. I may have been wrong.

CLERK. Women are blind as bats. Even if there were something good about me, they'd never see it. What's so good about me? My face? God, no. My figure? Not at all. Only my shadow. But of course you didn't notice that.

AGNES. Is that what you think? And when you leaned over to close the window, I suppose your shadow didn't lean over with you? And when you walked into the Vice-President's office, did you put your shadow away in a drawer? (*She strokes his shadow with her hand.*) How could I help noticing a shadow like that?

CLERK. You notice it now because I direct your attention to it.

AGNES. Have it your way. I thought I was looking at you, but what I saw was your shadow.

CLERK. Then you shouldn't say, what a handsome man. You should say, what a handsome shadow. (*He opens the window, the room is filled with music. It is still "La Seine."*)

AGNES. From now on, I shall say no more about it.

CLERK. (*Returning to desk*) Don't be angry, my dear. It's only because I'm a man of years and I have a right to warn you. I have a daughter of your age. I know what girls are. One day they see a fine shadow, and at once their heads are turned, the silly geese, and they think the man himself is handsome. Oh, I don't deny it, it's a rare thing, a fine shadow. And believe me it lasts—you don't keep your hair, you don't keep your skin, but your shadow lasts all your life. Even longer, they say. But that's not the point. These little fools invariably insist on confusing the shadow with the man, and if the idiot lets himself be talked into it, in a moment it's all over and they've ruined their lives for nothing, the nitwits. No, my dear. Heed an old man's warning.

You can't live your life among shadows. (*Man sticks out his head and lifts an admonishing finger.*)

AGNES. How handsome you are!

CLERK. You know why? It's because when I'm angry I show my teeth. And the fact is, they are rather good. My dentist says they're perfect. It's no credit to— It's because I eat hard foods. And when you— (*The buzzer sounds again.*) Ah—the Vice-President needs me again. Wait just a minute, my dear. I'll make sure that he sees you at once. I'll say it's my niece.

AGNES. (*As he bends over to close a drawer*) How beautiful it is, your shadow, when it leans over. One would say it belonged to Rodin's Thinker!

CLERK. (*Delighted*) Come, now, that will do. If you were my daughter, I'd give you a good slap on the— Sit down a minute. I'll get him for you. (*Crosses to the Vice-President's door and goes out.*)

(*Man comes out from behind the bust. The music stops.*)

MAN. Well, it's a start.

AGNES. I think I'm better with flies.

MAN. Because in your mind the idea of beauty is inseparable from the idea of the caress. Women have no sense of the abstract—a woman admiring the sky is a woman caressing the sky. In a woman's mind beauty is something she needs to touch. And you didn't want to touch the clerk, not even his shadow.

AGNES. No.

MAN. With my method, it's not your hands that must speak, nor your cheek, nor your lips— It's your brain.

AGNES. I had a narrow squeak. I almost lost him.

MAN. Yes, he had you there with his shadow. You're not ready to tackle a Vice-President. No. Not yet.

AGNES. But there's no time. What shall I do?

MAN. Practice. Practice on me.

AGNES. You expect me to tell you you're handsome?

MAN. Is it so difficult?

AGNES. Not at all. Only—

MAN. Think. Think before you speak.

AGNES. Oh, you're not bad at all, you know, when you tease one like this.

MAN. Very feeble. Why when I tease one like this? The rest of the time, I'm not handsome?

AGNES. Oh, yes. Always. Always.

MAN. Better. Now it's no longer your hands that are speaking.

AGNES. With you, all the same, they murmur a little something.

MAN. Good.

AGNES. The mass of your body is beautiful. The outline is beautiful. The face matters little.

MAN. What nonsense is this? My face matters little?

AGNES. (*Recovering quickly*) No more than the face of Rodin's Thinker.

MAN. In his case, doubtless the feet have more importance. Look here, Agnes, these little allusions to famous statues are ingenious. But is Rodin's Thinker the only one you know?

AGNES. Except for the Venus of Milo. But she wouldn't be much use to me with men.

MAN. That remains to be seen. In any case, we'd better extend your repertory. Forget The Thinker. Michelangelo's David is very good. Or his Moses. But best of all—the Apollo of Bellac—

AGNES. The Apollo of Bellac?

MAN. It doesn't exist. It will do perfectly.

AGNES. What does it look like?

MAN. A little like me, I think. I too come from Bellac. It's a little town in Limousin. I was born there.

AGNES. But they say the men of Limousin are so ugly. How does it happen that you are so handsome?

MAN. My father was a very handsome man, and he—Oh-oh. Good for you. (*He applauds.*)

AGNES. (*Pursuing her advantage*) Oh, never! Not with you! You taught me the secret. With you I could be no other than honest.

MAN. At last. You understand. (*The Vice-President's door opens.*) Here we are. (*Goes behind the bust*)

CLERK. (*Comes in, smiling tenderly*) The Vice-President will be out in a moment, my dear. No need to put yourself out. A shadow like his, you may see every day—in the zoo. (*He takes some papers from his desk and goes into where the Directors will meet.*)

AGNES. (*Whispers*) Help! Help! (*Man thrusts his head out.*) I feel faint!

MAN. Practice. Practice.

AGNES. (*Desperately*) On whom? On what?

MAN. On anything. The telephone.

AGNES. (*She speaks to the telephone.*) How handsome you are, my little telephone! (*She strokes it gently.*)

MAN. No! Not with the hands.

AGNES. But it's so much easier that way.

MAN. I know. Try the chandelier. That's one thing you can't touch.

AGNES. How handsome you are, my little, my great chandelier! (*The music begins again. Another tune.*) Only when you're lit up? Oh, don't say that. Other chandeliers, yes. Street lamps, store fixtures, yes. Not you. See— you are full of sunshine. You are the chandelier of the sun. A desk lamp needs to be lit. A planet needs to be lit. But you have radiance of your own. You are as beautiful as a galaxy of stars, even more beautiful, for a galaxy is only an imitation chandelier, a cluster of uncertain lights swinging precariously in the eternal darkness. But you are a creature of crystal with limbs of ivory and gold, a living miracle! (*The chandelier lights up by itself.*)

MAN. Bravo!

VICE-PRESIDENT. (*The door opens. The Vice-President comes in. His manner is important. His face is that of a gargoyle.*) My dear young lady, I have exactly two minutes to give you. (*He crosses to close the window.*)

AGNES. (*Whispering in awe*) Oh!

VICE-PRESIDENT. (*Stops and turns*) Why do you stare at me like that? You've seen me before?

AGNES. (*In a tone of wonder*) No! On the contrary.

VICE-PRESIDENT. And what does that mean, no, on the contrary?

AGNES. I was expecting to see the usual Vice-President, stoop-shouldered, paunchy, bald—And all at once, I see you! (*Vice-President freezes in his tracks. Man thrusts out his head. He raises a warning finger.*) (*Hastily*) How handsome you are!

VICE-PRESIDENT. What? (*He turns.*)

AGNES. Nothing. I beg your pardon.

VICE-PRESIDENT. I heard you distinctly. You said I was handsome. Don't deny it. (*He steps closer to her. Music swells up.*) You know, it gave me rather a shock to hear you say it. However, it can't be true. If I were really—what you said—wouldn't some woman have told me before this?

AGNES. Oh, the fools! The fools!

VICE-PRESIDENT. Whom are you calling fools, Mademoiselle? My sister, my mother, my niece?

AGNES. (*Giving up all at once. In a formal tone*) Mr. Vice-President, the truth is I am looking for a position. And I happened to hear through a friend of one of your directors, Mr. Lepédura— (*Man thrusts out his head.*)

VICE-PRESIDENT. Never mind Monsieur Lepédura. We are discussing me. As you probably know, I am one of the world's authorities in the fields of dreams. It is I who work with those who are able to invent only while they sleep, and I have been able to extract from their dreams such extraordinary devices as the book that reads itself and the adjustable Martini, wonders of modern science which without my help would have remained mere figments of the imagination. If you appeared to me in a dream and told me I was handsome, I should have understood at once. But we are in a waking state, or are we? One moment. (*He pinches himself.*) Ow! I am awake. Permit me. (*Pinches her*)

AGNES. Ow!

VICE-PRESIDENT. We're not dreaming, Mademoiselle. And now, my dear—(*He takes her hand.*) Why did you say I was handsome? To flatter me?—I can see you are incapable of such baseness. To make fun of me? No—your eye is gentle, your lips attract—Why did you say it, Mademoiselle?

AGNES. I say you are handsome because you are handsome. If your mother finds you ugly that's not my concern.

VICE-PRESIDENT. I cannot permit you to form so low an opinion of my mother's taste. Even when I was a boy, my mother used to say I had the hands of an artist.

AGNES. If your niece prefers Charles Boyer—

VICE-PRESIDENT. My niece? Only yesterday at dinner she was saying that my eyebrows could have been drawn by El Greco.

AGNES. If your sister—

VICE-PRESIDENT. My sister has never quite admitted that I am handsome, no, but she has always said that there was something distinctive about my face. A friend of hers, a history teacher, told her it's because in certain lights, I resemble Lodovico Sforza. (*He makes a deprecating gesture.*)

AGNES. Lodovico Sforza? Never. The Apollo of Bellac, yes.

VICE-PRESIDENT. The Apollo of Bellac?

AGNES. Wouldn't you say? Quite objectively?

VICE-PRESIDENT. Well—if you really think so—perhaps just a little. Although Lodovico Sforza, you know—I've seen engravings—

AGNES. When I say the Apollo of Bellac, I mean, naturally, the Apollo of Bellac in a beautifully tailored suit. You see, I am frank. I say what I think. Yes, Mr. Vice-President. You have the fault of all really handsome men—you dress carelessly.

VICE-PRESIDENT. (*Smiling*) What insolence! And this from a girl who tells every man she meets that he's handsome!

AGNES. I have said that to two men only in all my life. You are the second.

(*Clerk comes in.*)

VICE-PRESIDENT. What is it? Don't you see I'm busy?

CLERK. The Directors are on the way up, sir. It's time for the meeting.

VICE-PRESIDENT. I'll be right in. (*Clerk goes into the Directors' room.*) I'm sorry, Mademoiselle. I must go to this meeting. But we must certainly continue this wonderful conversation. Won't you come back and lunch with me? You know, my secretary is impossible. I'm having her transferred to the sales department. Now you're a first-rate typist, I'm told—

AGNES. I don't type. I play the piano.

VICE-PRESIDENT. Ah, that's wonderful. And you take dictation?

AGNES. In longhand, yes.

VICE-PRESIDENT. That's much the best way. That gives one time to think. Would you like to be my secretary?

AGNES. On one condition.

VICE-PRESIDENT. A condition?

AGNES. On condition that you never wear this awful jacket again. When I think of these wonderful shoulders in that ill-fitting suit—!

VICE-PRESIDENT. I have a beautiful blue silk suit. But it's for summer— It's a little light for the season.

AGNES. As you please.

VICE-PRESIDENT. I'll wear it tomorrow.

AGNES. Good-bye.

VICE-PRESIDENT. Don't forget. Lunch. (*He goes out, smiling, by way of the door to the Directors' room. The street music stops. Man peers out from behind the bust.*)

AGNES. I kept my hands behind my back the whole time. I pretended I had no hands. Now I can hardly move my fingers.

MAN. Here come the rest of the apes. Go to work.

AGNES. On the first?

MAN. On all. One after the other.

AGNES. But— (*Clerk throws open the doors of the Directors' room. The street music starts again. We have a glimpse of the Directors' table with chairs pulled back ready to receive the Directors. The Vice-President is seen inside. He is posturing in front of a bookcase in the glass door of which he sees himself reflected, and he is trying vainly to give a smartly tailored appearance to his coat. Clerk glances at him in astonishment, then he stands by the outer door to announce the Directors as they appear. They come in through the outer door and cross the length of the reception room, one by one in time to the music, which is a waltz.*)

CLERK. Mr. Cracheton.

   (*Mr. Cracheton comes in, a lugubrious type, stiff and melancholy.*)

AGNES. How handsome he is!

CRACHETON. (*He snaps his head about as if shot. His expression changes. He smiles. In a low voice*) Charming girl! (*He goes into the Directors' room, looking all the while over his shoulder.*)

CLERK. Mr. Lepédura.

LEPÉDURA. (*Appears. He has a face full of suspicion and worry. As he passes Agnes, he tips his derby perfunctorily, recognizing her.*) Good morning.

AGNES. How handsome you are!

LEPÉDURA. (*Stops dead*) Who says so?

AGNES. Your wife's friend, the Baroness Chagrobis. She thinks you're wonderful.

LEPÉDURA. (*A changed man, gallant and charming*) She thinks I'm wonderful? Well, well, give her my love when you see her. And tell her I mean to call her up shortly myself. She has a pretty thin time of it with the Baron, you know. We have to be nice to her. Is she still at the same address?

AGNES. Oh, yes. I'll tell her you're as handsome as ever.

LEPÉDURA. Now don't exaggerate, my dear. We don't want to disappoint her. (*He gives her a radiant smile, and goes in, fully six inches taller and many pounds lighter. To the Clerk*) Delightful girl!

CLERK. Mr. Rasemutte and Mr. Schultz.
(*They enter together, Mutt and Jeff.*)

AGNES. How handsome he is! (*Both stop as if at a signal.*)

RASEMUTTE. To which of us, Mademoiselle—

SCHULTZ. —Do you refer?

AGNES. Look at each other. You will see. (*They look at each other anxiously, and both smile radiantly.*)

RASEMUTTE. Charming creature!

SCHULTZ. Lovely girl! (*Schultz offers Rasemutte his arm. They walk into the Directors' room arm in arm like characters in "Alt Wien." Clerk blows Agnes a kiss, follows them in and closes the doors behind them. Man pokes his head out from behind Archimedes. He shakes his head ruefully.*)

AGNES. I'm not doing it well? You're sad?

MAN. You're doing it much too well. I'm frightened.

AGNES. You?

MAN. Like Frankenstein. (*The door of the Directors' room is flung open.*)

CLERK. The President! (*As the President enters the room, we catch a glimpse of the Directors. Each has a mirror in his hand. While one combs his hair into waves, another settles his tie. Another preens his whiskers. The Vice-President has taken off his jacket.*)

PRESIDENT. So you're the cause of it all, Miss— Miss—?

AGNES. Agnes

PRESIDENT. Miss Agnes, for fifteen years this organization has been steeped in melancholy, jealousy and suspicion. And now suddenly this morning, everything is changed. My reception clerk, ordinarily a species of hyena— (*The Clerk smiles affably.*) has become so affable he even bows to his own shadow on the wall— (*Clerk contemplates his silhouette in the sunshine with a nod of approval. It nods back.*) The First Vice-President, whose reputation for stuffiness and formality has never been seriously challenged, insists on sitting at the Directors' Meeting in his shirt sleeves, God knows why. In the Directors' Room, around the table, mirrors flash like sunbeams in a forest, and my Directors gaze into them with rapture. Mr. Lepédura contemplates with joy the Adam's apple of Mr. Lepédura. Mr. Rasemutte stares with pride at the nose of Mr. Rasemutte. They are in love with themselves and with each other. How in the world did you bring about this miracle, Miss Agnes? What was it you said to them?

AGNES. How handsome you are!

PRESIDENT. I beg your pardon?

AGNES. I said to them, to each of them, "How handsome you are!"

PRESIDENT. Ah! You conveyed it to them subtly by means of a smile, a wink, a promise—

AGNES. I said it in a loud clear voice. Like this: How handsome you are! (*In the Directors' Room, all heads turn suddenly. Clerk closes the doors.*)

PRESIDENT. I see. Like a child winding up a mechanical doll. Well, well! No wonder my mannikins are quivering with the joy of life. (*There is a round of applause from the Directors' Room.*) Listen to that. It's Mr. Cracheton proposing the purchase of a new three-way mirror for the men's room. Miss Agnes, I thank you. You have made a wonderful discovery.

AGNES. (*Modestly*) Oh, it was nothing.

PRESIDENT. And the President? How does it happen that you don't tell the President?

AGNES. How handsome he is?

PRESIDENT. He's not worth the trouble, is that it? (*She looks at him with a smile full of meaning.*) You've had enough of masculine vanity for one morning?

AGNES. Oh, Mr. President—you know the reason as well as I.

PRESIDENT. No. I assure you.

AGNES. But—I don't need to tell *you*. You *are* handsome.

PRESIDENT. (*Seriously*) Would you mind repeating that?

AGNES. You are handsome.

PRESIDENT. Think carefully, Miss Agnes. This is a serious matter. Are you quite sure that to you I seem handsome?

AGNES. You don't seem handsome. You are handsome.

PRESIDENT. You would be ready to repeat that before witnesses? Think. Much depends upon your answer. I have grave decisions to make today, and the outcome depends entirely upon you. Have you thought? Are you still of the same opinion?

AGNES. Completely.

PRESIDENT. Thank heaven. (*He goes to his private door, opens it and calls.*) Chevredent!

(*Chevredent comes in. She is a thin, sour woman with an insolent air. Her nose is pinched. Her chin is high. Her hair is drawn up tightly. When she opens her mouth she appears to be about to bite.*)

CHEVREDENT. Yes? (*She looks at Agnes and sniffs audibly.*)

PRESIDENT. Chevredent, how long have you been my private secretary?

CHEVREDENT. Three years and two months. Why?

PRESIDENT. In all that time there has never been a morning when the prospect of finding you in my office has not made me shudder.

CHEVREDENT. Thanks very much. Same to you.

PRESIDENT. I wouldn't have put up with you for ten minutes if it had ever occurred to me that I was handsome.

CHEVREDENT. Ha-ha.

PRESIDENT. But because I thought I was ugly, I took your meanness for generosity. Because I thought I was ugly, I assumed that your evil temper concealed a good heart. I thought it was kind of you even to look at me. For I am ugly, am I not? (*Chevredent sneers maliciously.*) Thank you. And now listen to me. This young lady seems to be far better equipped to see than you. Her eyelids are not red like yours, her pupils are clear, her glance is limpid. Miss Agnes, look at me. Am I ugly?

AGNES. You are beautiful. (*Chevredent shrugs.*)

PRESIDENT. This young lady's disinterested appraisal of my manly charms has no effect on your opinion?

CHEVREDENT. I never heard such rubbish in my life!

PRESIDENT. Quite so. Well, here is the problem that confronts us. I have the choice of spending my working time with an ugly old shrew who thinks I'm hideous or a delightful young girl who thinks I'm handsome. What do you advise?

CHEVREDENT. You intend to replace me with this little fool?

PRESIDENT. At once.

CHEVREDENT. We'll soon see about that, Mr. President. You may have forgotten, but your wife is inside in your office reading your mail. She should know about this.

PRESIDENT. She should. Tell her.

CHEVREDENT. With pleasure. (*She rushes into the President's office, slamming the door after her.*)

AGNES. I'm terribly sorry, Mr. President.

PRESIDENT. My dear, you come like an angel from heaven at the critical moment of my life. Today is my fifteenth wedding anniversary. My wife, with whose fury Chevredent threatens us, is going to celebrate the occasion by lunching with my Directors. I am going to present her with a gift. A diamond. (*He takes out a case and opens it.*) Like it?

AGNES. How handsome it is!

PRESIDENT. Extraordinary! You praised the diamond in exactly the same tone you used for me. Is it yellow, by any chance? Is it flawed?

AGNES. It is beautiful. Like you.

PRESIDENT. (*His door opens.*) We are about to become less so, both of us. (*He puts the case in his pocket.*) Here is my wife.

THERESE. (*Therese, the blonde lady, comes in with icy majesty. She looks Agnes up and down.*) So.

PRESIDENT. Therese, my dear, permit me to present—

THERESE. Quite unnecessary. That will be all, Mademoiselle. You may go.

PRESIDENT. Agnes is staying, my dear. She is replacing Chevredent.

THERESE. Agnes! So she is already Agnes!

PRESIDENT. Why not?

THERESE. And why is Agnes replacing Chevredent?

PRESIDENT. Because she thinks I'm handsome.

THERESE. Are you mad?

PRESIDENT. No. Handsome.

THERESE. (*To Agnes*) You think he's handsome?

AGNES. Oh, yes.

THERESE. He makes you think of Galahad? Of Lancelot?

AGNES. Oh, no. His type is classic. The Apollo of Bellac.

THERESE. The Apollo of Bellac?

PRESIDENT. Have you ever stopped to wonder, Therese, why the good Lord made women? Obviously they were not torn from our ribs in order to make life a torment for us. Women exist in order to tell men they are handsome. And those who say it the most are those who are most beautiful. Agnes tells me I'm handsome. It's because she's beautiful. You tell me I'm ugly. Why?

MAN. (*Appears. He applauds.*) Bravo! Bravo!

THERESE. Who is this maniac?

MAN. When one hears a voice which goes to the very heart of humanity, it is impossible to keep silent.

PRESIDENT. My friend—

MAN. From the time of Adam and Eve, of Samson and Delilah, of Antony and Cleopatra, the problem of man and woman has made an impenetrable barrier between man and woman. If, as it seems, we are able to solve this problem once and for all, it will be a work of immeasurable benefit to the human race.

THERESE. And you think we're getting somewhere with it today, is that it?

MAN. Oh, yes.

THERESE. You don't think the final solution could be deferred until tomorrow?

MAN. Till tomorrow? When the President has just posed the problem so beautifully?

AGNES. So beautifully!

THERESE. The beautiful man poses a beautiful problem, eh, Mademoiselle?

AGNES. I didn't say it. But I can say it. I say what I think.

THERESE. Little cheat!

PRESIDENT. I forbid you to insult Agnes!

THERESE. It's she who insults me!

PRESIDENT. When I'm called handsome, it's an insult to you—is that it?

THERESE. I'm no liar.

PRESIDENT. No. You show us the bottom of your heart.

MAN. Agnes is telling the President the truth, Madame. Just as Cleopatra told the truth, just as Isolt told the truth. The truth about men is, they are beautiful, every last one of them; and your husband is right, Madame, the woman who tells it to them never lies.

THERESE. So I am the liar!

MAN. (*Gently*) It's only because you don't see clearly. All you have to do to see the beauty of men is to watch as they breathe and move their limbs. Each has his special grace. His beauty of body. The heavy ones—how powerfully they hold the ground! The light ones—how well they hang from the sky! His beauty of position. A hunchback on the ridge of Notre Dame makes a masterpiece of Gothic sculpture. All you have to do is to get him up there. And, finally, his beauty of function. The steamfitter has the beauty of a steamfitter. The president has the beauty of a president. There is ugliness only when these beauties become confused—when the steamfitter has the beauty of a president, the president the beauty of a steamfitter.

AGNES. But there is no such confusion here.

THERESE. No. He has the beauty of a garbageman.

PRESIDENT. Thanks very much.

THERESE. My dear, I have known you too long to deceive you. You have many good qualities. But you're ugly.

PRESIDENT. Quiet!

THERESE. Yes. Yes. Ugly! This girl, whatever her motives, is just able to force her lips to whisper her lies. But with every part of me—my heart, my lungs, my arms, my eyes—I scream the truth at you. My legs! You're ugly! Do you hear?

PRESIDENT. I've heard nothing else for years.

THERESE. Because it's true.

MAN. There. And at last she's confessed.

THERESE. Confessed what? What have I confessed?

MAN. Your crime, Madame. You have injured this man. How could you expect him to be handsome in an environment that screamed at him constantly that he was ugly?

PRESIDENT. Ah! Now I understand!

THERESE. What do you understand? What's the matter with you all? What have I done?

PRESIDENT. Now I understand why I am always embarrassed not only in your presence, but in the presence of everything that belongs to you.

THERESE. Do you know what he is talking about?

PRESIDENT. The sight of your skirt on the back of a chair shortens my spine by three inches. Can you expect me to stand up like a man when you come in? Your stockings on the bureau tell me that I'm knock-kneed and thick-ankled. Is it any wonder if I stumble? Your nail file on my desk hisses at me that my fingers are thick and my gestures clumsy. What do you expect of me after that? And your onyx clock with the Dying Gaul on the mantelpiece—no wonder I always shiver when I go near the fire. Imagine—for fifteen years that Dying Gaul has been sneering at me in my own house, and I never realized why I was uncomfortable. Well, at last I understand. And this very evening—

THERESE. Don't you dare!

PRESIDENT. This very evening your Dying Gaul shall die. You will find him in the garbage with the rest of the conspiracy. Your Dresden china shepherd, your Arab sheik, your Directoire chairs with their scratchy bottoms—

THERESE. Those chairs belonged to my grandmother!

PRESIDENT. From now on they belong to the garbage. What are your chairs covered with, Agnes?

AGNES. Yellow satin.

PRESIDENT. I knew it. And the statues on your table?

AGNES. There is only a bowl of fresh flowers on my table. Today it is white carnations.

PRESIDENT. Of course. And over your fireplace?

AGNES. A mirror.

PRESIDENT. Naturally.

THERESE. I warn you, if you so much as touch my chairs, I'll leave you forever.

PRESIDENT. As you please, my dear.

THERESE. I see. So this is my anniversary gift after fifteen years of devotion. Very well. Only tell me, what have you to complain of? In all these years has it ever happened that your roast was too rare? Did I ever give you your coffee too cold, too hot, too light, too sweet? Thanks to me, you are known as a man whose handkerchief is always fresh, whose socks are always new. Have you ever known what it was to have a hole in your toe? Has anyone ever seen a spot on your vest? And yet how you splash in your gravy, my friend! How you go through your socks!

PRESIDENT. Tell me one thing. Do you say I am ugly because you think I am ugly or merely to spite me?

THERESE. Because you are ugly.

PRESIDENT. Thank you, Therese. Go on.

THERESE. Then this woman appears. And at the first glance we can guess the fate of the unhappy creature who marries her. We see it all—the slippers with the inner sole curled up in a scroll. The nightly battle over the newspaper. The pajamas without buttons and always too small. The headaches without aspirin, the soup without salt, the shower without towels—

PRESIDENT. Agnes, one question. Do you tell me I'm handsome because you think I'm handsome or only to make fun of me?

AGNES. Because you're handsome.

PRESIDENT. Thank you, Agnes.

THERESE. You mean because he's rich.

AGNES. If he were the richest man in the world, I'd still say he's handsome.

THERESE. Very well. Marry her if she thinks you're so handsome. Well? What are you waiting for?

PRESIDENT. Nothing.

THERESE. Take him, you, with my compliments. After fifteen years I've had enough. If you like to hear snoring at night—

AGNES. You snore? How wonderful!

THERESE. If you like bony knees—

AGNES. I like legs that have character.

THERESE. Look at that face! Now tell me he has the brow of a Roman Senator.

AGNES. No, Madame.

THERESE. No?

AGNES. The brow of a king.

THERESE. I give up. Good-bye.

PRESIDENT. Good-bye, my love.
       (*Therese rushes out through outer door.*)
And now, Agnes, in token of a happy future, accept this diamond. For me, one life has ended, and another begins. (*Clerk comes in and signs to him.*) Forgive me just one moment, Agnes. I must address the Directors. The Chairman of the Board is evidently not coming. I'll be right back. (*He crosses to the door. To the Clerk*) Send down to the florist. I want all the white carnations he has. Agnes, you have made me the happiest of men.

AGNES. The handsomest.
       (*The President goes out by his door, the Clerk by outer door.*)

MAN. Well, there you are, my dear. You have everything—a job, a husband and a diamond. I can leave?

AGNES. Oh, no! (*The street music starts afresh.*)

MAN. But what more do you want?

AGNES. Look at me. I have changed—haven't I?

MAN. Perhaps just a little. That can't be helped.

AGNES. It's your fault. I have told so many lies! I must tell the truth at last or I shall burst!

MAN. What truth do you want to tell?

AGNES. I want to tell someone who is really beautiful that he is beautiful. I want to tell the most beautiful man in the world that he is the most beautiful man in the world.

MAN. And to caress him, perhaps, just a little?

AGNES. Just a little.

MAN. There is the Apollo of Bellac.

AGNES. He doesn't exist.

MAN. What does it matter whether or not he exists? His beauty is the supreme beauty. Tell him.

AGNES. I can't. Unless I touch a thing I don't see it. You know that. I have no imagination.

MAN. Close your eyes.

AGNES. (*Closes them.*) Yes?

MAN. Suppose, Agnes, it were the God of Beauty himself who visited you this morning. Don't be astonished. Perhaps it's true. Where else could this terrible power have come from? Or this extraordinary emotion you feel? Or this sense of oppression? And suppose that now the god reveals himself?

AGNES. It is you?

MAN. Don't open your eyes. Suppose I stand before you now in all my truth and all my splendor.

AGNES. I see you.

MAN. Call me thou.

AGNES. I see thee.

MAN. How do I seem?

AGNES. You seem—

MAN. I am taller than mortal men. My head is small and fringed with golden ringlets. From the line of my shoulders, the geometricians derived the idea of the square. From my eyebrows the bowmen drew the concept of the arc. I am nude and this nudity inspired in the musicians the idea of harmony.

AGNES. Your heels are winged, are they not?

MAN. They are not. You are thinking of the Hermes of St. Yrieix.

AGNES. I don't see your eyes.

MAN. As for the eyes, it's as well you don't see them. The eyes of beauty are implacable. My eyeballs are silver. My pupils are graphite. From the eyes of beauty poets derived the idea of death. But the feet of beauty are enchanting. They are not feet that touch the ground. They are never soiled and never captive. The toes are slender, and from them artists derived the idea of symmetry. Do you see me now?

AGNES. You dazzle my eyes.

MAN. But your heart sees me.

AGNES. I'm not so sure. Do not count on me too much, God of Beauty. My life is small. My days are long, and when I come back to my room each evening, there are five flights to climb in the greasy twilight amid smells of cooking. These five flights mark the beginning and the end of every event of my life, and, oh, if you knew, Apollo, how lonely I am! Sometimes I find a cat waiting in a doorway. I kneel and stroke it for a moment, we purr together and it fills the rest of my day with joy. Sometimes I see a milk bottle that has fallen on its side. I set it right and the gesture comforts me. If I smell gas in the hallway I run and speak to the janitor. It is so good to speak to someone about something. Between the second story and the third, the steps sag. At this turning one abandons hope. At this turning one loses one's balance, and catches at the bannister, gasping with the anguish of those more fortunate ones who clutch at the rail on the heaving deck of a ship. This is my life, Apollo, a thing of shadows and tortured flesh. That is my conscience, Apollo, a staircase full of stale odors. If I hesitate to see you as you are, O beautiful god, it is because I need so much and I have so little and I must defend myself.

MAN. But I have rescued you, Agnes. You possess the secret.

AGNES. I know. From now on, my staircase will be new and full of light, the treads carpeted in velvet and adorned with initials. But to climb it with you would be unthinkable. Go away, God of Beauty. Leave me for always.

MAN. You wish that?

AGNES. If you were merely a handsome man, Apollo, thick and human in your flesh, with what joy I would take you in my arms! How I would love you! But you are too brilliant and too great for my staircase. I would do better to look at my diamond. Go, Apollo. Go away. Before I open my eyes, I implore you, vanish.

MAN. When I vanish, you will see before you an ordinary creature like yourself, covered with skin, covered with clothes.

AGNES. That is my destiny, and I prefer it. Let me kiss your lips, Apollo. And then—

MAN. (*He kisses her.*) Open your eyes, my dear. Apollo is gone. And I am going.

AGNES. How handsome you are!

MAN. Dear Agnes!

AGNES. Don't go. I will make you rich. I will order the President to buy your invention.

MAN. Which one?

AGNES. The Universal Vegetable. There must be a fortune in it.

MAN. I haven't quite got the hang of it yet. The roots don't hold the earth. I'll be back the moment I've perfected it.

AGNES. You promise?

MAN. We shall plant it together. And now—

AGNES. You are really leaving me? You think I shall marry the President?

MAN. No.

AGNES. Why not?

MAN. He's already married. And his wife has learned a lesson. You will see.

AGNES. Then whom shall I marry, if not the President?

CLERK. (*Enters. He crosses to the Directors' Room and throws open the door. Announces*) The Chairman of the Board!

(*The Chairman enters from outer door.*)

MAN. (*Whispers*) He is a bachelor.

AGNES. How handsome he is!

MAN. Yes.

(*He vanishes*)

CHAIRMAN. Mademoiselle—

PRESIDENT. (*The President comes in quickly great excitement.*) Agnes! Agnes! A miracle! My wife has just telephoned. I don't know what has come over her. She has thrown out the Dying Gaul and the china shepherd.

AGNES. Give her this diamond.

PRESIDENT. Thank you, Agnes. Thank you.

CHAIRMAN. (*Taking her hand*) And who is this charming girl who gives away diamonds?

AGNES. Her name is Agnes.

CHAIRMAN. Dear Agnes!

PRESIDENT. But what's happened to our friend? He isn't here?

AGNES. He is gone.

PRESIDENT. Call him back. He must have lunch with us. Do you know his name?

AGNES. He is gone.

PRESIDENT. (*Runs to the outer door*) Apollo! Apollo! (*The Directors come in, all adorned with white carnations.*) Gentlemen, gentlemen, let's call him! We can't let him go like that. Apollo! (*They each go to a door or a window save Agnes and the Chairman who remain standing hand in hand.*)

PRESIDENT AND DIRECTORS. Apollo! Apollo!

CHAIRMAN. But whom are they shouting at? Is Apollo here?

AGNES. No. He just passed by.

CURTAIN

Except for certain explicit indications of attitude written into the stage directions, the script of *The Apollo of Bellac* depends for its effects on the interchange of speech between characters. The stage directions function as narrative functions in prose fiction, except that they can be dispensed with as audible speech in the performance of the play. They are not, however, superfluous in the text. Without them the actors and the director of the play might miss certain implications that Giraudoux is anxious to underscore in the speeches. They are cues to interpretation of the play, cues to movement and gesture. They function as indications of tempo and tone function in the musical score. In this sense, reading the script of a play is like reading musical score. Many people, lacking in ability to visualize and finding the strain on the imagination too heavy, dislike reading play scripts, though they may thoroughly enjoy the performed play. On the other hand, the challenge of the play script becomes absorbing for the imaginative reader who is able to make use of all the cues it contains and who is sophisticated in his acquaintance with the functioning of literature.

The description of the scene informs us that a sense of opulence and elegance is necessary to the play. It is perhaps overopulent, this Bureau of Inventions, with its period desk and blotter, its elaborate chandelier, and its ivory telephone. There is a bust of Archimedes, the most famous of ancient mathematicians and an inventor of considerable importance. The title of the play has already told us that another classical figure, Apollo, is involved. Against all this we are given a clerk writing at the desk, though a clerk with the look of a Daumier caricature. (Can you find a picture by Daumier to tell you how this will look?) To him, timidly, walks Agnes as she enters.

Her first speech—the single word "Er—," involves the interpreter at once in gesture. What does "Er—" stand for? One cannot simply say "Er—" and let it go at that. The sound is partly a result of Agnes' timidity, partly a result of the fact that the Clerk does not even look up when she comes in.

The atmosphere is already a little like that of the fairy tale—the palace, the timid young girl, the ogre. Then in comes Therese, the equivalent of the beautiful, vain lady of the court (not the queen, for her husband is only the President, not the Chairman of the Board). She sweeps through the room and the conversation between Agnes and the Clerk continues—a kind of elaborate, nonsensical conversation, though matter-of-fact in manner. Then the Man from Bellac appears—not Apollo, though, as Valency puts it, he must "evoke Apollo." This is a fairy tale with a difference—no god in disguise here, no prince in peasant's clothing, but a poet-dreamer who is also a vagabond. He proceeds to talk in a way that astonishes Agnes and upsets (finally irritates) the Clerk, who leaves to answer the buzzer.

This has given us three small scenes: the first up to the entrance of Therese, the second up to the entrance of the Man, the third up to the departure of the Clerk. We now know something about the office, about the "importance" of its schedule and officers, about the scale and departmentalization of its interests. We also know something about the wife of its President. And however amusing the notion of the Universal Vegetable may be to us, we know that it is not beyond the imagination of the Clerk, who is used to grand inventions in this grand office. This is *serious* nonsense, the best kind!

Notice that everything to which we have been pointing is, in its way, part of the management of point of view in the dramatic mode. While we presumably are hearing characters speaking in their own right, all their language is controlled by the playwright (who in this sense is the "narrator" of the play, though the narrator seen this way differs in precise ways from the narrator in the epic mode.) Notice too that the words of the speaker, the text, are accompanied by what may be called subtext, the unspoken feelings, which may accompany or even contradict the words said aloud. The interpreter, working with the play as a whole, must ultimately decide how at any one moment the subtext governs, modifies, and conditions the thing spoken. Just as poem and reader must match, so subtext and text must match, must coalesce, in the final performance. The text should not be thought of as simply a "channel" to the subtext. Rather, the subtext should be thought of as giving solidity of specification to the text. The process is circular and fascinating in its circularity: text points to subtext (where else would we get it?), subtext draws specification from all that the interpreter knows and feels as a human being in his own right, and this specification in turn supports and enriches the text. Another way to put it is that the reader moves from outer to inner text, works out a viable coalescence between himself (inner and outer form of himself) and the inner text, and embodies it in the words of the outer text.

Through the first two scenes Agnes is central. Even when Therese sweeps through the room we think of her in terms of her contrast with Agnes. But in the third scene the Man becomes central. We begin by seeing him in terms of Agnes, but we end by seeing Agnes in terms of him. The locus has shifted. And it has shifted because, even without a narrator such as we find in prose fiction, this play has a perspective from which the tensions are manipulated, and the perspective that controls the whole of the action necessitates moving the Man to the central position for the time being. Is the Man, then, the playwright? No, he is the Man, and we must not automatically attribute his views to Giraudoux (even if we knew Giraudoux's views and those of the Man to be identical). This is the world of the play, not the world of Giraudoux.

Now there is a longer scene between the Man and Agnes. As the Man centers his attention on Agnes, as she begins to express her fears, she again becomes central. She is afraid of men, trembles when they speak to her. He tells her the secret of trembling before men: "Tell them they're handsome."

This brings us to the end of the play's first major movement. It is the first crisis of the action; it is also a preparation for the next. From this point up to the reentrance of the Clerk, we have the "argument" of the play. There is something extravagantly oversimplified about the argument, something amusing, something true. It is either seriously nonsensical or nonsensically serious or both. "Every man, even the ugliest, feels in his heart a secret alliance with beauty. When you tell him he's handsome, he will simply hear outwardly the voice he has been listening to inwardly all his life." Agnes, if she wishes, can become "the magic glass of truth, the princess of an enchanted world." There is something of the dispensing god in this shabby Apollo, holding out his vision of the world that can be. Agnes is a little frightened: "I'd better come back another day. I have to have training." She thinks she will go practice on her cousin. "No," says the Man, "try the monster" (by which he means the Clerk). In comes the Clerk; Agnes trembles (did you know that *Agnes* means "chaste" or "pure," and that the Latin word *agnus* means "lamb"?). "I can't," says Agnes. We have arrived at a climax. And then the Clerk fortunately leaves again.

Failure is averted. The climax turns out to be only a crisis, and we begin again, this time with the bust of Archimedes. No—with the fly. How handsome he is. Another crisis: the door of the Vice-President opens slowly . . . enter the Clerk. . . . Agnes (after an agony of indecision): "How handsome you are!" We wait. The Clerk isn't persuaded. Agnes almost gives up. Then, climax! He *is* persuaded after all, though it takes him a while to admit it. This is the hardest of Agnes' tasks; the others are to come easily, once she has the hang of it. "How handsome you are!"

But there are other things to learn, and the Man instructs her. She grows expert in the game, and it becomes not just a game but "the truth." Even the Man is swept up in it: "My father was a very handsome man, and he—Oh-oh. Good for you." It is fun, this game, and the world looks better through it. Even the chandelier is persuaded.

One crisis succeeds another now—the Vice-President, Mr. Cracheton, Mr. Lepédura, Mr. Rasemutte, and Mr. Schultz, the President himself. This last one gets serious. Agnes is on the verge of taking the lord away from his lady. Feelings and actions grow higher and quicker; complications grow. "Agnes," says the President, "you have made me the happiest of men." And he leaves to address the Directors.

Now we are again with Agnes and the Man. The scene grows quiet; the tensions alter. "Well, there you are, my dear. You have everything—a job, a husband, and a diamond." His errand is finished, but Agnes won't let him go. The scene becomes hieratic, visionary, as if the god Apollo himself had descended. As if. But oh, Agnes is after all a real young girl, not a fairy princess. She lives in a room five flights up, smelling of cooking—above the turning in the stair where one seems to abandon all hope. She is "a thing of shadows and tortured flesh," and her conscience is "a staircase full of stale odors." A god would be too much for such a girl. Nevertheless, in his way, the god has come and touched her life, and he has left her with her visions. Now she can say it: "Leave me for always." He seems a little reluctant to go. "You want me to?" "Yes," she does. The real crisis is past now; this is not to be a fairy story after all. And yet, there she is, as the play ends, clearly about to marry the king himself, the Chairman of the Board.

We have deliberately employed the words *crisis* and *climax* in ambiguous senses. We may think of the action of the play as residing in Agnes' growing assurance as she overcomes one obstacle after another in her search for the way to stop trembling before men. First the Clerk, then the Vice-President, then the President, in the order of ascending importance, with the winning of the President (away from his wife, it appears) the largest crisis, and the winning of the Chairman of the

Board as the climax. This is in part the story of a young girl who marries the Chairman of the Board of the International Bureau of Inventions. But this description of the action too largely ignores the Man from Bellac (where, incidentally, Giraudoux himself was born). Between the crisis and the climax comes that moving scene that verges on the supernatural. It not only conditions the climax (the winning of the Chairman); it serves as a second crisis, the action now being thought of as the relation between the Man and Agnes. For this second crisis, the climax is the departure of the man ("Apollo is not here") at the close.

These two actions are organically related; the one echoes the other. The one is a success story; the other is the story of a wonderful impossibility, recognized as impossible but beautifully near all the same. The real triumph of Agnes is not her marriage but her "conversion," and for this the Man from Bellac is responsible. But her conversion does not take her out of life; it plants her firmly in it. In some sense, Agnes has lost her innocence. It is a little sad; it is a little amusing. How realistic it is after all, this fairy tale.

This is the locus of the play, this tantalizing and curious hovering between the Apollonian vision of harmony and the darkness at the turning of the stair. It is a delicate balance that Giraudoux gives us and that the interpreter must maintain. Agnes must not be made of sugar candy and puff paste, but she must not smell too heavily of steaming cabbage. Remember that the period desk, the crystal chandelier, the opulence and elegance of that office are expensive. Agnes marries money; that will not displease her.

In describing the locus, we have been talking about the perspective, the angle of vision that determines the choice of episodes, the juxtaposition of actions, the arrangement of tensions, the nature of the coalescence. What is the relation of the street music to these matters? Why does it begin where it begins, return where it returns? What does the rapid sequence of entrances beginning with Mr. Cracheton have to do with the ordering of tensions? What does Chevredent ("goat tooth"), the wicked witch, have to do with the action? Why is the scene with the President much longer than the scene with the Chairman of the Board, though we have called the latter a climax?

No dramatic action can be static. Within this (seemingly) simple story there exist many shifts: in focus, in degree and quality of tensions, in attitude and gesture, tone and pacing. Giraudoux is disarming.

Valency makes a particular point of remarking that the Man is not Apollo, and should not look like Apollo. The eye tells us one thing, but the ear tells Agnes another as she listens to the Man in the crisis scene. What of Agnes herself? Should she be beautiful? What is the nature of her charm? What about Therese—how round a character is she? Is the Clerk a round character or a flat character? (What are the difficulties in answering these questions?)

In a solo reading, the interpreter may do nothing about the setting, the properties, or costumes. But when you consider Readers Theatre in the next section of this book, you may wish to discuss such matters in connection with group performances. Ask yourself then whether you would or would not want a chandelier.

Any section of the play will provide interesting questions for the interpreter. Let us take the speech by the man just before the first reentrance of the Clerk. Agnes has asked, "There are women then who already know this secret?" And the Man answers "Yes." Does the *yes* come quickly? Slowly? Matter-of-factly? Emphatically? And does the period after *yes* tell us anything about the relation between the word *yes* and the next sentence—"But they know it without really knowing it"? May one read it as if it were written, "Yes, but they know it. . . ."? What difference is there between the possibilities? Why does the third sentence begin with a conjunction (*And*) rather than with the word *usually?* Why not a period after *issue?* We must remember that we are dealing with a translation, and that we are talking about the English rather than the French text. The movement from sentence to sentence, from phrase to phrase within the sentence, from word to word within the phrase, even from syllable to syllable within the word is always significant movement. One can point to too much in it; one can point to too little. Is there greater "distance" between some sentences than between others in the speech? Where would you place the major transitions in it? What is the difference between the two dashes in the speech? (To what gestures do they point?) What weight is given to the last sentence because it is last in this speech? How does it differ in tensiveness from the sentence "They tell the hunchback he is generous, the walleyed that he's strong"? What is the difference in perspective in the two sentences?

These are questions that the actor and the interpreter ask constantly—or should ask. The mind of the speaker is never motionless; the "motionless" body is never without life. These things are as much a part of the plot as are the incidents; it is in the interaction between incident and character that the plot resides. The interpreter always wants to know how to manage his task. He must first ask why his task is what it is. As finely as you can define it, what is involved in your reading of the play? All answers to the question *How?* must arise from that. Unhappily, we all too often stop short of finding the full answers to the question of what is involved. An abstraction will not do. The interpreter's response must be in the best sense body response, the response of a body with a mind in it. The poise and heft of a sentence have more than conceptual qualities. In a play they carry the bodies of characters.

SPECIAL LITERARY KINDS AND MODES OF PERFORMANCE

Part **III**

Chapter 12

CHILDREN'S LITERATURE AND NONFICTIVE FORMS

Our discussion of literature has been restricted to the traditional literary kinds. Some mention must be made of other materials useful to the interpreter.

There is a great body of literature collected under the general name *children's literature*. It is made up of stories, plays, poems, fables, legends—even of selections from history, biography, and natural history. In general, the principles discussed with respect to traditional literary kinds will apply to the special kinds. Children's literature frequently exaggerates elements of sound and structure. The following poem, for example, emphasizes rhyme and rhythm by employing short lines and simple, parallel syntax:

CHILDREN'S LITERATURE

I had a little pony,
   His name was Dapple-grey.
I lent him to a lady
   To ride a mile away.

She whipped him, she slashed him,
   She rode him through the mire.
I would not lend my pony now
   For all the lady's hire.

Prosodically, the poem is a fascinating one. Do you think it is best described as foot prosody or stress prosody? How will your answer to this question affect your oral performance of the poem?

Children's literature may be read by children or by adults. It may be read to children or adults. The particular setting of a reading will affect the performance. How, for example, do you think you would distinguish between an adult audience and a child audience if you were reading "I had a little pony" to each in turn?

Young children like strong rhythmic effects. They like playing with the sounds of words and often do not care whether the words make sense; indeed, they may prefer it if the words do not make sense:

> One, two
> Button my shoe.
> Three, four,
> Shut the door.
> Five, six,
> Pick up sticks.
> Seven, eight,
> Lay them straight.
> Nine, ten,
> Big fat hen.

They are also likely to enjoy simple but large overt actions on the part of the oral reader—sudden clapping of the hands, sudden wide opening of the eyes and mouth, or sudden lunging of the body to stress a point. Children not only like but demand strong enthusiasm from the reader. Indeed, something might be said for the use of children's literature at the very beginning of a course in interpretation, for it necessitates total body involvement in a gross, obvious way and does not allow the reader to get lost in subtleties of lexical meaning. Notice how the following rhyme requires overt action if "this" is to make sense:

> This little pig went to market.
> This little pig stayed home.
> This little pig had roast beef.
> This little pig had none.
> This little pig cried 'Wee, wee, wee'
> All the way home.

It is not accidental that there are *five* little pigs!

When adults enjoy children's literature, they often enjoy it for reasons unfamiliar to children. Most children's literature is written by adults, and there is often an adult point of view existing beside a child-like one. In Lewis Carroll's "The Crocodile," irony is likely to outweigh the delight in nonsense for the adult reader:

> How doth the little crocodile
>   Improve his shining tail,
> And pour the waters of the Nile
>   On every golden scale!

How cheerfully he seems to grin!
  How neatly spread his claws,
And welcomes little fishes in
  With gently smiling jaws!

When the interpreter reads children's literature for adults, it is often not the same literature as when he reads the piece to children. The two differ in perspective, in tensiveness, in presence. One cannot always manage the two perspectives at once; when one does, the experience is likely to be both subtle and delightful.

In choosing between perspectives, the reader must be careful. It is likely to be a highly embarrassing experience to read to adults as if reading to children—embarrassing for the audience, even if not for the insensitive reader, a *dis*-location of the poem. However, if the reader treats an audience of children as if they were adults, he may very well bore the children to death. "But some children are on the verge of becoming adults," you will say. Very well, treat them as young adults. "What about a mixed audience?" you will ask in bewilderment. Ah, do you begin to see that the locus of a poem is a vastly complicated, therefore fascinating, thing? Never underestimate the power of a poem; never overestimate the powers of a reader. Since a poem is alive, it has the power to change; it is not necessarily the same today as it is tomorrow, any more than you are, even though you remain John Smith or Mary Jones and are still recognizable to your friends. (But we should be quite vexed to have John Smith confused with Mary Jones, though readers sometimes so browbeat a poem as to make it almost unrecognizable.) Never agree to read a poem "cold" for an audience, even though you have read it many times before for audiences. It should be reembodied for each occasion. Strangely enough, you may even find that the context (the other poems surrounding it in your performance) will alter your perspective and hence, subtly, your reading. In order that you may not be misled by the context, you must practice the reading in context—always, always.

TRANSITIONAL LITERARY FORMS

We have been concerned with the interpretation of works distinctly literary in kind. But certain forms lie somewhere between the strictly literary and the "nonliterary," with both an esthetic and a nonesthetic function, and the interpreter ought to take advantage of the appeal such forms may have for audiences.

The Essay

Essays are classified in various ways: personal or familiar, humorous, expository. One may give to essays the same designations often given to types of speeches: informative, persuasive, entertaining, commemorative, eulogistic, dedicatory. A general difference between the speech and the essay is that the essay is ordinarily not intended for oral delivery before a specific audience, and formally it need not follow the traditional arrangement of a speech (though it has a beginning, a middle, and an end). Nevertheless, in written form many speeches can be called essays. The essay is often lyrical in mode; it is direct communication between the author-in-the-work and the audience. It may closely resemble a short story (as in Charles Lamb's familiar essay "A Dissertation upon Roast Pig"), though when it does it tends to keep the personality of the narrator central in the story. Rather than creating a world of its own, as the literary work does, it tends to join the reader in the actual world to talk about something in which narrator and reader have a common interest—to create one side of a dialogue in which the reader supplies the other half.[1] Sometimes the actual world, as seen in the essay, is not really the actual world but a highly personalized or exaggerated version of it. The more gravely the narrator pretends to believe in his exaggerated picture, the more hilarious the essay may be, as if speaker and reader are together saying "Yes, this is the way things often are—but aren't they silly!"

The speech may acquire values from its author's mode of delivery; his own style of utterance will often add much that is not in the language itself. It is not unusual to find that a moving speech (or a moving sermon) when examined in print seems curiously unlike the performance we remember. To be a successful essay, the speech must contain within itself sufficient clues to the attitude, perspective, and tensions of the speaker. The world of the essay may be close to the actual world, but it must contain within itself the necessary clues for its reembodiment. A speech, on the other hand, may literally die with its delivery, except in the memory of those who have heard it.

One view of the essay suggests that it differs from other literary forms in taking as its center of reference a general rather than a particular situation or idea—comments about things rather than the presentation or bodying forth of things. An essay may be simply factual, and the personality of the speaker or writer may be almost totally submerged in the exposition. It is doubtful that such an essay is clearly literary, however.

The interpreter must decide, with such forms as the essay, whether the personality of the writer is a necessary part of the interpretation—and, if so, how far one ought to go in characterizing the writer. What difference is there between an interpretaiton of an essay by Lamb that makes Lamb the speaker and an interpretation that treats the speaker as nameless? (You may compare the problem of Matthew Arnold's poem "Dover Beach." Is the speaker Arnold or not? What difference does your answer make to your interpretation of the poem for an audience?) This is a complicated matter. We raise the question here but shall defer discussion of it until we come to diaries, letters, and journals.

History We do not think, nowadays, of history as a form of literature. In Shakespeare's time, the distinctions between the two forms were far from fixed. Much early history, indeed, is based on legend, myth, fancy. His-

[1] See the essay by Leigh Hunt on pp. 23–24.

tory was once thought of as a form of didactic literature—exempla for instruction in the ways of political thought and behavior. The story of Caedmon, included in Appendix A, is from Bede's *History,* but we may read it as literature rather than history.

Early Greek historians read their works aloud to audiences, and their books are filled with pieces that still rank high in literary value. Indeed, one Greek historian was accused of writing for audiences rather than recording facts.

A great deal of literature is based on history—Shakespeare's *Henry V,* for example, or historical novels such as George Eliot's *Romola* or poems such as Stephen Vincent Benét's *John Brown's Body.* These works often provide special problems for the interpreter. In a play about Abraham Lincoln, the interpreter must not behave like Henry VIII, and it would probably help if he did not look like Henry VIII in his own person, though we cannot (perhaps unfortunately) change our persons every time we change characters in reading! Theoretically, the interpreter need not be typecast for the thing he reads any more than the silent reader need be; in actual practice, however, interpreters find that audiences have limits of tolerance that make the reader's task difficult. Singers often face the same kind of problem. In a concert within memory, a distinguished soprano appeared before the audience dressed in what looked like burlap sacking. She was short, rotund—she waddled when she walked. She was to sing *"Depuis le jour"* from the opera *Louise,* a highly lyrical and romantic aria. She must have felt the audience's amusement keenly, since there was open laughter at her entrance, but she gave no sign of it. There was not the slightest sense of any irritation between her and her listeners. When she began to sing, concentrating wholly on the aria, it was easily possible for many in the audience to forget about her personal appearance and to become lost in the song itself. She was pure romance.

But not everyone in the audience managed this transfer from singer to song; only a consummate artist is able under such circumstances to carry the majority of the audience with him. There is a caveat here for interpreters: do not limit yourself narrowly to works of literature that suit your own person or you will never grow; on the other hand, it is suicidal to choose works for which you are unsuited unless you can withstand the opposition you may arouse. We are not talking here about class training, in which you will learn by tackling pieces you do not always do well, but about public performance.

If one is to read history, then, and to reembody historical figures, one is surely in part limited by the knowledge of his audience. In an operetta, audiences may be willing to accept a tall, slim, handsome Schubert—but no one will take the operetta Schubert for the real Schubert. In a history, such freedom is not always possible with figures who are known to us—Franklin Delano Roosevelt, for example, or John F. Kennedy, whose voices still sound clearly in many ears. Readers may find that while they are reading the words of such historical persons, audiences may be listening to another voice—the voice of the historical figure himself.

Much history, however, will not pose such problems for the reader. No one will worry about the actual historical figure of King Arthur of the Round Table—if indeed he ever existed. Nor about Pericles, or Mark Antony, or Charlemagne. The interpreter need only be concerned with these figures as they exist in the history he or she is reading, following such clues as are given there. Earlier history may be more easily cut off from its connections with the actual world than later history. It may be easy to read early history as fiction; it becomes more difficult to do so as we come closer to the present day.

Let the oral reader not overlook history, then, in choosing materials to read. Try putting a good historical account of the death of Lincoln on the same program with Whitman's poem about the dead Lincoln, and with passages from Carl Sandburg's biography of Lincoln. Or use Carlyle's *History of the French Revolution* as material for "locating" literature about the French Revolution—Dickens's *Tale of Two Cities,* perhaps. Newspaper accounts of events (that is, historical sources) may be effectively juxtaposed with poems or plays or stories based on the events. The possibilities are almost endless, and the interpreter will find it exciting to explore the differences in perspective and tension between the two kinds of handling of the same event. Too often interpreters have simply assumed, without much thought, that history is unsuitable for interpretation.

Biography

What we have been saying about history is largely true of biography. While every sound biography—as every sound piece of historical writing—is meant to give us an accurate notion of its subject, everyone knows that both biographical and historical writing involve perspective. Biographies of a single subject by two different writers will yield different views of the same man. Any biography can recover only a small fraction of the actual experience of its subject. The interpreter must look for the particular perspective of the biography from which he chooses to read, must examine its tensions, must seek to embody the subject it presents rather than the "same" subject as presented in another biography. One could build a fascinating program around the various views of a single human being as reflected in a series of studies or in writings of various kinds—biographies, letters, diaries, newspapers, political speeches, obituaries, and so on.

We are so used to Boswell's Johnson now that the "real" Johnson scarcely matters to many readers. The more "literary" a biography becomes—the more it cuts itself free from practical ties with the actual world and creates a world of its own with its own perspectives—the less accurate it may seem, from one point of view; but from another point of view such a biography may gain in accuracy. We have already said, for example, that an "accurate" description of a man (age, height, complexion, nationality, income, marital status) often succeeds simply in killing the man off, since we are interested in "what he looks like inside," which such statistics cannot give us. How free may a biography be, however, and remain biography? Shakespeare's *Richard III* is notoriously inaccurate as a biographical account, though it is highly effective as a historical melodrama.

Plutarch's *Lives* puports to be a biographical account of the lives of certain famous Romans; it is in part a history of their times. But it is highly imaginative in its depiction of details—often as much literature as fact. In the famous translation by North, Plutarch was used by Shakespeare as source material for his Roman plays; frequently Shakespeare simply "versified" the words of North. A recent university production of Shakespeare's *Antony and Cleopatra* employed a narrator who introduced the play with a prologue written by putting together passages from North. A comparison of North's account of Cleopatra on her barge and Shakespeare's famous speech by Enobarbus on the same subject makes it clear that the differences between biography and pure literature are often exceedingly hard to determine. (It will not do simply to say that Plutarch's object is truth while Shakespeare's object is pleasure. Why not?)

Let the oral reader not overlook biography.

Autobiography

Autobiography is biography in the lyrical mode. (Biography can be said to exist in the epic mode, with the writer acting as mediator between his subject and his audience.) It is frequently lyrical in a very special sense, however, for the writer, though he is writing about himself, may see himself almost as another person, so that the lyrical borders on the epic, though it never quite becomes that. He may be amused with himself, angry with himself, skeptical of himself. It is clear that one may have a perspective even when one is observing his own person. The locus of an autobiography is thus a highly complicated thing; it exists partly in the present, partly in the past—as an event and as the memory of an event. This puts the interpreter in a very different position from the position in reading a biography, play, or lyrical poem. In this sense, Joyce's "Araby" is an autobiography of the narrator and is lyrical in mode. Can you describe how this complication in locus might affect the tensions within the piece and within the reader seeking to embody the piece?

The autobiography leads us to a consideration of other forms of personal documents. We will now consider the question we raised with respect to the essay.

Journals, Letters, Diaries

The journal is a daily record of events in the life of the writer of the journal (compare the word *diurnal*). The journal is to the diary what annals are to history; as simply a record, it may lack a point of view and "feelings." But the two forms merge, and we shall not make any attempt here to keep them separate.

The diary is also a written record of events in the daily life of men or women. The entries may be daily, weekly, or completely unsystematic with regard to time. They are, in effect, the writers talking to themselves, though it is not uncommon for people to recognize that they may be writing for publication at some later date—and hence to exercise caution in what they set down. Diaries are often exceedingly frank and intimate—sometimes too intimate for reading in public.

The letter is likewise personal in its concern, but it always involves a recipient as well as a writer, and the character of the writer often seems to change as he writes first to one person and then to another. The letter of a poet writing to his publisher for an advance on royalties is likely to be very different in tone and perspective from a letter to his wife—just as a letter to his wife when he is happy and contented is very different in character from a letter to her when he is sick or angry. In some ways, a collection of all the letters a man ever wrote would show us his various selves better than his own autobiography could.

The so-called golden age of English letter writing was between 1750 and 1850. Many of the letters of that period are highly literary. With the coming of the telephone, quick transportation, and the telegram, many of us seem to have lost the art of letter writing—or at least to have lost interest and time for it. But audiences respond quickly to interesting letters, and richly entertaining evenings have been built upon such correspondence as that between Bernard Shaw and Mrs. Patrick Campbell, or Shaw and Ellen Terry, or Mr. and Mrs. Thomas Carlyle, or Samuel Johnson and Mrs. Piozzi, or D. H. Lawrence and his friends. Indeed, a correspondence between two lively writers often develops a story and can be arranged to produce a kind of play, as was recently done with the Shaw–Campbell letters. It would be an interesting project to take the letters of a single well-known figure (D. H. Lawrence, for example), cast separate readers for Lawrence and each of the recipients, and perform the various dialogues to show the many sides of Lawrence.

This brings us squarely to the problem we have been postponing. In reading personal documents, what obligation (if any) does the reader have to the historical personage writing the documents? In reading a letter written by Keats, does the reader imagine himself to be Keats? Does he try to dress as Keats might dress? Make himself up to look like Keats? In reading a letter by an Irishman, does he employ an Irish dialect? In reading a letter by a Black, does he appear in blackface? In reading a letter by a lame writer, will he appear to be lame? Will only a woman read a letter by Elizabeth Barrett Browning? It is possible to argue that there are at least two ways of looking at the answers to the questions.

There are related problems. In a performance of Gertrude Stein's short story *Melanctha,* in which a separate reader was being used as the narrator, the director thought for a long time about the person of the narrator. In the text of the story the narrator is nameless; nevertheless, the style of the story is pure Gertrude Stein, and it is almost impossible to imagine anyone else's having written it. The director raised the question whether it might not be a good idea to have the person who was to read the narration do so in the person of Miss Stein—in costume and makeup, since the story was being staged. Some of his colleagues felt that it would be worth trying; others were firmly opposed to the notion, arguing that since the story itself did not identify the narrator as Miss Stein the performance ought not to.

Again, in his performance of fiction by Charles Dickens, the actor Emlyn Williams took great pains to make himself up to look like Dickens, and used a replica of the reading desk actually used by Dickens. Dickens the writer thus became the narrator of each of his writings, in his "own" person.

The truth seems to be that there *is* no one answer to the questions we have raised. It is quite clear that a performance of *Melanctha* with Gertrude Stein as the narrator is not the same thing, in its effect, as a performance in which the narrator is nameless and unknown apart from the handling of the narration. Nor was the effect of Emlyn Williams's reading as Dickens the same as the effect would have been had Williams read in his own person. A letter read in the person of Keats will not be the same in its effect as the same letter read in the person of the reader. The locus shifts as the character of the reader shifts.

But Miss Stein's narration is characteristically Stein, Dickens's narration is characteristically Dickens, Keats's style is characteristically Keats. We would not want Dreiser to read Miss Stein's narration or Sinclair Lewis to read Dickens's narration or Dorothy Wordsworth to read Keats's.

Wouldn't we?

Perhaps we had better say that we would not want Dreiser to read Stein as if he were Dreiser or Lewis to read Dickens as if he were Lewis or Dorothy Wordsworth to read Keats as if she were Dorothy Wordsworth. But Drieser *is* Dreiser, isn't he? Lewis *is* Lewis, isn't he? Dorothy Wordsworth *is* Dorothy Wordsworth, isn't she?

This is really almost where we began. When Dreiser reads the narration in Dickens's writings, he must so accommodate himself to Dickens's style that he will not seem simply to be Dreiser. Lewis must not appear simply to be Lewis. Dorothy Wordsworth must not appear simply to be Dorothy Wordsworth. It is not that the reader turns into someone else—except metaphorically. And metaphorically he does. When Dreiser speaks the words of Dickens, if he really speaks them on their own terms, he is not being simply Dreiser, because Dreiser does not sound like Dickens. If, to the best of his ability, he tries to give body to the text of Dickens—and if he mangaes to keep our attention on that text—he will not seem to us simply to be Dreiser. He will be a particularization of the text of Dickens—a particularization which, because it is made up of a coalescence of two separate and distinct personalities, can never be duplicated. He will not be identical with Dickens reading Dickens or with anyone else reading Dickens. Ten readers may be equally good in reading Dickens, but they will not be the same.

The question for us now is this: Is Dickens reading Dickens necessarily the best way to read Dickens? Is the *man* Dickens identical with the *writer* Dickens? Is the writer identical with the nameless narrator in the work of fiction? Surely it is worthwhile to hear Dickens read Dickens—just as it was worthwhile to hear Auden read Auden, though many people think Auden read his own poems badly. Something in the reading by the author himself has value and cannot quite be duplicated. But the work of literature, we have argued constantly, has a life of its own; it is not tied to its creator any more than the child is tied to its mother once the umbilical cord has been cut. (Notice that we do not deny some relationship between the two. We simply deny identity.)

When we listen to a letter by Keats, it is possible to be interested solely or primarily in Keats himself. In that case, something is to be said for hearing the letter read by Keats in his own person. Lacking that, something is to be said for hearing the letter read by an actor playing the role of Keats. (The actor may read the letter more effectively; Keats might well be inhibited in a public reading.) Why do we say an actor rather than a reader? Simply because role playing, in costume, with prewritten dialogue is what we generally mean by acting.

What is the difference between actor and reader, then, since we have also said that the reader must embody the text? Probably this: *the locus of the text is not the same for the reader and the actor.* The actor keeps our mind on the visible character of the speaker; that is his job. The relationship between writer and audience, with the actor, is lyrical; the actor reading Keats's letter is Keats, insofar as he is able to be Keats. The relationship between writer and audience with the interpreter, on the other hand, is dramatic; the interpreter reading Keats's letter tries to disappear into the life of the letter itself. Doubtless it is puzzling to use the terms *lyrical* and *dramatic* with respect to the performer here, rather than with respect to the writer (as Aristotle used them). And it is even more puzzling to call the mode of the interpreter dramatic and the mode of the actor lyrical—but, alas, that is the way it seems. Mode and locus are related matters in this sense.

If what we have been saying is true, the interpreter does not read the letter of Keats in the person of Keats any more than he reads it in his own person. The style may be the inner man; it is not the outer man. He does read it in the *style* of Keats, which is another matter. The actor, however, reads it in the *person* of Keats. Quite likely, the art of the actor is in this respect considerably more complicated than the art of the interpreter—not therefore more valuable but simply more complicated and hence different. There are excellent interpreters who are not excellent actors; probably there is not an excellent actor who cannot learn to be an excellent reader. But when he interprets, he is not doing precisely the same thing as when he acts. The locus of the one art is not the locus of the other art; the appeal of the one art is not the appeal of the other art; the economy of the one art is not the economy of the other art.

What is to be said, then, of performances of letters, diaries, journals, and autobiographies in the person of the writers? This, at least: they have their own value, interest, and appeal. Should classes in acting deal with personal documents and not simply with plays, then? Why not?

In practice, classes in acting have enough to do with the scripts of plays, and other forms of literature are likely to be left to classes in interpretation. Furthermore, the training interpreters receive in attempting the acting of such characters will stand them in good stead in their reading of fiction and drama—even in their reading of poetry, since all these forms demand characterization. Notice that we have been careful not to say that the interpreter does not characterize. He does characterize when the text he is reading makes characterization explicit (as the dramatist makes it explicit); but he does no service to a novel if he makes an explicitly defined person of a narrator whom the novelist has deliberately chosen to leave impersonal or obscure. Biographical interest in Keats may cause the performer to present a letter of Keats in the person of Keats. But literary interest will probably cause the performer to present a letter of Keats as an interpreter—as an embodiment of the letter rather than of Keats. Both interests are worthwhile; each differs from the other. The eye of the actor is on the question, Who is speaking? The ear of the interpreter is on the question, What is being said? But the actor also has an ear and the interpreter has an eye—and the audience likewise has both. It will never do, therefore, to say that interpreters can simply be heard but actors must also be seen. The eye is not the ear and the ear is not the eye, but both organs are involved in the process of communication.

There is an abundance of literature devoted to travel. Some of it overlaps other kinds we have been discussing: diaries, letters, essays, even novels. Such literature offers the interpreter an interesting study in perspectives; it may be written from the point of view of a tourist, an anthropologist, a political analyst, a missionary, or a businessman—the possibilities are almost endless. There are fascinating studies of lands far from home and of the homeland itself. In many countries it would be possible to prepare a program of readings about various views of the country, a kind of kaleidoscope in words. Such a program might be combined with readings from history, anthropology, or pure literature— or with slide projections, music, or dance. The range of possible programs involving interpretation is limited only by the imagination of the interpreter.

The Literature of Travel

The purpose of this chapter has been to suggest materials that the interpreter might not readily associate with earlier discussions. Still other forms might be considered—sacred literature, for example: biblical and liturgical pieces, which many interpreters will surely find occasion to read. But, on the whole, the principles and elements already discussed will serve the reader for both pure and transitional forms of literature and we need not extend the list of types any further. In the practice materials that follow, you may find it of interest to see which pieces seem to you most literary and to try to describe why.

MATERIALS FOR PRACTICE

The selections below cannot possibly indicate the wide range of materials embraced by this chapter. Nevertheless, they may prove of interest in your examination of locus, perspective, and tensiveness, and in your study of structure.

AESOP'S FABLES

[*Aesop's* Fables *may or may not be regarded as children's literature. What difference does one's perspective make in the oral performance of a fable?*—Ed.]

1. *A Lion and a Mouse*

A mouse one day happened to run across the paws of a sleeping Lion and wakened him. The Lion, angry at being disturbed, grabbed the Mouse, and was about to swallow him, when the Mouse cried out, "Please, kind Sir, I didn't mean it; if you will let me go, I shall always be grateful; and, perhaps, I can help you some day." The idea that such a little thing as a Mouse could help him so amused the Lion that he let the Mouse go. A week later, the Mouse heard a Lion roaring loudly. He went closer to see what the trouble was and found his Lion caught in a hunter's net. Remembering his promise, the Mouse began to gnaw the ropes of the net and kept it up until the Lion could get free. The Lion then acknowledged that little friends might prove great friends.

2. *Belling the Cat*

One time the Mice were greatly bothered by a Cat; therefore, they decided to hold a meeting to talk over what could be done about the matter. During the meeting, a Young Mouse arose and suggested that a bell be put upon the Cat so that they could hear him coming. The suggestion was received with great applause, when an Old Mouse arose to speak. "That's all right," he said, "but who of us would dare to hang a bell around the Cat's neck?" Seeing their looks of fear, he added, "You know it is often much easier to suggest a plan than to carry it out."

THE NEW VESTMENTS[2]
—Edward Lear

There lived an old man in the Kingdom of Tess,
Who invented a purely original dress;
And when it was perfectly made and complete,
He opened the door, and walked into the street.

By way of a hat, he'd a loaf of Brown Bread,
In the middle of which he inserted his head;—
His Shirt was made up of no end of dead Mice,
The warmth of whose skins was quite fluffy and nice;—
His Drawers were of Rabbit-skins;—so were his Shoes;—
His Stockings were skins,—but it is not known whose;—
His Waistcoat and Trowsers were made of Pork Chops;—
His Buttons were Jujubes, and Chocolate Drops;—

[2] From *The Complete Nonsense of Edward Lear*, edited by Holbrook Jackson (New York: Dover Publications, 1951).

His Coat was all Pancakes with Jam for a border,
And a girdle of Biscuits to keep it in order;
And he wore over all, as a screen from bad weather,
A cloak of green Cabbage-leaves stitched all together.

He had walked a short way, when he heard a great noise,
Of all sorts of Beasticles, Birdlings, and Boys;—
And from every long street and dark lane in the town
Beasts, Birdles, and Boys in a tumult rushed down.
Two Cows and a half ate his Cabbage-leaf Cloak;—
Four Apes seized his Girdle, which vanished like smoke;—
Three Kids ate up half of his Pancaky Coat,—
And the tails were devour'd by an ancient He Goat;—
An army of Dogs in a twinkling tore *up* his
Pork Waistcoat and Trowsers to give to their Puppies;—
And while they were growling, and mumbling the Chops,
Ten Boys prigged the Jujubes and Chocolate Drops.—
He tried to run back to his house, but in vain,
For Scores of fat Pigs came again and again;—
They rushed out of stables and hovels and doors,—
They tore off his stockings, his shoes, and his drawers;—
And now from the housetops with screechings descend,
Striped, spotted, white, black, and gray Cats without end,
They jumped on his shoulders and knocked off his hat,—
When Crows, Ducks, and Hens made a mincemeat of that;—
They speedily flew at his sleeves in a trice,
And utterly tore up his Shirt of dead Mice;—
They swallowed the last of his Shirt with a squall,—
Whereon he ran home with no clothes on at all.

And he said to himself as he bolted the door,
"I will not wear a similar dress any more,
"Any more, any more, any more, never more!"

from MY MOTHER'S HOUSE AND SIDO
—Colette (trans. by Enid McLeod)

Behold me then . . .[3]

Alone! Really, one might think I was pitying myself for it!

"If you live all alone," said Brague, "it's because you really want to, isn't it?"

Certainly I "really" want to, and in fact I *want* to, quite simply. Only, well . . . there are days when solitude, for someone my age, is a heady wine that intoxicates you with freedom, others when it is a bitter tonic, and still others when it is a poison that makes you beat your head against the wall.

[3] From *Earthly Paradise*, Colette's autobiography drawn from her writings by Robert Phelps. Extracted from *My Mother's House and Sido* by Colette, translated by Enid McLeod; copyright 1953 by Farrar, Straus & Young (now Farrar, Straus & Giroux, Inc.). Reprinted by permission of Farrar, Straus & Giroux, Inc., and Martin Secker & Warburg Ltd.

This evening I would much prefer not to say which it is; all I want is to remain undecided, and not to be able to say whether the shiver that will seize me when I slip between the cold sheets comes from fear or contentment.

Alone . . . and for a long time past. The proof is that I am giving way to the habit of talking to myself and of holding conversations with my dog, and the fire, and my own reflection. It is an idiosyncrasy which recluses and old prisoners fall into; but I'm not like them, I'm free. And if I talk to myself it is because I have a writer's need to express my thoughts in rhythmical language.

Facing me from the other side of the looking glass, in that mysterious reflected room, is the image of "a woman of letters who has turned out badly." They also say of me that I'm "on the stage," but they never call me an actress. Why? The nuance is subtle, but there is certainly a polite refusal, on the part both of the public and of my friends themselves, to accord me any standing in this career which I have nevertheless adopted. A woman of letters who has turned out badly: that is what I must remain for everyone, I who no longer write, who deny myself the pleasure, the luxury of writing.

To write, to be able to write, what does it mean? It means spending long hours dreaming before a white page, scribbling unconsciously, letting your pen play around a blot of ink and nibble at a half-formed word, scratching it, making it bristle with darts, and adorning it with antennae and paws until it loses all resemblance to a legible word and turns into a fantastic insect or a fluttering creature half butterfly, half fairy.

To write is to sit and stare, hypnotized, at the reflection of the window in the silver inkstand, to feel the divine fever mounting to one's cheeks and forehead while the hand that writes grows blissfully numb upon the paper. It also means idle hours curled up in the hollow of the divan, and then the orgy of inspiration from which one emerges stupefied and aching all over, but already recompensed and laden with treasures that one unloads slowly on to the virgin page in the little round pool of light under the lamp.

To write is to pour one's innermost self passionately upon the tempting paper, at such frantic speed that sometimes one's hand struggles and rebels, overdriven by the impatient god who guides it—and to find, next day, in place of the golden bough that bloomed miraculously in that dazzling hour, a withered bramble and a stunted flower.

To write is the joy and torment of the idle. Oh, to write! From time to time I feel a need, sharp as thirst in summer, to note and to describe. And then I take up my pen again and attempt the perilous and elusive task of seizing and pinning down, under its flexible double-pointed nib, the many-hued, fugitive, thrilling adjective . . . The attack does not last long; it is but the itching of an old scar.

It takes up too much time to write. And the trouble is, I am no Balzac! The fragile story I am constructing crumbles away when the tradesman rings, or the shoemaker sends in his bill, when the solicitor, or one's counsel, telephones, or when the theatrical agent summons me to his office for "a social engagement at the house of some people of very good position but not in the habit of paying large fees."

The problem is, since I have been living alone, that I have had first to live, then to divorce, and then to go on living. To do all that demands incredible activity and persistence. And to get where? Is there, for me, no other haven than this commonplace room? Must I stay forever before this impenetrable mirror where I come up against myself, face to face?

from **MY APPRENTICESHIP**
—*Colette (trans. by Helen Beauclerk)*

Winter months . . .[4]

Winter months, summer months. . . . How long it seemed for June to come around again when I was young! Winter months, drenched with rain and Sunday concerts, while I wilted and grew pale; summer months that restored me to life with the hope that they would last forever. It was Champagnolle in the Jura, I remember, that saved me for another spell—in 1896? 1897?—from the salamander stove, gloom, and resignation. At Champagnolle the inn cost five francs a day.

For five francs we were allowed a room disgraced by mildewed wallpaper, peeling off and dangling in liana-like strips, by two iron bedsteads and some nasty little curtains fit for wrapping up abortions. But from noon onward the common table was covered with crayfish, quails, hares, partridges, all poached in the neighborhood. The mountain streams ran between cyclamen and wild strawberries, and my cheeks grew fresh and pink again.

From Champagnolle we went to Lons-le-Saulnier to stay with my husband's family. Before my marriage I had never "lived in someone's house," as I always called it, and it took me a long time to break down the constraint that kept me, not from loving the people who welcomed us, but from yielding to the simple pleasure of letting them see me as I was. Fortunately, the children got the better of me. Three here, four there, not to mention the more distant offshoots of the same stock. They soon found out what I was worth as a maker of flutes, a weaver of grasses, a gatherer of berries. With them I recovered my lost childhood; I told them the names of plants, of stones, lit them a fire using the punt of a bottle as a burning glass, caught grass snakes and let them go again, drove the little horse Mignon with proper care and precision, sang the magic formula that bids the snail put out its horns. A chain of quiet, disciplined children closed about me. Were they fond of me? Wherever I went, they followed. I never let them know how beautifully behaved I thought them, how easy of manner, nimble of mind, and how astonished I felt when I considered the difference between their childhood and mine. I, who had been broken in to an outward show of obedience, was as much impressed by the smooth, prompt deference they

[4] From *Earthly Paradise*, Colette's autobiography drawn from her writings by Robert Phelps. Extracted from *My Apprienticeship* by Colette, translated by Helen Beauclerk; copyright © 1957 by Martin Secker & Warburg Ltd. Reprinted by permission of Farrar, Straus & Giroux, Inc., and Martin Secker & Warburg Ltd.

could always display as by their tidy, well-brushed curls, their clean nails, their smell of English soap, their habit of crooking their little finger when eating a boiled egg. The sound of their voices calling along the paths of the cool little mountain, the name they chose to give me, the pleasure I felt at their taking to me so simply—something of all this comes back when I hear the voice, over the telephone, of Paule, who is a doctor, or her sister, the musician, or their cousin, the interior decorator: "Aunt Colette, tell me, Aunt Colette . . ." The children's company was very sweet to me. My stains and bruises were only superficial, and I was still very young. Perhaps what I needed, without knowing it, was a child born of my own body.

It was on our return from one of these visits to the Franche-Comté that M. Willy decided to tidy his writing desk. At least I think so, for the memory is linked in my mind with a sense of mourning for a lost, russet September, sweet with bunches of small, sugary grapes and hard, yellow peaches whose hearts were a deep, blood-stained purple. The odious piece of furniture, hideous in its red baize cover and sham ebony paint, was turned out; the whitewood drawers appeared, disgorging a compressed mass of papers; and there came to light the forgotten set of copybooks I had so industriously blackened: *Claudine à l'ecole.*

"Hello!" said M. Willy. "I thought I had chucked those away."

He opened one of the copybooks, turned the pages:

"It's rather nice."

He opened a second copybook and said no more. A third, a fourth.

"My God!" he muttered. "I am the bloodiest fool."

He swept up the scattered copybooks just as they were, grabbed his flat-brimmed top hat, and bolted to his publisher's. And that is how I became a writer.

from THE VAGABOND
—Colette (trans. by Enid McLeod)

My half-sister . . . [5]

My half-sister, the eldest of us all—the stranger in our midst—got engaged just when she seemed about to become an old maid. Plain though she was, with her Tibetan eyes she was not unpleasing. My mother did not dare to prevent this unfortunate marriage, but at least she made no secret of what she thought about it. From the rue de la Roche to Gerbaude, and from Bel-Air to Le Grand-Jeu, the talk was all of my sister's marriage.

"Is Juliette getting married?" a neighbor would ask my mother. "That's an event!"

"No, an accident," corrected Sido.

[5] From *Earthly Paradise,* Colette's autobiography drawn from her writings by Robert Phelps. Extracted from *The Vagabond* by Colette, translated by Enid McLeod; copyright © 1955 by Farrar, Straus & Young (now Farrar, Straus & Giroux, Inc.). Reprinted by permission of Farrar, Straus & Giroux, Inc., and Martin Secker & Warburg Ltd.

A few ventured acidly: "So Juliette's getting married at last! How unexpected! It almost seemed hopeless!"

"I should rather say desperate," retorted Sido, belligerently. "But there's no holding a girl of twenty-five."

"And who is she marrying?"

"Oh, some wretched upstart or other."

At heart she was full of pity for her lonely daughter, who spent her days in a fever of reading, her head stuffed with dreams. My brothers considered the "event" entirely from their own detached point of view. A year of medical studies in Paris had by no means tamed the elder; magnificent and aloof, he resented the glances of such women as he did not desire. The words "bridal train," "dress clothes," "wedding breakfast," "procession" fell on the two savages like drops of boiling pitch.

"I won't go to the wedding!" protested the younger, his eyes pale with indignation under his hair cropped close as a convict's, as usual. "I won't offer anyone my arm! I won't wear tails!"

"But you're your sister's best man," my mother pointed out to him.

"Well then, all she's got to do is not to marry! And for what she's marrying! A fellow who stinks of vermouth! Besides, she's always got along without us, so I can't see why she needs us to help her get married!"

Our handsome elder brother was less vocal, but we recognized that look on his face that he always wore when he was planning to leap over a wall and was measuring the obstacles. There were difficult days and recriminations which my father, full of anxiety himself and eager to avoid the malodorous intruder, was unable to quell. Then all at once the two boys appeared to agree to everything. Better still, they suggested that they themselves should organize a choral Mass, and Sido was so delighted that for a few hours she forgot her "upstart" of a son-in-law.

Our Aucher piano was carted along to the church and mingled its sweet but slightly tinny tone with the bleating of the harmonium. Bolting themselves in the empty church, the savages rehearsed the Suite from *L'Arlésienne*, something of Stradella's, and a piece by Saint-Saëns especially arranged for the nuptial ceremony.

Only when it was too late did my mother realize that her sons, each chained to his keyboard as a performer, would not appear for more than a moment at their sister's side. They played, I remember, like angel musicians, making the village Mass, and the bare church, which lacked even a belfry, radiant with music. I swaggered about, very proud of my eleven years, my long locks that made me look like a little Eve, and my pink dress, highly delighted with everything except when I looked at my sister. Very small and pale, weighed down with white silk and tulle and trembling with nervous weakness, she was gazing up at that unknown man with a swooning look of such submission on her strange, Mongolian face that the sight filled me with shame.

The violins for dancing put an end to the long meal, and at the mere sound of them the two boys quivered like wild horses. The younger, slightly tipsy, stayed where he was. But the elder, unable to bear any more, disappeared. Jumping over the wall of the rue des Vignes, he got into our garden, wandered around the closed house, broke a windowpane, and went to bed, where my mother found him when she returned, sad and weary, after handing her bewildered and trembling daughter over to the care of a man.

Long afterward she described to me that dust-gray, early dawn of summer, her empty house that felt as though it had been pillaged, her joyless fatigue, her dress with its beaded front, and the uneasy cats summoned home by her voice and the night. She told me how she had found her elder boy asleep, his arms folded on his breast, and how his fresh mouth and closed eyes, his whole body was eloquent of that sternness of his, the sternness of the pure savage.

"Just think of it, it was so that he could be alone, far from those sweating people, and sleep caressed by the night wind, that he broke the windowpane. Was there ever a child so wise?"

I have seen him, that wise one, vault through a window on a hundred occasions, as though by a reflex action, every time there was a ring at the bell which he did not expect. When he was growing gray and prematurely aged by overwork, he could still recover the elasticity of his youth to leap into the garden, and his little girls would laugh to see him. Gradually his fits of misanthropy, although he struggled against them, turned his face haggard. Captive as he was, did he perhaps find his prison yard daily more confined, and remember those escapes which once upon a time used to lead him to a childish bed where he slept half naked, chaste, and voluptuously alone?

from **DIVISION STREET: AMERICA**[6]
—*Studs Terkel*

Jan Powers, 24

She's on the staff of a magazine, popular with cool young men. Her job pays well and it's easy. She comes from a working-class family, and occasionally sees her mother and two younger brothers. She has an apartment of her own in a new high-rent high-rise on the Near North Side. She is engaged to Steven, a medical student.

I don't notice the world. I'm very bored. I really don't know how I feel. I'm nice and cordial but people sense something about me. I don't know, maybe I don't like them. Maybe I feel I'm above them. I can't think of anyone I love or respect. I can't be bothered with the news. I just can't get interested. I can't care less. I *should* care, it's terrible. (Laughs lightly.)

Vietnam? Isn't that a shame? (Laughs softly.) I saw a film on Vietnam, it showed the actual fighting. It looked ridiculous, just a bunch of kids. It was actually embarrassing to watch that, people were actually shooting and shouting. I saw Vietnam. I looked at a map once. I'm concerned with Vietnam if my brother has to go, otherwise, no.

My interest in life is me. It's a shame. I wish I could pick up a newspaper and read it. What I hear about things is heard from other people.

I hope I'll make it. I think it's marriage, to someone who is successful. Highland Park,* a couple of kids. I'm not too crazy about children, though. You're sitting in a room, and all of a sudden five kids'll come in and they'll go to another girl in the room. Same with dogs.

I'm worried about the next couple of years. Here I'm putting all this time and feeling into this relationship with Steve, and to have it not work out, it would be terrible. I don't know what I'd do. I'd probably find someone else and be just as happy.

Nothing touches me. I wonder why I don't care about these things. The Bomb doesn't bother me. I don't read the papers. There isn't much I can do about it, so I'm not worried. What is important now is my friend and me. The rest of the world can go.

If I were God, I'd make a world with a lot of me's in it. (Laughs.) No, no, I'd leave it the way it is. We have to have war, there's been wars through all the ages, apparently everyone gets enjoyment out of it. If we removed this part from man, it would be boring. Otherwise things would be sort of dull.

I love my building, I just love it. If I'm on a bus going to my mother's, I look at these people and get a nauseous feeling. On Michigan Avenue, I respect them more. Home gives me a sick feeling.

It's a shame Negroes don't like me and children don't like me and dogs don't run up to me.

Molly Rodriguez, 15

Mexican; one of eight children. She is seated on the sofa with her Anglo sister-in-law, seventeen-year-old Lorna, her brother Ernie's wife.

What do I do now? Nothing but laze around the house. That's all. My thoughts? Oh, my thoughts are a lot of things. Especially about school, and how it will be in the future. There won't hardly be any work because all the machines are taking over and you have to have a high-school education for this and ya have to have a college education for another thing. And that's just it, you ain't got it—well, you're just gonna sit there and just rot away.

Any hope? Oh, maybe that I get married and I find a boy that is not that smart, but at least he went to high school and he'll know what's happening and all that.

There's some colored people that are all right and there's some that are just no good. To me, they're like dirt. I just don't go for them. I'm actually *scared*. 'Cause you walk in their neighborhoods and what do they do? They throw rocks at you and all that. But then when they come walking

* An upper-middle-class suburb on the North Shore.

in ours, they just want you to sit there and do nothing about it. If it's that way, why do they do it to us? We can't go all over the world, because they're all over. I mean, we can't fly over them either.

What kind of world would I like to see? A world with all white people, no colored or nothing. That's all. I mean, I just put Mexicans and Italians and a couple of Irish people, that's all. I wouldn't put no colored people in there.

Frankie Rodriguez, 17

Molly's brother. He has been arrested several times; a dropout. In a parked car somewhere in the neighborhood, about one A.M.

Why should I worry about the world? I figure it this way: Who's gonna take care of you? Nobody! And you figure these people that don't wanna take care of you and you ain't got no education, what're you gonna do?

I wasn't learning nothing in this school, nothing at all. Just sit back, watch the teacher say something, and what not. He never asked me to say anything. He never told me to do nothing. Just as soon as the bell rings, go to another class. That was it. I even asked one teacher, "What's this?" You know. And he wouldn't even answer me. It was a drag.

What're you gonna do? You gonna be walkin' the street? So I figure like this: If I can't make money the right way, I'm sure gonna make it the wrong way. I'll be livin' in jail. (Half-laughs.) That's my home, that's my next home. Because look it, if I pull a job, I have it real nice, you know. If I get away with it. If I don't get away with it, I'm in jail.

What can I do in the street? I don't wanna be walkin' the street. Because you walk the street, and you see these young guys, like they wanna go bum-huntin'. Ha. They might just grab you one of these days and beat you up. So I figure like this: Why walk the street and look for your dimes and nickels and pennies on the sidewalk, when you can be robbin'. And if you rob and get away with it, you're lucky. But you can't be robbin' all your life, an' then don't get caught. So ya figure like this: You're gonna spend a couple of times in jail. But you ain't got no education, so that's it. It don't bother me. 'Cause I don't really care about the world, and the world don't care about me.

MOTHER TO SON[7]
—Langston Hughes

Well, son, I'll tell you,
Life for me ain't been no crystal stair.
It's had tacks in it.
And splinters,

CHILDREN'S LITERATURE AND NONFICTIVE FORMS   429

And boards torn up,
And places with no carpet on the floor—
Bare.
But all the time
I'se been a-climbin' on,
And reachin' landin's,
And turnin' corners,
And sometimes goin' in the dark
Where there ain't been no light.
So, boy, don't you turn back.
Don't you set down on the steps
'Cause you finds it kinder hard.
Don't you fall now—
For I'se still goin', honey,
I'se still climbin',
And life for me ain't been no crystal stair.

"TIN LIZZIE" from *U.S.A.*[8]
—*John Dos Passos*

"Mr. Ford the automobileer," the featurewriter wrote in 1900,

Mr. Ford the automobileer began by giving his steed three or four sharp jerks with the lever at the righthand side of the seat; that is, he pulled the lever up and down sharply in order, as he said, to mix air with gasoline and drive the charge into the exploding cylinder. . . . Mr. Ford slipped a small electric switch handle and there followed a puff, puff, puff. . . . The puffing of the machine assumed a higher key. She was flying along about eight miles an hour. The ruts in the road were deep, but the machine certainly went with a dreamlike smoothness. There was none of the bumping common even to a streetcar. . . . By this time the boulevard had been reached, and the automobileer, letting a lever fall a little, let her out. Whiz! She picked up speed with infinite rapidity. As she ran on there was a clattering behind, the new noise of the automobile."

For twenty years or more,

ever since he'd left his father's farm when he was sixteen to get a job in a Detroit machineshop, Henry had been nuts about machinery. First it was watches, then he designed a streamtractor, then he built a horseless carriage with an engine adapted from the Otto gasengine he'd read about in *The World of Science,* then a mechanical buggy with a onecylinder fourcycle motor, that would run forward but not back;

at last, ninetyeight, he felt he was far enough along to risk throwing up his job with the Detroit Edison Company, where he'd worked his way up from night fireman to chief engineer, to put all his time into working on a new gasoline engine, (in the late eighties he'd met Edison at a meeting of electric-light employees in Atlantic City. He'd gone up to Edison after Edison had delivered an address and asked him if he thought gasoline was practical as a motor fuel. Edison had said yes. If Edison said it, it was true. Edison was the great admiration of Henry Ford's Life);

and in driving his mechanical buggy, sitting there at the lever jauntily dressed in a tightbuttoned jacket and a high collar and a derby hat, back and forth over the level illpaved streets of Detroit,

scaring the big brewery horses and the skinny trotting horses and the sleekrumped pacers with the motor's loud explosions,

looking for men scatterbrained enough to invest money in a factory for building automobiles.

He was the eldest son of an Irish immigrant who during the Civil War had married the daughter of a prosperous Pennsylvania Dutch-farmer and settled down to farming near Dearborn in Wayne County, Michigan;

like plenty of other Americans, young Henry grew up hating the endless sogging through the mud about the chores, the hauling and pitching manure, the kerosene lamps to clean, the irk and sweat and solitude of the farm.

He was a slender, active youngster, a good skater, clever with his hands; what he liked was to tend the machinery and let the others do the heavy work. His mother had told him not to drink, smoke, gamble or go into debt, and he never did.

When he was in his early twenties his father tried to get him back from Detroit, where he was working as mechanic and repairman for the Drydock Engine Company that built engines for steamboats, by giving him forty acres of land.

Young Henry built himself an uptodate square white dwellinghouse with a false mansard roof and married and settled down on the farm,

but he let the hired men do the farming;

he bought himself a buzzsaw and rented a stationary engine and cut the timber off the woodlots.

He was a thrifty young man who never drank or smoked or gambled or coveted his neighbor's wife, but he couldn't stand living on a farm.

He moved to Detroit, and in the brick barn behind his house tinkered for years in his spare time with a mechanical buggy that would be light enough to run over the clayey wagonroads of Wayne County, Michigan.

By 1900 he had a practicable car to promote.

He was forty years old before the Ford Motor Company was started and production began to move.

Speed was the first thing the early automobile manufacturers went after. Races advertised the makes of cars.

Henry Ford himself hung up several records at the track at Grosse Pointe and on the ice on Lake St. Clair. In his 999 he did the mile in thirtynine and fourfifths seconds.

But it had always been his custom to hire others to do the heavy work. The speed he was busy with was speed in production, the records in efficient output. He hired Barney Oldfield, a stunt bicyclerider from Salt Lake City, to do the racing for him.

      Henry Ford had ideas about other things than the designing of motors, carburetors, magnetos, jigs and fixtures, punches and dies; he had ideas about sales,

      that the big money was in economical quantity production, quick turn-over, cheap interchangeable easily-replaced standardized parts;

      it wasn't until 1909, after years of arguing with his partners, that Ford put out the first Model T.

      Henry Ford was right.

      That season he sold more than ten thousand tin lizzies, ten years later he was selling almost a million a year.

      In these years the Taylor Plan was stirring up plantmanagers and manufacturers all over the country. Efficiency was the word. The same ingenuity that went into improving the performance of a machine could go into improving the performance of the workmen improving the machine.

      In 1913 they established the assemblyline at Ford's. That season the profits were something like twentyfive million dollars, but they had trouble in keeping the men on the job, machinists didn't seem to like it at Ford's.

      Henry Ford had ideas about other things than production.

      He was the largest automobile manufacturer in the world; he paid high wages; maybe if the steady workers thought they were getting a cut (a very small cut) in the profits, it would give trained men an inducement to stick to their jobs,

      wellpaid workers might save enough to buy a tin lizzie; the first day Ford's announced that cleancut properlymarried American workers who wanted jobs had a chance to make five bucks a day (of course it turned out that there were strings to it; always there were string to it)

      such an enormous crowd waited outside the Highland Park plant

      all through the zero January night

      that there was a riot when the gates were opened; cops broke heads, job-hunters threw bricks; property, Henry Ford's own property, was destroyed. The company dicks had to turn on the fire hose to beat back the crowd.

      The American Plan; automotive prosperity seeping down from above; it turned out there were strings to it.

      But that five dollars a day

      paid to good, clean American workmen

      who didn't drink or smoke cigarettes or read or think,

      and who didn't commit adultery

      and whose wives didn't take in boarders,

      made America once more the Yukon of the sweated workers of the world;

made all the tin lizzies and the automotive age, and incidentally,
    made Henry Ford the automobileer, the admirer of Edison, the bird-
lover,
    the great American of his time.

But Henry Ford had ideas about other things besides assemblylines
and the livinghabits of his employees. He was full of ideas. Instead of going
to the city to make his fortune, here was a country boy who'd made his
fortune by bringing the city out to the farm. The precepts he'd learned out
of McGuffey's Reader, his mother's prejudices and preconceptions, he had
preserved clean and unworn as freshprinted bills in the safe in a bank.

He wanted people to know about his ideas, so he bought the *Dearborn
Independent* and started a campaign against cigarettesmoking.

When war broke out in Europe, he had ideas about that too. (Suspicion of armymen and soldiering were part of the midwest farm tradition,
like thrift, stickativeness, temperance and sharp practice in money matters.)
Any intelligent American mechanic could see that if the Europeans hadn't
been a lot of ignorant underpaid foreigners who drank, smoked, were loose
about women and wasteful in their methods of production, the war could
never have happened.

When Rosika Schwimmer broke through the stockade of secretaries
and servicemen who surrounded Henry Ford and suggested to him he could
stop the war,
    he said sure they'd hire a ship and go over and get the boys out of the
trenches by Christmas.

He hired a steamboat, the *Oscar II*, and filled it up with pacifists and
social workers,
    to go over to explain to the princelings of Europe
    that what they were doing was vicious and silly.

It wasn't his fault that Poor Richard's commonsense no longer rules
the world and that most of the pacifists were nuts,
    goofy with headlines.

When William Jennings Bryan went over to Hoboken to see him off,
somebody handed William Jennings Bryan a squirrel in a cage; William
Jennings Bryan made a speech with the squirrel under his arm. Henry Ford
threw American Beauty roses to the crowd. The band played *I Didn't Raise
My Boy to Be a Soldier*. Practical jokers let loose more squirrels. An eloping
couple was married by a platoon of ministers in the saloon, and Mr. Zero,
the flophouse humanitarian, who reached the dock too late to sail,
    dove into the North River and swam after the boat.

The *Oscar II* was described as a floating Chautauqua; Henry Ford said
it felt like a middlewestern village, but by the time they reached Chris-
tiansand in Norway, the reporters had kidded him so that he had gotten cold
feet and gone to bed. The world was too crazy outside of Wayne County,
Michigan. Mrs. Ford and the management sent an Episcopal dean after him
who brought him home under wraps,
    and the pacifists had to speechify without him.

Two years later Ford's was manufacturing munitions, Eagle boats; Henry Ford was planning oneman tanks, and oneman submarines like the one tried out in the Revolutionary War. He announced to the press that he'd turn over his war profits to the government,
> but there's no record that he ever did.

One thing he brought back from his trip
was the Protocols of the Elders of Zion.
He started a campaign to enlighten the world in the *Dearborn Independent;* the Jews were why the world wasn't like Wayne County, Michigan, in the old horse and buggy days;
> the Jews had started the war, Bolshevism, Darwinism, Marxism, Nietzsche, short skirts and lipstick. They were behind Wall Street and the international bankers, and the whiteslave traffic and the movies and the Supreme Court and ragtime and the illegal liquor business.

Henry Ford denounced the Jews and ran for senator and sued the *Chicago Tribune* for libel,
> and was the laughingstock of the kept metropolitan press;
> but when the metropolitan bankers tried to horn in on his business he thoroughly outsmarted them.

In 1918 he had borowed on notes to buy out his minority stockholders for the picayune sum of seventyfive million dollars.
In February, 1920, he needed cash to pay off some of these notes that were coming due. A banker is supposed to have called on him and offered him every facility if the bankers' representative could be made a member of the board of directors. Henry Ford handed the banker his hat,
> and went about raising the money in his own way:
> he shipped every car and part he had in his plant to his dealers and demanded immediate cash payment. Let the other fellow do the borrowing had always been a cardinal principle. He shut down production and cancelled all orders from the supplyfirms. Many dealers were ruined, many supplyfirms failed, but when he reopened his plant,
> he owned it absolutely,
> the way a man owns an unmortgaged farm with the
> taxes paid up.

In 1922 there started the Ford boom for President (high wages, waterpower, industry scattered to the small towns) that was skillfully pricked behind the scenes
> by another crackerbarrel philosopher,
> Calvin Coolidge;
> but in 1922 Henry Ford sold one million three hundred and thirtytwo thousand two hundred and nine tin lizzies; he was the richest man in the world.

Good roads had followed the narrow ruts made in the mud by the Model T. The great automotive boom was on. At Ford's production was improving all the time; less waste, more spotters, strawbosses, stoolpigeons (fifteen minutes for lunch, three minutes to go to the toilet, the Taylorized speedup everywhere, reach under, adjust washer, screw down bolt, shove in cotterpin, reachunder adjustwasher, screwdown bolt, reachunderadjustscrewdownreachunderadjust until every ounce of life was sucked off into production and at night the workmen went home gray shaking husks).

Ford owned every detail of the process from the ore in the hills until the car rolled off the end of the assemblyline under its own power, the plants were rationalized to the last tenthousandth of an inch as measured by the Johansen scale;

in 1926 the production cycle was reduced to eightyone hours from the ore in the mine to the finished salable car proceeding under its own power,

but the Model T was obsolete.

New Era prosperity and the American Plan
(there were strings to it, always there were strings to it)
had killed Tin Lizzie.
Ford's was just one of many automobile plants.
When the stockmarket bubble burst,
Mr. Ford the crackerbarrel philosopher said jubilantly,
"I told you so.
Serves you right for gambling and getting in debt.
The country is sound."
But when the country on cracked shoes, in frayed trousers, belts tightened over hollow bellies,
idle hands cracked and chapped with the cold of that coldest March day of 1932,
started marching from Detroit to Dearborn, asking for work and the American plan, all they could think of at Ford's was machineguns.
The country was sound, but they mowed the marchers down.
They shot four of them dead.

Henry as an old man
is a passionate antiquarian,
(lives besieged on his father's farm embedded in an estate of thousands of millionaire acres, protected by an army of servicemen, secretaries, secret agents, dicks under orders of an English exprizefighter,
always afraid of the feet in broken shoes on the roads, afraid the gangs will kidnap his grandchildren,
that a crank will shoot him,
that Change and the idle hands out of work will break through the gates and the high fences;
protected by a private army against
the new American of starved children and hollow bellies and cracked shoes stamping on souplines,
that has swallowed up the old thrifty farmlands
of Wayne County, Michigan
as if they had never been).
Henry Ford as an old man
is a passionate antiquarian.

He rebuilt his father's farmhouse and put it back exactly in the state he remembered it in as a boy. He built a village of museums for buggies, sleighs, coaches, old plows, waterwheels, obsolete models of motorcars. He scoured the country for fiddlers to play oldfashioned squaredances.

Even old taverns he bought and put back into their original shape, as well as Thomas Edison's early laboratories.

When he bought the Wayside Inn near Sudbury, Massachusetts, he had the new highway where the newmodel cars roared and slithered and hissed oilily past (the new noise of the automobile),

moved away from the door,
put back the old bad road,
so that everything might be
the way it used to be,
in the days of horses and buggies.

from THE LETTERS OF MARY WORTLEY MONTAGU

[*Lady Mary Wortley Montagu died in 1762 at the age of seventy-three, a favorite of princes and poets. Her father was Lord Kingston; her husband, Edward Wortley Montagu. It is said that Lady Mary quarreled with her husband, very possibly deceived him, but that to the end of her life he remained the man whom she most esteemed. In 1739 she left England for more than twenty years. She never saw her husband again. But in 1710, the date of this letter, she and Mr. Wortley Montagu are not yet married. Ed.*]

[April 25, 1710]

To Mr. Wortley Montagu

I have this minute received your two letters. I know not how to direct to you, whether to London or the country; or, if in the country, to Durham or Wortley. 'T is very likely you'll never receive this. I hazard a great deal if it fall into other hands, and I write for all that. I wish with all my soul I thought as you do; I endeavor to convince myself by your arguments, and am sorry my reason is so obstinate not to be deluded into an opinion that 't is impossible a man can esteem a woman. I suppose I should then be very easy at your thoughts of me; I should thank you for the wit and beauty you give me, and not be angry at the follies and weaknesses; but to my infinite affliction I can believe neither one nor t' other so bad as you fancy it. Should we ever live together, you would be disappointed both ways; you would find an easy equality of temper you do not expect and a thousand faults you do not imagine. You think if you married me, I should be passionately fond of you one month, and of somebody else the next; neither would happen. I can esteem, I can be a friend, but I don't know whether I can love. Expect all that is complaisant and easy but never what is fond in me. You judge very wrong of my heart when you suppose me capable of views of interest, and that anything could oblige me to flatter anybody. Was I the most indigent creature in the world, I should answer you as I do now without adding or diminishing. I am incapable of art, and 't is because I will not be capable of it. Could I deceive one minute, I should never regain my own good opinion; and who could bear to live with one they despised? . . .

If you can resolve to live with a companion that will have all the deference due to your superiority of good sense, and if your proposals can be agreeable to those on whom I depend, I have nothing to say against them.

As to travelling, 't is what I should do with great pleasure, and could easily quit London upon your account; but a retirement in the country is not so disagreeable to me as I know a few months would make it tiresome to you. Where people are tied for life, 't is their mutual interest not to grow weary of one another. If I had all the personal charms that I want, a face is too slight a foundation for happiness. You would be soon tired with seeing every day the same thing. Where you saw nothing else, you would have leisure to remark all the defects,—which would increase in proportion as the novelty lessened, which is always a great charm. I should have the displeasure of seeing a coldness, which, though I could not reasonably blame you for, being involuntary, yet it would render me uneasy; and the more because I know a love may be revived which absence, inconstancy, or even infidelity has extinguished, but there is no returning from a *dégout* given by satiety.

I should not choose to live in a crowd. I could be very well pleased to be in London without making a great figure, or seeing above eight or nine agreeable people. Apartments, table, etc., are things that never come into my head. But I will never think of anything without the consent of my family, and advise you not to fancy a happiness in entire solitude which you would find only fancy.

Make no answer to this, if you can like me on my own terms. 'T is not to me you must make the proposals. If not, to what purpose is our correspondence?

However, preserve me your friendship, which I think of with a great deal of pleasure and some vanity. If ever you see me married, I flatter myself you'll see a conduct you would not be sorry your wife should imitate.

A CORRESPONDENCE BETWEEN THE FORD MOTOR COMPANY AND MISS MARIANNE MOORE[9]

October 19, 1955

Miss Marianne Moore
Cumberland Street
Brooklyn 5, New York

Dear Miss Moore:
    This is a morning we find ourselves with a problem which, strangely enough, is more in the field of words and the fragile meaning

of words than in car-making. And we just wonder whether you might be intrigued with it sufficiently to lend us a hand.

Our dilemma is a name for a rather important new series of cars.

We should like this name to be more than a label. Specifically, we should like it to have a compelling quality in itself and by itself. To convey, through association or other conjuration, some visceral feeling of elegance, fleetness, advanced features and design. A name, in short, that flashes a dramatically desirable picture in people's minds. (Another "Thunderbird" would be fine.)

Over the past few weeks this office has confected a list of three hundred-odd candidates which, it pains me to relate, are characterized by an embarrassing pedestrianism. We are miles short of our ambition. And so we are seeking the help of one who knows more about this sort of magic than we.

As to how we might go about this matter, I have no idea. But, in any event, all would depend on whether you find this overture of some challenge and interest.

Should we be so fortunate as to have piqued your fancy, we will be pleased to write more fully. And, of course, it is expected that our relations will be on a fee basis of an impeccably dignified kind.

Respectfully,
David Wallace
Special Products Division

October 21, 1955

Let me take it under advisement, Mr. Wallace. I am complimented to be recruited in this high matter.

I have seen and admired "Thunderbird" as a Ford designation. It would be hard to match; but let me, the coming week, talk with my brother, who would bring ardor and imagination to bear on the quest.

Sincerely yours,
Marianne Moore

October 27, 1955

Dear Mr. Wallace:

My brother thought most of the names I had considered suggesting to you for your new series too learned or too labored, but thinks I might ask if any of the following approximate the requirements:

THE FORD SILVER SWORD

This plant, of which the flower is a silver sword, I believe grows only on the Hawaiian Island Maui, on Mount Haleakala (House of the Sun); found at an altitude of from 9,500 to 10,000 feet. (The leaves—silver-white—surrounding the individual blossoms—have a pebbled texture that feels like Italian-twist backstitch all-over embroidery.)

My first thought was of a bird series—the swallow species—Hirundo, or phonetically, Aerundo. Malvina Hoffman is designing a device for the radiator of a made-to-order Cadillac, and said in her opinion the only term surpassing Thunderbird would be hurricane; and I then thought Hurricane Hirundo might be the first of a series such as Hurricane Aquila (eagle), Hurricane Accipiter (hawk), and so on. A species that takes its dinner on the wing ("swifts").

If these suggestions are not in character with the car, perhaps you could give me a sketch of its general appearance, or hint as to some of its exciting potentialities—though my brother reminds me that such information is highly confidential.

Sincerely yours,
Marianne Moore

November 4, 1955

Dear Miss Moore:

I'm delighted that your note implies that you are interested in helping us in our naming problem.

This being so, procedures in this rigorous business world dictate that we on this end at least document a formal arrangement with provision for a suitable fee or honorarium before pursuing the problem further.

One way might be for you to suggest a figure which could be considered for mutual acceptance. Once this is squared away, we will look forward to having you join us in the continuation of our fascinating search.

Sincerely yours,
David Wallace
Special Products Division

November 7, 1955

Dear Mr. Wallace:

It is handsome of you to consider remuneration for service merely enlisted. My fancy would be inhibited, however, by acknowledgment in advance of performance. If I could be of specific assistance, we could no doubt agree on some kind of honorarium for the service rendered.

I seem to exact participation; but if you could tell me how the suggestions submitted strayed—if obviously—from the ideal, I could then perhaps proceed more nearly in keeping with the Company's objective.

Sincerely yours,
Marianne Moore

November 11, 1955

Dear Miss Moore:

Our office philodendron has just benefited from an extra measure of water as, pacing about, I have sought words to respond to your recent generous note. Let me state my quandary thus. It is unspeakably contrary to procedure to accept counsel-even needed counsel-without a firm prior agreement of conditions (and, indeed, to follow the letter of things, without a Purchase Notice in quadruplicate and three Competitive Bids). But then, seldom has the auto business had occasion to indulge in so ethereal a matter as this. So, if you will risk a mutually satisfactory outcome with us, we should like to honor your wish for a fancy unencumbered.

As to wherein your earlier suggestions may have "strayed," as you put it—they did not at all. Shipment No. 1 was fine, and we would like to luxuriate in more of same—even those your brother regarded as over-learned or labored. For us to impose an ideal on your efforts would, I fear, merely defeat our purpose. We have sought your help to get an approach quite different from our own. In short, we should like suggestions that we ourselves would not have arrived at. And, in sober fact, have not.

Now we on this end must help you by sending some tangible representation of what we are talking about. Perhaps the enclosed sketches will serve the purpose. They are not IT, but they convey the feeling. At the very least, they may give you a sense of participation should your friend Malvina Hoffman break into brisk conversation on radiator caps.

Sincerely yours,
David Wallace
Special Products Division

November 13, 1955

Dear Mr. Wallace:

The sketches. They are indeed exciting; they have quality, and the toucan tones lend tremendous allure—confirmed by the wheels. Half the magic—sustaining effects of this kind. Looked at upside down, furthermore, there is a sense of fish buoyancy. Immediately your word "impeccable" sprang to mind. Might it be a possibility? The Impeccable. In any case, the baguette lapidary glamour you have achieved certainly spurs the imagination. Car-innovation is like launching a ship—"drama."

I am by no means sure that I can help you to the right thing, but performance with elegance casts a spell. Let me do some thinking in the direction of impeccable, symmechromatic, thunderbird. . . . (The exotics, if I can shape them a little.) Dearborn might come into one.

If the sketches should be returned at once, let me know. Otherwise, let me dwell on them for a time. I am, may I say, a trusty confidante.

I thank you for realizing that under contract esprit could not flower. You owe me nothing, specific or moral.

Sincerely,
Marianne Moore

November 19, 1955

Some other suggestions, Mr. Wallace, for the phenomenon:

THE RESILIENT BULLET
or Intelligent Bullet
or Bullet Cloisonné or Bullet Lavolta

(I have always had a fancy for THE INTELLIGENT WHALE—the little first Navy submarine, shaped like a sweet potato; on view in our Brooklyn Yard.)

THE FORD FABERGÉ

(That there is also a perfume Fabergé seems to me to do no harm, for here allusion is to the original silversmith.)

THE ARC-en-CIEL (the rainbow)
ARCENCIEL?

Please do not feel that memoranda from me need acknowledgment. I am not working day and night for you; I feel that etymological hits are partially accidental.

The bullet idea has possibilities, it seems to me, in connection with Mercury (with Hermes and Hermes Trismegistus) and magic (white magic).

Sincerely,
Marianne Moore

November 28, 1955

Dear Mr. Wallace:

MONGOOSE CIVIQUE
ANTICIPATOR
REGNA RACER (couronne à couronne) sovereign to sovereign
AEROTERRE
Fée Rapide (Aérofée, Aéro Faire, Fée Aiglette, Magi-faire)
Comme Il Faire
Tonnerre Alifère (winged thunder)
Aliforme Alifère (wing-slender, a-wing)
TURBOTORC (used as an adjective by Plymouth)
THUNDERBIRD Allié (Cousin Thunderbird)
THUNDER CRESTER
DEARBORN Diamante
MAGIGRAVURE
PASTELOGRAM
I shall be returning the sketches very soon.

M. M.

December 6, 1955

Dear Mr. Wallace:
Regina-rex
Taper Racer   Taper Acer
Varsity Stroke

Angelastro
Astranaut
Chaparral

Tir a l'arc (bull's eye)
Cresta Lark
Triskelion (three legs running)

Pluma Piluna (hairfine, feather-foot)

Andante con Moto (description of a good motor?)

My findings thin, so I terminate them and am returning the sketches. Two principles I have not been able to capture; 1, the topknot of the peacock and topnotcher of speed. 2, the swivel-axis (emphasized elsewhere), like the Captain's bed on the whaleship, Charles Morgan—balanced so that it levelled whatever the slant of the ship.

If I stumble on a hit, you shall have it. Anything so far has been pastime. Do not ponder appreciation, Mr. Wallace. That was embodied in the sketches.

M. M.

I cannot resist the temptation to disobey my brother and submit. TURCOTINGA (turquoise cotinga—the cotinga being a South-American finch or sparrow) solid indigo. (I have a three-volume treatise on flowers that might produce something but the impression given should certainly be unlabored).

December 8, 1955

Mr. Wallace:
    May I submit UTOPIAN TURTLETOP? Do not trouble to answer unless you like it.

Marianne Moore

December 23, 1955

MERRY CHRISTMAS TO OUR FAVORITE TURTLETOP-PER

David Wallace

December 26, 1955

Dear Mr. Wallace:
    An aspiring turtle is certain to glory in spiral eucalyptus, white pine straight from the forest, and innumerable scarlet roses almost too tall for close inspection. Of a temperament susceptible to shock though one may be, to be treated like royalty could not but induce sensations unprecedentedly august.

    Please know that a carfancyer's allegiance to the Ford automotive turtle—extending from the Model T Dynasty to the Wallace Utopian Dynasty—can never waver; impersonal gratitude surely becoming infinite when made personal. Gratitude to unmiserly Mr. Wallace and his idealistic associates.

Marianne Moore

November 8, 1956

Dear Miss Moore:
    Because you were so kind to us in our early days of looking for a suitable name, I feel a deep obligation to report on events that have ensued.

And I feel I must do so before the public announcement of same come Monday, November 19.

We have chosen a name out of the more than six thousand-odd candidates that we gathered. It fails somewhat of the resonance, gaiety, and zest we were seeking. But it has a personal dignity and meaning to many of us here. Our name, dear Miss Moore, is—Edsel.

I hope you will understand.

Cordially,
David Wallace
Special Products Division

THE PERSIAN WARS, II. 68-70
—Herodotus

The following are the peculiarities of the crocodile: During the four winter months they eat nothing; they are four-footed, and live indifferently on land or in the water. The female lays and hatches her eggs ashore, passing the greater portion of the day on dry land, but at night retiring to the river, the water of which is warmer than the night-air and the dew. Of all known animals this is the one which from the smallest size grows to be the greatest: for the egg of the crocodile is but little bigger than that of the goose, and the young crocodile is in proportion to the egg; yet when it is full grown the animal measures frequently twenty-five feet and even more. It has the eyes of a pig, teeth large and tusk-like, of a size proportioned to its frame; unlike any other animal, it is without a tongue; it cannot move its under-jaw, and in this respect too it is singular, being the only animal in the world which moves the upper-jaw but not the under. It has strong claws and a scaly skin, impenetrable upon the back. In the water it is blind, but on land it is very keen of sight. As it lives chiefly in the river, it has the inside of its mouth constantly covered with leeches; hence it happens that, while all the other birds and beasts avoid it, with the trochilus it lives at peace, since it owes much to that bird: for the cocodile, when he leaves the water and comes out upon the land, is in the habit of lying with his mouth wide open, facing the western breeze: at such times the trochilus goes into his mouth and devours the leeches. This benefits the crocodile, who is pleased, and takes care not to hurt the trochilus.

The crocodile is esteemed sacred by some of the Egyptians, by others he is treated as an enemy. Those who live near Thebes, and those who dwell around lake Moeris, regard them with especial veneration. In each of these places they keep one crocodile in particular, who is taught to be tame and tractable. They adorn his ears with ear-rings of molten stone or gold, and put bracelets on his forepaws, giving him daily a set portion of bread, with a certain number of victims; and after having thus treated him with the greatest possible attention while alive, they embalm him when he dies and bury him in a sacred repository. The people of Elephantine, on the other hand, are so far from considering these animals as sacred that they even eat their flesh. In the Egyptian language they are not called crocodiles, but champsae.

The name of crocodiles was given them by the Ionians, who remarked their resemblance to the lizards, which in Ionia live in the walls, and are called crocodiles.

The modes of catching the crocodile are many and various. I shall only describe the one which seems to me most worthy of mention. They bait a hook with a chine of pork and let the meat be carried out into the middle of the stream, while the hunter upon the bank holds a living pig, which he belabours. The crocodile hears its cries and, making for the sound, encounters the pork, which he instantly swallows down. The men on the shore haul, and when they have got him to land, the first thing the hunter does is to plaster his eyes with mud. This once accomplished, the animal is dispatched with ease, otherwise he gives great trouble.

NOBEL PRIZE ADDRESS[10]
—William Faulkner

(Delivered in Stockholm on December 10, 1950, in acceptance of the award of the Nobel Prize for Literature.)

I feel that this award was not made to me as a man, but to my work—a life's work in the agony and sweat of the human spirit, not for glory and least of all for profit, but to create out of the materials of the human spirit something which did not exist before. So this award is only mine in trust. It will not be difficult to find a dedication for the money part of it commensurate with the purpose and significance of its origin. But I would like to do the same with the acclaim too, by using this moment as a pinnacle from which I might be listened to by the young men and women already dedicated to the same anguish and travail, among whom is already that one who will some day stand here where I am standing.

Our tragedy today is a general and universal physical fear so long sustained by now that we can even bear it. There are no longer problems of the spirit. There is only the question: When will I be blown up? Because of this, the young man or woman writing today has forgotten the problems of the human heart in conflict with itself which alone can make good writing because only that is worth writing about, worth the agony and the sweat.

He must learn them again. He must teach himself that the basest of all things is to be afraid; and, teaching himself that, forget it forever, leaving no room in his workshop for anything but the old verities and truths of the heart, the old universal truths lacking which any story is ephemeral and doomed—love and honor and pity and pride and compassion and sacrifice. Until he does so, he labors under a curse. He writes not of love but of lust, of defeats in which nobody loses anything of value, of victories without hope and, worst of all, without pity or compassion. His griefs grieve on no universal bones, leaving no scars. He writes not of the heart but of the glands.

[10] Reprinted from *The Faulkner Reader*. Copyright 1954 by William Faulkner (New York: Random House, Inc.)

Until he relearns these things, he will write as though he stood among and watched the end of man. I decline to accept the end of man. It is easy enough to say that man is immortal simply because he will endure: that when the last ding-dong of doom has clanged and faded from the last worthless rock hanging tideless in the last red and dying evening, that even then there will still be one more sound: that of his puny inexhaustible voice, still talking. I refuse to accept this. I believe that man will not merely endure: he will prevail. He is immortal, not because he alone among creatures has an inexhaustible voice, but because he has a soul, a spirit capable of compassion and sacrifice and endurance. The poet's, the writer's, duty is to write about these things. It is his privilege to help man endure by lifting his heart, by reminding him of the courage and honor and hope and pride and compassion and pity and sacrifice which have been the glory of his past. The poet's voice need not merely be the record of man, it can be one of the props, the pillars to help him endure and prevail.

THE MAN OF PRINCIPLE[11]
—Ambrose Bierce

During a shower of rain the Keeper of a Zoölogical garden observed a Man of Principle crouching beneath the belly of the ostrich, which had drawn itself up to its full height to sleep.

"Why, my dear sir," said the Keeper, "if you fear to get wet, you'd better creep into the pouch of yonder female kangaroo—the *Saltarix mackintosha*—for if that ostrich wakes he will kick you to death in a minute."

"I can't help that," the Man of Principle replied, with that lofty scorn of practical considerations distinguishing his species. "He may kick me to death if he wish, but until he does he shall give me shelter from the storm. He has swallowed my umbrella."

RELIGIONS OF ERROR
—Ambrose Bierce

Hearing a sound of strife, a Christian in the Orient asked his Dragoman the cause of it.

"The Buddhists are cutting Mohammedan throats," the Dragoman replied, with oriental composure.

"I did not know," remarked the Christian, with scientific interest, "that that would make so much noise."

"The Mohammedans are cutting Buddhist throats, too," added the Dragoman.

"It is astonishing," mused the Christian, "how violent and how general are religious animosities. Everywhere in the world the devotees of each local

---

[11] This and the following fables by Bierce are from *Fantastic Fables*.

faith abhor the devotees of every other, and abstain from murder only so long as they dare not commit it. And the strangest thing about it is that all religions are erroneous and mischievous excepting mine. Mine, thank God is true and benign."

So saying he visibly smugged and went off to telegraph for a brigade of cutthroats to protect Christian interests.

RELIGIONS OF ERROR
—*Ambrose Bierce*

A married woman, whose lover was about to reform by running away, procured a pistol and shot him dead.

"Why did you do that, Madam?" inquired a Policeman sauntering by.

"Because," replied the Married Woman, "he was a wicked man, and had purchased a ticket to Chicago."

"My sister," said an adjacent Man of God, solemnly, "you cannot stop the wicked from going to Chicago by killing them."

THE INEFFECTIVE ROOTER
—*Ambrose Bierce*

A Drunken Man was lying in the road with a bleeding nose, upon which he had fallen, when a Pig passed that way.

"You wallow fairly well," said the Pig. "but my fine fellow, you have much to learn about rooting."

from THE COLOSSUS OF MAROUSSI[12]
—*Henry Miller*

It was dry in Athens, and unexpectedly hot. It was as though we were going back to Summer again. Now and then the wind blew down from the encircling mountains and then it was as chill as a knife blade. Mornings I would often walk to the Acropolis. I like the base of the Acropolis better than the Acropolis itself. I like the tumbledown shacks, the confusion, the erosion, the anarchic character of the landscape. The archaeologists have ruined the place; they have laid waste big tracts of land in order to uncover a mess of ancient relics which will be hidden away in museums. The whole base of the Acropolis resembles more and more a volcanic crater in which the loving hands of the archaeologists have laid out cemeteries of art. The tourist comes and looks down at these ruins, these scientifically created lava beds, with a moist eye. The live Greek walks about unnoticed or else is regarded

[12] Henry Miller, *Colossus of Maroussi*. Copyright 1941 by Henry Miller. Reprinted by permission of New Directions.

as an interloper. Meanwhile the new city of Athens covers almost the entire valley, is groping its way up the flanks of the surrounding mountains. For a country of only seven million inhabitants it is something of a phenomenon, the city of Athens. It is still in the throes of birth: it is awkward, confused, clumsy, unsure of itself; it has all the diseases of childhood and some of the melancholy and desolation of adolescence. But it has chosen a magnificent site in which to rear itself; in the sunlight it gleams like a jewel; at night it sparkles with a million twinkling lights which seem to be switching on and off with lightning-like speed. It is a city of startling atmospheric effects: it has not dug itself into the earth—it floats in a constantly changing light, beats with a chromatic rhythm. One is impelled to keep walking, to move on towards the mirage which is ever retreating. When one comes to the edge, to the great wall of mountains, the light becomes even more intoxicating; one feels as if one could bound up the side of the mountain in a few giant strides, and then—why then, if one did get to the top, one would race like mad along the smooth spine and jump clear into the sky, one clear headlong flight into the blue and Amen forever. Along the Sacred Way, from Daphni to the sea, I was on the point of madness several times. I actually did start running up the hillside only to stop midway, terror-stricken, wondering what had taken possession of me. On one side are stones and shrubs which stand out with microscopic clarity; on the other are trees such as one sees in Japanese prints, trees flooded with light, intoxicated, coryphantic trees which must have been planted by the gods in moments of drunken exaltation. One should not race along the Sacred Way in a motor car—it is sacrilege. One should walk, walk as the men of old walked, and allow one's whole being to become flooded with light. This is not a Christian highway: it was made by the feet of devout pagans on their way to initiation at Eleusis. There is no suffering, no martyrdom, no flagellation of the flesh connected with this processional artery. Everything here speaks now, as it did centuries ago, of illumination, of blinding, joyous illumination. Light acquires a transcendental quality: it is not the light of the Mediterranean alone, it is something more, something unfathomable, something holy. Here the light penetrates directly to the soul, opens the doors and windows of the heart, makes one naked, exposed, isolated in a metaphysical bliss which makes everything clear without being known. No analysis can go on in this light: here the neurotic is either instantly healed or goes mad. The rocks themselves are quite mad: they have been lying for centuries exposed to this divine illumination: they lie very still and quiet, nestling amid dancing coloured shrubs in a blood-stained soil, but they are mad, I say, and to touch them is to risk losing one's grip on everything which once seemed firm, solid and unshakable. One must glide through this gully with extreme caution, naked, alone, and devoid of all Christian humbug. One must throw off two thousand years of ignorance and superstition, of morbid, sickly subterranean living and lying. One must come to Eleusis stripped of the barnacles which have accumulated from centuries of lying in stagnant waters. At Eleusis one realizes, if never before, that there is no salvation in becoming adapted to a world which is crazy. At Eleusis one becomes adapted to the cosmos. Outwardly Eleusis may seem broken, disintegrated with the crumbled past; actually Eleusis is still intact and it is we who are broken, dispersed, crumbling to dust. Eleusis lives, lives eternally in the midst of a dying world.

from **DIVISIONS UPON GREEK GROUND**[13]
—Lawrence Durrell

> "No tongue: all eyes: be silent."
> *The Tempest*

Somewhere between Calabria and Corfu the blue really begins. All the way across Italy you find yourself moving through a landscape severely domesticated—each valley laid out after the architect's pattern, brilliantly lighted, human. But once you strike out from the flat and desolate Calabrian mainland towards the sea, you are aware of a change in the heart of things: aware of the horizon beginning to stain at the rim of the world: aware of *islands* coming out of the darkness to meet you.

In the morning you wake to the taste of snow on the air, and climbing the companion-ladder, suddenly enter the penumbra of shadow cast by the Albanian mountains—each wearing its cracked crown of snow—desolate and repudiating stone.

A peninsula nipped off while red hot and allowed to cool into an antarctica of lava. You are aware not so much of a landscape coming to meet you invisibly over those blue miles of water as of a climate. You enter Greece as one might enter a dark crystal; the form of things becomes irregular, refracted. Mirages suddenly swallow islands, and wherever you look the trembling curtain of the atmosphere deceives.

Other countries may offer you discoveries in manners or lore or landscape; Greece offers you something harder—the discovery of yourself.

. . .

5-7-37

Yesterday was a fisherman's holiday; first a great glistening turtle was washed up on the beach at the cliff edge. It was quite dead and its heavy yellow eyelids were drawn down over its eyes giving it a sinister and reptilian air of being half asleep. It must have weighed about as much as the dinghy. I expected the fishermen to make some use of the meat but nobody has touched it—except the village dogs which have been worrying its flippers.

More exciting was the killing of the eel. We were unhooking the boat when a small boy who was helping us cast off pointed to something in the water and exclaimed 'Zmyrna.' I was about to probe about with an oar—for I could see nothing in the shadow of the great rock—when Anastasius came running like a flash from the carpenter's shop. He held two heavy four-pronged tridents. For a moment or two he stared keenly down into the water; we could see nothing beyond the movements of marine life, the swaying of the seaweed fronds and the strange flickering passage of small fish. Then Anastasius lowered a piece of wood—simply the unshod shaft of a trident—into the darkest patch of the shadow. There was a small audible snap—as of a rat-trap closing—and his shoulders became rigid; maintaining his pressure on the wood he picked up a trident and lowering the point slowly into the water suddenly struck home at an angle. There was a sudden convulsion among the seaweed and the head of the eel emerged; it seemed to our terrified eyes about the size of a dog's head and infinitely more senseless and wicked. The trident had pierced the skull and while it was still dazed from the blow Anastasius strove to dislodge it from its perch. Help, too, was at hand. Old Father Nicholas came racing down with a couple of sharpened boat-hooks and these were driven into the meaty shoulders of the eel.

It took three of them to lug it on to the rock, and for a quarter of an hour on dry land it fought savagely, with two tridents piercing its brain and two more in its sides. I can hear the dry snapping of its jaws on the stick as I write. It had muscle on it like a wrestler, and its tail tapered into a great finned bolster of brown gristle—a turbine; altogether the whole fish looked more like an American invention than anything from the water-world; and it had the ferocity and determination of Satan. It was interesting to see how *afraid* its evil aspect made one; long after it was dead the peasants were driving their tridents into it with imprecations; and everyone gave it a wide berth until it stiffened with an unmistakable rigor.

Chapter **13**

ENSEMBLE PERFORMANCE
Choric Interpretation, Choreographed Interpretation, Readers Theatre, Chamber Theatre, Mixed Media

In earlier chapters we discussed interpretation largely in terms of the solo performer, who has been traditionally the center of training in courses in interpretation. Ensemble performance (a name that may be applied to all group performances of literature) provides problems of quite a different nature. Indeed, many ensemble performances nowadays can be distinguished only with difficulty (and sometimes not at all) from full-scale theatrical events.

Something is to be said for maintaining in ensemble performance the primacy of the text being performed, for insuring that the theatrical interest does not overwhelm the literary interest, since it is in the life which matches text and performer that interpretation resides. It is not true that adding costumes, lights, scenery, detailed stage movement will automatically add to the life of a text. Drama, as a literary form, normally *intends* these aids and may count on them in performance; other literary forms may suffer from having them imposed. Some Chamber Theatre performances, for example, forsake the novel for the play; turning the narrator into a dramatic character, they may distort his role in the structure of the fictive text, or may reduce it to make the novel more like a play. While we are not objecting to dramatization of novels, we *are* saying that the novel is not in itself a play and that Chamber Theatre (as defined by its originator, Robert Breen) does not permit forsaking the original form.

There are dangers in too simple an assumption that *more* in the way of theatrical aids is necessarily *better*. Even in the performance of drama, one can overload the stage. Nineteenth-century productions of Shakespeare, for example, often destroyed fluidity of action by saddling the play with detailed changes of scene. Contemporary productions of Shakespeare have wisely returned to simpler stage backings to keep the flow of the action uppermost.

It is important to recognize, however, that problems of definition ought not stand in the way of exploration. Ensemble interpretation has evoked widespread interest among students and audiences alike. Full-evening performances of novels, stories, long poems, composite texts, as well as plays, have become rather usual in schools and colleges. The range of materials open to interpreters in ensemble work is almost endless. All of the kinds discussed in Chapter 12 provide texts; there is no need to be restricted to traditional forms.

Certain things must be said at the outset: (1) Ensemble performances are not quick, easy ways of preparing public presentations. Most people find that a fully rehearsed performance in Readers Theatre or Chamber Theatre takes as long to prepare as a staged play, and it is not unusual to find that actors used to staged plays find the quality of concentration in interpretation difficult to master. (2) Reading performances should not be thought of as inexpensive ways to produce a play. Unless a play gains something by being performed as a reading, it should not be read. Readings of plays also lose certain things that are possible in fully staged productions. The two modes of performance differ from one another; each has something to offer, provided that the play chosen suits the medium. There is—or there ought to be—no sense of rivalry between them. Indeed, as we shall see, many performances choose to mix the modes, as playwrights and producers often themselves do now. (3) There are not set, inflexible rules for the various group modes, any more than there are for plays meant to be performed by actors. There are conventions (though they must not be rigid), and there are outer limits (though they are not easy to define).

The Problem of Defining Group Modes

It is impossible to find discrete terms for all possible modes of group performance. Even if we were to find terms for performances seen in the past, there are new performances to come. Furthermore, names of things are conventions, a contract between users to permit necessary dialogue. The attempt in this chapter is not to rule out viable ensemble performances but to make large distinctions that will hopefully prove useful. The acts of interpretation we have been discussing throughout this book apply equally to the various group modes to be discussed.

We shall not attempt to give a specific name to some kinds of group readings: group readings of expository prose, for example, in which lines are assigned to readers in terms of themes, tensions, weights, reader-qualities, and so on. We repeat: there is no attempt here to limit the modes of group performance. Nor should the conventions described in the discussion of Readers Theatre and Chamber Theatre be thought of as authoritative. They are conventions pragmatically derived; they must be tested pragmatically—if they do not carry weight in performance, they should be questioned and discarded. (This is not to say, of course, that everything that "works" in a performance is therefore necessarily good. A performer may delight an audience with effects that undermine the text being performed.)

Perhaps this is the place to introduce a matter that affects many other modes of presentation that we have discussed: intention of the performance. We have spoken as though the intention is always unvaried, that it is always to embody the literature in its own terms. But there is a special use to which performance may be put: it may deliberately be given a specific rhetorical or forensic slant; it may select one dominant attitude from a piece and emphasize that at the expense of others, to make a particular point a reader or a program may wish to stress. Remember that this is an exceptional, rather than the usual, mode of performance, but it has its own justification, and doubtless many interpreters will wish to use it from time to time.

FORENSIC USE OF LITERATURE (GROUP OR SOLO READING)

    Speakers often use literature to illustrate a point—using the literature not for itself but for a practical purpose. Often an interpretation program built around a theme will subordinate individual pieces to the role they play as representations of a theme. This may be a deliberate warping of texts, subordinating parts to other parts, even cutting parts out of texts, but why should it be frowned upon so long as the intention of the performance is clear? Such use of literature has, as a matter of fact, a long and honorable history. It is interpretation seen tangentially, but it is nevertheless interpretation.

    Many ensembles employ literature in this way, creating from a body of poems an effect that is larger than (and often rather different from) the effect of any one piece performed. That is, a program may itself have a point of view that modifies the perspective from which we see any one part of the program. There is a creative activity in programming; ignoring that fact may seriously limit the effectiveness of the performance. In group performances, as much care must be devoted to deciding which performer (or performers) will read a given piece as is given to the casting of characters in a drama. As careful attention should be devoted to the order of parts of the program as the playwright devotes to the order of the parts of his play.

Choric interpretation is just as much a mode of studying literature as any other form of interpretation. It involves, however, a particular difficulty not found in solo reading—a difficulty so great and formidable that many teachers shy away from choric work because of it: group readers must as an ensemble read as one. A clutter of uncoordinated

CHORIC INTERPRETATION

voices will drown out a reading, and an audience will be left bewildered and annoyed; a set of unrelated interpretations mouthed at one time will be equally distressing. But a good speech choir, fully rehearsed, in agreement on meanings, attitudes, and implications, moving in unison with the flow of the structure of a work of literature, can be a highly expressive instrument.

One of the famous choirs of our day is the Greek chorus that takes part each summer in the festival of Greek plays at Epidaurus. It demonstrates beyond any question that it is possible for a group of forty or fifty voices to speak as one, so that the relationship between a solo voice and the choir is much the same as that between a solo instrument and a full orchestra. In a modern performance of Euripides' *Hercules Furens* at Epidaurus, the choir not only spoke but moved and half chanted. Tall staves in the hands of the members of the chorus were used to punctuate the measured tread of the speakers' feet; they fell as one upon the earth, absolutely coordinated in time. While the voices differed in quality and pitch, they were as one in attacking and sustaining words and phrases. The effect was electric. The listener felt at once the strange position of the chorus in the play; actor and yet not actor; part of the action and yet not part of the action; human and yet not a human being but a force. This was orchestration in the fullest sense.

Anyone who has tried to train a group of readers to behave in this unified fashion knows how extremely difficult it is to succeed. The readers must agree on meanings—or compromises must be made to get unanimity—and the director of the choir will find that he or she must be genial, tactful, and firm all at once. Voices must be chosen carefully: a bad voice will stand out like a crow in a nest of robins; a too-loud voice will sound like a solo voice and destroy the wholeness of the choir; a voice noticeably higher or lower than the others will likewise call attention to itself. (We are not discussing solo parts, which may be used in conjunction with a choir, but the choral passages themselves.)

Does a choir read from a book? It may, it may not; this is a matter of taste. But if books are used by the members of the choir, this use must be as much a part of the rehearsal as any other aspect of the performance. There must be a locus for the group interpretation; it is distracting to find heads bobbing up and down at random to look at pages, just as it would be distracting to see members of the choir looking up at the ceiling or out the windows of the auditorium, or at a friend in the third row. All minds must seem to be in the same place, looking at the same thing.

Locus is also a problem in coordinating choral passages with solo passages in group presentation. An under-rehearsed choir will tend to finish a choral passage and then simply wait, at ease, until the solo reader has finished his lines; then they will plunge in again. The effect will be the same as when a single interpreter, reading a connected series of paragraphs, treats each paragraph as a unit in itself, seeming to say to himself as he finishes a paragraph. "There. That's done. Now for the next one." The interpreter must never fail to be aware both of the paragraph he is reading and of its relationship to the paragraphs before and after it. Unless he sustains this knowledge in his own mind and body, he cannot hope to create in his listeners an awareness of the wholeness of the work. So with the choir: it does not simply sit still while the solo reader is at work but stays with him in creating the sense of the presence of the literature, never deserting the locus of the piece, and when the choir begins again, the choral passage flows out of the solo passage that has preceded. When the bones of a body are really alive, a living substance knits them together. When a choral work is really alive, the choir never "dies" during solo passages.

There is considerable debate about the kind of material suited to choral performance. Some teachers feel that lyric poems (thought of as the subjective utterance of a single person—often the poet himself) should not be read by a group of readers, but not all lyrics are alike in the degree of their privacy. Keats's "When I have fears that I may cease to be" is rather unlike a sonnet by Gerard Manley Hopkins that sounds like a hymn in praise of God, and the hymn may actually gain power in a performance by a highly sensitive, thoroughly trained chorus of voices. The question of whether a choir will add to, detract from, or leave unchanged the effect of a work of literature is a complex and important one, and each choir director must take it seriously into account in choosing his material. It is likely that the effect of literature will always be changed; the question is whether the change will involve difference (as each reading differs in some respect from every other reading) or a radical warping of perspective and presence.

THE CHOIR DIRECTOR

We have mentioned the director of the choir. A choir must have a director, a coordinator who functions in much the same way as the director of an orchestra or of a play. It is often the sensitivity of the director that determines the success of the choir. The fineness of his or her awareness of all that we have discussed throughout the book will enter into the handling of the voices through which the poem is embodied. It is as if a single individual has been endowed with many voices rather than one. It goes without saying that the director is limited by the quality of the voices and minds to be coordinated.

It is usual to talk about "light" and "dark" voices in choric groups. Voices differ with respect to quality, pitch, strength. These differences are in part inherent, a result of physiological differences. Such differences are not the same as differences in habit, which drill and practice may alter. We do not refer to breathiness of voices, or to excessive nasality (though this *may* be physiological), or to lazy articulation. Assuming that voices are normal with respect to these factors, the former differences remain, so that voices will differ in "weight" just as instruments of the orchestra differ. Male voices are generally heavier than female voices—"darker," in other words. The director of the speech choir, in orchestrating a selection, may wish to divide the choir into groups according to weight and quality. A division into male and female groups will accomplish something, but further divisions are possible: contralto and bass voices may be played against soprano and tenor voices, and so on. There is no magic formula for making such divisions; everything depends on (1) the nature of the selection itself and (2) the sensibilities of the director.

In the selection that follows, the choir has been divided (1) according to sexes and (2) according to timbre. Try the arrangement with the full class, deciding how the soloists should be divided according to light and dark qualities. Be sure that you choose voices that will harmonize when put together. During your rehearsals, watch to see what changes might be made to make the arrangement more effective. (See, meanwhile, if you can determine why each of the present divisions was made.)

Psalm 90 from THE MODERN READERS BIBLE
—R. G. Moulton

FULL CHOIR.	Lord, thou hast been our dwelling place In all generations.
Male 1.	Before the mountains were brought forth,
Male 2.	Or ever thou hadst formed the earth and the world,
Male 1, 2.	Even from everlasting to everlasting,
Male Choir.	thou art God.
Female 1.	Thou turnest man to dust; And sayest, Return, ye children of men.
Female 2.	For a thousand years in thy sight Are but as yesterday when it passeth,
Female 1, 2.	And as a watch in the night.
Male 1, 2.	Thou carriest them away as with a flood;
Female 1, 2. Male 1, 2. }	They are as a sleep.
Female Choir.	In the morning they are like grass which groweth up:
Full Choir.	In the morning it flourisheth, and groweth up;
Male Choir.	In the evening it is cut down, and withereth.
Full Choir.	For we are consumed in thine anger, And in thy wrath are we troubled.
Female 1.	Thou hast set our iniquities before thee,
Male 1.	Our secret sins in the light of thy countenance.
Female 1. Male 1. }	—For all our days are passed away in thy wrath.
Female 1, 2.	We bring our years to an end as a tale that is told.
Female 1, 2. Male 1. }	—The days of our years are threescore years and ten,

Female 1, 2. ⎫ Male 1, 2. ⎭	—Or even by reason of strength fourscore years;
Female Choir.	Yet is their pride but labor and sorrow; For it is soon gone, and we fly away.
Male Choir.	Who knoweth the power of thine anger, And thy wrath according to the fear that is due unto thee?
Full Choir.	So teach us to number our days, That we may get us a heart of wisdom.
Female 1, 2.	Return, O Lord; how long?
Female Choir.	And let it repent thee concerning thy servants.
Male 1, 2.	O satisfy us in the morning with thy mercy;
Male Choir.	That we may rejoice and be glad all our days.
Female 1.	Make us glad according to the days wherein thou hast afflicted us,
Female 2.	And the years wherein we have seen evil.
Male 1.	Let thy work appear unto thy servants,
Male 2.	And thy glory upon their children.
Female Choir.	And let the beauty of the Lord our God be upon us:
Male Choir.	And establish thou the work of our hands upon us;
Full Choir.	Yes, the work of our hands establish thou it.

CHOREOGRAPHED INTERPRETATION

While anything like a helpful discussion of the dance is beyond the sphere of this volume, it may still be possible to speak usefully about choreographed interpretation, the bringing together into congruent form of interpretation and dancing, where the poem itself is still thought of as primary. (One must remember that this is a book on interpretation. In a book on dancing one might see the dance as primary and the poem as simply impetus or stimulus. The results of the two kinds of performance would not be identical.)

A single performer may both dance and speak. One performer may speak and another, or a group of others, may dance. A choir may read and dance, or a choir may read and a solo performer or group dance. All of these combinations are possible, though not every form is likely to succeed with every poem. The combination should be chosen to underscore and heighten the appeal of the poem to be performed.

First, some warnings: (1) Some poems will suffer from being combined with music and dance. (2) Care must be taken that, in combining appeals to the ear and eye, the visual element does not simply act as a distraction. (3) From the point of view of this book, at least, the performance ought not be a tour de force glorifying the performer.

With these reservations in mind, one must recognize that poems (specifically *poetry*) can benefit from the union. Poems are acts—and highly rhythmic acts, as we have seen. They involve the whole body and the musculature of the body; they must be felt. Interpretation gives body to the printed symbol, to experience. So does the dance, though usually mutely. Dance throws the human body, as an expressive instrument, totally into the foreground—through the movement of the body (though, it must be said, the body controlled by the operation of the whole personality), it says what it has to say, on the whole silently. It usually is accompanied by the rhythms and movement of sound in the music it employs as a score.

It may equally be accompanied by poems, in which the body itself may be thought of as the silent equivalent of sound, as "score" for the poem, the rhythms of the body providing a visible (rather than an aural) embodiment of the text. In serious poems it is usually wise to avoid literal dancing out of the words, though in comic poems literalness may be a virtue. More often than not, a very complicated poem that demands concentrated attention from the ear will not dance well, but this is not to say that a "dance poem" cannot have a strong degree of emotionality. A poem with a strong rhythmic design will be preferable to one in which the rhythmic pattern is slight or diffuse. Narrative poems often work well; rather fragile lyrics may become unforgettable in a carefully danced form. The range of choice is—as for choric interpretation—great, and it is limited ultimately only by the abilities and taste of the dance.

The essential question is this: In the dancing of a poem, what physical behaviors best match the text and the dancers? It is not a matter merely of "suiting the action to the word," of looking for movement which describes and literalizes (perhaps we should say *physicalizes*) the text *word by word*. There is a *trans*action involved as well as an action. The body cannot literally go everywhere language can go; nor can language literally duplicate the expressions of the body. But degrees of formality, degrees of grace, changes in tempi, patterns of movement, variations in proximity of members of the dance group, alterations in the size of the dancing space—all these are part of the vocabulary of the dance.

The body is a marvelous instrument; the dancer must learn to know it. The dancer as interpreter, the interpreter as dancer, needs to know equally well the instrument which is the voice. Needless to say, the mind accompanies both instruments! The journey from beginning to middle to end of the poem and the journey from beginning to middle to end of a dance both constitute acts. The interpreter and the dancer can be companions in the journey—but they must get their acts together. The voice never moves without movement within the body; in choreographed interpretation, the dancer never moves without a knowledge of the movement of the voice. That voice is the voice of the poem, embodied; it is also, in performance, the voice of the interpreter, embodied.

The size and extent of dance movements can do much to stress the qualities and degrees of tensions in poems. We said that language can be thought of as gesture. The dance too is gesture. When poem and dance are really congruent, when the one body matches the other, one cannot (to repeat Yeats once more) tell the dancer from the dance. The movement of the body through space and time, with or without music but with the presence of sounded language, which the moving body accepts as form and act—this is choreographed interpretation at its best. Not many performers can manage it by themselves. It is difficult even for more than a single performer. But try it—the training is excellent for the interpreter, whether or not he or she does it well enough to submit to the test of public performance.

The form of ensemble interpretation usually called Readers Theatre covers a variety of activities. Other terms are used: concert reading, interpreter's theatre, staged reading, theatre of the mind. Interest in the form has grown remarkably in the past few years; attempts to define it remain difficult.

> **READERS THEATRE**[1]

    In what follows, remember that we are more interested in describing possibilities than in prescribing limitations. Definitions are necessary and helpful, but they must not be allowed to stand in the way of enjoyment. Do not let the matter of definition spoil your pleasure in a performance. (Some people, for example, are so averse to the word *impersonation* that they cannot enjoy anything called by that name.) On the other hand, a plea for tolerance is not a plea for anarchy: it is probably not true that "anything goes."

    The term *Readers Theatre* is sometimes reserved for group performances of dramatic texts. It sometimes includes also the group reading of such narrative-dramatic poems as Browning's *The Ring and the Book* or a style of reading a short story or novel with several readers participating. It is possible to call the rendition of any kind of material by a group of readers by the name Readers Theatre; in this case our further classification, *Chamber Theatre,* would no longer be useful.

Hence we shall choose here to limit the term, to emphasize the word *theatre,* and to distinguish between Readers Theatre and Chamber Theatre. Readers Theatre, in our discussion, embraces the group reading of material involving delineated characters, with or without the presence of a narrator, in such a manner as to establish the usual locus of the piece not onstage with the readers but in the imagination of the audience. The reading of expository prose by a group of readers would not,

> **A Definition of Readers Theatre**

---

[1] There are profitable discussions of Readers Theatre and sample scripts in the following books: Leslie Irene Coger and Melvin R. White, *Readers Theatre Handbook,* 2nd ed. (Chicago: Scott, Foresman and Co., 1973); Beverly Whitaker Long, Lee Hudson, and Phillis Rienstra Jeffrey, *Group Performance of Literature* (Englewood Cliffs, N.J.: Prentice-Hall, Inc., 1977); Joanna Hawkins Maclay, *Readers Theatre: Toward a Grammar of Practice* (New York: Random House, Inc., 1971).

therefore, be included in our definition. The reading of biblical psalms by a group would not be included. But the reading of Browning's "Pied Piper of Hamelin," with readers taking the parts of the Mayor, the Piper, and the Little Lame Boy, would be included, provided that the usual locus was offstage. And clearly a reading of *King Lear* by a group of readers would be included—again provided that the locus was not on-stage. (We are not raising here the question of whether there should be one reader for each character or whether there may be doubling of parts.)

This sounds simple enough, but it is not. Thus far in this book, the interpreter has been thought of as locating his material outside himself, somewhere between himself and his audience, in the interest of establishing tension between the audience at one end of the taut line and himself at the other end. This is what we mean by the term *offstage* as opposed to *onstage*. The onstage locus serves to focus attention on the actor, on the visual element, the "here and now." The offstage locus serves what Brecht has called the "alienation effect," and gives a certain distancing to the performance, as the presence of the book does. (Observe the difference between the boy declaiming a poem onstage without book and the boy reading from a book as an interpreter. Or the orator speaking his own oration and the interpreter reading an oration.) We must be careful. Distancing here does not mean weakening. The effect may be equally powerful in the two cases—but it is not the same. Distance may, indeed, lend enchantment to the view!

Onstage Effects

But the problem is complicated. Drama is meant to be performed here and now; it is meant, usually, to make us feel that it is taking place at this very moment before our eyes. Certain things in the text of a play may require onstage explanation: the drawing of a dagger, the taking of a potion, if these are not explained in the words of the play itself; and surely it is futile to confuse an audience by refusing to give onstage explanations of this sort simply because we have defined Readers Theatre as having a locus offstage.

There is a rule of thumb to be followed. Whenever the text emphasizes something to be seen—rather than heard—Readers Theatre is usually required to put it onstage, lest its absence ruin the effect of the play. Does this mean that Readers Theatre moves back and forth between onstage and offstage locations, then? Yes, exactly that. This will seem to some people a confusion or denial of form, but it is not. We are used to seeing the movie or television camera shift focus in this way—we have said repeatedly that the locus of any literary piece shifts in many subtle ways within itself. The confusion, if there is any, is in the minds of those who seek to define Readers Theatre in so limiting a fashion as to leave it rigid and stultified. The locus is primarily offstage, but it is not—and cannot be—always there.

An illustration will help. In Shakespeare's *Othello* there is a scene in which Iago, amid great excitement among a group of men, runs up behind Roderigo, stabs him, and rushes from the stage. The physical commotion in the scene is highly important, and the text does not alone (without stage directions) make clear what has happened. One Readers Theatre performance of *Othello* placed this bit of business onstage, arguing that the thing seen was the important thing, not simply the words later referring to it, and that without the testimony of its own eyes the audience would miss much of the intended effect. On the other hand, this same performance placed Othello's strangling of Desdemona offstage rather than onstage, arguing that what mattered was the effect of the deed on the character of Othello, rather than the deed itself. In placing the scene offstage, the readers still had to indicate what was happening. Othello did strangle Desdemona, but his hands reached out toward the audience rather than toward her; she did respond, but she drew away from the audience rather than from the interpreter reading Othello, so that the physical impact on the faces and bodies of the readers showed fully to the audience—even while the appeal remained preeminently to the auditory imagination. One English teacher objected to Readers Theatre at this point, saying that the full-face agonies of the two characters were more than he could endure—but the director took this as a compliment rather than a criticism, since Shakespeare seems to mean the scene to be unbearable.

When esthetic effects can be heightened by the mixing of onstage and offstage locus, then definition alone should not stand in the way of freeing the form. Today, when much theatre moves toward free and mixed forms, Readers Theatre should participate in the freedom, not stifle literature by insisting on drawing rigid lines between kinds. There is something to be said for the reluctant suburban husband in the *New Yorker* cartoon who, sitting beside his "literary" wife at what was to be a concert reading and looking at the empty stools and music stands arranged in a row on the stage, said glumly, "I don't like it already." This is not to say that the classic form of Readers Theatre—readers with stools and lecterns facing the audience—need be static and dull. With a good performance it can be enormously exciting, highly concentrating the attention.

Eye Contact and Locus

Should the readers, with books in their hands, ever look at one another as they read? Or do they always place their scene out in the audience, as the single reader of a play does, establishing contact with the imagined character there? Readers Theatre faces a problem here with respect to audience expectations. With the solo reader, there is no objection to the placement of the character addressed in the audience (in the auditorium), since the alternative will engage the reader in the ludicrous activity of trying to fill the visual scene onstage all by himself. But when two or more people take part in a scene, by the convention of drama, we are used to seeing them look at one another. The strain of trying to

keep the convention of interpretation by asking all the readers to establish contact not onstage but offstage may be distracting to an audience.
(Audiences frequently have testified to this.) Both the unsophisticated
and the highly sophisticated audience are likely to accept the convention of interpretation in Readers Theatre, and when they do, the performance is often compelling. But the audience that is midway—and
this is perhaps the usual audience—may balk.

Furthermore, as we have already said, the scene sometimes ought
to be onstage. The test itself—not the convention of the medium—
should determine the answers to problems if we are not to permit the
medium to dictate the form of the piece. Granted that Readers Theatre
has chosen a text that is suitable for interpreters and flexible enough to
permit choices between onstage and offstage effects, it seems proper to
admit that the readers in Readers Theatre may indeed look at one another.

How, then, is the essential creation of an offstage scene, with a
primary auditory appeal, to be maintained? By a device that is very old
and that is itself a convention. Often in premodern drama there are long
conversations between characters that are meant to be delivered not so
much between character and character as between character and audience. Soliloquies are also sometimes so intended. Characters may sit
beside one another onstage and talk out to the audience, or they may
share something that both "see" in the audience. George Burns and
Gracie Allen, in their comedy sketches in vaudeville and on television,
managed to persuade audiences that they were talking to one another
even while they looked for the most part into the audience itself. The
effect would have been quite different if they had looked constantly at
each other.

Of course, we do not look constantly at one another even in face-
to-face talk. (Nothing is more disconcerting than to have someone stare
at you every minute you are talking with him.) The actor normally follows the practice of looking at the character to whom he is speaking
(though he is free to look away); the interpreter normally follows the
practice of looking toward the audience when he is speaking to another
character, though he is free also to look at the other character. The
difference between the two conventions (as in many of our examples) is
in emphasis and proportion. The interpreter, with his book and his
minimal visual aids, on the whole succeeds best when he keeps his
scene offstage; the actor, with his memorized lines and his fuller use of
visual aids, succeeds best, on the whole, when he presents his scene
onstage.

But movement between the two conventions should be free and
flexible. When characters speak to one another in Readers Theatre, particularly when they are very few in number so that the convention is not
awkward, they may look at one another from time to time to make their
conversing seem natural, though they should not simply place the scene
onstage. When there are as many as seven or eight characters on the

platform, and if they are placed on a line so that they cannot look at one another easily without bending forward and looking down the line, most audiences accept the limitation and feel easy about the offstage placement.

Again, notice that even within the same text the shifts from onstage to offstage location must be determined by the requirements of the scene itself, not simply by definition of the medium. A play like Thornton Wilder's *Our Town* moves constantly between the two forms. It employs memorized lines, costumes, onstage scenes; it also employs a narrator whose relation to the audience is that of the interpreter, minimal settings and properties, and many offstage scenes. How futile to criticize the play for being neither theatre nor interpretation (as some people once did) when its charm arises from the mixed nature of the form. A good deal of premodern drama falls into this mixed form— meant to be acted on the stage with much of the dialogue delivered more or less directly to the audience. For such drama, Readers Theatre underscores the literary text, but it cannot completely ignore the nonverbal requirements of the form.

Other Theatrical Effects

This description raises a host of questions: Should the "actors" in Readers Theatre use books? Should they use makeup? Should they be in costume? Should they be seated or standing? Should the whole cast remain onstage throughout, or should there be entrances and exits? Should lights be used for effects? Should music be used? Should scenery be used? Props? Where, finally, does one draw the line between Readers Theatre and fully staged performances?

Readers Theatre, as we have said, essentially locates its scene offstage. This is a primary distinction between it and conventional theatre—though we must recognize that this places Thornton Wilder's *Our Town* at least as much in the realm of Readers Theatre as in the realm of pure theatre. (Audiences are always quick to sense this difference in much of Wilder.) But one cannot make a sharp separation between the ear and the eye; vital organs are no longer vital when they have been severed in this fashion. Conventional theatre appeals to the ear as well as to the eye—but the eye is likely to be the dominant appeal. (One reason why some prefer conventional theatre to Readers Theatre may be that the eye is for most people the keenest of the sense organs.) Readers Theatre makes its appeal primarily to the ear, but whenever the eye may be made to serve the ear, Readers Theatre may properly serve the eye also. *Care must be taken that the appeal does not become always primarily visual, so that the scene of the reading is fixed onstage.* Perhaps we may put it this way: a blind man has less to lose in attending a performance in Readers Theatre than in attending a performance in conventional theatre. *This is not to say that he will lose nothing.* A deaf man has less to lose in attending a performance in conventional theatre than in attending a performance in Readers Theatre. *This is not to say that he will lose nothing.* What the blind man hears in Readers Theatre is perhaps the essence of interpretation; what the deaf man sees in conventional theatre is perhaps the essence of acting (notice that we do not say of *drama*). But both the eyes and the ears are needed for the appreciation of the effect the playwright seeks to achieve, and both the interpreter and the actor need to know how to speak and to move. The voice is no more independent of the body than the ear is independent of the eye in its contribution to total perception.

Hence Readers Theatre may indeed use costumes and makeup. It may employ entrances and exits. It may use lights, scenery, props. It ought often, we think, to use books for locating the performance, though this is a conservative position. It ought to limit costume, make-up, lights, scenery, and props in the interests of keeping the scene essentially offstage, though it should not prohibit them (as a matter of definition) and hence run the risk of impoverishing the experience of the audience.

Everything depends on the nature and quality of the text itself. Farces, depending heavily on stage business, are far less suitable for Readers Theatre than plays in which the reliance on such business is slight. Shakespeare's plays make dependence on scenery relatively slight: the orchard in *Romeo and Juliet* is given to us in all its essentials in the text itself, and the castle of Macbeth is far better in Shakespeare's own words than it often appears in fully staged productions (where it is likely to deny Shakespeare's description of it). So with makeup. If the character is clearly drawn in the language of the text, full character makeup is not economical in Readers Theatre and tends to keep the scene onstage. At the same time, it is not quite true that Readers Theatre frees the director from the necessity of choosing readers who resemble the characters they are portraying. For while he is doubtless freer than the director in a fully staged play, he cannot afford to overlook conventional expectations in the minds of his audience, who will balk at accepting a fat Juliet.

With respect to costumes, it may be difficult for an audience to accept a young man in blue jeans and open-necked wool shirt as Mirabel in *The Way of the World,* though it would probably accept him in modern evening dress. One cannot be explicit about such matters. A visitor at the rehearsal of a play does not expect to see the same thing as in a public performance—he may accept Hamlet in blue jeans in the one instance and balk at it in the other, because he knows that the eye is not fully served in the rehearsal of a play. In Readers Theatre, where the eye is never so fully served as in conventional theatre, his demands on the visual aspects of the performance will be fewer, but they will not be absent.

Lighting, strangely enough, seems to help the ear. The so-called color organ (in which the play of colors accompanies musical sounds) counts on this relationship. But lighting can also, overused, detract from auditory appeals by making too great visual demands on the attention of auditors. Music, auditory in its appeal, may be highly useful—or it may make competing demands for the attention of the ear and interfere with the projection of text.

Whether or not there are to be entrances and exits will depend on such things as the size of the platform, the number of readers, the kind of lighting, and—again and always—the nature of the text. If there are twenty-five readers in the cast (with no more than five, let us say, ever appearing at one time in a scene) and the stage platform is very small, it would be idle to squeeze all twenty-five readers onstage and keep them there throughout. On the other hand, a semicircle of twenty-five readers constantly onstage and stepping into scene when needed may provide a moving sense of keeping the whole play constantly in the presence of the audience. (It will also contribute to distancing.)

A play like Henry James's *The Other House* (successful in Readers Theatre though never staged in full performance) may make use of as few as eight readers, all of whom may be kept onstage and seated throughout. James's play depends heavily on dialogue—talk in the best Jamesian sense. Nothing is gained by moving the readers about. If they are seated on revolving stools (it helps the readers if there are back-rests!), they may make a half turn to enter or leave the scene. They may employ adjustable music stands for lecterns, adding to the formality of the visual element. The stage may be fully lit throughout the action.

Shakespeare's *Cymbeline,* however, with its villain popping out of a trunk, its headless body of Cloten, its mock battles, will require move-ment, props, certain bits of onstage business if it is to have its way with the audience. Dependence on the ear in *The Other House* is more nearly complete than it is in *Cymbeline. Cymbeline* must move toward the direction of the fully staged play. But to say, therefore, that *Cymbeline* can only be done, or can best be done, in fully staged form is to say more than can easily be defended. A Readers Theatre production of *Cymbeline* will not have an effect identical with that in a fully staged production of the play, but it may have an effect equally relevant, equally strong. Doubtless, Readers Theatre is at its best when it primarily serves the literary element in the play form, when the dramatic text is full and rich in language.

Doubling of Parts

In a play requiring many readers, some directors will assign a single reader to a number of roles. Two readers may even divide the cast of characters between them. But unless the readers are expert and capable of making sharp, clear distinctions between characters, the audience may be confused by such casting, particularly when there is little visual assistance (makeup, costuming). It is a mistake to assume too quickly that in a Readers Theatre performance one interpreter can easily handle many parts.

Entrances,
Exits, and
Use of
the Book

Sometimes, in an effort to avoid entrances and exits on the stage (in the belief that such movement tends to keep the performance located on the stage), the director will have readers turn their back to the audience when they are not in scene. This is, we think, a questionable practice. The human back is always tantalizing, since it conceals what is happening on the other side of the human figure, and the reader turned-about may well seem more in-scene than out-of-scene. The reader who simply drops out of character (without distracting movements) but remains facing the audience (fully or partially) will seem out-of-scene. He may close his book, lower his eyes, and so forth.

Will interpreters in Readers Theatre actually read their lines from the page? They will use their books, perhaps, but they must not be tied to them. Actors frequently find it difficult to use their scripts in Readers Theatre, but every good interpreter must know how to manage the book to good effect. If the book is simply held but never used—no pages turned, no reference made to lines—the audience is likely to resent the presence of the book as simply a gimmick. The sense of the book's being a part of the performance is important in Readers Theatre. At its best, the book may even seem a part of the character, built into the performance just as any prop would be. In a performance of Ibsen's *Ghosts,* books were employed in this fashion, each book bound in such a way as to underscore its relationship with the character. Mrs. Alving's book was bound in a material matching her costume; Pastor Manders's book looked like a Bible. Since much of the play is concerned with forms, conventions, and social laws, characters tended to "retreat" into their books (i.e., make the presence of the book markedly felt) whenever they hid behind conventions; they lowered them, even closed them, when they broke conventions. When Oswald had his attack at the close of the last act, his hands went limp and he dropped his book to the floor. The books were used—pages were turned, the raising and dropping of the texts was kept in character, the books' use was never aimless or arbitrary. The book should never function as a crutch, something there in case a line is forgotten—the audience should not be kept thinking "Oh, he didn't remember that speech," since such responses have the effect of constantly lowering the curtain on the scene. The use of the book must seem easy and effortless, though it will take constant practice for the interpreter to achieve such ease. (For an actor, this achievement in use of the book may at first seem impossible!)

Nothing is worse than a reading in which the readers simply look into their manuscripts without reference to the audience. The performer in Readers Theatre is bound, in this respect, by the same convention as the solo reader reading a lyric poem. He must be free enough from the book to establish the locus of the piece outside himself and to maintain that necessary tension between himself and audience—and yet he must keep the book in the performance. Unlike the actor, the interpreter has the written text as his immediate stimulus. Perhaps this is just a convention—but conventions are strong and real, and (perhaps more than we realize) we live by them. An actor reciting a poem by Baudelaire with a stage setting, costume, and movement will create quite a different effect from the interpreter reading the same poem from a book on the lectern, without setting and costume. (You might try the two forms in class and discuss the differences in effect.) One effect is not necessarily better than the other; they are simply different, and one is essentially the province of the actor and the other that of the interpreter. Material that is meant to be dramatic ought to make use of some of the conventions of the actor; material that is not essentially dramatic loses by being made dramatic. Everything depends on the nature of the material itself.

Appeals of Voice and Body

Neither the actor nor the interpreter can speak with the voice alone; the whole body speaks. But while the whole body of the actor is speaking (along with his voice), it is as if the playwright is saying "Look, look!" While the whole body of the interpreter is speaking, it is as if the writer is saying "Listen, listen!" In both cases we are both looking and listening.

It is occasionally argued that the ideal for the interpreter is the tape recording or the recorded disk, and that the ideal for the actor is the silent movie camera. Something is to be said for this view: the interpreter must be able to convey as much as possible through his voice, and the actor must be able to convey as much as possible through his body. But most people agree that the recorded reading is in some respects sterile, and probably no one wants to go back to the days of the silent film. Listening to a play broadcast on the radio, we are in no position to say whether the performers are interpreters or actors, since the voices are doing something that is an essential part of each of the two arts. But when performed on radio, the play faces all the problems Readers Theatre faces; it must ask how much can be done for the ear alone, and it is not free to do all that it might do onstage in a fully staged production. When it is done, however, in the actual presence of an audience it may (though with the presence of visual aids) still seek to rely primarily on the ear, or it may move the other way, in the direction of the actor's art.

Thus far we have talked mostly about the texts of plays. What about the text of a story, a novel, or a narrative poem? The same general rules hold. *Our Town* will serve as a model, since it is partially epic rather than purely dramatic in mode. The narrator in *Our Town* sometimes talks directly to the audience, sometimes directly to other characters within a scene, sometimes partly to the audience and partly within a scene. So in a story like Henry James's "The Beast in the Jungle" (which you will find in an adaptation at the end of the chapter), the narrator should probably place the scene in the audience—even look directly at the audience—but may, when he introduces the characters of the story or their dialogue, look at them or back and forth between them and the audience. And when the characters take over the scene and speak to one another, the narrator may see them onstage while they see one another essentially offstage. This is a way of breaking the direct contact between narrator and audience when the author wishes the narrator to retire. Since the narrator is thought of as controlling the perspective of the story, he ought not to drop out of the scene entirely by closing his book or turning away. When the characters retire, however, they probably ought to drop out of scene. Why?

CHAMBER THEATRE[2]

Chamber Theatre is a technique of staging prose fiction, retaining the text of the story or novel being performed but locating the scenes of the story onstage. It is not a dramatization, not a stage adaptation of prose fiction. It keeps the narrative form, the narrator, and the past tense in which most fiction is written, but it is like *Our Town* in moving, with the narrator, between the audience and the scenes onstage. Thus it gives fiction some of the immediacy of drama without sacrificing the epic mode in which it has been written.

A further refinement in Chamber Theatre as practiced by the scholar who has most fully served to define and develop it, Robert S. Breen, is that it treats as direct discourse certain parts of the text that are written as indirect discourse, assigning such passages to characters as if they were spoken aloud. This refinement will be illustrated later in the discussion.

Many people have testified to the vividness with which much fiction comes alive onstage. As written, stories and novels constantly move between scenes (in Phyllis Bentley's sense, in which we watch and listen as we might in a drama) and nonscenes, in which the author or narrator summarizes, describes, explains, or reflects—talking, as it were, directly to us, the silent readers. Chamber Theatre thus simply takes advantage of the dramatic moments to put them (as they seem to be) on the stage. In doing this, it tends perhaps more fully than Readers Theatre to make use of the conventions of stage performance: costumes, settings, character makeup. But it still tries to keep these elements to a minimum, and not to identify itself with the fully staged play, just as *Our Town* does. It is amazing what can be done with a chair, a table, and a spotlight.

Chamber Theatre does not alter (rewrite) the text of prose fiction, though it may cut and abridge in the interests of bringing a long text into manageable length for an evening's entertainment. Just as some texts are better suited than others for performance in Readers Theatre style, so some pieces of prose fiction are better suited than others for performance in Chamber Theatre style. On the whole, Chamber Theatre works best with fiction in which the interaction between narrator and characters is strong, and in which the psychological interest is high. In a story that is almost entirely in scene (not uncommon among modern

[2] For a full discussion, see Robert S. Breen, *Chamber Theatre* (Englewood Cliffs, N.J.: Prentice-Hall, 1978).

stories), Chamber Theatre begins to lose its identity and to resemble conventional drama, even though it may still take a more direct position toward the audience than is usual in conventional drama.

There is a danger in Chamber Theatre, as there is in practically everything. If it is not carefully handled, it tends to violate the temporal mode of fiction (normally past tense) by making the whole story too vividly present. There is a difference between the quality or feel of scenes in a novel (being read silently, or by a single reader who is reading both narrator and characters) and the quality of present-tense scenes onstage in which we have both narrator and characters. It is something like the difference between the following two passages:

from **THE KING OF THE GOLDEN RIVER**
—*John Ruskin*

Passage A:
"What did you keep us waiting in the rain for?" said Schwartz, as he walked in, throwing his umbrella in Gluck's face. "Ay! what for, indeed, you little vagabond?" said Hans, administering an educational box on the ear, as he followed his brother into the kitchen.

"Bless my soul!"said Schwartz when he opened the door.

"Amen," said the little gentleman, who had taken his cap off and was standing in the middle of the kitchen, bowing with the utmost possible velocity.

"Who's that?" said Schwartz, catching up a rolling-pin, and turning to Gluck with a fierce frown.

"I don't know, indeed, brother," said Gluck in great terror.

"How did he get in?" roared Schwartz.

"My dear brother," said Gluck, deprecatingly, "he was so *very* wet!"

Passage B:
SCHWARTZ. What did you keep us waiting in the rain for? (*Throwing his umbrella in Gluck's face*)

HANS. Ay! what for, indeed, you little vagabond? (*Boxing Gluck on the ear and following Schwartz into the kitchen*)

SCHWARTZ. (*Opening the door*) Bless my soul!

STRANGER. Amen! (*Bowing quickly*)

SCHWARTZ. Who's that? (*Catching up a rolling pin. Turning to Gluck with a fierce frown*)

GLUCK. (*Terrified*) I don't know, indeed, brother.

SCHWARTZ. How did he get in?

GLUCK. (*Deprecatingly*) My dear brother, he was so *very* wet!

This is not simply a matter of turning quotations into speeches; it is a transfer of mode from epic to dramatic. The tempo changes, the sense of "here and now" is much augmented. Passage B is drama; passage A is fiction. When Chamber Theatre makes the error of dramatizing (rather than staging) a prose fiction text, it sacrifices the very element it is presumably trying to capture, the vividness of the piece as prose fiction.

Hence the director of Chamber Theatre and the adapter of the text (they are often the same individual) must be careful to retain the narrator, though sometimes (as in the above passage) it is difficult. While it will seem like a mere confusion in terms to say that prose fiction offers present-tense scenes in the past tense, this is in effect what is usually does; if Chamber Theatre deliberately wipes out the past tense, it no longer serves the epic mode.

On the other hand, the narrator, mediating constantly between the onstage scene and the audience, keeps reminding us that the scenes are "as if," and that they are being seen through an intelligence not identical with the intelligence of the actors. He serves to distance the scenes. So do economies in staging. So do the offstage moments of the characters while they are in scene, since not all lines are directed to another character. And so, finally, does the assignment to the individual characters of indirect discourse treated as direct discourse. It is a virtue of Chamber Theatre that it vivifies narration and underscores the nature of point of view and the shifting locus of perspectives. It was in the interest of drawing the attention of students to the vitality of the narrator's voice, indeed, that Chamber Theatre was first created. It is usually not difficult for young interpreters to feel the necessity for rather full characterization of the speakers in dialogue scenes; often these same readers will brush over the narrative links, forgetting that the narrator to a large extent controls the perspectives within the dialogue. The narrator himself is normally the leading character in the text employed in a Chamber Theatre presentation—the leading character and, it must be said, the most difficult and complex character. The story is his story.

Adapting A Text

Turn again to the story "Araby," by James Joyce, in Chapter 3. Imagine, now, that we are staging it for a Chamber Theatre performance. Remember first of all that we have already decided that the story is divided between the boy's experience and the man's experience, since it is a story of memories. At times the man is predominant; at other times it is the boy. "Araby" provides an almost perfect text for Chamber Theatre, since Chamber Theatre provides us with a way of keeping the boy's experience from becoming too immediately present even when the boy is a character in a scene.

Imagine a dimly lighted stage. (Why should it be dimly lighted?) Imagine a man, the narrator, discovered on the stage, talking—quietly—directly to the audience. "North Richmond Street, being blind, was a quiet street except at the hour when the Christian Brothers' School set the boys free. An uninhabited house of two storeys stood at the blind end, detached from its neighbours in a square ground. The other houses

of the street, conscious of decent lives within them, gazed at one another with brown imperturbable faces." By this time, he may have located the house on the stage for us, walking to it. In the second paragraph, as he says "Among these I found a few paper-covered books,"
the imaginary house may be lighted with a dim spot, and a boy may be
discovered looking at the books. Boy and man together may observe the
wild garden behind the house; both may go into it, or perhaps the boy
alone may go, the man watching him and talking to us.

In the third paragraph the voices of boys at play may be introduced, and the boy's uncle and Mangan's sister, though never so vividly
as to drown out the narrator. Gradually the story settles down to less
summary, to more use of episode. In the fourth paragraph (though it
may be delayed till later) the entrance of the boy as a speaker becomes
possible:

THE MAN. Every morning I lay on the floor in the front parlour watching her door. *(The boy is pantomiming the action.)* The blind was pulled
down to within an inch of the sash so that I could not be seen. When she
came out on the doorstep my heart leaped.

THE BOY. *(The man watches him)* I ran to the hall, seized my books
and followed her. I kept her brown figure always in my eye. *(Mangan's
sister, entering the scene at "When she came out on the doorstep," walks
ahead of him)* and, when we came near the point at which our ways diverged, I quickened my pace and passed her. *(The boy and the girl disappear.)*

THE MAN. This happened morning after morning. I had never spoken
to her, except for a few casual words, and yet her name was like a summons
to all my foolish blood.

In the seventh paragraph, we begin to approach a scene:

THE BOY. At last she spoke to me. When she addressed the first words
to me, I was so confused that I did not know what to answer.

THE GIRL. She asked me was I going to Araby. *(To the boy)*

THE MAN. I forget whether I answered yes or no. *(To the audience)*

THE GIRL. *(To the boy)* It would be a splendid bazaar, she said she
would love to go.

THE BOY. And why can't you?

THE MAN. While she spoke she turned a silver bracelet round and
round her wrist.

THE GIRL. She could not go, she said, because there would be a retreat
that week in her convent.

THE MAN. Her brother and two other boys were fighting for their caps
and I was alone at the railings.

THE BOY. She held one of the spikes, bowing her head towards me.

THE MAN. (*Watching the boy responding to her*) The light from the lamp opposite our door caught the white curve of her neck, lit up her hair that rested there and, falling, lit up the hand upon the railing. It fell over one side of her dress and caught the white border of a petticoat, just visible as she stood at ease.

THE GIRL. It's well for you.

THE BOY. If I go, I will bring you something. (*They disappear as the light fades.*)

THE MAN. What innumerables follies laid waste my waking and sleeping thoughts after that evening! (And so on.)

Even so brief an example will suggest the possibilities for a rich, detailed examination of the movement of "Araby." It would be possible to keep the man and boy close together—even to let the man touch the boy and put an arm on his shoulder to suggest the warmth of his memory for the boy that he was. Also, this brief example suggests how excellent a medium Chamber Theatre is for the telling of prose fiction on television, where it is possible to fade into and out of scenes easily and to dissolve from characters to narrator with a minimum of effort.

It is probably clear that it would be a mistake to do too much in the way of placing properties and setting onstage. Not only are they remembered rather than quite present; they also come and go quickly and soundlessly. The problem might be quite different with a story in which the scene is kept solely and vividly within a single room, though such stories are few.

The question of who is to say what in Chamber Theatre is a question requiring a cautious, delicate answer. It is no simple matter of parceling out lines so that each character will get approximately an equal number! See if you can decide why the lines have been assigned as they have in the passages from "Araby." (There is no question about direct discourse; it is the passages in indirect discourse that require consideration.)

"Araby" is an Irish story by an Irish writer. Should the narrator and characters speak in an Irish dialect? Should they be costumed in the clothes these characters would wear in Dublin? What is involved in answering these questions?

Should the readers in Chamber Theatre use books? It is customary for them not to use books when they are characters in the scenes. The boy, Mangan's sister, and other characters in "Araby," since they function as actors function in a stage play for the most part, would not spoil that convention by reading from books, as if they were rehearsing a play. And since the narrator in "Araby" is a first-person narrator, himself a character in the story, probably he should not employ a book either, though in Readers Theatre all the characters might use books. (Chamber Theatre stages; Readers Theatre essentially does not.) The narrator in James's "The Beast in the Jungle," on the other hand, might use a book in Chamber Theatre even though the two characters in the story would not, since the narrator there is not really a character in the story but an observer—the author, as it were, reading his report to us. It is a question of the closeness of the tie between narrator and characters; the more involved the narrator is, the less likely he is to use a book. But the question should be left an open one, subject to examination with respect to each script, rather than made of matter of rule. It is related to the further question of the manipulation of the narrator onstage: does he remain separated from the action, to one side, as an observer, or does he (as in "Araby") literally step into the scene?

Quite apart from its use as a medium of performance, Chamber Theatre is an excellent way of teaching and understanding the complex issues involved in perspective within prose fiction. "Who is looking at what?" is a constant question for the adapter of the text. We have said that this is a vital question in determining the locus of any work of literature; Chamber Theatre constantly forces it upon us. Chamber Theatre guards against the too-easy dismissal of passages of description and exposition by reminding us that such passages are always being said by someone, and with something in mind.

READERS THEATRE, CHAMBER THEATRE, COMPOSITE SCRIPTS

All three of the forms named here are ensemble forms. We have said that Readers Theatre is the ensemble performance of any material involving delineated characters, with an essentially offstage locus; as texts it may include stories, poems, plays, novels, as well as many of the transitional forms considered in Chapter 12. Chamber Theatre is a particular technique for the staging of fiction. But there are many composite scripts which mix the various kinds, often in exciting ways.

Scripts may be documentary; they may represent variations on a given theme ("The Black Experience," for example); they may be biographical (the life of a writer and selections from his works, perhaps); they may make use of letters between famous individuals (Robert and Elizabeth Browning, for example); they may be polemic. There is literally no end to the kinds of scripts which can be imagined and produced.

One caveat is in order, however. Whatever the nature of the script, ensemble performance in interpretation ought to be concerned with the quality and significance of the script itself in performance. A vacuous text remains a vacuous text. This is not to say that a text must be "serious" or that it need be "great." Performance ought to be pleasurable, and there are various levels of pleasure. But a text ought to be worth the performers' and the audience's time, worth the effort which goes into careful preparation. Whether a solo or an ensemble performance, the performance in interpretation is not simply a theatrical event. Interest lies not simply in the performer; it is in the matching of the performer and the thing performed, in that double life, that significance will lie for the audience.

In ensemble performance, the group must function with the same dedication that solo performance requires of the single reader. To ask that a group learn to perform with the single-mindedness of an effective solo reader is to ask a great deal. It is *not* to ask too much.

PERFORMANCE AS METAPHOR

One view of ensemble performance suggests that the performance ought not simply "duplicate" the work in a literal way, but ought instead to provide a performance metaphor for the work. Rather than following out the concrete "stage directions" given by the author, the performance ought, in this view, to look for an extension or parallel that would underscore perspective rather than detail. In a novel in which the characters are seen as caught in an endless circle of behaviors, for example, the director might choose to use the wheel as a symbol for those behaviors—to locate characters on a wheel in the setting, to emphasize circularity in the movements of characters, perhaps to stage the work in the round to emphasize the point.

This is a justifiable view when the act of performance is seen as an act of criticism. Criticism is always reductive; in the reduction, it makes its point. Criticism is abstractive; in its abstraction, it also makes its point. But there is a danger in seeing the act of performance as an act of criticism, and in this book we distinguish between the two.

To create symbols for the performance of a work which is not in itself reaching clearly toward symbolism is to substitute the critic's work for the artist's. An implicit statement does not always gain by being made explicit. King Lear, as a character, is not a symbol, though through the character the playwright may indeed be reaching toward a symbolic statement about Lear's world. It is fatal, in our view, to reduce Lear himself to a symbol.

In the view we take, the aim of the performance is to keep the plenitude of the work, the multiplicity of its symbols, the concreteness as well as the abstraction through which it moves. The performer is a pluralist, seeking to embody all that he or she can. The best performance of a work is the most complex reading the work will sustain. It is possible to force into a work *more* than the work will contain, and that, too, is damaging; but most performances stop short of the complexities a work will profitably bear.

OTHER QUESTIONS FOR ENSEMBLE PERFORMANCE

In so brief a chapter we cannot hope to have covered the ground thoroughly. There are dozens of questions to be faced with each new group presentation in the various forms. Many questions must be left up to the director: Do the characters talking to one another offstage seem to be focusing on the same point (and hence to be talking with one another), or are they focusing on different points (appearing to miss seeing each other)? Are the characters who are not speaking at the moment responding to the offstage location of the character who is speaking, or are they looking in their manuscripts or waiting for their next speech? (*They should be responding.* Probably the worst time for a reader to drop his eyes to his manuscript is during the speech of another reader. He will appear to be hunting for his next lines.) In responding, is the silent character keeping his response minimal (though clear and sharp) so as not to steal the scene from the reader? Is the scene being placed far enough out in the audience so that the reading is reaching all the way to the back of the auditorium? Are the minimal actions large enough to carry? Are pantomimed actions properly motivated and carried through so that they avoid being ludicrous on the one hand and empty on the other?

These are typical questions. Those who are tempted to try group performances themselves—and we hope that many will be—will soon have a host of others to add to them.

We must add one additional consideration. There is a renewed interest in performances combining media—film clips, slides, music, dance, sounds (vocal and other), photography, painting. There is nothing very new about the notion of mixing media, but there are many more effects to mix than there used to be. While some such performances will seem too "souped-up," kitsch, or a tour de force (however exciting), others will succeed in heightening the appeal of the texts being used. A reading of James Agee's *Let Us Now Praise Famous Men,* for example, may be accompanied by blown-up versions of the photographs Walker Evans did for Agee's book. A program directed by Robert Breen dealing with London in a sequence of periods from Samuel Johnson to Virginia Woolf made effective use of slides detailing aspects of London life and of photographs of Virginia Woolf at various stages of her life. Music accompanied some scenes, and voices uttered the street cries familiar in London.

Electronic music may underscore modern texts making use of cacophonies and distortions. Dance, tableaus, vocal sound effects may extend and enlarge the meanings of concrete poetry. A reading of Dos Passos' *Tin Lizzie* (pages 429–435) may be intensified by the use of newsreel clips and sounds from the period about which Dos Passos writes.

One ought to consider whether one is employing the extra media simply as gimmicks or whether they are needed to achieve the rich effectiveness of a particular text. Or, again, the mixing of media may require that the literary text itself be simply an element (not necessarily the major element) in a performance with a rhetorical or forensic purpose. Or mixed media may exist for the sake of the mix itself—but some mixes are better than others, and some mixes spoil in the mixing. While there may be no accounting for tastes, in public performances tastes must ultimately be accounted for.

The evidence from artists themselves that media constitute an exciting new material may be demonstrated in comments made by a contemporary composer, Luciano Berio, who has written orchestral works, musical dramas, ballets, and electronic music. He seeks by the employ-

MIXED MEDIA PRESENTATIONS

ment of new forms to give music some of the immediacy of the theater. His *Sinfonia* (available on Columbia Records) makes use of the New York Philharmonic; the Swingle Singers; echoes of the music of Mahler and Debussy and Ravel; words from the writings of Joyce, Beckett, Levi-Strauss, and Martin Luther King; political slogans; and graffiti. Berio is quoted as saying: "I must transform things, and in order to make a transformation clear, you should deal with familiar objects. I'd use President Nixon if he were available."[3]

For Berio, according to Irving Kolodin's review of *Sinfonia,* words are necessary "as an associative element in the total thought process," and the use he makes of the Swingle Singers depends on "their enormous *facility* in the enunciation, as individuals and as a group, of verbal values." The human voices thus become one group of instruments in an orchestra. Kolodin closes his review by saying that the recording of *Sinfonia* "can be recommended to anyone thirsting for a new, valid musical experience and fed to here with the faddists, the fumblers, and the fakers. To close with one more quote: the novelty of Berio's *Sinfonia* reposes not in any specific innovation or deviation, but as Ravel said of *Le Sacre* (to Stravinsky's satisfaction), 'in the musical entity.'"[4]

Speaking of the same recording, Donal Henahan says, "There is, certainly, nothing in this that many a modern composer has not tried before—think only of Ives, or Cage, or Stockhausen. But, as Schoenberg asked in his Zennish way, 'A Chinese poet speaks Chinese, but what does he say?' What Berio has said in his *Sinfonia* is that old rigid separations—sounds versus music, poetry versus prose, and so on—are dead and should be buried."[5] The generalization attributed to Berio's music may be debatable, but surely the art of interpretation should be as much interested in the possibilities of mixed media as in the other group forms we have discussed. It may play a large or a minor part in the mix; but whatever part it plays, it must learn to play it well.

An interest in media presentations may, of course, go well beyond the interest upon which this book centers. The "interpreter" in some kinds of presentations becomes really a maker of "texts," and performance becomes a performance by the media themselves, as orchestrated by the "interpreter." Author and interpreter now become author-interpreter, and the electronic age brings us a new version of the ancient art of the rhapsode, where writer and performer were one.

MATERIALS FOR PRACTICE

You will find below scripts arranged for Readers Theatre and Chamber Theatre. The Readers Theatre script ("The Beast in the Jungle," by Henry

[3] *New York Times,* 15 February 1970.

[4] *Saturday Review,* 29 November 1969.

[5] *High Fidelity Magazine,* August 1969.

James) was prepared for a program of prescribed length for presentation at a national convention of the Speech Communication Association. A comparison of the script with the original James story will show that the story has been both cut and rearranged in the interest of the necessary condensation. This is a relatively free treatment of script, though, we think, faithful to the intention of the story. You will find it instructive as an exercise in cutting to compare the adaptation with the original. The Chamber Theatre script, on the other hand, involves no rearrangement and a minimum of cutting; the complete text is presented, with the cuts indicated. All speaker designations, in both scripts, are those of the adapters.

In the Chamber Theatre script, lines italicized are to be cut in performance or used as stage directions indicating action and business rather than spoken words. Two narrators have been employed rather than a single narrator, the second narrator being used to underscore the relationship between the boys and the puppies and to increase the tensions in the narration. The second narrator also imitates the sounds made by the puppies, since the puppies are imagined rather than present in the performance. Actions suggested in the story, when they involve characters in the production, are pantomimed: Ambo and Baldo fight on the ground, Baldo holds the imagined puppy and cuddles him, Nana Elang washes the imagined rice and prepares the imagined vegetables, Ambo eats the imagined banana, Tang Ciako kills the puppy. All these actions were carried out in the original performance of the story at the University of the Philippines under the direction of the adapter of the story.

THE BEAST IN THE JUNGLE[6]
—*Henry James*
(adapted by Natalie Cherry Baca)

NARRATOR. What determined the speech that startled John Marcher in the course of their encounter scarcely matters, being probably but some words spoken by himself quite without intention—spoken as they lingered and slowly moved together after their renewal of acquaintance. He had been conveyed by friends, that autumn day, for luncheon, to the house at which he was later to learn she was staying. They had sat, much separated, at a very long table—

JOHN. and when he first saw May Bartram, her face—a reminder, yet not quite a remembrance—had begun merely by troubling him rather pleasantly. It affected him as the sequel of something of which he had lost the beginning. He knew it, and for the time quite welcomed it, as a continuation—but didn't know what it continued.

He was also somehow aware—yet without a direct sign from her—that

---

[6] Reprinted by permission of the adapter. Copyright applied for.

the young woman herself had not lost the thread. She had not lost it, but she wouldn't give it back to him, he saw, without some putting forth of his hand for it.

NARRATOR. By the time they at last came to speech, they were alone in one of the rooms . . . and the charm of it was that even before they had spoken they had practically arranged with each other to stay behind for a talk.

JOHN. As soon as he heard her voice, the slight irony he divined in her attitude lost its advantage. He almost jumped at it to get there before her: "I met you years and years ago—7 years ago—in Rome; I remember all about it."

MAY. "I must confess I'm disappointed—I was so sure that you didn't. Particularly since it was more nearly 10 years—and it was not Rome, it was Naples—."

JOHN. "Oh yes—I had come up to Naples with the Pembles—."

MAY. "With the Boyers—."

JOHN. "You were with your—uncle and aunt . . . ?"

MAY. "My mother and brother—."

JOHN. "But I do remember the thunderstorm that drove us for refuge into an excavation at—ah—."

MAY. "Pompeii."

JOHN. He accepted her amendments, he enjoyed her corrections—and he only felt it as a drawback that when all was made comfortable to the truth there didn't appear much of anything left.

NARRATOR. There weren't apparently, all counted, more than a dozen little things that had succeeded in coming to pass between them—small possible germs, but too deeply buried—(too deeply, didn't it seem?)—to sprout after so many years.

JOHN. It was in vain to pretend she was an old friend, in spite of which it was as an old friend that he saw she would have suited him. He would have liked to invent something—get her to make-believe with him that some passage of a romantic or critical kind *had* originally occurred: He had, say, rendered her some service—saved her from a capsized boat in the Bay—or recovered her dressing bag, filched from her cab, in the streets of Naples, by a lazzarone with a stiletto. . . .

NARRATOR. He was really almost reaching out in imagination—as against time—for something that would do, when, just at the turn, she herself decided to take up the case and, as it were, save the situation.

MAY. "You know you told me something that I've never forgotten and that again and again has made me think of you since; it was that tremendously hot day when we went to Sorrento, across the bay, for the breeze. What I allude to was what you said to me, on the way back, as we sat, under the awning of the boat, enjoying the cool. . . . Have you forgotten?"

JOHN. "I try to think—but I give it up.—Yet I remember the Sorrento day."

MAY. "I'm not very sure you do, and I'm not very sure I ought to want you to. It's dreadful to bring a person back, at any time, to what he was ten years before. If you've lived away from it, so much the better."

JOHN. "Ah, if *you* haven't, why should I?"

MAY. "Lived away, you mean, from what I myself was?"

JOHN. "From what *I* was!—Besides, perhaps I haven't!"

MAY. "Perhaps. Yet if you haven't, I should suppose you would remember. It was about yourself.—Has it ever happened?"

JOHN. "Do you mean I told you—."

MAY. "It was something about yourself that it was natural one shouldn't forget—that is if one remembered you at all. That's why I ask you—if the thing you spoke of has ever come to pass?"

JOHN. Then he saw—

NARRATOR. but he was lost in wonder. After the first shock of it, her knowledge began, even if rather strangely, to taste sweet to him. She was the only other person in the world then who would have it, and she had had it all these years, while the fact of his having so breathed his secret had unaccountably faded from him.

JOHN. No wonder they couldn't have met as if nothing had happened! "I judge that I know what you mean. Only I had strangely enough lost the consciousness of having taken you so far into my confidence."

MAY. "Is it because you've taken so many others as well?"

JOHN. "I've taken nobody. Not a creature since then."

MAY. "So that I'm the only person who knows?"

JOHN. "The only person in the world."

MAY. "Well, I myself have never spoken. I've never, never repeated of you what you told me—and I never will—."

JOHN. She looked at him so that he perfectly believed her—. "Please don't then. We're just right as it is."

MAY. "Oh, I am, if you are!—Then you do still feel the same way?"

JOHN. It all kept coming as a sort of revelation. He had thought of himself so long as abominably alone, and, lo, he wasn't alone a bit. He hadn't been, it appeared, for an hour—since those moments on the Sorrento boat. It was she who had been alone.—To tell her what he told her—! What had it been but to ask something of her? Something that she had given in her charity, without his having so much as thanked her. He had endless gratitude to make up. Only for that he must see just how he had figured to her: "And what, exactly, was the account I gave—?"

MAY. "Of the way you did feel? Well, it was very simple. You said you had had from your earliest time, as the deepest thing within you, the sense of being kept for something rare and strange, possibly prodigious and terrible, that was sooner or later to happen to you, that you had in your bones the foreboding and the conviction of, and that would perhaps overwhelm you."

JOHN. "Do you call that very simple?"

MAY. "It was perhaps because I seemed, as you spoke, to understand it."

JOHN. "You do understand it?"

MAY. "You still have the belief?"

JOHN. "Oh!"

MAY. "Whatever it is to be, it hasn't yet come."

JOHN. "It hasn't yet come. Only, you know, it isn't anything I'm to do—."

MAY. "It's to be something you're merely to suffer?"

JOHN. "Well, say to wait for—to have to meet, to face, to see suddenly break out in my life; possibly destroying all further consciousness, possibly annihilating me; possibly, on the other hand, only altering everything, striking at the root of all my world and leaving me to the consequences, however they shape themselves."

MAY. "Isn't what you describe but the expectation—or, at any rate, the sense of danger, familiar to so many people—of falling in love?"

JOHN. "Did you ask me that before?"

MAY. "No—I wasn't so free-and-easy then. But it's what strikes me now."

JOHN. "Of course it strikes you. Of course it strikes *me*. Of course what's in store for me may be no more than that. The only thing is that I think if it had been that, I should by this time know."

MAY. "Do you mean because you've *been* in love? . . . You've been in love, and it hasn't meant such a cataclysm, hasn't proved the great affair?"

JOHN. "Here I am, you see. It hasn't been overwhelming."

MAY. "Then it hasn't been love."

JOHN. "Well, I at least thought it was. I took it for that—I've taken it till now. It was agreeable, it was delightful, it was miserable. But it wasn't strange. It wasn't what *my* affair's to be."

MAY. "Is it a sense of coming violence?"

JOHN. "I don't think of it as—when it does come—necessarily violent. I only think of it as natural and as, of course, above all, unmistakable."

MAY. "Then how will it appear strange?"

JOHN. "It won't—to *me*."

MAY. "To whom then?"

JOHN. "Well—say to you."

MAY. "Oh then, I'm to be present?"

JOHN. "Why you *are* present—since you know."

MAY. "I see. . . . But I mean at the catastrophe."

JOHN. "It will depend on yourself—if you'll watch with me."

MAY. "Are you afraid?"

JOHN. "Don't leave me *now*."

MAY. "Are you afraid?"

JOHN. "Do you think me simply out of my mind? Do I merely strike you as a harmless lunatic?"

MAY. "No. I understand you. I believe you."

JOHN. "You mean you feel how my obsession—poor old thing!—may correspond to some possible reality?"

MAY. "To some possible reality."

JOHN. "Then you *will* watch with me?"

MAY. "Are you afraid?"

JOHN. "Did I tell you I was—at Naples?"

MAY. "No, you said nothing about it."

JOHN. "Then I don't know. And I should *like* to know.—You'll tell me yourself whether you think so. If you'll watch with me you'll see."

MAY. "Very well then.—I'll watch with you."

NARRATOR. The fact that she "knew"—knew and neither chaffed him nor betrayed him—in a short time began to constitute between them a sensible bond, which became more marked, during the years that followed, as their meetings flourished and multiplied. They went to the National Gallery—to the South Kensington museum—and, as often as a dozen nights in the month, the season permitting, to the opera. Seeing her home at such times, he occasionally went in with her to finish, as he called it, the evening, and to sit down to the always careful little supper that awaited his pleasure. Her piano at hand and each of them familiar with it, at such hours they went over passages of the opera together. They were, to Marcher's sense, no longer hovering about the headwaters of their stream, but had felt their boat pushed sharply off and down the current. They were, now, literally afloat together.

JOHN. And the fortunate cause of it was just the buried treasure of her knowledge. It had never entered into his plan that anyone should "know," but since a mysterious fate had opened his mouth in youth, he would count that a compensation and profit by it to the utmost. That the right person *should* know tempered the asperity of his secret, and May Bartram was clearly right, because—well, because there she was. Her knowledge simply settled it; he would have been sure enough by this time had she been wrong.

NARRATOR. As for May Bartram's position, well, he was quite ready to be selfish just a little—since, surely, no more charming occasion for it had come to him.

JOHN. Nevertheless, he would be quite careful not to be in the least coercive, and he would keep well before him the lines on which consideration for her—the very highest—ought to proceed. . . . The real form it should have taken, of course, on the basis that stood out large, was the form of their marrying. But the devil in this was that the very basis itself put marrying out of the question. His conviction, his apprehension, his obsession, in short, was not a condition he could invite a woman to share; and that consequence of it was precisely what was the matter with him. Something or other lay in wait for him, amid the twists and the turns of the months and the years, like a crouching beast in the jungle. It signified little whether the beast were destined to slay him or to be slain. The definite point was the inevitable spring of the creature; and the definite lesson from that was that a man didn't cause himself to be accompanied by a lady on a tiger-hunt.

NARRATOR. He was, at all events, destined to become aware little by little, as time went by, that May Bartram was all the while looking at his life, judging it, measuring it, in the light of the thing she knew, which grew to be at last, with the consecration of the years, never mentioned between them save as "the real truth" about him. . . . *She* at least never spoke of the secret of his life except as "the real truth about you," and she had in fact a wonderful way of making it seem, as such, the secret of her own life too.

And so, while they grew older together, she watched with him, and she let this association give shape and colour to her entire existence. Beneath her forms, as well, detachment had learned to sit, and behaviour had become for her, in the social sense, a false account of herself. They had, from an early time, made up their minds that society was, luckily, unintelligent, and the margin that this gave them had fairly become one of their commonplaces. Yet there were still moments when the situation turned almost fresh—usually under the effect of some expression drawn from herself. Her expressions doubtless repeated themselves, but her intervals were generous—.

MAY. "What saves us, you know, is that we answer so completely to so usual an appearance: that of the man and woman whose friendship has become such a daily habit, or almost, as to be at last indispensable. . . . Our habit saves you, at least, don't you see? because it makes you, after all, for the vulgar, indistinguishable from other men. . . . What's the most inveterate mark of men in general? Why, the capacity to spend endless time with dull women—to spend it, I won't say without being bored, but without minding that they are—without being driven off at a tangent by it; which comes to the same thing. I'm your dull woman, a part of the daily bread for which you pray at church. That covers your tracks more than anything."

JOHN. "And what covers yours? . . . I see of course what you mean by your saving me, in one way and another, so far as other people are concerned—I've seen it all along. Only, what is it that saves *you*? I often think, you know, of that."

MAY. "Where other people, you mean, are concerned?"

JOHN. "Well, you're really so in with me, you know—as a sort of result of my being so in with yourself. What is it that saves *you*?"

MAY. "I never said that it hadn't made me talked about."

JOHN. "Ah well then, you're not 'saved'."

MAY. "It has not been a question for me. If you've had your woman, I've had my man."

JOHN. "And you mean that makes you all right?"

MAY. "I don't know why it shouldn't make me—humanly, which is what we're speaking of—as right as it makes you."

JOHN. "I see. 'Humanly,' no doubt, as showing that you're living for something. Not, that is, just for me and my secret."

MAY. "I don't pretend it exactly shows that I'm not living for you. It's my intimacy with you that's in question."

JOHN. "Yes, but since, as you say, I'm only, so far as people make out, ordinary, you're—aren't you?—no more than ordinary either. You help me to pass for a man like another. So if I *am*, as I understand you, you're not compromised. Is that it?"

MAY. "That's it. It's all that concerns me—to help you pass for a man like another."

JOHN. "How kind, how beautiful, you are to me! How shall I ever repay you?"

MAY. "By going on as you are."

JOHN. "I sometimes ask myself if it's quite fair. Fair I mean to have so involved and—since one may say it—interested you. I almost feel as if you hadn't really had time to do anything else."

MAY. "Anything else but be interested?—Ah, what else does one ever want to be? If I've been 'watching' with you, as we long ago agreed that I was to do, watching is always in itself an absorption."

JOHN. "Oh, certainly, if you hadn't had your curiosity—! Only, doesn't it sometimes come to you, as time goes on, that your curiosity is not being particularly repaid?"

MAY. "Do you ask that, by any chance, because you feel at all that yours isn't? I mean because you have to wait so long?"

JOHN. "For the thing to happen that never does happen? For the beast to jump out? No, I'm just where I was about it. One's in the hands of one's law—there one is. As to the form the law will take, the way it will operate, that's its own affair."

MAY. "Yes, of course, one's fate is coming, of course it *has* come, in its own form and its own way, all the while. Only, you know, the form and the way in your case were to have been—well, something so exceptional and, as one may say, so particularly *your* own."

JOHN. "You say 'were to *have* been,' as if in your heart you had begun to doubt."

MAY. "Oh!"

JOHN. "As if you believed that nothing will now take place."

MAY. "You're far from my thought."

JOHN. "What then is the matter with you?"

MAY. "Well, the matter with me is simply that I'm more sure than ever my 'curiosity,' as you call it, will be but too well repaid."

JOHN. "You know something I don't. You know what's to happen. You know, and you're afraid to tell me. It's so bad that you're afraid I'll find out."

MAY. "You'll never find out."

NARRATOR. And so it was into his "going on as he was" that their relationship relapsed, and really for so long a time that the day inevitably came for a further sounding of their depths. A difference had been made, once for all, by the fact that she had, all this while, not appeared to feel the need of rebutting his charge of an idea within her that she didn't dare to express.

JOHN. He circled about the idea at a distance that alternately narrowed and widened and that yet was not much affected by the consciousness in him that there was nothing she could "know," after all, any better than he did—except of course that she might have finer nerves. That was what women had where they were interested; they made out things, where people were concerned, that the people often couldn't have made out for themselves—and the beauty of May Bartram was in particular that she had given herself so to his case.

He felt in these days what, oddly enough, he had never felt before, the growth of a dread of losing her by some catastrophe—some catastrophe that yet wouldn't at all be *the* catastrophe: partly because she had, almost of a sudden, begun to strike him as useful to him as never yet, and partly by reason of an appearance of uncertainty in her health, coincident and equally new.

NARRATOR. When the day came that she confessed to him her fear of a deep disorder in her blood, he felt the shadow of a change and the chill of a shock.

She kept to the house, now, as she had never done—he had to go to her to see her—she could meet him nowhere, though there was scarce a corner of their loved old London in which she had not in the past, at one time or another, done so.

He had gone in late, one day, to see her, but evening had not settled and she was presented to him in that long, fresh light of waning April days which affects us often with a sadness sharper than the greyest hours of autumn. May Bartram sat, for the first time in the year, without a fire, a fact that, to Marcher's sense, gave the scene of which she formed part, a smooth and ultimate look, an air of knowing, in its immaculate order and its cold, meaningless cheer, that it would never see a fire again.

JOHN. He caught himself wondering if the great accident would take form now as nothing more than his being condemned to see this charming woman, this admirable friend, pass away from him. He had never so unreservedly qualified her as while confronted in thought with such a possibility; in spite of which there was small doubt for him that as an answer to his long riddle the mere effacement of even so fine a feature of his situation would be an abject anti-climax. It would represent, as connected with his past attitude, a drop of dignity under the shadow of which his existence could only become the most grotesque of failures.—But what did everything mean—what, that is, did *she* mean, she and her vain waiting and her probable death and the soundless admonition of it all—unless that, at this time of day, it was simply, it was overwhelmingly too late? . . . Oh, he didn't care now what awful crash might overtake him, with what ignominy or what monstrosity he might yet be associated—since he wasn't, after all, too utterly old to suffer—if it would only be decently proportionate to the posture he had kept, all his life, in the promised presence of it.

This was why he felt the strongest need, on this occasion, to ask her again, though indirectly, what she knew: "What do you regard as the very worst that, at this time of day, *can* happen to me?"

MAY. "I've repeatedly thought, only it always seemed to me of old that I couldn't quite make up my mind. I thought of dreadful things, between which it was difficult to choose; and so must you have done."

JOHN. "Rather! I feel now as if I had scarce done anything else. I appear to myself to have spent my life in thinking of nothing *but* dreadful things.—Ah, yes, there were times when we did go far."

MAY. "Oh, far—!"

JOHN. "Do you mean you're prepared to go further?"

MAY. "Do you consider that we went so far?"

JOHN. "Why, I thought it the point you were just making—that we *had* looked most things in the face."

MAY. "Including each other?—But you're quite right. We've had together great imaginations, often great fears; but some of them have been unspoken."

JOHN. "Then the worst—we haven't faced that. I *could* face it, I believe, if I knew what you think it. I feel as if I had lost my power to conceive such things. It's spent."

MAY. "Then why do you assume that mine isn't?"

JOHN. "Because you've given me signs to the contrary. It isn't a question for you of conceiving, imagining, comparing. It isn't a question now of choosing.—You know something that I don't. You've shown me that before."

MAY. "I've shown you, my dear, nothing."

JOHN. "You can't hide it."

MAY. "Oh, oh!"

JOHN. "You admitted it months ago, when I spoke of it to you as of something you were afraid I would find out. Your answer was that I couldn't, that I wouldn't, and I don't pretend I have. But you had something therefore in mind, and I see now that it must have been, that it still is, the possibility that, of all possibilities, has settled itself for you as the worst. This is why I appeal to you. I'm only afraid of ignorance now—I'm not afraid of knowledge."

MAY. "It *would* be the worst. I mean the thing that I've said.—What we're speaking of, remember, is only my idea."

JOHN. "It's your belief. That's enough for me. If, having it, you give me no more light on it, you abandon me."

MAY. "No, no!—I'm with you—don't you see?—still. I haven't forsaken you."

JOHN. "Then tell me if I shall consciously suffer."

MAY. "Never."

JOHN. "Well, what's better than that? Do you call that the worst?"

MAY. "You think nothing is better?"

JOHN. ". . . It isn't that it's all a mistake?"

MAY. "A mistake?—Oh, no, it's nothing of that sort. You've been right."

JOHN. "Are you telling me the truth, so that I sha'n't have been a bigger idiot that I can bear to know? I *haven't* lived with a vain imagination? I haven't waited but to see the door shut in my face?"

MAY. "However the case stands *that* isn't the truth. Whatever the reality, it *is* a reality.—But the door isn't shut. . . . The door's open—."

JOHN. "Then something's to come?"

MAY. "It's never too late—."

JOHN. ". . . But—you don't tell me. . . ."

MAY. "I'm afraid I'm too ill."

JOHN. "Too ill to tell me?"

MAY. "Don't you know, now?"

JOHN. "'Now'—. I know nothing".

MAY. "Oh!"

JOHN. "Are you in pain?"

MAY. "No."

JOHN. "What then has happened?"

MAY. "What *was* to. . . . You've nothing to wait for more. It *has* come."

JOHN. "But come in the night—come and passed me by?"

MAY. "Oh no, it hasn't passed you by!"

JOHN. "But I haven't been aware of it, and it hasn't touched me?"

MAY. "Ah, your not being aware of it—your not being aware of it is the strangeness *in* the strangeness. It's the wonder *of* the wonder.—It *has* touched you. It has done its office. It has made you all its own."

JOHN. "So utterly without my knowing it?"

MAY. "So utterly without your knowing it.—It's enough if *I* know it. . . . Did we ever dream, with all our dreams, that we should sit and talk of it thus?"

JOHN. "It might have been that we couldn't talk?"

MAY. "Well, not from this side. This, you see, is the *other* side. We've got across . . . we're *here*. It's past—it's behind. Before—."

JOHN. "Before . . .?"

MAY. "Before, you see, it was always to *come*. That kept it present."

JOHN. "Oh, I don't care what comes now! It seems to me I liked it better present, as you say, that I can like it absent with *your* absence—with the absence of everything—."

MAY. "I would live for you still—if I could.—But I can't—."

NARRATOR. They had parted forever in that strange talk. Access to her chamber of pain, rigidly guarded, was almost wholly forbidden him; he was feeling now, moreover, in the face of doctors, nurses, the two or three relatives, how few were the rights, as they were called in such cases, that he had to put forward, and how odd it might even seem that their intimacy shouldn't have given him more of them. A woman might have been, as it were, everything to him, and it might yet present him in no connection that anyone appeared obliged to recognize.

If this was the case in these closing weeks, it was the case more sharply on the occasion of the last offices rendered, in the great grey London cemetery, to what had been mortal, to what had been precious in his friend.

JOHN. He saw himself treated as scarce more nearly concerned with her than if there had been a thousand others. He couldn't quite have said what he expected, but he had somehow not expected this approach to a double privation. There were moments, as the weeks went by, when he would have liked, by some almost aggressive act, to take his stand on the intimacy of his loss, in order that it *might* be questioned and his retort, to the relief of his spirit, so recorded. But an irritation more helpless followed fast on this—a moment during which, turning things over and with a good conscience but with a bare horizon—he found himself wondering if he oughtn't to have begun, so to speak, further back.

NARRATOR. He found himself wondering indeed at many things, and this last speculation had others to keep it company. What it presently came to in truth was that poor Marcher waded through the beaten grass of his jungle, where no life stirred, where no breath sounded, where no evil eye seemed to gleam from a possible lair, very much as if vaguely looking for the Beast, and still more as if missing it. He walked about in an existence that had grown strangely more spacious, and, stopping fitfully in places where the undergrowth of life struck him as closer, asked himself yearningly, wondered secretly and sorely, if it would have lurked here or there. The lost stuff of consciousness became thus for him as a strayed or stolen child to an unappeasable father; he hunted it up and down very much as if he were knocking at doors and inquiring of the police.—This was the spirit in which, inevitably, he envisioned for himself a journey—a journey that was to be as long and as far as he could make it—.

JOHN. Before he quitted London, however, he made a pilgrimage, once more, to May Bartram's grave, took his way to it through the endless avenues of the grim suburban necropolis, sought it out in the wilderness of tombs, and, though he had come but for the renewal of the act of farewell, found himself, when he at last stood by it, beguiled into long intensities.— *This* was the open page—*here* were the facts of the past, here the truth of his life, here the backward reaches in which he could lose himself. With this light before him, he knew that even of late his ache had only been smothered. It was strangely drugged, but it throbbed; at the touch it began to bleed.

NARRATOR. And the touch, in the event, was the face of a fellow-mortal. This face looked into Marcher's own, through the gray autumn afternoon, with the leaves thick in the alleys, with an expression like the cut of a blade. The person who so mutely assaulted him was a figure he had vaguely noticed, on reaching his own goal, absorbed by an apparently fresh grave a short distance away. A middle-aged man, in mourning, whose bowed back, among the clustered monuments and mortuary yews, was constantly presented. Marcher rested, with a heaviness he had not yet known, on the low stone table that bore May Bartram's name. He rested without power to move, as if some spring in him, some spell vouchsafed, had suddenly been broken forever.

JOHN. If he could have done that moment as he wanted he would simply have stretched himself on the slab that was ready to take him, treating it as a placed prepared to receive his last sleep. What in all the wide world had he now to keep awake for? He stared before him with the question, and it was then that he caught the shock of the face.

NARRATOR. His neighbor was now advancing along the path on his way to one of the gates. This brought him near, and his pace was slow, so that—and all the more as there was a kind of hunger in his look—the two men were for a minute directly confronted.—He felt him on the spot as one of the deeply stricken—

JOHN. —a perception so sharp that nothing else in the picture lived for it—nothing but the deep ravage of the features that he showed.

NARRATOR. What he was conscious of, in the first place, was that the image of scarred passion presented to him was conscious too—of something that profaned the air; and, in the second, that roused, startled, shocked, he was yet the next moment looking after it, as it went, with envy. The stranger passed, but the raw glare of his grief remained.

JOHN. What had the man *had* to make him, by the loss of it, so bleed and yet live? Something that *he*, John Marcher, hadn't; . . . No passion had ever touched him, for this was what passion meant. He had survived and maundered and pined, but where had been *his* deep ravage? The sight that had just met his eyes named to him, as in letters of quick flame, something he had utterly, insanely missed! He had seen *outside* his life—not learned it within—the way a woman was mourned when she had been loved for herself.—

NARRATOR. And what he presently stood there gazing at was the sounded void of his life.—The name on the table smote him as the passage of his neighbour had done, . . .

JOHN. . . . and what it said to him, full in the face, was that *she* was what he had missed.

NARRATOR. This was the awful thought, the answer to all the past, the vision at the dread clearness of which he turned as cold as the stone beneath. The fate he had been marked for he had met with a vengeance—he had emptied the cup to the lees; he had been the man of his time, *the* man to whom nothing on earth was to have happened!

JOHN. She had seen it—had, at a given moment, perceived, and she had then offered him the chance to baffle his doom. The escape would have been to love her; then, *then* he would have lived. *She* had lived, since she had loved him for himself; whereas he had never thought of her but in the chill of his egotism and the light of her use.

Her spoken words came back to him, and the chain stretched and stretched. The beast had lurked indeed, and the beast, at its hour, had sprung; it had sprung in that twilight of the cold April when, pale, ill, wasted, but all beautiful, and perhaps even then recoverable, she had risen from the chair to stand before him and let him imaginably guess. It had sprung as he didn't guess; it had sprung as she hopelessly turned from him, and the mark, by the time he left her, had fallen where it *was* to fall.

He saw the Jungle of his life and saw the lurking beast; then while he looked, perceived it, as by a stir of the air, rise, huge and hideous, for the leap that was to settle him.—It was close; and turning, to avoid it, he flung himself, on his face, on the tomb.

NOTE: Mrs. Baca appends the following production comment to the adaptation:

Reading stands and stools work best here; scripts, preferably in looseleaf covers and with the text on both pages, rest on the stands. Each script may thus be individualized: Long speeches unbroken, page turning at the most effective points for each reader. May Bartram and John Marcher, side by side, place the scene somewhere in the rear of the room and maintain that placement throughout. The narrator is placed about five feet stage right; as James's central intelligence, he is not restricted to the characters' scene placement although he observes it: He is free to look directly at characters as he seems to introduce them; he confides in the audience without relinquishing esthetic distance; he is immersed in the emotional content of the narrative at the same time that he suggests psychological and moral implications.

MORNING IN NAGREBCAN[7]
from HOW MY BROTHER LEON BROUGHT HOME A WIFE
—*Manuel E. Arguilla*
(adapted by Wallace A. Bacon)

NARRATOR 1. It was sunrise in Nagrebcan.
The fine, bluish mist, low over the tobacco fields, was lifting and thinning moment by moment. A ragged strip of it, pulled away by the morning

[7] Reprinted by permission of Lydia Arguilla Salas.

breeze, had caught on the clumps of bamboo along the banks of the stream that flowed to one side of the barrio.[8]

Before long the sun would top the Katayagan hills, but as yet no people were around. In the gray shadow of the hills, the barrio was gradually awaking. Roosters crowed and strutted on the ground while hens hesitated on their perches among the branches of the camachile trees. Stray goats nibbled the weeds on the sides of the road, and the bull carabaos tugged restively against their stakes.

NARRATOR 2. In the early morning the puppies lay curled up together between their mother's paws under the ladder of the house. Four were all white like the mother. The fifth had a big black spot like a saddle on its back.

The opening of the sawali door, its uneven bottom dragging noisily against the bamboo flooring, aroused the mother dog and she got up and stretched and shook herself, scattering dust and loose white hair. A rank doggy smell rose in the cool morning air.

The bitch took a quick leap forward, cleared the puppies which had begun to whine about her, wanting to suckle; she trotted away and disappeared beyond the house of a neighbor.

The puppies sat back on their rumps, whining. After a little while they lay down and went back to sleep, the black-spotted puppy climbing on top of the four.

NARRATOR 1. Baldo stood at the threshold and rubbed his sleep-heavy eyes with his fists. He must have been about ten years old, small for his age, but compactly built, and he stood straight on his bony legs. He wore one of his father's discarded cotton undershirts.

The boy descended the ladder, leaning heavily on the single bamboo pole that served as a railing. He sat on the lowest step of the ladder, yawning and rubbing his eyes one after the other.

NARRATOR 2. Bending down, he reached between his legs for the black-spotted puppy. He held it to him, stroked its soft, warm body.

He blew on its nose. The puppy stuck out a small red tongue, lapping the air. It whined eagerly. Baldo laughed—a low gurgle.

He rubbed his face against that of the dog. He said softly

BALDO. "My puppy. My puppy."

NARRATOR 2. He said it many times.

BALDO. The puppy licked his ears, his cheeks. When it licked his mouth, Baldo straightened up, raised the puppy on a level with his eyes.

"You are a foolish puppy," *he said laughing.* "Foolish, foolish, foolish," *he said, rolling the puppy in his lap so that it began to snarl.*

NARRATOR 2. The four other puppies awoke and came scrambling about Baldo's legs.

NARRATOR 1. He put down the black-spotted puppy and ran to the narrow foot-bridge of woven split-bamboo, spanning the roadside ditch.

[8] Small settlement.

When it rained, water from the roadway flowed under the makeshift bridge, but it had not rained for a long time and the ground was dry and sandy.

Baldo sat on the bridge, digging his bare feet into the sand, feeling the cool particles escaping between his toes. He whistled, *a toneless whistle with a curious trilling to it produced by placing the tip of the tongue against the lower teeth and then moving it up and down.*

Narrator 2. The whistle excited the puppies; they ran to the boy as fast as their unsteady legs could carry them, barking choppy little barks.

Narrator 1. Nana Elang, the mother of Baldo, now appeared in the doorway with a handful of ricestraw. She called Baldo and told him to get some live coals from their neighbor.

Nana Elang. "Get two or three burning coals and bring them home on the rice straw," *she said.* "Do not wave the straw in the wind. If you do, it will catch fire before you get home."

She watched him run toward Ca Ikkao's house where already smoke was rising through the nipa roofing into the misty air.

Narrator 1. One or two empty carromatas drawn by sleepy little ponies rattled along the pebbly street, bound for the railroad station. Nana Elang was a thin, wispy woman, with bony hands and arms. Her cheekbones seemed on the point of bursting through the dry, yellowish-brown skin.

Above a gray-checkered skirt, she wore a single wide-sleeved cotton blouse that ended below her flat breasts. Sometimes when she stooped or reached up for anything, a glimpse of the flesh at her waist showed in a dark, purplish band where the skirt had been tied so often.

Nana Elang. She turned from the doorway into the small, untidy kitchen, tying her straight, graying hair into a tight knot at the back of her head.

She washed the rice and put it in a pot which she placed on the cold clay-stove. She made ready the other pot for the mess of vegetables and dried fish.

Narrator 1. Baldo came back with the rice straw and burning coals

Nana Elang. and she told him to start a fire in the stove, while she cut the ampalaya tendrils and sliced the eggplant.

Narrator 2. When the fire finally flamed inside the stove, Baldo's eyes were smarting from the smoke of the rice straw.

Baldo. "There's the fire, Mother," *he said.* "Is Father awake already?"
Nana Elang shook her head.

Narrator 1. Baldo went out slowly on tiptoe.

Baldo. There were already many people going about. Several fishermen wearing coffee-coloured shirts and trousers and hats made from the rind of white pumpkins passed by.[9] The smoke of their home-made cigars floated behind them like shreds of the morning mist.

[9] As Baldo watches, Narrator 1 (male) crosses the stage wearing a pumpkin-rind hat and smoking an Ilocano cigar. As Baldo describes the women, Narrator 2 (female) crosses the stage carrying a tobacco basket.

Women carrying big empty baskets were going to the tobacco fields.

NARRATOR 1. Day was quickly growing older. The east flamed redly and Baldo called to his mother.

BALDO. "Look, Mother, God also cooks his breakfast."

NARRATOR 2. He played with the puppies. He sat on the bridge and took them on his lap one by one, searching for fleas which he crushed between his thumb-nails.

BALDO. "You puppy. You puppy," *he murmured softly.*

NARRATOR 2. When he held the black-spotted puppy, he said,

BALDO. "My puppy. My puppy."

NARRATOR 1. Ambo, his seven-year-old brother, had awakened.

NANA ELANG. Nana Elang could be heard patiently calling him to the kitchen.

NARRATOR 2. Later he came down with a ripe banana in his hand. Ambo was almost as tall as his brother and he had stout, husky legs. He ate the banana without peeling it.

BALDO. "You foolish boy, remove the skin," *Baldo said.*

AMBO. "I will not," *Ambo said.* "It is not your banana." *He took a big bite and swallowed it with exaggerated relish.*

BALDO. "But the skin is tart. It tastes bad."

AMBO. "You are not eating it," *Ambo said. The rest of the banana vanished into his mouth.*

NARRATOR 2. He sat down beside Baldo and both played with the puppies.

The mother dog had not yet returned and the puppies were becoming hungry and restless.

AMBO. They sniffed the hands of Ambo, licked his fingers. They tried to scramble up his breast to lick his mouth, but he brushed them down.
Baldo laughed.

BALDO. [Baldo] held the black-spotted puppy closely, fondled it lovingly.
"My puppy," *he said.* "My puppy."

AMBO. Ambo played with the other puppies, but he soon tired of them. He wanted the black-spotted one.

NARRATOR 2. He sidled close to Baldo and put out a hand to caress the puppy nestling contentedly in the crook of his brother's arm.
Baldo struck the hand away.

BALDO. "Don't touch my puppy," *he said.* "My puppy."

AMBO. Ambo begged to be allowed to hold the black-spotted puppy.

BALDO. But Baldo said he would not let him hold the black-spotted puppy because he would not peel the banana.

AMBO. Ambo then said that he would obey his older brother next time, for all time.

BALDO. Baldo would not believe him; he refused to let him touch the puppy.

AMBO. Ambo rose to his feet. He looked longingly at the black-spotted puppy in Baldo's arms.

NARRATOR 2. Suddenly he bent down and tried to snatch the puppy away.

NARRATOR 1. But Baldo sent him sprawling in the dust with a deft push.

AMBO. Ambo did not cry. He came up with a fistful of sand which he flung into his brother's face.

BALDO. But as he started to flee, Baldo thrust out his leg and tripped him.

NARRATOR 1. In complete silence, Ambo slowly got up from the dust, getting to his feet with both hands full of sand which again he cast at his older brother.

NARRATOR 2. Baldo put down the puppy and sprang upon Ambo.

NARRATOR 1. They grappled and rolled in the sand.
Ambo kicked and bit and scratched in silence.

NARRATOR 2. He caught hold of Baldo's ear and hair and tugged with all his might.

NARRATOR 1. They rolled over and over

NARRATOR 2. and then Baldo was sitting on Ambo's back, pummeling him with his fists.

NARRATOR 1. He accompanied every blow with a curse.

BALDO. "I hope you die, you little demon," *he said between sobs; he was crying; he could hardly see.*

NARRATOR 1. Ambo wriggled and struggled and tried to bite Baldo's legs. Failing, he buried his face in the sand and bawled at the top of his voice.

NANA ELANG. Nana Elang called out in her tired, patient voice that if they didn't stop their noise, they'd wake up their father and he'd whip them.

BALDO. Baldo now left Ambo and ran to the black-spotted puppy which he caught up in his arms, holding it against his throat.

AMBO. Ambo followed, crying out threats and curses. He grabbed the tail of the puppy, jerked it hard.

BALDO. The puppy howled shrilly and Baldo had to let go of it,

AMBO. but Ambo kept hold of the tail as the dog fell to the ground.

NARRATOR 2. It turned around and snapped at the hand holding its tail. Its sharp little teeth sank into the fleshy edge of Ambo's palm.

AMBO. With a cry, Ambo snatched away his hand from the mouth of the enraged puppy.

NARRATOR 1. At that moment the window of the house facing the street was pushed violently open and the boys' father, Tang Ciako, poked out his head.

TANG CIAKO. He saw the blood from the toothmarks on Ambo's hand. *He called out inarticulately and*

NARRATOR 1. the two brothers looked up in surprise and fear.

AMBO. Ambo hid his bitten hand behind him.

BALDO. Baldo stooped to pick up the black-spotted puppy,

TANG CIAKO. but Tang Ciako shouted hoarsely to him not to touch the dog.

NARRATOR 2. At Tang Ciako's angry voice, the puppy had crouched back snarling, its pink lips drawn back, the hair on its back rising.

TANG CIAKO. "The dog has gone mad," *the man cried, coming down hurriedly.*

By the kitchen stove, he stopped to get a sizable piece of firewood, throwing an angry look and a curse at Nana Elang for letting her sons play with the dogs. He removed a splinter or two, then hurried down the ladder, cursing in a loud angry voice.

NANA ELANG. Nana Elang ran to the doorway and stood there silently, fingering her skirt.

NARRATOR 1. Baldo and Ambo awaited the coming of their father, fear written on their faces.

TANG CIAKO. Tang Ciako approached, the piece of firewood held firmly in one hand.

NARRATOR 1. He was a big, gaunt man with thick bony wrists and stooped shoulders. His short pants showed his bony-kneed, hard-muscled legs covered with black hair.

He was a carpenter. Now and then he drank great quantities of basi[10] and came home at night and beat his wife and children.

TANG CIAKO. "You are a whore,"

NARRATOR 1. *he roared at his wife, and as he beat his children, he shouted,*

TANG CIAKO. "I will kill you both, you bastards."

NANA ELANG. *If Nana Elang ventured to remonstrate, he beat them harder and cursed her for an interfering whore.*

TANG CIAKO. "I am king in my own house," he said.

NARRATOR 1. Now, as he approached the two, Ambo cowered behind his elder brother, keeping his wounded hand behind his back, unable to remove his gaze from his father's close-set, red-specked eyes.

NARRATOR 2. The puppy slunk between Baldo's legs.

BALDO. Baldo looked at the dog, avoiding his father's eyes.

NARRATOR 1. Tang Ciako roared at them to get away from the dog.

TANG CIAKO. "Fools! Don't you see that it's mad?"

BALDO. Baldo laid a hand on Ambo as they moved back hastily.

---

[10] A brown Ilocano wine made of sugar-cane juice.

NARRATOR 2. The puppy attempted to follow them,

NARRATOR 1. but Tang Ciako caught it with a sweeping blow of the piece of firewood.

TANG CIAKO. The puppy was flung into the air.

NARRATOR 2. It rolled over once before it fell, howling weakly.

TANG CIAKO. Again the chunk of firewood descended, Tang Ciako grunting with the effort he put into the blow, and the puppy ceased to howl.

NARRATOR 2. It lay on its side, feebly moving its jaws from which dark blood oozed.

TANG CIAKO. Once more Tang Ciako raised his arm,

NARRATOR 1. but Baldo suddenly clung to it with both hands and begged him to stop.

BALDO. "Enough, Father, enough. Don't beat it any more," *he entreated. Tears flowed down his upraised face.*

TANG CIAKO. Tang Ciako shook him off with an oath.

NARRATOR 1. Baldo fell on his face in the dust. He did not rise, but cried and sobbed and tore his hair. The rays of the rising sun fell brightly upon him, turning to gold the dust that he raised with his kicking feet.

TANG CIAKO. Tang Ciako dealt the battered puppy another blow and at last it lay limply still. He kicked it over and watched for a sign of life.

NARRATOR 2. The puppy did not move where it lay twisted on its side.
He turned his attention to Baldo.

TANG CIAKO. "Get up," *he said hoarsely, pushing the boy with his foot.*

NARRATOR 1. Baldo was deaf. He went on crying and kicking in the dust.

TANG CIAKO. Tang Ciako struck him with the piece of firewood in his hand and again told him to get up.

NARRATOR 1. Baldo writhed and cried harder, clasping his hands over the back of his head.

TANG CIAKO. Tang Ciako took hold of one of the boy's arms and jerked him to his feet. Then he began to beat him.

BALDO. Baldo encircled his head with his loose arm and strove to free himself, running around his father, plunging backward, ducking and twisting.

TANG CIAKO. "Shameless son of a whore," *Tang Ciako roared.* "Stand still. I'll teach you to obey me."
He shortened his grip on the arm of Baldo and laid on his blows.

BALDO. Baldo fell to his knees, screaming for mercy. He called on his mother to help him.

NANA ELANG. Nana Elang came down, but she hesitated at the foot of the ladder.

AMBO. Ambo ran up to her.

TANG CIAKO. "You, too," *Tang Ciako cried, and struck at the fleeing Ambo.*

NARRATOR 1. The piece of firewood caught him behind the knees and he fell on his face.

NANA ELANG. Nana Elang ran to the fallen boy and picked him up, brushed his clothes with her hands to shake off the dust.

TANG CIAKO. Tang Ciako pushed Baldo toward her.

NARRATOR 1. The boy tottered forward weakly, dazed and trembling. He had ceased to cry aloud, but he shook with hard, spasmodic sobs which he tried vainly to stop.

TANG CIAKO. "Here, take your child," *Tang Ciako said, thickly*. He faced the curious children and neighbors who had gathered by the side of the road. He yelled at them to go away. He said it was none of their business if he killed his children.

"They are mine," *he shouted*. "I feed them and I can do anything I like with them."

NARRATOR 1. The children ran home. the neighbors returned to their work.

TANG CIAKO. Tang Ciako went to the house, cursing in a loud voice. Passing the dead puppy, he picked it up by its hind legs and flung it away.

NARRATOR 2. The black and white body soared through the sunlit air, fell among the tall corn behind the house.

TANG CIAKO. Tang Ciako still cursing and grumbling strode upstairs. He threw the chunk of firewood beside the stove. He squatted by the low table and began eating the breakfast his wife had prepared for him.

NANA ELANG. Nana Elang knelt by her children and dusted their clothes.

She passed her hand over the red welts on Baldo's body.

BALDO. But Baldo shook himself away.

NANA ELANG. He was still trying to stop sobbing, wiping his tears away with his forearm.

Nana Elang put one arm around Ambo. She sucked the wound in his hand.

NARRATOR 1. She was crying silently.

NARRATOR 2. When the mother of the puppies returned, she licked the remaining four by the small bridge of woven split-bamboo. She lay down in the dust and suckled her young. She did not seem to miss the black-spotted puppy.

NARRATOR 1. Afterward Baldo and Ambo searched among the tall corn for the body of the dead puppy.

NANA ELANG. Tang Ciako had gone to work and would not be back till nightfall.

In the house, Nana Elang was busy washing the breakfast dishes.

NARRATOR 2. Later she came down and fed the mother dog.

NARRATOR 1. The two brothers were entirely hidden by the tall corn plants. As they moved about among the slender stalks, the cornflowers shook agitatedly. Pollen scattered like gold dust in the sun, falling on the fuzzy green leaves.

NARRATOR 2. When they found the dead dog, they buried it in the corner of the field.

NARRATOR 1. Baldo dug the grave with a sharp-pointed stake. Ambo stood silently by, holding the dead puppy.

NARRATOR 2. They covered the dog with soft earth and stamped on the grave until the disturbed ground was flat and hard again.

NARRATOR 1. With difficulty they rolled the big stone on top of the grave.

Then Baldo placed an arm around the shoulders of Ambo; they hurried up to the house.

NARRATORS 1 AND 2 TOGETHER. The sun had risen high above the Katayagan hills, and warm, golden sunlight filled Nagrebcan. The mist on the tobacco fields had completely dissolved.

NOTE: In the performance of this story at the University of the Philippines, the rear of the stage was ramped up to a platform about three feet in height and about fifty inches in depth. Behind the platform was a nipa house in stylized silhouette. Bamboo and banana trees were grouped against a sky cyclorama. The platform rather than the house itself was used for scenes within the house and the area behind it for the cornfield where the children searched for the dead puppy. The forestage was used for the remainder of the action of the story, carried out as described in the text.

The two narrators began the story at opposite sides of the stage, talking to the audience and describing to them the scene as it unfolded, moving back and forth between the imagined scene and the audience. As the story proceeded, they sometimes mingled with the characters in the scene, sometimes withdrew to the sides and front of the stage, depending on the degree of intimacy that each episode called for between narrators and actors.

THE AUDIENCE AND CRITICISM

Part **IV**

Chapter **14**

THE AUDIENCE

The audience may have seemed peripheral to our discussion of interpretation. It is not. The discussion has centered upon the performer and the text because it is the matching of those two forms which is the center of the audience's attention. While distortion of the text simply to gain an audience's approval is here discountenanced, and hence too early and simple a concern with audience response discouraged, it remains true probably that the interpreter's awareness from the beginning that he or she is going to perform for an audience has something to do, in a positive way, with response to the text to be performed. Kaplan and Mohrmann provide evidence that the *nature* of the audience makes a difference. ". . . readers who anticipated that the audience was thoroughly familiar with the literature formed more detailed and complex impressions of the materials," and importantly, "perceptual differences start to arise at the very outset"; "the expectation of performance shapes the initial impression of the literature."[1]

These findings support the theoretical position which this book has taken—that the study of literature through the medium of performance, where the performance (i.e., the matching of text and performer) is held

THE CLASS AS AUDIENCE

[1] Stuart J. Kaplan and G. P. Mohrmann, "Reader, Text, Audience: Oral Interpretation and Cognitive Tuning," *Quarterly Journal of Speech*, 63 (1977), 59–65.

up to the audience as the embodied text, results in a particularly meaningful experience. In the classroom in interpretation, the class members, as audience, at their best provide the interpreter with that condition which fosters the fullest perception of the text. That is why many teachers ask all students in the class to be familiar with the material being performed. Knowing the material, they become not only the best critics but the best audience for the performer. The audience is not, then, peripheral to the study of interpretation but ultimately (and initially) significant.

There is, of course, an audience *within* the work, often. The definition and location of that audience is part of the establishment of the work's presence and perspective, part of the work's locus, and the performer must face the task of making that audience operational in performance. But we are talking here about the audience for which the interpreter performs. We have said earlier that the performer may be his or her own audience. The interpreter who is accustomed to reading for an audience doubtless becomes a very special audience for his or her own reading and is likely, we think, to profit from the "audience sense" in the way Kaplan and Mohrmann describe. In this way, the study of literature through performance remains useful throughout the student's life, whether or not he or she ever performs publicly beyond the classroom. But in our immediate context, in the class in which the art of interpretation is being studied, there is always an audience beyond the performer himself, and that audience is an integral part of our concern.

COMMUNION AND COMMUNICATION

For one thing, the audience enters into communion with the performer; each moves toward that central concern which is the embodied text. In communion, communication occurs. It is not primarily a matter of sending and receiving messages; it is rather a common participation in the experience of a created world, a life form set free by the writer and now actualized by the interpreter. In this sense, the audience, too, performs, though silently. This silent audience in part resembles the silent reader who reads a text to himself, but it also in part differs from that reader since it is a group and the text is an embodied text. Just as the interpreter fills in, from the written text, kinds of details often not made explicit by the writer (gestures, movements—paralinguistic material that accompanies the written language), so the audience members contribute their sum to the text-in-process in performance. An image, for example, may have one particular referent for the writer (Wordsworth's tree, to which we have referred elsewhere), another for the interpreter, still others for members of the audience. But the good writer controls the lengths to which these extensions can go; good text may be tolerant, but it says what it wants to say. Not *everything* goes—but more goes than we are sometimes willing to permit. The poem in performance before an audience is a large study of unity in variety.

Any interpreter knows that the degree and quality of response from the audience affects the performance. It may assist, it may interfere; it may augment, it may reduce. Some kinds of audience response lead the performer away from the text, and that is likely to have negative results; other kinds intensify the sense of the poem's body, and this is likely to have positive effects. While it seems to us not true that the performance to the public audience ought to be the goal of a course in interpretation (not many students will continue to perform publicly), it is certainly true that the public performance is a pleasurable, profitable, useful event and hence significant. One's goal ought not be *simply* "to please an audience," but the hope is that a good performance will indeed please. In rehearsals, the interpreter must accept the fact that there is going to be, in the classroom, an audience. He does not rehearse as if no one will ever hear. For some performers, the public event will augment, enlarge the private response; for others, the public event will subdue and refine responses that in private might be more fully indulged. In rehearsal, one may indeed reread two or three times, simply for the pleasure of it, a passage of which the performer is particularly fond, whereas in the public performance such indulgence will be rare. One may afford, in rehearsal, to laugh aloud at a comic touch achieved in matching the text, but in public performance what could seem to be self-congratulation might be fatal.

Our point of view has been, steadily, that interpretation is concerned with the process of matching text and performer, that the process is a way of knowing—a very special way of knowing. It is that kind of knowledge which we take to be the aim of classes in interpretation, for we are, after all, talking here about a subject of study. But the matching of text and performer, in the classroom, must include an awareness that the audience in the classroom in its turn matches the embodied text. That is why, presumably, so much time is devoted in the classroom to discussions of the performance. We shall devote our attention to that issue in the next chapter. The interpreter learns to perform in part by hearing others perform; their experience becomes his or her experience to some degree.

It is futile to argue about whether there *need* be an audience other than the reader's self. It is futile to argue about whether interpretation is or is not communication. Ultimately, these are matters of definition, not of truth. Performance for oneself is not the same as performance for a public audience. *Both*, we would say, can be seen as interpretation. Interpretation can be seen profitably as communion; that is not to argue that it is not communication. The either/or argument is ultimately stultifying. But it seems clear enough that Beverly Whitaker Long is sensible in suggesting that "the greatest value for student performers and their fellow class members occurs when the audience is well enough acquainted with the literature to act as critics or (incipient) performers." She writes:

AUDIENCE RESPONSE AS AFFECTIVE

We speak so often of the interrelationships a performance in-volves—text, performer, audience. I believe a "knowing" audience (including the instructor) *informs* the performer and is in a position to *be* informed in a particularly rich way by the performed text.[2]

CONTINUUM: STUDENT, CLASS, PUBLIC

We are not through, however. Presumably, ensemble performances are prepared, more often than not, for public performance. They are cer-tainly not *normally* prepared for the performers themselves, though they of course may be. They tend to move the act of performance out of the classroom, to confront a different text-audience relationship; they are more immediately like theatrical events. It is at this point that some teachers of interpretation demur; they may be unwilling to see their work as preparation for public performance, and that demurrer is both understandable and defensible. But that stance is again a matter of defi-nition, not of truth. Other teachers will be quite willing to undertake the added challenge of public performance and to find that it does not run counter to their view of their profession. There is a difference be-tween seeing interpretation as a pedagogical act and seeing it as an art of performance; on the other hand, there is no *necessary* inconsistency between the two views. Indeed, in this book we would have it both ways. For us, interpretation is an art of performance; but it is an art we are engaged in studying, and in the study we have concentrated on the performer who is studying and the text which is being performed. We are willing to view the performer himself as ultimately the only *required* audience (though while the student is studying he or she must have another audience to report on the progress of the study!). But we are also willing to view the additional audience in the classroom or in a public situation as a pleasant and useful part of the process, and as audience members we know that the performance *can* be a wonderfully instructive and pleasurable event. It is our position that the whole range of situations is significant, but not everything of significance can be studied at once. Nor, in the present state of our knowledge, are we in any position to be dogmatic about performer-audience relationships. It is possible that we never shall arrive at a sensible dogma. It is important that we seek answers; it is important that we not find them too early or too easily. The world will not necessarily be more pleasurable when all answers have been discovered. Happily, that unhappy day is likely never to arrive.

POEM, SPEAKER, PERFORMER

A poem (i.e., a literary work of any sort) in some sense speaks. It uses language. It intends. It is constituted in the act of speaking. Unlike most scientific discourse, it also tells us how it feels as it speaks. It tends to reify the phenomenal world rather than to escape from it. But while the poem speaks, there are poems which may be called speakerless in the

[2] Beverly Whitaker Long, in *Issues in Interpretation,* II, 2, n.p.

sense that there is not a clearly defined *person* who speaks. Concrete poems very often have no sense of issuing from *a* speaker. Japanese haiku (at least in the original language) often seem brush paintings or photographs rather than "something spoken." But interpreters *do* speak (though speech is not the whole of their activity, by any means). An interpretative act may be a soliloquy—there is no audience in the soliloquy, frequently, other than the self who speaks; but when the interpreter performs, there is certainly an audience that hears, even if it be only the interpreter's self. Hence we must be very careful about asking questions of a text as we prepare to perform it. Such a question as "Who is speaking?" may *not* be a useful question unless one is prepared to accept such an answer as "No *person* is speaking."

The point is simply that the usual discussions of speaker–audience relationships are often too simple for the interpreter, who must cope with "no speaker" poems, "no audience" poems at the same time he or she must cope with the fact that the interpreter *is* someone speaking, and he or she is always speaking to someone. It is wonderfully ironic— and a marvelous challenge—to find that one must somehow embody a disembodied speaker, or to say to someone something which a speaker never intends to be heard. The opposite end of the continuum is the clearly defined personality who has a clearly defined audience in mind, whether within or outside the work. There is *no* way in which the interpreter can finally afford to disclaim an interest in the audience.

Chapter 15

CRITICISM OF PERFORMANCE

Criticism, too, is an act. In preparation for the act of performing, and in the course of rehearsing, we have looked critically at the many elements that make up works of literature and have sought ways to make them fund the process by which interpreter and text are brought together. While the act of performance itself seems to us not critical but creative (the act of criticism always in some sense distances the critic from the text; the act of performance seeks to eliminate distance, except such distancing as is built into the text itself), it is clear enough that after an initial, receptive response to a literary work the interpreter will profit from a critical examination of it. The appreciative response and the critical act are not simply separable, but neither are they identical. One must shift gears, so to speak, in moving from one act to the other.

The *discussion* of performance *is* a critical act, and many of you doubtless can testify that it is one thing simply to respond to the text in performance and another to begin talking about it. As the interpreter's critical activity prior to performance can assist him or her, so can criticism by the class and the instructor subsequent to performance. We have said that the class constitutes a particularly effective audience for an interpreter; at its best, it can constitute an effective body of critics.

Criticism is often a delicate matter. It is also clear enough that while there are standards of criticism, critical estimates will vary; there is no way of eliminating all subjectivity in criticism, just as there is no way of eliminating all variations in readers' responses to literary texts. Hence the performer in the classroom must tolerate differences, listen as carefully as possible, and ultimately make his or her own judgment of criticisms. Some criticisms are clearly better than others.

It is helpful if the members of the class begin their criticism of a performance by talking about what they actually heard and saw. (You will find that initially many people are not very close observers!) If the performance involves characterization, what kind of character (or characters) did you get? What in the way of tempo, posture, gesture, articulation, movement, locus, tension—in short, what in the *presence* of the character created the impression made upon you? Were there things which you could not put together—was there a failure in the coalescence of the various performing acts which prevented clear communication of meaning? If the performance is of a lyric poem, what condition in the speaker was conveyed by the performer? If the performance involves narration, what seemed to you the locus of the narrator with respect to the story and to the audience?

What elements of the performance kept the text in process—i.e., not static but evolving? Were you aware of transitions; if so, how were they handled? How would you describe the tone of the performance? If the text intended a specific kind of setting, what kind of setting did you get? In what ways did the behavior of the performer convey a sense of setting? In short, one may ask, of all the many elements which we have talked about in the structures of literary works, how did this particular performance handle them? (For any one performance, of course, you will have to single out dominant elements; there is never time for everything. The better the performance, the finer the distinctions that can be made.)

After you have talked about what you actually saw and heard (and you will not all have seen and heard the same things), it is important to ask whether these acts matched the text. If the performance contradicts the text in terms of specific evidence (if, for example, a young girl is made to sound like an old woman), something has gone wrong and you must say why. If a poem is written in Scottish dialect and the performer uses a Georgia drawl, something has gone wrong—everyone will know why. If characters in a play scene cannot be distinguished, if they all sound alike, reasons must be found for distinguishing between them, and those reasons should arise from the text. If the speaker is intended to be ironic and the performer presents you with no sense of irony, something has gone wrong. What? Try, for example, reading the following line in different ways—first as an expression of genuine longing, second as ironic, third as highly amused:

I can hardly wait for him to come!

DESCRIPTIVE CRITICISM

EVALUATIVE CRITICISM

How can you describe the differences between the three readings? What does the voice contribute, specifically? What changes occur in relationships between speaker and auditor?

One can go farther in making distinctions. Try reading that same line now as genuine longing, but first with eagerness, then with anxiety. Again, how do you specify the differences between the readings? Or still another possibility—read the line as if you mean to say "I can't possibly wait that long, because I have other things to do!" What further modifications can you point to in performance behavior?

What one must ask, ultimately, if that line actually occurs in a text, is: Which of the various possible readings of the line will match the intention of the text? Surely not all of them will be possible, though more than one may. Think of the body of the text—what is *that* body trying to say? And how can you, as performer, match your body with that? If your intention is not what the class audience tells you it saw as intention, where did you fail? (If half the class sees your intention and half does not, you must decide whether only half the class was a "good" audience or whether your behavior was perhaps too subtle. If you modify what you did, will you hold on to the half you initially persuaded and still reach the other half?)

A class can be very useful in pointing out in your performance personal mannerisms that you carry over from one reading to the next without being aware of it. *Some* of these mannerisms you may perhaps wish to eliminate or modify. There is no way for you *literally* to be a different person from reading to reading, but it is possible to *seem* different if you are not overburdened with mannerisms. The point is: How do you make yourself capable of reading more than one kind of text? Part of the answer lies in discovering what in the text needs to be matched; the other part lies in discovering what in you hinders or helps the matching.

RATINGS Some instructors like to use rating sheets for readings, with a list of items you check off (evaluate) for every performance. Such sheets have their use. More useful forms might be progressive, with the items to be evaluated changing throughout the course of instruction, perhaps getting down to finer and finer distinctions.

On the whole, however, it seems wiser to eschew ratings of this sort—to let each reading provide its own questions, since each text is always in some ways unique. The instructor can determine what questions may be the most profitable at any give time for any given student. Not all students are ready for precisely the same questions at any one time. A comment useful for one student is not useful for another; a comment not useful this week for a particular student may be highly useful a week hence. While not every possible variation can be taken into account in the classroom, good instructors must temper the criticism to the student performer, and good critics must temper their comments to the fellow student who has read.

Criticism can be thoughtlessly cruel. It ought to be constructive and helpful. Performance is a very personal matter for many students. If one really believes that interpretation is the matching of performer and text, remember that criticism of the performance is a criticism of both bodies. Nothing is less helpful than a boorish "I didn't like it at all." Nor is it much more helpful to have one student's "I didn't like it" followed immediately by another's "I did; I loved it." Every performer would like everyone to enjoy the performance, but for the critic "Did you like it?" is *not* the best place to begin. Never mind whether you liked it or didn't, to begin with. What did you get, specifically? Did it match the intention of the text? Did it enlarge and extend the text—and if so, how? Did it circumscribe and limit the text—and if so, how? Even if it did not seem properly to match the text, was it clear within the intentions of the performer? What evidence in the text would suggest that the performer's intentions might be changed to good advantage?

CONSTRUCTIVE CRITICISM

One of the most usual forms of critical questioning has been called dramatistic. It involves asking, with respect to a piece of literature (and hence with respect to the conveyance of the embodied text in performance), such questions as Who is speaking? To whom? Where and when? Why? In what way? About what? These are useful questions, always. But remember that any set of critical questions will provide answers only to those questions. One must have as many sets of questions as possible to explore fully any very complex literary work. The dramatistic method tends, for example, to leave out of account the possibility of "speakerless" poems and tends to throw into high relief the sense of a clearly defined character. Hence throughout this book we have sought to raise as many critical questions as possible without setting forth a *particular* method of inquiry. Systems generalize, whereas literary works are unique. Make use of any critical system that will lead to useful answers, but do not subscribe simply to one.

THE DRAMATISTIC VIEW

It is possible to say, of a given performance, that it is *wrong*. If, for example, an interpreter performed Stevens's "A Postcard from the Volcano" (pp. 261–262) as if a child were speaking, he would be wrong. Why? On the other hand, if the interpreter decided that the speaker was a woman rather than a man, the interpretation would not be wrong, despite the use of the pronoun *he* in the penultimate stanza. Why? Would it be right, wrong, or neither if the interpreter decided to make the speaker (a) an urban Mexican, (b) a New England farmer, (c) A

POSSIBILITIES

Missouri villager? What are the poem's limits of tolerance? When do we move from clear evidence to possibilities to improbabilities, or from improbabilities to error? As we have said throughout this book, the matching of text and performer is a creative, mutual endeavor. It is not a matter of a performer's "reproducing" a text. Neither the performer nor the text is finally the object of criticism, but the text embodied, in performance. Where do the performer's and the poem's energies begin to come into conflict? When the two bodies do not match but quarrel, something is wrong—unless, of course, one intends a comic effect, when the quarrel may be highly functional.

Criticism in the classroom can be, should be, instructive both to performer and to audience. The art of interpretation and the act of criticism share alike in helping to create better readers, whether silent or oral, of what others have written. Literature makes possible the experiencing of the inexpressible; the great writer uncovers for us the deepest springs of our own experience, makes manifest in language and in symbolic action experiences we could never otherwise explore or endure, extends our horizons and stretches our spirits, gives wings to words and spurs to thoughts. The writer communes with the world in which he or she lives and communicates to us that unique act of communion in which he or she engages. In literature, language is used at its most human levels, in the exploration of the most human gestures. The interpreter shares in that exploration in a very special way. As performer, he literally embodies language, accepting both the limitations placed upon him by the text and the possibilities opened to him by it. Together, text and performer reach out to others. It is the critic's task to say by what art or craft and with what degree of success that union and communion are accomplished. We have constantly asked the performer to be modest, to yield to the intentions of the text. We must ask the critic, in turn, to listen carefully with open heart, before yielding the role of sympathetic listener to take on the role of judge. The performer, too, wants love.

IN CONCLUSION

We shall not cease from exploration
And the end of all our exploring
Will be to arrive where we started
And know the place for the first time.

—*T. S. Eliot*
from Little Gidding[1]

Repeatedly, in a variety of ways, we have been seeking for answers to the question, How does a literary work feel when it speaks? This is the basic question for the interpreter, who must put himself in the position of the poem rather than in the position of a viewer of the poem if he is to let us see and hear the poem rather than himself. He must have some sense of the "antecedents" of the poem, the state of mind out of which it arises, so that even at the outset he gives us not himself but the work. In this respect, he is much like the writer, who, as Eliot has said, escapes

[1] From "Little Gidding" in *Four Quarters,* copyright, 1943, by T. S. Eliot; renewed, 1971, by Esme Valerie Eliot. Reprinted by permission of Harcourt Brace Jovanovich, Inc. and Faber and Faber, Ltd. See further notice on copyright page.

from the confines of his own personality by entering into the thing being created. It is a paradox, and a happy one, that our own growth results in part from this concentration on growth outside us. It is not alone the writer who aspires, or the reader; literature itself aspires, speaks, and the interpreter becomes language in its full and most significant sense. He is not a horn through which the poet calls, not a vacuum simply transmitting speech, but the embodiment of speech.

Emphasis has been on the process of becoming. For a time during the process, the tensions observable in the experience of interpreting will seem more the tensions of the reader than of the poem; the presence and perspective frequently will be those of the reader. But practice will help the interpreter to channel his own tensions into the tensions of the poem—or, where they are not functional within the poem, to eliminate them. It is a difficult and demanding art, the art of interpretation, but it has rich rewards, including, but certainly not stopping with, the pleasure of reading.

A literary structure, within the limits of its materials, is what it is because it tries to become what it wants to be. Emphasis here too is on the process of becoming. Once *becoming* has ripened into full *being,* once the realization is complete, no more is to be done. Some literary works set their goals very low, and we find it difficult to sustain interest in them; other works set their goals very high—sometimes so high that they are doomed to defeat. Sometimes the goal is barely beyond reach and constantly exhilarating; sometimes the goal is almost fully achieved. Almost. It is never completely achieved; complete ripeness is possible only on the verge of decay—and, indeed, some poems are overripe. The reader too may set his goals too high or too low, but his overripeness is likely to be an overripeness of techniques thought of as ends in themselves, a lack of congruence between his body and the body of the poem—all the virtues of life except significant purpose.

Like the poem, the interpreter, within the limits of his capacities, is what he is because he tries to become what he wants to be. Hence our emphasis has been first on what he should want to be and second on the means by which he tries to achieve his goal. We have looked first at the body of the poem (what the interpreter want to be), then at the interpreter (who wants to be the poem). This is not to say that our primary interest is the poem, for the two things together ultimately constitute our single interest; the ultimate goal can be achieved more completely by looking first at the poem rather than at the student.

We have been wary of rules, though not of suggestions. It is better to say "Let's see whether" than to say "You must never." We are not so much interested in confining as in defining possibilities. Our responsibility, finally, is to be responsive.

This view has placed interpretation squarely in the liberal arts context. Interpretation is the study of literature through the medium of oral performance, where the medium is itself a process of defining. The essential educational value of interpretation as a separate and distinct aspect of speech and of literary study lies in its emphasis on the bringing together into an organic relationship of student and poem.

The art of interpretation is an art of performance. A performance involves an audience, and the audience becomes, in its way and in its turn, a participant in the total act of interpretation. There is interaction between reader and poem; there is interaction between reader and audience. In the intricate process of matching, all three elements of the transaction are significant.

It is to the process of matching—of bringing one's own life form for the moment into congruence with the life form of the poem—that the interpreter first and foremost devotes attention. The process of matching is also a process of maturation; one grows by giving in to the otherness of the life of the text by extending oneself, by reaching out, by loving. It is this exercising of the spirit in the act of understanding that the liberal arts have always cherished. There is a kind of paradox— the kind that Browning said comforts even while it mocks—in the fact that growth of the self depends on one's willingness to look beyond the self.

The tensive life of literature, its relationship with the life of the interpreter, and the relationship between these two lives and the life of the audience have been the center of our study throughout this volume. The total process of enactment is highly complex, as are all life acts; we have only begun, doubtless, to touch on many of the matters involved in it. Difficult though the art of interpretation may be, its pleasures, like the pleasures of literature, are many, varied, and richly rewarding. They do not come automatically. Readers who want to become interpreters must actively try to become the interpreters they want to become. Let them reach out, gladly, to the poems they read.

THE STORY OF CAEDMON
from THE ECCLESIASTICAL
HISTORY OF THE ENGLISH NATION

—VENERABLE BEDE

In the monastery of this abbess [Hild, 614–680] there was a certain brother made notable by a grace of God specially given, for that he was wont to make songs fit for religion and godliness; insomuch that, whatsoever of the divine writings he learned by them that expounded them, he set it forth after a little time with poetical language, put together with very great sweetness and pricking of the heart, in his own, that is to say, the English tongue. With whose songs the minds of many men were oft inflamed to the contempt of the world and desire of the heavenly life. And indeed other too among the English people after him assayed to make religious poems; but no man could match his cunning. For he himself learned the art of singing without being taught of men nor of men's help; but he received the gift of singing freely by the aid of God. And therefore he could never make any fond or vain poem, but only such as belonging to religion befitted his religious mouth. For as long time as he was settled in secular life, until he was well stricken in age, he had at no time learned any songs. And so it was that sometimes at the table, when the company was set to be merry and had agreed that each man should sing in his course, he, when he saw the harp to be coming near him, would rise up at midst of supper and going out get him back to his own house. And as he did so on a certain time, and leaving the house of feasting had gone out to the stable of the beasts which had been appointed him to look to that night, and there at the fitting hour had bestowed his limbs to rest, there stood by him a certain man in a dream and bade him God speed, and calling him by his name said to him: "Caedmon, sing me something!" Whereupon he answering said: "I know not how to sing for that too is the matter why I came out from the table to this place apart, because I could not sing." "But yet," quoth he again that spake with him, "thou hast to sing to me." "What," quoth he, "should I sing?" Whereupon the other said: "Sing the beginning of the creatures!" At which answer he began forthwith to sing in praise of God the Creator verses which he had never heard before, of which the sense is this: "Now ought we to praise the Maker of the heavenly kingdom, the power of the Creator and His counsel, the acts of the Father of glory; how He, being God eternal, was the author of all miracles; which first created unto the children of men heaven for the top of their dwelling-place, and thereafter the almighty Keeper of mankind created the earth." This is the sense but not the selfsame order of the words which he sang in his sleep: for songs, be they never so well made, cannot be turned of one tongue into another, word for word, without loss to their grace and worthiness. Now in rising from slumber he remembered still all the things that he had sung in his sleep, and did by and by join thereto in the same measure more words of the songs worthy of God.

And coming on the morrow to the town reeve under whom he was, he shewed unto him what gift he had received; and being brought to the abbess, he was commanded in the presence of many learned men to tell his dream and rehearse the song, that it might by the judgment of them all be tried what or whence the thing was which he reported. And it seemed to them all, that a heavenly grace was granted him of the Lord. And they recited unto him the process of a holy story or lesson, bidding him, if he could, to turn the same into metre and verse. Whereupon he undertaking so to do went his way, and on the morrow came again and brought the same which they had required of him, made in very good verse. Whereupon by and by the abbess embracing the grace of God in the man, instructed him to forsake the secular habit and take upon him the monastical vow, and when he had so done she placed him in the company of the brethren with all them that were with her, and gave commandment for him to be instructed in the regular course of holy history. But he by thinking again with himself upon all that he could hear and learn, and chewing thereon as a clean beast cheweth the cud, would turn it into very sweet song; and by melodiously singing the same again would make his teachers to become in their turn his hearers [auditores]. Now he sang of the creation of the world, and beginning of mankind, and all the story of Genesis, of the going of Israel out of Egypt, and their entering in the land of promise, and of very many other histories of Holy Scripture, of the incarnation of the Lord, of His passion, resurrection and ascension into heaven, of the coming of the Holy Ghost, and the teaching of the apostles. Also he would make many songs of the dread of judgment to come, of the terror of the pains of hell, and of the sweetness of the kingdom of heaven; moreover, many other songs of the divine benefits and judgments, in all which his endeavour was to pull men away from the love of wickedness and stir them up to the love and readiness to do well. For he was a man very devout and humbly obedient to the discipline of the rules; but very zealous and fervently inflamed against them that would do otherwise: wherefore too he closed his life with a goodly end.

For when the hour of his departing was at hand, he was taken before with bodily sickness which was heavy upon him fourteen days; and yet so temperately, that he might all that time both speak and walk. Now there was thereby a building wherein they that were sick, and such as seemed near to die, were wont to be brought. He desired, therefore, him that served him, at the falling of evening on the night that he was to depart from the world, to provide him a place to rest in that building: and the other marvelling why he desired this, he seemed nothing likely to die yet, nevertheless did as he was bid. And when they were laid in the same place, and were having some merry talking and sporting among themselves and them that were there before, and the season of midnight was now passed, he asked whether they had the sacrament there within. They answered: "What need is there of the sacrament, for your time is not come to die yet, and art so merrily talking with us as a man in good health." "And yet," quoth he again, "do ye bring me hither the sacrament." Which when he had taken in his hand, he asked them, whether they were all of a quiet mind toward him, and without complaint of quarrel and bitterness. They answered all that they were very peaceably disposed toward him and were far from wrath: and they asked him in their turn to have a quiet mind toward them. And he forthwith answered: "I do bear, my dear children, a quiet mind toward all God's servants." And so arming himself with the heavenly voyage-provision he made him ready to enter into the other life; and asked how nigh the hour was at which the brethren should be roused to say their night lauds to the Lord. "It is not far off," answered they. "Well then," quoth he thereat, "let us tarry for that hour." And signing himself with the sign of the holy cross, he laid his head on the bolster, and falling a little in slumber so ended his life in silence. And thus was it brought about that, even as he had served the Lord with a simple and pure mind and peaceful devoutness, so likewise leaving the world with a peaceful death he might come to His sight, and that tongue, which had framed so many wholesome words in the praise of the Creator, might also close up its last words in His praise, by the signing of himself and commending his spirit into His hands; and by these things that we have told it appeareth also that he had known beforehand of his departing.

APPENDIX **B**

A GLOSSARY OF USEFUL TERMS

All the terms in this Glossary will be helpful to the interpreter in the study of literature in performance. While the list is far from exhaustive, it includes the most frequently encountered terms as well as many special terms having particular relevance to oral reading. Teachers will find the Glossary useful as a source for additional discussion and for written exercises.

The following check list will be convenient. The category GENERAL includes terms used with reference to more than a single literary genre and certain terms (marked with an asterisk) specifically concerned with oral performance. Under DRAMA, FICTION, and POETRY are listed those terms having particular bearing on the study of one form. Some terms are listed more than once. All terms printed in small capitals within definitions have separate Glossary entries.

The general index to the volume does not cross-index all the terms on this list, but only those terms to which extended treatment is given in the text.

Check List	GENERAL	DRAMA	FICTION	POETRY
	act	act	action	accent
	action	action	allegory	acrostic scrambling
	affective fallacy	antagonist	climax	bling

GENERAL	DRAMA	FICTION	POETRY
allegory	anticlimax	conflict	Alexandrine
allusion	catharsis	crisis	alliteration
anticlimax	character	denouement	amphibrach
antithesis	chronicle play	description	amphimacer
apostrophe	climax	direct discourse	anacrusis
* articulation	comedy	epic (mode)	anapest
atmosphere	comedy of man-	episode	antistrophe
bathos	ners	epistolary novel	apocope
burlesque	comic relief	exemplum	assonance
cacophony	comical satire	fable	augmentation
cadence	conflict	figures (see GEN-	ballad
character	crisis	ERAL)	ballade
chiasmus	denouement	flashback	ballad stanza
circumlocution	deus ex machina	flat characters	blank verse
classic	discovery	foreshadow	cacophony
cliché	drama	Gothic	cadence
climax	dramatic irony	indirect dis-	caesura
* communication	episode	course	catalexis
* communion	exposition	invocation	closed couplet
conceit	expressionism	motivation	conceit
conflict	farce	narration	concrete poetry
connotation	figures (see GEN-	narrative	consonance
* consonantal	ERAL)	narrator	consonantal cog-
cognates	flashback	novel	nates
conventional	flat characters	novella	counterpoint
symbol	foreshadow	parable	couplet
crisis	French scene	pastoral	dactyl
dead metaphor	heroic play	picaresque novel	diaeresis
decorum	high comedy	or tale	dimeter
denotation	history play	plot	diminution
description	irony	point of view	dipody
deus ex machina	low comedy	prose	double rhyme
* diction	masque	protagonist	dramatic lyric
didactic litera-	melodrama	rhythm	dramatic mono-
ture	miracle play	romance	logue
direct discourse	morality play	round characters	eclogue
dramatic (mode)	motivation	scene	elegy
emotive lan-	mystery play	setting	elision
guage	pastoral	short story	end rhyme
* empathy	pathos	stock situations	end-stopped
epic (mode)	peripety	stream of con-	enjambement
epigram	plot	ciousness	epic
episode	problem play	summary	epigram
essay	prose	suspense	equivalence
* esthetic dis-	protagonist		euphony
tance	romantic comedy		exact rhyme
euphemism	round characters		eye rhyme
euphony	scene		falling rhythm
Euphuism	sentimental com-		feet
existentialism	edy		feminine ending

GENERAL	DRAMA	FICTION	POETRY
exposition	setting		feminine rhyme
expressionism	slapstick		figures (see GEN-
fallacies	soliloquy		ERAL)
figures of com-	stichomythia		foot prosody
parison	stock characters		free verse
figures of conti-	stock situations		full rhyme
guity	suspense		half rhyme
figures of rhet-	tragedy		heptameter
oric	tragicomedy		heroic couplet
figures of sense	tragic relief		hexameter
figures of sound			hiatus
flashback			hypercatalexis
flat characters			iambus
* focus			ictus
foreshadow			image
genre			Imagists
Gothic			incremental rep-
hyperbole			etition
image			internal rhyme
imagery			invocation
impression			isochronous
indirect dis-			verse
course			isosyntactical
* inflection			verse
intentional fal-			lyric
lacy			masculine end-
* intonation			ing
invocation			masculine rhyme
irony			measures
* kinesics			metaphysical
* kinesthesis			meter
lampoon			metrical tale
litotes			mock epic
* locus			octameter
lyric			octave
materials			ode
meiosis			onomatopoeia
metaphor			ottava rima
metaphysical			pastoral
metonymy			pause
motivation			pentameter
* muscle tone			Pindaric ode
myth			poetry
narration			prosody
narrative			pyrrhic
narrator			quantitative
naturalism			verse

GENERAL	DRAMA	FICTION	POETRY
negative emo- tions			quatrain
Neoclassic			quintet
* offstage			refrain
onomatopoeia			rhyme
* onstage			rhythm
organic unity			rime
overstatement			rime royal
oxymoron			rising rhythm
paradox			rocking rhythm
* paralanguage			romance
parody			rondeau
paronomasia			rondel
pathos			run-on
* pause			scansion
peripety			septet
periphrasis			sestet
personification			sestina
* perspective			slant rhyme
plot			song
poem			sonnet
point of view			Spenserian
* presence			stanza
* projection			spondee
* pronunciation			sprung rhythm
prose			stanza
pun			stress
realism			stress prosody
referential lan- guage			syllabic prosody
Romantic			synaerisis
round characters			syncopation
sarcasm			syncope
satire			synizesis
sententia			tercet
simile			terminal rhyme
steno language			terza rima
stock characters			tetrameter
stream of con- sciousness			tone color
structure			trimeter
style			triolet
suggestion			triple rhyme
suspense			triplet
symbol			trochee
sympathy			truncation
synecdoche			verse
			vers libre
			villanelle
			visual prosody

GENERAL	DRAMA	FICTION	POETRY
synesthesia			weak ending
tenor and vehicle			weak rhyme
* tensiveness			
texture			
tone			
* tone color			
trompe l'oeil			
trope			
understatement			
vehicle			
* vowel triangle			
zeugma			

ACCENT.   The habitual stress placed, in pronouncing, on a particular syllable or syllables of a word containing more than one syllable. See p. 224

ACROSTIC SCRAMBLING.   A figure of sound in which sounds are repeated but in a scrambled order. For example, "later rate," in which the sounds represented by *a, t,* and *er* are repeated in the order *r, a, t.* The figure is functional only when the repetitions are close enough together to be caught by the ear. (This term, and the terms AUGMENTATION and DIMINUTION, are borrowed from Kenneth Burke.)

ACT.   A major division in a play. Plays generally contain one, three, or five acts, though there are plays of two, four, and more than five acts. Whatever the reason for act division, and there are many (shift in time, shift in setting, change of focus, and so on), each act is likely to have an "ending" of its own, though only the final ending is a "real" ending. For *act* in a more special sense, see p. 37 and pp. 156–160.

ACTION.   Although sometimes identified with PLOT, action can be distinguished from it. Action is an aspect of plot—what is done, or thought; a progression of events, whether interior or exterior. There is mental as well as physical action. A plot is an articulated series of actions involving characters. All stories have action.

AFFECTIVE FALLACY.   see FALLACIES.

ALEXANDRINE.   A line of six feet, normally in iambics. The SPENSERIAN STANZA illustrates the Alexandrine in its last line. For example, here are the last two lines of such a stanza, the second being an Alexandrine:

> And all at once they sang, "Our island home
> Is far beyond the wave; we will no longer roam."

ALLEGORY.   A narrative in which the characters, setting, and action are representative of general concepts or ideas. Bunyan's *Pilgrim's Progress,* a classic example of the type, presents the progress of a Christian's trials in seeking salvation in the allegorical form of a search of the character named Christian for the Celestial City; en route, Christian meets such characters as Faithful and Despair, and visits such places as the Slough of Despond and the Valley of the Shadow of Death. Allegories may be written in prose (*Pilgrim's Progress*), poetry (Spenser's *Faerie Queene*), or dramatic form (*Everyman*). See MORALITY PLAY.

ALLITERATION.   The repetition of the same consonant sound in close succession. *Full alliteration* is the repetition of such sounds at the beginning of stressed syllables:

> *F*ull *f*athom *f*ive thy *f*ather lies (Shakespeare)

Hidden alliteration is the repetition of such sounds involving unstressed syllables or positions other than initial positions:

> After li*f*e's fit*f*ul fever (Shakespeare)

(Notice that in this example we have full alliteration in *f*it- and in *f*ever, which serves to lift the hidden alliteration to the attention of the ear.) *Para-alliteration* is the use of related consonant sounds in an effect close to that of full alliteration:

> *t*ired and *d*irty   *p*ill *b*ox

where the first sound in each pair is the voiceless equivalent of the voiced second sound in the pair. (Notice the reverse of this condition in tire*d* and dir*ty*, and the hidden alliteration in the *r* sounds.) *Transverse alliteration* is an arrangement of alliterating sounds in which the pattern is *abab:*

> *R*elieve my *l*anguish and *r*estore the *l*ight (Samuel Daniel)

Inverse alliteration is an arrangement in which the pattern is *abba;*

> *B*rother to *d*eath, in silent *d*arkness *b*orn (Samuel Daniel)

ALLUSION.   Considered here allusion is reference (ordinarily brief) to a person, place, or occurrence thought to be of general knowledge, and employed to heighten or expand the point for which the reference is made:

> Ask me no more if east or west
> The Phoenix builds her spicy nest;
> For unto you at last she flies,
> And in your fragrant bosom dies. (Thomas Carew)

Here the allusion to the mythical Phoenix is meant to heighten the tribute which the poet is paying to his mistress.

AMPHIBRACH.   A metrical foot of three syllables, the second being the most conspicuous, normally because it receives greater stress (although marked changes in pitch, duration, chest pulsation may also be causes). Normally marked thus: x / x

AMPHIMACER.   A metrical foot of three syllables, the first and third being the most conspicuous, normally because they receive greater stress (although marked changes in pitch, duration, chest pulsation may also be causes). Normally marked thus: / x /

ANACRUSIS.   The addition of an extra syllable or syllables at the beginning of a line of poetry

> x / x / x /   x
> I never never liked her

where the line is thought of as being trochaic with anacrusis. See also CATALEXIS and HYPERCATALEXIS.

ANAPEST.   A metrical foot of three syllables, the last being the most conspicuous, normally because it receives greater stress (although marked changes in pitch, duration, chest pulsation may also be causes). Normally marked thus: x x / See also DACTYL.

ANTAGONIST.   a term used particularly in the criticism of drama to designate the character against whom the hero is pitted in the action of the play. It may be used with respect to other forms as well. See PROTAGONIST.

ANTICLIMAX.   If one thinks of climax as the most important in a series of items—the highest point in some respect—one may describe anticlimax as a point after the climax that is presented as if it were actually higher than the climax but that fails to achieve this distinction. An anticlimax may be intentional on the writer's part or unintentional. The intended climax of Shakespeare's *Pericles,* for example, is anticlimactic because it is overshadowed by an earlier climax in Act 5. Used intentionally, anticlimax often provides comic effects, as in the following example:

> To confess an honest truth, a pig is one of those things I could never think of sending away. Teals, widgeons, snipes, barn-door fowls, ducks, geese, . . . Welsh mutton, collars of brawn, sturgeon, fresh or pickled, your potted char, Swiss cheeses, French pies, early grapes, muscadines, I impart as freely unto my friends as to myself . . . but pigs are pigs, and I myself therein am nearest to myself. (Charles Lamb)

See also CLIMAX.

ANTISTROPHE.   See ODE.

ANTITHESIS.   Balance or parallelism of structure combined with opposition in meaning. Antithesis is a figure frequently found in the HEROIC COUPLET, as in the following example from Pope:

> Fortune in men has some small diff'rence made,
> One flaunts in rags, one flutters in brocade.

APOCOPE.   Omission of the last sound or syllable of a word: *th' open* for *the open.* A form of ELISION. See also HIATUS.

APOSTROPHE.   A FIGURE OF SENSE in which (1) an absent person is addressed as though present or (2) an inanimate object or thing is addressed as if it were capable of hearing. The first use is related to ALLUSION, the second to PERSONIFICATION.

> (1) Milton! thou should'st be living at this hour (Wordsworth)
> (2) Death, be not proud (John Donne)

see also INVOCATION.

ARTICULATION.   The production of sound through the manipulation of the parts of the speech mechanism. Strictly speaking, ENUNCIATION refers to the sounding and articulation to the activity resulting in sound, though the two may be used synonymously. See also DICTION and PRONUNCIATION.

ASSONANCE.   A FIGURE OF SOUND employing the repetition of vowel sounds. Full assonance is the repetition of such sounds in stressed syllables (though not necessarily in initial positions such as in *all off*). For example:

> That d*ea*d men r*i*se up n*e*ver (Swinburne)

It may be paired with ALLITERATION:

> He too with *dea*th shall *dwe*ll (Swinburne)

(Notice, however, that the pair *rowing-sowing* constitutes RHYME rather than simple assonance.) *Hidden assonance* is the repetition of vowels in unstressed positions:

—Fair as a star, when only one
*I*s shin*i*ng *i*n the sky (Wordsworth)

Hidden assonance is often uncovered by being paired with other effects (here, for example, with the repeated nasal sound).

The repetition of related rather than identical vowel sounds has been given the unhappy name of *half assonance,* which may be called by the graver name *semiassonance,* though that sounds like an evasion. For example:

To m*e*n that m*i*x and m*ee*t her (Swinburne)

where we have front vowels drawn into a sequence (underscored by the alliterating *m's*) by virtue of the fact that they steadily rise in placement: ε, ɪ, i. For placement of vowel sounds, see VOWEL TRIANGLE. Vowel sequences may be patterned (whether identical or related vowels) just as consonant sequences are patterned in ALLITERATION to produce *transverse* or *inverse* arrangements. Here, for example, is a subtle transverse pattern of related vowels in Swinburne, who is especially fond of assonantal effects such as this:

N*o*t kn*o*wn of the cl*i*ffs and the f*i*elds and the s*ea*

F*i*elds and s*ea* produce full assonance; but the other stressed words also form a pattern "N*o*t kn*o*wn" gives us two vowels whose relation to one another is that of lower to higher; "cl*i*ffs" and "f*i*elds-s*ea*" gives us a pair with the same relationship. Furthermore, both sounds in the second pair are higher than the sounds in the first pair. The pattern may be written thus: abAB. In Swinburne, such effects count in the sound values of the poems; but see, under FIGURES OF SOUND, the warning against too ingenious analysis of sound patterns.

ATMOSPHERE.   The aura within a work of literature, the feeling that pervades it. Atmosphere arises from details of SETTING, CHARACTERIZATION, ACTION, and so forth, but it is not identical with any of these. Nor is it to be identified with TONE, which points to authorial attitudes. It is possible, within a dark and gloomy atmosphere, to have a tone of amusement. The comic sometimes achieves its effect by such incongruous juxtapositions of atmosphere and tone.

AUGMENTATION.   A FIGURE OF SOUND in which sounds are repeated but with an increase in the distance between them: "slow sail," where *sl* is repeated as *s—l.* See DIMINUTION.

BALLAD.   A poem, originally intended to be sung, which tells a story. It is either epic or dramatic in mode, simple in form, strong in effect, "objective" in treatment. Normally ballads employ repetition or refrain. Subject matter is likely to be broadly universal, often with supernatural or magical elements. The *popular ballad* is anonymous, preserved originally by oral tradition; the so-called *literary* or *artistic ballad* is an imitation of the popular ballad form by a known poet.

BALLADE.   A French poetic form popular in the time of Chaucer and occasionally revived. It may consist of three stanzas of either eight or ten lines, followed by an envoy of four or five lines. The last line of the opening stanza becomes the refrain and last line of each subsequent stanza and of the envoy.

BALLAD STANZA.   See QUATRAIN, on p. 244.

BATHOS.   The opposite of sublimity—the descent, by accident, of a writer into the ludicrous when he attempts the sublime.

BLANK VERSE.   Verse written in lines of unrhymed iambic pentameter.

BURLESQUE.   A form of the comic in which the humor resides in the incongruous imitation of people, actions, events, ideas, customs. Burlesque involves a perspective which may be called satirical (see SATIRE), though the satire may be either heavy or slight. PARODY, the MOCK EPIC, and travesty are forms of burlesque, as are caricature and the LAMPOON. Anna Russell, in concert and on records, has treated her audiences to musical burlesques of such composers as Wagner and Sullivan. The libretti of W. S. Gilbert are often burlesques. Byron's *Don Juan* is a celebrated burlesque in verse.

CACOPHONY.   Discordant or harsh sound, as opposed to EUPHONY. Cacophony is often deliberate, for effect; occasionally it results from carelessness on the writer's part.

CADENCE.   Literally, a "fall"; a sense unit accompanied by a terminal pause, whether or not accompanied by falling inflection. *Primary cadences* are complete logical units; *secondary cadences* are speech phrases within the primary cadences. Variations in the handling of secondary cadences account for many differences between oral readings of the same work by different readers. Both prose and poetry are cadenced, since the English language is cadenced, but the cadences of poetry are likely to be patterned temporally by METER. FREE VERSE may relate cadences and syllable count, or cadences and number of stresses per line, or cadences and syntactical units, but cadence by itself cannot produce sufficient patterning to yield poetic rhythm. See p. 240 for further discussion.

CAESURA.   A clearly discernible pause within a line of verse. Often the name is restricted to the dominant pause within the line. The caesura is likely to be about the middle of the line; there may be more than one caesura within a single line. In the following line, there is a single caesura marked by the comma:

> I held it truth, with him who sings (Tennyson)

In the next example, however, there are three:

> Why linger, why turn back, why shrink, my Heart? (Shelley)

Perhaps in the third example, the pauses ought not to be called caesuras at all:

> 'tis naught
> That ages, empires, and religions there
> Lie buried in the ravage . . . (Shelley)

The caesura, as employed by such poets as Pope and Dryden, is an integral part of the effect of the heroic couplet. See HEROIC COUPLET.

CATALEXIS.   The omission of an unaccented or unstressed syllable at the conclusion of a line of poetry:

> / x x   / x x / x
> This is the day of the locust.

(The term is useful only if one imagines the line to consist of three dactyls. If one describes the line as being composed of two dactyls and one trochee, there is no missing syllable. Another example:

　　/　x　　/　　x　/　　　x　/
　　This is where the road begins

in which the line is thought of as trochaic; but if the line is read as iambic, the line will illustrate the term TRUNCATION.

　　A caution: It is not arbitrary whether the line is called one kind of meter or another. The individual line must be seen in the context of the metrical pattern of the whole poem. See also HYPERCATALEXIS. A line that is complete is said to be acatalectic (i.e., without catalexis).

CATHARSIS.　A difficult term derived from Aristotle's *Poetics,* catharsis means "purgation" and points to the effect of a cleansing of the emotions felt upon witnessing a tragedy. The action of a tragedy, according to Aristotle, does not depress but rather relieves (purges) an audience of the tragic emotions of pity and fear, producing an effect of greater emotional health. See TRAGEDY.

CHARACTER.　A person participating in the PLOT of a story, whether in verse or in prose and whether in lyric, epic, or dramatic mode. Characters may be ROUND or FLAT, may be fully developed personalities or sketched in briefest outline, depending on their part in the plot. Distinct from the word *character* thought of as describing moral qualities (such as a "good man" or a "villain"). See also STOCK CHARACTERS.

CHIASMUS.　A FIGURE OF SENSE that employs phrases parallel in syntax but given first in one order and then in a reversed order, as in this example:

　　Calm without rage; without o'erflowing full (Denham)

where the adjective precedes the prepositional phrase before the CAESURA and follows it after the caesura. Chiasmus is frequently combined with sound patterns, as in the following line, where it is accompanied by *transverse* ALLITERATION:

　　Each *s*trengthens *r*eason, and *s*elf-love *r*estrains (Pope)

(The normal order here would be "Each strengthens reason and restrains self-love.")

CHRONICLE PLAY.　A form of drama brought into popularity in the sixteenth century in England, consisting of the loose dramatization of historical materials taken from chronicle histories and making use of pageantry, wars, and spectacles for effect. Marlowe and Shakespeare unified such loose actions in the interests of CHARACTER and PLOT, and their tighter plays are sometimes called HISTORY PLAYS to distinguish them from the earlier chronicle plays.

CIRCUMLOCUTION　A roundabout way of expressing something. Circumlocution may be employed for comic effects. It may be a way of being tactful. It may be an indication of modesty or embarrassment or delicacy of feeling. It may be a sign of prudery. A particular aspect of circumlocution, the attempt to employ a "nicer" or "more genteel" expression for a less delicate expression, is called EUPHEMISM. For example, instead of saying "She died yesterday," one may say "She passed away yesterday." Speakers sometimes employ circumlocution to avoid repetition, often with comic effects. In speaking of Shakespeare, for example, a lecturer may refer to him once as Shakespeare, and then emply such circumlocutions as "the Bard of Stratford," "the Swan of Stratford-upon-Avon," "the author of *Hamlet,*" and "the greatest master of the English tongue." Much of what Wordsworth and Coleridge objected to in the language of eighteenth century poetry was really circumlocution.

CLASSIC.   Used in several senses: (1) a work of the greatest literary merit; (2) a work adhering to classical rules and models (see sense 3); (3) in the plural, the literature of ancient Greece and Rome; (4) a work serving as a pattern or model of expression. See NEOCLASSIC. Shakespeare's *King Lear* may be called a classic in sense 1; the epigrams of Elizabethan scholar-poets may be called classic in sense 2, in their imitation of the Roman poets Horace, Martial, Juvenal; "the classics" (sense 3) are the great works of ancient Greece and Rome; the speech by Ulysses on degree in Shakespeare's *Troilus and Cressida* may be called a classic statement (sense 4) of the concept of order and degree.

CLICHE.   A too-familiar expression, hackneyed by use: "toe the mark," "fish or cut bait," "sharp as a tack," "thin as a rail," "dead as a doornail." It is not always easy to decide when an expression has passed into the realm of cliché; it may become a cliché more quickly for one person than for another or may at one period be a cliché and not at another period. Clichés are often dead figurative expressions.

CLIMAX.   (For its particular reference to drama, see p. 295.) In some sense, the high point of an action, that to which everything else leads. In Shakespeare's *King Lear,* for example, the climax is the death of Lear himself; in *The Taming of the Shrew,* it is Kate's speech to the assembly at the end of Act 5. The climax may or may not be the peak of emotion. It describes a moment or point in the structure rather than a moment of emotion. The term is frequently useful in discussing poetry, usually useful in discussing prose fiction, almost always useful in discussing drama. Some critics use this word for the point we choose to call the CRISIS. Any work may contain a series of climaxes, but each minor climax leads in turn toward the major climax.

CLOSED COUPLET.   See HEROIC COUPLET.

COALESCENCE.   In literature and the performance of literature, the term refers to the growing together or unification of parts; assimilation of details. Meanings do not exist independently of one another but reinforce and alter one another; their relations are tensive. Sounds, gestures, silences are, as parts of meaning, parts of this coalescence. The performance of a poem in which the reader has not put back together the elements he has analyzed will exist in fragments; a dramatic scene that is not put back together will seem not to "go anyplace"; a scene from fiction that remains fragmented will seem not to have a clear point of view. The question—a large one—is whether the interpreter can at the same time keep a value in all the elements and yet make them serve the full *act* of the literary work, with no one element receiving more than its due emphasis.

COMEDY.   One of the two major classes of drama (the other is TRAGEDY). Comedy and tragedy are distinct from one another not so much by virtue of their incidents as by virtue of their perspective. Comic perspective usually stresses the incongruous and takes care not to involve too deeply the sympathies of the audience. It normally holds a strong sense of proprieties and conventions. Beyond such simple distinctions as this (even these are not really simple), the problem of defining comedy is fraught with peril. Comedies, as opposed to tragedies, end more or less happily for the central characters.

The comic may appear in verse and prose as well as in drama, but the term *comedy* is normally reserved for drama. See also BURLESQUE, COMEDY OF MANNERS, COMICAL SATIRE, FARCE, HIGH COMEDY, LAMPOON, LOW COMEDY, PARODY, ROMANTIC COMEDY, SENTIMENTAL COMEDY.

COMEDY OF MANNERS. Particularly applied to the English comedy of the Restoration period, comedy of manners points to comedy concerned with the social actions and behavior of members of a highly sophisticated, upper-class society. Low-class characters are normally subordinate in interest or are played against the foibles of their "betters." Such comedy emphasizes wit, whether true or false, and more often than not takes an arch view of the love game.

COMIC RELIEF. The use of comic scenes, characters, or events to alter the tension of a serious or tragic action. Ideally, comic relief should at the same time underscore the tragic action rather than for the moment dismiss it—should be organic rather than irrelevant or digressive. The drunken porter in *Macbeth* illustrates such an organic comic character, for he underscores the hellish quality of Macbeth's castle and deed and the general malaise of Macbeth's world even while he provides laughter. The gravediggers in *Hamlet* provide a sharp counterpoint in the theme of death and dying. It is not usual to talk about tragic relief (the use of serious scenes, characters, or events to alter the tension in a comic action), but such a thing exists often in the comedies of Shakespeare.

COMICAL SATIRE. A term employed in the English Renaissance to describe comedies heavily satirical in vein. Ben Jonson is perhaps the most famous of the playwrights employing the form (though the phrase might also be used to describe such a playwright as Aristophanes). Comical satire deals with breaches of moral and social decorum and often with contrasts between so-called truewits (bright, sophisticated young men) and falsewits (their gulls and dupes).

COMMUNICATION and COMMUNION. While we recognize that literature, in being lifted to the conscious level, communicates something to its readers and that if the reader is successful he makes the literature meaningful to an audience (i.e., communicates), we nevertheless prefer the terms *commune* and *communion* to *communicate* and *communication*. A speech, for example, exists primarily to communicate, to persuade. It uses language in a *mediating* fashion, as a tool. But a literary work, while it does communicate, exists also as a thing created, using language in an *immediate* fashion as material to construct a form that parallels other life forms, having value in and of itself. When the interpreter reads a speech to an audience, his primary task is that of embodying, but he can never simply become identical with the poem, since he is an autonomous being. He establishes with it a relationship that can be called communion—a feeling of togetherness existing along with a certain distancing. It is a "holding in common," a "showing" rather than an "instructing" or "telling." When the interpreter adequately projects this communion, the responsive audience shares in it.

CONCEIT. An ingenious or witty comparison (see FIGURES OF COMPARISON). The METAPHYSICAL CONCEIT (from its use by the "Metaphysical poets" of the school of Donne) is noted for strong intellectuality as well as for its novelty—the comparison, for example, of the souls of two lovers with a pair of compasses in Donne's "A Valediction Forbidding Mourning":

> If they be two, they are two so
>> As stiff twin compasses are two:
> Thy soul, the fixed foot, makes no show
>> To move, but doth if the other do.
>
> And though it in the center sit,
>> Yet, when the other far doth roam,
> It leans, and hearkens after it,
>> And grows erect as that comes home.

CONCRETE POETRY.   Poetry that juxtaposes words and optical signs to produce "tension of object-words in the time-space continuum; dynamic structures; multiplicity of concomitant movements." See pp. 246–253 for a fuller discussion.

CONFLICT.   A term that points to an aspect of TENSIVENESS; the strain set up between two characters or two forces, between a character and his environment, or between two or more tendencies within a single personality that begins to shape PLOT. Conflict applies particularly to the plots of plays and to the relation of PROTAGONIST to ANTAGONIST, but it is present in all stories.

CONNOTATION.   Overtones and associations in addition to the DENOTATION of a word. Compare the largely denotative meaning of *brothers* with the connotations of *brethren* or the modern spelling of *daisy* with the original *day's eye* (which is figurative).

CONSONANCE.   A FIGURE OF SOUND employing the repetition of a pattern of consonants with a change of intervening vowels. Examples in catch phrases are *sing song, pitter, patter, shilly shally, tick tock*. (Notice that these are also examples of ALLITERATION.) Subtler examples are the following:

> "Out of this house"—said *rider* to *reader,*
> Yours never will"—said *farer* to *fearer,*
> "They're looking for you"—said *hearer* to *horror,*
> As he left them there, as he left them there. (Auden)

The term is sometimes used for words in rhyme positions beginning or ending in the same consonant sound, but this is really a mode of alliteration functioning as semirhyme:

> . . . shrie*k*
> . . . crac*k*
> . . . *f*ire
> . . . *f*lint

CONSONANTAL COGNATES.   Vowels are compared on the VOWEL TRIANGLE with respect to their placement in utterance; consonant sounds may be compared too with respect to their utterance, as follows:

> 1. *Plosives* or *stops* (sounds made by first blocking and then releasing the breath stream)—

	Voiceless	Voiced	
labial	p	b	(stoppage by lips)
dental	t	d	(stoppage by tongue and alveolar ridge)
palatal	k	g	(stoppage by tongue and hard palate)

2. *Nasals* (sounds made with the voice issuing wholly or partly through the nose)—m, n, ŋ
3. *Fricatives* (sounds in which the "rub"—from *fricāre,* to rub—results from the forcing of air through the aperture to produce the sound)—

Voiceless	Voiced	Glottal
f	v	h
s	z	
θ	ð	
ʃ	ʒ	

4. *Affricates* (sounds beginning with a stop and ending with a fricative—from *affricātus,* to rub against)—

Voiceless	Voiced
t ʃ	**dʒ**

5. *Glides* (transitional sounds, including semivowels)—r, j, w, ʍ
6. *Lateral* (sounds made with the breath passing beside the tongue)—l

The sounds *r* and *l* are frequently paired as *liquids* (sounds that are frictionless and capable of sustention like vowels).

FIGURES OF SOUND often pair related consonant sounds, so that *t* and *d* in the phrase *t*ired and *d*irty may be said to illustrate PARA-ALLITER-ATION (or paralliteration).

CONVENTIONAL SYMBOL   See SYMBOL.

COUNTERPOINT.   The employment of plural meters in verse, one meter enhancing another. In prose, the playing of one element against another—a theme against a theme, a tone against a tone, a setting against a setting. In Shelley's "The Cloud," two rising meters (iambic and anapestic) combine to produce a rhythmic effect which may be described as counterpoint. Compare SYNCOPATION.

COUPLET.   Two rhyming lines of verse. See also p. 243.

CRISIS.   Sometimes useful in discussing other forms, this term is particularly applicable to drama. As distinguished from major CLIMAX, the major crisis is a turning point—somewhere near the middle of a five-act play or toward the close of the the second act of a three-act play, generally speaking—after which the possibilites of the action are clearly limited. In *Romeo and Juliet,* the major crisis is the killing of Tybalt by Romeo, which leads to Romeo's exile, Juliet's taking of the potion, and ultimately the deaths of the two young lovers. It is not accurate to say that after the crisis the ending is inevitable, if by that one means that one can foretell the climax at the moment of crisis. Often one can distinguish the crisis only by looking backward from the climax of the play. Crisis is a structural term, not a description of something the audience necessarily recognizes at the moment of its happening, though it may do so. It is sometimes said that the action up to the crisis is *rising action,* and the action after the crisis *falling action;* but "falling action" has the unhappy connotation of action that becomes less interesting, which is surely not descriptive of dramatic action in a successful play.

DACTYL.   A metrical foot of three syllables, the first being the most conspicuous, normally because it receives greater stress (although marked changes in pitch, duration, chest pulsation may also be causes). Normally marked thus: / xx See also ANAPEST.

DEAD METAPHOR.   see METAPHOR.

DECORUM.   Agreement among style, speaker, situation, and literary mode. The oral interpreter may employ the term to describe the necessary congruence between himself, the literary work he reads, and the situation within which he is reading.

DENOTATION.   The referential aspect of a word; the exact thing a word signifies. Purely denotative words are transparent—they do not carry values in themselves. The word *boat,* insofar as it simply points to the kind of structure we mean when we use the word, is denotative. The word *barque,* which also points to a kind of structure employed upon the water, has overtones and associations beyond its denotation (see CONNOTATION). A word of caution: it is not necessarily true that a word rich in connotation is better in verse than a word essentially denotative, any more than it is true that a word essentially denotative need be devoid of connotative meaning. The denotative value of a word is essentially the same for any number of readers, whereas the connotative value of a word is only in part subject to the user's control. Literary works are more than usually successful in deciding when and to what extent such values are to be controlled.

DENOUEMENT.   Sometimes called the *resolution* and used particularly with respect to the play form. The final unraveling of the story; not synonymous with the CLIMAX. In *Romeo and Juliet,* the death of the lovers may be called the climax; the denouement is the subsequent explanation of events involving Friar Laurence.

DESCRIPTION.   In Phyllis Bentley's sense, an aspect of rhythm in prose fiction. It is the slowest tempo, as a narrator moves very slowly to convey in words the appearance of someone or something. See pp. 282–284.

DEUS EX MACHINA.   A phrase derived from the ancient practice of lowering a god from above in a stage machine; used now to refer to any arbitrary solution to an impasse, as when in desperation an author calls in an earthquake to bring his story to an end.

DIAERESIS.   The resolution of one syllable into two: *Aërial* for *aerial, mediaeval* for *medieval.* The opposite of SYNAERESIS.

DICTION.   The words employed in discourse; in general, the vocabulary of a work. Sometimes used as synonymous with ARTICULATION.

DIDACTIC LITERATURE   Literature that seeks to instruct and inform. Many critics rule out of consideration as "pure literature" literature that has as its primary purpose the presentation of a thesis, but such a way of delimiting literature proves difficult. A work may be written with didactic intent and still remain alive long after interest in the outside issue has died away. It becomes a question of defining intent and of distinguishing between the intent of the writer and the intent of the piece he has written. A playwright may (as a playwright has done) write a play about seagoing men, with his purpose the reform of certain laws affecting the safety of shipping; if his play is more than the presentation of a thesis (if it is also a play), it will invest its characters and action with sufficient interest to ensure its life *after* the reform of the laws. Much literature of eighteenth century England has been ruled out of consideration too easily by being labeled didactic. Didactic literature and pure literature overlap frequently and complexly. See, for example, SATIRE, ALLEGORY, FABLE. Indeed, there is no final quarrel between instruction and pleasure as proper ends of literature. Perhaps the term *propaganda* ought to be employed to describe the kind of work that has a specific, immediate, and sociological position to which it attempts to sway a reader apart from concern with *literary* form (though one cannot say "apart from *any* concern with form").

DIMETER.   A verse written in two feet.

DIMINUTION   A FIGURE OF SOUND in which sounds are repeated with a decrease in the distance between them: *sail slow.* See AUGMENTATION.

DIPODY.   Dipodic measures are composed of two FEET, and the run of a line seems to pair feet rather than to measure them separately. The ballad stanza often divides the line thus, as in the following stanza (lines 1 and 3) from Coleridge's *Rime of the Ancient Mariner,* an artistic ballad:

> And every tongue, through utter drought,
>   Was withered at the root;
> We could not speak, no more than if
>   We had been choked with soot.

The medial CAESURA in lines 1 and 3 breaks each line into two halves, each composed of two iambs. It is more descriptive of the effect of the lines to speak of them as iambic and dipodic than to speak of them as composed of four iambs each. For an extended example, see the popular ballad "Lord Randal."

DIRECT DISCOURSE.   The direct words of a speaker—the language one ordinarily finds within quotation marks as the speech of a character in a story. Quotation marks need not be used, as in the following example, though by conventional rules they are thought "proper":

> She's dying, he thought to himself with a shock.
> She's dying and there's nothing I can do about it.

See INDIRECT DISCOURSE.

DISCOVERY.   A term applied (from Aristotle) to a change on the part of the hero from ignorance to discovery, often coupled with a PERIPETY. Such a discovery is Macbeth's learning that Macduff fulfills the prophecy of the weird sisters that he will be slain by one not of woman born.

DOUBLE RHYME.   Another name for FEMININE RHYME; rhyme in which the rhyming syllables precede the final syllables of the line: *greater, later.*

DRAMA.   See pp. 122–136 and 291–297. That form of literary work intended for performance onstage by actors (whether or not actually performed), written in the dramatic mode, in either prose or verse. It embraces COMEDY, TRAGEDY, TRAGICOMEDY, HISTORY PLAY, CHRONICLE PLAY, COMICAL SATIRE, MASQUE, MELODRAMA, MIRACLE PLAY, MORALITY PLAY, MYSTERY PLAY, PASTORAL PLAY. The term is sometimes used loosely to describe a serious play that does not fit comfortably the descriptions of either comedy or tragedy, a play that ends in a state that cannot be easily described as either happy or tragic.

DRAMATIC.   Here used to define the literary mode (see also LYRIC and EPIC) in which the writer-speaker is concealed from view by speaking through characters rather than in his own person or in the person of a narrator. Plays are largely dramatic in mode; poems are sometimes dramatic in mode; prose fiction is sometimes dramatic in mode, though normally it is in the mixed or intermediate mode described as epic.

DRAMATIC IRONY.   Awareness within a dramatic action that the effect to be achieved is, or is likely to be, the opposite of the effect expected or desired. Lady Macbeth's statement to her husband immediately after his murder of Duncan ("A little water clears us of this deed") is ironical, since the blood can never be washed from their hands. The fate of King Oedipus is ironical, since he builds the case for his own undoing. Dramatic irony achieves its effect by granting the audience an awareness denied to at least certain of the characters in the action. While the term has particular reference to the play as a form, it may apply to other forms as well. See also IRONY.

DRAMATIC LYRIC.   A characteristic modern form, the dramatic lyric is lyrical in attitude, center, and musicality and dramatic in mode. Written in verse, it gives us a character speaking within a defined situation and may involve a story or action. See also DRAMATIC MONOLOGUE.

DRAMATIC MONOLOGUE.   A poem dramatic in mode (speaker, situation, action) but less lyrical in tone than the DRAMATIC LYRIC and normally suggesting the presence of other characters within the poem. Often written in blank verse. Tennyson's "Ulysses" and Browning's "My Last Duchess" are among the most popular examples of the type.

ECLOGUE.   See PASTORAL.

ELEGY.   Originally employed to designate any poem written in the elegiac meter in classical poetry, the term has now come to apply to subject matter and attitude rather than to form. It refers generally to poems expressing grief from a point of view that is subjective, meditative, often lyrical, but it may be formal and even impersonal. It may be combined with pastoral elements (as in Milton's *Lycidas*). The formal elegy may begin with personal sadness and rise thence to a concern with more far-reaching issues, as in Gray's famous "Elegy in a Country Churchyard."

ELISION.   Suppression of a sound for metrical reasons. See SYNCOPE, APOCOPE, SYNAERESIS, HIATUS, all of which are related terms.

EMOTIVE LANGUAGE.   An awkward term, but see STENO LANGUAGE. "Emotive" here does not mean "loose" or "irrational."

EMPATHY.   The state of "feeling into," physical responsivity to feelings, sensations, motions outside oneself. When one empathizes with a tree blowing in the wind, he seems to sway with the tree; when one empathizes with Othello, he feels to some degree what Othello feels; when one winces when he sees another person struck, he is empathizing with the suffering of the one struck. This is a key term for the interpreter, who is intimately concerned with the question of physical relationship between oral reader and text. It is related to, but not at all identical with, the term *imaging*. See SYMPATHY.

END RHYME.   See TERMINAL RHYME.

END-STOPPED.   A line of verse that has a clearly marked pause at its termination. See RUN-ON and PAUSE.

ENJAMBEMENT.   See RUN-ON.

EPIC.   Do not confuse the term *epic* used as the name of a genre with the same term used as the name of a mode, as we have used it in this book. As a genre (a literary type defined by subject matter, form, or style), *epic* refers to a long narrative in verse dealing with heroic characters and events, usually racial or tribal or national in scope. Exalted in style, intricate in its arrangement of episodes, it may be either popular or literary (anonymous and composite in authorship or by a known poet). The MOCK EPIC (of which Pope's *Rape of the Lock* is a well-known example) is a BURLESQUE of the epic form, involving high-flown treatment of trivial matter.

For a discussion of epic as a mode, see pp. 244–245. As distinguished from LYRIC and DRAMATIC, it is that mixed mode in which the writer-speaker seems at some times to speak directly in his own person (lyric mode) or in the person of a narrator and at other times to disappear behind or into characters who speak in their own persons (dramatic mode).

EPIGRAM. A short, terse, witty statement, whether in prose or verse. Ordinarily the epigram leads to an amusing or ingenious turn:

> I am unable, yonder beggar cries,
> To stand or move; if he say true, he *lies*. (Donne)

Epigrams may be elegiac, eulogistic, amatory, paradoxical, anecdotal, satiric, reflective. They are defined in terms of their length and perspective rather than in terms of subject matter.

EPISODE. A single incident in a series of actions. The killing of Polonius, for example, is an episode in the plot of *Hamlet*. A story is said to be episodic when its episodes lack successful articulation as a plot and remain loosely tied together. See PLOT.

EPISTOLARY NOVEL. A novel written in the form of exchanged letters. Richardson's *Pamela* and *Clarissa Harlowe* are two famous English examples of the form.

EQUIVALENCE. The equation of one poetic FOOT with another. In terms of duration, for example, it is said that the IAMBUS and the TROCHEE are equivalent feet, though their pattern of stresses is reversed. Or on the assumption that the ANAPEST is a "quick-running foot," it may be taken as the equivalent of an IAMBUS. In general, any foot that seems to read "smoothly" with another (as measured by the ear) may be called its equivalent, though the theory is full of difficulties. A really rigid prosodist might deny that any foot other than an identical foot is the equivalent of another, and his position would have some merit.

ESSAY. A "transitional form," the essay is a short composition dealing with a particular subject, situation, or idea but more concerned with talking about it than with embodying it. While essays are normally in prose, there are essays in poetic form: Pope's *Essay on Criticism, Essay on Man*. Horace's essay on poetics is written in the form of a verse letter. See pp. 411–412.

ESTHETIC DISTANCE. A difficult term, esthetic distance points to the relationship between work and audience in terms of the work's degree of "objectivity" and hence the audience's degree of "detachment." We may illustrate three degrees of distancing by singling out a letter by Keats, a play by Shakespeare, and a play by Thornton Wilder. The letter by Keats (highly personal, involving intimate emotion) runs the risk in performance of involving an audience too intimately, so that the listeners may feel either ashamed or embarrassed to be eavesdropping at so naked a display of a man's heart. The play by Shakespeare is, by contrast, more "objective," since we feel that it is not Shakespeare himself but fictitious characters who are speaking. The play *Our Town,* by Wilder, will increase such "objectivity" by having the narrator break in on the scene and say, for example, "Thank you, ladies. Thank you very much"—whereupon Mrs. Gibbs and Mrs. Webb stop talking and leave the stage, so that the sense of "play acting" is increased. We may say that the esthetic distance is least in the Keats letter and greatest in the Wilder play. The presence of the book is likely to affect distance; there is generally greater distance in the performance of the interpreter than in that of the actor. A word of caution: distance does not refer to the *strength* of impact of a literary work on the audience; it refers to the nature and quality of it. Esthetic distance affects the audience's perspective. A literary work creates its own distance, in part; interpreters must be wary of increasing or decreasing the distance too much, lest they destroy the intended perspective. (Locus is involved for the oral reader.)

EUPHEMISM.   See CIRCUMLOCUTION.

EUPHONY.   The quality of sounding pleasant to the ear; musicality of sound, as opposed to CACOPHONY.

EUPHUISM.   The highly artificial prose style popularized by John Lyly (and deriving its name from his romance entitled *Euphues*). Euphuistic prose is elaborately balanced, replete with alliteration, figures, antitheses, *sententiae.* Often burlesqued by other writers because of its self-consciousness.

EXACT RHYME.   The repetition of identical *accented* vowel sounds in combination with identical succeeding sounds but different preceding sounds; *big, pig; many, penny; quality, jollity.*

EXEMPLUM.   A short narrative illustrating a particular text, especially the text of a sermon.

EXISTENTIALISM.   A philosophical doctrine that is also a literary doctrine: the view (somewhere between materialism and idealism) that stresses the identity of the external world and the world within the mind and that focuses on man's problem of choice within a universe that lacks purpose and plan. Sartre is a chief exponent of the doctrine. The so-called doctrine of the absurd (as in the phrase *theatre of the absurd*) is a reductive view of existentialism, as the restricted sense of REALISM is a reductive view of realism.

EXPOSITION.   Explanation needed for further understanding of the course of an action or the nature or a character of event. Though used with particular reference to drama (the initial scenes in a play contain much information needed to adjust the audience to the story), exposition is also found in other story forms in prose or poetry.

EXPRESSIONISM.   A literary doctrine and method aimed at uncovering the inner life of characters rather than in displaying their outer reality; often involved in the presentation of struggles between abstract forces rather than between people. Often exemplified in the work of German dramatists at the time of World War I. At the opposite pole from PHOTOGRAPHIC REALISM.

EYE RHYME.   The pairing of words in rhyme position that look like rhyming words but do not sound like rhyme: *rough, bough;* or *new, sew.*

FABLE.   A short narrative in which animals are personified and in which the story illustrates a moral. See the fables by Aesop, p. 420.

FALLACIES.   False, erroneous, or unsound views. We have specified two fallacious ways of seeing relationships between literary works and readers. The AFFECTIVE FALLACY confuses the poem and its results, judging worth by the intensity of emotional response where the response may in fact arise largely from causes other than the work. The INTENTIONAL FALLACY confuses the poem with the cause of the poem. A caution: Wimsatt and Beardsley, who employ the terms, are not implying either that a reader's emotion is always irrelevant or that poets' views of their poems should be disregarded. See the discussion on pp. 196–198.

FALLING RHYTHM.   Rhythms composed predominantly of trochaic and dactylic meters, where the feet may be said to "fall" from the stressed or conspicuous syllables. Doubtless the word *falling* here indicates the customary view that accented or stressed syllables are likely to have a higher pitch, though this is by no means always the case.

FARCE.   A form of comedy typically involving FLAT CHARACTERS, STOCK SITUATIONS, and physical action that is often LOW COMEDY or BURLESQUE. Farce emphasizes the incongruous, the ludicrous, the improbable, but plays classified as farces may depart from this typical scheme to give us round characters, a high degree of wit, and a minimum of horseplay. Shakespeare's *Comedy of Errors,* for example, though in many respects a typical farce, includes a romantic frame tale and a love story; Molière's farces often have the verbal polish of HIGH COMEDY; Oscar Wilde's *The Importance of Being Earnest* is an interesting blend of FARCE, BURLESQUE, HIGH COMEDY, and ROMANTIC or SENTIMENTAL COMEDY.

FEET.   The units of measurement in metered poetry. Feet are made up of syllables combined so as to indicate an alternation of contrasting values, usually seen as contrast of stresses, though such things as pitch, duration, and chest pulsation are involved. In the view of many prosodists, feet are thought of as *isochronous,* equal in time of pronunciation. In English poetry the usual feet are the IAMB, the TROCHEE, the ANAPEST, the DACTYL, the SPONDEE, and the PYRRHIC. See pp. 226–229 for a fuller discussion.

FEMININE ENDING.   The addition of extra "light" syllables at the end of a line of poetry (also called *weak ending*). "Tomorrow and tomorrow and tomorrow," for example, if the line is thought of as pentameter and decasyllabic, although there are eleven syllables by count, and if the added syllable is unstressed or unaccented. See HYPERCATALEXIS.

FEMININE RHYME.   See DOUBLE RHYME.

FIGURES OF COMPARISON.   A class of FIGURES OF SENSE embracing METAPHOR and SIMILE.

FIGURES OF CONTIGUITY.   A class of FIGURES OF SENSE embracing SYNECDOCHE and METONYMY.

FIGURES OF RHETORIC.   See FIGURES OF SENSE.

FIGURES OF SENSE.   Devices or arrangements of language by which a writer seeks, in escaping from the direct and literal use of language, to speak more strikingly, more picturesquely, or more accurately. Some figures of sense (the FIGURES OF COMPARISON and of CONTIGUITY) underscore meaning by extending the sense; others (ANTITHESIS, PARALLELISM, CHIASMUS) underscore meaning by calling attention to the syntax in which the statement is made. Still others enlarge the realm of experience by giving life to nonliving things (PERSONIFICATION), by calling into the present things not actually present (APOSTROPHE), or by invoking other known experiences (ALLUSION). See the

discussion on pp. 202–204 as well as the Glossary entries for ALLUSION, AN-
TITHESIS, APOSTROPHE, CHIASMUS, HYPERBOLE, IRONY, LITOTES, PARADOX, PARALLEL-
ISM, PERSONIFICATION, ZEUGMA. (Compare with FIGURES OF SOUND.)

Figures of sense are sometimes divided into *tropes* and *figures of rhetoric;* figures of rhetoric include those figures in which the effect is achieved
by the arrangement of words, and tropes include those figures in which a
radical change in meaning is involved. The distinctions are not sharp however; indeed, such figures as *antithesis* surely involve even appeals to the
ear. It seems simpler for our purposes to limit ourselves to the two terms
FIGURES OF SENSE and FIGURES OF SOUND, recognizing that problems exist also
with these terms.

FIGURES OF SOUND.   Arrangements of language that seek to promote aural
effects of language through the creation of sound patterns. See pp. 206–208,
as well as the Glossary entries for ACROSTIC SCRAMBLING, ALLITERATION, ASSO-
NANCE, AUGMENTATION, CONSONANCE, DIMINUTION, ONOMATOPOEIA, RHYME,
TONE COLOR. A general warning: since language is composed of a limited
number of sounds, *all* sounds undergo repetition. Probably only those patterns raised to the level of the listener's awareness are to be counted as
figures of sound, though it must be confessed that some listeners have
better ears than others. (See the discussion of ASSONANCE.)

FLASHBACK.   A return within the course of a story to events taking place at an
earlier time. Arthur Miller's *Death of a Salesman,* for example, keeps recur-
ring to events in the history of Willy Loman prior to the time of the opening
of the play.

FLAT CHARACTERS.   Characters that seem to possess a single dominant and
unchanging trait. Caricature presents such traits in a ludicrously exaggerated fashion, but not all flat characters are caricatures by any means. In
some works, a flat character may serve an author better than a ROUND CHAR-
ACTER.

FOCUS.   Sharpness of definition; central point of attention. One may speak of
the focus of the reader, of the poem, or of the reader's placement and
location of the poem.

FOOT.   See FEET.

FOOT PROSODY.   The metrical system in which poetry is arranged into FEET,
q.v. See also pages 226–229.

FORESHADOW.   A hint of things to come in a story. The prologue of *Romeo
and Juliet* foreshadows the deaths of the young lovers.

FREE VERSE.   Poetry written without a fixed metrical pattern, though frequently
with an abstract meter lurking in the background. Free verse is often highly
cadenced. See pages 238–243.

FRENCH SCENE.   See SCENE.

FULL RHYME.   See EXACT RHYME.

GENRE.   A type or kind. Genre criticism seeks to define works by classifying
them according to type. The term is a difficult one because there are various
schemes for determining types. Works may be classified by subject matter
(PASTORAL), perspective (LYRIC), metrical form (HEROIC COUPLET), stanzaic pattern (SONNET), and so on. Genres are not necessarily mutually exclusive.

GOTHIC.   Deriving from Horace Walpole's novel *The Castle of Otranto,* 1764,
this term describes tales in gloomy settings, often medieval, filled with
specters, sensational events, and horrors. The popular *Dracula* movies and
stories are Gothic in tone, as are certain stories by such widely differing
authors as Poe and Faulkner.

HALF RHYME.   Also called SLANT RHYME. Rhyme in which the vowels in the accented syllables are similar but not identical; in some views, *any* vowel may be thought of as "similar to" another: *márry, shérry; déad, sháde.*

HEPTAMETER.   A verse written in seven feet.

HEROIC COUPLET.   See p. 243. The heroic couplet at its "purest" insists on decasyllabic lines in strict iambic feet (limited substitutions), end-stopped lines, and frequent use of strong medial CAESURAS; furthermore, the second line of the couplet ideally closes the sense—hence called a *closed couplet.* Favorite rhetorical patterns accompanying the form are ANTITHESIS, INVERSION, PARALLELISM, CHIASMUS, ZEUGMA. The most famous illustration of the formal heroic couplet is undoubtedly that by John Denham in *Cooper's Hill:*

> O could I flow like thee, and make thy stream
> My great example, as it is my theme!
> Though deep, yet clear; though gentle, yet not dull;
> Strong without rage; without o'erflowing full.

HEROIC PLAY.   A form of tragedy written in the Restoration period, concerned with the double themes of love and honor, usually written in HEROIC COUPLETS, and aspiring to be epic in size of subject. Dryden's *All for Love* is a retelling, in a heroic play, of Shakespeare's *Antony and Cleopatra.*

HEXAMETER.   A verse written in six feet. (See ALEXANDRINE.)

HIATUS.   Vowel gaping: an opening or gap necessary to keep separate vowel sounds from being pronounced as one: *Co-op* as opposed to *coop.* The term is used with reference to successive words, one ending in a vowel and the next beginning with a vowel; Pope's phrase "oft the *ear* the *o*pen vowels tire" illustrates hiatus, which Pope (and many others in his time) disliked. Neoclassic poets often eliminated hiatus by APOCOPE (a form of ELISION)—*th'ear* for *the ear.* Such elision is an essential part of much neoclassic prosody.

HIGH COMEDY.   George Meredith's term for the kind of COMEDY OF MANNERS that places a premium on wit and the amusement of the mind in beholding the spectacle of man's foibles. S. N. Behrman is sometimes pointed to as the sole American playwright capable of continued success in writing this form of comedy.

HISTORY PLAY.   See CHRONICLE PLAY.

HYPERBOLE.   A FIGURE OF SENSE involving overstatement, exaggeration for effect—"He was a regular bear this morning."

HYPERCATALEXIS.   The presence of one or two extra syllables in a poetic line; an eleven-syllable or twelve-syllable line of blank verse is thus hypercatalectic. See also CATALEXIS.

IAMBUS (IAMB).   A metrical foot composed of two syllables, the second of which is more conspicuous because it receives greater stress or greater emphasis in terms of pitch or duration. Normally marked thus: x/ (See also TROCHEE.)

ICTUS.   The beat employed to distinguish one syllable from another by the application of greater force or loudness of utterance.

IMAGE, IMAGERY.   The reconstitution of experience, in the mind, in the absence of the original stimulus. For ways of classifying images, see the discussion on p. 162 and pp. 204–206.

IMAGISTS.   A group of poets who, in the first quarter of the present century, rebelled against certain tendencies in nineteenth century poetry and issued a manifesto (1915) proclaiming the freedom of poets to choose their own subjects and forms. Imagism championed free verse and what John Crowe Ransom has called "physical poetry," which attempts to create the physical presence of things in words by the use of concrete, sharply etched images. Ezra Pound and Amy Lowell were among the leaders of Imagism.

IMPRESSIONISM.   A literary doctrine and method interested in the depiction of moods, feelings, tone (through the use of selective detail) rather than in the presentation of objective reality. Interest in what a thing "feels like" rather than what a thing "is."

INCREMENTAL REPETITION.   Repetition with a change that forwards the story. See the repetition in the popular ballad "Lord Randal" for an excellent instance.

INDIRECT DISCOURSE.   The reporting of a speaker's words indirectly rather than directly, and hence with greater esthetic distance. The two forms (direct and indirect) can be illustrated as follows:

> *Direct:* "I feel sick," he said.
> *Indirect:* He said that he felt sick.

It is more difficult to classify such language as the following:

> He wanted to run to her and say, I'm lonely and I'm sick, but he resisted doing it.

The oral interpreter can read this as direct discourse (with the same distancing he would employ in direct speech: "I'm lonely and I'm sick") or as indirect discourse (less immediate, more distanced). The context alone will tell him which of these choices is to be preferred. The choice involves *locus.*

INFLECTION.   Change in pitch or loudness in vocal utterance. Inflection refers to the modulation itself, whereas INTONATION refers to the melody resulting from inflection.

INTENTIONAL FALLACY.   See FALLACIES.

INTERNAL RHYME.   Rhyme within, rather than between, lines of poetry. In the line "I bring fresh *shówers* for the thirsting *flówers*," the italicized words illustrate internal rhyme.

INTONATION.   Speech melody thought of with reference to changes in pitch (and sometimes in loudness also). The intonation pattern (the unit of speech melody) reveals the attitudes and feelings of a speaker. The phrase "She is dead," for example, depending on the intonation pattern employed, can express sorrow, anger, horror, disbelief, unconcern, although the words themselves (the diction) do not change. Intonation patterns are a primary concern of the interpreter; they indicate to a listener what the grammatical structure of the phrase *really* is.

INVOCATION.   An APOSTROPHE addressed to a god or muse calling for assistance in the penning of a work:

> Of Man's first disobedience, and the fruit
> Of that forbidden tree whose mortal taste
> Brought death into the World, and all our woe,
> With loss of Eden, till one greater Man
> Restore us, and regain the blissful seat,

Sing, Heavenly Muse, that, on the secret top
Of Oreb, or of Sinai, didst inspire
That Shepherd who first taught the chosen seed
In the beginning how the heavens and earth
Rose out of Chaos. . . .   (Milton)

IRONY.   *Verbal irony* is a FIGURE OF SENSE in which the thing said is the opposite
of the thing meant. When Mark Antony calls Brutus an "honorable man,"
he is employing irony, since he really thinks Brutus dishonorable. In Swift's
A Modest Proposal, irony is used as a vehicle for SATIRE. Irony frequently
points to incongruities which mock us—the irony in the fate of the lover of
roses, for example, who dies from the infection resulting from his being
pricked by a rose thorn. Or there is *comic irony* in the situation of the
practical joker who accidentally upsets on his own head the pail of water
he has set over a door to empty onto the head of another person. For
instances of *tragic irony,* see DRAMATIC IRONY. Related to irony are other
modes: SARCASM, which is irony strongly caustic or biting in tone; UNDER-
STATEMENT (*meiosis*), which is frequently comic in its effect, as in Mark
Twain's "The reports of my death are greatly exaggerated"; and DRAMATIC
IRONY. The term IRONY is also employed widely among certain modern critics to refer to tensiveness, the strain produced when things pull two ways at
once; indeed, the term is sometimes used as if irony were the whole mark
of literary life, but such a use is so general as to blot out the technical use of
irony as a figure of sense.

ISOCHRONOUS VERSE.   Verse in which the feet are thought to be equal in
time, performed in equal intervals of time.

ISOSYNTACTICAL VERSE.   Verse in which an identity in syntactical patterns
functions as a primary prosodic device. See pp. 239–240.

KINESICS.   The science of bodily motion in relation to speech. A wave of the
hand, a lift of an eyebrow, a blush, an elevation of the shoulders are all
involved in the study of kinesics. Studies of such movement may be quali-
tative, quantitative, or positional. For the interpreter, kinesics is an aspect of
the whole role of gesture in performance.

KINESTHESIS.   The sense of body movement, position, and tension.

LAMPOON.   A form of the comic in which an individual is subjected to abu-
sive ridicule.

LITOTES.   A FIGURE OF SENSE that is a form of understatement, as opposed to
figures of overstatement (see HYPERBOLE). In litotes, an affirmative position is
taken by stating the negative of its opposite. For example, the statement
"She's no mean actress," meaning "She's a good actress."

LOCUS.   "Place," the location of a thing. In literature and the performance of
literature, it involves the relationship between reader and poem and between reader and audience. (For the audience, it involves the relationship
between audience, reader, and poem.) With reference to the audience, the
situation may be open, closed, or mixed. With reference to the poem, "location" involves point of view and perspective and includes such questions
as onstage-offstage placement and shifts in time and place. Essentially,
physical space is always involved, though the space may be either real or
imagined. See the discussion in Chapter 4.

LOW COMEDY.   A general term covering such modes as SLAPSTICK, FARCE, and
BURLESQUE. More interested in belly laughs than in cerebration, though one
must be careful in saying so (Molière, noted for his farces, has a strong

intellectual appeal). It is useful to remember that low comedy may include farce, but that not all farces are low comedy. There may be nonfarcical elements in farce. See also FARCE.

LYRIC.   Do not confuse the term *lyric* used as the name of a GENRE with the same term used as the name of a mode, as we have used it in this book. As a genre, lyric refers to a brief poem that is subjective in attitude, single in emotional center, and musical in its use of language. The lyric is a large class embracing SONG, SONNET, many ODES, and a number of French forms such as the BALLADE, the RONDEAU, the RONDEL, the TRIOLET, and the VILLANELLE. See also DRAMATIC LYRIC.

Lyric is also that mode in which the writer-speaker seems to speak most directly to the audience in his own person rather than through characters or a narrator. See pp. 244–245 for a discussion of modes.

MASCULINE ENDING.   Also called *strong ending:* a poetic line ending in a stressed or accented syllable, as opposed to a FEMININE ENDING.

MASCULINE RHYME.   Rhyme in which the rhyming syllables are the final and stressed syllables of the line. See p. 222.

MASQUE.   A form dramatic in mode, frequently allegorical in nature, combining elements from drama, poetry, music, and dance. During the reign of James I of England, the masque achieved enormous popularity as a form of royal and courtly entertainment, and two of its most famous figures were Ben Jonson, the writer, and Inigo Jones, the designer (who did not get along with each other). The masque often served to compliment honored guests in the audience through its allegory; it often ended with the presentation of a gift to the special guest and an invitation to the lords and ladies of the audience to join in dancing. Lavishness characterized the spectacle; slightness of dramatic plot was favored over strong and detailed story line. Elements of the masque were occasionally woven into other plays—for example, the masque in *The Tempest,* Act 4, where Prospero afterwards speaks of a quality typical of such entertainments, the sense of illusion with which they ended.

MATERIALS.   See STRUCTURE.

MEASURES.   See FEET.

MEIOSIS.   See IRONY.

MELODRAMA.   A form of "low tragedy" or TRAGIC COMEDY typified by the early movies portraying spotless young heroines, deep-dyed villains, and pure-hearted heroes engaging in hair-raising adventures while the pianist in the pit pounded out mood music, which tinkled over romance, wept with the dying old mother, roared as the express train came bearing down on the innocent damsel tied to the rails, and so on. (The Greek word for *song* is *melos.*) Melodrama is more often than not highly moral in its perspective. It is comparable to sentimentality in this respect: each represents an excess of emotional appeal over rationality.

Many literary works that are not melodramas nevertheless employ melodramatic elements (just as many works that are not farces employ elements of farce). Reduced to their story alone, for example, many of Henry James's finest works seem melodramatic, sensational. The term *melodrama* need not be (though it usually is) employed pejoratively.

METAPHOR.   See pp. 202–203. One further issue should be raised here. When one says "She is as white as a sheet," the question as to whether this is or is not metaphor (specifically, SIMILE) depends on the felt comparison. If the expression is taken to compare whiteness with whiteness, it is not a metaphor, since no dissimilarities are involved. If it is taken to compare *she* and *sheet* with respect to the fact that they both are white, the statement *is* a metaphor, since more than color alone is involved. It is important to observe that in FIGURES OF COMPARISON both the similarities and the dissimilarities are functional, the "miraculism" (Ransom's term) residing precisely in the coalescence of the contraries.

The DEAD METAPHOR is a metaphor that has become a cliché, so worn with use that its metaphorical value has been forgotten—"She is a jewel."

The metaphor is often found in combination with other figures; it may be exceedingly complex within itself. In the expression "A wholesome tongue is a tree of life" (Proverbs 15:4), the tongue is compared with a tree, it implies a wholesome speaker, the "goodness" of its speech is compared with a state of health in the body, health is related to growth, and "tree of life" contains a reference. It is even not too fanciful to sense the tongue as having roots like a tree, its source of life buried within.

METAPHYSICAL.   See CONCEIT.

METER.   The arrangement of verse into measures composed of patterned elements of contrasting values, usually thought of as greater and lesser stresses. See pp. 223–229. Meter in English tends to make the measures equal or approximately equal in duration.

METONYMY.   See pp. 203–204. This FIGURE OF CONTIGUITY entails the use of one thing for another logically related to it. It covers, for example, the relationship between the container and the thing contained ("five bottles" for "five bottles of pop"), the sign and the thing signified ("my flag" for "my country"), the cause and the effect ("he died of a draft" for "he died as the result of an illness caused by a draft"), all of which are relationships of contiguity (of things in continuous connection). "He is addicted to the bottle" is a metonymic way of saying "He likes liquor." "He holds the scepter" is a way of saying "He rules." Notice that the bottle-drink relationship is not the same as the relationship of *ship* to *sail:* "I saw ten sails" is SYNECDOCHE, not metonymy. The sail is a part of the ship, but the drink is not a part of the bottle. Nevertheless, the two kinds of relationship are so close that the term SYNECDOCHE is often used to cover both of these figures of contiguity.

METRICAL TALE.   A story in the epic mode told in verse; a short story in metrical form. Tales may be grouped into collections (as in Chaucer's *Canterbury Tales* or Tennyson's *Idylls of the King*) or may exist singly; they may be told from a single point of view (as are Tennyson's) or from several points of view (as are Chaucer's), or there may be a single tale told from the points of view of a number of speakers (as in Browning's *The Ring and the Book*). There is no set meter for such tales.

MIRACLE PLAY.   A play form defined by its subject matter—the legends of saints. See also MYSTERY PLAY.

MOCK EPIC.   See EPIC.

MORALITY PLAY.   A Christian allegory in play form employing as characters vices and virtues personified and contending for mastery over the soul of man. See ALLEGORY.

MOTIVATION.   A term to describe causation in analyzing the behavior of characters in a work of literature: the explanation for actions of characters.

MUSCLE TONE.   Elasticity of the muscle system that controls the state of tension of the body. It is a continuous state as a result of which the organism is kept ready for response to stimulation; health of the muscle system.

MYSTERY PLAY. A play form defined by its subject matter—scenes and events from the Old and the New Testament. Sometimes the mystery and MIRACLE are known collectively as MIRACLE PLAYS. Biblical plays were often grouped in cycles—the Wakefield, York, and Coventry cycles in England, for example—and performed in a series by guilds during religious festivals. See also MORALITY.

MYTH. Used in two general senses: (1) a short narrative, epic in mode, explaining actions, events, and forces in the world in terms of the behavior of supernatural beings, and (2) a system of stories providing a "world" scheme within which events can be presented and explained. The first sense is illustrated in the myth which explains the rising and setting of the sun in terms of Apollo's driving his chariot across the heavens; the second is illustrated in the work of Blake or Yeats or Faulkner, all of whom invented myths within which to write.

The term is also used widely in modern criticism (particularly psychological and archetypal criticism) in senses too complex to be summarized here though pointing to a *collective belief* (the log-cabin myth in American politics) or to *subconscious activity* (the Oedipus myth in Freudian thinking, Jung's view of dream figures). A well-known illustration of such criticism is the Ernest Jones interpretation of Shakespeare's *Hamlet,* which treats the play as an example of the Oedipus story and in this sense as part of a collective myth.

NARRATION. Broadly speaking, the term means "storytelling"—as in "the narration of the Christmas story." More narrowly, it is used to designate those sections of a story given in the language of the storyteller or speaker within the story, as opposed to those sections presented in the dialogue of characters. See NARRATOR.

NARRATIVE. Broadly speaking, any running account that tells a story, whether in verse or prose, whether dramatic or nondramatic. The story may be episodic or fragmentary; it may be a fully developed plot. More strictly used, it may refer to stories in verse or in prose rather than in play form, or simply to stories in prose. See also NARRATION and METRICAL TALE.

NARRATOR. The teller of a story, not to be simply identified with the author of the story. The "speaker" from whose point of view or perspective the account is presented. In Chamber Theatre, and in nondramatic material in Readers Theatre, the narrator speaks the NARRATION (in the strict sense), though those parts of the narration thought of as intimately reflecting the thoughts of characters may be assigned to characters as if they were DIRECT DISCOURSE. The narrator may or may not himself be a character in the story he tells. He may be given a specific personality and visual appearance or he may be concealed and presented only in terms of his state of mind. He may be emotionally involved in the action or detached and objective about it (though in either case, of course, EMPATHY is involved). He may be in complete control of the story, or he may share with an unnamed and nonpersonalized speaker who is thought of as being the author. The nature of the narrator is a crucial question for the interpreter.

NATURALISM. In one sense, an aspect of REALISM—unselective presentation of real life. In another sense, naturalism as a literary doctrine emphasizes the role of heredity and environment in the development of human life and actions. Émile Zola is an exponent of naturalism in this second sense.

NEGATIVE EMOTIONS.   Emotions normally offensive or repulsive to audience taste but employed by a writer for calculated effects. The work of Swift often illustrates such use of negative emotions.

NEOCLASSIC.   A large term, but frequently used to refer to the period in England extending from about 1660 to 1780 during which rules, order, decorum, and general nature appealed above the expression of individual passions and nature unconfined. The neoclassic poet typically cared more to write about Man in Love than to write about one distinct individual in love, and was concerned more with the ways in which men move according to common laws than with ways in which each man lives a solitary and unique life. Neoclassicism employed the HEROIC COUPLET as its typical metrical form, and the HEROIC PLAY was its typical tragic form. See also ROMANTIC.

NOVEL.   A long work of prose fiction employing a PLOT. Essentially EPIC in mode, it may be heavily LYRIC (as in the novels of Virginia Woolf) or heavily DRAMATIC (as in some of the work of Hemingway). Some extended verse narratives have been called novels, but the word has never been fully accepted with respect to verse. Novels may be classified according to subject matter (GOTHIC), form (EPISTOLARY), or function (propagandistic). Other classifications, involving point of view and perspective, cut across these classes: comic, tragic, regional, realistic. See also pp. 287–288.

NOVELLA.   A short tale in prose, highly condensed and often realistic in treatment. Boccaccio's *Decameron* is the classic example of the novella (pl., *novelle*).

OCTAMETER.   A verse written in eight FEET.

OCTAVE.   A batch of eight lines. In the Italian (and sometimes in the English) SONNET, the octave constitutes the first major division of the poem, followed by a sestet. See p. 244.

ODE.   A long poetic form, complex in pattern, dealing with a dignified or impressive theme, often public rather than private in nature. The PINDARIC ODE, named after the Greek lyricist Pindar, consists of an arrangement of three kinds of stanzas—*strophe, antistrophe,* and *epode.* It has usually proved too complicated for successful imitation in English. The *Horatian Ode,* free and irregular, is sometimes called the *False Pindaric.* Two famous examples in English are Dryden's "Alexander's Feast" and Wordsworth's "Intimations of Immortality." The odes of Keats are highly lyrical in nature.

OFFSTAGE.   The placement of a reading in the realm of the audience, "out front," as opposed to placement onstage, on the principle that the locus of a reading is in the imaginations of the audience. See the discussion on pp. 458–459 in connection with Readers Theatre.

ONOMATOPOEIA.   A FIGURE OF SOUND embracing the use of words whose sound is said to suggest their sense (the "bang" of a gun, the "buzz" of a bee). Actually, the associations are conventional rather than real. A rooster, for example, does not give the same sound in French, English, and Korean. See also TONE COLOR for a different but related effect, in which the sounding of the word attempts to duplicate or suggest the sense.

ONSTAGE.   The placement of a reading onstage with the reader, as if in a staged production of a play, rather than "out front" in an imagined scene. See the discussion on pp. 458–459 in connection with Readers Theatre.

ORGANIC UNITY.   A phrase describing the unity of a work of art in terms of life form—that is, the work of art grows from within as the plant grows from the seed and consists of a series of interrelated parts. In this analogy, the whole is greater than the sum of its parts by virtue of the fact that no mere collection of the various parts will produce the life of the whole. Furthermore, the work of art seen as possessing organic unity will not contain within it any elements unrelated to the organism, unless it is to be judged defective with respect to its form. The work of art as an organic unity has a proper beginning, middle, and end: a beginning without *necessary* antecedent, a middle issuing out of the beginning and leading to the end, and an end without *necessary* sequel. For example, *Hamlet* may properly begin where it does—we do not need to be shown Hamlet as a babe in arms or as a schoolboy; and it may properly end where it does—we do not need to wait for the inevitable death of Horatio before the play is ended.

OTTAVA RIMA.   See p. 244.

OVERSTATEMENT.   See HYPERBOLE.

OXYMORON.   A FIGURE OF SENSE in which a paradoxical statement involves the use of terms normally thought of as contraries in themselves: cruel kindness, loving hate, a something nothing. See PARADOX.

PARABLE.   A short narrative illustrating a moral thesis, but not (like ALLEGORY) through the PERSONIFICATION of abstractions or (like the FABLE) through personification of animals. The parable is so closely associated with biblical literature that it is often thought of as a specifically Christian narrative, though it need not be. (See the parable of the Sower, or of the Good Samaritan, or of the Wise and Foolish Virgins in the Bible.)

PARADOX.   A FIGURE OF SENSE; a seemingly self-contradictory statement or proposition; a statement in which both halves of a set of contradictory assertions prove true. The striking quality of the paradox lies in its harmonizing of opposites; in this respect, it resembles FIGURES OF COMPARISON, which emphasize the similarity in things strikingly dissimilar. But both paradox and figures of comparison depend also on the striking quality of differences; simple similarity would produce neither kind of figure. Paradox may be expressed in METAPHOR and metaphor may be yoked with paradox, but the figures are essentially distinct.

> *Paradox*
>> For hence,—a paradox
>> Which comforts while it mocks,—
>> Shall life succeed in that it seems to fail:
>> What I aspired to be,
>> And was not, comforts me . . . (Browning)

> *Paradox combined with metaphor*
>> The earth that's nature's mother is her tomb.
>> What is her burying grave, that is her womb. (Shakespeare)

The second example also involves PERSONIFICATION and a combination of PARALLELISM with ANTITHESIS. See also OXYMORON.

PARALANGUAGE.   The voice qualities involved in sounding language. Such elements as *control* of pitch, rhythm, resonance, tempo, and intensity distinguish one speaker from another; they are distinct from elements of pitch, stress, and juncture thought of as dictated by the structure of the language itself. For example, such vocal qualities as loudness, softness, drawl, hesitancy, tremolo, whine, stridency, breathiness are elements of paralanguage.

It is helpful to think of language (as a structural system), paralanguage, and kinesics as forming a triad, with each member significant in the act of communication. (See also KINESICS.)

PARODY.   A form of the comic that derives its humor from the burlesque imitation of the style of a work or author. See BURLESQUE.

PARONOMASIA.   See PUN.

PASTORAL.   A term describing subject matter rather than fixed form. Pastorals are found in prose fiction, in verse, and in drama; they may be realistic or outrageously romantic, direct or allegorical, sympathetic or critical and satirical. The subject matter of the pastoral is rural life: shepherds and shepherdesses, simple rustic or peasant folk, country scenes; often the characters are people of high estate (lords and ladies, for example) masquerading as country folk. As a type, the pastoral often seems to modern readers too artificial to be appealing. Famous examples are Spenser's *The Shepheardes Calender,* Sidney's *Arcadia,* the Greek Romance *Daphnis and Chloë, aspects of Shakespeare's As You Like It,* the fourth act of *The Winter's Tale.*

PATHOS.   The pitful (as opposed, often, to the tragic). The evocation of gentle sorrow, sadness, sympathy over unhappiness or suffering. The deaths of Romeo and Juliet may be said to be pathetic rather than tragic insofar as we see the two young lovers as being crushed by forces beyond their control, or as dying because of the accidental miscarrying of a letter.

PAUSE.   A matter of pervasive importance to all speakers is that of pause. While each literary work dictates its own qualites of pausing, the interpreter may find certain general comments helpful.

A pause is a temporary cessation of speech. Punctuation normally (but not always) indicates the necessity or desirability of pausing. It is customary to think of the comma, the semicolon, and the period as marking pauses of different length, though one must be careful about ascribing fixed quantities to pauses. The dash, the dots indicating ellipsis, the colon, quotation marks, parentheses, the hyphen, the apostrophe, and brackets—all these, too, involve degrees and varieties of pause, though it is futile (and wrong) to reduce them to inflexible rule. But pauses are not always marked by punctuation. The interpreter will find that the timing of utterance with the help of all possible clues to pausation is one of the central techniques for embodying the presence of a work of literature. Pauses indicate grammatical relationship, rhetorical divisions, metrical breaks. They also indicate attitudes accompanying or lying behind the language uttered. A meaningful pause often says more than words. The reader who reads everything at the same rate of utterance is a speech machine, not an interpreter.

It will be a useful exercise to examine specific pieces with respect to pausation. In Wordsworth's "I Wandered Lonely as a Cloud," on p. 22, what happens if one introduces a sustained pause after "lonely" in line 1? Or after "saw" in line 3? What ambiguity is introduced if one pauses after "saw I" in line 11? Compare the nature of the pause at the end of line 2 with that of the pause at the end of lines 3 and 4. What is the difference in the "feel" of these pauses? Would you pause at the end of the first line in stanza 2? What difference would it make if you converted the comma at the end of line 2 in the second stanza to a semicolon? What difference would it make if you took out the first dash in line 5 of the third stanza? Do you get any feeling that certain of the pauses in the poem tend to emphasize the idea *before* the pause, while others tend to emphasize the idea *following* the pause? The handling of pausation clearly conditions the weight and tone of lines.

Metrical pause is a complex matter. (See END-STOPPED.) The poet builds into his sound pattern certain necessary pauses—you cannot ride over the pause after *not* in the lines "We will grieve not, rather find / Strength in what remains behind," and the pause conditions the utterance of both *not* and *rather*. But compare the following lines thought of first as two-stress lines and then as three-stress lines:

> O joy! that in our embers
> Is something that doth live,
> That nature yet remembers
> What was so fugitive!

The lines may be thought of as hovering between two and three stresses (at least taken in isolation this way); this is part of the tension in the prosodic surface, and it clearly affects pausation. How, for example, does your choice of a two-stress or a three-stress line affect your handling of the exclamation point in line 1? (The two stresses would presumably fall on the word *joy* and on the first syllable of *embers;* the third stress, if employed, would be the lighter stress on *in,* promoted by the abstract meter.) How does your choice affect the quality of the rhyme in line 4? Is line 1 end-stopped? There is no mark of punctuation, and yet the prepositional phrase (adverbial in its function) at the end of the line is the kind of phrase frequently followed by a pause. We can all agree that the pause (if there is one) is less than the pause at the end of line 2, but we will differ in our handling of the pause at the end of line 1. If it seems to you clearly marked (not by punctuation, but by rhetorical purpose), the line is for you end-stopped; if you think it is either vaguely or not at all marked, the line is for you run-on. This may seem to be an evasion of the answer, but it is not meant to be. Readers will differ with respect to such pausation, and the differences seem to us legitimate. Pausation is of many degrees—an almost infinite number. The terms RUN-ON and END-STOPPED are gross terms incapable of marking all the degrees possible. Does the rhythm of the poem remain unaltered as a result of these differing readings? Clearly not; the rhythm is affected even though the meter is not. Some poets control rhythmic effects loosely; some control them tightly. The difference is not necessarily a difference between good and bad, nor between better and worse. Too tightly controlled rhythm may be a fault; too loosely controlled rhythm also may be a fault. Poets such as Poe and Swinburne tend to control rhythms tightly; a poet like Whitman deliberately employs loose rhythms.

PENTAMETER.   A verse written in five FEET.

PERIPETY.   A reversal: applied (from Aristotle) to the change in the hero's fortune in tragedy. In *Macbeth,* there is a peripety coupled with a DISCOVERY when, learning that Macduff was ripped untimely from his mother's womb (and hence fulfills the prophecy of the weird sisters), Macbeth suddenly realizes that his doom is upon him. (In comedy, there is often a reversal of the other sort—from distress to happiness; in Wilde's *The Importance of Being Earnest,* such a reversal is coupled with discovery when all is put to rights by Jack's discovering that his name is really Earnest after all.)

PERIPHRASIS.   See CIRCUMLOCUTION.

PERSONIFICATION.   A FIGURE OF SENSE in which nonliving things are given life or in which nonhuman creatures are given human attributes. "Death, be not proud" exemplifies the first of these classes; "'Not I,' said the bird" illustrates the second. The figure is often combined with other figures— here, for example, with metaphor: "The snake wore a robe of diamonds," where personification consists in the snake's being dressed as a human being and metaphor consists in the snake's skin's being compared with a jeweled gown. While more than a single figure may be employed at once, the effectiveness of the combination resides in the coalescence of the kinds. (Also called *prosopopoeia*, the Greek name.)

PERSPECTIVE.   The attitude, the angle of vision of a literary work. The dominant perspective is called the POINT OF VIEW, but any work may have more than a single perspective. Furthermore, the interpreter himself has a unique perspective, which conditions his view of other perspectives, including those in the work he reads. Perspective is an aspect of LOCUS.

PICARESQUE NOVEL OR TALE.   A *picaro* is a rogue, and the picaresque novel or tale has a rogue as its hero. The picaresque tale achieved great popularity in Spain before it spread to other European countries. Fielding's *Tom Jones* is a descendant of the type.

PINDARIC ODE.   See ODE.

PLOT.   A difficult term, plot refers to the articulation of episodes in a story and to the structuring of relationships between characters and events. While sometimes CHARACTER and ACTION are separated, there is a sense in which they cannot be, since in a fine work of literature the characters tend to shape the movement of the story just as the story tends to shape the characters. A character acts as he does partly because of the nature of the situation he is in; but in acting as he does, he also affects the situation. Probably plot should be used to cover both these aspects of STRUCTURE. One way (awkward, perhaps) to distinguish the two things would be to refer to events and to personalities or persons, keeping story (or action) and characters for the articulation or knitting together of events and persons.

POEM, POETRY.   The word *poem* is often used, traditionally, to mean any work of imaginative literature, stemming from the Greek word ποίημα, or póiēma, which means "to make." A poet is a maker. This general sense of the word is usually employed in this volume. But the word also refers more specifically (as does the word *poetry*) to imaginative works in language that is arranged on the principle of *return*—language given a prosodic structure (foot, stress, syllable, syntax, rhyme, stanza, cadence, time are typical elements of the arrangement) and usually enriched more than is usual in prose with FIGURES, both of sound and of sense. The phrase "prose poem" is sometimes used to designate a work in prose that is closely cadenced or that is exceptionally rich in figures or both. For an extended discussion, see Chapter 9.

POINT OF VIEW.   The major perspective from which a story is seen and told. Used particularly with reference to prose fiction (novel, short story), but useful also with respect to other forms, though it is not usually employed for the play form. There are many ways of cataloging points of view (see pp. 278–282), but for the oral interpreter the essential consideration is that several perspectives always function together in a literary work: the point of view of a narrator, of the author who may be looking over the shoulder of the narrator, and of the various characters involved. While the major point of view, the shaping point of view, is central, the reader cannot ignore the more limited perspective (limited by the major point of view) of each individual character with whom he must deal in his reading. Tensiveness results in part from this interlocking of perspectives. The locus shifts as we move from character to character speaking, and while we listen to the character speaking we may for the moment be unconscious of the narrator, though later we return to him.

PRESENCE.   As used in this volume, PRESENCE refers to the overall tensive quality of a work as felt by the reader—a sense of the work's objective being, of an embodied self, of its existence as a living thing. It is a sense of the "otherness" of the work that elicits response from the reader.

PROBLEM PLAY.   That kind of play that treats seriously some general human problem, centering not so much on the private conduct of its characters as on their role in society. Many Ibsen plays are problem plays, as are such Shakespearean plays as *Troilus and Cressida, Measure for Measure,* and *All's Well That Ends Well.* The term PROBLEM PLAY cuts across distinctions between comedy and tragedy; problem plays are often tragicomedies.

PROJECTION.   (1) In psychology, the act of ascribing to another feelings present only in oneself. Readers guilty of projection thus tend to substitute their own feelings for those in the literature. (2) In performance, the act of making a reading sufficiently overt and tensive so that it is shareable with an audience. It is probably helpful to see projection in this sense as in large part a mental act, not simply a matter of loudness.

PRONUNCIATION.   The "correct" sounding of a word in terms of its accents and phonemic values. A dictionary lists pronunciations of words. See ENUNCIATION and ARTICULATION.

PROSE.   As distinct from poetry, prose is language employed in its "normal" manner, without prosodic arrangement, though it may of course be highly arranged in other respects: inverse sentence order, periodic structure, use of strongly marked cadences, employment of figures, and so on. In general, prose is *less* densely figured than poetry, and it eschews rhyme and meter. It is said that even in prose, the English language tends to move in temporal equivalents between *primary* stresses (i.e., the greatest degree of stress in sentences), but these temporal groups are so long and so complex in their rhythmic structures that they are not ordinarily felt, by the ear, as "measures," as they are in poetry.

PROSODY.   The art or science of patterning in poetry. See also FOOT PROSODY, FREE VERSE, ISOCHRONOUS VERSE, ISOSYNTACTICAL VERSE, RHYME, STRESS PROSODY, SYLLABIC PROSODY, VISUAL PROSODY. While the patterning of imagery is not usually thought of as a prosodic matter, it *can* be and perhaps should be.

PROTAGONIST.   The leading character (hero or heroine) of a work, against whom is often pitted an ANTAGONIST.

PUN.   (The Greek name is *paronomasia.*) A FIGURE OF SENSE that involves a play on words. It may play upon two words identical (or similar) in sound but distinctly different in meaning, or it may make use of a single word having two distinct meanings that are both relevant. The first case is illustrated in the pun of the cobbler in *Julius Caesar:* "All that I live by is my *awl.*" The second case is illustrated in the Joycean pun concerning the priest who died a failure: "His life was *crossed.*" Shakespeare's *Hamlet* illustrates the pun on words similar in sound: "A little more than *kin* and less than *kind.*"

As these examples show, it is a mistake always to think of the pun as simply humorous.

PYRRHIC. A metrical FOOT composed of two syllables, both "light" or inconspicuous. See p. 227. Proponents of the "equal time" theory deny the existence of the pyrrhic as a foot, since no two light syllables are likely to be the equal of a foot containing at least one heavy or stressed syllable. In the views of such prosodists, the pyrrhic is absorbed into another kind of patterning of the line.

QUANTITATIVE VERSE. Verse, such as Latin and Greek, that is made up of poetic feet determined by length of utterance, and in which a short syllable (the smallest metrical unit) is one-half the length of a long syllable in duration. In such a scheme, the spondee and the dactyl agree in length, though a spondee and an iambus never can. In the sixteenth century there was an attempt by Sidney and other scholarly poets to write quantitative verse in English, but it soon failed, since English could not be measured as Latin was presumed to have been partly because of the number of monosyllables in English, partly because of the fluctuations in English spelling, and particularly because English is accentual rather than quantitative in nature. For example, by classical rule the word *carpenter* should be accented on the second syllable in English (a vowel followed by two consonants, *ent*, makes a syllable long), whereas it is actually accented on the first syllable.

QUATRAIN. A batch or stanza of four lines. See p. 244.

QUINTET. A five-line stanza.

REALISM. The literary doctrine that holds that art should be faithful to nature and real life. *Photographic realism* would show life exactly as it is. The term is made obscure by the fact that what life "really is" seems to differ from person to person. In a somewhat restricted sense, realism often means a particular concern with trivial, unpleasant, or sordid aspects of life. See also NATURALISM.

REFERENTIAL LANGUAGE. See STENO LANGUAGE.

REFRAIN. One or more lines of a poem repeated at intervals in the poem, often with certain changes. See INCREMENTAL REPETITION.

RHYME. The repetition of identical (FULL or EXACT RHYME) or similar (HALF or SLANT RHYME) accented vowel sounds in combination with identical *succeeding* sounds but different *preceding* sounds. Exact rhyme: *fúll, púll; báby, máybe.* Slant rhyme: *fúll, páll, báby, tábby.* See also MASCULINE RHYME, FEMININE RHYME, WEAK RHYME, DOUBLE RHYME, TRIPLE RHYME. For an additional term, see CONSONANCE.

RHYTHM. With respect to poetry, rhythm is the tension produced in the prosodic surface of a poem by the recurrence of a pattern of sound interrupted or varied by substitutions in the meter, by pauses, by inflections, or by any aspect of sound other than the simple recurrence of the basic prosodic unit. The orchestration of sound patterns. (See also COUNTERPOINT, RISING RHYTHM, FALLING RHYTHM.) All organisms, including literary organisms, are dynamic, having a tension-release cycle that moves from imbalance to balance to imbalance. Rugg quotes Whitehead: "The essence of rhythm is the fusion of sameness and novelty. . . ." With respect to prose, rhythm refers more generally to fluctuations in the temporal, pitch, and force patterns of the language between *primary* stresses (SEE PROSE).

RIME. See RHYME.

RIME ROYAL. See SEPTET.

RISING RHYTHM. Rhythms composed predominantly of IAMBIC and ANAPESTIC meters, in which the feet may be said to "rise" toward the stressed or conspicuous syllables. Doubtless the word *rising* here indicates the customary view that accented or stressed syllables are likely to have a higher pitch.

ROCKING RHYTHM. An effect achieved by catching the ear between two simple meters. For example,

x/x| x/x | x/x | x/x

The poetic foot here, an AMPHIBRACH, catches the ear between IAMBUS and TROCHEE to produce a rocking or galloping effect, illustrated in Browning's "How They Brought the Good News":

I sprang to the stirrup, and Jeris, and he;
I galloped, Dirck galloped, we galloped all three;

in which the meter *might* but probably *should not* be described as mixed iambic and anapestic, since the AMPHIBRACH better fits the rhetorical arrangement of the lines. In considering the lines to be amphibrachic, one takes the last feet ("and he," "all three") to be catalectic, the missing light syllable taken care of by the pause that the punctuation indicates. For further discussion of rocking rhythm in a poem by Shelley, see p. 235.

ROMANCE. Originally, a story of love and adventure involving the persons of kings, knights, and ladies, fanciful rather than realistic. The *pastoral romance* portrayed rural scenes. Probably the first Western romances were the *Greek romances* of Heliodorus, Achilles Tatius, Longus, and others—long and longwinded, often ingenious in their structuring, heavily rhetorical, full of spectacle and incredible actions—roughly between the first and sixth centuries A.D. Many later romances were in verse form. In subsequent prose fiction, the term ROMANCE is often used to designate a story of love and adventure cut free from the realistic world.

ROMANTIC. A term paired with NEOCLASSIC to present the other side of the coin, the interest in individual feelings and thoughts, freedom of expression, the use of everyday diction, varied meters; an interest in the natural as opposed to the formal and the ordered in the animal, mineral, and vegetable worlds. The Romantics cared more for the tutelage of the intuitive faculty than for the tutelage of authority. Not to be confused with the adjective derived from ROMANCE.

ROMANTIC COMEDY. Often not broadly comic, except in the sense that it ends happily for the hero and heroine, romantic comedy tells the story of lovers for whom the course of true love never does run smooth, though it ends well. Romantic comedies are frequently sad or pathetic in tone, and often run the risk of being sentimental. The most famous examples of the kind are Shakespeare's, as illustrated in *Much Ado About Nothing, As You Like It,* and *Twelfth Night.* The first of these has elements of farce, high comedy, and tragicomedy; the second has elements of the pastoral, farce, and masque; the third has a strong low-comedy subplot, as well as a shipwreck-and-separation motif drawn from Greek romance.

RONDEAU. A French poetic form consisting of thirteen lines employing only two rhymes, with an unrhymed refrain (consisting of the beginning of the first line) repeated after lines 8 and 13, making a total of fifteen lines altogether. A popular example is John McCrae's "In Flanders Fields," in which the form is aabba/aab-refrain/aabba-refrain, with the phrase "In Flanders fields" functioning as the refrain.

RONDEL.   A French poetic form consisting of thirteen or fourteen lines employing only two rhymes. The first two lines are repeated as the refrain in lines 7 and 8, and either one or both of the lines reappear at the close (the choice determining whether the poem has thirteen or fourteen lines). Pattern: *ABbaabAB abbaA(B)*.

ROUND CHARACTERS.   Characters who seem to have the fullness of dimension, the dynamism, of people in real life, as opposed to FLAT or STOCK CHARACTERS.

RUN-ON.   A run-on line of verse is one in which there is no definite pause at the end of the line and in which the sense unit continues without break to the succeeding line. Also called ENJAMBEMENT. While there may be (some critics think there should be) a hold or suspension even at the end of a run-on line, the effect should never be to cut the line off from its successor. Clearly, those who argue for the "hold" at the end of the run-on line have difficulty in illustrating the steady development of such a writer as Shakespeare from his early use of end-stopped lines to his later softening of the end-stopping and his ultimate strongly run-on lines, when his verse begins to approach the freedom of strongly rhythmical prose (though it remains verse, and admirably so). It is probably a mistake to make a general rule about line endings; doubtless the poet should have the right to determine the amount of end-stopping he wishes. Compare the two following passages:

Passage A
His sceptre shows the force of temporal power,
The attribute to awe and majesty,
Wherein doth sit the dread and fear of kings;
But mercy is above this sceptred sway,
It is enthroned in the hearts of kings,
It is an attribute to God himself.
And earthly power doth then show likest God's
When mercy seasons justice.   (*The Merchant of Venice*)

Passage B
Nay, but this dotage of our general's
O'erflows the measure; those his goodly eyes,
That o'er the files and musters of the war
Have glowed like plated Mars, now bend, now turn
The office and devotion of their view
Upon a tawny front. . . .   (*Antony and Cleopatra*)

The first passage is heavily end-stopped; the second, heavily run-on, with strong medial CAESURAS working against the division into lines. The second should not be read as prose, but it must not be end-stopped to sound like the first passage, or the reader defeats the very effects for which the poet has worked.

SARCASM.   See IRONY.

SATIRE.   Satire is a term describing attitude and purpose rather than fixed form or subject matter. It may be written in verse (Dryden's *Absalom and Achitophel*) or in prose (Swift's *Gulliver's Travels*), and it may cover a wide range of tones—angry, humorous, contemptuous, bantering, superior, hostile, and so on; but it has at its center a critical purpose and a desire to castigate, ridicule, or laugh at vices, foibles, manners, conventions, excesses. Satire frequently finds outlet in drama (as in the plays of Aristophanes, Molière, Jonson). There are often satirical elements in pieces that cannot be called satire.

SCANSION.   (Literally, "climbing," "proceeding by steps") The division of poetic lines into their component FEET. The verb form is *scan*.

SCENE.   See also SCENE (IN DRAMA). Used to refer to setting or, in this volume, to moments in any narrative when we have dialogue and "stage business," as opposed to SUMMARY or DESCRIPTION. See pp. 282–284.

SCENE (IN DRAMA).   A division of a play, smaller than an ACT; *French scenes* are numbered according to the movement onstage and offstage of characters in the play, each entrance or exit beginning a new scene. The general practice, however, is to begin new scenes only with a shift in setting, time or event.

SENTENTIA.   (Pl., *sententiae*) A "sentence" defined not as a grammatical unit but as a concise and pithy statement of a general thought or maxim. Thus, Shakespeare's plays are full of "sentences," such as those in Polonius' advice to Laertes in *Hamlet*.

SENTIMENTAL COMEDY.   Sometimes called "weeping comedy" (*comédie larmoyante*). A term referring to certain eighteenth-century comedies (Steele's *The Conscious Lovers* is a famous example), sentimental and moralistic in vein, in which middle-class heroes and heroines behave and talk in a manner so noble and selfless as to evoke tears from their beholders. To modern audiences, such characters may appear either incredible or insufferable.

SEPTET.   A seven-line stanza, including the special form known as *rime royal* (iambic pentameter, rhyming *ababbcc*).

SESTET.   A six-line stanza. Also the term designating the second half of the Italian (and frequently of the English) sonnet, of which the first half is an OCTAVE.

SESTINA.   A poem written in six-line stanzas, the last word in each of the six lines repeated in a different order in each stanza, and a three-line envoy using all six of these words. See Auden's poem on pp. 255–256 as an example.

SETTING.   The locale of a narrative and the placement of the locale in time. In a play, the setting is the visible scene onstage.

SHORT STORY.   A short work of prose fiction employing a PLOT and essentially EPIC in mode. It differs from the novel in length and in "breadth"—it is more concentrated, more single in its effect. The short story is to the novel as the one-act play is to the long play. Early forms allied to the short story but differing from it by offering less elaboration of either PLOT or CHARACTER (or both) are the NOVELLA, the PARABLE, the FABLE, the folk tale.

SIMILE.   A FIGURE OF COMPARISON in which an *expressed* comparison is made between two things which are in some respects dissimilar: She looks like a patchwork quilt. See p. 202.

SLANT RHYME.   See HALF RHYME.

SLAPSTICK.   A form of LOW COMEDY (or low comedy stage business) that depends on "horseplay," broad physical action that derives its humor from its ludicrousness—the custard pie in the face, the pratfall, the dive into the empty swimming pool.

SOLILOQUY.   A speech in which a character utters his thoughts aloud but to himself rather than to another character. (A soliloquy may, depending on its nature, be delivered to the audience, however.) Distinct from the DRAMATIC MONOLOGUE, in which a character addresses another person or persons who remain silent. In this sense, O'Neill's one-act play *Before Breakfast* is a dramatic monologue, not a soliloquy, with the nagging wife addressing an offstage husband.

SONG.   Lyric in mode, the song is a musical expression of simple and universal emotion. Such poets as Tennyson, Shakespeare, Burns, and Campion have excelled in the writing of songs. Songs are musical in a double sense; they must be capable of being sung, and they must be rich in tone color.

SONNET.   A lyric of fourteen lines, usually in iambic pentameter. The whole poem is contained in the fourteen lines, though sonnets may be linked in cycles. The two conventional forms are the *Italian,* or *Petrarchan,* and the *English,* or *Shakespearean.* The Italian sonnet has an OCTAVE rhyming *abbaabba* introducing a thought developed by a SESTET varying in rhyme scheme but employing either two or three rhymes. The English sonnet has three QUATRAINS rhyming *ababcdcdefef* and a concluding couplet rhyming *gg.* Many sonnets vary from these strict forms; originally the sonnet was not restricted to fourteen lines in length but referred simply to a short, single-stanza lyric, the subject of which was romantic love. A famous modern sonnet sequence, *Modern Love* by George Meredith, is made up of sonnets of sixteen lines.

SPENSERIAN STANZA.   A nine-line stanza consisting of eight lines of iambic pentameter followed by an ALEXANDRINE, rhyming *ababbcbcc.*

SPONDEE.   A metrical FOOT composed of two syllables, both stressed or conspicuous. See p. 227.

SPRUNG RHYTHM.   A difficult term made famous by Gerard Manley Hopkins, who used it to describe rhythmic effects derived from mixed meters based preeminently on stress, in which a single stress might exist independently or be combined with one, two, or three unstressed or "slack" syllables.

STANZA.   A "batch" of lines of poetry. A poem may consist of a single stanza (a SONNET) or may contain several batches or groupings of lines. In regular verse, stanzas are composed of more or less regularly patterned lines; in FREE VERSE, the stanzas may be freely arranged. (Some regular verse, however, is irregular in its stanzaic structure—for example, the ENGLISH OR FREE ODE). The verse paragraph in a long work (as in *Paradise Lost*) is not a stanza. Some critics restrict *stanza* to batches of more than three lines, arguing that the distich or COUPLET is a distinct category.

STENO LANGUAGE.   Language that as neutrally as possible simply points to the thing for which it stands. Called REFERENTIAL LANGUAGE for this reason. Steno language contrasts with so-called EMOTIVE LANGUAGE, which, rather than being neutral or transparent, calls attention to values in itself beyond simple reference. For example:

> *Steno language:* It is cold today.
> *Emotive language:* It is a biting day today.

Clearly the terms relate to problems of DENOTATION and CONNOTATION. A word of warning is in order, however: literature makes heavy use of emotive language but nevertheless points to what it really wishes to say. Be careful of thinking of steno language as precise language and literary language as imprecise language. For some uses, steno language is far less precise than the language of literature.

STICHOMYTHIA.   Alternating lines of dialogue, often found in highly formal or passionate exchanges between characters, as in Greek drama. In Shakespeare, it is frequently coupled with the use of rhyme, as in the following passage from *The Comedy of Errors:*

> ADRIANA. This servitude makes you to keep unwed.
> LUCIANA. Not this, but troubles of the marriage-bed.
> ADRIANA. But were you wedded, you would bear some sway.
> LUCIANA. Ere I learn love, I'll practise to obey.
> ADRIANA. How if your husband start some other where?
> LUCIANA. Till he come home again, I would forbear.

STOCK CHARACTERS.   FLAT characters who are also familiar types (the rustic, the braggart, the witty servant, the jealous husband, etc.).

STOCK SITUATIONS.   Conventional, repeated situations readily recognized by readers or audiences as usual or trite, though they may be given fresh treatment. They are to situations what flat characters are to characterization. The rise of the poor boy from a log cabin to the White House is a stock situation in American lore.

STREAM OF CONSCIOUSNESS.   A technique with a long history, but one which has achieved both renown and notoriety with the development of psychological interests. It is the attempt to express psychological states by presenting interior monologues—setting down words, thoughts, intuitions, associations, feelings as they occur in the mind, in all their helter-skelter. Actually, the technique always involves selection and arrangement on the part of the writer. Joyce's *Ulysses* is a classic example in English; the novels of Virginia Woolf represent a more apparent selection and arrangement using the same general technique.

STRESS.   The ICTUS, or beat, employed to distinguish one syllable from another by the application of greater force or loudness of utterance. In English, nouns, verbs, and adjectives normally receive stress; articles, personal pronouns, prepositions, conjunctions, and *auxiliary* verbs normally do not—but one must be very cautious in making such a generalization. Everything depends, in the last analysis, on context. A "cándy vendor" is not the same thing as a "candy véndor," though one recognizes that the first syllable of *vendor* receives greater stress than the second in both examples, as does the first syllable of *candy.* In fact, English has at least four and maybe five, six, or more degrees of stress, though the ear may have difficulty hearing more than three. Furthermore, differences in stress are accompanied by changes in intonation, and the change in the intonation pattern may be "heard" by the speaker as a change in stress. The point is that English tends to set up *contrasts* in the degree of stress in a chain of utterance; when we get a regular alternation of degrees in poetry we mark the arrangement x/x/ (etc.) when the first degree is lesser than the second. But if we mark the syllables in terms of the *specific* degree (primary: /; secondary: ∧; tertiary: \; weak ∪), we get such a series as this for the word *anticipate*: \ / ∪ ∧. Such contrast rather than a simple alternation of two degrees of loudness is operative in prosody. A poet's stress pattern may be, in certain instances, the primary clue to meaning.

ACCENT is an aspect of stress. It is the habitual stress placed in pronouncing on one or more syllables of a word of more than one syllable. Monosyllables may have stress; they cannot have accent; words of more than one syllable have at least one accent. Accents may be primary (*typic*al) or secondary (t*ypic*álity).

STRESS PROSODY.   A kind of patterning of sound in poetry that is based on the count of stresses per line. See p. 226.

STRUCTURE.   The inclusive term for the architecture of a literary work of art, including all the elements that have been given esthetic purpose and function by participating in form. The elements so shaped may be called MATERIALS prior to their participation in structure. (See p. 219.) Wellek and Warren have suggested these terms (MATERIALS, STRUCTURE) as alternatives to another pair of words often used to get at these distinctions: *form* and *content*. The difficulty with the latter pair of words is that they unhappily suggest too separable a relationship within the work of art.

STYLE.   The "voice," or manner, of a writer or work, described in terms of diction, grammar, syntax, figuration, texture, melody, and tone. An analysis of style is essentially an analysis of what we have called the presence of a work, involving perspective and tensiveness. It was fashionable at one time to distinguish between three general levels of style—high, middle, and low—and to relate level of style to social level of characters and setting in terms of DECORUM.

SUGGESTION.   A technique by which the writer says more than he seems to be saying; a form of economy in the handling of words paralleling the economy of a Japanese painting, in which simple strokes stand for detailed objects and scenes. Statement by indirection rather than by direction, with implicit rather than explicit pointing. See pp. 199–200.

SUMMARY.   In Phyllis Bentley's sense, an aspect of tempo in prose fiction. The rapid narration of information on which the narrator does not wish to spend much time; often used in EXPOSITION. A brief, compact statement or restatement of things in which time is much reduced. See pp. 282–284.

SUSPENSE.   An aspect of PLOT; the creation of interest by arousing concern as to the outcome of an action.

SYLLABIC PROSODY.   A kind of patterning in poetry based on the count of syllables per line. See p. 229.

SYMBOL.   One thing that stands for another but also has value in itself. (See FIGURES OF SENSE.) In *The Dead,* Joyce introduces the snow first on a nonsymbolic, realistic level but gradually makes us aware that it stands for death. All words are, of course, symbols—the word *cat* stands for the animal called by that name—but in literary use symbols are figurative, and a comparison is involved. Broadly speaking, such symbols are metaphorical. They may be *conventional* (love is a red rose, life is a weary river, death is a skeleton, black is evil) or they may be *nonconventional* or *created,* as in the snow in Joyce's story. The conventional symbol is immediately recognized as a symbol by the reader; the nonconventional symbol must be established by the writer before it acquires symbolical value. The *emblem* is a kind of conventional symbol, an object or picture that stands for a quality, state, or class—the flag, which stands for a country or for patriotism; the cross, which stands for Christianity; a crest designating a family; the old man with the hourglass, who stands for Time.

SYMPATHY.   Feeling *with,* as distinct from feeling *into,* which is EMPATHY. One may empathize with both Iago and Othello, but one is likely to sympathize with Othello—to be on his side, accept his attitudes rather than Iago's as proper—or, in the smothering of Desdemona, whereas we may empathize

with both husband and wife, we are more likely to sympathize with Desdemona. Neither sympathy nor empathy is quite synonymous with *identification;* both recognize a difference between the beholder and the person or
thing beheld. Identification is to be discouraged in the esthetic experience,
though complete alienation or detachment is likewise to be discouraged.

SYNAERESIS.   Also called *synizesis.* A crushing together of two like vowel
sounds into one syllable; *seest* for *see-est.* The opposite of DIAERESIS.

SYNCOPATION.   An effect achieved in verse by defeating the ear's expectation
of a continuing metrical pattern—for example, by inserting a trochee in the
midst of an iambic line or vice versa. Syncopation sometimes involves the
end of one line and the beginning of the next. Hopkins especially makes
use of such effects of syncopation, as in the following:

<pre>
           x   x   /   x   /
It gathers to a greatness like the ooze of oil

    /
Crushed. . . .
</pre>

SYNCOPE.   The loss or omission of a sound or sounds in the middle of a word:
heav'n, ne'er. See also APOCOPE.

SYNECDOCHE.   A FIGURE OF CONTIGUITY. See pp. 203–204.

SYNESTHESIA.   The interpretation of one sense in terms of another ("A loud
red poppy," where the sight is given sound value). See also p. 205.

SYNIZESIS.   See SYNAERESIS.

TENOR AND VEHICLE.   Terms introduced by I. A. Richards to distinguish between the primary and secondary subjects of metaphor. In the metaphor
"She is a social butterfly," *she* is the tenor and *butterfly* is the vehicle. In the
metaphor "The social butterfly left the party," *butterfly* is still the vehicle,
but the tenor is implied rather than expressed. See METAPHOR.

TENSIVENESS OR TENSION.   In living organisms, the quality of resistance to
stretch, the normal tension of the tissues by virtue of which the parts are
kept in shape, alert, and ready to function. In literature, it is the quality of
elasticity, of tautness, that produces the sense of the ongoing act. It results
from the interplay of meanings involved in the word-symbols: connotations, denotations, images, contrasts, oppositions, figures of speech; it involves also such things as rhythm, pitch levels, pausing—everything, in fact,
entering into the ebb and flow of literary works and participating in the
cycle of tension and release, which is the life of texts. The interpreter, in his
felt sensing of this state of tensiveness in the text, seeks to embody it in oral
performance. For a fuller discussion see Chapter 6.

TERCET.   Three rhyming lines of verse. Also called TRIPLET.

TERMINAL RHYME.   Rhyme that falls at line endings (as contrasted with INTER-
NAL RHYME.) See p. 221.

TERZA RIMA.   Tercets in a pattern rhyming as follows: *aba bcb cdc ded* (etc.)

TETRAMETER.   A verse written in four FEET.

TEXTURE.   A term pointing to the closeness (*close texture*) or openness (*open
texture*) of the "weave" of a literary work. A closely textured work calls for
closer scrutiny because it is more detailed and complex in verbal patterning
(its employment of figures, tone coloring, syntactical arrangement, symbolism) than a work of open texture. A work may be closely textured though
loosely plotted, or open textured though closely plotted.

TONE.   A term made popular by I. A. Richards, who uses it to point to attitudes adopted within a work of literature toward its subject matter, and hence pointing to responses proper to its audience. The tone of a work may be warm, cold, sympathetic, ironical, detached, and so forth.

TONE COLOR (TIMBRE).   The resonance quality of voiced sounds, dependent on the size and shape of the air column and resonating cavities, and the texture of the walls of the throat. For an extended discussion, see Gray and Wise, *The Bases of Speech,* 3d ed. (New York and London, 1959), pp. 110–116; they specify that while changes in the tenseness and laxness of the throat are necessary to produce the full range of tones from high and sharp (tense walls) to heavy and dull (lax walls), a certain degree of tensiveness is necessary to a full, rich voice. Hence tone color is another aspect of TENSIVE-NESS and one of considerable importance to the interpreter, who indicates qualities of feeling in part by his employment of tone coloration. It is important that he avoid the play of sound for its own sake, which results in the kind of reader who is said to be in love with the sound of his own voice, but no reader of literature can read successfully without proper attention to timbre. The question is whether the coloring and the literary work match.

TRAGEDY.   One of the two major classes of drama (the other being COMEDY). (The term *tragic* may apply to other literary forms, but TRAGEDY is normally reserved for the play form.) Comedy and tragedy are distinct from one another not so much in incident as in perspective. The PLOT of tragedy is serious, involving the PROTAGONIST in a catastrophe that may or may not be of his own making. Aristotle, who in his *Poetics* began serious discussion of the tragic form, suggested that the hero shoud be good, though not perfect, and that the actions involving him should purge the audience of such tragic emotions as pity and fear (see CATHARSIS). Later critics ask whether Shakespeare's Macbeth is indeed a good man and whether Aristotle's theory is not too exclusive. Should a tragedy result from some choice or disposition on the part of the hero himself, or may it arise through no fault of the protagonist? Need tragedy leave an audience with the cleansed state suggested by the term catharsis? Clearly, there is more than one answer to such questions.

In *Shakespearean tragedy,* the catastrophe always includes the death of the protagonist, though it need not in so-called *modern tragedy,* such as Ibsen's *Ghosts.* In *medieval tragedies* (not always dramatic in form) the catastrophe always involved the fall of a great man, the "eminent but erring" statesman. In *Senecan tragedy* (named after the Roman playwright Seneca, who established the type) the tragic action is cast in heavily rhetorical dialogue and lavishly ornamented with ghosts, blood, revenge, dismemberment, and crime. The English *revenge play,* of which *Hamlet* is thought to be a modified example, is a form derived from the Senecan model. *Romantic tragedy* is a story of thwarted love, such as *Romeo and Juliet.* A special variety of tragedy is the HEROIC PLAY. In such English writers as Otway we find a kind of tragedy sometimes called *she-tragedy,* after the fact that the protagonist is a woman. *Domestic tragedy* is tragedy involving domestic problems; in part, both *Othello* and *King Lear* are domestic tragedies. The phrase *domestic tragedy* or *bourgeois tragedy* is also used specifically to point to such plays as George Lillo's *George Barnwell,* which in the middle eighteenth century were popular plays of a serious nature based on the fall of a middle-class or lower-class hero for "everyday" reasons. See also MELO-DRAMA or TRAGICOMEDY.

TRAGICOMEDY.   A term used to designate the kind of play that is serious and often near-tragic, but which issues in a more or less happy ending, for the PROTAGONIST. A mixed form, involving both comic and tragic elements. The so-called *dramatic romances* of Shakespeare (*Pericles, Cymbeline, The Winter's Tale*) are tragicomedies; *The Tempest,* often classified with them, is a combination of tragicomedy and masque, though this will not describe its full effect. See MASQUE and PROBLEM PLAY.

TRAGIC RELIEF.   See COMIC RELIEF.

TRIMETER.   A verse written in three FEET.

TRIOLET.   A French poetic form consisting of eight lines employing only two rhymes. Lines 1 and 2 are repeated as lines 7 and 8; line 1 is repeated as line 4: *ABaAabAB.*

TRIPLE RHYME.   Rhyme falling on the antepenult, the third syllable from the end of a rhyme group: *beáutiful, dútiful.* (Often used for comic effects: *bétter for, métaphor.*)

TRIPLET.   See TERCET.

TROCHEE.   A metrical FOOT composed of two syllables, the first being the more conspicuous because it receives greater stress or greater emphasis in terms of pitch or duration. Normally marked thus: / x See also IAMBUS.

TROMPE L'OEIL.   Literally, "deception of the eye." In painting the term means making the unnatural natural through the use of minute detail or sensory values (making a still life look real when the arrangement is actually quite unreal). In literature the term refers also to making the esthetic illusion seem real by the use of devices that heighten the reality of the imaginary— for example, the play-within-a-play in *Hamlet* heightens the reality of the characters watching the play; or, in *Antony and Cleopatra,* Cleopatra's reference to being "boyed" (acted by a boy) on the public stage tends to conceal the fact that she is at that very moment being "boyed" by the Elizabethan actor playing the role.

TROPE.   See FIGURES OF SENSE.

TRUNCATION.   The omission of an unstressed or unaccented syllable at the beginning of a line of poetry:

          x /   x x   / x x   /
          Today is the day of the bee.

(The term is useful here only if one thinks of the line as being composed of three anapests, the first incomplete.) See also CATALEXIS.

UNDERSTATEMENT.   See IRONY and LITOTES.

VEHICLE.   See TENOR.

VERSE.   Used in at least three general senses: (1) a *line* of poetry, (2) anything written in poetic form (whether metered or not), or (3) pejoratively, poetry of slight content or merit.

VERS LIBRE.   See FREE VERSE.

VILLANELLE.   A French poetic form consisting of six stanzas, five containing three lines each and the final one containing four, employing only two rhymes throughout the form. The first line functions as the refrain and is repeated as lines 6, 12, and 18. The third line is a second refrain, repeated as lines 9, 15, and 19. So tightly restricted a form will often seem, in execution, a *tour de force.* Pattern: AbA abA abA abA abA abAA.

VISUAL PROSODY. Not all critics will admit this as a form of poetic patterning, since it normally seems to make its appeal primarily to the eye. It consists of the creating of forms and pictures out of words, in type. Such modern poets as Dylan Thomas and e. e. cummings have made use of visual prosody, writing poems in the form of diamonds, smoke rising from a locomotive, and so forth. Thomas's "Vision and Prayer" makes use of two designs, one for the vision and one for the prayer. The question is always whether the finished work is or is not a poem and whether the "prosodic" arrangement is functional. Medieval poets were ingenious in designing such forms, creating poems (or verse) that could be read forward and backward, up and down, diagonally, and so on.

VOWEL TRIANGLE. A diagrammatic representation of the placement of vowel sounds during their production, with respect to tension in the tongue and the relation of the tongue to the roof of the mouth. The example given below lists the bulk of General American vowel sounds in the symbols of the I.P.A. (See CONSONANTAL COGNATES.)

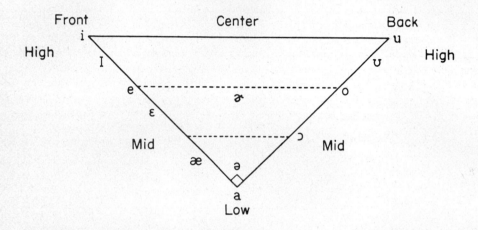

WEAK ENDING. See FEMININE ENDING.

WEAK RHYME. Rhyming of unstressed syllables:

> . . .charac*ter*
> . . .grandmo*ther*

ZEUGMA. Literally translated, "yoking," this involves the use of a term in the same grammatical relationship with other terms but with a switch in meaning. For example:

> Here thou, Great Anna! whom three realms obey,
> Dost sometimes counsel take—and sometimes tea.　　(Pope)

in which the verb *take* means one thing in the phrase "take counsel" and another in "take tea."

GENERAL INDEX

INDEX OF SELECTIONS BY AUTHOR AND TITLE[1]

[1] Excerpts from longer works are indicated by an asterisk following the listing.